# Core Java®

## Volume II—Advanced Features

### Ninth Edition

# Core Java®

## Volume II—Advanced Features

### Ninth Edition

**Cay S. Horstmann**
**Gary Cornell**

PRENTICE
HALL

Upper Saddle River, NJ • Boston • Indianapolis • San Francisco
New York • Toronto • Montreal • London • Munich • Paris • Madrid
Capetown • Sydney • Tokyo • Singapore • Mexico City

The publisher offers excellent discounts on this book when ordered in quantity for bulk purchases or special sales, which may include electronic versions and/or custom covers and content particular to your business, training goals, marketing focus, and branding interests. For more information, please contact:

U.S. Corporate and Government Sales
(800) 382-3419
corpsales@pearsontechgroup.com

For sales outside the United States, please contact:

International Sales
international@pearson.com

Visit us on the Web: informit.com/ph

*Library of Congress Cataloging-in-Publication Data:*

Horstmann, Cay S., 1959-
  Core Java / Cay S. Horstmann, Gary Cornell.—Ninth edition.
    pages cm
  Includes index.
  ISBN 978-0-13-708189-9 (v. 1 : pbk. : alk. paper)  1.  Java (Computer program language)  I. Cornell, Gary. II. Title.
  QA76.73.J38H6753 2013
  005.13'3—dc23
                                                    2012035397

ISBN-13: 978-0-13-708160-8
ISBN-10:     0-13-708160-X
Text printed in the United States on recycled paper at Edwards Brothers Malloy in Ann Arbor, Michigan.
First printing, February 2013

# Contents

# Preface

## To the Reader

The book you have in your hands is the second volume of the ninth edition of *Core Java*®, fully updated for Java SE 7. The first volume covers the essential features of the language; this volume deals with the advanced topics that a programmer needs to know for professional software development. Thus, as with the first volume and the previous editions of this book, we are still targeting programmers who want to put Java technology to work on real projects.

Please note: If you are an experienced developer who is comfortable with advanced language features such as inner classes and generics, you need not have read the first volume in order to benefit from this volume. While we do refer to sections of the previous volume when appropriate (and, of course, hope you will buy or have bought Volume I), you can find all the background material you need in any comprehensive introductory book about the Java platform.

Finally, as is the case with any book, errors and inaccuracies are inevitable. Should you find any in this book, we would very much like to hear about them. Of course, we would prefer to hear about them only once. For this reason, we have put up a web site at http://horstmann.com/corejava with a FAQ, bug fixes, and workarounds. Strategically placed at the end of the bug report web page (to encourage you to read the previous reports) is a form that you can use to report bugs or problems and to send suggestions for improvements to future editions.

## About This Book

The chapters in this book are, for the most part, independent of each other. You should be able to delve into whatever topic interests you the most and read the chapters in any order.

The topic of **Chapter 1** is input and output handling (I/O). In Java, all I/O is handled through so-called streams. Streams let you deal, in a uniform manner, with communications among various sources of data, such as files, network connections, or memory blocks. We include detailed coverage of the reader and writer classes that make it easy to deal with Unicode. We show you what goes on under the hood when you use the object serialization mechanism, which makes saving and loading objects easy and convenient. We then move on to regular expressions and the NIO2 library of Java SE 7, which makes common operations (such as reading all lines in a file) very convenient.

**Chapter 2** covers XML. We show you how to parse XML files, how to generate XML, and how to use XSL transformations. As a useful example, we show you how to specify the layout of a Swing form in XML. We also discuss the XPath API, which makes "finding needles in XML haystacks" much easier.

**Chapter 3** covers the networking API. Java makes it phenomenally easy to do complex network programming. We show you how to make network connections to servers, how to implement your own servers, and how to make HTTP connections.

**Chapter 4** covers database programming. The main focus is on JDBC, the Java database connectivity API that lets Java programs connect to relational databases. We show you how to write useful programs to handle realistic database chores, using a core subset of the JDBC API. (A complete treatment of the JDBC API would require a book almost as long as this one.) We finish the chapter with a brief introduction into hierarchical databases and discuss JNDI (the Java Naming and Directory Interface) and LDAP (the Lightweight Directory Access Protocol).

**Chapter 5** discusses a feature that we believe can only grow in importance: internationalization. The Java programming language is one of the few languages designed from the start to handle Unicode, but the internationalization support in the Java platform goes much further. As a result, you can internationalize Java applications so that they not only cross platforms but cross country boundaries as well. For example, we show you how to write a retirement calculator that uses either English, German, or Chinese languages.

**Chapter 6** contains all the Swing material that didn't make it into Volume I, especially the important but complex tree and table components. We show the basic uses of editor panes, the Java implementation of a "multiple document" interface, progress indicators used in multithreaded programs, and "desktop integration features" such as splash screens and support for the system tray. Again, we focus on the most useful constructs that you are likely to encounter in practical programming because an encyclopedic coverage of the entire Swing library would fill several volumes and would only be of interest to dedicated taxonomists.

**Chapter 7** covers the Java 2D API, which you can use to create realistic drawings and special effects. The chapter also covers some advanced features of the AWT (Abstract Windowing Toolkit) that seemed too specialized for coverage in Volume I but should, nonetheless, be part of every programmer's toolkit. These features include printing and the APIs for cut-and-paste and drag-and-drop.

**Chapter 8** explains what you need to know about the component API for the Java platform—JavaBeans. We show you how to write your own beans that other programmers can manipulate in integrated builder environments. We conclude this chapter by showing you how you can use JavaBeans persistence to store your data in a format that—unlike object serialization—is suitable for long-term storage.

**Chapter 9** takes up the Java security model. The Java platform was designed from the ground up to be secure, and this chapter takes you under the hood to see how this design is implemented. We show you how to write your own class loaders and security managers for special-purpose applications. Then, we take up the security API that allows for such important features as message and code signing, authorization and authentication, and encryption. We conclude with examples that use the AES and RSA encryption algorithms.

**Chapter 10** covers distributed objects. We cover RMI (Remote Method Invocation) in detail. This API lets you work with Java objects that are distributed over multiple machines.

**Chapter 11** discusses three techniques for processing code. The scripting and compiler APIs allow your program to call code in scripting languages such as JavaScript or Groovy, and to compile Java code. Annotations allow you to add arbitrary information (sometimes called metadata) to a Java program. We show you how annotation processors can harvest these annotations at the source or class file level, and how annotations can be used to influence the behavior of classes at runtime. Annotations are only useful with tools, and we hope that our discussion will help you select useful annotation processing tools for your needs.

**Chapter 12** takes up native methods, which let you call methods written for a specific machine such as the Microsoft Windows API. Obviously, this feature is controversial: Use native methods, and the cross-platform nature of the Java platform vanishes. Nonetheless, every serious programmer writing Java applications for specific platforms needs to know these techniques. At times, you need to turn to the operating system's API for your target platform when you interact with a device or service that is not supported by Java. We illustrate this by showing you how to access the registry API in Windows from a Java program.

As always, all chapters have been completely revised for the latest version of Java. Outdated material has been removed, and the new APIs of Java SE 7 are covered in detail.

## Conventions

As is common in many computer books, we use monospace type to represent computer code.

**NOTE:** Notes are tagged with "note" icons that look like this.

 **TIP:** Tips are tagged with "tip" icons that look like this.

 **CAUTION:** When there is danger ahead, we warn you with a "caution" icon.

 **C++ NOTE:** There are a number of C++ notes that explain the difference between the Java programming language and C++. You can skip them if you aren't interested in C++.

Java comes with a large programming library, or Application Programming Interface (API). When using an API call for the first time, we add a short summary description at the end of the section. These descriptions are a bit more informal but, we hope, also a little more informative than those in the official online API documentation. The names of interfaces are in italics, just like in the official documentation. The number after a class, interface, or method name is the JDK version in which the feature was introduced.

```
Application Programming Interface 1.2
```

Programs whose source code is included in the companion code for this book are listed as examples; for instance,

```
Listing 1.1  ScriptTest.java
```

You can download the companion code from http://horstmann.com/corejava.

# Acknowledgments

Writing a book is always a monumental effort, and rewriting doesn't seem to be much easier, especially with such a rapid rate of change in Java technology. Making a book a reality takes many dedicated people, and it is my great pleasure to acknowledge the contributions of the entire Core Java team.

A large number of individuals at Prentice Hall provided valuable assistance, but they managed to stay behind the scenes. I'd like them all to know how much I appreciate their efforts. As always, my warm thanks go to my editor, Greg Doench, for steering the book through the writing and production process, and for allowing me to be blissfully unaware of the existence of all those folks behind the scenes. I am very grateful to Julie Nahil for production support, and to Dmitry Kirsanov and Alina Kirsanova for copyediting and typesetting the manuscript.

Thanks to the many readers of earlier editions who reported embarrassing errors and made lots of thoughtful suggestions for improvement. I am particularly grateful to the excellent reviewing team that went over the manuscript with an amazing eye for detail and saved me from many more embarrassing errors.

Reviewers of this and earlier editions include Chuck Allison (Contributing Editor, C/C++ Users Journal), Lance Anderson (Oracle), Alec Beaton (PointBase, Inc.), Cliff Berg (iSavvix Corporation), Joshua Bloch, David Brown, Corky Cartwright, Frank Cohen (PushToTest), Chris Crane (devXsolution), Dr. Nicholas J. De Lillo (Manhattan College), Rakesh Dhoopar (Oracle), Robert Evans (Senior Staff, The Johns Hopkins University Applied Physics Lab), David Geary (Sabreware), Jim Gish (Oracle), Brian Goetz (Principal Consultant, Quiotix Corp.), Angela Gordon, Dan Gordon, Rob Gordon, John Gray (University of Hartford), Cameron Gregory (olabs.com), Marty Hall (The Johns Hopkins University Applied Physics Lab), Vincent Hardy, Dan Harkey (San Jose State University), William Higgins (IBM), Vladimir Ivanovic (PointBase), Jerry Jackson (ChannelPoint Software), Tim Kimmet (Preview Systems), Chris Laffra, Charlie Lai, Angelika Langer, Doug Langston, Hang Lau (McGill University), Mark Lawrence, Doug Lea (SUNY Oswego), Gregory Longshore, Bob Lynch (Lynch Associates), Philip Milne (consultant), Mark Morrissey (The Oregon Graduate Institute), Mahesh Neelakanta (Florida Atlantic University), Hao Pham, Paul Philion, Blake Ragsdell, Ylber Ramadani (Ryerson University), Stuart Reges (University of Arizona), Rich Rosen (Interactive Data Corporation), Peter Sanders

(ESSI University, Nice, France), Dr. Paul Sanghera (San Jose State University and Brooks College), Paul Sevinc (Teamup AG), Devang Shah, Richard Slywczak (NASA/Glenn Research Center), Bradley A. Smith, Steven Stelting, Christopher Taylor, Luke Taylor (Valtech), George Thiruvathukal, Kim Topley (author of *Core JFC, Second Edition*), Janet Traub, Paul Tyma (consultant), Peter van der Linden, Burt Walsh, Joe Wang (Oracle), and Dan Xu (Oracle).

*Cay Horstmann*
*San Francisco, California*
*December 2012*

CHAPTER

# Streams and Files

**In this chapter:**

In this chapter, we will cover the Java Application Programming Interfaces (APIs) for input and output. You will learn how to access files and directories and how to read and write data in binary and text format. This chapter also shows you the object serialization mechanism that lets you store objects as easily as you can store text or numeric data. Next, we will turn to several improvements that were made in the "new I/O" package java.nio, introduced in Java SE 1.4, and the "new new I/O" enhancements of Java 7. We finish the chapter with a discussion of regular expressions, even though they are not actually related to streams and files. We couldn't find a better place to handle that topic, and apparently neither could the Java team—the regular expression API specification was attached to the specification request for the "new I/O" features.

# 1.1 Streams

In the Java API, an object from which we can read a sequence of bytes is called an *input stream*. An object to which we can write a sequence of bytes is called an *output stream*. These sources and destinations of byte sequences can be—and often are—files, but they can also be network connections and even blocks of memory. The abstract classes InputStream and OutputStream form the basis for a hierarchy of input/output (I/O) classes.

Byte-oriented streams are inconvenient for processing information stored in Unicode (recall that Unicode uses multiple bytes per character). Therefore, a separate hierarchy provides classes for processing Unicode characters that inherit from the abstract Reader and Writer classes. These classes have read and write operations that are based on two-byte Unicode code units rather than on single-byte characters.

## 1.1.1 Reading and Writing Bytes

The InputStream class has an abstract method:

```
abstract int read()
```

This method reads one byte and returns the byte that was read, or -1 if it encounters the end of the input source. The designer of a concrete input stream class overrides this method to provide useful functionality. For example, in the FileInputStream class, this method reads one byte from a file. System.in is a predefined object of a subclass of InputStream that allows you to read information from the keyboard.

The InputStream class also has nonabstract methods to read an array of bytes or to skip a number of bytes. These methods call the abstract read method, so subclasses need to override only one method.

Similarly, the OutputStream class defines the abstract method

```
abstract void write(int b)
```

which writes one byte to an output location.

Both the read and write methods *block* until the byte is actually read or written. This means that if the stream cannot immediately be accessed (usually because of a busy network connection), the current thread blocks. This gives other threads the chance to do useful work while the method is waiting for the stream to become available again.

The available method lets you check the number of bytes that are currently available for reading. This means a fragment like the following is unlikely to block:

```
int bytesAvailable = in.available();
if (bytesAvailable > 0)
{
   byte[] data = new byte[bytesAvailable];
   in.read(data);
}
```

When you have finished reading or writing to a stream, close it by calling the close method. This call frees up the operating system resources that are in limited supply. If an application opens too many streams without closing them, system resources can become depleted. Closing an output stream also *flushes* the buffer used for the output stream: Any characters that were temporarily placed in a buffer so that they could be delivered as a larger packet are sent off. In particular, if you do not close a file, the last packet of bytes might never be delivered. You can also manually flush the output with the flush method.

Even if a stream class provides concrete methods to work with the raw read and write functions, application programmers rarely use them. The data that you are interested in probably contain numbers, strings, and objects, not raw bytes.

Java gives you many stream classes derived from the basic InputStream and OutputStream classes that let you work with data in the forms that you usually use, not with bytes.

---

**java.io.InputStream** 1.0

- abstract int read()
  reads a byte of data and returns the byte read; returns -1 at the end of the stream.
- int read(byte[] b)
  reads into an array of bytes and returns the actual number of bytes read, or -1 at the end of the stream; this method reads at most b.length bytes.
- int read(byte[] b, int off, int len)
  reads into an array of bytes and returns the actual number of bytes read, or -1 at the end of the stream.

  | *Parameters:* | b | The array into which the data is read |
  | --- | --- | --- |
  | | off | The offset into b where the first bytes should be placed |
  | | len | The maximum number of bytes to read |

- long skip(long n)
  skips n bytes in the input stream, returns the actual number of bytes skipped (which may be less than n if the end of the stream was encountered).

---

*(Continues)*

---

**java.io.InputStream**  1.0  *(Continued)*

---

- `int available()`
  returns the number of bytes available, without blocking (recall that blocking means that the current thread loses its turn).
- `void close()`
  closes the input stream.
- `void mark(int readlimit)`
  puts a marker at the current position in the input stream (not all streams support this feature). If more than `readlimit` bytes have been read from the input stream, the stream is allowed to forget the marker.
- `void reset()`
  returns to the last marker. Subsequent calls to `read` reread the bytes. If there is no current marker, the stream is not reset.
- `boolean markSupported()`
  returns `true` if the stream supports marking.

---

**java.io.OutputStream**  1.0

---

- `abstract void write(int n)`
  writes a byte of data.
- `void write(byte[] b)`
- `void write(byte[] b, int off, int len)`
  writes all bytes or a range of bytes in the array `b`.

  *Parameters:*     b      The array from which to write the data

                 off     The offset into `b` to the first byte that will be written

                 len     The number of bytes to write
- `void close()`
  flushes and closes the output stream.
- `void flush()`
  flushes the output stream—that is, sends any buffered data to its destination.

## 1.1.2 The Complete Stream Zoo

Unlike C, which gets by just fine with a single type `FILE*`, Java has a whole zoo of more than 60 (!) different stream types (see Figures 1.1 and 1.2).

Let's divide the animals in the stream class zoo by how they are used. There are separate hierarchies for classes that process bytes and characters. As you saw,

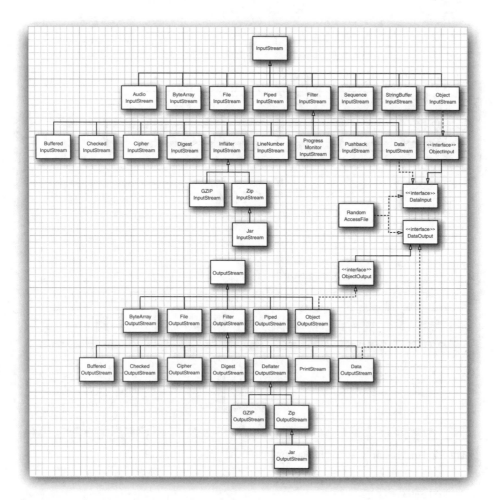

**Figure 1.1** Input and output stream hierarchy

the InputStream and OutputStream classes let you read and write individual bytes and arrays of bytes. These classes form the basis of the hierarchy shown in Figure 1.1. To read and write strings and numbers, you need more capable subclasses. For example, DataInputStream and DataOutputStream let you read and write all the primitive Java types in binary format. Finally, there are streams that do useful stuff; for example, the ZipInputStream and ZipOutputStream let you read and write files in the familiar ZIP compression format.

For Unicode text, on the other hand, you can use subclasses of the abstract classes Reader and Writer (see Figure 1.2). The basic methods of the Reader and Writer classes are similar to those for InputStream and OutputStream.

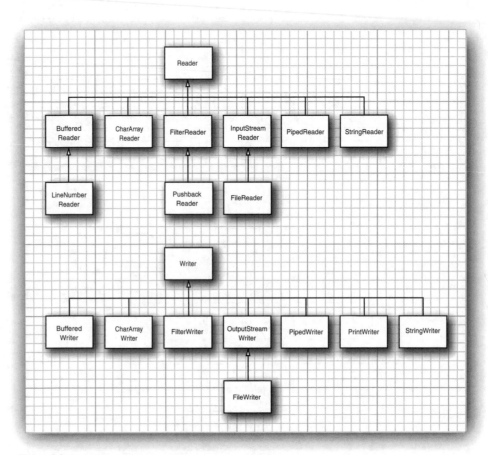

**Figure 1.2** Reader and writer hierarchy

```
abstract int read()
abstract void write(int c)
```

The read method returns either a Unicode code unit (as an integer between 0 and 65535) or -1 when you have reached the end of the file. The write method is called with a Unicode code unit. (See Volume I, Chapter 3 for a discussion of Unicode code units.)

There are four additional interfaces: Closeable, Flushable, Readable, and Appendable (see Figure 1.3). The first two interfaces are very simple, with methods

```
void close() throws IOException
```

and

```
void flush()
```

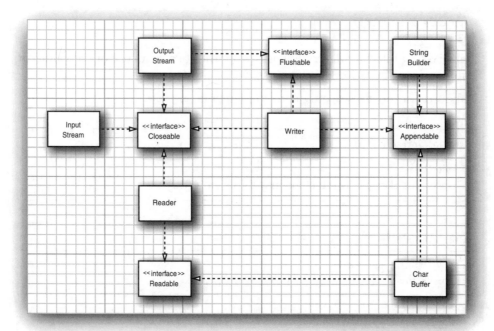

**Figure 1.3** The Closeable, Flushable, Readable, and Appendable interfaces

respectively. The classes InputStream, OutputStream, Reader, and Writer all implement the Closeable interface.

---

 **NOTE:** The java.io.Closeable interface extends the java.lang.AutoCloseable interface. Therefore, you can use the try-with-resources statement with any Closeable. Why have two interfaces? The close method of the Closeable interface only throws an IOException, whereas the AutoCloseable.close method may throw any exception.

---

OutputStream and Writer implement the Flushable interface.

The Readable interface has a single method

```
int read(CharBuffer cb)
```

The CharBuffer class has methods for sequential and random read/write access. It represents an in-memory buffer or a memory-mapped file. (See Section 1.7.1, "The Buffer Data Structure," on p. 77 for details.)

The Appendable interface has two methods for appending single characters and character sequences:

```
Appendable append(char c)
Appendable append(CharSequence s)
```

The CharSequence interface describes basic properties of a sequence of char values. It is implemented by String, CharBuffer, StringBuilder, and StringBuffer.

Of the stream zoo classes, only Writer implements Appendable.

---

**java.io.Closeable**  5.0

- void close()
  closes this Closeable. This method may throw an IOException.

---

**java.io.Flushable**  5.0

- void flush()
  flushes this Flushable.

---

**java.lang.Readable**  5.0

- int read(CharBuffer cb)
  attempts to read as many char values into cb as it can hold. Returns the number of values read, or -1 if no further values are available from this Readable.

---

**java.lang.Appendable**  5.0

- Appendable append(char c)
- Appendable append(CharSequence cs)
  appends the given code unit, or all code units in the given sequence, to this Appendable; returns this.

---

**java.lang.CharSequence**  1.4

- char charAt(int index)
  returns the code unit at the given index.
- int length()
  returns the number of code units in this sequence.

*(Continues)*

---

> *java.lang.CharSequence* 1.4 *(Continued)*
>
> - `CharSequence subSequence(int startIndex, int endIndex)`
>   returns a `CharSequence` consisting of the code units stored at index `startIndex` to `endIndex` - 1.
> - `String toString()`
>   returns a string consisting of the code units of this sequence.

## 1.1.3 Combining Stream Filters

`FileInputStream` and `FileOutputStream` give you input and output streams attached to a disk file. You need to pass the file name or full path name of the file to the constructor. For example,

```
FileInputStream fin = new FileInputStream("employee.dat");
```

looks in the user directory for a file named `employee.dat`.

 **TIP:** All the classes in `java.io` interpret relative path names as starting from the user's working directory. You can get this directory by a call to `System.getProperty("user.dir")`.

 **CAUTION:** Since the backslash character is the escape character in Java strings, be sure to use `\\` for Windows-style path names (for example, `C:\\Windows\\win.ini`). In Windows, you can also use a single forward slash (`C:/Windows/win.ini`) because most Windows file-handling system calls will interpret forward slashes as file separators. However, this is not recommended—the behavior of the Windows system functions is subject to change. Instead, for portable programs, use the file separator character for the platform on which your program runs. It is available as the constant string `java.io.File.separator`.

Like the abstract `InputStream` and `OutputStream` classes, these classes support only reading and writing at the byte level. That is, we can only read bytes and byte arrays from the object `fin`.

```
byte b = (byte) fin.read();
```

As you will see in the next section, if we just had a `DataInputStream`, we could read numeric types:

```
DataInputStream din = . . .;
double s = din.readDouble();
```

But just as the FileInputStream has no methods to read numeric types, the DataInputStream has no method to get data from a file.

Java uses a clever mechanism to separate two kinds of responsibilities. Some streams (such as the FileInputStream and the input stream returned by the openStream method of the URL class) can retrieve bytes from files and other more exotic locations. Other streams (such as the DataInputStream and the PrintWriter) can assemble bytes into more useful data types. The Java programmer has to combine the two. For example, to be able to read numbers from a file, first create a FileInputStream and then pass it to the constructor of a DataInputStream.

```
FileInputStream fin = new FileInputStream("employee.dat");
DataInputStream din = new DataInputStream(fin);
double s = din.readDouble();
```

If you look at Figure 1.1 again, you can see the classes FilterInputStream and FilterOutputStream. The subclasses of these classes are used to add capabilities to raw byte streams.

You can add multiple capabilities by nesting the filters. For example, by default streams are not buffered. That is, every call to read asks the operating system to dole out yet another byte. It is more efficient to request blocks of data instead and store them in a buffer. If you want buffering *and* the data input methods for a file, you need to use the following rather monstrous sequence of constructors:

```
DataInputStream din = new DataInputStream(
    new BufferedInputStream(
        new FileInputStream("employee.dat")));
```

Notice that we put the DataInputStream *last* in the chain of constructors because we want to use the DataInputStream methods, and we want *them* to use the buffered read method.

Sometimes you'll need to keep track of the intermediate streams when chaining them together. For example, when reading input, you often need to peek at the next byte to see if it is the value that you expect. Java provides the PushbackInputStream for this purpose.

```
PushbackInputStream pbin = new PushbackInputStream(
    new BufferedInputStream(
        new FileInputStream("employee.dat")));
```

Now you can speculatively read the next byte

```
int b = pbin.read();
```

and throw it back if it isn't what you wanted.

```
if (b != '<') pbin.unread(b);
```

However, reading and unreading are the *only* methods that apply to a pushback input stream. If you want to look ahead and also read numbers, then you need both a pushback input stream and a data input stream reference.

```
DataInputStream din = new DataInputStream(
   pbin = new PushbackInputStream(
      new BufferedInputStream(
         new FileInputStream("employee.dat"))));
```

Of course, in the stream libraries of other programming languages, niceties such as buffering and lookahead are automatically taken care of, so it is a bit of a hassle to resort, in Java, to combining stream filters. However, the ability to mix and match filter classes to construct truly useful sequences of streams does give you an immense amount of flexibility. For example, you can read numbers from a compressed ZIP file by using the following sequence of streams (see Figure 1.4):

```
ZipInputStream zin = new ZipInputStream(new FileInputStream("employee.zip"));
DataInputStream din = new DataInputStream(zin);
```

(See Section 1.4, "ZIP Archives," on p. 33 for more on Java's handling of ZIP files.)

---

**java.io.FileInputStream** 1.0

- `FileInputStream(String name)`
- `FileInputStream(File file)`
  creates a new file input stream using the file whose path name is specified by the name string or the file object. (The File class is described at the end of this chapter.) Path names that are not absolute are resolved relative to the working directory that was set when the VM started.

---

**java.io.FileOutputStream** 1.0

- `FileOutputStream(String name)`
- `FileOutputStream(String name, boolean append)`
- `FileOutputStream(File file)`
- `FileOutputStream(File file, boolean append)`
  creates a new file output stream specified by the name string or the file object. (The File class is described at the end of this chapter.) If the append parameter is true, an existing file with the same name will not be deleted and data will be added at the end of the file. Otherwise, this method deletes any existing file with the same name.

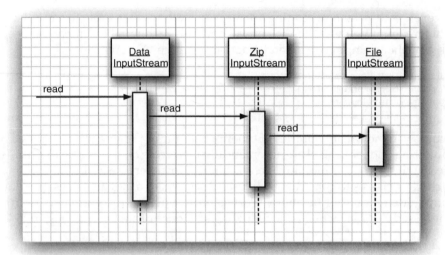

**Figure 1.4** A sequence of filtered streams

---

**java.io.BufferedInputStream** 1.0

- BufferedInputStream(InputStream in)
  creates a buffered stream. A buffered input stream reads bytes from a stream without causing a device access every time. When the buffer is empty, a new block of data is read into the buffer.

---

**java.io.BufferedOutputStream** 1.0

- BufferedOutputStream(OutputStream out)
  creates a buffered stream. A buffered output stream collects bytes to be written without causing a device access every time. When the buffer fills up or when the stream is flushed, the data are written.

---

**java.io.PushbackInputStream** 1.0

- PushbackInputStream(InputStream in)
- PushbackInputStream(InputStream in, int size)
  constructs a stream with one-byte lookahead or a pushback buffer of specified size.
- void unread(int b)
  pushes back a byte, which is retrieved again by the next call to read.
  *Parameters:*    b    The byte to be read again

## 1.2 Text Input and Output

When saving data, you have the choice between binary and text formats. For example, if the integer 1234 is saved in binary, it is written as the sequence of bytes 00 00 04 D2 (in hexadecimal notation). In text format, it is saved as the string "1234". Although binary I/O is fast and efficient, it is not easily readable by humans. We first discuss text I/O and cover binary I/O in Section 1.3, "Reading and Writing Binary Data," on p. 25.

When saving text strings, you need to consider the *character encoding*. In the UTF-16 encoding, the string "1234" is encoded as 00 31 00 32 00 33 00 34 (in hex). However, many programs expect that text files are encoded in a different encoding. In ISO 8859-1, the encoding most commonly used in the United States and Western Europe, the string would be written as 31 32 33 34, without the zero bytes.

The OutputStreamWriter class turns a stream of Unicode code units into a stream of bytes, using a chosen character encoding. Conversely, the InputStreamReader class turns an input stream that contains bytes (specifying characters in some character encoding) into a reader that emits Unicode code units.

For example, here is how you make an input reader that reads keystrokes from the console and converts them to Unicode:

```
InputStreamReader in = new InputStreamReader(System.in);
```

This input stream reader assumes the default character encoding used by the host system, such as the ISO 8859-1 encoding in Western Europe. You can choose a different encoding by specifying it in the constructor for the InputStreamReader, for example:

```
InputStreamReader in = new InputStreamReader(new FileInputStream("kremlin.dat"), "ISO8859_5");
```

See Section 1.2.4, "Character Sets," on p. 20 for more information on character encodings.

### 1.2.1 How to Write Text Output

For text output, use a PrintWriter. That class has methods to print strings and numbers in text format. There is even a convenience constructor to link a PrintWriter to a FileWriter. The statement

```
PrintWriter out = new PrintWriter("employee.txt");
```

is equivalent to

```
PrintWriter out = new PrintWriter(new FileWriter("employee.txt"));
```

To write to a print writer, use the same print, println, and printf methods that you used with System.out. You can use these methods to print numbers (int, short, long, float, double), characters, boolean values, strings, and objects.

For example, consider this code:

```
String name = "Harry Hacker";
double salary = 75000;
out.print(name);
out.print(' ');
out.println(salary);
```

This writes the characters

```
Harry Hacker 75000.0
```

to the writer out. The characters are then converted to bytes and end up in the file employee.txt.

The println method adds the correct end-of-line character for the target system ("\r\n" on Windows, "\n" on UNIX) to the line. This is the string obtained by the call System.getProperty("line.separator").

If the writer is set to *autoflush mode,* all characters in the buffer are sent to their destination whenever println is called. (Print writers are always buffered.) By default, autoflushing is *not* enabled. You can enable or disable autoflushing by using the PrintWriter(Writer out, boolean autoFlush) constructor:

```
PrintWriter out = new PrintWriter(new FileWriter("employee.txt"), true); // autoflush
```

The print methods don't throw exceptions. You can call the checkError method to see if something went wrong with the stream.

**NOTE:** Java veterans might wonder whatever happened to the PrintStream class and to System.out. In Java 1.0, the PrintStream class simply truncated all Unicode characters to ASCII characters by dropping the top byte. (At the time, Unicode was still a 16-bit encoding.) Clearly, that was not a clean or portable approach, and it was fixed with the introduction of readers and writers in Java 1.1. For compatibility with existing code, System.in, System.out, and System.err are still streams, not readers and writers. But now the PrintStream class internally converts Unicode characters to the default host encoding in the same way as the PrintWriter does. Objects of type PrintStream act exactly like print writers when you use the print and println methods, but unlike print writers they allow you to output raw bytes with the write(int) and write(byte[]) methods.

---

**java.io.PrintWriter 1.1**

- PrintWriter(Writer out)
- PrintWriter(Writer out, boolean autoFlush)
  creates a new PrintWriter.

  *Parameters:*  out             A character-output writer

  autoflush      If true, the println methods will flush the output
                 buffer (default: false).

- PrintWriter(OutputStream out)
- PrintWriter(OutputStream out, boolean autoflush)
  creates a new PrintWriter from an existing OutputStream by creating the necessary
  intermediate OutputStreamWriter.

- PrintWriter(String filename)
- PrintWriter(File file)
  creates a new PrintWriter that writes to the given file by creating the necessary
  intermediate FileWriter.

- void print(Object obj)
  prints an object by printing the string resulting from toString.

  *Parameters:*  obj             The object to be printed

- void print(String s)
  prints a string containing Unicode code units.

- void println(String s)
  prints a string followed by a line terminator. Flushes the stream if the stream is in
  autoflush mode.

- void print(char[] s)
  prints all Unicode code units in the given array.

- void print(char c)
  prints a Unicode code unit.

- void print(int i)
- void print(long l)
- void print(float f)
- void print(double d)
- void print(boolean b)
  prints the given value in text format.

- void printf(String format, Object... args)
  prints the given values as specified by the format string. See Volume I, Chapter 3
  for the specification of the format string.

*(Continues)*

---

**java.io.PrintWriter** 1.1 *(Continued)*

- boolean checkError()
  returns true if a formatting or output error occurred. Once the stream has encountered an error, it is tainted and all calls to checkError return true.

---

## 1.2.2  How to Read Text Input

You already know that:

- To write data in binary format, you use a DataOutputStream.
- To write in text format, you use a PrintWriter.

Therefore, you might expect that there is an analog to the DataInputStream that lets you read data in text format. The closest analog is the Scanner class that we used extensively in Volume I. However, before Java SE 5.0, the only game in town for processing text input was the BufferedReader class with the readLine method that lets you read a line of text. You need to combine a buffered reader with an input source.

```
BufferedReader in = new BufferedReader(
    new InputStreamReader(new FileInputStream("employee.txt"), "UTF-8));
```

The readLine method returns null when no more input is available. A typical input loop, therefore, looks like this:

```
String line;
while ((line = in.readLine()) != null)
{
    do something with line
}
```

However, a BufferedReader has no methods for reading numbers. We suggest that you use a Scanner for reading text input.

## 1.2.3  Saving Objects in Text Format

In this section, we walk you through an example program that stores an array of Employee records in a text file. Each record is stored in a separate line. Instance fields are separated from each other by delimiters. We use a vertical bar (|) as our delimiter. (A colon (:) is another popular choice. Part of the fun is that everyone uses a different delimiter.) Naturally, we punt on the issue of what might happen if a | actually occurred in one of the strings we save.

Here is a sample set of records:

```
Harry Hacker|35500|1989|10|1
Carl Cracker|75000|1987|12|15
Tony Tester|38000|1990|3|15
```

Writing records is simple. Since we write to a text file, we use the PrintWriter class. We simply write all fields, followed by either a | or, for the last field, a \n. This work is done in the following writeData method that we add to our Employee class:

```java
public void writeData(PrintWriter out) throws IOException
{
   GregorianCalendar calendar = new GregorianCalendar();
   calendar.setTime(hireDay);
   out.println(name + "|"
      + salary + "|"
      + calendar.get(Calendar.YEAR) + "|"
      + (calendar.get(Calendar.MONTH) + 1) + "|"
      + calendar.get(Calendar.DAY_OF_MONTH));
}
```

To read records, we read in a line at a time and separate the fields. We use a scanner to read each line and then split the line into tokens with the String.split method.

```java
public void readData(Scanner in)
{
   String line = in.nextLine();
   String[] tokens = line.split("\\|");
   name = tokens[0];
   salary = Double.parseDouble(tokens[1]);
   int y = Integer.parseInt(tokens[2]);
   int m = Integer.parseInt(tokens[3]);
   int d = Integer.parseInt(tokens[4]);
   GregorianCalendar calendar = new GregorianCalendar(y, m - 1, d);
   hireDay = calendar.getTime();
}
```

The parameter of the split method is a regular expression describing the separator. We discuss regular expressions in more detail at the end of this chapter. As it happens, the vertical bar character has a special meaning in regular expressions, so it needs to be escaped with a \ character. That character needs to be escaped by another \, yielding the "\\|" expression.

The complete program is in Listing 1.1. The static method

```java
void writeData(Employee[] e, PrintWriter out)
```

first writes the length of the array, then writes each record. The static method

```java
Employee[] readData(BufferedReader in)
```

first reads in the length of the array, then reads in each record. This turns out to be a bit tricky:

```
int n = in.nextInt();
in.nextLine(); // consume newline
Employee[] employees = new Employee[n];
for (int i = 0; i < n; i++)
{
   employees[i] = new Employee();
   employees[i].readData(in);
}
```

The call to nextInt reads the array length but not the trailing newline character. We must consume the newline so that the readData method can get the next input line when it calls the nextLine method.

**Listing 1.1** textFile/TextFileTest.java

```
 1  package textFile;
 2
 3  import java.io.*;
 4  import java.util.*;
 5
 6  /**
 7   * @version 1.13 2012-05-30
 8   * @author Cay Horstmann
 9   */
10  public class TextFileTest
11  {
12     public static void main(String[] args) throws IOException
13     {
14        Employee[] staff = new Employee[3];
15
16        staff[0] = new Employee("Carl Cracker", 75000, 1987, 12, 15);
17        staff[1] = new Employee("Harry Hacker", 50000, 1989, 10, 1);
18        staff[2] = new Employee("Tony Tester", 40000, 1990, 3, 15);
19
20        // save all employee records to the file employee.dat
21        try (PrintWriter out = new PrintWriter("employee.dat", "UTF-8"))
22        {
23           writeData(staff, out);
24        }
25
26        // retrieve all records into a new array
27        try (Scanner in = new Scanner(
28              new FileInputStream("employee.dat"), "UTF-8"))
29        {
30           Employee[] newStaff = readData(in);
```

```
31          // print the newly read employee records
32          for (Employee e : newStaff)
33              System.out.println(e);
34      }
35  }
36
37  /**
38   * Writes all employees in an array to a print writer
39   * @param employees an array of employees
40   * @param out a print writer
41   */
42  private static void writeData(Employee[] employees, PrintWriter out) throws IOException
43  {
44      // write number of employees
45      out.println(employees.length);
46
47      for (Employee e : employees)
48          writeEmployee(out, e);
49  }
50
51  /**
52   * Reads an array of employees from a scanner
53   * @param in the scanner
54   * @return the array of employees
55   */
56  private static Employee[] readData(Scanner in)
57  {
58      // retrieve the array size
59      int n = in.nextInt();
60      in.nextLine(); // consume newline
61
62      Employee[] employees = new Employee[n];
63      for (int i = 0; i < n; i++)
64      {
65          employees[i] = readEmployee(in);
66      }
67      return employees;
68  }
69
70  /**
71   * Writes employee data to a print writer
72   * @param out the print writer
73   */
74  public static void writeEmployee(PrintWriter out, Employee e)
75  {
76      GregorianCalendar calendar = new GregorianCalendar();
77      calendar.setTime(e.getHireDay());
78      out.println(e.getName() + "|" + e.getSalary() + "|" + calendar.get(Calendar.YEAR) + "|"
79          + (calendar.get(Calendar.MONTH) + 1) + "|" + calendar.get(Calendar.DAY_OF_MONTH));
80  }
```

*(Continues)*

**Listing 1.1** *(Continued)*

```
81  /**
82   * Reads employee data from a buffered reader
83   * @param in the scanner
84   */
85  public static Employee readEmployee(Scanner in)
86  {
87     String line = in.nextLine();
88     String[] tokens = line.split("\\|");
89     String name = tokens[0];
90     double salary = Double.parseDouble(tokens[1]);
91     int year = Integer.parseInt(tokens[2]);
92     int month = Integer.parseInt(tokens[3]);
93     int day = Integer.parseInt(tokens[4]);
94     return new Employee(name, salary, year, month, day);
95  }
96 }
```

## 1.2.4 Character Sets

In the past, international character sets have been handled rather unsystematically throughout the Java library. The java.nio package—introduced in Java SE 1.4—unifies character set conversion with the Charset class. (Note that the s is lowercase.)

A character set maps between sequences of Unicode characters and byte sequences used in a local character encoding. A popular character encoding is ISO 8859-1, a single-byte encoding of the first 256 Unicode characters. Gaining in importance is ISO 8859-15, which replaces some of the less useful characters of ISO 8859-1 with accented letters used in French and Finnish, and, more importantly, replaces the "international currency" character ¤ with the Euro symbol (€) in code point 0xA4. Other examples of character encodings are the variable-byte encodings commonly used for Japanese and Chinese.

The Charset class uses the character set names standardized in the IANA Character Set Registry (www.iana.org/assignments/character-sets). These names differ slightly from those used in previous versions. For example, the "official" name of ISO 8859-1 is now "ISO-8859-1" and no longer "ISO8859_1" which was the preferred name up to Java SE 1.3.

For compatibility with other naming conventions, each character set can have a number of aliases. For example, ISO 8859-1 has aliases

```
ISO8859-1
ISO_8859_1
ISO8859_1
```

```
ISO_8859-1
ISO_8859-1:1987
8859_1
latin1
l1
csISOLatin1
iso-ir-100
cp819
IBM819
IBM-819
819
```

The `aliases` method returns a `Set` of the aliases. Here is the code to iterate through the aliases:

```
Set<String> aliases = cset.aliases();
for (String alias : aliases)
    System.out.println(alias);
```

Character set names are case-insensitive.

To obtain a `Charset`, call the static `forName` method with either the official name or one of its aliases:

```
Charset cset = Charset.forName("ISO-8859-1");
```

---

 **NOTE:** An excellent reference for the "ISO 8859 alphabet soup" is http://czyborra.com/charsets/iso8859.html.

---

To find out which character sets are available in a particular implementation, call the static `availableCharsets` method. Use this code to find out the names of all available character sets:

```
Map<String, Charset> charsets = Charset.availableCharsets();
for (String name : charsets.keySet())
    System.out.println(name);
```

Table 1.1 lists the character encodings that every Java implementation is required to have. Table 1.2 lists the encoding schemes that the Java Development Kit (JDK) installs by default. The character sets in Table 1.3 are installed only on operating systems that use non-European languages.

Local encoding schemes cannot represent all Unicode characters. If a character cannot be represented, it is transformed to a ?.

Once you have a character set, you can use it to convert between Java strings (which contain Unicode code units) and encoded byte sequences. Here is how you encode a Java string:

**Table 1.1** Required Character Encodings

| Charset Standard Name | Legacy Name | Description |
|---|---|---|
| US-ASCII | ASCII | American Standard Code for Information Interchange |
| ISO-8859-1 | ISO8859_1 | ISO 8859-1, Latin alphabet No. 1 |
| UTF-8 | UTF8 | Eight-bit Unicode Transformation Format |
| UTF-16 | UTF-16 | Sixteen-bit Unicode Transformation Format, byte order specified by an optional initial byte-order mark |
| UTF-16BE | UnicodeBigUnmarked | Sixteen-bit Unicode Transformation Format, big-endian byte order |
| UTF-16LE | UnicodeLittleUnmarked | Sixteen-bit Unicode Transformation Format, little-endian byte order |

**Table 1.2** Basic Character Encodings

| Charset Standard Name | Legacy Name | Description |
|---|---|---|
| ISO8859-2 | ISO8859_2 | ISO 8859-2, Latin alphabet No. 2 |
| ISO8859-4 | ISO8859_4 | ISO 8859-4, Latin alphabet No. 4 |
| ISO8859-5 | ISO8859_5 | ISO 8859-5, Latin/Cyrillic alphabet |
| ISO8859-7 | ISO8859_7 | ISO 8859-7, Latin/Greek alphabet |
| ISO8859-9 | ISO8859_9 | ISO 8859-9, Latin alphabet No. 5 |
| ISO8859-13 | ISO8859_13 | ISO 8859-13, Latin alphabet No. 7 |
| ISO8859-15 | ISO8859_15 | ISO 8859-15, Latin alphabet No. 9 |
| windows-1250 | Cp1250 | Windows Eastern European |
| windows-1251 | Cp1251 | Windows Cyrillic |
| windows-1252 | Cp1252 | Windows Latin-1 |
| windows-1253 | Cp1253 | Windows Greek |
| windows-1254 | Cp1254 | Windows Turkish |
| windows-1257 | Cp1257 | Windows Baltic |

**Table 1.3** Extended Character Encodings

| Charset Standard Name | Legacy Name | Description |
| --- | --- | --- |
| Big5 | Big5 | Big5, Traditional Chinese |
| Big5-HKSCS | Big5_HKSCS | Big5 with Hong Kong extensions, Traditional Chinese |
| EUC-JP | EUC_JP | JIS X 0201, 0208, 0212, EUC encoding, Japanese |
| EUC-KR | EUC_KR | KS C 5601, EUC encoding, Korean |
| GB18030 | GB18030 | Simplified Chinese, PRC Standard |
| GBK | GBK | GBK, Simplified Chinese |
| ISCII91 | ISCII91 | ISCII91 encoding of Indic scripts |
| ISO-2022-JP | ISO2022JP | JIS X 0201, 0208 in ISO 2022 form, Japanese |
| ISO-2022-KR | ISO2022KR | ISO 2022 KR, Korean |
| ISO8859-3 | ISO8859_3 | ISO 8859-3, Latin alphabet No. 3 |
| ISO8859-6 | ISO8859_6 | ISO 8859-6, Latin/Arabic alphabet |
| ISO8859-8 | ISO8859_8 | ISO 8859-8, Latin/Hebrew alphabet |
| Shift_JIS | SJIS | Shift-JIS, Japanese |
| TIS-620 | TIS620 | TIS620, Thai |
| windows-1255 | Cp1255 | Windows Hebrew |
| windows-1256 | Cp1256 | Windows Arabic |
| windows-1258 | Cp1258 | Windows Vietnamese |
| windows-31j | MS932 | Windows Japanese |
| x-EUC-CN | EUC_CN | GB2312, EUC encoding, Simplified Chinese |
| x-EUC-JP-LINUX | EUC_JP_LINUX | JIS X 0201, 0208, EUC encoding, Japanese |
| x-EUC-TW | EUC_TW | CNS11643 (Plane 1–3), EUC encoding, Traditional Chinese |
| x-MS950-HKSCS | MS950_HKSCS | Windows Traditional Chinese with Hong Kong extensions |
| x-mswin-936 | MS936 | Windows Simplified Chinese |
| x-windows-949 | MS949 | Windows Korean |
| x-windows-950 | MS950 | Windows Traditional Chinese |

```
String str = . . .;
ByteBuffer buffer = cset.encode(str);
byte[] bytes = buffer.array();
```

Conversely, to decode a byte sequence, you need a byte buffer. Use the static `wrap` method of the `ByteBuffer` class to turn a byte array into a byte buffer. The result of the `decode` method is a `CharBuffer`. Call its `toString` method to get a string.

```
byte[] bytes = . . .;
ByteBuffer bbuf = ByteBuffer.wrap(bytes, offset, length);
CharBuffer cbuf = cset.decode(bbuf);
String str = cbuf.toString();
```

---

**java.nio.charset.Charset** 1.4

- static SortedMap availableCharsets()
  gets all available character sets for this virtual machine. Returns a map whose keys are character set names and whose values are character sets.

- static Charset forName(String name)
  gets a character set for the given name.

- Set aliases()
  returns the set of alias names for this character set.

- ByteBuffer encode(String str)
  encodes the given string into a sequence of bytes.

- CharBuffer decode(ByteBuffer buffer)
  decodes the given byte sequence. Unrecognized inputs are converted to the Unicode "replacement character" ('\uFFFD').

---

**java.nio.ByteBuffer** 1.4

- byte[] array()
  returns the array of bytes that this buffer manages.

- static ByteBuffer wrap(byte[] bytes)
- static ByteBuffer wrap(byte[] bytes, int offset, int length)
  returns a byte buffer that manages the given array of bytes or the given range.

---

**java.nio.CharBuffer**

- char[] array()
  returns the array of code units that this buffer manages.

*(Continues)*

---

**java.nio.CharBuffer** *(Continued)*

---

- char charAt(int index)

  returns the code unit at the given index.

- String toString()

  returns a string consisting of the code units that this buffer manages.

---

## 1.3 Reading and Writing Binary Data

The DataOutput interface defines the following methods for writing a number, a character, a boolean value, or a string in binary format:

```
writeChars
writeByte
writeInt
writeShort
writeLong
writeFloat
writeDouble
writeChar
writeBoolean
writeUTF
```

For example, writeInt always writes an integer as a 4-byte binary quantity regardless of the number of digits, and writeDouble always writes a double as an 8-byte binary quantity. The resulting output is not human-readable, but the space needed will be the same for each value of a given type and reading it back in will be faster than parsing text.

 **NOTE:** There are two different methods of storing integers and floating-point numbers in memory, depending on the processor you are using. Suppose, for example, you are working with a 4-byte int, say the decimal number 1234, or 4D2 in hexadecimal (1234 = 4 × 256 + 13 × 16 + 2). This value can be stored in such a way that the first of the four bytes in memory holds the most significant byte (MSB) of the value: 00 00 04 D2. This is the so-called big-endian method. Or, we can start with the least significant byte (LSB) first: D2 04 00 00. This is called, naturally enough, the little-endian method. For example, the SPARC uses big-endian; the Pentium, little-endian. This can lead to problems. When a C or C++ file is saved, the data are saved exactly as the processor stores them. That makes it challenging to move even the simplest data files from one platform to another. In Java, all values are written in the big-endian fashion, regardless of the processor. That makes Java data files platform-independent.

**Table 1.4** UTF-8 Encoding

| Character Range | Encoding |
|---|---|
| 0...7F | $0a_6a_5a_4a_3a_2a_1a_0$ |
| 80...7FF | $110a_{10}a_9a_8a_7a_6 \; 10a_5a_4a_3a_2a_1a_0$ |
| 800...FFFF | $1110a_{15}a_{14}a_{13}a_{12} \; 10a_{11}a_{10}a_9a_8a_7a_6 \; 10a_5a_4a_3a_2a_1a_0$ |
| 10000...10FFFF | $11110a_{20}a_{19}a_{18} \; 10a_{17}a_{16}a_{15}a_{14}a_{13}a_{12} \; 10a_{11}a_{10}a_9a_8a_7a_6 \; 10a_5a_4a_3a_2a_1a_0$ |

**Table 1.5** UTF-16 Encoding

| Character Range | Encoding |
|---|---|
| 0...FFFF | $a_{15}a_{14}a_{13}a_{12}a_{11}a_{10}a_9a_8 \; a_7a_6a_5a_4a_3a_2a_1a_0$ |
| 10000...10FFFF | $110110b_{19}b_{18} \; b_{17}b_{16}a_{15}a_{14}a_{13}a_{12}a_{11}a_{10} \; 110111a_9a_8 \; a_7a_6a_5a_4a_3a_2a_1a_0$ <br> where $b_{19}b_{18}b_{17}b_{16} = a_{20}a_{19}a_{18}a_{17}a_{16} - 1$ |

The writeUTF method writes string data using a modified version of 8-bit Unicode Transformation Format. Instead of simply using the standard UTF-8 encoding (which is shown in Table 1.4), sequences of Unicode code units are first represented in UTF-16 (see Table 1.5) and then the result is encoded using the UTF-8 rules. This modified encoding is different for characters with codes higher than 0xFFFF. It is used for backward compatibility with virtual machines that were built when Unicode had not yet grown beyond 16 bits.

Since nobody else uses this modification of UTF-8, you should only use the writeUTF method to write strings intended for a Java virtual machine—for example, in a program that generates bytecodes. Use the writeChars method for other purposes.

 **NOTE:** See RFC 2279 (http://ietf.org/rfc/rfc2279.txt) and RFC 2781 (http://ietf.org/rfc/rfc2781.txt) for definitions of UTF-8 and UTF-16.

To read the data back in, use the following methods defined in the DataInput interface:

```
readInt
readShort
readLong
readFloat
```

```
readDouble
readChar
readBoolean
readUTF
```

The `DataInputStream` class implements the `DataInput` interface. To read binary data from a file, combine a `DataInputStream` with a source of bytes such as a `FileInputStream`:

```
DataInputStream in = new DataInputStream(new FileInputStream("employee.dat"));
```

Similarly, to write binary data, use the `DataOutputStream` class that implements the `DataOutput` interface:

```
DataOutputStream out = new DataOutputStream(new FileOutputStream("employee.dat"));
```

---

### *java.io.DataInput* 1.0

- `boolean readBoolean()`
- `byte readByte()`
- `char readChar()`
- `double readDouble()`
- `float readFloat()`
- `int readInt()`
- `long readLong()`
- `short readShort()`
  reads in a value of the given type.
- `void readFully(byte[] b)`
  reads bytes into the array b, blocking until all bytes are read.

  *Parameters:*    b        The buffer into which the data are read
- `void readFully(byte[] b, int off, int len)`
  reads bytes into the array b, blocking until all bytes are read.

  *Parameters:*    b        The buffer into which the data are read

  off      The start offset of the data

  len      The maximum number of bytes to read
- `String readUTF()`
  reads a string of characters in the "modified UTF-8" format.
- `int skipBytes(int n)`
  skips n bytes, blocking until all bytes are skipped.

  *Parameters:*    n        The number of bytes to be skipped

---

---

**java.io.DataOutput  1.0**

- void writeBoolean(boolean b)
- void writeByte(int b)
- void writeChar(int c)
- void writeDouble(double d)
- void writeFloat(float f)
- void writeInt(int i)
- void writeLong(long l)
- void writeShort(int s)

  writes a value of the given type.

- void writeChars(String s)

  writes all characters in the string.

- void writeUTF(String s)

  writes a string of characters in the "modified UTF-8" format.

---

## 1.3.1  Random-Access Files

The RandomAccessFile class lets you read or write data anywhere in a file. Disk files are random-access, but streams of data from a network are not. You can open a random-access file either for reading only or for both reading and writing; specify the option by using the string "r" (for read access) or "rw" (for read/write access) as the second argument in the constructor.

```
RandomAccessFile in = new RandomAccessFile("employee.dat", "r");
RandomAccessFile inOut = new RandomAccessFile("employee.dat", "rw");
```

When you open an existing file as a RandomAccessFile, it does not get deleted.

A random-access file has a *file pointer* that indicates the position of the next byte to be read or written. The seek method sets the file pointer to an arbitrary byte position within the file. The argument to seek is a long integer between zero and the length of the file in bytes.

The getFilePointer method returns the current position of the file pointer.

The RandomAccessFile class implements both the DataInput and DataOutput interfaces. To read and write from a random-access file, use methods such as readInt/writeInt and readChar/writeChar that we discussed in the preceding section.

Let's walk through an example program that stores employee records in a random-access file. Each record will have the same size. This makes it easy to read an arbitrary record. Suppose you want to position the file pointer to the third record. Simply set the file pointer to the appropriate byte position and start reading.

```
long n = 3;
in.seek((n - 1) * RECORD_SIZE);
Employee e = new Employee();
e.readData(in);
```

If you want to modify the record and save it back into the same location, remember to set the file pointer back to the beginning of the record:

```
in.seek((n - 1) * RECORD_SIZE);
e.writeData(out);
```

To determine the total number of bytes in a file, use the length method. The total number of records is the length divided by the size of each record.

```
long nbytes = in.length(); // length in bytes
int nrecords = (int) (nbytes / RECORD_SIZE);
```

Integers and floating-point values have a fixed size in binary format, but we have to work harder for strings. We provide two helper methods to write and read strings of a fixed size.

The writeFixedString writes the specified number of code units, starting at the beginning of the string. If there are too few code units, the method pads the string, using zero values.

```
public static void writeFixedString(String s, int size, DataOutput out)
   throws IOException
{
   for (int i = 0; i < size; i++)
   {
      char ch = 0;
      if (i < s.length()) ch = s.charAt(i);
      out.writeChar(ch);
   }
}
```

The readFixedString method reads characters from the input stream until it has consumed size code units or until it encounters a character with a zero value. Then, it skips past the remaining zero values in the input field. For added efficiency, this method uses the StringBuilder class to read in a string.

```
public static String readFixedString(int size, DataInput in)
   throws IOException
{
   StringBuilder b = new StringBuilder(size);
   int i = 0;
   boolean more = true;
   while (more && i < size)
   {
      char ch = in.readChar();
      i++;
      if (ch == 0) more = false;
      else b.append(ch);
   }
   in.skipBytes(2 * (size - i));
   return b.toString();
}
```

We placed the `writeFixedString` and `readFixedString` methods inside the `DataIO` helper class.

To write a fixed-size record, we simply write all fields in binary.

```
DataIO.writeFixedString(e.getName(), Employee.NAME_SIZE, out);
out.writeDouble(e.getSalary());
GregorianCalendar calendar = new GregorianCalendar();
calendar.setTime(e.getHireDay());
out.writeInt(calendar.get(Calendar.YEAR));
out.writeInt(calendar.get(Calendar.MONTH) + 1);
out.writeInt(calendar.get(Calendar.DAY_OF_MONTH));
```

Reading the data back is just as simple.

```
String name = DataIO.readFixedString(Employee.NAME_SIZE, in);
double salary = in.readDouble();
int y = in.readInt();
int m = in.readInt();
int d = in.readInt();
```

Let us compute the size of each record. We will use 40 characters for the name strings. Therefore, each record contains 100 bytes:

- 40 characters = 80 bytes for the name
- 1 `double` = 8 bytes for the salary
- 3 `int` = 12 bytes for the date

The program shown in Listing 1.2 writes three records into a data file and then reads them from the file in reverse order. To do this efficiently requires random access—we need to get at the last record first.

**Listing 1.2** randomAccess/RandomAccessTest.java

```
1  package randomAccess;
2
3  import java.io.*;
4  import java.util.*;
5  /**
6   * @version 1.12 2012-05-30
7   * @author Cay Horstmann
8   */
9  public class RandomAccessTest
10 {
11    public static void main(String[] args) throws IOException
12    {
13       Employee[] staff = new Employee[3];
14
15       staff[0] = new Employee("Carl Cracker", 75000, 1987, 12, 15);
16       staff[1] = new Employee("Harry Hacker", 50000, 1989, 10, 1);
17       staff[2] = new Employee("Tony Tester", 40000, 1990, 3, 15);
18
19       try (DataOutputStream out = new DataOutputStream(new FileOutputStream("employee.dat")))
20       {
21          // save all employee records to the file employee.dat
22          for (Employee e : staff)
23             writeData(out, e);
24       }
25
26       try (RandomAccessFile in = new RandomAccessFile("employee.dat", "r"))
27       {
28          // retrieve all records into a new array
29
30          // compute the array size
31          int n = (int)(in.length() / Employee.RECORD_SIZE);
32          Employee[] newStaff = new Employee[n];
33
34          // read employees in reverse order
35          for (int i = n - 1; i >= 0; i--)
36          {
37             newStaff[i] = new Employee();
38             in.seek(i * Employee.RECORD_SIZE);
39             newStaff[i] = readData(in);
40          }
41
42          // print the newly read employee records
43          for (Employee e : newStaff)
44             System.out.println(e);
45       }
46    }
```

*(Continues)*

**Listing 1.2** *(Continued)*

```
47   /**
48      Writes employee data to a data output.
49      @param out the data output
50      @param e the employee
51   */
52   public static void writeData(DataOutput out, Employee e) throws IOException
53   {
54      DataIO.writeFixedString(e.getName(), Employee.NAME_SIZE, out);
55      out.writeDouble(e.getSalary());
56
57      GregorianCalendar calendar = new GregorianCalendar();
58      calendar.setTime(e.getHireDay());
59      out.writeInt(calendar.get(Calendar.YEAR));
60      out.writeInt(calendar.get(Calendar.MONTH) + 1);
61      out.writeInt(calendar.get(Calendar.DAY_OF_MONTH));
62   }
63
64   /**
65      Reads employee data from a data input.
66      @param in the data input
67      @return the employee
68   */
69   public static Employee readData(DataInput in) throws IOException
70   {
71      String name = DataIO.readFixedString(Employee.NAME_SIZE, in);
72      double salary = in.readDouble();
73      int y = in.readInt();
74      int m = in.readInt();
75      int d = in.readInt();
76      return new Employee(name, salary, y, m - 1, d);
77   }
78 }
```

---

**java.io.RandomAccessFile 1.0**

- RandomAccessFile(String file, String mode)
- RandomAccessFile(File file, String mode)

| | | |
|---|---|---|
| *Parameters:* | file | The file to be opened |
| | mode | "r" for read-only mode, "rw" for read/write mode, "rws" for read/write mode with synchronous disk writes of data and metadata for every update, and "rwd" for read/write mode with synchronous disk writes of data only |

*(Continues)*

---

**java.io.RandomAccessFile**  1.0  *(Continued)*

---

- `long getFilePointer()`
  returns the current location of the file pointer.
- `void seek(long pos)`
  sets the file pointer to `pos` bytes from the beginning of the file.
- `long length()`
  returns the length of the file in bytes.

---

# 1.4  ZIP Archives

ZIP archives store one or more files in (usually) compressed format. Each ZIP archive has a header with information such as the name of each file and the compression method that was used. In Java, you can use a `ZipInputStream` to read a ZIP archive. You need to look at the individual *entries* in the archive. The `getNextEntry` method returns an object of type `ZipEntry` that describes the entry. The `read` method of the `ZipInputStream` is modified to return -1 at the end of the current entry (instead of just at the end of the ZIP file). You must then call `closeEntry` to read the next entry. Here is a typical code sequence to read through a ZIP file:

```
ZipInputStream zin = new ZipInputStream(new FileInputStream(zipname));
ZipEntry entry;
while ((entry = zin.getNextEntry()) != null)
{
   analyze entry
   read the contents of zin
   zin.closeEntry();
}
zin.close();
```

To read the contents of a ZIP entry, you will rarely want to use the raw `read` method; usually, you will use the methods of a more competent stream filter. For example, to read a text file inside a ZIP file, use the following loop:

```
Scanner in = new Scanner(zin);
while (in.hasNextLine())
   do something with in.nextLine()
```

---

 **CAUTION:** Do not close the ZIP input stream after reading a single ZIP entry, and don't pass it to a method that would close it. Otherwise, you won't be able to read subsequent entries.

---

To write a ZIP file, use a `ZipOutputStream`. For each entry that you want to place into the ZIP file, create a `ZipEntry` object. Pass the file name to the `ZipEntry` constructor; it sets the other parameters such as file date and decompression method. You can override these settings if you like. Then, call the `putNextEntry` method of the `ZipOutputStream` to begin writing a new file. Send the file data to the ZIP stream. When you are done, call `closeEntry`. Repeat for all the files you want to store. Here is a code skeleton:

```
FileOutputStream fout = new FileOutputStream("test.zip");
ZipOutputStream zout = new ZipOutputStream(fout);
for all files
{
    ZipEntry ze = new ZipEntry(filename);
    zout.putNextEntry(ze);
    send data to zout
    zout.closeEntry();
}
zout.close();
```

**NOTE:** JAR files (which were discussed in Volume I, Chapter 10) are simply ZIP files with a special entry, the so-called manifest. Use the `JarInputStream` and `JarOutputStream` classes to read and write the manifest entry.

ZIP streams are a good example of the power of the stream abstraction. When you read data stored in compressed form, you don't need to worry that the data are being decompressed as they are being requested. Moreover, the source of the bytes in a ZIP stream need not be a file—the ZIP data can come from a network connection. In fact, whenever the class loader of an applet reads a JAR file, it reads and decompresses data from the network.

**NOTE:** Section 1.6.7, "ZIP File Systems," on p. 67 shows how to access a ZIP archive without a special API, using the `FileSystem` class of Java SE 7.

---

`java.util.zip.ZipInputStream`  1.1

- `ZipInputStream(InputStream in)`
  creates a `ZipInputStream` that allows you to inflate data from the given `InputStream`.

- `ZipEntry getNextEntry()`
  returns a `ZipEntry` object for the next entry, or `null` if there are no more entries.

- `void closeEntry()`
  closes the current open entry in the ZIP file. You can then read the next entry by using `getNextEntry()`.

---

### java.util.zip.ZipOutputStream 1.1

- ZipOutputStream(OutputStream out)

  creates a ZipOutputStream that you can use to write compressed data to the specified OutputStream.

- void putNextEntry(ZipEntry ze)

  writes the information in the given ZipEntry to the stream and positions the stream for the data. The data can then be written to the stream by write().

- void closeEntry()

  closes the currently open entry in the ZIP file. Use the putNextEntry method to start the next entry.

- void setLevel(int level)

  sets the default compression level of subsequent DEFLATED entries. The default value is Deflater.DEFAULT_COMPRESSION. Throws an IllegalArgumentException if the level is not valid.

  *Parameters:*   level   A compression level, from 0 (NO_COMPRESSION) to 9 (BEST_COMPRESSION)

- void setMethod(int method)

  sets the default compression method for this ZipOutputStream for any entries that do not specify a method.

  *Parameters:*   method   The compression method, either DEFLATED or STORED

---

### java.util.zip.ZipEntry 1.1

- ZipEntry(String name)

  constructs a zip entry with a given name.

  *Parameters:*   name   The name of the entry

- long getCrc()

  returns the CRC32 checksum value for this ZipEntry.

- String getName()

  returns the name of this entry.

- long getSize()

  returns the uncompressed size of this entry, or -1 if the uncompressed size is not known.

- boolean isDirectory()

  returns true if this entry is a directory.

- void setMethod(int method)

  *Parameters:*   method   The compression method for the entry; must be either DEFLATED or STORED

*(Continues)*

---

**java.util.zip.ZipEntry** 1.1 *(Continued)*

- void setSize(long size)
  sets the size of this entry. Only required if the compression method is STORED.

  *Parameters:*  size  The uncompressed size of this entry

- void setCrc(long crc)
  sets the CRC32 checksum of this entry. Use the CRC32 class to compute this checksum. Only required if the compression method is STORED.

  *Parameters:*  crc  The checksum of this entry

---

**java.util.zip.ZipFile** 1.1

- ZipFile(String name)
- ZipFile(File file)
  creates a ZipFile for reading from the given string or File object.

- Enumeration entries()
  returns an Enumeration object that enumerates the ZipEntry objects that describe the entries of the ZipFile.

- ZipEntry getEntry(String name)
  returns the entry corresponding to the given name, or null if there is no such entry.

  *Parameters:*  name  The entry name

- InputStream getInputStream(ZipEntry ze)
  returns an InputStream for the given entry.

  *Parameters:*  ze  A ZipEntry in the ZIP file

- String getName()
  returns the path of this ZIP file.

---

# 1.5 Object Streams and Serialization

Using a fixed-length record format is a good choice if you need to store data of the same type. However, objects that you create in an object-oriented program are rarely all of the same type. For example, you might have an array called staff that is nominally an array of Employee records but contains objects that are actually instances of a subclass such as Manager.

It is certainly possible to come up with a data format that allows you to store such polymorphic collections—but fortunately, we don't have to. The Java language supports a very general mechanism, called *object serialization*, that makes it possible to write any object to a stream and read it again later. (You will see later in this chapter where the term "serialization" comes from.)

To save object data, you first need to open an ObjectOutputStream object:

```
ObjectOutputStream out = new ObjectOutputStream(new FileOutputStream("employee.dat"));
```

Now, to save an object, simply use the writeObject method of the ObjectOutputStream class as in the following fragment:

```
Employee harry = new Employee("Harry Hacker", 50000, 1989, 10, 1);
Manager boss = new Manager("Carl Cracker", 80000, 1987, 12, 15);
out.writeObject(harry);
out.writeObject(boss);
```

To read the objects back in, first get an ObjectInputStream object:

```
ObjectInputStream in = new ObjectInputStream(new FileInputStream("employee.dat"));
```

Then, retrieve the objects in the same order in which they were written, using the readObject method.

```
Employee e1 = (Employee) in.readObject();
Employee e2 = (Employee) in.readObject();
```

There is, however, one change you need to make to any class that you want to save to and restore from an object stream. The class must implement the Serializable interface:

```
class Employee implements Serializable { . . . }
```

The Serializable interface has no methods, so you don't need to change your classes in any way. In this regard, it is similar to the Cloneable interface that we discussed in Volume I, Chapter 6. However, to make a class cloneable, you still had to override the clone method of the Object class. To make a class serializable, you do not need to do anything else.

 **NOTE:** You can write and read only *objects* with the writeObject/readObject methods. For primitive type values, use methods such as writeInt/readInt or writeDouble/readDouble. (The object stream classes implement the DataInput/DataOutput interfaces.)

Behind the scenes, an ObjectOutputStream looks at all the fields of the objects and saves their contents. For example, when writing an Employee object, the name, date, and salary fields are written to the output stream.

However, there is one important situation that we need to consider: What happens when one object is shared by several objects as part of its state?

To illustrate the problem, let us make a slight modification to the `Manager` class. Let's assume that each manager has a secretary:

```
class Manager extends Employee
{
   private Employee secretary;
   . . .
}
```

Each `Manager` object now contains a reference to the `Employee` object that describes the secretary. Of course, two managers can share the same secretary, as is the case in Figure 1.5 and the following code:

```
harry = new Employee("Harry Hacker", . . .);
Manager carl = new Manager("Carl Cracker", . . .);
carl.setSecretary(harry);
Manager tony = new Manager("Tony Tester", . . .);
tony.setSecretary(harry);
```

Saving such a network of objects is a challenge. Of course, we cannot save and restore the memory addresses for the secretary objects. When an object is reloaded, it will likely occupy a completely different memory address than it originally did.

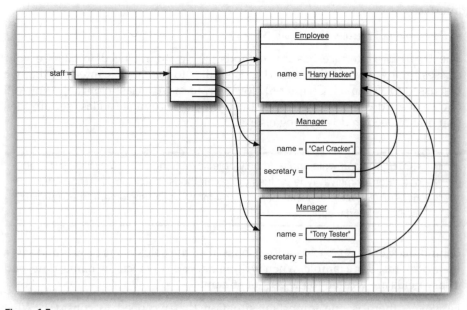

**Figure 1.5** Two managers can share a mutual employee.

Instead, each object is saved with a *serial number*, hence the name *object serialization* for this mechanism. Here is the algorithm:

1.  Associate a serial number with each object reference that you encounter (as shown in Figure 1.6).

2.  When encountering an object reference for the first time, save the object data to the stream.

3.  If it has been saved previously, just write "same as the previously saved object with serial number *x*."

When reading back the objects, the procedure is reversed.

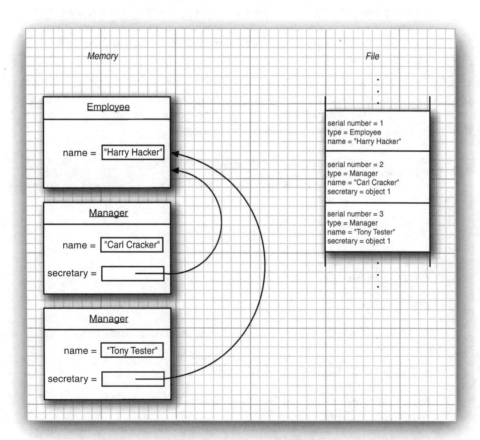

**Figure 1.6** An example of object serialization

1. When an object is specified in the stream for the first time, construct it, initialize it with the stream data, and remember the association between the serial number and the object reference.

2. When the tag "same as the previously saved object with serial number $x$" is encountered, retrieve the object reference for the sequence number.

 **NOTE:** In this chapter, we will use serialization to save a collection of objects to a disk file and retrieve it exactly as we stored it. Another very important application is the transmittal of a collection of objects across a network connection to another computer. Just as raw memory addresses are meaningless in a file, they are also meaningless when communicating with a different processor. By replacing memory addresses with serial numbers, serialization permits the transport of object collections from one machine to another. We study that use of serialization when discussing remote method invocation in Chapter 5.

Listing 1.3 is a program that saves and reloads a network of Employee and Manager objects (some of which share the same employee as a secretary). Note that the secretary object is unique after reloading—when newStaff[1] gets a raise, that is reflected in the secretary fields of the managers.

**Listing 1.3** objectStream/ObjectStreamTest.java

```
1   package objectStream;
2
3   import java.io.*;
4
5   /**
6    * @version 1.10 17 Aug 1998
7    * @author Cay Horstmann
8    */
9   class ObjectStreamTest
10  {
11     public static void main(String[] args) throws IOException, ClassNotFoundException
12     {
13        Employee harry = new Employee("Harry Hacker", 50000, 1989, 10, 1);
14        Manager carl = new Manager("Carl Cracker", 80000, 1987, 12, 15);
15        carl.setSecretary(harry);
16        Manager tony = new Manager("Tony Tester", 40000, 1990, 3, 15);
17        tony.setSecretary(harry);
18
19        Employee[] staff = new Employee[3];
```

```
20      staff[0] = carl;
21      staff[1] = harry;
22      staff[2] = tony;
23
24      // save all employee records to the file employee.dat
25      try (ObjectOutputStream out = new ObjectOutputStream(new FileOutputStream("employee.dat")))
26      {
27         out.writeObject(staff);
28      }
29
30      try (ObjectInputStream in = new ObjectInputStream(new FileInputStream("employee.dat")))
31      {
32         // retrieve all records into a new array
33
34         Employee[] newStaff = (Employee[]) in.readObject();
35
36         // raise secretary's salary
37         newStaff[1].raiseSalary(10);
38
39         // print the newly read employee records
40         for (Employee e : newStaff)
41            System.out.println(e);
42      }
43   }
44 }
```

---

**java.io.ObjectOutputStream** 1.1

- ObjectOutputStream(OutputStream out)
  creates an ObjectOutputStream so that you can write objects to the specified OutputStream.

- void writeObject(Object obj)
  writes the specified object to the ObjectOutputStream. This method saves the class of the object, the signature of the class, and the values of any nonstatic, nontransient fields of the class and its superclasses.

---

**java.io.ObjectInputStream** 1.1

- ObjectInputStream(InputStream in)
  creates an ObjectInputStream to read back object information from the specified InputStream.

*(Continues)*

---

`java.io.ObjectInputStream`   **1.1**   *(Continued)*

- `Object readObject()`
  reads an object from the `ObjectInputStream`. In particular, this method reads back the class of the object, the signature of the class, and the values of the nontransient and nonstatic fields of the class and all its superclasses. It does deserializing to allow multiple object references to be recovered.

---

## 1.5.1  Understanding the Object Serialization File Format

Object serialization saves object data in a particular file format. Of course, you can use the `writeObject`/`readObject` methods without having to know the exact sequence of bytes that represents objects in a file. Nonetheless, we found studying the data format extremely helpful for gaining insight into the object streaming process. As the details are somewhat technical, feel free to skip this section if you are not interested in the implementation.

Every file begins with the two-byte "magic number"

```
AC ED
```

followed by the version number of the object serialization format, which is currently

```
00 05
```

(We use hexadecimal numbers throughout this section to denote bytes.) Then, it contains a sequence of objects, in the order in which they were saved.

String objects are saved as

| 74 | two-byte length | characters |

For example, the string "Harry" is saved as

```
74 00 05 Harry
```

The Unicode characters of the string are saved in the "modified UTF-8" format.

When an object is saved, the class of that object must be saved as well. The class description contains

- The name of the class
- The *serial version unique ID*, which is a fingerprint of the data field types and method signatures
- A set of flags describing the serialization method
- A description of the data fields

The fingerprint is obtained by ordering the descriptions of the class, superclass, interfaces, field types, and method signatures in a canonical way, and then applying the so-called Secure Hash Algorithm (SHA) to that data.

SHA is a fast algorithm that gives a "fingerprint" to a larger block of information. This fingerprint is always a 20-byte data packet, regardless of the size of the original data. It is created by a clever sequence of bit operations on the data that makes it essentially 100 percent certain that the fingerprint will change if the information is altered in any way. (For more details on SHA, see, for example, *Cryptography and Network Security, Fifth Edition*, by William Stallings, Prentice Hall, 2011.) However, the serialization mechanism uses only the first eight bytes of the SHA code as a class fingerprint. It is still very likely that the class fingerprint will change if the data fields or methods change.

When reading an object, its fingerprint is compared against the current fingerprint of the class. If they don't match, it means the class definition has changed after the object was written, and an exception is generated. Of course, in practice, classes do evolve, and it might be necessary for a program to read in older versions of objects. We will discuss this in Section 1.5.4, "Versioning," on p. 52.

Here is how a class identifier is stored:

72
2-byte length of class name
Class name
8-byte fingerprint
1-byte flag
2-byte count of data field descriptors
Data field descriptors
78 (end marker)
Superclass type (70 if none)

The flag byte is composed of three bit masks, defined in `java.io.ObjectStreamConstants`:

```
static final byte SC_WRITE_METHOD = 1;
   // class has a writeObject method that writes additional data
static final byte SC_SERIALIZABLE = 2;
   // class implements the Serializable interface
static final byte SC_EXTERNALIZABLE = 4;
   // class implements the Externalizable interface
```

We discuss the Externalizable interface later in this chapter. Externalizable classes supply custom read and write methods that take over the output of their instance fields. The classes that we write implement the Serializable interface and will have a flag value of 02. The serializable java.util.Date class defines its own readObject/writeObject methods and has a flag of 03.

Each data field descriptor has the format:

1-byte type code

2-byte length of field name

Field name

Class name (if the field is an object)

The type code is one of the following:

| | |
|---|---|
| B | byte |
| C | char |
| D | double |
| F | float |
| I | int |
| J | long |
| L | object |
| S | short |
| Z | boolean |
| [ | array |

When the type code is L, the field name is followed by the field type. Class and field name strings do not start with the string code 74, but field types do. Field types use a slightly different encoding of their names—namely, the format used by native methods.

For example, the salary field of the Employee class is encoded as:

```
D 00 06 salary
```

Here is the complete class descriptor of the Employee class:

```
72 00 08 Employee
      E6 D2 86 7D AE AC 18 1B 02          Fingerprint and flags
      00 03                               Number of instance fields
      D 00 06 salary                      Instance field type and name
      L 00 07 hireDay                     Instance field type and name
      74 00 10 Ljava/util/Date;           Instance field class name: Date
      L 00 04 name                        Instance field type and name
      74 00 12 Ljava/lang/String;         Instance field class name: String
      78                                  End marker
      70                                  No superclass
```

These descriptors are fairly long. If the *same* class descriptor is needed again in the file, an abbreviated form is used:

> 71            4-byte serial number

The serial number refers to the previous explicit class descriptor. We discuss the numbering scheme later.

An object is stored as

> 73            class descriptor          object data

For example, here is how an Employee object is stored:

```
40 E8 6A 00 00 00 00 00               salary field value—double
73                                     hireDay field value: new object
      71 00 7E 00 08                   Existing class java.util.Date
      77 08 00 00 00 91 1B 4E B1 80 78 External storage (details later)
74 00 0C Harry Hacker                  name field value: String
```

As you can see, the data file contains enough information to restore the Employee object.

Arrays are saved in the following format:

> 75            class descriptor          4-byte number of          entries
>                                         entries

The array class name in the class descriptor is in the same format as that used by native methods (which is slightly different from the format used by class names in other class descriptors). In this format, class names start with an L and end with a semicolon.

For example, an array of three Employee objects starts out like this:

| | |
|---|---|
| 75 | Array |
| 72 00 0B [LEmployee; | New class, string length, class name Employee[] |
| FC BF 36 11 C5 91 11 C7 02 | Fingerprint and flags |
| 00 00 | Number of instance fields |
| 78 | End marker |
| 70 | No superclass |
| 00 00 00 03 | Number of array entries |

Note that the fingerprint for an array of Employee objects is different from a fingerprint of the Employee class itself.

All objects (including arrays and strings) and all class descriptors are given serial numbers as they are saved in the output file. The numbers start at 00 7E 00 00.

We already saw that a full class descriptor for any given class occurs only once. Subsequent descriptors refer to it. For example, in our previous example, a repeated reference to the Date class was coded as

```
71 00 7E 00 08
```

The same mechanism is used for objects. If a reference to a previously saved object is written, it is saved in exactly the same way; that is, 71 followed by the serial number. It is always clear from the context whether the particular serial reference denotes a class descriptor or an object.

Finally, a null reference is stored as

```
70
```

Here is the commented output of the ObjectRefTest program of the preceding section. Run the program, look at a hex dump of its data file employee.dat, and compare it with the commented listing. The important lines toward the end of the output show a reference to a previously saved object.

| | |
|---|---|
| AC ED 00 05 | File header |
| 75 | Array staff (serial #1) |
| 72 00 0B [LEmployee; | New class, string length, class name Employee[] (serial #0) |
| FC BF 36 11 C5 91 11 C7 02 | Fingerprint and flags |
| 00 00 | Number of instance fields |
| 78 | End marker |
| 70 | No superclass |
| 00 00 00 03 | Number of array entries |
| 73 | staff[0]—new object (serial #7) |
| 72 00 07 Manager | New class, string length, class name (serial #2) |
| 36 06 AE 13 63 8F 59 B7 02 | Fingerprint and flags |

| | |
|---|---|
| 00 01 | Number of data fields |
| L 00 09 secretary | Instance field type and name |
| 74 00 0A LEmployee; | Instance field class name: String (serial #3) |
| 78 | End marker |
| 72 00 08 Employee | Superclass: new class, string length, class name (serial #4) |
| E6 D2 86 7D AE AC 18 1B 02 | Fingerprint and flags |
| 00 03 | Number of instance fields |
| D 00 06 salary | Instance field type and name |
| L 00 07 hireDay | Instance field type and name |
| 74 00 10 Ljava/util/Date; | Instance field class name: String (serial #5) |
| L 00 04 name | Instance field type and name |
| 74 00 12 Ljava/lang/String; | Instance field class name: String (serial #6) |
| 78 | End marker |
| 70 | No superclass |
| 40 F3 88 00 00 00 00 00 | salary field value: double |
| 73 | hireDay field value: new object (serial #9) |
| 72 00 0E java.util.Date | New class, string length, class name (serial #8) |
| 68 6A 81 01 4B 59 74 19 03 | Fingerprint and flags |
| 00 00 | No instance variables |
| 78 | End marker |
| 70 | No superclass |
| 77 08 | External storage, number of bytes |
| 00 00 00 83 E9 39 E0 00 | Date |
| 78 | End marker |
| 74 00 0C Carl Cracker | name field value: String (serial #10) |
| 73 | secretary field value: new object (serial #11) |
| 71 00 7E 00 04 | existing class (use serial #4) |
| 40 E8 6A 00 00 00 00 00 | salary field value: double |
| 73 | hireDay field value: new object (serial #12) |
| 71 00 7E 00 08 | Existing class (use serial #8) |
| 77 08 | External storage, number of bytes |
| 00 00 00 91 1B 4E B1 80 | Date |
| 78 | End marker |
| 74 00 0C Harry Hacker | name field value: String (serial #13) |
| 71 00 7E 00 0B | staff[1]: existing object (use serial #11) |
| 73 | staff[2]: new object (serial #14) |
| 71 00 7E 00 02 | Existing class (use serial #2) |
| 40 E3 88 00 00 00 00 00 | salary field value: double |

| | |
|---|---|
| 73 | hireDay field value: new object (serial #15) |
| 71 00 7E 00 08 | Existing class (use serial #8) |
| 77 08 | External storage, number of bytes |
| 00 00 00 94 6D 3E EC 00 00 | Date |
| 78 | End marker |
| 74 00 0B Tony Tester | name field value: String (serial #16) |
| 71 00 7E 00 0B | secretary field value: existing object (use serial #11) |

Of course, studying these codes can be about as exciting as reading the average phone book. It is not important to know the exact file format (unless you are trying to create an evil effect by modifying the data), but it is still instructive to know that the object stream has a detailed description of all the objects that it contains, with sufficient detail to allow reconstruction of both objects and arrays of objects.

What you should remember is this:

- The object stream output contains the types and data fields of all objects.
- Each object is assigned a serial number.
- Repeated occurrences of the same object are stored as references to that serial number.

## 1.5.2 Modifying the Default Serialization Mechanism

Certain data fields should never be serialized—for example, integer values that store file handles or handles of windows that are only meaningful to native methods. Such information is guaranteed to be useless when you reload an object at a later time or transport it to a different machine. In fact, improper values for such fields can actually cause native methods to crash. Java has an easy mechanism to prevent such fields from ever being serialized. Mark them with the keyword transient. You also need to tag fields as transient if they belong to nonserializable classes. Transient fields are always skipped when objects are serialized.

The serialization mechanism provides a way for individual classes to add validation or any other desired action to the default read and write behavior. A serializable class can define methods with the signature

```
private void readObject(ObjectInputStream in)
    throws IOException, ClassNotFoundException;
private void writeObject(ObjectOutputStream out)
    throws IOException;
```

Then, the data fields are no longer automatically serialized, and these methods are called instead.

Here is a typical example. A number of classes in the java.awt.geom package, such as Point2D.Double, are not serializable. Now, suppose you want to serialize a class LabeledPoint that stores a String and a Point2D.Double. First, you need to mark the Point2D.Double field as transient to avoid a NotSerializableException.

```
public class LabeledPoint implements Serializable
{
    private String label;
    private transient Point2D.Double point;
    . . .
}
```

In the writeObject method, we first write the object descriptor and the String field, label, by calling the defaultWriteObject method. This is a special method of the ObjectOutputStream class that can only be called from within a writeObject method of a serializable class. Then we write the point coordinates, using the standard DataOutput calls.

```
private void writeObject(ObjectOutputStream out)
    throws IOException
{
    out.defaultWriteObject();
    out.writeDouble(point.getX());
    out.writeDouble(point.getY());
}
```

In the readObject method, we reverse the process:

```
private void readObject(ObjectInputStream in)
    throws IOException
{
    in.defaultReadObject();
    double x = in.readDouble();
    double y = in.readDouble();
    point = new Point2D.Double(x, y);
}
```

Another example is the java.util.Date class that supplies its own readObject and writeObject methods. These methods write the date as a number of milliseconds from the epoch (January 1, 1970, midnight UTC). The Date class has a complex internal representation that stores both a Calendar object and a millisecond count to optimize lookups. The state of the Calendar is redundant and does not have to be saved.

The readObject and writeObject methods only need to save and load their data fields. They should not concern themselves with superclass data or any other class information.

Instead of letting the serialization mechanism save and restore object data, a class can define its own mechanism. To do this, a class must implement the `Externalizable` interface. This, in turn, requires it to define two methods:

```
public void readExternal(ObjectInputStream in)
   throws IOException, ClassNotFoundException;
public void writeExternal(ObjectOutputStream out)
   throws IOException;
```

Unlike the `readObject` and `writeObject` methods that were described in the preceding section, these methods are fully responsible for saving and restoring the entire object, *including the superclass data*. The serialization mechanism merely records the class of the object in the stream. When reading an externalizable object, the object stream creates an object with the no-argument constructor and then calls the `readExternal` method. Here is how you can implement these methods for the `Employee` class:

```
public void readExternal(ObjectInput s)
   throws IOException
{
   name = s.readUTF();
   salary = s.readDouble();
   hireDay = new Date(s.readLong());
}

public void writeExternal(ObjectOutput s)
   throws IOException
{
  s.writeUTF(name);
  s.writeDouble(salary);
  s.writeLong(hireDay.getTime());
}
```

 **CAUTION:** Unlike the `readObject` and `writeObject` methods, which are private and can only be called by the serialization mechanism, the `readExternal` and `writeExternal` methods are public. In particular, `readExternal` potentially permits modification of the state of an existing object.

## 1.5.3 Serializing Singletons and Typesafe Enumerations

You have to pay particular attention to serializing and deserializing objects that are assumed to be unique. This commonly happens when you are implementing singletons and typesafe enumerations.

If you use the `enum` construct of the Java language, you need not worry about serialization—it just works. However, suppose you maintain legacy code that contains an enumerated type such as

```
public class Orientation
{
    public static final Orientation HORIZONTAL = new Orientation(1);
    public static final Orientation VERTICAL  = new Orientation(2);

    private int value;

    private Orientation(int v) { value = v; }
}
```

This idiom was common before enumerations were added to the Java language. Note that the constructor is private. Thus, no objects can be created beyond `Orientation.HORIZONTAL` and `Orientation.VERTICAL`. In particular, you can use the == operator to test for object equality:

```
if (orientation == Orientation.HORIZONTAL) . . .
```

There is an important twist that you need to remember when a typesafe enumeration implements the `Serializable` interface. The default serialization mechanism is not appropriate. Suppose we write a value of type `Orientation` and read it in again:

```
Orientation original = Orientation.HORIZONTAL;
ObjectOutputStream out = . . .;
out.write(original);
out.close();
ObjectInputStream in = . . .;
Orientation saved = (Orientation) in.read();
```

Now the test

```
if (saved == Orientation.HORIZONTAL) . . .
```

will fail. In fact, the `saved` value is a completely new object of the `Orientation` type that is not equal to any of the predefined constants. Even though the constructor is private, the serialization mechanism can create new objects!

To solve this problem, you need to define another special serialization method, called `readResolve`. If the `readResolve` method is defined, it is called after the object is deserialized. It must return an object which then becomes the return value of the `readObject` method. In our case, the `readResolve` method will inspect the `value` field and return the appropriate enumerated constant:

```
protected Object readResolve() throws ObjectStreamException
{
    if (value == 1) return Orientation.HORIZONTAL;
    if (value == 2) return Orientation.VERTICAL;
    return null; // this shouldn't happen
}
```

Remember to add a `readResolve` method to all typesafe enumerations in your legacy code and to all classes that follow the singleton design pattern.

## 1.5.4 Versioning

If you use serialization to save objects, you will need to consider what happens when your program evolves. Can version 1.1 read the old files? Can the users who still use 1.0 read the files that the new version is producing? Clearly, it would be desirable if object files could cope with the evolution of classes.

At first glance, it seems that this would not be possible. When a class definition changes in any way, its SHA fingerprint also changes, and you know that object streams will refuse to read in objects with different fingerprints. However, a class can indicate that it is *compatible* with an earlier version of itself. To do this, you must first obtain the fingerprint of the *earlier* version of the class. Use the stand-alone `serialver` program that is part of the JDK to obtain this number. For example, running

```
serialver Employee
```

prints

```
Employee: static final long serialVersionUID = -1814239825517340645L;
```

If you start the `serialver` program with the `-show` option, the program brings up a graphical dialog box (see Figure 1.7).

All *later* versions of the class must define the `serialVersionUID` constant to the same fingerprint as the original.

```
class Employee implements Serializable // version 1.1
{
    . . .
    public static final long serialVersionUID = -1814239825517340645L;
}
```

When a class has a static data member named `serialVersionUID`, it will not compute the fingerprint manually but will use that value instead.

Once that static data member has been placed inside a class, the serialization system is now willing to read in different versions of objects of that class.

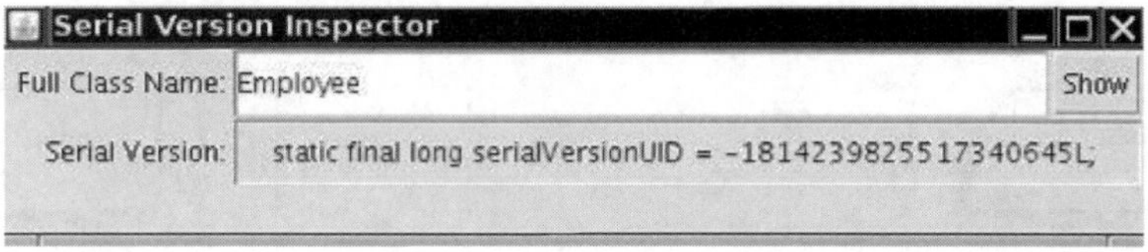

Full Class Name: Employee    Show

Serial Version:    static final long serialVersionUID = –1814239825517340645L;

**Figure 1.7** The graphical version of the serialver program

If only the methods of the class change, there is no problem with reading the new object data. However, if the data fields change, you may have problems. For example, the old file object may have more or fewer data fields than the one in the program, or the types of the data fields may be different. In that case, the object stream makes an effort to convert the stream object to the current version of the class.

The object stream compares the data fields of the current version of the class with those of the version in the stream. Of course, the object stream considers only the nontransient and nonstatic data fields. If two fields have matching names but different types, the object stream makes no effort to convert one type to the other—the objects are incompatible. If the object in the stream has data fields that are not present in the current version, the object stream ignores the additional data. If the current version has data fields that are not present in the streamed object, the added fields are set to their default (null for objects, zero for numbers, and false for boolean values).

Here is an example. Suppose we have saved a number of employee records on disk, using the original version (1.0) of the class. Now we change the Employee class to version 2.0 by adding a data field called department. Figure 1.8 shows what

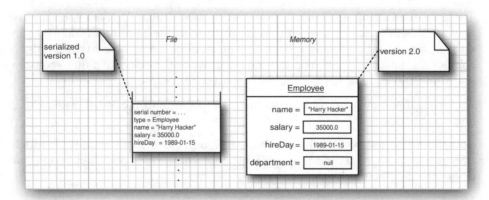

**Figure 1.8** Reading an object with fewer data fields

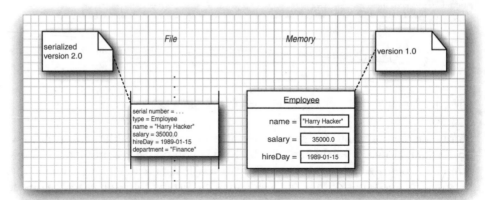

**Figure 1.9** Reading an object with more data fields

happens when a 1.0 object is read into a program that uses 2.0 objects. The department field is set to null. Figure 1.9 shows the opposite scenario: A program using 1.0 objects reads a 2.0 object. The additional department field is ignored.

Is this process safe? It depends. Dropping a data field seems harmless—the recipient still has all the data that it knew how to manipulate. Setting a data field to null might not be so safe. Many classes work hard to initialize all data fields in all constructors to non-null values, so that the methods don't have to be prepared to handle null data. It is up to the class designer to implement additional code in the readObject method to fix version incompatibilities or to make sure the methods are robust enough to handle null data.

## 1.5.5  Using Serialization for Cloning

There is an amusing use for the serialization mechanism: It gives you an easy way to clone an object, provided the class is serializable. Simply serialize it to an output stream and then read it back in. The result is a new object that is a deep copy of the existing object. You don't have to write the object to a file—you can use a ByteArrayOutputStream to save the data into a byte array.

As Listing 1.4 shows, to get clone for free, simply extend the SerialCloneable class, and you are done.

You should be aware that this method, although clever, will usually be much slower than a clone method that explicitly constructs a new object and copies or clones the data fields.

**Listing 1.4** serialClone/SerialCloneTest.java

```
 1  package serialClone;
 2
 3  /**
 4     @version 1.20 17 Aug 1998
 5     @author Cay Horstmann
 6  */
 7
 8  import java.io.*;
 9  import java.util.*;
10
11  public class SerialCloneTest
12  {
13     public static void main(String[] args)
14     {
15        Employee harry = new Employee("Harry Hacker", 35000, 1989, 10, 1);
16        // clone harry
17        Employee harry2 = (Employee) harry.clone();
18
19        // mutate harry
20        harry.raiseSalary(10);
21
22        // now harry and the clone are different
23        System.out.println(harry);
24        System.out.println(harry2);
25     }
26  }
27
28  /**
29     A class whose clone method uses serialization.
30  */
31  class SerialCloneable implements Cloneable, Serializable
32  {
33     public Object clone()
34     {
35        try
36        {
37           // save the object to a byte array
38           ByteArrayOutputStream bout = new ByteArrayOutputStream();
39           ObjectOutputStream out = new ObjectOutputStream(bout);
40           out.writeObject(this);
41           out.close();
42
43           // read a clone of the object from the byte array
44           ByteArrayInputStream bin = new ByteArrayInputStream(bout.toByteArray());
45           ObjectInputStream in = new ObjectInputStream(bin);
```

*(Continues)*

**Listing 1.4** *(Continued)*

```
46          Object ret = in.readObject();
47          in.close();
48
49          return ret;
50      }
51      catch (Exception e)
52      {
53          return null;
54      }
55    }
56  }
57
58  /**
59     The familiar Employee class, redefined to extend the
60     SerialCloneable class.
61  */
62  class Employee extends SerialCloneable
63  {
64      private String name;
65      private double salary;
66      private Date hireDay;
67
68      public Employee(String n, double s, int year, int month, int day)
69      {
70          name = n;
71          salary = s;
72          GregorianCalendar calendar = new GregorianCalendar(year, month - 1, day);
73          hireDay = calendar.getTime();
74      }
75
76      public String getName()
77      {
78          return name;
79      }
80
81      public double getSalary()
82      {
83          return salary;
84      }
85
86      public Date getHireDay()
87      {
88          return hireDay;
89      }
```

```
90    public void raiseSalary(double byPercent)
91    {
92       double raise = salary * byPercent / 100;
93       salary += raise;
94    }
95
96    public String toString()
97    {
98       return getClass().getName()
99          + "[name=" + name
100         + ",salary=" + salary
101         + ",hireDay=" + hireDay
102         + "]";
103   }
104 }
```

## 1.6  Working with Files

You have learned how to read and write data from a file. However, there is more
to file management than reading and writing. The Path and Files classes encapsulate the functionality required to work with the file system on the user's machine.
For example, use the Files class to remove or rename the file, or to find out when
a file was last modified. In other words, the stream classes are concerned with
the contents of files, whereas the classes that we discuss here are concerned
with the storage of files on a disk.

The Path and Files classes were added in Java SE 7. They are much more convenient
to use than the File class which dates back all the way to JDK 1.0. We expect them
to be very popular with Java programmers and discuss them in-depth.

### 1.6.1  Paths

A Path is a sequence of directory names, optionally followed by a file name. The
first component of a path may be a *root component* such as / or C:\. The permissible
root components depend on the file system. A path that starts with a root component is *absolute*. Otherwise, it is *relative*. For example, here we construct an absolute and a relative path. For the absolute path, we assume a computer running a
UNIX-like file system.

```
Path absolute = Paths.get("/home", "cay");
Path relative = Paths.get("myprog", "conf", "user.properties");
```

The static Paths.get method receives one or more strings, which it joins with the
path separator of the default file system (/ for a UNIX-like file system, \ for
Windows). It then parses the result, throwing an InvalidPathException if the result is
not a valid path in the given file system. The result is a Path object.

The get method can get a single string containing multiple components. For example, you can read a path from a configuration file like this:

```
String baseDir = props.getProperty("base.dir")
    // May be a string such as /opt/myprog or c:\Program Files\myprog
Path basePath = Paths.get(baseDir); // OK that baseDir has separators
```

> **NOTE:** A path does not have to correspond to a file that actually exists. It is merely an abstract sequence of names. As you will see in the next section, when you want to create a file, you first make a path and then call a method to create the corresponding file.

It is very common to combine or *resolve* paths. The call p.resolve(q) returns a path according to these rules:

- If q is absolute, then the result is q.
- Otherwise, the result is "p then q", according to the rules of the file system.

For example, suppose your application needs to find its working directory relative to a given base directory that is read from a configuration file, as in the preceding example.

```
Path workRelative = Paths.get("work");
Path workPath = basePath.resolve(workRelative);
```

There is a shortcut for the resolve method that takes a string instead of a path:

```
Path workPath = basePath.resolve("work");
```

There is a convenience method resolveSibling that resolves against a path's parent, yielding a sibling path. For example, if workPath is /opt/myapp/work, the call

```
Path tempPath = workPath.resolveSibling("temp")
```

creates /opt/myapp/temp.

The opposite of resolve is relativize. The call p.relativize(r) yields the path q which, when resolved with q, yields r. For example, relativizing "/home/cay" against "/home/fred/myprog" yields "../fred/myapp". Here, we assume that .. denotes the parent directory in the file system.

The normalize method removes any redundant . and .. components (or whatever the file system may deem redundant). For example, normalizing the path /home/cay/../fred/./myprog yields /home/fred/myprog.

The toAbsolutePath method yields the absolute path of a given path, starting at a root component.

The Path class has many useful methods for taking paths apart and combining them with other paths. This code sample shows some of the most useful ones:

```
Path p = Paths.get("/home", "cay", "myprog.properties");
Path parent = p.getParent(); // the path /home/cay
Path file = p.getFileName(); // the path myprog.properties
Path root = p.getRoot(); // the path /
```

**NOTE:** Occasionally, you may need to interoperate with legacy APIs that use the File class instead of the Path class. The Path class has a toFile method, and the File class has a toPath method.

---

**java.nio.file.Paths** 7

- static Path get(String first, String... more)
  makes a path by joining the given strings.

---

**java.nio.file.Path** 7

- Path resolve(Path other)
- Path resolve(String other)
  if other is absolute, returns other; otherwise, returns the path obtained from joining this and other.
- Path resolveSibling(Path other)
- Path resolveSibling(String other)
  if other is absolute, returns other; otherwise, returns the path obtained from joining the parent of this and other.
- Path relativize(Path other)
  returns the relative path that, when resolved with this, yields other.
- Path normalize()
  removes redundant path elements such as . and ..
- Path toAbsolutePath()
  returns an absolute path that is equivalent to this path.
- Path getParent()
  returns the parent, or null if this path has no parent.
- Path getFileName()
  returns the last component of this path, or null if this path has no components.
- Path getRoot()
  returns the root component of this path, or null if this path has no root components.
- toFile()
  makes a File from this path.

---

**java.io.File** 1.0

- Path toPath() 7

  makes a Path from this file.

---

## 1.6.2 Reading and Writing Files

The Files class makes quick work of common file operations. For example, you can easily read the entire contents of a file:

```
byte[] bytes = Files.readAllBytes(path);
```

If you want to read the file as a string, call readAllBytes followed by

```
String content = new String(bytes, charset);
```

But if you want the file as a sequence of lines, call

```
List<String> lines = Files.readAllLines(path, charset);
```

Conversely, if you want to write a string, call

```
Files.write(path, content.getBytes(charset));
```

To append to a given file, use

```
Files.write(path, content.getBytes(charset), StandardOpenOption.APPEND);
```

You can also write a collection of lines with

```
Files.write(path, lines);
```

These simple methods are intended for dealing with text files of moderate length. If your files are large or binary, you can still use the familiar streams or readers/writers:

```
InputStream in = Files.newInputStream(path);
OutputStream out = Files.newOutputStream(path);
Reader in = Files.newBufferedReader(path, charset);
Writer out = Files.newBufferedWriter(path, charset);
```

These convenience methods save you from dealing with FileInputStream, FileOutputStream, BufferedReader, or BufferedWriter.

---

java.nio.file.Files 7

- static byte[] readAllBytes(Path path)
- static List<String> readAllLines(Path path, Charset charset)
  reads the contents of a file.
- static Path write(Path path, byte[] contents, OpenOption... options)
- static Path write(Path path, Iterable<? extends CharSequence> contents, OpenOption options)
  writes the given contents to a file and returns path.
- static InputStream newInputStream(Path path, OpenOption... options)
- static OutputStream newOutputStream(Path path, OpenOption... options)
- static BufferedReader newBufferedReader(Path path, Charset charset)
- static BufferedWriter newBufferedWriter(Path path, Charset charset, OpenOption... options)
  opens a file for reading or writing.

---

## 1.6.3 Copying, Moving, and Deleting Files

To copy a file from one location to another, simply call

```
Files.copy(fromPath, toPath);
```

To move the file (that is, copy and delete the original), call

```
Files.move(fromPath, toPath);
```

The copy or move will fail if the target exists. If you want to overwrite an existing target, use the REPLACE_EXISTING option. If you want to copy all file attributes, use the COPY_ATTRIBUTES option. You can supply both like this:

```
Files.copy(fromPath, toPath, StandardCopyOption.REPLACE_EXISTING,
    StandardCopyOption.COPY_ATTRIBUTES);
```

You can specify that a move should be atomic. Then you are assured that either the move completed successfully, or the source continues to be present. Use the ATOMIC_MOVE option:

```
Files.move(fromPath, toPath, StandardCopyOption.ATOMIC_MOVE);
```

Finally, to delete a file, simply call

```
Files.delete(path);
```

This method throws an exception if the file doesn't exist, so instead you may want to use

```
boolean deleted = Files.deleteIfExists(path);
```

The deletion methods can also be used to remove an empty directory.

---

**java.nio.file.Files  7**

- static Path copy(Path from, Path to, CopyOption... options)
- static Path move(Path from, Path to, CopyOption... options)
  copies or moves from to the given target location and returns to.
- static void delete(Path path)
- static boolean deleteIfExists(Path path)
  deletes the given file or empty directory. The first method throws an exception if the file or directory doesn't exist. The second method returns false in that case.

---

## 1.6.4  Creating Files and Directories

To create a new directory, call

```
Files.createDirectory(path);
```

All but the last component in the path must already exist. To create intermediate directories as well, use

```
Files.createDirectories(path);
```

You can create an empty file with

```
Files.createFile(path);
```

The call throws an exception if the file already exists. The check for existence and creation are atomic. If the file doesn't exist, it is created before anyone else has a chance to do the same.

There are convenience methods for creating a temporary file or directory in a given or system-specific location.

```
Path newPath = Files.createTempFile(dir, prefix, suffix);
Path newPath = Files.createTempFile(prefix, suffix);
Path newPath = Files.createTempDirectory(dir, prefix);
Path newPath = Files.createTempDirectory(prefix);
```

Here, dir is a Path, and prefix/suffix are strings which may be null. For example, the call Files.createTempFile(null, ".txt") might return a path such as /tmp/1234405522364837194.txt.

When you create a file or directory, you can specify attributes, such as owners or permissions. However, the details depend on the file system, and we won't cover them here.

---

```
java.nio.file.Files  7
```
- static Path createFile(Path path, FileAttribute<?>... attrs)
- static Path createDirectory(Path path, FileAttribute<?>... attrs)
- static Path createDirectories(Path path, FileAttribute<?>... attrs)

  creates a file or directory. The createDirectories method creates any intermediate directories as well.
- static Path createTempFile(String prefix, String suffix, FileAttribute<?>... attrs)
- static Path createTempFile(Path parentDir, String prefix, String suffix, FileAttribute<?>... attrs)
- static Path createTempDirectory(String prefix, FileAttribute<?>... attrs)
- static Path createTempDirectory(Path parentDir, String prefix, FileAttribute<?>... attrs)

  creates a temporary file or directory, in a location suitable for temporary files or in the given parent directory. Returns the path to the created file or directory.

---

## 1.6.5 Getting File Information

The following static methods return a boolean value to check a property of a path:

- exists
- isHidden
- isReadable, isWritable, isExecutable
- isRegularFile, isDirectory, isSymbolicLink

The size method returns the number of bytes in a file.

```
long fileSize = Files.size(path);
```

The getOwner method returns the owner of the file, as an instance of java.nio.file.attribute.UserPrincipal.

All file systems report a set of basic attributes, encapsulated by the BasicFileAttributes interface, which partially overlaps with that information. The basic file attributes are

- The times at which the file was created, last accessed, and last modified, as instances of the class java.nio.file.attribute.FileTime
- Whether the file is a regular file, a directory, a symbolic link, or none of these
- The file size
- The file key—an object of some class, specific to the file system, that may or may not uniquely identify a file

To get these attributes, call

```
BasicFileAttributes attributes = files.readAttributes(path, BasicFileAttributes.class);
```

If you know that the user's file system is POSIX-compliant, you can instead get an instance of `PosixFileAttributes`:

```
PosixFileAttributes attributes = files.readAttributes(path, PosixFileAttributes.class);
```

Then you can find out the group owner and the owner, group, and world access permissions. We won't dwell on the details since so much of this information is not portable across operating systems.

---

**`java.nio.file.Files` 7**

- `static boolean exists(Path path)`
- `static boolean isHidden(Path path)`
- `static boolean isReadable(Path path)`
- `static boolean isWritable(Path path)`
- `static boolean isExecutable(Path path)`
- `static boolean isRegularFile(Path path)`
- `static boolean isDirectory(Path path)`
- `static boolean isSymbolicLink(Path path)`
  checks for the given property of the file given by the path.
- `static long size(Path path)`
  gets the size of the file in bytes.
- `A readAttributes(Path path, Class<A> type, LinkOption... options)`
  reads the file attributes of type A.

---

**`java.nio.file.attribute.BasicFileAttributes` 7**

- `FileTime creationTime()`
- `FileTime lastAccessTime()`
- `FileTime lastModifiedTime()`
- `boolean isRegularFile()`
- `boolean isDirectory()`
- `boolean isSymbolicLink()`
- `long size()`
- `Object fileKey()`
  gets the requested attribute.

---

## 1.6.6 Iterating over the Files in a Directory

The old `File` class had a method for getting an array of all files in a directory, but that led to poor performance with directories holding huge numbers of files. For that reason, the `Files` class has a method that yields an `Iterable` object instead. Here is how you use it:

```
try (DirectoryStream<Path> entries = Files.newDirectoryStream(dir))
{
    for (Path entry : entries)
        Process entries
}
```

The try-with-resources block ensures that the directory stream is properly closed.

There is no specific order in which the directory entries are visited.

You can filter the files with a glob pattern:

```
try (DirectoryStream<Path> entries = Files.newDirectoryStream(dir, "*.java"))
```

Table 1.6 shows all glob patterns.

**CAUTION:** If you use the glob syntax on Windows, you have to escape backslashes *twice*: once for the glob syntax, and once for the Java string syntax: `Files.newDirectoryStream(dir, "C:\\\\")`

If you want to visit all descendants of a directory, call the `walkFileTree` method instead and supply an object of type `FileVisitor`. That object gets notified

- When a file or directory is encountered: `FileVisitResult visitFile(T path, BasicFileAttributes attrs)`
- Before a directory is processed: `FileVisitResult preVisitDirectory(T dir, IOException ex)`
- After a directory is processed: `FileVisitResult postVisitDirectory(T dir, IOException ex)`
- When an error occurred trying to visit a file or directory, such as trying to open a directory without the necessary permissions: `FileVisitResult visitFileFailed(T path, IOException ex)`

In each case, you can specify whether you want to

- Continue visiting the next file: `FileVisitResult.CONTINUE`
- Continue the walk, but without visiting the entries in this directory: `FileVisitResult.SKIP_SUBTREE`
- Continue the walk, but without visiting the siblings of this file: `FileVisitResult.SKIP_SIBLINGS`
- Terminate the walk: `FileVisitResult.TERMINATE`

If any of the methods throws an exception, the walk is also terminated, and that exception is thrown from the `walkFileTree` method.

**Table 1.6** Glob Patterns

| Pattern | Description | Example |
|---------|-------------|---------|
| * | Matches zero or more characters of a path component | `*.java` matches all Java files in the current directory |
| ** | Matches zero or more characters, crossing directory boundaries | `**.java` matches all Java files in any subdirectory |
| ? | Matches one character | `????.java` matches all four-character Java files (not counting the extension) |
| [...] | Matches a set of characters. You can use hyphens [0-9] and negation [!0-9]. | `Test[0-9A-F].java` matches `Testx.java`, where $x$ is one hexadecimal digit. |
| {...} | Matches alternatives, separated by commas | `*.{java,class}` matches all Java and class files |
| \ | Escapes any of the above | `*\**` matches all files with a * in their name |

 **NOTE:** The `FileVisitor` interface is a generic type, but it isn't likely that you'll ever want something other than a `FileVisitor<Path>`. The `walkFileTree` method is willing to accept a `FileVisitor<? super Path>`, but `Path` does not have an abundance of supertypes.

A convenience class `SimpleFileVisitor` implements the `FileVisitor` interface. All but the `visitFileFailed` method do nothing and continue. The `visitFileFailed` method throws the exception that caused the failure, thereby terminating the visit.

For example, here is how you can print out all subdirectories of a given directory.

```java
Files.walkFileTree(dir, new SimpleFileVisitor<Path>()
    {
        public FileVisitResult visitFile(Path path, BasicFileAttributes attrs) throws IOException
        {
            if (attrs.isDirectory())
                System.out.println(path);
            return FileVisitResult.CONTINUE;
        }
        public FileVisitResult visitFileFailed(Path path, IOException exc) throws IOException
        {
            return FileVisitResult.CONTINUE;
        }
    });
```

Note that we need to override `visitFileFailed`. Otherwise, the visit would fail as soon as it encounters a directory that it's not allowed to open.

Also note that the attributes of the path are passed as a parameter. The `walkFileTree` already had to make an OS call to get the attributes, since it needs to distinguish between files and directories. This way, you don't need to make another call.

The other methods of the `FileVisitor` interface are useful if you need to do some work when entering or leaving a directory. For example, when you make a copy of a directory tree, you need to copy the current directory before you add file copies to it. When you delete a directory tree, you need to remove the current directory after you have removed all of its files.

---

**`java.nio.file.Files` 7**

- `DirectoryStream<Path> newDirectoryStream(Path path)`
- `DirectoryStream<Path> newDirectoryStream(Path path, String glob)`

  gets an iterator over the files and directories in a given directory. The second method only accepts those entries matching the given glob pattern.

- `Path walkFileTree(Path start, FileVisitor<? super Path> visitor)`

  walks all descendants of the given path, applying the visitor to all descendants.

---

**`java.nio.file.SimpleFileVisitor<T>` 7**

- `FileVisitResult visitFile(T path, BasicFileAttributes attrs)`

  is called when a file or directory is visited, returns one of `CONTINUE`, `SKIP_SUBTREE`, `SKIP_SIBLINGS`, or `TERMINATE`. The default implementation does nothing and continues.

- `FileVisitResult preVisitDirectory(T dir, BasicFileAttributes attrs)`
- `FileVisitResult postVisitDirectory(T dir, BasicFileAttributes attrs)`

  are called before and after visiting a directory. The default implementation does nothing and continues.

- `FileVisitResult visitFileFailed(T path, IOException exc)`

  is called if an exception was thrown in an attempt to get information about the given file. The default implementation rethrows the exception, which causes the visit to terminate with that exception. Override the method if you want to continue.

---

## 1.6.7 ZIP File Systems

The `Paths` class looks up paths in the default file system—the files on the user's local disk. You can have other file systems. One of the more useful ones is a *ZIP file system*. If `zipname` is the name of a ZIP file, then the call

```
FileSystem fs = FileSystems.newFileSystem(Paths.get(zipname), null);
```

establishes a file system that contains all files in the ZIP archive. It's an easy matter to copy a file out of that archive if you know its name:

```
Files.copy(fs.getPath(sourceName), targetPath);
```

Here, fs.getPath is the analog of Paths.get for an arbitrary file system.

To list all files in a ZIP archive, walk the file tree:

```
FileSystem fs = FileSystems.newFileSystem(Paths.get(zipname), null);
Files.walkFileTree(fs.getPath("/"), new SimpleFileVisitor<Path>()
   {
      public FileVisitResult visitFile(Path file, BasicFileAttributes attrs) throws IOException
      {
         System.out.println(file);
         return FileVisitResult.CONTINUE;
      }
   });
```

That is nicer than the API described in Section 1.4, "ZIP Archives," on p. 33 which required a set of new classes just to deal with ZIP archives.

---

**java.nio.file.FileSystems 7**

---

- `static FileSystem newFileSystem(Path path, ClassLoader loader)`
  iterates over the installed file system providers and, provided that loader is not null, the file systems that the given class loader can load. Returns the file system that is created by the first file system provider that accepts the given path. By default, there is a provider for ZIP file systems that accepts files whose names end in .zip or .jar.

---

**java.nio.file.FileSystem 7**

---

- `static Path getPath(String first, String... more)`
  makes a path by joining the given strings.

---

## 1.7 Memory-Mapped Files

Most operating systems can take advantage of the virtual memory implementation to "map" a file, or a region of a file, into memory. Then the file can be accessed as if it were an in-memory array, which is much faster than the traditional file operations.

**Table 1.7** Timing Data for File Operations

| Method | Time |
| --- | --- |
| Plain input stream | 110 seconds |
| Buffered input stream | 9.9 seconds |
| Random access file | 162 seconds |
| Memory-mapped file | 7.2 seconds |

At the end of this section, you can find a program that computes the CRC32 checksum of a file using traditional file input and a memory-mapped file. On one machine, we got the timing data shown in Table 1.7 when computing the checksum of the 37MB file rt.jar in the jre/lib directory of the JDK.

As you can see, on this particular machine, memory mapping is a bit faster than using buffered sequential input and dramatically faster than using a RandomAccessFile.

Of course, the exact values will differ greatly from one machine to another, but it is obvious that the performance gain, compared to random access, can be substantial. For sequential reading of files of moderate size, on the other hand, there is no reason to use memory mapping.

The java.nio package makes memory mapping quite simple. Here is what you do.

First, get a *channel* for the file. A channel is an abstraction for a disk file that lets you access operating system features such as memory mapping, file locking, and fast data transfers between files.

```
FileChannel channel = FileChannel.open(path, options);
```

Then, get a ByteBuffer from the channel by calling the map method of the FileChannel class. Specify the area of the file that you want to map and a *mapping mode*. Three modes are supported:

- FileChannel.MapMode.READ_ONLY: The resulting buffer is read-only. Any attempt to write to the buffer results in a ReadOnlyBufferException.
- FileChannel.MapMode.READ_WRITE: The resulting buffer is writable, and the changes will be written back to the file at some time. Note that other programs that have mapped the same file might not see those changes immediately. The exact behavior of simultaneous file mapping by multiple programs depends on the operating system.
- FileChannel.MapMode.PRIVATE: The resulting buffer is writable, but any changes are private to this buffer and not propagated to the file.

Once you have the buffer, you can read and write data using the methods of the `ByteBuffer` class and the `Buffer` superclass.

Buffers support both sequential and random data access. A buffer has a *position* that is advanced by `get` and `put` operations. For example, you can sequentially traverse all bytes in the buffer as

```
while (buffer.hasRemaining())
{
   byte b = buffer.get();
   . . .
}
```

Alternatively, you can use random access:

```
for (int i = 0; i < buffer.limit(); i++)
{
   byte b = buffer.get(i);
   . . .
}
```

You can also read and write arrays of bytes with the methods

```
get(byte[] bytes)
get(byte[], int offset, int length)
```

Finally, there are methods

```
getInt
getLong
getShort
getChar
getFloat
getDouble
```

to read primitive type values that are stored as *binary* values in the file. As we already mentioned, Java uses big-endian ordering for binary data. However, if you need to process a file containing binary numbers in little-endian order, simply call

```
buffer.order(ByteOrder.LITTLE_ENDIAN);
```

To find out the current byte order of a buffer, call

```
ByteOrder b = buffer.order()
```

 **CAUTION:** This pair of methods does not use the `set`/`get` naming convention.

To write numbers to a buffer, use one of the methods

```
putInt
putLong
putShort
putChar
putFloat
putDouble
```

At some point, and certainly when the channel is closed, these changes are written back to the file.

Listing 1.5 computes the 32-bit cyclic redundancy checksum (CRC32) of a file. That quantity is a checksum that is often used to determine whether a file has been corrupted. Corruption of a file makes it very likely that the checksum has changed. The java.util.zip package contains a class CRC32 that computes the checksum of a sequence of bytes, using the following loop:

```
CRC32 crc = new CRC32();
while (more bytes)
    crc.update(next byte)
long checksum = crc.getValue();
```

 **NOTE:** For a nice explanation of the CRC algorithm, see www.relisoft.com/ Science/CrcMath.html.

The details of the CRC computation are not important. We just use it as an example of a useful file operation.

Run the program as

```
java memoryMap.MemoryMapTest filename
```

**Listing 1.5** memoryMap/MemoryMapTest.java

```
1  package memoryMap;
2
3  import java.io.*;
4  import java.nio.*;
5  import java.nio.channels.*;
6  import java.nio.file.*;
7  import java.util.zip.*;
8  /**
9   * This program computes the CRC checksum of a file in four ways. <br>
10  * Usage: java memoryMap.MemoryMapTest filename
11  * @version 1.01 2012-05-30
12  * @author Cay Horstmann
13  */
```

*(Continues)*

**Listing 1.5** *(Continued)*

```java
14  public class MemoryMapTest
15  {
16     public static long checksumInputStream(Path filename) throws IOException
17     {
18        try (InputStream in = Files.newInputStream(filename))
19        {
20           CRC32 crc = new CRC32();
21
22           int c;
23           while ((c = in.read()) != -1)
24              crc.update(c);
25           return crc.getValue();
26        }
27     }
28
29     public static long checksumBufferedInputStream(Path filename) throws IOException
30     {
31        try (InputStream in = new BufferedInputStream(Files.newInputStream(filename)))
32        {
33           CRC32 crc = new CRC32();
34
35           int c;
36           while ((c = in.read()) != -1)
37              crc.update(c);
38           return crc.getValue();
39        }
40     }
41
42     public static long checksumRandomAccessFile(Path filename) throws IOException
43     {
44        try (RandomAccessFile file = new RandomAccessFile(filename.toFile(), "r"))
45        {
46           long length = file.length();
47           CRC32 crc = new CRC32();
48
49           for (long p = 0; p < length; p++)
50           {
51              file.seek(p);
52              int c = file.readByte();
53              crc.update(c);
54           }
55           return crc.getValue();
56        }
57     }
58
59     public static long checksumMappedFile(Path filename) throws IOException
60     {
```

```
61      try (FileChannel channel = FileChannel.open(filename))
62      {
63         CRC32 crc = new CRC32();
64         int length = (int) channel.size();
65         MappedByteBuffer buffer = channel.map(FileChannel.MapMode.READ_ONLY, 0, length);
66
67         for (int p = 0; p < length; p++)
68         {
69            int c = buffer.get(p);
70            crc.update(c);
71         }
72         return crc.getValue();
73      }
74   }
75
76   public static void main(String[] args) throws IOException
77   {
78      System.out.println("Input Stream:");
79      long start = System.currentTimeMillis();
80      Path filename = Paths.get(args[0]);
81      long crcValue = checksumInputStream(filename);
82      long end = System.currentTimeMillis();
83      System.out.println(Long.toHexString(crcValue));
84      System.out.println((end - start) + " milliseconds");
85
86      System.out.println("Buffered Input Stream:");
87      start = System.currentTimeMillis();
88      crcValue = checksumBufferedInputStream(filename);
89      end = System.currentTimeMillis();
90      System.out.println(Long.toHexString(crcValue));
91      System.out.println((end - start) + " milliseconds");
92
93      System.out.println("Random Access File:");
94      start = System.currentTimeMillis();
95      crcValue = checksumRandomAccessFile(filename);
96      end = System.currentTimeMillis();
97      System.out.println(Long.toHexString(crcValue));
98      System.out.println((end - start) + " milliseconds");
99
100      System.out.println("Mapped File:");
101      start = System.currentTimeMillis();
102      crcValue = checksumMappedFile(filename);
103      end = System.currentTimeMillis();
104      System.out.println(Long.toHexString(crcValue));
105      System.out.println((end - start) + " milliseconds");
106   }
107 }
```

---

**java.io.FileInputStream** 1.0

- `FileChannel getChannel()` **1.4**
  returns a channel for accessing this stream.

---

**java.io.FileOutputStream** 1.0

- `FileChannel getChannel()` **1.4**
  returns a channel for accessing this stream.

---

**java.io.RandomAccessFile** 1.0

- `FileChannel getChannel()` **1.4**
  returns a channel for accessing this file.

---

**java.nio.channels.FileChannel** 1.4

- `static FileChannel open(Path path, OpenOption... options)` **7**
  opens a file channel for the given path. By default, the channel is opened for reading.

  | *Parameters:* | path | The path to the file on which to open the channel |
  | | options | Values `WRITE`, `APPEND`, `TRUNCATE_EXISTING`, `CREATE` in the `StandardOpenOption` enumeration |

- `MappedByteBuffer map(FileChannel.MapMode mode, long position, long size)`
  maps a region of the file to memory.

  | *Parameters:* | mode | One of the constants `READ_ONLY`, `READ_WRITE`, or `PRIVATE` in the `FileChannel.MapMode` class |
  | | position | The start of the mapped region |
  | | size | The size of the mapped region |

---

**java.nio.Buffer** 1.4

- `boolean hasRemaining()`
  returns `true` if the current buffer position has not yet reached the buffer's limit position.

*(Continues)*

---

`java.nio.Buffer` 1.4 *(Continued)*

---

- `int limit()`

  returns the limit position of the buffer—that is, the first position at which no more values are available.

---

`java.nio.ByteBuffer` 1.4

---

- `byte get()`

  gets a byte from the current position and advances the current position to the next byte.

- `byte get(int index)`

  gets a byte from the specified index.

- `ByteBuffer put(byte b)`

  puts a byte at the current position and advances the current position to the next byte. Returns a reference to this buffer.

- `ByteBuffer put(int index, byte b)`

  puts a byte at the specified index. Returns a reference to this buffer.

- `ByteBuffer get(byte[] destination)`
- `ByteBuffer get(byte[] destination, int offset, int length)`

  fills a byte array, or a region of a byte array, with bytes from the buffer, and advances the current position by the number of bytes read. If not enough bytes remain in the buffer, then no bytes are read, and a `BufferUnderflowException` is thrown. Returns a reference to this buffer.

  | *Parameters:* | destination | The byte array to be filled |
  | --- | --- | --- |
  | | offset | The offset of the region to be filled |
  | | length | The length of the region to be filled |

- `ByteBuffer put(byte[] source)`
- `ByteBuffer put(byte[] source, int offset, int length)`

  puts all bytes from a byte array, or the bytes from a region of a byte array, into the buffer, and advances the current position by the number of bytes read. If not enough bytes remain in the buffer, then no bytes are written, and a `BufferOverflowException` is thrown. Returns a reference to this buffer.

  | *Parameters:* | source | The byte array to be written |
  | --- | --- | --- |
  | | offset | The offset of the region to be written |
  | | length | The length of the region to be written |

*(Continues)*

---

**java.nio.ByteBuffer** 1.4 *(Continued)*

- *Xxx* get*Xxx*()
- *Xxx* get*Xxx*(int index)
- ByteBuffer put*Xxx*(*Xxx* value)
- ByteBuffer put*Xxx*(int index, *Xxx* value)

  gets or puts a binary number. *Xxx* is one of Int, Long, Short, Char, Float, or Double.

- ByteBuffer order(ByteOrder order)
- ByteOrder order()

  sets or gets the byte order. The value for order is one of the constants BIG_ENDIAN or LITTLE_ENDIAN of the ByteOrder class.

- static ByteBuffer allocate(int capacity)

  constructs a buffer with the given capacity.

- static ByteBuffer wrap(byte[] values)

  constructs a buffer that is backed by the given array.

- CharBuffer asCharBuffer()

  constructs a character buffer that is backed by this buffer. Changes to the character buffer will show up in this buffer, but the character buffer has its own position, limit, and mark.

---

**java.nio.CharBuffer** 1.4

- char get()
- CharBuffer get(char[] destination)
- CharBuffer get(char[] destination, int offset, int length)

  gets one char value, or a range of char values, starting at the buffer's position and moving the position past the characters that were read. The last two methods return this.

- CharBuffer put(char c)
- CharBuffer put(char[] source)
- CharBuffer put(char[] source, int offset, int length)
- CharBuffer put(String source)
- CharBuffer put(CharBuffer source)

  puts one char value, or a range of char values, starting at the buffer's position and advancing the position past the characters that were written. When reading from a CharBuffer, all remaining characters are read. All methods return this.

### 1.7.1 The Buffer Data Structure

When you use memory mapping, you make a single buffer that spans the entire file or the area of the file that you're interested in. You can also use buffers to read and write more modest chunks of information.

In this section, we briefly describe the basic operations on Buffer objects. A buffer is an array of values of the same type. The Buffer class is an abstract class with concrete subclasses ByteBuffer, CharBuffer, DoubleBuffer, FloatBuffer, IntBuffer, LongBuffer, and ShortBuffer.

**NOTE:** The StringBuffer class is not related to these buffers.

In practice, you will most commonly use ByteBuffer and CharBuffer. As shown in Figure 1.10, a buffer has

- A *capacity* that never changes
- A *position* at which the next value is read or written
- A *limit* beyond which reading and writing is meaningless
- Optionally, a *mark* for repeating a read or write operation

These values fulfill the condition

$$0 \leq mark \leq position \leq limit \leq capacity$$

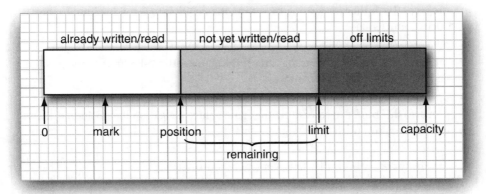

**Figure 1.10** A buffer

The principal purpose of a buffer is a "write, then read" cycle. At the outset, the buffer's position is 0 and the limit is the capacity. Keep calling put to add values to the buffer. When you run out of data or reach the capacity, it is time to switch to reading.

Call flip to set the limit to the current position and the position to 0. Now keep calling get while the remaining method (which returns *limit – position*) is positive. When you have read all values in the buffer, call clear to prepare the buffer for the next writing cycle. The clear method resets the position to 0 and the limit to the capacity.

If you want to reread the buffer, use rewind or mark/reset (see the API notes for details).

To get a buffer, call a static method such as ByteBuffer.allocate or ByteBuffer.wrap.

Then, you can fill a buffer from a channel, or write its contents to a channel. For example,

```
ByteBuffer buffer = ByteBuffer.allocate(RECORD_SIZE);
channel.read(buffer);
channel.position(newpos);
buffer.flip();
channel.write(buffer);
```

This can be a useful alternative to using a random-access file.

---

**java.nio.Buffer** 1.4

- Buffer clear()
  prepares this buffer for writing by setting the position to 0 and the limit to the capacity; returns this.

- Buffer flip()
  prepares this buffer for reading after writing, by setting the limit to the position and the position to 0; returns this.

- Buffer rewind()
  prepares this buffer for rereading the same values by setting the position to 0 and leaving the limit unchanged; returns this.

- Buffer mark()
  sets the mark of this buffer to the position; returns this.

- Buffer reset()
  sets the position of this buffer to the mark, thus allowing the marked portion to be read or written again; returns this.

---

*(Continues)*

---

**java.nio.Buffer** 1.4 *(Continued)*

- `int remaining()`
  returns the remaining number of readable or writable values—that is, the difference between the limit and position.
- `int position()`
- `void position(int newValue)`
  gets and sets the position of this buffer.
- `int capacity()`
  returns the capacity of this buffer.

---

## 1.7.2 File Locking

When multiple simultaneously executing programs need to modify the same file, they need to communicate in some way, or the file can easily become damaged. File locks can solve this problem. A file lock controls access to a file or a range of bytes within a file.

Suppose your application saves a configuration file with user preferences. If a user invokes two instances of the application, it could happen that both of them want to write the configuration file at the same time. In that situation, the first instance should lock the file. When the second instance finds the file locked, it can decide to wait until the file is unlocked or simply skip the writing process.

To lock a file, call either the `lock` or `tryLock` methods of the `FileChannel` class.

```
FileChannel = FileChannel.open(path);
FileLock lock = channel.lock();
```

or

```
FileLock lock = channel.tryLock();
```

The first call blocks until the lock becomes available. The second call returns immediately, either with the lock or with `null` if the lock is not available. The file remains locked until the channel is closed or the `release` method is invoked on the lock.

You can also lock a portion of the file with the call

```
FileLock lock(long start, long size, boolean shared)
```

or

```
FileLock tryLock(long start, long size, boolean shared)
```

The shared flag is false to lock the file for both reading and writing. It is true for a *shared* lock, which allows multiple processes to read from the file, while preventing any process from acquiring an exclusive lock. Not all operating systems support shared locks. You may get an exclusive lock even if you just asked for a shared one. Call the isShared method of the FileLock class to find out which kind you have.

 **NOTE:** If you lock the tail portion of a file and the file subsequently grows beyond the locked portion, the additional area is not locked. To lock all bytes, use a size of Long.MAX_VALUE.

Be sure to unlock the lock when you are done. As always, this is best done with a try-with-resources statement:

```
try (FileLock lock = channel.lock())
{
    access the locked file or segment
}
```

Keep in mind that file locking is system-dependent. Here are some points to watch for:

- On some systems, file locking is merely *advisory*. If an application fails to get a lock, it may still write to a file that another application has currently locked.
- On some systems, you cannot simultaneously lock a file and map it into memory.
- File locks are held by the entire Java virtual machine. If two programs are launched by the same virtual machine (such as an applet or application launcher), they can't each acquire a lock on the same file. The lock and tryLock methods will throw an OverlappingFileLockException if the virtual machine already holds another overlapping lock on the same file.
- On some systems, closing a channel releases all locks on the underlying file held by the Java virtual machine. You should therefore avoid multiple channels on the same locked file.
- Locking files on a networked file system is highly system-dependent and should probably be avoided.

---

**java.nio.channels.FileChannel** 1.4

- FileLock lock()
  acquires an exclusive lock on the entire file. This method blocks until the lock is acquired.

*(Continues)*

---

**java.nio.channels.FileChannel**  1.4  *(Continued)*

- FileLock tryLock()
  acquires an exclusive lock on the entire file, or returns null if the lock cannot be acquired.
- FileLock lock(long position, long size, boolean shared)
- FileLock tryLock(long position, long size, boolean shared)
  acquires a lock on a region of the file. The first method blocks until the lock is acquired, and the second method returns null if the lock cannot be acquired.

  | *Parameters:* | position | The start of the region to be locked |
  | --- | --- | --- |
  | | size | The size of the region to be locked |
  | | shared | true for a shared lock, false for an exclusive lock |

---

**java.nio.channels.FileLock**  1.4

- void close()  1.7
  releases this lock.

---

# 1.8  Regular Expressions

Regular expressions are used to specify string patterns. You can use regular expressions whenever you need to locate strings that match a particular pattern. For example, one of our sample programs locates all hyperlinks in an HTML file by looking for strings of the pattern <a href="...">.

Of course, for specifying a pattern, the ... notation is not precise enough. You need to specify exactly what sequence of characters is a legal match, using a special syntax to describe a pattern.

Here is a simple example. The regular expression

    [Jj]ava.+

matches any string of the following form:

- The first letter is a J or j.
- The next three letters are ava.
- The remainder of the string consists of one or more arbitrary characters.

For example, the string "javanese" matches this particular regular expression, but the string "Core Java" does not.

As you can see, you need to know a bit of syntax to understand the meaning of a regular expression. Fortunately, for most purposes, a few straightforward constructs are sufficient.

- A *character class* is a set of character alternatives, enclosed in brackets, such as [Jj], [0-9], [A-Za-z], or [^0-9]. Here the - denotes a range (all characters whose Unicode values fall between the two bounds), and ^ denotes the complement (all characters except those specified).

- To include a - inside a character class, make it the first or last item. To include a [, make it the first item. To include a ^, put it anywhere but the beginning. You only need to escape [ and \.

- There are many predefined character classes such as \d (digits) or \p{Sc} (Unicode currency symbol). See Tables 1.8 and 1.9.

- Most characters match themselves, such as the ava characters in the preceding example.

- The . symbol matches any character (except possibly line terminators, depending on flag settings).

- Use \ as an escape character, for example, \. matches a period and \\ matches a backslash.

- ^ and $ match the beginning and end of a line, respectively.

- If *X* and *Y* are regular expressions, then *XY* means "any match for *X* followed by a match for *Y*". *X* | *Y* means "any match for *X* or *Y*".

- You can apply *quantifiers* X+ (1 or more), X* (0 or more), and X? (0 or 1) to an expression *X*.

- By default, a quantifier matches the largest possible repetition that makes the overall match succeed. You can modify that behavior with suffixes ? (reluctant, or stingy, match: match the smallest repetition count) and + (possessive, or greedy, match: match the largest count even if that makes the overall match fail).

  For example, the string cab matches [a-z]*ab but not [a-z]*+ab. In the first case, the expression [a-z]* only matches the character c, so that the characters ab match the remainder of the pattern. But the greedy version [a-z]*+ matches the characters cab, leaving the remainder of the pattern unmatched.

- You can use *groups* to define subexpressions. Enclose the groups in ( ), for example, ([+-]?)([0-9]+). You can then ask the pattern matcher to return the match of each group or to refer back to a group with \n where *n* is the group number, starting with \1.

**Table 1.8** Regular Expression Syntax

| Syntax | Explanation |
|---|---|
| **Characters** | |
| c | The character $c$ |
| \u*nnnn*, \x*nn*, \0*n*, \0*nn*, \0*nnn* | The code unit with the given hex or octal value |
| \t, \n, \r, \f, \a, \e | The control characters tab, newline, return, form feed, alert, and escape |
| \c*c* | The control character corresponding to the character $c$ |
| **Character Classes** | |
| [$C_1 C_2$...] | Any of the characters represented by $C_1$, $C_2$, ... The $Ci$ are characters, character ranges ($c_1$-$c_2$), or character classes |
| [^...] | Complement of character class |
| [ ... && ... ] | Intersection of two character classes |
| **Predefined Character Classes** | |
| . | Any character except line terminators (or any character if the DOTALL flag is set) |
| \d | A digit [0-9] |
| \D | A nondigit [^0-9] |
| \s | A whitespace character [ \t\n\r\f\x0B] |
| \S | A nonwhitespace character |
| \w | A word character [a-zA-Z0-9_] |
| \W | A nonword character |
| \p{*name*} | A named character class (see Table 1.9) |
| \P{*name*} | The complement of a named character class |
| **Boundary Matchers** | |
| ^ $ | Beginning, end of input (or beginning, end of line in multiline mode) |
| \b | A word boundary |

*(Continues)*

**Table 1.8** *(Continued)*

| Syntax | Explanation |
| --- | --- |
| \B | A nonword boundary |
| \A | Beginning of input |
| \z | End of input |
| \Z | End of input, except final line terminator |
| \G | End of previous match |
| **Quantifiers** | |
| $X?$ | Optional $X$ |
| $X*$ | $X$ repeated 0 or more times |
| $X+$ | $X$ repeated 1 or more times |
| $X\{n\}$ $X\{n,\}$ $X\{n,m\}$ | $X$ $n$ times, at least $n$ times, between $n$ and $m$ times |
| **Quantifier Suffixes** | |
| ? | Turn the default (greedy) match into reluctant match |
| + | Turn the default (greedy) match into possessive match |
| **Set Operations** | |
| $XY$ | Any string from $X$, followed by any string from $Y$ |
| $X\|Y$ | Any string from $X$ or $Y$ |
| **Grouping** | |
| $(X)$ | Capture the string matching $X$ as a group |
| \n | The match of the $n$th group |
| **Escapes** | |
| \c | The character $c$ (must not be an alphabetic character) |
| \Q ... \E | Quote ... verbatim |
| (? ... ) | Special construct—see API notes for the Pattern class |

**Table 1.9** Predefined Character Class Names

| Character Class Name | Explanation |
| --- | --- |
| Lower | ASCII lower case [a-z] |
| Upper | ASCII upper case [A-Z] |
| Alpha | ASCII alphabetic [A-Za-z] |
| Digit | ASCII digits [0-9] |
| Alnum | ASCII alphabetic or digits [A-Za-z0-9] |
| XDigit | Hex digits [0-9A-Fa-f] |
| Print or Graph | Printable ASCII character [\x21-\x7E] |
| Punct | ASCII nonalpha or digit [\p{Print}&&\P{Alnum}] |
| ASCII | All ASCII [\x00-\x7F] |
| Cntrl | ASCII Control character [\x00-\x1F] |
| Blank | Space or tab [ \t] |
| Space | Whitespace [ \t\n\r\f\0x0B] |
| javaLowerCase | Lowercase, as determined by Character.isLowerCase() |
| javaUpperCase | Uppercase, as determined by Character.isUpperCase() |
| javaWhitespace | Whitespace, as determined by Character.isWhitespace() |
| javaMirrored | Mirrored, as determined by Character.isMirrored() |
| In*Block* | *Block* is the name of a Unicode character block, with spaces removed, such as Arrows or Latin1Supplement. |
| Is*Script* | *Script* is the name of a Unicode script, with spaces removed, such as Common. |
| *Category* or Is*Category* | *Category* is the name of a Unicode character category such as L (letter) or Sc (currency symbol). |
| Is*Property* | *Property* is one of Alphabetic, Ideographic, Letter, Lowercase, Uppercase, Titlecase, Punctuation, Control, White_Space, Digit, Hex_Digit, Noncharacter_Code_Point, Assigned |

For example, here is a somewhat complex but potentially useful regular expression that describes decimal or hexadecimal integers:

```
[+-]?[0-9]+|0[Xx][0-9A-Fa-f]+
```

Unfortunately, the regular expression syntax is not completely standardized between various programs and libraries; there is a consensus on the basic constructs but many maddening differences in the details. The Java regular expression classes use a syntax that is similar to, but not quite the same as, the one used in the Perl language. Table 1.8 shows all constructs of the Java syntax. For more information on the regular expression syntax, consult the API documentation for the Pattern class or the book *Mastering Regular Expressions* by Jeffrey E. F. Friedl (O'Reilly and Associates, 2006).

The simplest use for a regular expression is to test whether a particular string matches it. Here is how you program that test in Java. First, construct a Pattern object from a string containing the regular expression. Then, get a Matcher object from the pattern and call its matches method:

```
Pattern pattern = Pattern.compile(patternString);
Matcher matcher = pattern.matcher(input);
if (matcher.matches()) . . .
```

The input of the matcher is an object of any class that implements the CharSequence interface, such as a String, StringBuilder, or CharBuffer.

When compiling the pattern, you can set one or more flags, for example:

```
Pattern pattern = Pattern.compile(patternString,
    Pattern.CASE_INSENSITIVE + Pattern.UNICODE_CASE);
```

The following six flags are supported:

- CASE_INSENSITIVE: Match characters independently of the letter case. By default, this flag takes only US ASCII characters into account.
- UNICODE_CASE: When used in combination with CASE_INSENSITIVE, use Unicode letter case for matching.
- MULTILINE: ∧ and $ match the beginning and end of a line, not the entire input.
- UNIX_LINES: Only recognize '\n' as a line terminator when matching ∧ and $ in multiline mode.
- DOTALL: Make the . symbol match all characters, including line terminators.
- CANON_EQ: Take canonical equivalence of Unicode characters into account. For example, u followed by ¨ (diaeresis) matches ü.

If the regular expression contains groups, the Matcher object can reveal the group boundaries. The methods

```
int start(int groupIndex)
int end(int groupIndex)
```

yield the starting index and the past-the-end index of a particular group.

You can simply extract the matched string by calling

```
String group(int groupIndex)
```

Group 0 is the entire input; the group index for the first actual group is 1. Call the `groupCount` method to get the total group count.

Nested groups are ordered by the opening parentheses. For example, given the pattern

```
((1?[0-9]):([0-5][0-9]))[ap]m
```

and the input

```
11:59am
```

the matcher reports the following groups

| Group Index | Start | End | String |
|---|---|---|---|
| 0 | 0 | 7 | 11:59am |
| 1 | 0 | 5 | 11:59 |
| 2 | 0 | 2 | 11 |
| 3 | 3 | 5 | 59 |

Listing 1.6 prompts for a pattern, then for strings to match. It prints out whether or not the input matches the pattern. If the input matches and the pattern contains groups, the program prints the group boundaries as parentheses, such as

```
((11):(59))am
```

**Listing 1.6** regex/RegexTest.java

```java
1  package regex;
2
3  import java.util.*;
4  import java.util.regex.*;
5
6  /**
7     This program tests regular expression matching. Enter a pattern and strings to match,
8     or hit Cancel to exit. If the pattern contains groups, the group boundaries are displayed
9     in the match.
10    @version 1.02 2012-06-02
11    @author Cay Horstmann
12  */
```

*(Continues)*

**Listing 1.6**  *(Continued)*

```
13  public class RegexTest
14  {
15     public static void main(String[] args) throws PatternSyntaxException
16     {
17        Scanner in = new Scanner(System.in);
18        System.out.println("Enter pattern: ");
19        String patternString = in.nextLine();
20
21        Pattern pattern = Pattern.compile(patternString);
22
23        while (true)
24        {
25           System.out.println("Enter string to match: ");
26           String input = in.nextLine();
27           if (input == null || input.equals("")) return;
28           Matcher matcher = pattern.matcher(input);
29           if (matcher.matches())
30           {
31              System.out.println("Match");
32              int g = matcher.groupCount();
33              if (g > 0)
34              {
35                 for (int i = 0; i < input.length(); i++)
36                 {
37                    // Print any empty groups
38                    for (int j = 1; j <= g; j++)
39                       if (i == matcher.start(j) && i == matcher.end(j))
40                          System.out.print("()");
41                    // Print ( for non-empty groups starting here
42                    for (int j = 1; j <= g; j++)
43                       if (i == matcher.start(j) && i != matcher.end(j))
44                          System.out.print('(');
45                    System.out.print(input.charAt(i));
46                    // Print ) for non-empty groups ending here
47                    for (int j = 1; j <= g; j++)
48                       if (i + 1 != matcher.start(j) && i + 1 == matcher.end(j))
49                          System.out.print(')');
50                 }
51                 System.out.println();
52              }
53           }
54           else
55              System.out.println("No match");
56        }
57     }
58  }
```

Usually, you don't want to match the entire input against a regular expression, but to find one or more matching substrings in the input. Use the find method of the Matcher class to find the next match. If it returns true, use the start and end methods to find the extent of the match.

```
while (matcher.find())
{
    int start = matcher.start();
    int end = matcher.end();
    String match = input.substring(start, end);
    . . .
}
```

Listing 1.7 puts this mechanism to work. It locates all hypertext references in a web page and prints them. To run the program, supply a URL on the command line, such as

```
java HrefMatch http://www.horstmann.com
```

**Listing 1.7**  match/HrefMatch.java

```
1  package match;
2
3  import java.io.*;
4  import java.net.*;
5  import java.util.regex.*;
6
7  /**
8   * This program displays all URLs in a web page by matching a regular expression that describes the
9   * <a href=...> HTML tag. Start the program as <br>
10  * java match.HrefMatch URL
11  * @version 1.01 2004-06-04
12  * @author Cay Horstmann
13  */
14 public class HrefMatch
15 {
16    public static void main(String[] args)
17    {
18       try
19       {
20          // get URL string from command line or use default
21          String urlString;
22          if (args.length > 0) urlString = args[0];
23          else urlString = "http://java.sun.com";
24
25          // open reader for URL
26          InputStreamReader in = new InputStreamReader(new URL(urlString).openStream());
```

*(Continues)*

**Listing 1.7**   *(Continued)*

```
27          // read contents into string builder
28          StringBuilder input = new StringBuilder();
29          int ch;
30          while ((ch = in.read()) != -1)
31             input.append((char) ch);
32
33          // search for all occurrences of pattern
34          String patternString = "<a\\s+href\\s*=\\s*(\"[^\"]*\"|[^\\s>]*)\\s*>";
35          Pattern pattern = Pattern.compile(patternString, Pattern.CASE_INSENSITIVE);
36          Matcher matcher = pattern.matcher(input);
37
38          while (matcher.find())
39          {
40             int start = matcher.start();
41             int end = matcher.end();
42             String match = input.substring(start, end);
43             System.out.println(match);
44          }
45       }
46       catch (IOException e)
47       {
48          e.printStackTrace();
49       }
50       catch (PatternSyntaxException e)
51       {
52          e.printStackTrace();
53       }
54    }
55 }
```

The `replaceAll` method of the `Matcher` class replaces all occurrences of a regular expression with a replacement string. For example, the following instructions replace all sequences of digits with a # character.

```
Pattern pattern = Pattern.compile("[0-9]+");
Matcher matcher = pattern.matcher(input);
String output = matcher.replaceAll("#");
```

The replacement string can contain references to the groups in the pattern: $n is replaced with the *n*th group. Use \$ to include a $ character in the replacement text.

If you have a string that may contain $ and \, and you don't want them to be interpreted as group replacements, call `matcher.replaceAll(Matcher.quoteReplacement(str))`.

The `replaceFirst` method replaces only the first occurrence of the pattern.

Finally, the `Pattern` class has a `split` method that splits an input into an array of strings, using the regular expression matches as boundaries. For example, the following instructions split the input into tokens, where the delimiters are punctuation marks surrounded by optional whitespace.

```
Pattern pattern = Pattern.compile("\\s*\\p{Punct}\\s*");
String[] tokens = pattern.split(input);
```

---

**java.util.regex.Pattern** 1.4

- static Pattern compile(String expression)
- static Pattern compile(String expression, int flags)

  compiles the regular expression string into a pattern object for fast processing of matches.

  *Parameters:*     expression   The regular expression

  flags        One or more of the flags CASE_INSENSITIVE, UNICODE_CASE, MULTILINE, UNIX_LINES, DOTALL, and CANON_EQ

- Matcher matcher(CharSequence input)

  returns a matcher object that you can use to locate the matches of the pattern in the input.

- String[] split(CharSequence input)
- String[] split(CharSequence input, int limit)

  splits the input string into tokens, where the pattern specifies the form of the delimiters. Returns an array of tokens. The delimiters are not part of the tokens.

  *Parameters:*     input    The string to be split into tokens

  limit    The maximum number of strings to produce. If `limit` - 1 matching delimiters have been found, then the last entry of the returned array contains the remaining unsplit input. If `limit` is   0, then the entire input is split. If `limit` is 0, then trailing empty strings are not placed in the returned array.

---

**java.util.regex.Matcher** 1.4

- boolean matches()

  returns `true` if the input matches the pattern.

- boolean lookingAt()

  returns `true` if the beginning of the input matches the pattern.

*(Continues)*

---

`java.util.regex.Matcher`   1.4 *(Continued)*

- `boolean find()`
- `boolean find(int start)`

  attempts to find the next match and returns `true` if another match is found.

  *Parameters:*    start     The index at which to start searching

- `int start()`
- `int end()`

  returns the start or past-the-end position of the current match.

- `String group()`

  returns the current match.

- `int groupCount()`

  returns the number of groups in the input pattern.

- `int start(int groupIndex)`
- `int end(int groupIndex)`

  returns the start or past-the-end position of a given group in the current match.

  *Parameters:*    groupIndex     The group index (starting with 1), or 0 to indicate the entire match

- `String group(int groupIndex)`

  returns the string matching a given group.

  *Parameters:*    groupIndex     The group index (starting with 1), or 0 to indicate the entire match

- `String replaceAll(String replacement)`
- `String replaceFirst(String replacement)`

  returns a string obtained from the matcher input by replacing all matches, or the first match, with the replacement string.

  *Parameters:*    replacement     The replacement string. It can contain references to pattern groups as $n. Use \$ to include a $ symbol.

- `static String quoteReplacement(String str)`   **5.0**

  quotes all \ and $ in str.

- `Matcher reset()`
- `Matcher reset(CharSequence input)`

  resets the matcher state. The second method makes the matcher work on a different input. Both methods return `this`.

---

You have now seen how to carry out input and output operations in Java, and had an overview of the regular expression package that was a part of the "new I/O" specification. In the next chapter, we turn to the processing of XML data.

# XML

## In this chapter:

The preface of the book *Essential XML* by Don Box et al. (Addison-Wesley, 2000) states only half-jokingly: "The Extensible Markup Language (XML) has replaced Java, Design Patterns, and Object Technology as the software industry's solution to world hunger." Indeed, as you will see in this chapter, XML is a very useful technology for describing structured information. XML tools make it easy to process and transform that information. However, XML is not a silver bullet. You need domain-specific standards and code libraries to use it effectively. Moreover, far from making Java technology obsolete, XML works very well with Java. Since the late 1990s, IBM, Apache, and others have been instrumental in producing high-quality Java libraries for XML processing. Many of these libraries have now been integrated into the Java platform.

This chapter introduces XML and covers the XML features of the Java library. As always, we'll point out along the way when the hype surrounding XML is justified—and when you have to take it with a grain of salt and try solving your problems the old-fashioned way, through good design and code.

## 2.1 Introducing XML

In Chapter 10 of Volume I, you have seen the use of *property files* to describe the configuration of a program. A property file contains a set of name/value pairs, such as

```
fontname=Times Roman
fontsize=12
windowsize=400 200
color=0 50 100
```

You can use the Properties class to read in such a file with a single method call. That's a nice feature, but it doesn't really go far enough. In many cases, the information you want to describe has more structure than the property file format can comfortably handle. Consider the fontname/fontsize entries in the example. It would be more object-oriented to have a single entry:

```
font=Times Roman 12
```

But then, parsing the font description gets ugly as you have to figure out when the font name ends and the font size starts.

Property files have a single flat hierarchy. You can often see programmers work around that limitation with key names, such as

```
title.fontname=Helvetica
title.fontsize=36
body.fontname=Times Roman
body.fontsize=12
```

Another shortcoming of the property file format is the requirement that keys must be unique. To store a sequence of values, you need another workaround, such as

```
menu.item.1=Times Roman
menu.item.2=Helvetica
menu.item.3=Goudy Old Style
```

The XML format solves these problems. It can express hierarchical structures and is thus more flexible than the flat table structure of a property file.

An XML file for describing a program configuration might look like this:

```
<configuration>
   <title>
      <font>
         <name>Helvetica</name>
         <size>36</size>
      </font>
   </title>
   <body>
      <font>
         <name>Times Roman</name>
         <size>12</size>
      </font>
   </body>
   <window>
      <width>400</width>
      <height>200</height>
   </window>
   <color>
      <red>0</red>
      <green>50</green>
      <blue>100</blue>
   </color>
   <menu>
      <item>Times Roman</item>
      <item>Helvetica</item>
      <item>Goudy Old Style</item>
   </menu>
</configuration>
```

The XML format allows you to express the hierarchy and record repeated elements without contortions.

The format of an XML file is straightforward. It looks similar to an HTML file. There is a good reason for that—both the XML and HTML formats are descendants of the venerable Standard Generalized Markup Language (SGML).

SGML has been around since the 1970s for describing the structure of complex documents. It has been used with success in some industries that require ongoing maintenance of massive documentation—in particular, the aircraft industry. However, SGML is quite complex, so it has never caught on in a big way. Much of that complexity arises because SGML has two conflicting goals. SGML wants to make sure that documents are formed according to the rules for their document type, but it also wants to make data entry easy by allowing shortcuts that reduce typing. XML was designed as a simplified version of SGML for use on the Internet. As is often true, simpler is better, and XML has enjoyed the immediate and enthusiastic reception that has eluded SGML for so long.

**NOTE:** You can find a very nice version of the XML standard, with annotations by Tim Bray, at www.xml.com/axml/axml.html.

Even though XML and HTML have common roots, there are important differences between the two.

- Unlike HTML, XML is case-sensitive. For example, `<H1>` and `<h1>` are different XML tags.

- In HTML, you can omit end tags, such as `</p>` or `</li>`, if it is clear from the context where a paragraph or list item ends. In XML, you can never omit an end tag.

- In XML, elements that have a single tag without a matching end tag must end in a /, as in `<img src="coffeecup.png"/>`. That way, the parser knows not to look for a `</img>` tag.

- In XML, attribute values must be enclosed in quotation marks. In HTML, quotation marks are optional. For example, `<applet code="MyApplet.class" width=300 height=300>` is legal HTML but not legal XML. In XML, you have to use quotation marks: `width="300"`.

- In HTML, you can have attribute names without values, such as `<input type="radio" name="language" value="Java" checked>`. In XML, all attributes must have values, such as `checked="true"` or (ugh) `checked="checked"`.

## 2.1.1 The Structure of an XML Document

An XML document should start with a header such as

```
<?xml version="1.0"?>
```

or

```
<?xml version="1.0" encoding="UTF-8"?>
```

Strictly speaking, a header is optional, but it is highly recommended.

 **NOTE:** Since SGML was created for processing of real documents, XML files are called *documents* even though many of them describe data sets that one would not normally call documents.

The header can be followed by a *document type definition* (DTD), such as

```
<!DOCTYPE web-app PUBLIC
   "-//Sun Microsystems, Inc.//DTD Web Application 2.2//EN"
   "http://java.sun.com/j2ee/dtds/web-app_2_2.dtd">
```

DTDs are an important mechanism to ensure the correctness of a document, but they are not required. We will discuss them later in this chapter.

Finally, the body of the XML document contains the *root element*, which can contain other elements. For example,

```
<?xml version="1.0"?>
<!DOCTYPE configuration . . .>
<configuration>
   <title>
      <font>
         <name>Helvetica</name>
         <size>36</size>
      </font>
   </title>
   . . .
</configuration>
```

An element can contain *child elements*, text, or both. In the preceding example, the font element has two child elements, name and size. The name element contains the text "Helvetica".

---

 **TIP:** It is best to structure your XML documents so that an element contains *either* child elements *or* text. In other words, you should avoid situations such as

```
<font>
   Helvetica
   <size>36</size>
</font>
```

This is called *mixed content* in the XML specification. As you will see later in this chapter, you can simplify parsing if you avoid mixed content.

---

XML elements can contain attributes, such as

```
<size unit="pt">36</size>
```

There is some disagreement among XML designers about when to use elements and when to use attributes. For example, it would seem easier to describe a font as

```
<font name="Helvetica" size="36"/>
```

than

```
<font>
    <name>Helvetica</name>
    <size>36</size>
</font>
```

However, attributes are much less flexible. Suppose you want to add units to the size value. If you use attributes, you will have to add the unit to the attribute value:

```
<font name="Helvetica" size="36 pt"/>
```

Ugh! Now you have to parse the string `"36 pt"`, just the kind of hassle that XML was designed to avoid. Adding an attribute to the size element is much cleaner:

```
<font>
    <name>Helvetica</name>
    <size unit="pt">36</size>
</font>
```

A commonly used rule of thumb is that attributes should be used only to modify the interpretation of a value, not to specify values. If you find yourself engaged in metaphysical discussions about whether a particular setting is a modification of the interpretation of a value or not, just say "no" to attributes and use elements throughout. Many useful XML documents don't use attributes at all.

 **NOTE:** In HTML, the rule for attribute usage is simple: If it isn't displayed on the web page, it's an attribute. For example, consider the hyperlink

```
<a href="http://java.sun.com">Java Technology</a>
```

The string Java Technology is displayed on the web page, but the URL of the link is not a part of the displayed page. However, the rule isn't all that helpful for most XML files because the data in an XML file aren't normally meant to be viewed by humans.

Elements and text are the "bread and butter" of XML documents. Here are a few other markup instructions that you might encounter:

- *Character references* have the form &#*decimalValue*; or &#x*hexValue*;. For example, the character can be denoted with either of the following:

    &#233; &#xE9;

- *Entity references* have the form &*name*;. The entity references

    &lt; &gt; &amp; &quot; &apos;

have predefined meanings: the less-than, greater-than, ampersand, quotation mark, and apostrophe characters. You can define other entity references in a DTD.

- *CDATA sections* are delimited by `<![CDATA[` and `]]>`. They are a special form of character data. You can use them to include strings that contain characters such as `< > &` without having them interpreted as markup, for example:

  ```
  <![CDATA[< & > are my favorite delimiters]]>
  ```

  CDATA sections cannot contain the string `]]>`. Use this feature with caution! It is too often used as a back door for smuggling legacy data into XML documents.

- *Processing instructions* are instructions for applications that process XML documents. They are delimited by `<?` and `?>`, for example

  ```
  <?xml-stylesheet href="mystyle.css" type="text/css"?>
  ```

  Every XML document starts with a processing instruction

  ```
  <?xml version="1.0"?>
  ```

- *Comments* are delimited by `<!--` and `-->`, for example

  ```
  <!-- This is a comment. -->
  ```

  Comments should not contain the string `--`. Comments should only be information for human readers. They should never contain hidden commands; use processing instructions for commands.

## 2.2 Parsing an XML Document

To process an XML document, you need to *parse* it. A parser is a program that reads a file, confirms that the file has the correct format, breaks it up into the constituent elements, and lets a programmer access those elements. The Java library supplies two kinds of XML parsers:

- Tree parsers, such as the Document Object Model (DOM) parser, that read an XML document into a tree structure.
- Streaming parsers, such as the Simple API for XML (SAX) parser, that generate events as they read an XML document.

The DOM parser is easier to use for most purposes, and we explain it first. You may consider a streaming parser if you process very long documents whose tree structures would use up a lot of memory, or if you are only interested in a few elements and don't care about their context. For more information, see Section 2.6, "Streaming Parsers," on p. 150.

The DOM parser interface is standardized by the World Wide Web Consortium (W3C). The `org.w3c.dom` package contains the definitions of interface types such as `Document` and `Element`. Different suppliers, such as the Apache Organization and IBM, have written DOM parsers whose classes implement these interfaces. The Java API for XML Processing (JAXP) library actually makes it possible to plug in any of these parsers. But the JDK also comes with a DOM parser. We will use that parser in this chapter.

To read an XML document, you need a `DocumentBuilder` object that you get from a `DocumentBuilderFactory` like this:

```
DocumentBuilderFactory factory = DocumentBuilderFactory.newInstance();
DocumentBuilder builder = factory.newDocumentBuilder();
```

You can now read a document from a file:

```
File f = . . .
Document doc = builder.parse(f);
```

Alternatively, you can use a URL:

```
URL u = . . .
Document doc = builder.parse(u);
```

You can even specify an arbitrary input stream:

```
InputStream in = . . .
Document doc = builder.parse(in);
```

---

 **NOTE:** If you use an input stream as an input source, the parser will not be able to locate other files that are referenced relative to the location of the document, such as a DTD in the same directory. You can install an "entity resolver" to overcome that problem.

---

The `Document` object is an in-memory representation of the tree structure of the XML document. It is composed of objects whose classes implement the `Node` interface and its various subinterfaces. Figure 2.1 shows the inheritance hierarchy of the subinterfaces.

Start analyzing the contents of a document by calling the `getDocumentElement` method. It returns the root element.

```
Element root = doc.getDocumentElement();
```

For example, if you are processing a document

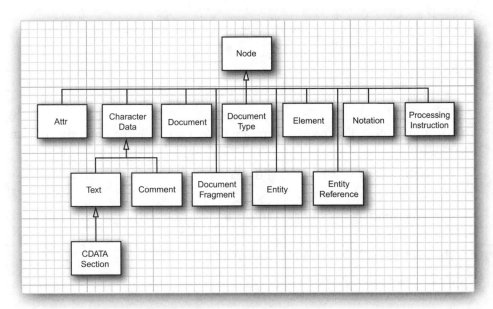

**Figure 2.1** The Node interface and its subinterfaces

```
<?xml version="1.0"?>
<font>
   . . .
</font>
```

then calling getDocumentElement returns the font element.

The getTagName method returns the tag name of an element. In the preceding example, root.getTagName() returns the string "font".

To get the element's children (which may be subelements, text, comments, or other nodes), use the getChildNodes method. That method returns a collection of type NodeList. That type was invented before the standard Java collections, and it has a different access protocol. The item method gets the item with a given index, and the getLength method gives the total count of the items. Therefore, you can enumerate all children like this:

```
NodeList children = root.getChildNodes();
for (int i = 0; i < children.getLength(); i++)
{
   Node child = children.item(i);
   . . .
}
```

Be careful when analyzing the children. Suppose, for example, that you are processing the document

```
<font>
   <name>Helvetica</name>
   <size>36</size>
</font>
```

You would expect the font element to have two children, but the parser reports five:

- The whitespace between <font> and <name>
- The name element
- The whitespace between </name> and <size>
- The size element
- The whitespace between </size> and </font>

Figure 2.2 shows the DOM tree.

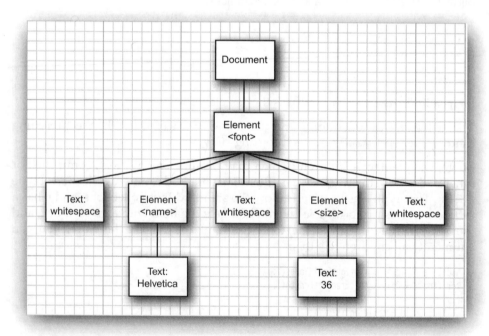

**Figure 2.2** A simple DOM tree

If you expect only subelements, you can ignore the whitespace:

```
for (int i = 0; i < children.getLength(); i++)
{
   Node child = children.item(i);
   if (child instanceof Element)
   {
      Element childElement = (Element) child;
      . . .
   }
}
```

Now you look at only two elements, with tag names name and size.

As you will see in the next section, you can do even better if your document has a DTD. Then the parser knows which elements don't have text nodes as children, and it can suppress the whitespace for you.

When analyzing the name and size elements, you want to retrieve the text strings that they contain. Those text strings are themselves contained in child nodes of type Text. You know that these Text nodes are the only children, so you can use the getFirstChild method without having to traverse another NodeList. Then, use the getData method to retrieve the string stored in the Text node.

```
for (int i = 0; i < children.getLength(); i++)
{
   Node child = children.item(i);
   if (child instanceof Element)
   {
      Element childElement = (Element) child;
      Text textNode = (Text) childElement.getFirstChild();
      String text = textNode.getData().trim();
      if (childElement.getTagName().equals("name"))
         name = text;
      else if (childElement.getTagName().equals("size"))
         size = Integer.parseInt(text);
   }
}
```

 **TIP:** It is a good idea to call trim on the return value of the getData method. If the author of an XML file puts the beginning and the ending tags on separate lines, such as

```
<size>
   36
</size>
```

then the parser includes all line breaks and spaces in the text node data. Calling the trim method removes the whitespace surrounding the actual data.

You can also get the last child with the getLastChild method, and the next sibling of a node with getNextSibling. Therefore, another way of traversing a set of child nodes is

```
for (Node childNode = element.getFirstChild();
   childNode != null;
   childNode = childNode.getNextSibling())
{
   . . .
}
```

To enumerate the attributes of a node, call the getAttributes method. It returns a NamedNodeMap object that contains Node objects describing the attributes. You can traverse the nodes in a NamedNodeMap in the same way as a NodeList. Then, call the getNodeName and getNodeValue methods to get the attribute names and values.

```
NamedNodeMap attributes = element.getAttributes();
for (int i = 0; i < attributes.getLength(); i++)
{
   Node attribute = attributes.item(i);
   String name = attribute.getNodeName();
   String value = attribute.getNodeValue();
   . . .
}
```

Alternatively, if you know the name of an attribute, you can retrieve the corresponding value directly:

```
String unit = element.getAttribute("unit");
```

You have now seen how to analyze a DOM tree. The program in Listing 2.1 puts these techniques to work. You can use the File —> Open menu option to read in an XML file. A DocumentBuilder object parses the XML file and produces a Document object. The program displays the Document object as a tree (see Figure 2.3).

The tree display shows clearly how child elements are surrounded by text containing whitespace and comments. For greater clarity, the program displays newline and return characters as \n and \r. (Otherwise, they would show up as hollow boxes—the default symbol for a character that Swing cannot draw in a string.)

In Chapter 6, you will learn the techniques that this program uses to display the tree and the attribute tables. The DOMTreeModel class implements the TreeModel interface. The getRoot method returns the root element of the document. The getChild method gets the node list of children and returns the item with the requested index. The tree cell renderer displays the following:

• For elements, the element tag name and a table of all attributes

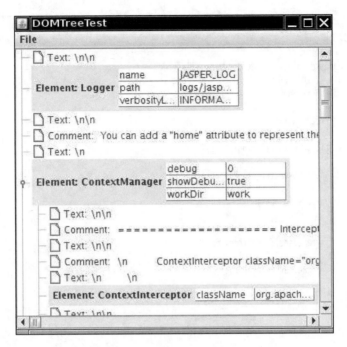

**Figure 2.3** A parse tree of an XML document

- For character data, the interface (Text, Comment, or CDATASection), followed by the data, with newline and return characters replaced by \n and \r
- For all other node types, the class name followed by the result of toString

**Listing 2.1** dom/TreeViewer.java

```
 1  package dom;
 2
 3  import java.awt.*;
 4  import java.awt.event.*;
 5  import java.io.*;
 6  import javax.swing.*;
 7  import javax.swing.event.*;
 8  import javax.swing.table.*;
 9  import javax.swing.tree.*;
10  import javax.xml.parsers.*;
11  import org.w3c.dom.*;
12  import org.w3c.dom.CharacterData;
```

*(Continues)*

**Listing 2.1** *(Continued)*

```java
13  /**
14   * This program displays an XML document as a tree.
15   * @version 1.12 2012-06-03
16   * @author Cay Horstmann
17   */
18  public class TreeViewer
19  {
20     public static void main(String[] args)
21     {
22        EventQueue.invokeLater(new Runnable()
23           {
24              public void run()
25              {
26                 JFrame frame = new DOMTreeFrame();
27                 frame.setTitle("TreeViewer");
28                 frame.setDefaultCloseOperation(JFrame.EXIT_ON_CLOSE);
29                 frame.setVisible(true);
30              }
31           });
32     }
33  }
34
35  /**
36   * This frame contains a tree that displays the contents of an XML document.
37   */
38  class DOMTreeFrame extends JFrame
39  {
40     private static final int DEFAULT_WIDTH = 400;
41     private static final int DEFAULT_HEIGHT = 400;
42
43     private DocumentBuilder builder;
44
45     public DOMTreeFrame()
46     {
47        setSize(DEFAULT_WIDTH, DEFAULT_HEIGHT);
48
49        JMenu fileMenu = new JMenu("File");
50        JMenuItem openItem = new JMenuItem("Open");
51        openItem.addActionListener(new ActionListener()
52           {
53              public void actionPerformed(ActionEvent event)
54              {
55                 openFile();
56              }
57           });
58        fileMenu.add(openItem);
59
60        JMenuItem exitItem = new JMenuItem("Exit");
```

```
61        exitItem.addActionListener(new ActionListener()
62           {
63              public void actionPerformed(ActionEvent event)
64              {
65                 System.exit(0);
66              }
67           });
68        fileMenu.add(exitItem);
69
70        JMenuBar menuBar = new JMenuBar();
71        menuBar.add(fileMenu);
72        setJMenuBar(menuBar);
73     }
74
75     /**
76      * Open a file and load the document.
77      */
78     public void openFile()
79     {
80        JFileChooser chooser = new JFileChooser();
81        chooser.setCurrentDirectory(new File("dom"));
82
83        chooser.setFileFilter(new javax.swing.filechooser.FileFilter()
84           {
85              public boolean accept(File f)
86              {
87                 return f.isDirectory() || f.getName().toLowerCase().endsWith(".xml");
88              }
89
90              public String getDescription()
91              {
92                 return "XML files";
93              }
94           });
95        int r = chooser.showOpenDialog(this);
96        if (r != JFileChooser.APPROVE_OPTION) return;
97        final File file = chooser.getSelectedFile();
98
99        new SwingWorker<Document, Void>()
100          {
101             protected Document doInBackground() throws Exception
102             {
103                if (builder == null)
104                {
105                   DocumentBuilderFactory factory = DocumentBuilderFactory.newInstance();
106                   builder = factory.newDocumentBuilder();
107                }
108                return builder.parse(file);
109             }
```

*(Continues)*

**Listing 2.1**  *(Continued)*

```
110            protected void done()
111            {
112               try
113               {
114                  Document doc = get();
115                  JTree tree = new JTree(new DOMTreeModel(doc));
116                  tree.setCellRenderer(new DOMTreeCellRenderer());
117
118                  setContentPane(new JScrollPane(tree));
119                  validate();
120               }
121               catch (Exception e)
122               {
123                  JOptionPane.showMessageDialog(DOMTreeFrame.this, e);
124               }
125            }
126         }.execute();
127   }
128
129 }
130
131 /**
132  * This tree model describes the tree structure of an XML document.
133  */
134 class DOMTreeModel implements TreeModel
135 {
136    private Document doc;
137
138    /**
139     * Constructs a document tree model.
140     * @param doc the document
141     */
142    public DOMTreeModel(Document doc)
143    {
144       this.doc = doc;
145    }
146
147    public Object getRoot()
148    {
149       return doc.getDocumentElement();
150    }
151
152    public int getChildCount(Object parent)
153    {
154       Node node = (Node) parent;
155       NodeList list = node.getChildNodes();
156       return list.getLength();
157    }
```

```
158    public Object getChild(Object parent, int index)
159    {
160        Node node = (Node) parent;
161        NodeList list = node.getChildNodes();
162        return list.item(index);
163    }
164
165    public int getIndexOfChild(Object parent, Object child)
166    {
167        Node node = (Node) parent;
168        NodeList list = node.getChildNodes();
169        for (int i = 0; i < list.getLength(); i++)
170            if (getChild(node, i) == child) return i;
171        return -1;
172    }
173
174    public boolean isLeaf(Object node)
175    {
176        return getChildCount(node) == 0;
177    }
178
179    public void valueForPathChanged(TreePath path, Object newValue)
180    {
181    }
182
183    public void addTreeModelListener(TreeModelListener l)
184    {
185    }
186
187    public void removeTreeModelListener(TreeModelListener l)
188    {
189    }
190
191 }
192
193 /**
194  * This class renders an XML node.
195  */
196 class DOMTreeCellRenderer extends DefaultTreeCellRenderer
197 {
198    public Component getTreeCellRendererComponent(JTree tree, Object value, boolean selected,
199            boolean expanded, boolean leaf, int row, boolean hasFocus)
200    {
201        Node node = (Node) value;
202        if (node instanceof Element) return elementPanel((Element) node);
203
204        super.getTreeCellRendererComponent(tree, value, selected, expanded, leaf, row, hasFocus);
```

*(Continues)*

**Listing 2.1** *(Continued)*

```
205        if (node instanceof CharacterData) setText(characterString((CharacterData) node));
206        else setText(node.getClass() + ": " + node.toString());
207        return this;
208    }
209
210    public static JPanel elementPanel(Element e)
211    {
212        JPanel panel = new JPanel();
213        panel.add(new JLabel("Element: " + e.getTagName()));
214        final NamedNodeMap map = e.getAttributes();
215        panel.add(new JTable(new AbstractTableModel()
216            {
217                public int getRowCount()
218                {
219                    return map.getLength();
220                }
221
222                public int getColumnCount()
223                {
224                    return 2;
225                }
226
227                public Object getValueAt(int r, int c)
228                {
229                    return c == 0 ? map.item(r).getNodeName() : map.item(r).getNodeValue();
230                }
231            }));
232        return panel;
233    }
234
235    public static String characterString(CharacterData node)
236    {
237        StringBuilder builder = new StringBuilder(node.getData());
238        for (int i = 0; i < builder.length(); i++)
239        {
240            if (builder.charAt(i) == '\r')
241            {
242                builder.replace(i, i + 1, "\\r");
243                i++;
244            }
245            else if (builder.charAt(i) == '\n')
246            {
247                builder.replace(i, i + 1, "\\n");
248                i++;
249            }
```

```
250        else if (builder.charAt(i) == '\t')
251        {
252            builder.replace(i, i + 1, "\\t");
253            i++;
254        }
255    }
256    if (node instanceof CDATASection) builder.insert(0, "CDATASection: ");
257    else if (node instanceof Text) builder.insert(0, "Text: ");
258    else if (node instanceof Comment) builder.insert(0, "Comment: ");
259
260    return builder.toString();
261    }
262 }
```

---

**javax.xml.parsers.DocumentBuilderFactory**  1.4

- `static DocumentBuilderFactory newInstance()`
  returns an instance of the `DocumentBuilderFactory` class.

- `DocumentBuilder newDocumentBuilder()`
  returns an instance of the `DocumentBuilder` class.

---

**javax.xml.parsers.DocumentBuilder**  1.4

- `Document parse(File f)`
- `Document parse(String url)`
- `Document parse(InputStream in)`
  parses an XML document from the given file, URL, or input stream and returns
  the parsed document.

---

**org.w3c.dom.Document**  1.4

- `Element getDocumentElement()`
  returns the root element of the document.

---

**org.w3c.dom.Element**  1.4

- `String getTagName()`
  returns the name of the element.

- `String getAttribute(String name)`
  returns the value of the attribute with the given name, or the empty string if there
  is no such attribute.

---

**org.w3c.dom.Node** 1.4

- NodeList getChildNodes()
  returns a node list that contains all children of this node.
- Node getFirstChild()
- Node getLastChild()
  gets the first or last child node of this node, or null if this node has no children.
- Node getNextSibling()
- Node getPreviousSibling()
  gets the next or previous sibling of this node, or null if this node has no siblings.
- Node getParentNode()
  gets the parent of this node, or null if this node is the document node.
- NamedNodeMap getAttributes()
  returns a node map that contains Attr nodes that describe all attributes of this node.
- String getNodeName()
  returns the name of this node. If the node is an Attr node, the name is the attribute name.
- String getNodeValue()
  returns the value of this node. If the node is an Attr node, the value is the attribute value.

---

**org.w3c.dom.CharacterData** 1.4

- String getData()
  returns the text stored in this node.

---

**org.w3c.dom.NodeList** 1.4

- int getLength()
  returns the number of nodes in this list.
- Node item(int index)
  returns the node with the given index. The index is between 0 and getLength() - 1.

---

**org.w3c.dom.NamedNodeMap** 1.4

- int getLength()
  returns the number of nodes in this map.
- Node item(int index)
  returns the node with the given index. The index is between 0 and getLength() - 1.

## 2.3 Validating XML Documents

In the preceding section, you saw how to traverse the tree structure of a DOM document. However, if you simply follow that approach, you'll find that you will have to perform quite a bit of tedious programming and error checking. Not only do you have to deal with whitespace between elements, but you also need to check whether the document contains the nodes that you expect. For example, suppose you are reading an element:

```
<font>
   <name>Helvetica</name>
   <size>36</size>
</font>
```

You get the first child. Oops . . . it is a text node containing whitespace "\n ". You skip text nodes and find the first element node. Then, you need to check that its tag name is "name" and that it has one child node of type Text. You move on to the next nonwhitespace child and make the same check. What if the author of the document switched the order of the children or added another child element? It is tedious to code all this error checking, but reckless to skip the checks.

Fortunately, one of the major benefits of an XML parser is that it can automatically verify that a document has the correct structure. Then, parsing becomes much simpler. For example, if you know that the font fragment has passed validation, you can simply get the two grandchildren, cast them as Text nodes, and get the text data, without any further checking.

To specify the document structure, you can supply a DTD or an XML Schema definition. A DTD or schema contains rules that explain how a document should be formed, by specifying the legal child elements and attributes for each element. For example, a DTD might contain a rule:

```
<!ELEMENT font (name,size)>
```

This rule expresses that a font element must always have two children, which are name and size elements. The XML Schema language expresses the same constraint as

```
<xsd:element name="font">
   <xsd:sequence>
      <xsd:element name="name" type="xsd:string"/>
      <xsd:element name="size" type="xsd:int"/>
   </xsd:sequence>
</xsd:element>
```

XML Schema can express more sophisticated validation conditions (such as the fact that the size element must contain an integer) than can DTDs. Unlike the DTD syntax, the XML Schema syntax uses XML, which is a benefit if you need to process schema files.

The XML Schema language was designed to replace DTDs. However, as we write this chapter, DTDs are still very much alive. XML Schema is very complex and far from universally adopted. In fact, some XML users are so annoyed by the complexity of XML Schema that they use alternative validation languages. The most common choice is Relax NG (www.relaxng.org).

In the next section, we will discuss DTDs in detail, then briefly cover the basics of XML Schema support. Finally, we will present a complete application that demonstrates how validation simplifies XML programming.

## 2.3.1 Document Type Definitions

There are several methods for supplying a DTD. You can include a DTD in an XML document like this:

```
<?xml version="1.0"?>
<!DOCTYPE configuration [
   <!ELEMENT configuration . . .>
   more rules
   . . .
]>
<configuration>
   . . .
</configuration>
```

As you can see, the rules are included inside a DOCTYPE declaration, in a block delimited by [. . .]. The document type must match the name of the root element, such as configuration in our example.

Supplying a DTD inside an XML document is somewhat uncommon because DTDs can grow lengthy. It makes more sense to store the DTD externally. The SYSTEM declaration can be used for that purpose; specify a URL that contains the DTD, for example:

```
<!DOCTYPE configuration SYSTEM "config.dtd">
```

or

```
<!DOCTYPE configuration SYSTEM "http://myserver.com/config.dtd">
```

**CAUTION:** If you use a relative URL for the DTD (such as "config.dtd"), give the parser a File or URL object, not an InputStream. If you must parse from an input stream, supply an entity resolver (see the following note).

Finally, the mechanism for identifying well-known DTDs has its origin in SGML. Here is an example:

```
<!DOCTYPE web-app
  PUBLIC "-//Sun Microsystems, Inc.//DTD Web Application 2.2//EN"
  "http://java.sun.com/j2ee/dtds/web-app_2_2.dtd">
```

If an XML processor knows how to locate the DTD with the public identifier, it need not go to the URL.

**NOTE:** If you use a DOM parser and would like to support a PUBLIC identifier, call the setEntityResolver method of the DocumentBuilder class to install an object of a class that implements the EntityResolver interface. That interface has a single method, resolveEntity. Here is the outline of a typical implementation:

```
class MyEntityResolver implements EntityResolver
{
    public InputSource resolveEntity(String publicID,
        String systemID)
    {
        if (publicID.equals(a known ID))
            return new InputSource(DTD data);
        else
            return null; // use default behavior
    }
}
```

You can construct the input source from an InputStream, a Reader, or a string.

Now that you have seen how the parser locates the DTD, let us consider the various kinds of rules.

The ELEMENT rule specifies what children an element can have. Specify a regular expression, made up of the components shown in Table 2.1.

Here are several simple but typical examples. The following rule states that a menu element contains 0 or more item elements:

```
<!ELEMENT menu (item)*>
```

This set of rules states that a font is described by a name followed by a size, each of which contain text:

```
<!ELEMENT font (name,size)>
<!ELEMENT name (#PCDATA)>
<!ELEMENT size (#PCDATA)>
```

**Table 2.1** Rules for Element Content

| Rule | Meaning |
|---|---|
| $E*$ | 0 or more occurrences of $E$ |
| $E+$ | 1 or more occurrences of $E$ |
| $E?$ | 0 or 1 occurrences of $E$ |
| $E_1 \mid E_2 \mid . . . \mid E_n$ | One of $E_1, E_2, . . ., E_n$ |
| $E_1, E_2, . . ., E_n$ | $E_1$ followed by $E_2, . . ., E_n$ |
| #PCDATA | Text |
| $(\#PCDATA \mid E_1 \mid E_2 \mid . . . \mid E_n)*$ | 0 or more occurrences of text and $E_1, E_2, . . ., E_n$ in any order (mixed content) |
| ANY | Any children allowed |
| EMPTY | No children allowed |

The abbreviation PCDATA denotes *parsed character data*. It is "parsed" because the parser interprets the text string, looking for < characters that denote the start of a new tag, or & characters that denote the start of an entity.

An element specification can contain regular expressions that are nested and complex. For example, here is a rule that describes the makeup of a chapter in this book:

```
<!ELEMENT chapter (intro,(heading,(para|image|table|note)+)+)>
```

Each chapter starts with an introduction, which is followed by one or more sections consisting of a heading and one or more paragraphs, images, tables, or notes.

However, in one common case you can't define the rules to be as flexible as you might like. Whenever an element can contain text, there are only two valid cases. Either the element contains nothing but text, such as

```
<!ELEMENT name (#PCDATA)>
```

or the element contains *any combination of text and tags in any order*, such as

```
<!ELEMENT para (#PCDATA|em|strong|code)*>
```

It is not legal to specify any other types of rules that contain #PCDATA. For example, the following is illegal:

```
<!ELEMENT captionedImage (image,#PCDATA)>
```

You have to rewrite such a rule, either by introducing another caption element or by allowing any combination of image elements and text.

This restriction simplifies the job of the XML parser when parsing *mixed content* (a mixture of tags and text). Since you lose some control by allowing mixed content, it is best to design DTDs so that all elements contain either other elements or nothing but text.

 **NOTE:** Actually, it isn't quite true that you can specify arbitrary regular expressions of elements in a DTD rule. An XML parser may reject certain complex rule sets that lead to nondeterministic parsing. For example, a regular expression $((x,y)|(x,z))$ is nondeterministic. When the parser sees x, it doesn't know which of the two alternatives to take. This expression can be rewritten in a deterministic form as $(x,(y|z))$. However, some expressions can't be reformulated, such as $((x,y)*|x?)$. The Sun parser gives no warnings when presented with an ambiguous DTD; it simply picks the first matching alternative when parsing, which causes it to reject some correct inputs. Of course, the parser is well within its rights to do so because the XML standard allows a parser to assume that the DTD is unambiguous.

In practice, this isn't an issue over which you should lose sleep, because most DTDs are so simple that you will never run into ambiguity problems.

You can also specify rules to describe the legal attributes of elements. The general syntax is

<!ATTLIST *element attribute type default*>

Table 2.2 shows the legal attribute types, and Table 2.3 shows the syntax for the defaults.

**Table 2.2** Attribute Types

| Type | Meaning |
| --- | --- |
| CDATA | Any character string |
| $(A_1|A_2| \ldots |A_n)$ | One of the string attributes $A_1, A_2, \ldots, A_n$ |
| NMTOKEN, NMTOKENS | One or more name tokens |
| ID | A unique ID |
| IDREF, IDREFS | One or more references to a unique ID |
| ENTITY, ENTITIES | One or more unparsed entities |

**Table 2.3** Attribute Defaults

| Default | Meaning |
| --- | --- |
| #REQUIRED | Attribute is required. |
| #IMPLIED | Attribute is optional. |
| *A* | Attribute is optional; the parser reports it to be *A* if it is not specified. |
| #FIXED *A* | The attribute must either be unspecified or *A*; in either case, the parser reports it to be *A*. |

Here are two typical attribute specifications:

```
<!ATTLIST font style (plain|bold|italic|bold-italic) "plain">
<!ATTLIST size unit CDATA #IMPLIED>
```

The first specification describes the style attribute of a font element. There are four legal attribute values, and the default value is plain. The second specification expresses that the unit attribute of the size element can contain any character data sequence.

 **NOTE:** We generally recommend the use of elements, not attributes, to describe data. Following that recommendation, the font style should be a separate element, such as <font><style>plain</style>. . .</font>. However, attributes have an undeniable advantage for enumerated types because the parser can verify that the values are legal. For example, if the font style is an attribute, the parser checks that it is one of the four allowed values, and supplies a default if no value was given.

The handling of a CDATA attribute value is subtly different from the processing of #PCDATA that you have seen before, and quite unrelated to the <![CDATA[...]]> sections. The attribute value is first *normalized*—that is, the parser processes character and entity references (such as &#233; or &lt;) and replaces whitespace with spaces.

An NMTOKEN (or name token) is similar to CDATA, but most nonalphanumeric characters and internal whitespace are disallowed, and the parser removes leading and trailing whitespace. NMTOKENS is a whitespace-separated list of name tokens.

The ID construct is quite useful. An ID is a name token that must be unique in the document—the parser checks the uniqueness. You will see an application in the next sample program. An IDREF is a reference to an ID that exists in the same document, which the parser also checks. IDREFS is a whitespace-separated list of ID references.

An ENTITY attribute value refers to an "unparsed external entity." That is a holdover from SGML that is rarely used in practice. The annotated XML specification at www.xml.com/axml/axml.html has an example.

A DTD can also define *entities*, or abbreviations that are replaced during parsing. You can find a good example for the use of entities in the user interface descriptions for the Mozilla/Netscape 6 browser. Those descriptions are formatted in XML and contain entity definitions such as

```
<!ENTITY back.label "Back">
```

Elsewhere, text can contain an entity reference, for example:

```
<menuitem label="&back.label;"/>
```

The parser replaces the entity reference with the replacement string. To internationalize the application, only the string in the entity definition needs to be changed. Other uses of entities are more complex and less commonly used; look at the XML specification for details.

This concludes the introduction to DTDs. Now that you have seen how to use DTDs, you can configure your parser to take advantage of them. First, tell the document builder factory to turn on validation:

```
factory.setValidating(true);
```

All builders produced by this factory validate their input against a DTD. The most useful benefit of validation is ignoring whitespace in element content. For example, consider the XML fragment

```
<font>
   <name>Helvetica</name>
   <size>36</size>
</font>
```

A nonvalidating parser reports the whitespace between the font, name, and size elements because it has no way of knowing if the children of font are

```
(name,size)
(#PCDATA,name,size)*
```

or perhaps

```
ANY
```

Once the DTD specifies that the children are (name,size), the parser knows that the whitespace between them is not text. Call

```
factory.setIgnoringElementContentWhitespace(true);
```

and the builder will stop reporting the whitespace in text nodes. That means you can now *rely on* the fact that a font node has two children. You no longer need to program a tedious loop:

```
for (int i = 0; i < children.getLength(); i++)
{
    Node child = children.item(i);
    if (child instanceof Element)
    {
        Element childElement = (Element) child;
        if (childElement.getTagName().equals("name")) . . .
        else if (childElement.getTagName().equals("size")) . . .
    }
}
```

Instead, you can simply access the first and second child:

```
Element nameElement = (Element) children.item(0);
Element sizeElement = (Element) children.item(1);
```

That is why DTDs are so useful. You don't overload your program with rule checking code—the parser has already done that work by the time you get the document.

 **TIP:** Many programmers who start using XML are uncomfortable with validation and end up analyzing the DOM tree on the fly. If you need to convince colleagues of the benefit of using validated documents, show them the two coding alternatives—it should win them over.

When the parser reports an error, your application will want to do something about it—log it, show it to the user, or throw an exception to abandon the parsing. Therefore, you should install an error handler whenever you use validation. Supply an object that implements the ErrorHandler interface. That interface has three methods:

```
void warning(SAXParseException exception)
void error(SAXParseException exception)
void fatalError(SAXParseException exception)
```

Install the error handler with the setErrorHandler method of the DocumentBuilder class:

```
builder.setErrorHandler(handler);
```

---

**javax.xml.parsers.DocumentBuilder** 1.4

- void setEntityResolver(EntityResolver resolver)
  sets the resolver to locate entities that are referenced in the XML documents to be parsed.
- void setErrorHandler(ErrorHandler handler)
  sets the handler to report errors and warnings that occur during parsing.

---

**org.xml.sax.EntityResolver** 1.4

- public InputSource resolveEntity(String publicID, String systemID)
  returns an input source that contains the data referenced by the given ID(s), or null to indicate that this resolver doesn't know how to resolve the particular name. The publicID parameter may be null if no public ID was supplied.

---

**org.xml.sax.InputSource** 1.4

- InputSource(InputStream in)
- InputSource(Reader in)
- InputSource(String systemID)
  constructs an input source from a stream, reader, or system ID (usually a relative or absolute URL).

---

**org.xml.sax.ErrorHandler** 1.4

- void fatalError(SAXParseException exception)
- void error(SAXParseException exception)
- void warning(SAXParseException exception)
  Override these methods to provide handlers for fatal errors, nonfatal errors, and warnings.

---

**org.xml.sax.SAXParseException** 1.4

- int getLineNumber()
- int getColumnNumber()
  returns the line and column number of the end of the processed input that caused the exception.

---

**`javax.xml.parsers.DocumentBuilderFactory`** 1.4

- `boolean isValidating()`
- `void setValidating(boolean value)`

  gets or sets the `validating` property of the factory. If set to `true`, the parsers that this factory generates validate their input.

- `boolean isIgnoringElementContentWhitespace()`
- `void setIgnoringElementContentWhitespace(boolean value)`

  gets or sets the `ignoringElementContentWhitespace` property of the factory. If set to `true`, the parsers that this factory generates ignore whitespace between element nodes that don't have mixed content (i.e., a mixture of elements and #PCDATA).

---

## 2.3.2 XML Schema

XML Schema is quite a bit more complex than the DTD syntax, so we will only cover the basics. For more information, we recommend the tutorial at www.w3.org/TR/xmlschema-0.

To reference a Schema file in a document, add attributes to the root element, for example:

```
<?xml version="1.0"?>
<configuration xmlns:xsi="http://www.w3.org/2001/XMLSchema-instance"
    xsi:noNamespaceSchemaLocation="config.xsd">
    . . .
</configuration>
```

This declaration states that the schema file `config.xsd` should be used to validate the document. If your document uses namespaces, the syntax is a bit more complex—see the XML Schema tutorial for details. (The prefix xsi is a *namespace alias*; see Section 2.5, "Using Namespaces," on p. 147 for more information.)

A schema defines a *type* for each element. The type can be a *simple type*—a string with formatting restrictions—or a *complex type*. Some simple types are built into XML Schema, including

```
xsd:string
xsd:int
xsd:boolean
```

---

 **NOTE:** We use the prefix xsd: to denote the XML Schema Definition namespace. Some authors use the prefix xs: instead.

---

You can define your own simple types. For example, here is an enumerated type:

```
<xsd:simpleType name="StyleType">
   <xsd:restriction base="xsd:string">
      <xsd:enumeration value="PLAIN" />
      <xsd:enumeration value="BOLD" />
      <xsd:enumeration value="ITALIC" />
      <xsd:enumeration value="BOLD_ITALIC" />
   </xsd:restriction>
</xsd:simpleType>
```

When you define an element, you specify its type:

```
<xsd:element name="name" type="xsd:string"/>
<xsd:element name="size" type="xsd:int"/>
<xsd:element name="style" type="StyleType"/>
```

The type constrains the element content. For example, the elements

```
<size>10</size>
<style>PLAIN</style>
```

will validate correctly, but the elements

```
<size>default</size>
<style>SLANTED</style>
```

will be rejected by the parser.

You can compose types into complex types, for example:

```
<xsd:complexType name="FontType">
   <xsd:sequence>
      <xsd:element ref="name"/>
      <xsd:element ref="size"/>
      <xsd:element ref="style"/>
   </xsd:sequence>
</xsd:complexType>
```

A FontType is a sequence of name, size, and style elements. In this type definition, we use the ref attribute and refer to definitions that are located elsewhere in the schema. You can also nest definitions, like this:

```
<xsd:complexType name="FontType">
   <xsd:sequence>
      <xsd:element name="name" type="xsd:string"/>
      <xsd:element name="size" type="xsd:int"/>
      <xsd:element name="style" type="StyleType">
         <xsd:simpleType>
            <xsd:restriction base="xsd:string">
               <xsd:enumeration value="PLAIN" />
               <xsd:enumeration value="BOLD" />
```

```
                    <xsd:enumeration value="ITALIC" />
                    <xsd:enumeration value="BOLD_ITALIC" />
                </xsd:restriction>
            </xsd:simpleType>
        </xsd:element>
    </xsd:sequence>
</xsd:complexType>
```

Note the *anonymous type definition* of the `style` element.

The `xsd:sequence` construct is the equivalent of the concatenation notation in DTDs. The `xsd:choice` construct is the equivalent of the | operator. For example,

```
<xsd:complexType name="contactinfo">
    <xsd:choice>
        <xsd:element ref="email"/>
        <xsd:element ref="phone"/>
    </xsd:choice>
</xsd:complexType>
```

This is the equivalent of the DTD type `email|phone`.

To allow repeated elements, use the `minoccurs` and `maxoccurs` attributes. For example, the equivalent of the DTD type `item*` is

```
<xsd:element name="item" type=". . ." minoccurs="0" maxoccurs="unbounded">
```

To specify attributes, add `xsd:attribute` elements to `complexType` definitions:

```
<xsd:element name="size">
    <xsd:complexType>
        . . .
        <xsd:attribute name="unit" type="xsd:string" use="optional" default="cm"/>
    </xsd:complexType>
</xsd:element>
```

This is the equivalent of the DTD statement

```
<!ATTLIST size unit CDATA #IMPLIED "cm">
```

Enclose element and type definitions of your schema inside an `xsd:schema` element:

```
<xsd:schema xmlns:xsd="http://www.w3.org/2001/XMLSchema">
    . . .
</xsd:schema>
```

Parsing an XML file with a schema is similar to parsing a file with a DTD, but with three differences:

1.  You need to turn on support for namespaces, even if you don't use them in your XML files.

    ```
    factory.setNamespaceAware(true);
    ```

2.  You need to prepare the factory for handling schemas, with the following magic incantation:

```
final String JAXP_SCHEMA_LANGUAGE = "http://java.sun.com/xml/jaxp/properties/schemaLanguage";
final String W3C_XML_SCHEMA = "http://www.w3.org/2001/XMLSchema";
factory.setAttribute(JAXP_SCHEMA_LANGUAGE, W3C_XML_SCHEMA);
```

3.  The parser *does not discard element content whitespace*. This is a definite annoyance, and there is disagreement whether or not it is an actual bug. See the code in Listing 2.4 on p. 135 for a workaround.

## 2.3.3 A Practical Example

In this section, we work through a practical example that shows the use of XML in a realistic setting. Recall from Volume I, Chapter 9 that the GridBagLayout is the most useful layout manager for Swing components. However, it is feared not just for its complexity but also for the programming tedium. It would be much more convenient to put the layout description into a text file instead of producing large amounts of repetitive code. In this section, you will see how to use XML to describe a grid bag layout and how to parse the layout files.

A grid bag is made up of rows and columns, very similar to an HTML table. Similar to an HTML table, we describe it as a sequence of rows, each of which contains cells:

```
<gridbag>
   <row>
      <cell>...</cell>
      <cell>...</cell>
      . . .
   </row>
   <row>
      <cell>...</cell>
      <cell>...</cell>
      . . .
   </row>
   . . .
</gridbag>
```

The gridbag.dtd specifies these rules:

```
<!ELEMENT gridbag (row)*>
<!ELEMENT row (cell)*>
```

Some cells can span multiple rows and columns. In the grid bag layout, that is achieved by setting the gridwidth and gridheight constraints to values larger than 1. We will use attributes of the same name:

```
<cell gridwidth="2" gridheight="2">
```

Similarly, we can use attributes for the other grid bag constraints `fill`, `anchor`, `gridx`, `gridy`, `weightx`, `weighty`, `ipadx`, and `ipady`. (We don't handle the `insets` constraint because its value is not a simple type, but it would be straightforward to support it.) For example,

```
<cell fill="HORIZONTAL" anchor="NORTH">
```

For most of these attributes, we provide the same defaults as the no-argument constructor of the `GridBagConstraints` class:

```
<!ATTLIST cell gridwidth CDATA "1">
<!ATTLIST cell gridheight CDATA "1">
<!ATTLIST cell fill (NONE|BOTH|HORIZONTAL|VERTICAL) "NONE">
<!ATTLIST cell anchor (CENTER|NORTH|NORTHEAST|EAST
   |SOUTHEAST|SOUTH|SOUTHWEST|WEST|NORTHWEST) "CENTER">
. . .
```

The `gridx` and `gridy` values get special treatment because it would be tedious and somewhat error-prone to specify them by hand. Supplying them is optional:

```
<!ATTLIST cell gridx CDATA #IMPLIED>
<!ATTLIST cell gridy CDATA #IMPLIED>
```

If they are not supplied, the program determines them according to the following heuristic: In column 0, the default `gridx` is 0. Otherwise, it is the preceding `gridx` plus the preceding `gridwidth`. The default `gridy` is always the same as the row number. Thus, you don't have to specify `gridx` and `gridy` in the most common cases where a component spans multiple rows. However, if a component spans multiple columns, you must specify `gridx` whenever you skip over that component.

**NOTE:** Grid bag experts might wonder why we don't use the `RELATIVE` and `REMAINDER` mechanism to let the grid bag layout automatically determine the `gridx` and `gridy` positions. We tried, but no amount of fussing would produce the layout of the font dialog example of Figure 2.4. Reading through the `GridBagLayout` source code, it is apparent that the algorithm just won't do the heavy lifting required to recover the absolute positions.

The program parses the attributes and sets the grid bag constraints. For example, to read the grid width, the program contains a single statement:

```
constraints.gridwidth = Integer.parseInt(e.getAttribute("gridwidth"));
```

The program need not worry about a missing attribute because the parser automatically supplies the default value if no other value was specified in the document.

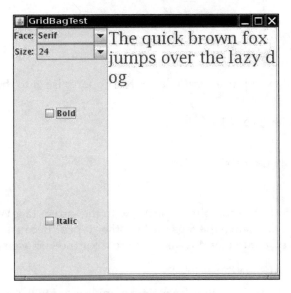

**Figure 2.4** A font dialog defined by an XML layout

To test whether a `gridx` or `gridy` attribute was specified, we call the `getAttribute` method and check if it returns the empty string:

```
String value = e.getAttribute("gridy");
if (value.length() == 0) // use default
    constraints.gridy = r;
else
    constraints.gridy = Integer.parseInt(value);
```

We found it convenient to allow arbitrary objects inside cells. That lets us specify noncomponent types such as borders. We only require that the objects belong to a class that follows the JavaBeans convention to have a no-argument constructor and to have properties that are given by getter/setter pairs. (We will discuss JavaBeans in more detail in Chapter 8.)

A bean is defined by a class name and zero or more properties:

```
<!ELEMENT bean (class, property*)>
<!ELEMENT class (#PCDATA)>
```

A property contains a name and a value:

```
<!ELEMENT property (name, value)>
<!ELEMENT name (#PCDATA)>
```

The value is an integer, `boolean`, string, or another bean:

```
<!ELEMENT value (int|string|boolean|bean)>
<!ELEMENT int (#PCDATA)>
<!ELEMENT string (#PCDATA)>
<!ELEMENT boolean (#PCDATA)>
```

Here is a typical example, a JLabel whose text property is set to the string "Face: ":

```
<bean>
  <class>javax.swing.JLabel</class>
  <property>
    <name>text</name>
    <value><string>Face: </string></value>
  </property>
</bean>
```

It seems like a bother to surround a string with the <string> tag. Why not just use #PCDATA for strings and leave the tags for the other types? Because then we would need to use mixed content and weaken the rule for the value element to

```
<!ELEMENT value (#PCDATA|int|boolean|bean)*>
```

However, that rule would allow an arbitrary mixture of text and tags.

The program sets a property by using the BeanInfo class. BeanInfo enumerates the property descriptors of the bean. We search for the property with the matching name, and then call its setter method with the supplied value.

When our program reads in a user interface description, it has enough information to construct and arrange the user interface components. But, of course, the interface is not alive—no event listeners have been attached. To add event listeners, we have to locate the components. For that reason, we support an optional attribute of type ID for each bean:

```
<!ATTLIST bean id ID #IMPLIED>
```

For example, here is a combo box with an ID:

```
<bean id="face">
  <class>javax.swing.JComboBox</class>
</bean>
```

Recall that the parser checks that IDs are unique.

A programmer can attach event handlers like this:

```
gridbag = new GridBagPane("fontdialog.xml");
setContentPane(gridbag);
JComboBox face = (JComboBox) gridbag.get("face");
face.addListener(listener);
```

**NOTE:** In this example, we only use XML to describe the component layout and leave it to programmers to attach the event handlers in the Java code. You could go a step further and add the code to the XML description. The most promising approach is to use a scripting language such as JavaScript for the code. If you want to add that enhancement, check out the Rhino interpreter at www.mozilla.org/rhino.

The program in Listing 2.2 shows how to use the GridBagPane class to do all the boring work of setting up the grid bag layout. The layout is defined in Listing 2.4; Figure 2.4 shows the result. The program only initializes the combo boxes (which are too complex for the bean property-setting mechanism that the GridBagPane supports) and attaches event listeners. The GridBagPane class in Listing 2.3 parses the XML file, constructs the components, and lays them out. Listing 2.5 shows the DTD.

The program can also process a schema instead of a DTD if you choose a file that contains the string -schema.

Listing 2.6 contains the schema.

This example is a typical use of XML. The XML format is robust enough to express complex relationships. The XML parser adds value by taking over the routine job of validity checking and supplying defaults.

---

**Listing 2.2**  read/GridBagTest.java

```
1  package read;
2
3  import java.awt.*;
4  import java.awt.event.*;
5  import java.io.*;
6  import javax.swing.*;
7  /**
8   * This program shows how to use an XML file to describe a gridbag layout.
9   * @version 1.11 2012-06-03
10   * @author Cay Horstmann
11   */
12  public class GridBagTest
13  {
14     public static void main(String[] args)
15     {
16        EventQueue.invokeLater(new Runnable()
17           {
18              public void run()
19              {
```

*(Continues)*

**Listing 2.2** *(Continued)*

```
20                JFileChooser chooser = new JFileChooser("read");
21                chooser.showOpenDialog(null);
22                File file = chooser.getSelectedFile();
23                JFrame frame = new FontFrame(file);
24                frame.setTitle("GridBagTest");
25                frame.setDefaultCloseOperation(JFrame.EXIT_ON_CLOSE);
26                frame.setVisible(true);
27             }
28          });
29       }
30 }
31
32 /**
33  * This frame contains a font selection dialog that is described by an XML file.
34  * @param filename the file containing the user interface components for the dialog.
35  */
36 class FontFrame extends JFrame
37 {
38    private GridBagPane gridbag;
39    private JComboBox<String> face;
40    private JComboBox<String> size;
41    private JCheckBox bold;
42    private JCheckBox italic;
43
44    @SuppressWarnings("unchecked")
45    public FontFrame(File file)
46    {
47       gridbag = new GridBagPane(file);
48       add(gridbag);
49
50       face = (JComboBox<String>) gridbag.get("face");
51       size = (JComboBox<String>) gridbag.get("size");
52       bold = (JCheckBox) gridbag.get("bold");
53       italic = (JCheckBox) gridbag.get("italic");
54
55       face.setModel(new DefaultComboBoxModel<String>(new String[] { "Serif",
56          "SansSerif", "Monospaced", "Dialog", "DialogInput" }));
57
58       size.setModel(new DefaultComboBoxModel<String>(new String[] { "8",
59          "10", "12", "15", "18", "24", "36", "48" }));
60
61       ActionListener listener = new ActionListener()
62          {
63             public void actionPerformed(ActionEvent event)
64             {
65                setSample();
66             }
67          };
```

```
68      face.addActionListener(listener);
69      size.addActionListener(listener);
70      bold.addActionListener(listener);
71      italic.addActionListener(listener);
72
73      setSample();
74      pack();
75   }
76
77   /**
78    * This method sets the text sample to the selected font.
79    */
80   public void setSample()
81   {
82      String fontFace = face.getItemAt(face.getSelectedIndex());
83      int fontSize = Integer.parseInt(size.getItemAt(size.getSelectedIndex()));
84      JTextArea sample = (JTextArea) gridbag.get("sample");
85      int fontStyle = (bold.isSelected() ? Font.BOLD : 0)
86            + (italic.isSelected() ? Font.ITALIC : 0);
87
88      sample.setFont(new Font(fontFace, fontStyle, fontSize));
89      sample.repaint();
90   }
91 }
```

**Listing 2.3**  read/GridBagPane.java

```
1  package read;
2
3  import java.awt.*;
4  import java.beans.*;
5  import java.io.*;
6  import java.lang.reflect.*;
7  import javax.swing.*;
8  import javax.xml.parsers.*;
9  import org.w3c.dom.*;
10
11 /**
12  * This panel uses an XML file to describe its components and their grid bag layout positions.
13  */
14 public class GridBagPane extends JPanel
15 {
16    private GridBagConstraints constraints;
17
18    /**
19     * Constructs a grid bag pane.
20     * @param filename the name of the XML file that describes the pane's components and their
21     * positions
22     */
```

*(Continues)*

**Listing 2.3** *(Continued)*

```java
23   public GridBagPane(File file)
24   {
25      setLayout(new GridBagLayout());
26      constraints = new GridBagConstraints();
27
28      try
29      {
30         DocumentBuilderFactory factory = DocumentBuilderFactory.newInstance();
31         factory.setValidating(true);
32
33         if (file.toString().contains("-schema"))
34         {
35            factory.setNamespaceAware(true);
36            final String JAXP_SCHEMA_LANGUAGE =
37               "http://java.sun.com/xml/jaxp/properties/schemaLanguage";
38            final String W3C_XML_SCHEMA = "http://www.w3.org/2001/XMLSchema";
39            factory.setAttribute(JAXP_SCHEMA_LANGUAGE, W3C_XML_SCHEMA);
40         }
41
42         factory.setIgnoringElementContentWhitespace(true);
43
44         DocumentBuilder builder = factory.newDocumentBuilder();
45         Document doc = builder.parse(file);
46         parseGridbag(doc.getDocumentElement());
47      }
48      catch (Exception e)
49      {
50         e.printStackTrace();
51      }
52   }
53
54   /**
55    * Gets a component with a given name.
56    * @param name a component name
57    * @return the component with the given name, or null if no component in this grid bag
58    * pane has the given name
59    */
60   public Component get(String name)
61   {
62      Component[] components = getComponents();
63      for (int i = 0; i < components.length; i++)
64      {
65         if (components[i].getName().equals(name)) return components[i];
66      }
67      return null;
68   }
```

```
69  /**
70   * Parses a gridbag element.
71   * @param e a gridbag element
72   */
73  private void parseGridbag(Element e)
74  {
75     NodeList rows = e.getChildNodes();
76     for (int i = 0; i < rows.getLength(); i++)
77     {
78        Element row = (Element) rows.item(i);
79        NodeList cells = row.getChildNodes();
80        for (int j = 0; j < cells.getLength(); j++)
81        {
82           Element cell = (Element) cells.item(j);
83           parseCell(cell, i, j);
84        }
85     }
86  }
87
88  /**
89   * Parses a cell element.
90   * @param e a cell element
91   * @param r the row of the cell
92   * @param c the column of the cell
93   */
94  private void parseCell(Element e, int r, int c)
95  {
96     // get attributes
97
98     String value = e.getAttribute("gridx");
99     if (value.length() == 0) // use default
100    {
101       if (c == 0) constraints.gridx = 0;
102       else constraints.gridx += constraints.gridwidth;
103    }
104    else constraints.gridx = Integer.parseInt(value);
105
106    value = e.getAttribute("gridy");
107    if (value.length() == 0) // use default
108    constraints.gridy = r;
109    else constraints.gridy = Integer.parseInt(value);
110
111    constraints.gridwidth = Integer.parseInt(e.getAttribute("gridwidth"));
112    constraints.gridheight = Integer.parseInt(e.getAttribute("gridheight"));
113    constraints.weightx = Integer.parseInt(e.getAttribute("weightx"));
114    constraints.weighty = Integer.parseInt(e.getAttribute("weighty"));
115    constraints.ipadx = Integer.parseInt(e.getAttribute("ipadx"));
116    constraints.ipady = Integer.parseInt(e.getAttribute("ipady"));
```

*(Continues)*

**Listing 2.3** *(Continued)*

```
117      // use reflection to get integer values of static fields
118      Class<GridBagConstraints> cl = GridBagConstraints.class;
119
120      try
121      {
122         String name = e.getAttribute("fill");
123         Field f = cl.getField(name);
124         constraints.fill = f.getInt(cl);
125
126         name = e.getAttribute("anchor");
127         f = cl.getField(name);
128         constraints.anchor = f.getInt(cl);
129      }
130      catch (Exception ex) // the reflection methods can throw various exceptions
131      {
132         ex.printStackTrace();
133      }
134
135      Component comp = (Component) parseBean((Element) e.getFirstChild());
136      add(comp, constraints);
137   }
138
139   /**
140    * Parses a bean element.
141    * @param e a bean element
142    */
143   private Object parseBean(Element e)
144   {
145      try
146      {
147         NodeList children = e.getChildNodes();
148         Element classElement = (Element) children.item(0);
149         String className = ((Text) classElement.getFirstChild()).getData();
150
151         Class<?> cl = Class.forName(className);
152
153         Object obj = cl.newInstance();
154
155         if (obj instanceof Component) ((Component) obj).setName(e.getAttribute("id"));
156
157         for (int i = 1; i < children.getLength(); i++)
158         {
159            Node propertyElement = children.item(i);
160            Element nameElement = (Element) propertyElement.getFirstChild();
161            String propertyName = ((Text) nameElement.getFirstChild()).getData();
162
163            Element valueElement = (Element) propertyElement.getLastChild();
```

```
164            Object value = parseValue(valueElement);
165            BeanInfo beanInfo = Introspector.getBeanInfo(cl);
166            PropertyDescriptor[] descriptors = beanInfo.getPropertyDescriptors();
167            boolean done = false;
168            for (int j = 0; !done && j < descriptors.length; j++)
169            {
170               if (descriptors[j].getName().equals(propertyName))
171               {
172                  descriptors[j].getWriteMethod().invoke(obj, value);
173                  done = true;
174               }
175            }
176         }
177         return obj;
178      }
179      catch (Exception ex) // the reflection methods can throw various exceptions
180      {
181         ex.printStackTrace();
182         return null;
183      }
184   }
185
186   /**
187    * Parses a value element.
188    * @param e a value element
189    */
190   private Object parseValue(Element e)
191   {
192      Element child = (Element) e.getFirstChild();
193      if (child.getTagName().equals("bean")) return parseBean(child);
194      String text = ((Text) child.getFirstChild()).getData();
195      if (child.getTagName().equals("int")) return new Integer(text);
196      else if (child.getTagName().equals("boolean")) return new Boolean(text);
197      else if (child.getTagName().equals("string")) return text;
198      else return null;
199   }
200 }
```

**Listing 2.4**  read/fontdialog.xml

```
1 <?xml version="1.0"?>
2 <!DOCTYPE gridbag SYSTEM "gridbag.dtd">
3 <gridbag>
4    <row>
5       <cell anchor="EAST">
6          <bean>
7             <class>javax.swing.JLabel</class>
```

*(Continues)*

**Listing 2.4** *(Continued)*

```
8              <property>
9                  <name>text</name>
10                 <value><string>Face: </string></value>
11             </property>
12         </bean>
13     </cell>
14     <cell fill="HORIZONTAL" weightx="100">
15         <bean id="face">
16             <class>javax.swing.JComboBox</class>
17         </bean>
18     </cell>
19     <cell gridheight="4" fill="BOTH" weightx="100" weighty="100">
20         <bean id="sample">
21             <class>javax.swing.JTextArea</class>
22             <property>
23                 <name>text</name>
24                 <value><string>The quick brown fox jumps over the lazy dog</string></value>
25             </property>
26             <property>
27                 <name>editable</name>
28                 <value><boolean>false</boolean></value>
29             </property>
30             <property>
31                 <name>lineWrap</name>
32                 <value><boolean>true</boolean></value>
33             </property>
34             <property>
35                 <name>border</name>
36                 <value>
37                     <bean>
38                         <class>javax.swing.border.EtchedBorder</class>
39                     </bean>
40                 </value>
41             </property>
42         </bean>
43     </cell>
44 </row>
45 <row>
46     <cell anchor="EAST">
47         <bean>
48             <class>javax.swing.JLabel</class>
49             <property>
50                 <name>text</name>
51                 <value><string>Size: </string></value>
52             </property>
53         </bean>
54     </cell>
```

```
55      <cell fill="HORIZONTAL" weightx="100">
56         <bean id="size">
57            <class>javax.swing.JComboBox</class>
58         </bean>
59      </cell>
60   </row>
61   <row>
62      <cell gridwidth="2" weighty="100">
63         <bean id="bold">
64            <class>javax.swing.JCheckBox</class>
65            <property>
66               <name>text</name>
67               <value><string>Bold</string></value>
68            </property>
69         </bean>
70      </cell>
71   </row>
72   <row>
73      <cell gridwidth="2" weighty="100">
74         <bean id="italic">
75            <class>javax.swing.JCheckBox</class>
76            <property>
77               <name>text</name>
78               <value><string>Italic</string></value>
79            </property>
80         </bean>
81      </cell>
82   </row>
83 </gridbag>
```

---

**Listing 2.5**  read/gridbag.dtd

```
1  <!ELEMENT gridbag (row)*>
2  <!ELEMENT row (cell)*>
3  <!ELEMENT cell (bean)>
4
5  <!ATTLIST cell gridx CDATA #IMPLIED>
6  <!ATTLIST cell gridy CDATA #IMPLIED>
7  <!ATTLIST cell gridwidth CDATA "1">
8  <!ATTLIST cell gridheight CDATA "1">
9  <!ATTLIST cell weightx CDATA "0">
10 <!ATTLIST cell weighty CDATA "0">
11 <!ATTLIST cell fill (NONE|BOTH|HORIZONTAL|VERTICAL) "NONE">
12 <!ATTLIST cell anchor
13    (CENTER|NORTH|NORTHEAST|EAST|SOUTHEAST|SOUTH|SOUTHWEST|WEST|NORTHWEST) "CENTER">
14 <!ATTLIST cell ipadx CDATA "0">
15 <!ATTLIST cell ipady CDATA "0">
```

*(Continues)*

---

**Listing 2.5**  *(Continued)*

```
16  <!ELEMENT bean (class, property*)>
17  <!ATTLIST bean id ID #IMPLIED>
18
19  <!ELEMENT class (#PCDATA)>
20  <!ELEMENT property (name, value)>
21  <!ELEMENT name (#PCDATA)>
22  <!ELEMENT value (int|string|boolean|bean)>
23  <!ELEMENT int (#PCDATA)>
24  <!ELEMENT string (#PCDATA)>
25  <!ELEMENT boolean (#PCDATA)>
```

---

**Listing 2.6**  read/gridbag.xsd

```
1   <xsd:schema xmlns:xsd="http://www.w3.org/2001/XMLSchema">
2
3     <xsd:element name="gridbag" type="GridBagType"/>
4
5     <xsd:element name="bean" type="BeanType"/>
6
7     <xsd:complexType name="GridBagType">
8       <xsd:sequence>
9         <xsd:element name="row" type="RowType" minOccurs="0" maxOccurs="unbounded"/>
10      </xsd:sequence>
11    </xsd:complexType>
12
13    <xsd:complexType name="RowType">
14      <xsd:sequence>
15        <xsd:element name="cell" type="CellType" minOccurs="0" maxOccurs="unbounded"/>
16      </xsd:sequence>
17    </xsd:complexType>
18
19    <xsd:complexType name="CellType">
20      <xsd:sequence>
21        <xsd:element ref="bean"/>
22      </xsd:sequence>
23      <xsd:attribute name="gridx" type="xsd:int" use="optional"/>
24      <xsd:attribute name="gridy" type="xsd:int" use="optional"/>
25      <xsd:attribute name="gridwidth" type="xsd:int" use="optional" default="1" />
26      <xsd:attribute name="gridheight" type="xsd:int" use="optional" default="1" />
27      <xsd:attribute name="weightx" type="xsd:int" use="optional" default="0" />
28      <xsd:attribute name="weighty" type="xsd:int" use="optional" default="0" />
29      <xsd:attribute name="fill" use="optional" default="NONE">
30        <xsd:simpleType>
31          <xsd:restriction base="xsd:string">
32            <xsd:enumeration value="NONE" />
33            <xsd:enumeration value="BOTH" />
```

```
34          <xsd:enumeration value="HORIZONTAL" />
35          <xsd:enumeration value="VERTICAL" />
36        </xsd:restriction>
37      </xsd:simpleType>
38    </xsd:attribute>
39    <xsd:attribute name="anchor" use="optional" default="CENTER">
40      <xsd:simpleType>
41        <xsd:restriction base="xsd:string">
42          <xsd:enumeration value="CENTER" />
43          <xsd:enumeration value="NORTH" />
44          <xsd:enumeration value="NORTHEAST" />
45          <xsd:enumeration value="EAST" />
46          <xsd:enumeration value="SOUTHEAST" />
47          <xsd:enumeration value="SOUTH" />
48          <xsd:enumeration value="SOUTHWEST" />
49          <xsd:enumeration value="WEST" />
50          <xsd:enumeration value="NORTHWEST" />
51        </xsd:restriction>
52      </xsd:simpleType>
53    </xsd:attribute>
54    <xsd:attribute name="ipady" type="xsd:int" use="optional" default="0" />
55    <xsd:attribute name="ipadx" type="xsd:int" use="optional" default="0" />
56  </xsd:complexType>
57
58  <xsd:complexType name="BeanType">
59    <xsd:sequence>
60      <xsd:element name="class" type="xsd:string"/>
61      <xsd:element name="property" type="PropertyType" minOccurs="0" maxOccurs="unbounded"/>
62    </xsd:sequence>
63    <xsd:attribute name="id" type="xsd:ID" use="optional" />
64  </xsd:complexType>
65
66  <xsd:complexType name="PropertyType">
67    <xsd:sequence>
68      <xsd:element name="name" type="xsd:string"/>
69      <xsd:element name="value" type="ValueType"/>
70    </xsd:sequence>
71  </xsd:complexType>
72
73  <xsd:complexType name="ValueType">
74    <xsd:choice>
75      <xsd:element ref="bean"/>
76      <xsd:element name="int" type="xsd:int"/>
77      <xsd:element name="string" type="xsd:string"/>
78      <xsd:element name="boolean" type="xsd:boolean"/>
79    </xsd:choice>
80  </xsd:complexType>
81 </xsd:schema>
```

## 2.4  Locating Information with XPath

If you want to locate a specific piece of information in an XML document, it can be a bit of a hassle to navigate the nodes of the DOM tree. The XPath language makes it simple to access tree nodes. For example, suppose you have this XML document:

```
<configuration>
   . . .
   <database>
      <username>dbuser</username>
      <password>secret</password>
      . . .
   </database>
</configuration>
```

You can get the database user name by evaluating the XPath expression

```
/configuration/database/username
```

That's a lot simpler than the plain DOM approach:

1.  Get the document node.
2.  Enumerate its children.
3.  Locate the database element.
4.  Get its first child, the username element.
5.  Get its first child, a text node.
6.  Get its data.

An XPath can describe *a set of nodes* in an XML document. For example, the XPath

```
/gridbag/row
```

describes the set of all row elements that are children of the gridbag root element. You can select a particular element with the [] operator:

```
/gridbag/row[1]
```

is the first row. (The index values start at 1.)

Use the @ operator to get attribute values. The XPath expression

```
/gridbag/row[1]/cell[1]/@anchor
```

describes the anchor attribute of the first cell in the first row. The XPath expression

```
/gridbag/row/cell/@anchor
```

describes all anchor attribute nodes of cell elements within row elements that are children of the gridbag root node.

There are a number of useful XPath functions. For example,

```
count(/gridbag/row)
```

returns the number of row children of the gridbag root. There are many more elaborate XPath expressions; see the specification at www.w3c.org/TR/xpath or the nifty online tutorial at www.zvon.org/xxl/XPathTutorial/General/examples.html.

Java SE 5.0 added an API to evaluate XPath expressions. First, create an XPath object from an XPathFactory:

```
XPathFactory xpfactory = XPathFactory.newInstance();
path = xpfactory.newXPath();
```

Then, call the evaluate method to evaluate XPath expressions:

```
String username = path.evaluate("/configuration/database/username", doc);
```

You can use the same XPath object to evaluate multiple expressions.

This form of the evaluate method returns a string result. It is suitable for retrieving text, such as the text of the username node in the preceding example. If an XPath expression yields a node set, make a call such as the following:

```
NodeList nodes = (NodeList) path.evaluate("/gridbag/row", doc, XPathConstants.NODESET);
```

If the result is a single node, use XPathConstants.NODE instead:

```
Node node = (Node) path.evaluate("/gridbag/row[1]", doc, XPathConstants.NODE);
```

If the result is a number, use XPathConstants.NUMBER:

```
int count = ((Number) path.evaluate("count(/gridbag/row)", doc, XPathConstants.NUMBER)).intValue();
```

You don't have to start the search at the document root; you can start at any node or node list. For example, if you have a node from a previous evaluation, you can call

```
result = path.evaluate(expression, node);
```

The program in Listing 2.7 demonstrates the evaluation of XPath expressions. Load an XML file and type an expression. Select the expression type and click the Evaluate button. The result of the expression is displayed at the bottom of the frame (see Figure 2.5).

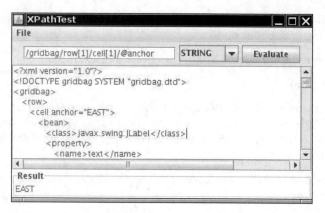

**Figure 2.5** Evaluating XPath expressions

**Listing 2.7**  xpath/XPathTester.java

```
1  package xpath;
2
3  import java.awt.*;
4  import java.awt.event.*;
5  import java.io.*;
6  import java.nio.file.*;
7  import javax.swing.*;
8  import javax.swing.border.*;
9  import javax.xml.namespace.*;
10 import javax.xml.parsers.*;
11 import javax.xml.xpath.*;
12 import org.w3c.dom.*;
13 import org.xml.sax.*;
14
15 /**
16  * This program evaluates XPath expressions.
17  * @version 1.01 2007-06-25
18  * @author Cay Horstmann
19  */
20 public class XPathTester
21 {
22    public static void main(String[] args)
23    {
24       EventQueue.invokeLater(new Runnable()
25          {
26             public void run()
27             {
28                JFrame frame = new XPathFrame();
29                frame.setTitle("XPathTest");
```

```
30          frame.setDefaultCloseOperation(JFrame.EXIT_ON_CLOSE);
31          frame.setVisible(true);
32       }
33    });
34  }
35 }
36
37 /**
38  * This frame shows an XML document, a panel to type an XPath expression, and a text field to
39  * display the result.
40  */
41 class XPathFrame extends JFrame
42 {
43    private DocumentBuilder builder;
44    private Document doc;
45    private XPath path;
46    private JTextField expression;
47    private JTextField result;
48    private JTextArea docText;
49    private JComboBox<String> typeCombo;
50
51    public XPathFrame()
52    {
53       JMenu fileMenu = new JMenu("File");
54       JMenuItem openItem = new JMenuItem("Open");
55       openItem.addActionListener(new ActionListener()
56          {
57             public void actionPerformed(ActionEvent event)
58             {
59                openFile();
60             }
61          });
62       fileMenu.add(openItem);
63
64       JMenuItem exitItem = new JMenuItem("Exit");
65       exitItem.addActionListener(new ActionListener()
66          {
67             public void actionPerformed(ActionEvent event)
68             {
69                System.exit(0);
70             }
71          });
72       fileMenu.add(exitItem);
73
74       JMenuBar menuBar = new JMenuBar();
75       menuBar.add(fileMenu);
76       setJMenuBar(menuBar);
```

*(Continues)*

**Listing 2.7** *(Continued)*

```
77      ActionListener listener = new ActionListener()
78         {
79            public void actionPerformed(ActionEvent event)
80            {
81               evaluate();
82            }
83         };
84      expression = new JTextField(20);
85      expression.addActionListener(listener);
86      JButton evaluateButton = new JButton("Evaluate");
87      evaluateButton.addActionListener(listener);
88
89      typeCombo = new JComboBox<String>(new String[] {
90         "STRING", "NODE", "NODESET", "NUMBER", "BOOLEAN" });
91      typeCombo.setSelectedItem("STRING");
92
93      JPanel panel = new JPanel();
94      panel.add(expression);
95      panel.add(typeCombo);
96      panel.add(evaluateButton);
97      docText = new JTextArea(10, 40);
98      result = new JTextField();
99      result.setBorder(new TitledBorder("Result"));
100
101     add(panel, BorderLayout.NORTH);
102     add(new JScrollPane(docText), BorderLayout.CENTER);
103     add(result, BorderLayout.SOUTH);
104
105     try
106     {
107        DocumentBuilderFactory factory = DocumentBuilderFactory.newInstance();
108        builder = factory.newDocumentBuilder();
109     }
110     catch (ParserConfigurationException e)
111     {
112        JOptionPane.showMessageDialog(this, e);
113     }
114
115     XPathFactory xpfactory = XPathFactory.newInstance();
116     path = xpfactory.newXPath();
117     pack();
118  }
119
120  /**
121   * Open a file and load the document.
122   */
```

```
123   public void openFile()
124   {
125      JFileChooser chooser = new JFileChooser();
126      chooser.setCurrentDirectory(new File("xpath"));
127
128      chooser.setFileFilter(new javax.swing.filechooser.FileFilter()
129         {
130            public boolean accept(File f)
131            {
132               return f.isDirectory() || f.getName().toLowerCase().endsWith(".xml");
133            }
134
135            public String getDescription()
136            {
137               return "XML files";
138            }
139         });
140      int r = chooser.showOpenDialog(this);
141      if (r != JFileChooser.APPROVE_OPTION) return;
142      File file = chooser.getSelectedFile();
143      try
144      {
145         docText.setText(new String(Files.readAllBytes(file.toPath())));
146         doc = builder.parse(file);
147      }
148      catch (IOException e)
149      {
150         JOptionPane.showMessageDialog(this, e);
151      }
152      catch (SAXException e)
153      {
154         JOptionPane.showMessageDialog(this, e);
155      }
156   }
157
158   public void evaluate()
159   {
160      try
161      {
162         String typeName = (String) typeCombo.getSelectedItem();
163         QName returnType = (QName) XPathConstants.class.getField(typeName).get(null);
164         Object evalResult = path.evaluate(expression.getText(), doc, returnType);
165         if (typeName.equals("NODESET"))
166         {
167            NodeList list = (NodeList) evalResult;
168            StringBuilder builder = new StringBuilder();
169            builder.append("{");
```

*(Continues)*

**Listing 2.7**  *(Continued)*

```
170              for (int i = 0; i < list.getLength(); i++)
171              {
172                 if (i > 0) builder.append(", ");
173                 builder.append("" + list.item(i));
174              }
175              builder.append("}");
176              result.setText("" + builder);
177           }
178           else result.setText("" + evalResult);
179        }
180        catch (XPathExpressionException e)
181        {
182           result.setText("" + e);
183        }
184        catch (Exception e) // reflection exception
185        {
186           e.printStackTrace();
187        }
188     }
189 }
```

---

**javax.xml.xpath.XPathFactory** 5.0

- static XPathFactory newInstance()
  returns an XPathFactory instance for creating XPath objects.

- XPath newXpath()
  constructs an XPath object for evaluating XPath expressions.

---

*javax.xml.xpath.XPath* 5.0

- String evaluate(String expression, Object startingPoint)
  evaluates an expression, beginning at the given starting point. The starting point
  can be a node or node list. If the result is a node or node set, the returned string
  consists of the data of all text node children.

- Object evaluate(String expression, Object startingPoint, QName resultType)
  evaluates an expression, beginning at the given starting point. The starting point
  can be a node or node list. The resultType is one of the constants STRING, NODE, NODESET,
  NUMBER, or BOOLEAN in the XPathConstants class. The return value is a String, Node, NodeList,
  Number, or Boolean.

## 2.5 Using Namespaces

The Java language uses packages to avoid name clashes. Programmers can use the same name for different classes as long as they aren't in the same package. XML has a similar *namespace* mechanism for element and attribute names.

A namespace is identified by a Uniform Resource Identifier (URI), such as

```
http://www.w3.org/2001/XMLSchema
uuid:1c759aed-b748-475c-ab68-10679700c4f2
urn:com:books-r-us
```

The HTTP URL form is the most common. Note that the URL is just used as an identifier string, not as a locator for a document. For example, the namespace identifiers

```
http://www.horstmann.com/corejava
http://www.horstmann.com/corejava/index.html
```

denote *different* namespaces, even though a web server would serve the same document for both URLs.

There need not be any document at a namespace URL—the XML parser doesn't attempt to find anything at that location. However, as a help to programmers who encounter a possibly unfamiliar namespace, it is customary to place a document explaining the purpose of the namespace at the URL location. For example, if you point your browser to the namespace URL for the XML Schema namespace (`http://www.w3.org/2001/XMLSchema`), you will find a document describing the XML Schema standard.

Why use HTTP URLs for namespace identifiers? It is easy to ensure that they are unique. If you choose a real URL, the host part's uniqueness is guaranteed by the domain name system. Your organization can then arrange for the uniqueness of the remainder of the URL. This is the same rationale that underlies the use of reversed domain names in Java package names.

Of course, although long namespace identifiers are good for uniqueness, you don't want to deal with long identifiers any more than you have to. In the Java programming language, you use the `import` mechanism to specify the long names of packages, and then use just the short class names. In XML, there is a similar mechanism:

```
<element xmlns="namespaceURI">
    children
</element>
```

The element and its children are now part of the given namespace.

A child can provide its own namespace, for example:

```
<element xmlns="namespaceURI1">
    <child xmlns="namespaceURI2">
        grandchildren
    </child>
    more children
</element>
```

Then the first child and the grandchildren are part of the second namespace.

This simple mechanism works well if you need only a single namespace or if the namespaces are naturally nested. Otherwise, you will want to use a second mechanism that has no analog in Java. You can have a *prefix* for a namespace—a short identifier that you choose for a particular document. Here is a typical example—the xsd prefix in an XML Schema file:

```
<xsd:schema xmlns:xsd="http://www.w3.org/2001/XMLSchema">
    <xsd:element name="gridbag" type="GridBagType"/>
    . . .
</xsd:schema>
```

The attribute

```
xmlns:prefix="namespaceURI"
```

defines a namespace and a prefix. In our example, the prefix is the string xsd. Thus, xsd:schema really means schema in the namespace http://www.w3.org/2001/XMLSchema.

---

 **NOTE:** Only child elements inherit the namespace of their parent. Attributes without an explicit prefix are never part of a namespace. Consider this contrived example:

```
<configuration xmlns="http://www.horstmann.com/corejava"
    xmlns:si="http://www.bipm.fr/enus/3_SI/si.html">
    <size value="210" si:unit="mm"/>
    . . .
</configuration>
```

In this example, the elements configuration and size are part of the namespace with URI http://www.horstmann.com/corejava. The attribute si:unit is part of the namespace with URI http://www.bipm.fr/enus/3_SI/si.html. However, the attribute value is not part of any namespace.

---

You can control how the parser deals with namespaces. By default, the Sun DOM parser is not namespace-aware.

To turn on namespace handling, call the setNamespaceAware method of the DocumentBuilderFactory:

```
factory.setNamespaceAware(true);
```

Now, all builders the factory produces support namespaces. Each node has three properties:

- The *qualified name*, with a prefix, returned by getNodeName, getTagName, and so on
- The namespace URI, returned by the getNamespaceURI method
- The *local name*, without a prefix or a namespace, returned by the getLocalName method

Here is an example. Suppose the parser sees the following element:

```
<xsd:schema xmlns:xsd="http://www.w3.org/2001/XMLSchema">
```

It then reports the following:

- Qualified name = xsd:schema
- Namespace URI = http://www.w3.org/2001/XMLSchema
- Local name = schema

---

 **NOTE:** If namespace awareness is turned off, getNamespaceURI and getLocalName return null.

---

**org.w3c.dom.Node** 1.4

- String getLocalName()
  returns the local name (without prefix), or null if the parser is not namespace-aware.
- String getNamespaceURI()
  returns the namespace URI, or null if the node is not part of a namespace or if the parser is not namespace-aware.

**javax.xml.parsers.DocumentBuilderFactory** 1.4

- boolean isNamespaceAware()
- void setNamespaceAware(boolean value)
  gets or sets the namespaceAware property of the factory. If set to true, the parsers that this factory generates are namespace-aware.

## 2.6 Streaming Parsers

The DOM parser reads an XML document in its entirety into a tree data structure. For most practical applications, DOM works fine. However, it can be inefficient if the document is large and if your processing algorithm is simple enough that you can analyze nodes on the fly, without having to see all of the tree structure. In these cases, you should use a streaming parser.

In the following sections, we discuss the streaming parsers supplied by the Java library: the venerable SAX parser and the more modern StAX parser that was added to Java SE 6. The SAX parser uses event callbacks, and the StAX parser provides an iterator through the parsing events. The latter is usually a bit more convenient.

### 2.6.1 Using the SAX Parser

The SAX parser reports events as it parses the components of the XML input, but it does not store the document in any way—it is up to the event handlers to build a data structure. In fact, the DOM parser is built on top of the SAX parser. It builds the DOM tree as it receives the parser events.

Whenever you use a SAX parser, you need a handler that defines the event actions for the various parse events. The `ContentHandler` interface defines several callback methods that the parser executes as it parses the document. Here are the most important ones:

- `startElement` and `endElement` are called each time a start tag or end tag is encountered.
- `characters` is called whenever character data are encountered.
- `startDocument` and `endDocument` are called once each, at the start and the end of the document.

For example, when parsing the fragment

```
<font>
   <name>Helvetica</name>
   <size units="pt">36</size>
</font>
```

the parser makes the following callbacks:

1. `startElement`, element name: `font`
2. `startElement`, element name: `name`
3. `characters`, content: `Helvetica`

4.   `endElement`, element name: `name`

5.   `startElement`, element name: `size`, attributes: `units="pt"`

6.   `characters`, content: `36`

7.   `endElement`, element name: `size`

8.   `endElement`, element name: `font`

Your handler needs to override these methods and have them carry out whatever action you want to carry out as you parse the file. The program at the end of this section prints all links `<a href="...">` in an HTML file. It simply overrides the `startElement` method of the handler to check for links with name `a` and an attribute with name `href`. This is potentially useful for implementing a "web crawler"—a program that reaches more and more web pages by following links.

---

 **NOTE:** HTML doesn't have to be valid XML, and many web pages deviate so much from proper XML that the example programs will not be able to parse them. However, most pages authored by the W3C are written in XHTML (an HTML dialect that is proper XML). You can use those pages to test the example program. For example, if you run

```
java SAXTest http://www.w3.org/MarkUp
```

you will see a list of the URLs of all links on that page.

---

The sample program is a good example for the use of SAX. We don't care at all in which context the `a` elements occur, and there is no need to store a tree structure.

Here is how you get a SAX parser:

```
SAXParserFactory factory = SAXParserFactory.newInstance();
SAXParser parser = factory.newSAXParser();
```

You can now process a document:

```
parser.parse(source, handler);
```

Here, `source` can be a file, URL string, or input stream. The `handler` belongs to a subclass of `DefaultHandler`. The `DefaultHandler` class defines do-nothing methods for the four interfaces:

```
ContentHandler
DTDHandler
EntityResolver
ErrorHandler
```

The example program defines a handler that overrides the startElement method of the ContentHandler interface to watch out for a elements with an href attribute:

```
DefaultHandler handler = new
   DefaultHandler()
   {
      public void startElement(String namespaceURI, String lname, String qname, Attributes attrs)
         throws SAXException
      {
         if (lname.equalsIgnoreCase("a") && attrs != null)
         {
            for (int i = 0; i < attrs.getLength(); i++)
            {
               String aname = attrs.getLocalName(i);
               if (aname.equalsIgnoreCase("href"))
                  System.out.println(attrs.getValue(i));
            }
         }
      }
   };
```

The startElement method has three parameters that describe the element name. The qname parameter reports the qualified name of the form prefix:localname. If namespace processing is turned on, then the namespaceURI and lname parameters provide the namespace and local (unqualified) name.

As with the DOM parser, namespace processing is turned off by default. To activate namespace processing, call the setNamespaceAware method of the factory class:

```
SAXParserFactory factory = SAXParserFactory.newInstance();
factory.setNamespaceAware(true);
SAXParser saxParser = factory.newSAXParser();
```

In this program, we cope with another common issue. An XHTML file starts with a tag that contains a DTD reference, and the parser will want to load it. Understandably, the W3C isn't too happy to serve billions of copies of files such as www.w3.org/TR/xhtml11/DTD/xhtml1-strict.dtd. At one point, they refused altogether, but at the time of this writing, they serve the DTD at a glacial pace. If you don't need to validate the document, just call

```
factory.setFeature("http://apache.org/xml/features/nonvalidating/load-external-dtd", false);
```

Listing 2.8 contains the code for the web crawler program. Later in this chapter, you will see another interesting use of SAX. An easy way of turning a non-XML data source into XML is to report the SAX events that an XML parser would report. See Section 2.8, "XSL Transformations," on p. 173 for details.

**Listing 2.8**  sax/SAXTest.java

```
 1  package sax;
 2
 3  import java.io.*;
 4  import java.net.*;
 5  import javax.xml.parsers.*;
 6  import org.xml.sax.*;
 7  import org.xml.sax.helpers.*;
 8
 9  /**
10   * This program demonstrates how to use a SAX parser. The program prints all hyperlinks of an
11   * XHTML web page.<br>
12   * Usage: java SAXTest url
13   * @version 1.00 2001-09-29
14   * @author Cay Horstmann
15   */
16  public class SAXTest
17  {
18     public static void main(String[] args) throws Exception
19     {
20        String url;
21        if (args.length == 0)
22        {
23           url = "http://www.w3c.org";
24           System.out.println("Using " + url);
25        }
26        else url = args[0];
27
28        DefaultHandler handler = new DefaultHandler()
29           {
30              public void startElement(String namespaceURI, String lname, String qname,
31                 Attributes attrs)
32              {
33                 if (lname.equals("a") && attrs != null)
34                 {
35                    for (int i = 0; i < attrs.getLength(); i++)
36                    {
37                       String aname = attrs.getLocalName(i);
38                       if (aname.equals("href")) System.out.println(attrs.getValue(i));
39                    }
40                 }
41              }
42           };
43
44        SAXParserFactory factory = SAXParserFactory.newInstance();
45        factory.setNamespaceAware(true);
46        factory.setFeature("http://apache.org/xml/features/nonvalidating/load-external-dtd", false);
```

*(Continues)*

**Listing 2.8** *(Continued)*

```
47      SAXParser saxParser = factory.newSAXParser();
48      InputStream in = new URL(url).openStream();
49      saxParser.parse(in, handler);
50    }
51  }
```

---

**javax.xml.parsers.SAXParserFactory** 1.4

- static SAXParserFactory newInstance()

  returns an instance of the SAXParserFactory class.

- SAXParser newSAXParser()

  returns an instance of the SAXParser class.

- boolean isNamespaceAware()
- void setNamespaceAware(boolean value)

  gets or sets the namespaceAware property of the factory. If set to true, the parsers that this factory generates are namespace-aware.

- boolean isValidating()
- void setValidating(boolean value)

  gets or sets the validating property of the factory. If set to true, the parsers that this factory generates validate their input.

---

**javax.xml.parsers.SAXParser** 1.4

- void parse(File f, DefaultHandler handler)
- void parse(String url, DefaultHandler handler)
- void parse(InputStream in, DefaultHandler handler)

  parses an XML document from the given file, URL, or input stream and reports parse events to the given handler.

---

*org.xml.sax.ContentHandler* 1.4

- void startDocument()
- void endDocument()

  is called at the start or the end of the document.

- void startElement(String uri, String lname, String qname, Attributes attr)
- void endElement(String uri, String lname, String qname)

  is called at the start or the end of an element.

*(Continues)*

---

**org.xml.sax.ContentHandler** 1.4 *(Continued)*

| *Parameters:* | uri | The URI of the namespace (if the parser is namespace-aware) |
| | lname | The local name without prefix (if the parser is namespace-aware) |
| | qname | The element name if the parser is not namespace-aware, or the qualified name with prefix if the parser reports qualified names in addition to local names |

- void characters(char[] data, int start, int length)
  is called when the parser reports character data.

| *Parameters:* | data | An array of character data |
| | start | The index of the first character in the data array that is a part of the reported characters |
| | length | The length of the reported character string |

---

**org.xml.sax.Attributes** 1.4

- int getLength()
  returns the number of attributes stored in this attribute collection.
- String getLocalName(int index)
  returns the local name (without prefix) of the attribute with the given index, or the empty string if the parser is not namespace-aware.
- String getURI(int index)
  returns the namespace URI of the attribute with the given index, or the empty string if the node is not part of a namespace or if the parser is not namespace-aware.
- String getQName(int index)
  returns the qualified name (with prefix) of the attribute with the given index, or the empty string if the qualified name is not reported by the parser.
- String getValue(int index)
- String getValue(String qname)
- String getValue(String uri, String lname)
  returns the attribute value from a given index, qualified name, or namespace URI + local name. Returns null if the value doesn't exist.

## 2.6.2 Using the StAX Parser

The StAX parser is a "pull parser." Instead of installing an event handler, you simply iterate through the events, using this basic loop:

```
InputStream in = url.openStream();
XMLInputFactory factory = XMLInputFactory.newInstance();
XMLStreamReader parser = factory.createXMLStreamReader(in);
while (parser.hasNext())
{
   int event = parser.next();
   Call parser methods to obtain event details
}
```

For example, when parsing the fragment

```
<font>
   <name>Helvetica</name>
   <size units="pt">36</size>
</font>
```

the parser yields the following events:

1.  START_ELEMENT, element name: font
2.  CHARACTERS, content: white space
3.  START_ELEMENT, element name: name
4.  CHARACTERS, content: Helvetica
5.  END_ELEMENT, element name: name
6.  CHARACTERS, content: white space
7.  START_ELEMENT, element name: size
8.  CHARACTERS, content: 36
9.  END_ELEMENT, element name: size
10. CHARACTERS, content: white space
11. END_ELEMENT, element name: font

To analyze the attribute values, call the appropriate methods of the XMLStreamReader class. For example,

```
String units = parser.getAttributeValue(null, "units");
```

gets the units attribute of the current element.

By default, namespace processing is enabled. You can deactivate it by modifying the factory:

```
XMLInputFactory factory = XMLInputFactory.newInstance();
factory.setProperty(XMLInputFactory.IS_NAMESPACE_AWARE, false);
```

Listing 2.9 contains the code for the web crawler program implemented with the StAX parser. As you can see, the code is simpler than the equivalent SAX code because you don't have to worry about event handling.

---

**Listing 2.9**  stax/StAXTest.java

```java
1  package stax;
2
3  import java.io.*;
4  import java.net.*;
5  import javax.xml.stream.*;
6
7  /**
8   * This program demonstrates how to use a StAX parser. The program prints all hyperlinks
9   * of an XHTML web page.<br>
10  * Usage: java StAXTest url
11  * @author Cay Horstmann
12  * @version 1.0 2007-06-23
13  */
14 public class StAXTest
15 {
16    public static void main(String[] args) throws Exception
17    {
18       String urlString;
19       if (args.length == 0)
20       {
21          urlString = "http://www.w3c.org";
22          System.out.println("Using " + urlString);
23       }
24       else urlString = args[0];
25       URL url = new URL(urlString);
26       InputStream in = url.openStream();
27       XMLInputFactory factory = XMLInputFactory.newInstance();
28       XMLStreamReader parser = factory.createXMLStreamReader(in);
29       while (parser.hasNext())
30       {
31          int event = parser.next();
32          if (event == XMLStreamConstants.START_ELEMENT)
33          {
34             if (parser.getLocalName().equals("a"))
35             {
36                String href = parser.getAttributeValue(null, "href");
37                if (href != null)
38                   System.out.println(href);
39             }
40          }
41       }
42    }
43 }
```

---

**`javax.xml.stream.XMLInputFactory`** 6

- `static XMLInputFactory newInstance()`
  returns an instance of the XMLInputFactory class.

- `void setProperty(String name, Object value)`
  sets a property for this factory, or throws an IllegalArgumentException if the property
  is not supported or cannot be set to the given value. The Java SE implementation
  supports the following Boolean-valued properties:

  | | |
  |---|---|
  | "javax.xml.stream.isValidating" | When false (the default), the document is not validated. Not required by the specification. |
  | "javax.xml.stream.isNamespaceAware" | When true (the default), namespaces are processed. Not required by the specification. |
  | "javax.xml.stream.isCoalescing" | When false (the default), adjacent character data are not coalesced. |
  | "javax.xml.stream.isReplacingEntityReferences" | When true (the default), entity references are replaced and reported as character data. |
  | "javax.xml.stream.isSupportingExternalEntities" | When true (the default), external entities are resolved. The specification gives no default for this property. |
  | "javax.xml.stream.supportDTD" | When true (the default), DTDs are reported as events. |

- `XMLStreamReader createXMLStreamReader(InputStream in)`
- `XMLStreamReader createXMLStreamReader(InputStream in, String characterEncoding)`
- `XMLStreamReader createXMLStreamReader(Reader in)`
- `XMLStreamReader createXMLStreamReader(Source in)`
  creates a parser that reads from the given stream, reader, or JAXP source.

---

**`javax.xml.stream.XMLStreamReader`** 6

- `boolean hasNext()`
  returns true if there is another parse event.

- `int next()`
  sets the parser state to the next parse event and returns one of the following constants: START_ELEMENT, END_ELEMENT, CHARACTERS, START_DOCUMENT, END_DOCUMENT, CDATA, COMMENT,
  SPACE (ignorable whitespace), PROCESSING_INSTRUCTION, ENTITY_REFERENCE, DTD.

*(Continues)*

---

*javax.xml.stream.XMLStreamReader*  **6**  *(Continued)*

- `boolean isStartElement()`
- `boolean isEndElement()`
- `boolean isCharacters()`
- `boolean isWhiteSpace()`

  returns true if the current event is a start element, end element, character data, or whitespace.

- `QName getName()`
- `String getLocalName()`

  gets the name of the element in a START_ELEMENT or END_ELEMENT event.

- `String getText()`

  returns the characters of a CHARACTERS, COMMENT, or CDATA event, the replacement value for an ENTITY_REFERENCE, or the internal subset of a DTD.

- `int getAttributeCount()`
- `QName getAttributeName(int index)`
- `String getAttributeLocalName(int index)`
- `String getAttributeValue(int index)`

  gets the attribute count and the names and values of the attributes, provided the current event is START_ELEMENT.

- `String getAttributeValue(String namespaceURI, String name)`

  gets the value of the attribute with the given name, provided the current event is START_ELEMENT. If namespaceURI is null, the namespace is not checked.

---

## 2.7  Generating XML Documents

You now know how to write Java programs that read XML. Let us now turn to the opposite process: producing XML output. Of course, you could write an XML file simply by making a sequence of print calls, printing the elements, attributes, and text content, but that would not be a good idea. The code is rather tedious, and you can easily make mistakes if you don't pay attention to special symbols (such as " or <) in the attribute values and text content.

A better approach is to build up a DOM tree with the contents of the document and then write out the tree contents. The following sections discuss the details.

### 2.7.1  Documents without Namespaces

To build a DOM tree, you start out with an empty document. You can get an empty document by calling the newDocument method of the DocumentBuilder class:

```
Document doc = builder.newDocument();
```

Use the `createElement` method of the `Document` class to construct the elements of your document:

```
Element rootElement = doc.createElement(rootName);
Element childElement = doc.createElement(childName);
```

Use the `createTextNode` method to construct text nodes:

```
Text textNode = doc.createTextNode(textContents);
```

Add the root element to the document, and add the child nodes to their parents:

```
doc.appendChild(rootElement);
rootElement.appendChild(childElement);
childElement.appendChild(textNode);
```

As you build up the DOM tree, you may also need to set element attributes. Simply call the `setAttribute` method of the `Element` class:

```
rootElement.setAttribute(name, value);
```

## 2.7.2 Documents with Namespaces

If you use namespaces, the procedure for creating a document is slightly different.

First, set the builder factory to be namespace-aware, then create the builder:

```
DocumentBuilderFactory factory = DocumentBuilderFactory.newInstance();
factory.setNamespaceAware(true);
builder = factory.newDocumentBuilder();
```

Then use `createElementNS` instead of `createElement` to create any nodes:

```
String namespace = "http://www.w3.org/2000/svg";
Element rootElement = doc.createElementNS(namespace, "svg");
```

If your node has a qualified name, with a namespace prefix, then any necessary `xmlns`-prefixed attributes are created automatically. For example, if you need SVG inside XHTML, you can construct an element like this:

```
Element svgElement = doc.createElement(namespace, "svg:svg")
```

When the element is written, it turns into

```
<svg:svg xmlns:svg="http://www.w3.org/2000/svg">
```

If you need to set element attributes whose names are in a namespace, use the `setAttributeNS` method of the `Element` class:

```
rootElement.setAttributeNS(namespace, qualifiedName, value);
```

### 2.7.3 Writing Documents

Somewhat curiously, it is not so easy to write a DOM tree to an output stream. The easiest approach is to use the Extensible Stylesheet Language Transformations (XSLT) API. For more information about XSLT, turn to Section 2.8, "XSL Transformations," on p. 173. Right now, consider the code that follows a magic incantation to produce XML output.

We apply the do-nothing transformation to the document and capture its output. To include a DOCTYPE node in the output, we also need to set the SYSTEM and PUBLIC identifiers as output properties.

```
// construct the do-nothing transformation
Transformer t = TransformerFactory.newInstance().newTransformer();
// set output properties to get a DOCTYPE node
t.setOutputProperty(OutputKeys.DOCTYPE_SYSTEM, systemIdentifier);
t.setOutputProperty(OutputKeys.DOCTYPE_PUBLIC, publicIdentifier);
// set indentation
t.setOutputProperty(OutputKeys.INDENT, "yes");
t.setOutputProperty(OutputKeys.METHOD, "xml");
t.setOutputProperty("{http://xml.apache.org/xslt}indent-amount", "2");
// apply the do-nothing transformation and send the output to a file
t.transform(new DOMSource(doc), new StreamResult(new FileOutputStream(file)));
```

Another approach is to use the LSSerializer interface. To get an instance, you have to use the following magic incantation:

```
DOMImplementation impl = doc.getImplementation();
DOMImplementationLS implLS = (DOMImplementationLS) impl.getFeature("LS", "3.0");
LSSerializer ser = implLS.createLSSerializer();
```

If you want spaces and line breaks, set this flag:

```
ser.getDomConfig().setParameter("format-pretty-print", true);
```

Then it's simple enough to convert a document to a string:

```
String str = ser.writeToString(doc);
```

If you want to write the output directly to a file, you need an LSOutput:

```
LSOutput out = implLS.createLSOutput();
out.setEncoding("UTF-8");
out.setByteStream(Files.newOutputStream(path));
ser.write(doc, out);
```

### 2.7.4 An Example: Generating an SVG File

Listing 2.10 on p. 165 is a typical program that produces XML output. The program draws a modernist painting—a random set of colored rectangles (see

Figure 2.6). To save a masterpiece, we use the Scalable Vector Graphics (SVG) format. SVG is an XML format to describe complex graphics in a device-independent fashion. You can find more information about SVG at www.w3c.org/Graphics/SVG. To view SVG files, simply use any modern browser.

We don't need to go into details about SVG; for our purposes, we just need to know how to express a set of colored rectangles. Here is a sample:

```
<?xml version="1.0" encoding="UTF-8"?>
<!DOCTYPE svg PUBLIC "-//W3C//DTD SVG 20000802//EN"
   "http://www.w3.org/TR/2000/CR-SVG-20000802/DTD/svg-20000802.dtd">
<svg xmlns="http://www.w3.org/2000/svg" width="300" height="150">
<rect x="231" y="61" width="9" height="12" fill="#6e4a13"/>
<rect x="107" y="106" width="56" height="5" fill="#c406be"/>
. . .
</svg>
```

As you can see, each rectangle is described as a rect node. The position, width, height, and fill color are attributes. The fill color is an RGB value in hexadecimal.

---

**NOTE:** SVG uses attributes heavily. In fact, some attributes are quite complex. For example, here is a path element:

```
<path d="M 100 100 L 300 100 L 200 300 z">
```

The M denotes a "moveto" command, L is "lineto," and z is "closepath" (!). Apparently, the designers of this data format didn't have much confidence in using XML for structured data. In your own XML formats, you might want to use elements instead of complex attributes.

---

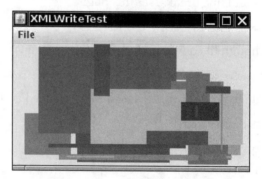

**Figure 2.6** Generating modern art

---

**javax.xml.parsers.DocumentBuilder**  1.4

- `Document newDocument()`
  returns an empty document.

---

**org.w3c.dom.Document**  1.4

- `Element createElement(String name)`
- `Element createElementNS(String uri, String qname)`
  creates an element with the given name.
- `Text createTextNode(String data)`
  creates a text node with the given data.

---

**org.w3c.dom.Node**  1.4

- `Node appendChild(Node child)`
  appends a node to the list of children of this node. Returns the appended node.

---

**org.w3c.dom.Element**  1.4

- `void setAttribute(String name, String value)`
- `void setAttributeNS(String uri, String qname, String value)`
  sets the attribute with the given name to the given value.

  | *Parameters:* | uri | The URI of the namespace, or `null` |
  | | qname | The qualified name. If it has an alias prefix, then `uri` must not be `null`. |
  | | value | The attribute value |

---

**javax.xml.transform.TransformerFactory**  1.4

- `static TransformerFactory newInstance()`
  returns an instance of the `TransformerFactory` class.
- `Transformer newTransformer()`
  returns an instance of the `Transformer` class that carries out an identity (do-nothing) transformation.

---

**javax.xml.transform.Transformer** 1.4

- void setOutputProperty(String name, String value)

  sets an output property. See www.w3.org/TR/xslt#output for a listing of the standard output properties. The most useful ones are shown here:

  | | |
  |---|---|
  | doctype-public | The public ID to be used in the DOCTYPE declaration |
  | doctype-system | The system ID to be used in the DOCTYPE declaration |
  | indent | "yes" or "no" |
  | method | "xml", "html", "text", or a custom string |

- void transform(Source from, Result to)

  transforms an XML document.

---

**javax.xml.transform.dom.DOMSource** 1.4

- DOMSource(Node n)

  constructs a source from the given node. Usually, n is a document node.

---

**javax.xml.transform.stream.StreamResult** 1.4

- StreamResult(File f)
- StreamResult(OutputStream out)
- StreamResult(Writer out)
- StreamResult(String systemID)

  constructs a stream result from a file, stream, writer, or system ID (usually a relative or absolute URL).

---

## 2.7.5 Writing an XML Document with StAX

In the preceding section, you saw how to produce an XML document by writing a DOM tree. If you have no other use for the DOM tree, that approach is not very efficient.

The StAX API lets you write an XML tree directly. Construct an XMLStreamWriter from an OutputStream:

```
XMLOutputFactory factory = XMLOutputFactory.newInstance();
XMLStreamWriter writer = factory.createXMLStreamWriter(out);
```

To produce the XML header, call

```
writer.writeStartDocument()
```

Then call

```
writer.writeStartElement(name);
```

Add attributes by calling

```
writer.writeAttribute(name, value);
```

Now you can add child elements by calling writeStartElement again, or write characters with

```
writer.writeCharacters(text);
```

When you have written all child nodes, call

```
writer.writeEndElement();
```

This causes the current element to be closed.

To write an element without children (such as <img. . ./>), use the call

```
writer.writeEmptyElement(name);
```

Finally, at the end of the document, call

```
writer.writeEndDocument();
```

This call closes any open elements.

As with the DOM/XSLT approach, you don't have to worry about escaping characters in attribute values and character data. However, it is possible to produce malformed XML, such as a document with multiple root nodes. Also, the current version of StAX has no support for producing indented output.

The program in Listing 2.10 shows you both approaches for writing XML. Listings 2.11 and 2.12 show the frame and component classes for the rectangle painting.

---

**Listing 2.10** write/XMLWriteTest.java

```
1  package write;
2
3  import java.awt.*;
4  import javax.swing.*;
5
6  /**
7   * This program shows how to write an XML file. It saves a file describing a modern drawing in SVG
8   * format.
9   * @version 1.11 2012-01-26
10  * @author Cay Horstmann
11  */
```

*(Continues)*

**Listing 2.10** *(Continued)*

```
12  public class XMLWriteTest
13  {
14     public static void main(String[] args)
15     {
16        EventQueue.invokeLater(new Runnable()
17           {
18              public void run()
19              {
20                 JFrame frame = new XMLWriteFrame();
21                 frame.setTitle("XMLWriteTest");
22                 frame.setDefaultCloseOperation(JFrame.EXIT_ON_CLOSE);
23                 frame.setVisible(true);
24              }
25           });
26     }
27  }
```

**Listing 2.11** write/XMLWriteFrame.java

```
1  package write;
2
3  import java.awt.event.*;
4  import java.beans.*;
5  import java.io.*;
6  import java.nio.file.*;
7  import javax.swing.*;
8  import javax.xml.stream.*;
9  import javax.xml.transform.*;
10 import javax.xml.transform.dom.*;
11 import javax.xml.transform.stream.*;
12 import org.w3c.dom.*;
13
14 /**
15  * A frame with a component for showing a modern drawing.
16  */
17 public class XMLWriteFrame extends JFrame
18 {
19    private RectangleComponent comp;
20    private JFileChooser chooser;
21
22    public XMLWriteFrame()
23    {
24       chooser = new JFileChooser();
25
26       // add component to frame
27       comp = new RectangleComponent();
28       add(comp);
```

```
29        // set up menu bar
30        JMenuBar menuBar = new JMenuBar();
31        setJMenuBar(menuBar);
32
33        JMenu menu = new JMenu("File");
34        menuBar.add(menu);
35
36        JMenuItem newItem = new JMenuItem("New");
37        menu.add(newItem);
38        newItem.addActionListener(EventHandler.create(ActionListener.class, comp, "newDrawing"));
39
40        JMenuItem saveItem = new JMenuItem("Save with DOM/XSLT");
41        menu.add(saveItem);
42        saveItem.addActionListener(EventHandler.create(ActionListener.class, this, "saveDocument"));
43
44        JMenuItem saveStAXItem = new JMenuItem("Save with StAX");
45        menu.add(saveStAXItem);
46        saveStAXItem.addActionListener(EventHandler.create(ActionListener.class, this, "saveStAX"));
47
48        JMenuItem exitItem = new JMenuItem("Exit");
49        menu.add(exitItem);
50        exitItem.addActionListener(new ActionListener()
51           {
52              public void actionPerformed(ActionEvent event)
53              {
54                 System.exit(0);
55              }
56           });
57        pack();
58    }
59
60    /**
61     * Saves the drawing in SVG format, using DOM/XSLT
62     */
63    public void saveDocument() throws TransformerException, IOException
64    {
65        if (chooser.showSaveDialog(this) != JFileChooser.APPROVE_OPTION) return;
66        File file = chooser.getSelectedFile();
67        Document doc = comp.buildDocument();
68        Transformer t = TransformerFactory.newInstance().newTransformer();
69        t.setOutputProperty(OutputKeys.DOCTYPE_SYSTEM,
70              "http://www.w3.org/TR/2000/CR-SVG-20000802/DTD/svg-20000802.dtd");
71        t.setOutputProperty(OutputKeys.DOCTYPE_PUBLIC, "-//W3C//DTD SVG 20000802//EN");
72        t.setOutputProperty(OutputKeys.INDENT, "yes");
73        t.setOutputProperty(OutputKeys.METHOD, "xml");
74        t.setOutputProperty("{http://xml.apache.org/xslt}indent-amount", "2");
75        t.transform(new DOMSource(doc), new StreamResult(Files.newOutputStream(file.toPath())));
76    }
```

*(Continues)*

**Listing 2.11** *(Continued)*

```
77      /**
78       * Saves the drawing in SVG format, using StAX
79       */
80      public void saveStAX() throws IOException, XMLStreamException
81      {
82          if (chooser.showSaveDialog(this) != JFileChooser.APPROVE_OPTION) return;
83          File file = chooser.getSelectedFile();
84          XMLOutputFactory factory = XMLOutputFactory.newInstance();
85          XMLStreamWriter writer = factory.createXMLStreamWriter(Files.newOutputStream(file.toPath()));
86          try
87          {
88              comp.writeDocument(writer);
89          }
90          finally
91          {
92              writer.close(); // Not autocloseable
93          }
94      }
95  }
```

**Listing 2.12** write/RectangleComponent.java

```
1   package write;
2
3   import java.awt.*;
4   import java.awt.geom.*;
5   import java.util.*;
6   import javax.swing.*;
7   import javax.xml.parsers.*;
8   import javax.xml.stream.*;
9   import org.w3c.dom.*;
10
11  /**
12   * A component that shows a set of colored rectangles
13   */
14  public class RectangleComponent extends JComponent
15  {
16      private static final int DEFAULT_WIDTH = 300;
17      private static final int DEFAULT_HEIGHT = 200;
18
19      private java.util.List<Rectangle2D> rects;
20      private java.util.List<Color> colors;
21      private Random generator;
22      private DocumentBuilder builder;
```

```
23   public RectangleComponent()
24   {
25      rects = new ArrayList<>();
26      colors = new ArrayList<>();
27      generator = new Random();
28
29      DocumentBuilderFactory factory = DocumentBuilderFactory.newInstance();
30      factory.setNamespaceAware(true);
31      try
32      {
33         builder = factory.newDocumentBuilder();
34      }
35      catch (ParserConfigurationException e)
36      {
37         e.printStackTrace();
38      }
39   }
40
41   /**
42    * Create a new random drawing.
43    */
44   public void newDrawing()
45   {
46      int n = 10 + generator.nextInt(20);
47      rects.clear();
48      colors.clear();
49      for (int i = 1; i <= n; i++)
50      {
51         int x = generator.nextInt(getWidth());
52         int y = generator.nextInt(getHeight());
53         int width = generator.nextInt(getWidth() - x);
54         int height = generator.nextInt(getHeight() - y);
55         rects.add(new Rectangle(x, y, width, height));
56         int r = generator.nextInt(256);
57         int g = generator.nextInt(256);
58         int b = generator.nextInt(256);
59         colors.add(new Color(r, g, b));
60      }
61      repaint();
62   }
63
64   public void paintComponent(Graphics g)
65   {
66      if (rects.size() == 0) newDrawing();
67      Graphics2D g2 = (Graphics2D) g;
68
69      // draw all rectangles
```

*(Continues)*

**Listing 2.12** *(Continued)*

```
70      for (int i = 0; i < rects.size(); i++)
71      {
72         g2.setPaint(colors.get(i));
73         g2.fill(rects.get(i));
74      }
75   }
76
77   /**
78    * Creates an SVG document of the current drawing.
79    * @return the DOM tree of the SVG document
80    */
81   public Document buildDocument()
82   {
83      String namespace = "http://www.w3.org/2000/svg";
84      Document doc = builder.newDocument();
85      Element svgElement = doc.createElementNS(namespace, "svg");
86      doc.appendChild(svgElement);
87      svgElement.setAttribute("width", "" + getWidth());
88      svgElement.setAttribute("height", "" + getHeight());
89      for (int i = 0; i < rects.size(); i++)
90      {
91         Color c = colors.get(i);
92         Rectangle2D r = rects.get(i);
93         Element rectElement = doc.createElementNS(namespace, "rect");
94         rectElement.setAttribute("x", "" + r.getX());
95         rectElement.setAttribute("y", "" + r.getY());
96         rectElement.setAttribute("width", "" + r.getWidth());
97         rectElement.setAttribute("height", "" + r.getHeight());
98         rectElement.setAttribute("fill", colorToString(c));
99         svgElement.appendChild(rectElement);
100     }
101     return doc;
102  }
103
104  /**
105   * Writes an SVG document of the current drawing.
106   * @param writer the document destination
107   */
108  public void writeDocument(XMLStreamWriter writer) throws XMLStreamException
109  {
110     writer.writeStartDocument();
111     writer.writeDTD("<!DOCTYPE svg PUBLIC \"-//W3C//DTD SVG 20000802//EN\" "
112        + "\"http://www.w3.org/TR/2000/CR-SVG-20000802/DTD/svg-20000802.dtd\">");
113     writer.writeStartElement("svg");
114     writer.writeDefaultNamespace("http://www.w3.org/2000/svg");
```

```
115      writer.writeAttribute("width", "" + getWidth());
116      writer.writeAttribute("height", "" + getHeight());
117      for (int i = 0; i < rects.size(); i++)
118      {
119         Color c = colors.get(i);
120         Rectangle2D r = rects.get(i);
121         writer.writeEmptyElement("rect");
122         writer.writeAttribute("x", "" + r.getX());
123         writer.writeAttribute("y", "" + r.getY());
124         writer.writeAttribute("width", "" + r.getWidth());
125         writer.writeAttribute("height", "" + r.getHeight());
126         writer.writeAttribute("fill", colorToString(c));
127      }
128      writer.writeEndDocument(); // closes svg element
129   }
130
131   /**
132    * Converts a color to a hex value.
133    * @param c a color
134    * @return a string of the form #rrggbb
135    */
136   private static String colorToString(Color c)
137   {
138      StringBuffer buffer = new StringBuffer();
139      buffer.append(Integer.toHexString(c.getRGB() & 0xFFFFFF));
140      while (buffer.length() < 6)
141         buffer.insert(0, '0');
142      buffer.insert(0, '#');
143      return buffer.toString();
144   }
145
146   public Dimension getPreferredSize() { return new Dimension(DEFAULT_WIDTH, DEFAULT_HEIGHT); }
147 }
```

---

**javax.xml.stream.XMLOutputFactory** 6

- static XMLOutputFactory newInstance()
  returns an instance of the XMLOutputFactory class.

- XMLStreamWriter createXMLStreamWriter(OutputStream in)
- XMLStreamWriter createXMLStreamWriter(OutputStream in, String characterEncoding)
- XMLStreamWriter createXMLStreamWriter(Writer in)
- XMLStreamWriter createXMLStreamWriter(Result in)
  creates a writer that writes to the given stream, writer, or JAXP result.

---

*javax.xml.stream.XMLStreamWriter* 6

- void writeStartDocument()
- void writeStartDocument(String xmlVersion)
- void writeStartDocument(String encoding, String xmlVersion)

  writes the XML processing instruction at the top of the document. Note that the encoding parameter is only used to write the attribute. It does not set the character encoding of the output.

- void setDefaultNamespace(String namespaceURI)
- void setPrefix(String prefix, String namespaceURI)

  sets the default namespace or the namespace associated with a prefix. The declaration is scoped to the current element or, if no element has been written, to the document root.

- void writeStartElement(String localName)
- void writeStartElement(String namespaceURI, String localName)

  writes a start tag, replacing the namespaceURI with the associated prefix.

- void writeEndElement()

  closes the current element.

- void writeEndDocument()

  closes all open elements.

- void writeEmptyElement(String localName)
- void writeEmptyElement(String namespaceURI, String localName)

  writes a self-closing tag, replacing the namespaceURI with the associated prefix.

- void writeAttribute(String localName, String value)
- void writeAttribute(String namespaceURI, String localName, String value)

  writes an attribute for the current element, replacing the namespaceURI with the associated prefix.

- void writeCharacters(String text)

  writes character data.

- void writeCData(String text)

  writes a CDATA block.

- void writeDTD(String dtd)

  writes the dtd string, which is assumed to contain a DOCTYPE declaration.

- void writeComment(String comment)

  writes a comment.

- void close()

  closes this writer.

---

## 2.8  XSL Transformations

The XSL Transformations (XSLT) mechanism allows you to specify rules for transforming XML documents into other formats, such as plain text, XHTML, or any other XML format. XSLT is commonly used to translate from one machine-readable XML format to another, or to translate XML into a presentation format for human consumption.

You need to provide an XSLT stylesheet that describes the conversion of XML documents into some other format. An XSLT processor reads an XML document and the stylesheet and produces the desired output (see Figure 2.7).

Here is a typical example. We want to transform XML files with employee records into HTML documents. Consider this input file:

```
<staff>
   <employee>
      <name>Carl Cracker</name>
      <salary>75000</salary>
      <hiredate year="1987" month="12" day="15"/>
   </employee>
   <employee>
      <name>Harry Hacker</name>
      <salary>50000</salary>
      <hiredate year="1989" month="10" day="1"/>
   </employee>
   <employee>
      <name>Tony Tester</name>
      <salary>40000</salary>
      <hiredate year="1990" month="3" day="15"/>
   </employee>
</staff>
```

The desired output is an HTML table:

```
<table border="1">
<tr>
<td>Carl Cracker</td><td>$75000.0</td><td>1987-12-15</td>
</tr>
<tr>
<td>Harry Hacker</td><td>$50000.0</td><td>1989-10-1</td>
</tr>
<tr>
<td>Tony Tester</td><td>$40000.0</td><td>1990-3-15</td>
</tr>
</table>
```

The XSLT specification is quite complex, and entire books have been written on the subject. We can't possibly discuss all the features of XSLT, so we will just

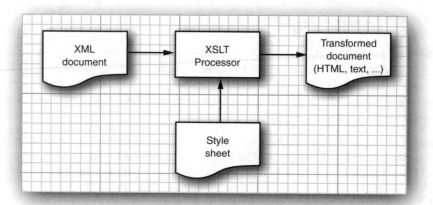

**Figure 2.7** Applying XSL transformations

work through a representative example. You can find more information in the book *Essential XML* by Don Box et al. The XSLT specification is available at www.w3.org/TR/xslt.

A stylesheet with transformation templates has this form:

```
<?xml version="1.0" encoding="ISO-8859-1"?>
<xsl:stylesheet
   xmlns:xsl="http://www.w3.org/1999/XSL/Transform"
   version="1.0">
   <xsl:output method="html"/>
   template₁


   template₂
   . . .
</xsl:stylesheet>
```

In our example, the `xsl:output` element specifies the method as HTML. Other valid method settings are `xml` and `text`.

Here is a typical template:

```
<xsl:template match="/staff/employee">
   <tr><xsl:apply-templates/></tr>
</xsl:template>
```

The value of the `match` attribute is an XPath expression. The template states: Whenever you see a node in the XPath set `/staff/employee`, do the following:

1. Emit the string `<tr>`.
2. Keep applying templates as you process its children.

3.   Emit the string </tr> after you are done with all children.

In other words, this template generates the HTML table row markers around every employee record.

The XSLT processor starts processing by examining the root element. Whenever a node matches one of the templates, it applies the template. (If multiple templates match, the best matching one is used; see the specification at www.w3.org/ TR/xslt for the gory details.) If no template matches, the processor carries out a default action. For text nodes, the default is to include the contents in the output. For elements, the default action is to create no output but to keep processing the children.

Here is a template for transforming name nodes in an employee file:

```
<xsl:template match="/staff/employee/name">
  <td><xsl:apply-templates/></td>
</xsl:template>
```

As you can see, the template produces the <td>. . .</td> delimiters, and it asks the processor to recursively visit the children of the name element. There is just one child, the text node. When the processor visits that node, it emits the text contents (provided, of course, that there is no other matching template).

You have to work a little harder if you want to copy attribute values into the output. Here is an example:

```
<xsl:template match="/staff/employee/hiredate">
  <td><xsl:value-of select="@year"/>-<xsl:value-of
  select="@month"/>-<xsl:value-of select="@day"/></td>
</xsl:template>
```

When processing a hiredate node, this template emits

1.   The string <td>
2.   The value of the year attribute
3.   A hyphen
4.   The value of the month attribute
5.   A hyphen
6.   The value of the day attribute
7.   The string </td>

The xsl:value-of statement computes the string value of a node set. The node set is specified by the XPath value of the select attribute. In this case, the path is relative to the currently processed node. The node set is converted to a string by concatenation of the string values of all nodes. The string value of an attribute node is its value. The string value of a text node is its contents. The string value of an element node is the concatenation of the string values of its child nodes (but not its attributes).

Listing 2.13 contains the stylesheet for turning an XML file with employee records into an HTML table.

**Listing 2.13** transform/makehtml.xsl

```
1  <?xml version="1.0" encoding="ISO-8859-1"?>
2
3  <xsl:stylesheet
4     xmlns:xsl="http://www.w3.org/1999/XSL/Transform"
5     version="1.0">
6
7     <xsl:output method="html"/>
8
9     <xsl:template match="/staff">
10        <table border="1"><xsl:apply-templates/></table>
11     </xsl:template>
12
13     <xsl:template match="/staff/employee">
14        <tr><xsl:apply-templates/></tr>
15     </xsl:template>
16
17     <xsl:template match="/staff/employee/name">
18        <td><xsl:apply-templates/></td>
19     </xsl:template>
20
21     <xsl:template match="/staff/employee/salary">
22        <td>$<xsl:apply-templates/></td>
23     </xsl:template>
24
25     <xsl:template match="/staff/employee/hiredate">
26        <td><xsl:value-of select="@year"/>-<xsl:value-of
27        select="@month"/>-<xsl:value-of select="@day"/></td>
28     </xsl:template>
29
30  </xsl:stylesheet>
```

Listing 2.14 shows a different set of transformations. The input is the same XML file, and the output is plain text in the familiar property file format:

```
employee.1.name=Carl Cracker
employee.1.salary=75000.0
employee.1.hiredate=1987-12-15
employee.2.name=Harry Hacker
employee.2.salary=50000.0
employee.2.hiredate=1989-10-1
employee.3.name=Tony Tester
```

employee.3.salary=40000.0
employee.3.hiredate=1990-3-15

**Listing 2.14** transform/makeprop.xsl

```
1  <?xml version="1.0"?>
2
3  <xsl:stylesheet
4     xmlns:xsl="http://www.w3.org/1999/XSL/Transform"
5     version="1.0">
6
7     <xsl:output method="text" omit-xml-declaration="yes"/>
8
9     <xsl:template match="/staff/employee">
10  employee.<xsl:value-of select="position()"
11  />.name=<xsl:value-of select="name/text()"/>
12  employee.<xsl:value-of select="position()"
13  />.salary=<xsl:value-of select="salary/text()"/>
14  employee.<xsl:value-of select="position()"
15  />.hiredate=<xsl:value-of select="hiredate/@year"
16  />-<xsl:value-of select="hiredate/@month"
17  />-<xsl:value-of select="hiredate/@day"/>
18     </xsl:template>
19
20  </xsl:stylesheet>
```

That example uses the position() function which yields the position of the current node as seen from its parent. We thus get an entirely different output simply by switching the stylesheet. This means you can safely use XML to describe your data; if some applications need the data in another format, just use XSLT to generate the alternative format.

It is extremely simple to generate XSL transformations in the Java platform. Set up a transformer factory for each stylesheet. Then, get a transformer object and tell it to transform a source to a result:

```
File styleSheet = new File(filename);
StreamSource styleSource = new StreamSource(styleSheet);
Transformer t = TransformerFactory.newInstance().newTransformer(styleSource);
t.transform(source, result);
```

The parameters of the transform method are objects of classes that implement the Source and Result interfaces. Several classes implement the Source interface:

```
DOMSource
SAXSource
StAXSource
StreamSource
```

You can construct a StreamSource from a file, stream, reader, or URL, and a DOMSource from the node of a DOM tree. For example, in the preceding section, we invoked the identity transformation as

```
t.transform(new DOMSource(doc), result);
```

In our example program, we do something slightly more interesting. Instead of starting out with an existing XML file, we produce a SAX XML reader that gives the illusion of parsing an XML file by emitting appropriate SAX events. Actually, our XML reader reads a flat file, as described in Chapter 1. The input file looks like this:

```
Carl Cracker|75000.0|1987|12|15
Harry Hacker|50000.0|1989|10|1
Tony Tester|40000.0|1990|3|15
```

Our XML reader generates SAX events as it processes the input. Here is a part of the parse method of the EmployeeReader class that implements the XMLReader interface:

```
AttributesImpl attributes = new AttributesImpl();
handler.startDocument();
handler.startElement("", "staff", "staff", attributes);
while ((line = in.readLine()) != null)
{
   handler.startElement("", "employee", "employee", attributes);
   StringTokenizer t = new StringTokenizer(line, "|");
   handler.startElement("", "name", "name", attributes);
   String s = t.nextToken();
   handler.characters(s.toCharArray(), 0, s.length());
   handler.endElement("", "name", "name");
   . . .
   handler.endElement("", "employee", "employee");
}
handler.endElement("", rootElement, rootElement);
handler.endDocument();
```

The SAXSource for the transformer is constructed from the XML reader:

```
t.transform(new SAXSource(new EmployeeReader(),
   new InputSource(new FileInputStream(filename))), result);
```

This is an ingenious trick to convert non-XML legacy data into XML. Of course, most XSLT applications will already have XML input data, and you can simply invoke the transform method on a StreamSource:

```
t.transform(new StreamSource(file), result);
```

The transformation result is an object of a class that implements the Result interface. The Java library supplies three classes:

```
DOMResult
SAXResult
StreamResult
```

To store the result in a DOM tree, use a `DocumentBuilder` to generate a new document node and wrap it into a `DOMResult`:

```
Document doc = builder.newDocument();
t.transform(source, new DOMResult(doc));
```

To save the output in a file, use a `StreamResult`:

```
t.transform(source, new StreamResult(file));
```

Listing 2.15 contains the complete source code.

---

**Listing 2.15** transform/TransformTest.java

```
 1  package transform;
 2
 3  import java.io.*;
 4  import java.nio.file.*;
 5  import java.util.*;
 6  import javax.xml.transform.*;
 7  import javax.xml.transform.sax.*;
 8  import javax.xml.transform.stream.*;
 9  import org.xml.sax.*;
10  import org.xml.sax.helpers.*;
11
12  /**
13   * This program demonstrates XSL transformations. It applies a transformation to a set of employee
14   * records. The records are stored in the file employee.dat and turned into XML format. Specify
15   * the stylesheet on the command line, e.g.
16   * java TransformTest makeprop.xsl
17   * @version 1.02 2012-06-04
18   * @author Cay Horstmann
19   */
20  public class TransformTest
21  {
22     public static void main(String[] args) throws Exception
23     {
24        Path path;
25        if (args.length > 0) path = Paths.get(args[0]);
26        else path = Paths.get("transform", "makehtml.xsl");
27        try (InputStream styleIn = Files.newInputStream(path))
28        {
29           StreamSource styleSource = new StreamSource(styleIn);
```

*(Continues)*

**Listing 2.15** *(Continued)*

```
30          Transformer t = TransformerFactory.newInstance().newTransformer(styleSource);
31          t.setOutputProperty(OutputKeys.INDENT, "yes");
32          t.setOutputProperty(OutputKeys.METHOD, "xml");
33          t.setOutputProperty("{http://xml.apache.org/xslt}indent-amount", "2");
34
35          try (InputStream docIn = Files.newInputStream(Paths.get("transform", "employee.dat")))
36          {
37             t.transform(new SAXSource(new EmployeeReader(), new InputSource(docIn)),
38                new StreamResult(System.out));
39          }
40       }
41    }
42 }
43
44 /**
45  * This class reads the flat file employee.dat and reports SAX parser events to act as if it was
46  * parsing an XML file.
47  */
48 class EmployeeReader implements XMLReader
49 {
50    private ContentHandler handler;
51
52    public void parse(InputSource source) throws IOException, SAXException
53    {
54       InputStream stream = source.getByteStream();
55       BufferedReader in = new BufferedReader(new InputStreamReader(stream));
56       String rootElement = "staff";
57       AttributesImpl atts = new AttributesImpl();
58
59       if (handler == null) throw new SAXException("No content handler");
60
61       handler.startDocument();
62       handler.startElement("", rootElement, rootElement, atts);
63       String line;
64       while ((line = in.readLine()) != null)
65       {
66          handler.startElement("", "employee", "employee", atts);
67          StringTokenizer t = new StringTokenizer(line, "|");
68
69          handler.startElement("", "name", "name", atts);
70          String s = t.nextToken();
71          handler.characters(s.toCharArray(), 0, s.length());
72          handler.endElement("", "name", "name");
73
74          handler.startElement("", "salary", "salary", atts);
75          s = t.nextToken();
76          handler.characters(s.toCharArray(), 0, s.length());
```

```
77          handler.endElement("", "salary", "salary");
78
79          atts.addAttribute("", "year", "year", "CDATA", t.nextToken());
80          atts.addAttribute("", "month", "month", "CDATA", t.nextToken());
81          atts.addAttribute("", "day", "day", "CDATA", t.nextToken());
82          handler.startElement("", "hiredate", "hiredate", atts);
83          handler.endElement("", "hiredate", "hiredate");
84          atts.clear();
85
86          handler.endElement("", "employee", "employee");
87       }
88
89       handler.endElement("", rootElement, rootElement);
90       handler.endDocument();
91    }
92
93    public void setContentHandler(ContentHandler newValue)
94    {
95       handler = newValue;
96    }
97
98    public ContentHandler getContentHandler()
99    {
100      return handler;
101   }
102
103   // the following methods are just do-nothing implementations
104   public void parse(String systemId) throws IOException, SAXException
105   {
106   }
107
108   public void setErrorHandler(ErrorHandler handler)
109   {
110   }
111
112   public ErrorHandler getErrorHandler()
113   {
114      return null;
115   }
116
117   public void setDTDHandler(DTDHandler handler)
118   {
119   }
120
121   public DTDHandler getDTDHandler()
122   {
123      return null;
124   }
```

*(Continues)*

---

**Listing 2.15** *(Continued)*

```
125    public void setEntityResolver(EntityResolver resolver)
126    {
127    }
128
129    public EntityResolver getEntityResolver()
130    {
131       return null;
132    }
133
134    public void setProperty(String name, Object value)
135    {
136    }
137
138    public Object getProperty(String name)
139    {
140       return null;
141    }
142
143    public void setFeature(String name, boolean value)
144    {
145    }
146
147    public boolean getFeature(String name)
148    {
149       return false;
150    }
151 }
```

---

**javax.xml.transform.TransformerFactory** 1.4

- Transformer newTransformer(Source styleSheet)
  returns an instance of the Transformer class that reads a stylesheet from the given source.

---

**javax.xml.transform.stream.StreamSource** 1.4

- StreamSource(File f)
- StreamSource(InputStream in)
- StreamSource(Reader in)
- StreamSource(String systemID)
  constructs a stream source from a file, stream, reader, or system ID (usually a relative or absolute URL).

---

**javax.xml.transform.sax.SAXSource** 1.4

- SAXSource(XMLReader reader, InputSource source)
  constructs a SAX source that obtains data from the given input source and uses the given reader to parse the input.

---

**org.xml.sax.XMLReader** 1.4

- void setContentHandler(ContentHandler handler)
  sets the handler that is notified of parse events as the input is parsed.

- void parse(InputSource source)
  parses the input from the given input source and sends parse events to the content handler.

---

**javax.xml.transform.dom.DOMResult** 1.4

- DOMResult(Node n)
  constructs a source from the given node. Usually, n is a new document node.

---

**org.xml.sax.helpers.AttributesImpl** 1.4

- void addAttribute(String uri, String lname, String qname, String type, String value)
  adds an attribute to this attribute collection.

  | *Parameters:* | uri | The URI of the namespace |
  |---|---|---|
  | | lname | The local name without prefix |
  | | qname | The qualified name with prefix |
  | | type | The type, one of "CDATA", "ID", "IDREF", "IDREFS", "NMTOKEN", "NMTOKENS", "ENTITY", "ENTITIES", or "NOTATION" |
  | | value | The attribute value |

- void clear()
  removes all attributes from this attribute collection.

---

This example concludes our discussion of XML support in the Java library. You should now have a good perspective on the major strengths of XML—in particular, for automated parsing and validation and as a powerful transformation mechanism. Of course, all this technology is only going to work for you if you design your XML formats well. You need to make sure that the formats are rich enough to express all your business needs, that they are stable over time, and that your business partners are willing to accept your XML documents. Those issues can be far more challenging than dealing with parsers, DTDs, or transformations.

In the next chapter, we will discuss network programming on the Java platform, starting with the basics of network sockets and moving on to higher level protocols for e-mail and the World Wide Web.

CHAPTER **3**

# Networking

### In this chapter:

We begin this chapter by reviewing basic networking concepts, then move on to writing Java programs that connect to network services. We will show you how network clients and servers are implemented. Finally, you will see how to send e-mail from a Java program and how to harvest information from a web server.

## 3.1 Connecting to a Server

Before writing our first network program, let's discuss a great debugging tool for network programming that you already have—namely, telnet. Telnet is pre-installed on most systems. You should be able to launch it by typing telnet from a command shell.

**NOTE:** In Windows Vista, telnet is installed but deactivated by default. To activate it, go to the Control Panel, select Programs, click "Turn Windows Features On or Off", and select the "Telnet client" checkbox. The Windows firewall also blocks quite a few network ports that we use in this chapter; you might need an administrator account to unblock them.

You may have used telnet to connect to a remote computer, but you can use it to communicate with other services provided by Internet hosts as well. Here is an example of what you can do. Type

```
telnet time-A.timefreq.bldrdoc.gov 13
```

As Figure 3.1 shows, you should get back a line like this:

```
54276 07-06-25 21:37:31 50 0 0 659.0 UTC(NIST) *
```

What is going on? You have connected to the "time of day" service that most UNIX machines constantly run. The particular server that you connected to is operated by the National Institute of Standards and Technology in Boulder, Colorado, and gives the measurement of a Cesium atomic clock. (Of course, the reported time is not completely accurate due to network delays.)

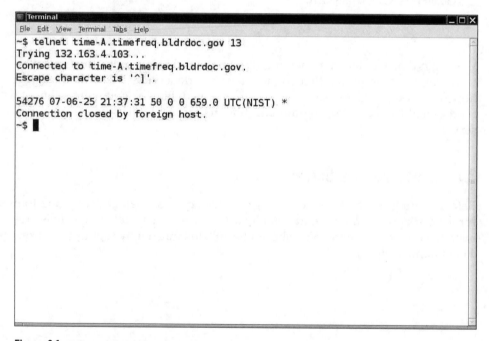

**Figure 3.1** Output of the "time of day" service

By convention, the "time of day" service is always attached to "port" number 13.

 **NOTE:** In network parlance, a port is not a physical device, but an abstraction facilitating communication between a server and a client (see Figure 3.2).

The server software is continuously running on the remote machine, waiting for any network traffic that wants to chat with port 13. When the operating system on the remote computer receives a network package that contains a request to connect to port number 13, it wakes up the listening server process and establishes the connection. The connection stays up until it is terminated by one of the parties.

When you began the telnet session with `time-A.timefreq.bldrdoc.gov` at port 13, a piece of network software knew enough to convert the string `"time-A. timefreq.bldrdoc.gov"` to its correct Internet Protocol (IP) address, 132.163.4.103. The telnet software then sent a connection request to that address, asking for a connection to port 13. Once the connection was established, the remote program sent back a line of data and closed the connection. In general, of course, clients and servers engage in a more extensive dialog before one or the other closes the connection.

Here is another experiment along the same lines—but a bit more interesting. Type

```
telnet horstmann.com 80
```

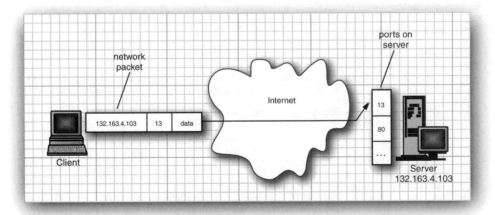

**Figure 3.2** A client connecting to a server port

Then type very carefully the following:

```
GET / HTTP/1.1
Host: horstmann.com
blank line
```

That is, hit the Enter key twice at the end.

Figure 3.3 shows the response. It should look eerily familiar—you got a page of HTML-formatted text, namely Cay Horstmann's home page.

This is exactly the same process that your web browser goes through to get a web page. It uses HTTP to request web pages from servers. Of course, the browser displays the HTML code more nicely.

 **NOTE:** The `Host` key/value pair is required when you connect to a web server that hosts multiple domains with the same IP address. You can omit it if the server hosts a single domain.

Our first network program in Listing 3.1 will do the same thing we did using telnet—connect to a port and print out what it finds.

```
~$ telnet horstmann.com 80
Trying 67.210.118.65...
Connected to horstmann.com.
Escape character is '^]'.
GET / HTTP/1.1
Host: horstmann.com

HTTP/1.1 200 OK
Date: Sun, 26 Jun 2011 01:05:27 GMT
Server: Apache/1.3.42 (Unix) Sun-ONE-ASP/4.0.2 mod_fastcgi/2.4.6 mod_log_bytes/1
.2 mod_bwlimited/1.4 mod_auth_passthrough/1.8 FrontPage/5.0.2.2635 mod_ssl/2.8.3
1 OpenSSL/0.9.7a
Last-Modified: Sun, 22 May 2011 08:11:15 GMT
ETag: "305e572-189f-4dd8c523"
Accept-Ranges: bytes
Content-Length: 6303
Content-Type: text/html

<?xml version="1.0" encoding="us-ascii"?>
<!DOCTYPE html PUBLIC "-//W3C//DTD XHTML 1.0 Strict//EN"
     "http://www.w3.org/TR/xhtml1/DTD/xhtml1-strict.dtd">
<html xmlns="http://www.w3.org/1999/xhtml">
<head>
  <title>Cay Horstmann's Home Page</title>
```

**Figure 3.3** Using telnet to access an HTTP port

---

**Listing 3.1** socket/SocketTest.java

```java
1  package socket;
2
3  import java.io.*;
4  import java.net.*;
5  import java.util.*;
6
7  /**
8   * This program makes a socket connection to the atomic clock in Boulder, Colorado, and prints
9   * the time that the server sends.
10  *
11  * @version 1.20 2004-08-03
12  * @author Cay Horstmann
13  */
14  public class SocketTest
15  {
16     public static void main(String[] args) throws IOException
17     {
18        try (Socket s = new Socket("time-A.timefreq.bldrdoc.gov", 13))
19        {
20           InputStream inStream = s.getInputStream();
21           Scanner in = new Scanner(inStream);
22
23           while (in.hasNextLine())
24           {
25              String line = in.nextLine();
26              System.out.println(line);
27           }
28        }
29     }
30  }
```

---

The key statements of this simple program are as follows:

```java
Socket s = new Socket("time-A.timefreq.bldrdoc.gov", 13);
InputStream inStream = s.getInputStream();
```

The first line opens a *socket*, which is a network software abstraction that enables communication out of and into this program. We pass the remote address and the port number to the socket constructor. If the connection fails, an UnknownHostException is thrown. If there is another problem, an IOException occurs. Since UnknownHostException is a subclass of IOException and this is a sample program, we just catch the superclass.

Once the socket is open, the getInputStream method in java.net.Socket returns an InputStream object that you can use just like any other stream. Once you have grabbed the stream, this program simply prints each input line to standard output. This process continues until the stream is finished and the server disconnects.

This program works only with very simple servers, such as a "time of day" service. In more complex networking programs, the client sends request data to the server, and the server might not immediately disconnect at the end of a response. You will see how to implement that behavior in several examples throughout this chapter.

The Socket class is pleasant and easy to use because the Java library hides the complexities of establishing a networking connection and sending data across it. The java.net package essentially gives you the same programming interface you would use to work with a file.

 **NOTE:** In this book, we cover only the Transmission Control Protocol (TCP). The Java platform also supports the User Datagram Protocol (UDP), which can be used to send packets (also called *datagrams*) with much less overhead than that of TCP. The drawback is that packets need not be delivered in sequential order to the receiving application and can even be dropped altogether. It is up to the recipient to put the packets in order and to request retransmission of missing packets. UDP is well suited for applications in which missing packets can be tolerated—for example, for audio or video streams or continuous measurements.

---

**java.net.Socket** 1.0

- Socket(String host, int port)
  constructs a socket to connect to the given host and port.
- InputStream getInputStream()
- OutputStream getOutputStream()
  gets the stream to read data from the socket or write data to the socket.

---

## 3.1.1 Socket Timeouts

Reading from a socket blocks until data are available. If the host is unreachable, your application waits for a long time and you are at the mercy of the underlying operating system to eventually time out.

You can decide what timeout value is reasonable for your particular application. Then, call the setSoTimeout method to set a timeout value (in milliseconds).

```
Socket s = new Socket(. . .);
s.setSoTimeout(10000); // time out after 10 seconds
```

If the timeout value has been set for a socket, all subsequent read and write operations throw a `SocketTimeoutException` when the timeout has been reached before the operation has completed its work. You can catch that exception and react to the timeout.

```
try
{
   InputStream in = s.getInputStream(); // read from in
   . . .
}
catch (InterruptedIOException exception)
{
   react to timeout
}
```

There is one additional timeout issue that you need to address. The constructor

```
Socket(String host, int port)
```

can block indefinitely until an initial connection to the host is established.

You can overcome this problem by first constructing an unconnected socket and then connecting it with a timeout:

```
Socket s = new Socket();
s.connect(new InetSocketAddress(host, port), timeout);
```

See Section 3.3, "Interruptible Sockets," on p. 202 for how to allow users to interrupt the socket connection at any time.

---

**java.net.Socket** 1.0

- `Socket()` **1.1**
  creates a socket that has not yet been connected.
- `void connect(SocketAddress address)` **1.4**
  connects this socket to the given address.
- `void connect(SocketAddress address, int timeoutInMilliseconds)` **1.4**
  connects this socket to the given address, or returns if the time interval expired.
- `void setSoTimeout(int timeoutInMilliseconds)` **1.1**
  sets the blocking time for read requests on this socket. If the timeout is reached, an `InterruptedIOException` is raised.
- `boolean isConnected()` **1.4**
  returns `true` if the socket is connected.
- `boolean isClosed()` **1.4**
  returns `true` if the socket is closed.

## 3.1.2 Internet Addresses

Usually, you don't have to worry too much about Internet addresses—the numerical host addresses that consist of 4 bytes (or, with IPv6, 16 bytes) such as 132.163.4.102. However, you can use the InetAddress class if you need to convert between host names and Internet addresses.

The java.net package supports IPv6 Internet addresses, provided the host operating system does.

The static getByName method returns an InetAddress object of a host. For example,

```
InetAddress address = InetAddress.getByName("time-A.timefreq.b1drdoc.gov");
```

returns an InetAddress object that encapsulates the sequence of four bytes 132.163.4.104. You can access the bytes with the getAddress method.

```
byte[] addressBytes = address.getAddress();
```

Some host names with a lot of traffic correspond to multiple Internet addresses, to facilitate load balancing. For example, at the time of this writing, the host name google.com corresponds to twelve different Internet addresses. One of them is picked at random when the host is accessed. You can get all hosts with the getAllByName method.

```
InetAddress[] addresses = InetAddress.getAllByName(host);
```

Finally, you sometimes need the address of the local host. If you simply ask for the address of localhost, you always get the local loopback address 127.0.0.1, which cannot be used by others to connect to your computer. Instead, use the static getLocalHost method to get the address of your local host.

```
InetAddress address = InetAddress.getLocalHost();
```

Listing 3.2 is a simple program that prints the Internet address of your local host if you do not specify any command-line parameters, or all Internet addresses of another host if you specify the host name on the command line, such as

```
java inetAddress/InetAddressTest www.horstmann.com
```

**Listing 3.2**  inetAddress/InetAddressTest.java

```
1  package inetAddress;
2
3  import java.io.*;
4  import java.net.*;
```

```
 5  /**
 6   * This program demonstrates the InetAddress class. Supply a host name as command-line argument,
 7   * or run without command-line arguments to see the address of the local host.
 8   * @version 1.02 2012-06-05
 9   * @author Cay Horstmann
10   */
11  public class InetAddressTest
12  {
13     public static void main(String[] args) throws IOException
14     {
15        if (args.length > 0)
16        {
17           String host = args[0];
18           InetAddress[] addresses = InetAddress.getAllByName(host);
19           for (InetAddress a : addresses)
20              System.out.println(a);
21        }
22        else
23        {
24           InetAddress localHostAddress = InetAddress.getLocalHost();
25           System.out.println(localHostAddress);
26        }
27     }
28  }
```

---

**java.net.InetAddress** 1.0

- static InetAddress getByName(String host)
- static InetAddress[] getAllByName(String host)

  constructs an InetAddress, or an array of all Internet addresses, for the given host name.

- static InetAddress getLocalHost()

  constructs an InetAddress for the local host.

- byte[] getAddress()

  returns an array of bytes that contains the numerical address.

- String getHostAddress()

  returns a string with decimal numbers, separated by periods, for example "132.163.4.102".

- String getHostName()

  returns the host name.

## 3.2 Implementing Servers

Now that we have implemented a basic network client that receives data from the Internet, let's program a simple server that can send information to clients. Once you start the server program, it waits for a client to attach to its port. We chose port number 8189, which is not used by any of the standard services. The ServerSocket class establishes a socket. In our case, the command

```
ServerSocket s = new ServerSocket(8189);
```

establishes a server that monitors port 8189. The command

```
Socket incoming = s.accept();
```

tells the program to wait indefinitely until a client connects to that port. Once someone connects to this port by sending the correct request over the network, this method returns a Socket object that represents the connection that was made. You can use this object to get input and output streams, as is shown in the following code:

```
InputStream inStream = incoming.getInputStream();
OutputStream outStream = incoming.getOutputStream();
```

Everything that the server sends to the server output stream becomes the input of the client program, and all the output from the client program ends up in the server input stream.

In all the examples in this chapter, we transmit text through sockets. We therefore turn the streams into scanners and writers.

```
Scanner in = new Scanner(inStream);
PrintWriter out = new PrintWriter(outStream, true /* autoFlush */);
```

Let's send the client a greeting:

```
out.println("Hello! Enter BYE to exit.");
```

When you use telnet to connect to this server program at port 8189, you will see the preceding greeting on the terminal screen.

In this simple server, we just read the client input, a line at a time, and echo it. This demonstrates that the program receives the client's input. An actual server would obviously compute and return an answer depending on the input.

```
String line = in.nextLine();
out.println("Echo: " + line);
if (line.trim().equals("BYE")) done = true;
```

In the end, we close the incoming socket.

```
incoming.close();
```

That is all there is to it. Every server program, such as an HTTP web server, continues performing this loop:

1. It receives a command from the client ("get me this information") through an incoming data stream.
2. It decodes the client command.
3. It gathers the information that the client requested.
4. It sends the information to the client through the outgoing data stream.

Listing 3.3 is the complete program.

---

**Listing 3.3** server/EchoServer.java

```
 1  package server;
 2
 3  import java.io.*;
 4  import java.net.*;
 5  import java.util.*;
 6  /**
 7   * This program implements a simple server that listens to port 8189 and echoes back all client
 8   * input.
 9   * @version 1.21 2012-05-19
10   * @author Cay Horstmann
11   */
12  public class EchoServer
13  {
14     public static void main(String[] args) throws IOException
15     {
16        // establish server socket
17        try (ServerSocket s = new ServerSocket(8189))
18        {
19           // wait for client connection
20           try (Socket incoming = s.accept())
21           {
22              InputStream inStream = incoming.getInputStream();
23              OutputStream outStream = incoming.getOutputStream();
24
25              try (Scanner in = new Scanner(inStream))
26              {
27                 PrintWriter out = new PrintWriter(outStream, true /* autoFlush */);
28
29                 out.println("Hello! Enter BYE to exit.");
30
31                 // echo client input
32                 boolean done = false;
```

*(Continues)*

---

**Listing 3.3** *(Continued)*

```
33              while (!done && in.hasNextLine())
34              {
35                 String line = in.nextLine();
36                 out.println("Echo: " + line);
37                 if (line.trim().equals("BYE")) done = true;
38              }
39           }
40        }
41     }
42  }
43 }
```

---

To try it out, compile and run the program. Then use telnet to connect to the server localhost (or IP address 127.0.0.1) and port 8189.

If you are connected directly to the Internet, anyone in the world can access your echo server, provided they know your IP address and the magic port number.

When you connect to the port, you will see the message shown in Figure 3.4:

```
Hello! Enter BYE to exit.
```

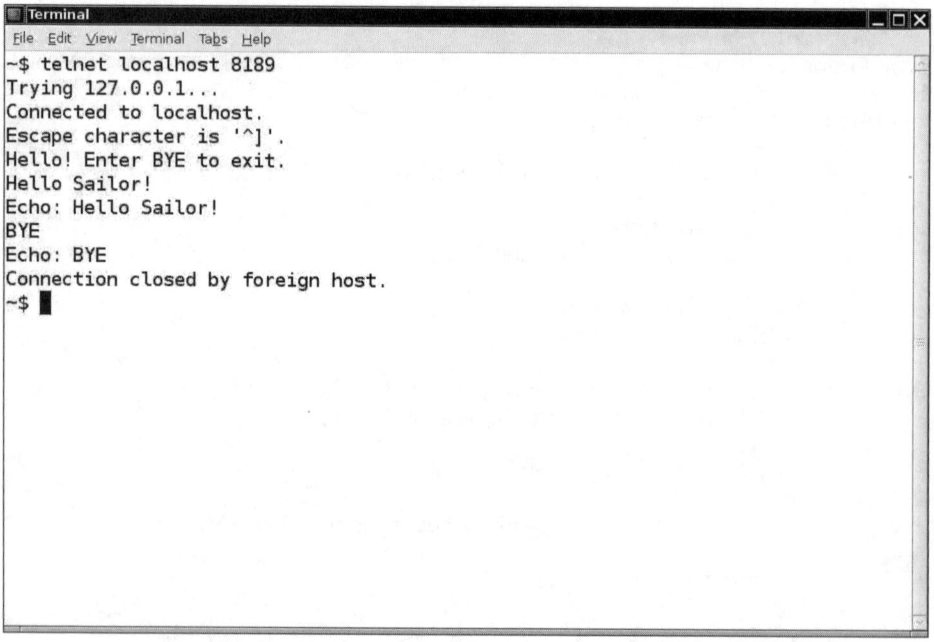

```
Terminal                                                    _ □ ×
File  Edit  View  Terminal  Tabs  Help
~$ telnet localhost 8189
Trying 127.0.0.1...
Connected to localhost.
Escape character is '^]'.
Hello! Enter BYE to exit.
Hello Sailor!
Echo: Hello Sailor!
BYE
Echo: BYE
Connection closed by foreign host.
~$ ▮
```

**Figure 3.4** Accessing an echo server

Type anything and watch the input echo on your screen. Type BYE (all uppercase letters) to disconnect. The server program will terminate as well.

---

**java.net.ServerSocket** 1.0

- ServerSocket(int port)
  creates a server socket that monitors a port.

- Socket accept()
  waits for a connection. This method blocks (i.e., idles) the current thread until the connection is made. The method returns a Socket object through which the program can communicate with the connecting client.

- void close()
  closes the server socket.

---

## 3.2.1 Serving Multiple Clients

There is one problem with the simple server in the preceding example. Suppose we want to allow multiple clients to connect to our server at the same time. Typically, a server runs constantly on a server computer, and clients from all over the Internet might want to use it at the same time. Rejecting multiple connections allows any one client to monopolize the service by connecting to it for a long time. We can do much better through the magic of threads.

Every time we know the program has established a new socket connection—that is, every time the call to accept() returns a socket—we will launch a new thread to take care of the connection between the server and *that* client. The main program will just go back and wait for the next connection. For this to happen, the main loop of the server should look like this:

```
while (true)
{
   Socket incoming = s.accept();
   Runnable r = new ThreadedEchoHandler(incoming);

   Thread t = new Thread(r);
   t.start();
}
```

The ThreadedEchoHandler class implements Runnable and contains the communication loop with the client in its run method.

```
class ThreadedEchoHandler implements Runnable
{
   . . .
   public void run()
   {
      try
      {
         InputStream inStream = incoming.getInputStream();
         OutputStream outStream = incoming.getOutputStream();
         Process input and send response
         incoming.close();
      }
      catch(IOException e)
      {
         Handle exception
      }
   }
}
```

When each connection starts a new thread, multiple clients can connect to the server at the same time. You can easily check this out.

1. Compile and run the server program (Listing 3.4).

2. Open several telnet windows as we have in Figure 3.5.

3. Switch between windows and type commands. Note that you can communicate through all of them simultaneously.

4. When you are done, switch to the window from which you launched the server program and use Ctrl+C to kill it.

---

 **NOTE:** In this program, we spawn a separate thread for each connection. This approach is not satisfactory for high-performance servers. You can achieve greater server throughput by using features of the java.nio package. See www.ibm.com/developerworks/java/library/j-javaio for more information.

---

**Listing 3.4** threaded/ThreadedEchoServer.java

```
1  package threaded;
2
3  import java.io.*;
4  import java.net.*;
5  import java.util.*;
```

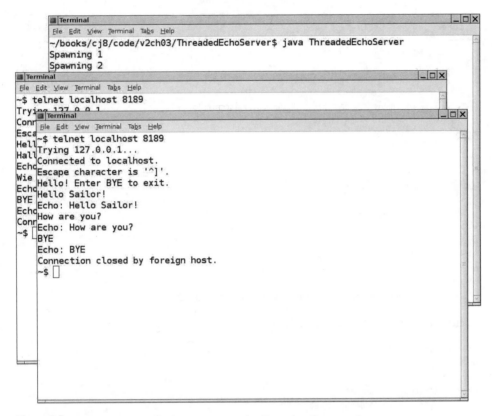

**Figure 3.5** Several telnet windows communicating simultaneously

```
6   /**
7      This program implements a multithreaded server that listens to port 8189 and echoes back
8      all client input.
9      @author Cay Horstmann
10     @version 1.21 2012-06-04
11  */
12  public class ThreadedEchoServer
13  {
14     public static void main(String[] args )
15     {
16        try
17        {
18           int i = 1;
19           ServerSocket s = new ServerSocket(8189);
```

*(Continues)*

**Listing 3.4** *(Continued)*

```
20          while (true)
21          {
22              Socket incoming = s.accept();
23              System.out.println("Spawning " + i);
24              Runnable r = new ThreadedEchoHandler(incoming);
25              Thread t = new Thread(r);
26              t.start();
27              i++;
28          }
29      }
30      catch (IOException e)
31      {
32          e.printStackTrace();
33      }
34   }
35 }
36
37 /**
38    This class handles the client input for one server socket connection.
39 */
40 class ThreadedEchoHandler implements Runnable
41 {
42    private Socket incoming;
43
44    /**
45       Constructs a handler.
46       @param i the incoming socket
47    */
48    public ThreadedEchoHandler(Socket i)
49    {
50       incoming = i;
51    }
52
53    public void run()
54    {
55       try
56       {
57          try
58          {
59             InputStream inStream = incoming.getInputStream();
60             OutputStream outStream = incoming.getOutputStream();
61
62             Scanner in = new Scanner(inStream);
63             PrintWriter out = new PrintWriter(outStream, true /* autoFlush */);
64
65             out.println( "Hello! Enter BYE to exit." );
```

```
66          // echo client input
67          boolean done = false;
68          while (!done && in.hasNextLine())
69          {
70             String line = in.nextLine();
71             out.println("Echo: " + line);
72             if (line.trim().equals("BYE"))
73                done = true;
74          }
75       }
76       finally
77       {
78          incoming.close();
79       }
80    }
81    catch (IOException e)
82    {
83       e.printStackTrace();
84    }
85  }
86 }
```

## 3.2.2 Half-Close

The *half-close* provides the ability for one end of a socket connection to terminate its output while still receiving data from the other end.

Here is a typical situation. Suppose you transmit data to the server but you don't know at the outset how much data you have. With a file, you'd just close the file at the end of the data. However, if you close a socket, you immediately disconnect from the server and cannot read the response.

The half-close overcomes this problem. You can close the output stream of a socket, thereby indicating to the server the end of the requested data, but keep the input stream open.

The client side looks like this:

```
Socket socket = new Socket(host, port);
Scanner in = new Scanner(socket.getInputStream());
PrintWriter writer = new PrintWriter(socket.getOutputStream());
// send request data
writer.print(. . .);
writer.flush();
socket.shutdownOutput();
// now socket is half-closed
// read response data
while (in.hasNextLine() != null) { String line = in.nextLine(); . . . }
socket.close();
```

The server side simply reads input until the end of the input stream is reached. Then it sends the response.

Of course, this protocol is only useful for one-shot services such as HTTP where the client connects, issues a request, catches the response, and then disconnects.

---

**java.net.Socket** 1.0

- void shutdownOutput() 1.3
  sets the output stream to "end of stream."
- void shutdownInput() 1.3
  sets the input stream to "end of stream."
- boolean isOutputShutdown() 1.4
  returns true if output has been shut down.
- boolean isInputShutdown() 1.4
  returns true if input has been shut down.

---

## 3.3 Interruptible Sockets

When you connect to a socket, the current thread blocks until the connection has been established or a timeout has elapsed. Similarly, when you read or write data through a socket, the current thread blocks until the operation is successful or has timed out.

In interactive applications, you would like to give users an option to simply cancel a socket connection that does not appear to produce results. However, if a thread blocks on an unresponsive socket, you cannot unblock it by calling interrupt.

To interrupt a socket operation, use a SocketChannel, a feature of the java.nio package. Open the SocketChannel like this:

```
SocketChannel channel = SocketChannel.open(new InetSocketAddress(host, port));
```

A channel does not have associated streams. Instead, it has read and write methods that make use of Buffer objects. (See Chapter 1 for more information about NIO buffers.) These methods are declared in the interfaces ReadableByteChannel and WritableByteChannel.

If you don't want to deal with buffers, you can use the Scanner class to read from a SocketChannel because Scanner has a constructor with a ReadableByteChannel parameter:

```
Scanner in = new Scanner(channel);
```

To turn a channel into an output stream, use the static `Channels.newOutputStream` method.

```
OutputStream outStream = Channels.newOutputStream(channel);
```

That's all you need to do. Whenever a thread is interrupted during an open, read, or write operation, the operation does not block, but is terminated with an exception.

The program in Listing 3.5 contrasts interruptible and blocking sockets. A server sends numbers and pretends to be stuck after the tenth number. Click on either button, and a thread is started that connects to the server and prints the output. The first thread uses an interruptible socket; the second thread uses a blocking socket. If you click the Cancel button within the first ten numbers, you can interrupt either thread.

However, after the first ten numbers, you can only interrupt the first thread. The second thread keeps blocking until the server finally closes the connection (see Figure 3.6).

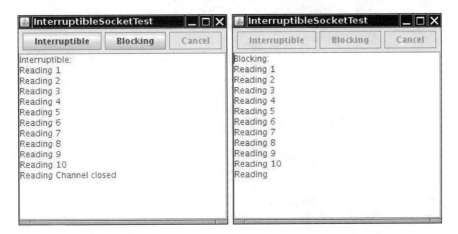

**Figure 3.6** Interrupting a socket

**Listing 3.5** interruptible/InterruptibleSocketTest.java

```
1  package interruptible;
2
3  import java.awt.*;
4  import java.awt.event.*;
5  import java.util.*;
6  import java.net.*;
7  import java.io.*;
```

*(Continues)*

**Listing 3.5**  *(Continued)*

```
 8  import java.nio.channels.*;
 9  import javax.swing.*;
10
11  /**
12   * This program shows how to interrupt a socket channel.
13   * @author Cay Horstmann
14   * @version 1.03 2012-06-04
15   */
16  public class InterruptibleSocketTest
17  {
18     public static void main(String[] args)
19     {
20        EventQueue.invokeLater(new Runnable()
21           {
22              public void run()
23              {
24                 JFrame frame = new InterruptibleSocketFrame();
25                 frame.setTitle("InterruptibleSocketTest");
26                 frame.setDefaultCloseOperation(JFrame.EXIT_ON_CLOSE);
27                 frame.setVisible(true);
28              }
29           });
30     }
31  }
32
33  class InterruptibleSocketFrame extends JFrame
34  {
35     public static final int TEXT_ROWS = 20;
36     public static final int TEXT_COLUMNS = 60;
37
38     private Scanner in;
39     private JButton interruptibleButton;
40     private JButton blockingButton;
41     private JButton cancelButton;
42     private JTextArea messages;
43     private TestServer server;
44     private Thread connectThread;
45
46     public InterruptibleSocketFrame()
47     {
48        JPanel northPanel = new JPanel();
49        add(northPanel, BorderLayout.NORTH);
50
51        messages = new JTextArea(TEXT_ROWS, TEXT_COLUMNS);
52        add(new JScrollPane(messages));
53
54        interruptibleButton = new JButton("Interruptible");
55        blockingButton = new JButton("Blocking");
```

```
56      northPanel.add(interruptibleButton);
57      northPanel.add(blockingButton);
58
59      interruptibleButton.addActionListener(new ActionListener()
60         {
61            public void actionPerformed(ActionEvent event)
62            {
63               interruptibleButton.setEnabled(false);
64               blockingButton.setEnabled(false);
65               cancelButton.setEnabled(true);
66               connectThread = new Thread(new Runnable()
67                  {
68                     public void run()
69                     {
70                        try
71                        {
72                           connectInterruptibly();
73                        }
74                        catch (IOException e)
75                        {
76                           messages.append("\nInterruptibleSocketTest.connectInterruptibly: " + e);
77                        }
78                     }
79                  });
80               connectThread.start();
81            }
82         });
83
84      blockingButton.addActionListener(new ActionListener()
85         {
86            public void actionPerformed(ActionEvent event)
87            {
88               interruptibleButton.setEnabled(false);
89               blockingButton.setEnabled(false);
90               cancelButton.setEnabled(true);
91               connectThread = new Thread(new Runnable()
92                  {
93                     public void run()
94                     {
95                        try
96                        {
97                           connectBlocking();
98                        }
99                        catch (IOException e)
100                       {
101                          messages.append("\nInterruptibleSocketTest.connectBlocking: " + e);
102                       }
103                    }
104                 });
```

*(Continues)*

**Listing 3.5** *(Continued)*

```
105              connectThread.start();
106          }
107       });
108
109    cancelButton = new JButton("Cancel");
110    cancelButton.setEnabled(false);
111    northPanel.add(cancelButton);
112    cancelButton.addActionListener(new ActionListener()
113       {
114          public void actionPerformed(ActionEvent event)
115          {
116             connectThread.interrupt();
117             cancelButton.setEnabled(false);
118          }
119       });
120    server = new TestServer();
121    new Thread(server).start();
122    pack();
123 }
124
125 /**
126  * Connects to the test server, using interruptible I/O
127  */
128 public void connectInterruptibly() throws IOException
129 {
130    messages.append("Interruptible:\n");
131    try (SocketChannel channel = SocketChannel.open(new InetSocketAddress("localhost", 8189)))
132    {
133       in = new Scanner(channel);
134       while (!Thread.currentThread().isInterrupted())
135       {
136          messages.append("Reading ");
137          if (in.hasNextLine())
138          {
139             String line = in.nextLine();
140             messages.append(line);
141             messages.append("\n");
142          }
143       }
144    }
145    finally
146    {
147       EventQueue.invokeLater(new Runnable()
148       {
149          public void run()
150          {
```

```
151              messages.append("Channel closed\n");
152              interruptibleButton.setEnabled(true);
153              blockingButton.setEnabled(true);
154           }
155        });
156     }
157  }
158
159  /**
160   * Connects to the test server, using blocking I/O
161   */
162  public void connectBlocking() throws IOException
163  {
164     messages.append("Blocking:\n");
165     try (Socket sock = new Socket("localhost", 8189))
166     {
167        in = new Scanner(sock.getInputStream());
168        while (!Thread.currentThread().isInterrupted())
169        {
170           messages.append("Reading ");
171           if (in.hasNextLine())
172           {
173              String line = in.nextLine();
174              messages.append(line);
175              messages.append("\n");
176           }
177        }
178     }
179     finally
180     {
181        EventQueue.invokeLater(new Runnable()
182        {
183           public void run()
184           {
185              messages.append("Socket closed\n");
186              interruptibleButton.setEnabled(true);
187              blockingButton.setEnabled(true);
188           }
189        });
190     }
191  }
192
193  /**
194   * A multithreaded server that listens to port 8189 and sends numbers to the client, simulating
195   * a hanging server after 10 numbers.
196   */
```

*(Continues)*

**Listing 3.5** *(Continued)*

```
197   class TestServer implements Runnable
198   {
199      public void run()
200      {
201         try
202         {
203            ServerSocket s = new ServerSocket(8189);
204
205            while (true)
206            {
207               Socket incoming = s.accept();
208               Runnable r = new TestServerHandler(incoming);
209               Thread t = new Thread(r);
210               t.start();
211            }
212         }
213         catch (IOException e)
214         {
215            messages.append("\nTestServer.run: " + e);
216         }
217      }
218   }
219
220   /**
221    * This class handles the client input for one server socket connection.
222    */
223   class TestServerHandler implements Runnable
224   {
225      private Socket incoming;
226      private int counter;
227
228      /**
229       * Constructs a handler.
230       * @param i the incoming socket
231       */
232      public TestServerHandler(Socket i)
233      {
234         incoming = i;
235      }
236
237      public void run()
238      {
239         try
240         {
241            try
242            {
```

```
243            OutputStream outStream = incoming.getOutputStream();
244            PrintWriter out = new PrintWriter(outStream, true /* autoFlush */);
245            while (counter < 100)
246            {
247               counter++;
248               if (counter <= 10) out.println(counter);
249               Thread.sleep(100);
250            }
251         }
252         finally
253         {
254            incoming.close();
255            messages.append("Closing server\n");
256         }
257      }
258      catch (Exception e)
259      {
260         messages.append("\nTestServerHandler.run: " + e);
261      }
262   }
263 }
264 }
```

---

**java.net.InetSocketAddress**   1.4

- `InetSocketAddress(String hostname, int port)`
  constructs an address object with the given host and port, resolving the host name during construction. If the host name cannot be resolved, the address object's `unresolved` property is set to `true`.

- `boolean isUnresolved()`
  returns `true` if this address object could not be resolved.

---

**java.nio.channels.SocketChannel**   1.4

- `static SocketChannel open(SocketAddress address)`
  opens a socket channel and connects it to a remote address.

---

**java.nio.channels.Channels**   1.4

- `static InputStream newInputStream(ReadableByteChannel channel)`
  constructs an input stream that reads from the given channel.

- `static OutputStream newOutputStream(WritableByteChannel channel)`
  constructs an output stream that writes to the given channel.

## 3.4 Getting Web Data

To access web servers in a Java program, you will want to work at a higher level than making a socket connection and issuing HTTP requests. In the following sections, we discuss the classes that the Java library provides for this purpose.

### 3.4.1 URLs and URIs

The URL and URLConnection classes encapsulate much of the complexity of retrieving information from a remote site. You can construct a URL object from a string:

```
URL url = new URL(urlString);
```

If you simply want to fetch the contents of the resource, use the openStream method of the URL class. This method yields an InputStream object. Use it in the usual way, for example, to construct a Scanner:

```
InputStream inStream = url.openStream();
Scanner in = new Scanner(inStream);
```

The java.net package makes a useful distinction between URLs (uniform resource *locators*) and URIs (uniform resource *identifiers*).

A URI is a purely syntactical construct that contains the various parts of the string specifying a web resource. A URL is a special kind of URI, namely, one with sufficient information to *locate* a resource. Other URIs, such as

```
mailto:cay@horstmann.com
```

are not locators—there is no data to locate from this identifier. Such a URI is called a URN (uniform resource *name*).

In the Java library, the URI class has no methods for accessing the resource that the identifier specifies—its sole purpose is parsing. In contrast, the URL class can open a stream to the resource. For that reason, the URL class only works with schemes that the Java library knows how to handle, such as http:, https:, ftp:, the local file system (file:), and JAR files (jar:).

To see why parsing is not trivial, consider how complex URIs can be. For example,

```
http://maps.yahoo.com/py/maps.py?csz=Cupertino+CA
ftp://username:password@ftp.yourserver.com/pub/file.txt
```

The URI specification gives the rules for the makeup of these identifiers. A URI has the syntax

[*scheme* :] *schemeSpecificPart* [*#fragment*]

Here, the [. . .] denotes an optional part, and the : and # are included literally in the identifier.

If the *scheme*: part is present, the URI is called *absolute*. Otherwise, it is called *relative*.

An absolute URI is *opaque* if the *schemeSpecificPart* does not begin with a / such as

```
mailto:cay@horstmann.com
```

All absolute nonopaque URIs and all relative URIs are *hierarchical*. Examples are

```
http://horstmann.com/index.html
../../java/net/Socket.html#Socket()
```

The *schemeSpecificPart* of a hierarchical URI has the structure

```
[//authority][path][?query]
```

where, again, [. . .] denotes optional parts.

For server-based URIs, the *authority* part has the form

```
[user-info@]host[:port]
```

The *port* must be an integer.

RFC 2396, which standardizes URIs, also supports a registry-based mechanism by which the *authority* has a different format, but this is not in common use.

One of the purposes of the URI class is to parse an identifier and break it up into its components. You can retrieve them with the methods

```
getScheme
getSchemeSpecificPart
getAuthority
getUserInfo
getHost
getPort
getPath
getQuery
getFragment
```

The other purpose of the URI class is the handling of absolute and relative identifiers. If you have an absolute URI such as

```
http://docs.mycompany.com/api/java/net/ServerSocket.html
```

and a relative URI such as

```
../../java/net/Socket.html#Socket()
```

then you can combine the two into an absolute URI.

```
http://docs.mycompany.com/api/java/net/Socket.html#Socket()
```

This process is called *resolving* a relative URL.

The opposite process is called *relativization*. For example, suppose you have a *base* URI

```
http://docs.mycompany.com/api
```

and a URI

```
http://docs.mycompany.com/api/java/lang/String.html
```

Then the relativized URI is

```
java/lang/String.html
```

The URI class supports both of these operations:

```
relative = base.relativize(combined);
combined = base.resolve(relative);
```

## 3.4.2 Using a URLConnection to Retrieve Information

If you want additional information about a web resource, then you should use the URLConnection class, which gives you much more control than the basic URL class.

When working with a URLConnection object, you must carefully schedule your steps:

1. Call the openConnection method of the URL class to obtain the URLConnection object:

   ```
   URLConnection connection = url.openConnection();
   ```

2. Set any request properties, using the methods

   ```
   setDoInput
   setDoOutput
   setIfModifiedSince
   setUseCaches
   setAllowUserInteraction
   setRequestProperty
   setConnectTimeout
   setReadTimeout
   ```

   We discuss these methods later in this section and in the API notes.

3. Connect to the remote resource by calling the connect method.

   ```
   connection.connect();
   ```

   Besides making a socket connection to the server, this method also queries the server for *header information*.

4.  After connecting to the server, you can query the header information. Two methods, `getHeaderFieldKey` and `getHeaderField`, enumerate all fields of the header. The method `getHeaderFields` gets a standard `Map` object containing the header fields. For your convenience, the following methods query standard fields:

    ```
    getContentType
    getContentLength
    getContentEncoding
    getDate
    getExpiration
    getLastModified
    ```

5.  Finally, you can access the resource data. Use the `getInputStream` method to obtain an input stream for reading the information. (This is the same input stream that the `openStream` method of the `URL` class returns.) The other method, `getContent`, isn't very useful in practice. The objects that are returned by standard content types such as `text/plain` and `image/gif` require classes in the `com.sun` hierarchy for processing. You could register your own content handlers, but we do not discuss that technique in this book.

---

**CAUTION:** Some programmers form the wrong mental image when using the `URLConnection` class, thinking that the `getInputStream` and `getOutputStream` methods are similar to those of the `Socket` class. But that isn't quite true. The `URLConnection` class does quite a bit of magic behind the scenes, in particular, the handling of request and response headers. For that reason, it is important that you follow the setup steps for the connection.

---

Let us now look at some of the `URLConnection` methods in detail. Several methods set properties of the connection before connecting to the server. The most important ones are `setDoInput` and `setDoOutput`. By default, the connection yields an input stream for reading from the server but no output stream for writing. If you want an output stream (for example, for posting data to a web server), you need to call

```
connection.setDoOutput(true);
```

Next, you may want to set some of the request headers. The request headers are sent together with the request command to the server. Here is an example:

```
GET www.server.com/index.html HTTP/1.0
Referer: http://www.somewhere.com/links.html
Proxy-Connection: Keep-Alive
User-Agent: Mozilla/5.0 (X11; U; Linux i686; en-US; rv:1.8.1.4)
Host: www.server.com
Accept: text/html, image/gif, image/jpeg, image/png, */*
Accept-Language: en
```

```
Accept-Charset: iso-8859-1,*,utf-8
Cookie: orangemilano=192218887821987
```

The `setIfModifiedSince` method tells the connection that you are only interested in data that have been modified since a certain date.

The `setUseCaches` and `setAllowUserInteraction` methods should only be called inside applets. The `setUseCaches` method directs the browser to first check the browser cache. The `setAllowUserInteraction` method allows an applet to pop up a dialog box for querying the user name and password for password-protected resources (see Figure 3.7).

Finally, you can use the catch-all `setRequestProperty` method to set any name/value pair that is meaningful for the particular protocol. For the format of the HTTP request headers, see RFC 2616. Some of these parameters are not well-documented and are passed around by word of mouth from one programmer to the next. For example, if you want to access a password-protected web page, you must do the following:

1.  Concatenate the user name, a colon, and the password.

    ```
    String input = username + ":" + password;
    ```

2.  Compute the Base64 encoding of the resulting string. (The Base64 encoding encodes a sequence of bytes into a sequence of printable ASCII characters.)

    ```
    String encoding = base64Encode(input);
    ```

3.  Call the `setRequestProperty` method with a name of `"Authorization"` and the value `"Basic "` + encoding:

    ```
    connection.setRequestProperty("Authorization", "Basic " + encoding);
    ```

---

 **TIP:** You just saw how to access a password-protected web page. To access a password-protected file by FTP, use an entirely different method: Simply construct a URL of the form

```
ftp://username:password@ftp.yourserver.com/pub/file.txt
```

---

Once you call the `connect` method, you can query the response header information. First, let's see how to enumerate all response header fields. The implementors of this class felt a need to express their individuality by introducing yet another iteration protocol. The call

```
String key = connection.getHeaderFieldKey(n);
```

gets the `n`th key from the response header, where `n` starts from 1! It returns `null` if `n` is zero or greater than the total number of header fields. There is no method to

**Figure 3.7** A network password dialog box

return the number of fields; you simply keep calling getHeaderFieldKey until you get null. Similarly, the call

```
String value = connection.getHeaderField(n);
```

returns the nth value.

The method getHeaderFields returns a Map of response header fields.

```
Map<String,List<String>> headerFields = connection.getHeaderFields();
```

Here is a set of response header fields from a typical HTTP request:

```
Date: Wed, 27 Aug 2008 00:15:48 GMT
Server: Apache/2.2.2 (Unix)
Last-Modified: Sun, 22 Jun 2008 20:53:38 GMT
Accept-Ranges: bytes
Content-Length: 4813
Connection: close
Content-Type: text/html
```

As a convenience, six methods query the values of the most common header types and convert them to numeric types when appropriate. Table 3.1 shows these convenience methods. The methods with return type `long` return the number of seconds since January 1, 1970 GMT.

The program in Listing 3.6 lets you experiment with URL connections. Supply a URL and an optional user name and password on the command line when running the program, for example:

```
java urlConnection.URLConnectionTest http://www.yourserver.com user password
```

The program prints

- All keys and values of the header
- The return values of the six convenience methods in Table 3.1
- The first ten lines of the requested resource

The program is straightforward, except for the computation of the Base64 encoding. There is an undocumented class, `sun.misc.BASE64Encoder`, that you can use instead of the one that we provide in the example program. Simply replace the call to `base64Encode` with

```
String encoding = new sun.misc.BASE64Encoder().encode(input.getBytes());
```

However, we supplied our own class because we do not like to rely on undocumented classes.

 **NOTE:** The `javax.mail.internet.MimeUtility` class in the JavaMail standard extension package also has a method for Base64 encoding. The JDK has a class `java.util.prefs.Base64` for the same purpose, but it is not public, so you cannot use it in your code.

**Table 3.1** Convenience Methods for Response Header Values

| Key Name | Method Name | Return Type |
|---|---|---|
| Date | getDate | long |
| Expires | getExpiration | long |
| Last-Modified | getLastModified | long |
| Content-Length | getContentLength | int |
| Content-Type | getContentType | String |
| Content-Encoding | getContentEncoding | String |

**Listing 3.6** urlConnection/URLConnectionTest.java

```
1  package urlConnection;
2
3  import java.io.*;
4  import java.net.*;
5  import java.util.*;
6
7  /**
8   * This program connects to an URL and displays the response header data and the first 10 lines of
9   * the requested data.
10  *
11  * Supply the URL and an optional username and password (for HTTP basic authentication) on the
12  * command line.
13  * @version 1.11 2007-06-26
14  * @author Cay Horstmann
15  */
16 public class URLConnectionTest
17 {
18    public static void main(String[] args)
19    {
20       try
21       {
22          String urlName;
23          if (args.length > 0) urlName = args[0];
24          else urlName = "http://horstmann.com";
25
26          URL url = new URL(urlName);
27          URLConnection connection = url.openConnection();
28
29          // set username, password if specified on command line
30          if (args.length > 2)
31          {
32             String username = args[1];
33             String password = args[2];
34             String input = username + ":" + password;
35             String encoding = base64Encode(input);
36             connection.setRequestProperty("Authorization", "Basic " + encoding);
37          }
38
39          connection.connect();
40
41          // print header fields
42          Map<String, List<String>> headers = connection.getHeaderFields();
43          for (Map.Entry<String, List<String>> entry : headers.entrySet())
44          {
45             String key = entry.getKey();
```

*(Continues)*

**Listing 3.6** *(Continued)*

```
46              for (String value : entry.getValue())
47                  System.out.println(key + ": " + value);
48          }
49
50          // print convenience functions
51          System.out.println("----------");
52          System.out.println("getContentType: " + connection.getContentType());
53          System.out.println("getContentLength: " + connection.getContentLength());
54          System.out.println("getContentEncoding: " + connection.getContentEncoding());
55          System.out.println("getDate: " + connection.getDate());
56          System.out.println("getExpiration: " + connection.getExpiration());
57          System.out.println("getLastModified: " + connection.getLastModified());
58          System.out.println("----------");
59
60          Scanner in = new Scanner(connection.getInputStream());
61
62          // print first ten lines of contents
63          for (int n = 1; in.hasNextLine() && n <= 10; n++)
64              System.out.println(in.nextLine());
65          if (in.hasNextLine()) System.out.println(". . .");
66      }
67      catch (IOException e)
68      {
69          e.printStackTrace();
70      }
71  }
72
73  /**
74   * Computes the Base64 encoding of a string.
75   * @param s a string
76   * @return the Base64 encoding of s
77   */
78  public static String base64Encode(String s)
79  {
80      ByteArrayOutputStream bOut = new ByteArrayOutputStream();
81      Base64OutputStream out = new Base64OutputStream(bOut);
82      try
83      {
84          out.write(s.getBytes());
85          out.flush();
86      }
87      catch (IOException e)
88      {
89      }
90      return bOut.toString();
91  }
92 }
```

```
93   /**
94    * This stream filter converts a stream of bytes to their Base64 encoding.
95    *
96    * Base64 encoding encodes 3 bytes into 4 characters. |11111122|22223333|33444444| Each set of 6
97    * bits is encoded according to the toBase64 map. If the number of input bytes is not a multiple
98    * of 3, then the last group of 4 characters is padded with one or two = signs. Each output line
99    * is at most 76 characters.
100   */
101  class Base64OutputStream extends FilterOutputStream
102  {
103     private static char[] toBase64 = { 'A', 'B', 'C', 'D', 'E', 'F', 'G', 'H', 'I', 'J', 'K', 'L',
104        'M', 'N', 'O', 'P', 'Q', 'R', 'S', 'T', 'U', 'V', 'W', 'X', 'Y', 'Z', 'a', 'b', 'c', 'd',
105        'e', 'f', 'g', 'h', 'i', 'j', 'k', 'l', 'm', 'n', 'o', 'p', 'q', 'r', 's', 't', 'u', 'v',
106        'w', 'x', 'y', 'z', '0', '1', '2', '3', '4', '5', '6', '7', '8', '9', '+', '/' };
107
108     private int col = 0;
109     private int i = 0;
110     private int[] inbuf = new int[3];
111
112     /**
113      * Constructs the stream filter.
114      * @param out the stream to filter
115      */
116     public Base64OutputStream(OutputStream out)
117     {
118        super(out);
119     }
120
121     public void write(int c) throws IOException
122     {
123        inbuf[i] = c;
124        i++;
125        if (i == 3)
126        {
127           if (col >= 76)
128           {
129              super.write('\n');
130              col = 0;
131           }
132           super.write(toBase64[(inbuf[0] & 0xFC) >> 2]);
133           super.write(toBase64[((inbuf[0] & 0x03) << 4) | ((inbuf[1] & 0xF0) >> 4)]);
134           super.write(toBase64[((inbuf[1] & 0x0F) << 2) | ((inbuf[2] & 0xC0) >> 6)]);
135           super.write(toBase64[inbuf[2] & 0x3F]);
136           col += 4;
137           i = 0;
138        }
139     }
```

*(Continues)*

---

**Listing 3.6** *(Continued)*

```
140    public void flush() throws IOException
141    {
142       if (i > 0 && col >= 76)
143       {
144          super.write('\n');
145          col = 0;
146       }
147       if (i == 1)
148       {
149          super.write(toBase64[(inbuf[0] & 0xFC) >> 2]);
150          super.write(toBase64[(inbuf[0] & 0x03) << 4]);
151          super.write('=');
152          super.write('=');
153       }
154       else if (i == 2)
155       {
156          super.write(toBase64[(inbuf[0] & 0xFC) >> 2]);
157          super.write(toBase64[((inbuf[0] & 0x03) << 4) | ((inbuf[1] & 0xF0) >> 4)]);
158          super.write(toBase64[(inbuf[1] & 0x0F) << 2]);
159          super.write('=');
160       }
161    }
162 }
```

---

**java.net.URL 1.0**

- InputStream openStream()
  opens an input stream for reading the resource data.

- URLConnection openConnection();
  returns a URLConnection object that manages the connection to the resource.

---

**java.net.URLConnection 1.0**

- void setDoInput(boolean doInput)
- boolean getDoInput()
  If doInput is true, the user can receive input from this URLConnection.

- void setDoOutput(boolean doOutput)
- boolean getDoOutput()
  If doOutput is true, the user can send output to this URLConnection.

*(Continues)*

---

**java.net.URLConnection** 1.0 *(Continued)*

- void setIfModifiedSince(long time)
- long getIfModifiedSince()
  The ifModifiedSince property configures this URLConnection to fetch only data modified since a given time. The time is given in seconds since midnight, GMT, January 1, 1970.

- void setUseCaches(boolean useCaches)
- boolean getUseCaches()
  If useCaches is true, data can be retrieved from a local cache. Note that the URLConnection itself does not maintain such a cache. The cache must be supplied by an external program such as a browser.

- void setAllowUserInteraction(boolean allowUserInteraction)
- boolean getAllowUserInteraction()
  If allowUserInteraction is true, the user can be queried for passwords. Note that the URLConnection itself has no facilities for executing such a query. The query must be carried out by an external program such as a browser or browser plug-in.

- void setConnectTimeout(int timeout)  **5.0**
- int getConnectTimeout()  **5.0**
  sets or gets the timeout for the connection (in milliseconds). If the timeout has elapsed before a connection was established, the connect method of the associated input stream throws a SocketTimeoutException.

- void setReadTimeout(int timeout)  **5.0**
- int getReadTimeout()  **5.0**
  sets or gets the timeout for reading data (in milliseconds). If the timeout has elapsed before a read operation was successful, the read method throws a SocketTimeoutException.

- void setRequestProperty(String key, String value)
  sets a request header field.

- Map<String,List<String>> getRequestProperties()  **1.4**
  returns a map of request properties. All values for the same key are placed in a list.

- void connect()
  connects to the remote resource and retrieves response header information.

- Map<String,List<String>> getHeaderFields()  **1.4**
  returns a map of response headers. All values for the same key are placed in a list.

- String getHeaderFieldKey(int n)
  gets the key for the nth response header field, or null if n is ≤ 0 or greater than the number of response header fields.

*(Continues)*

---

**java.net.URLConnection** 1.0 *(Continued)*

- `String getHeaderField(int n)`
  gets value of the nth response header field, or `null` if n is ≤ 0 or greater than the number of response header fields.
- `int getContentLength()`
  gets the content length if available, or -1 if unknown.
- `String getContentType()`
  gets the content type, such as `text/plain` or `image/gif`.
- `String getContentEncoding()`
  gets the content encoding, such as `gzip`. This value is not commonly used, because the default `identity` encoding is not supposed to be specified with a `Content-Encoding` header.
- `long getDate()`
- `long getExpiration()`
- `long getLastModifed()`
  gets the date of creation, expiration, and last modification of the resource. The dates are specified as seconds since midnight, GMT, January 1, 1970.
- `InputStream getInputStream()`
- `OutputStream getOutputStream()`
  returns a stream for reading from the resource or writing to the resource.
- `Object getContent()`
  selects the appropriate content handler to read the resource data and convert it into an object. This method is not useful for reading standard types such as `text/plain` or `image/gif` unless you install your own content handler.

## 3.4.3 Posting Form Data

In the preceding section, you saw how to read data from a web server. Now we will show you how your programs can send data back to a web server and to programs that the web server invokes.

To send information from a web browser to the web server, a user fills out a *form*, like the one in Figure 3.8.

When the user clicks the Submit button, the text in the text fields and the settings of the checkboxes and radio buttons are sent back to the web server. The web server invokes a program that processes the user input.

Many technologies enable web servers to invoke programs. Among the best known ones are Java servlets, JavaServer Faces, Microsoft Active Server Pages

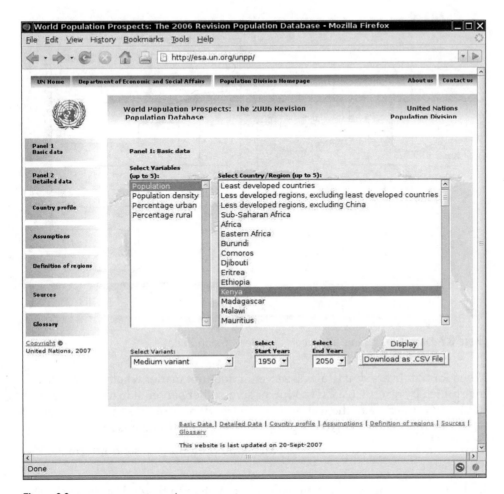

**Figure 3.8** An HTML form

(ASP), and Common Gateway Interface (CGI) scripts. For simplicity, we use the generic term *script* for a server-side program, no matter what technology is used.

The server-side script processes the form data and produces another HTML page that the web server sends back to the browser. This sequence is illustrated in Figure 3.9. The response page can contain new information (for example, in an information-search program) or just an acknowledgment. The web browser then displays the response page.

We do not discuss the implementation of server-side scripts in this book. Our interest is merely in writing client programs that interact with existing server-side scripts.

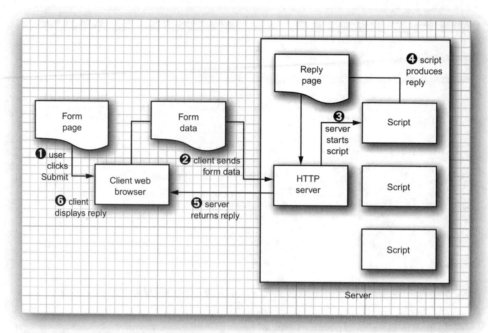

**Figure 3.9** Data flow during execution of a server-side script

When form data are sent to a web server, it does not matter whether the data are interpreted by a servlet, a CGI script, or some other server-side technology. The client sends the data to the web server in a standard format, and the web server takes care of passing it on to the program that generates the response.

Two commands, called GET and POST, are commonly used to send information to a web server.

In the GET command, you simply attach parameters to the end of the URL. The URL has the form

    http://*host*/*script*?*parameters*

Each parameter has the form *name=value*. Parameters are separated by & characters. Parameter values are encoded using the *URL encoding* scheme, following these rules:

- Leave the characters A through Z, a through z, 0 through 9, and . - ~ _ unchanged.
- Replace all spaces with + characters.
- Encode all other characters into UTF-8 and encode each byte by a %, followed by a two-digit hexadecimal number.

For example, to transmit *New York, NY*, you use New+York%2c+NY, as the hexadecimal number 2c (or decimal 44) is the ASCII code of the ',' character.

This encoding keeps any intermediate programs from messing with spaces and interpreting other special characters.

For example, at the time of this writing the Yahoo! web site has a script, py/maps.py, at the host maps.yahoo.com. The script requires two parameters with names addr and csz. To get a map of 1 Market Street, San Francisco, CA, use the following URL:

```
http://maps.yahoo.com/py/maps.py?addr=1+Market+Street&csz=San+Francisco+CA
```

The GET command is simple, but it has a major limitation that makes it relatively unpopular: Most browsers have a limit on the number of characters that you can include in a GET request.

In the POST command, you do not attach parameters to a URL. Instead, you get an output stream from the URLConnection and write name/value pairs to the output stream. You still have to URL-encode the values and separate them with & characters.

Let us look at this process in detail. To post data to a script, first establish a URLConnection:

```
URL url = new URL("http://host/script");
URLConnection connection = url.openConnection();
```

Then, call the setDoOutput method to set up the connection for output:

```
connection.setDoOutput(true);
```

Next, call getOutputStream to get a stream through which you can send data to the server. If you are sending text to the server, it is convenient to wrap that stream into a PrintWriter.

```
PrintWriter out = new PrintWriter(connection.getOutputStream());
```

Now you are ready to send data to the server:

```
out.print(name1 + "=" + URLEncoder.encode(value1, "UTF-8") + "&");
out.print(name2 + "=" + URLEncoder.encode(value2, "UTF-8"));
```

Close the output stream.

```
out.close();
```

Finally, call getInputStream and read the server response.

Let's run through a practical example. The web site at http://esa.un.org/unpd/ wpp/unpp/panel_population.htm contains a form to request population data (see Figure 3.8 on p. 223). If you look at the HTML source, you will see the following HTML tag:

```
<form method="post" onSubmit="return checksubmit(. . .)" . . .>
```

When you look inside the JavaScript code of the checksubmit function, you will see that the CSV download causes the following:

```
document.menuForm.action ="p2k0data_script.asp";
```

This tells us the name of the script that processes the POST action.

Next, you need to find out the field names that the script expects. Look at the user interface components. Each of them has a name attribute, for example

```
<select name="Variable">
<option value="12;">Population</option>
more options  . . .
</select>
```

This tells you that the name of the field is Variable. This field specifies the population table type. If you specify the table type "12;", you will get a table of the total population estimates. If you look further, you will also find a field name Location with values such as 900 for the entire world and 404 for Kenya.

There are several other fields that need to be set. To get the population estimates of Kenya from 1950 to 2050, construct this string:

```
Panel=1&Variable=12%3b&Location=404&Varient=2&StartYear=1950&EndYear=2050;
```

Send the string to the URL:

```
http://esa.un.org/unpd/wpp/unpp/p2k0data.asp
```

The script sends back the following reply:

```
"Country","Variable","Variant","Year","Value"
"Kenya","Population (thousands)","Medium variant","1950",6077
"Kenya","Population (thousands)","Medium variant","1955",6984
"Kenya","Population (thousands)","Medium variant","1960",8115
"Kenya","Population (thousands)","Medium variant","1965",9524
. . .
```

As you can see, this particular script sends back a comma-separated data file. That is the reason we picked it as an example—it is easy to see what happens with this script, whereas the complex sets of HTML tags that other scripts produce might be confusing to decipher.

The program in Listing 3.7 sends POST data to any script. Place the data into a .properties file such as the following:

```
url=http://esa.un.org/unpd/wpp/unpp/p2k0data_script.asp
Panel=1
Variable=12;
Location=404
Varient=2
StartYear=1950
EndYear=2050
```

The program removes the url entry and sends all others to the doPost method.

In the doPost method, we first open the connection, call setDoOutput(true), and open the output stream. We then enumerate all keys and values. For each of them, we send the key, = character, value, and & separator character:

```
out.print(key);
out.print('=');
out.print(URLEncoder.encode(value, "UTF-8"));
if (more pairs) out.print('&');
```

Finally, we read the response from the server.

There is one twist with reading the response. If a script error occurs, the call to connection.getInputStream() throws a FileNotFoundException. However, the server still sends an error page back to the browser (such as the ubiquitous "Error 404 — page not found"). To capture this error page, cast the URLConnection object to the HttpURLConnection class and call its getErrorStream method:

```
InputStream err = ((HttpURLConnection) connection).getErrorStream();
```

More for curiosity's sake than for practical use, you might like to know exactly what information the URLConnection sends to the server in addition to the data that you supply.

The URLConnection object first sends a request header to the server. When posting form data, the header includes

```
Content-Type: application/x-www-form-urlencoded
```

The header for a POST must also include the content length, for example

```
Content-Length: 124
```

The end of the header is indicated by a blank line. Then, the data portion follows. The web server strips off the header and routes the data portion to the server-side script.

Note that the URLConnection object buffers all data that you send to the output stream because it must first determine the total content length.

The technique that this program displays is useful whenever you need to query information from an existing web site. Simply find out the parameters that you need to send (usually by inspecting the HTML source of a web page that carries out the same query), and then strip out the HTML tags and other unnecessary information from the reply.

**Listing 3.7** post/PostTest.java

```
1  package post;
2
3  import java.io.*;
4  import java.net.*;
5  import java.nio.file.*;
6  import java.util.*;
7
8  /**
9   * This program demonstrates how to use the URLConnection class for a POST request.
10  * @version 1.30 2012-06-04
11  * @author Cay Horstmann
12  */
13 public class PostTest
14 {
15    public static void main(String[] args) throws IOException
16    {
17       Properties props = new Properties();
18       try (InputStream in = Files.newInputStream(Paths.get(args[0])))
19       {
20          props.load(in);
21       }
22       String url = props.remove("url").toString();
23       String result = doPost(url, props);
24       System.out.println(result);
25    }
26
27    public static String doPost(String urlString, Map<Object, Object> nameValuePairs)
28          throws IOException
29    {
30       URL url = new URL(urlString);
31       URLConnection connection = url.openConnection();
32       connection.setDoOutput(true);
33
34       try (PrintWriter out = new PrintWriter(connection.getOutputStream()))
35       {
36          boolean first = true;
37          for (Map.Entry<Object, Object> pair : nameValuePairs.entrySet())
38          {
39             if (first) first = false;
40             else out.print('&');
41
42             String name = pair.getKey().toString();
```

```
43          String value = pair.getValue().toString();
44          out.print(name);
45          out.print('=');
46          out.print(URLEncoder.encode(value, "UTF-8"));
47       }
48    }
49
50    StringBuilder response = new StringBuilder();
51    try (Scanner in = new Scanner(connection.getInputStream()))
52    {
53       while (in.hasNextLine())
54       {
55          response.append(in.nextLine());
56          response.append("\n");
57       }
58    }
59    catch (IOException e)
60    {
61       if (!(connection instanceof HttpURLConnection)) throw e;
62       InputStream err = ((HttpURLConnection) connection).getErrorStream();
63       if (err == null) throw e;
64       Scanner in = new Scanner(err);
65       response.append(in.nextLine());
66       response.append("\n");
67    }
68
69    return response.toString();
70 }
71 }
```

---

**java.net.HttpURLConnection** 1.0

- InputStream getErrorStream()
  returns a stream from which you can read web server error messages.

---

**java.net.URLEncoder** 1.0

- static String encode(String s, String encoding) 1.4
  returns the URL-encoded form of the string s, using the given character encoding scheme. (The recommended scheme is "UTF-8".) In URL encoding, the characters 'A'–'Z', 'a'–'z', '0'–'9', '-', '_', '.', and '~' are left unchanged. Space is encoded into '+', and all other characters are encoded into sequences of encoded bytes of the form "%XY", where 0xXY is the hexadecimal value of the byte.

---

> **java.net.URLDecoder** 1.2
>
> * static string decode(String s, String encoding) 1.4
>   returns the decoding of the URL encoded string s under the given character encoding scheme.

## 3.5 Sending E-Mail

In the past, it was simple to write a program that sends e-mail by making a socket connection to port 25, the SMTP port. The Simple Mail Transport Protocol (SMTP) describes the format for e-mail messages. Once you are connected to the server, send a mail header (in the SMTP format, which is easy to generate), followed by the mail message.

Here are the details:

1. Open a socket to your host.

   ```
   Socket s = new Socket("mail.yourserver.com", 25); // 25 is SMTP
   PrintWriter out = new PrintWriter(s.getOutputStream());
   ```

2. Send the following information to the print stream:

   ```
   HELO sending host
   MAIL FROM: sender e-mail address
   RCPT TO: recipient e-mail address
   DATA
   Subject: subject
   (blank line)
   mail message (any number of lines)
   .
   QUIT
   ```

The SMTP specification (RFC 821) states that lines must be terminated with \r followed by \n.

It used to be that SMTP servers were routinely willing to route e-mail from anyone. However, in these days of spam floods, most servers have built-in checks and only accept requests from users or IP address ranges that they trust. Authentication usually happens over secure socket connections.

Implementing these authentication schemes manually would be very tedious. Instead, we will show you how to use the JavaMail API to send e-mail from a Java program.

Download JavaMail from www.oracle.com/technetwork/java/javamail and unzip it somewhere on your hard disk.

To use JavaMail, you need to set up some properties that depend on your mail server. For example, with GMail, you use

```
mail.transport.protocol=smtps
mail.smtps.auth=true
mail.smtps.host=smtp.gmail.com
mail.smtps.user=cayhorstmann@gmail.com
```

Our sample program reads these from a property file.

For security reasons, we don't put the password into the property file but instead prompt for it.

Read in the property file, then get a mail session like this:

```
Session mailSession = Session.getDefaultInstance(props);
```

Make a message with the desired sender, recipient, subject, and message text:

```
MimeMessage message = new MimeMessage(mailSession);
message.setFrom(new InternetAddress(from));
message.addRecipient(RecipientType.TO, new InternetAddress(to));
message.setSubject(subject);
message.setText(builder.toString());
```

Then send it off:

```
Transport tr = mailSession.getTransport();
tr.connect(null, password);
tr.sendMessage(message, message.getAllRecipients());
tr.close();
```

The program in Listing 3.8 reads the message from a text file of the format

*Sender*
*Recipient*
*Subject*
*Message text (any number of lines)*

To run the program, type

```
java -classpath .:path/to/mail.jar path/to/message.txt
```

Here, `mail.jar` is the JAR file that came with the JavaMail distribution. (Windows users: Remember to type a semicolon instead of a colon in the classpath.)

At the time of this writing, GMail does not check the veracity of the information—you can supply any sender you like. (Keep this in mind the next time you get an e-mail message from president@whitehouse.gov inviting you to a black-tie affair on the front lawn.)

**TIP:** If you can't figure out why your mail connection isn't working, call

mailSession.setDebug(true);

and check out the messages. Also, the JavaMail API FAQ has some useful hints.

**Listing 3.8** mail/MailTest.java

```java
1  package mail;
2
3  import java.io.*;
4  import java.nio.charset.*;
5  import java.nio.file.*;
6  import java.util.*;
7  import javax.mail.*;
8  import javax.mail.internet.*;
9  import javax.mail.internet.MimeMessage.RecipientType;
10
11 /**
12  * This program shows how to use JavaMail to send mail messages.
13  * @author Cay Horstmann
14  * @version 1.00 2012-06-04
15  */
16 public class MailTest
17 {
18    public static void main(String[] args) throws MessagingException, IOException
19    {
20       Properties props = new Properties();
21       try (InputStream in = Files.newInputStream(Paths.get("mail", "mail.properties")))
22       {
23          props.load(in);
24       }
25       List<String> lines = Files.readAllLines(Paths.get(args[0]), Charset.forName("UTF-8"));
26
27       String from = lines.get(0);
28       String to = lines.get(1);
29       String subject = lines.get(2);
30
31       StringBuilder builder = new StringBuilder();
32       for (int i = 3; i < lines.size(); i++)
33       {
34          builder.append(lines.get(i));
35          builder.append("\n");
36       }
37
38       Console console = System.console();
39       String password = new String(console.readPassword("Password: "));
40
41       Session mailSession = Session.getDefaultInstance(props);
```

```
42      // mailSession.setDebug(true);
43      MimeMessage message = new MimeMessage(mailSession);
44      message.setFrom(new InternetAddress(from));
45      message.addRecipient(RecipientType.TO, new InternetAddress(to));
46      message.setSubject(subject);
47      message.setText(builder.toString());
48      Transport tr = mailSession.getTransport();
49      try
50      {
51         tr.connect(null, password);
52         tr.sendMessage(message, message.getAllRecipients());
53      }
54      finally
55      {
56         tr.close();
57      }
58   }
59 }
```

In this chapter, you have seen how to write network clients and servers in Java and how to harvest information from web servers. The next chapter covers database connectivity. You will learn how to work with relational databases in Java, using the JDBC API. The chapter also has a brief introduction to hierarchical databases (such as LDAP directories) and the JNDI API.

CHAPTER

# 4

# Database Programming

## In this chapter:

In 1996, Sun released the first version of the JDBC API. This API lets programmers connect to a database to query or update it using the Structured Query Language (SQL). (SQL, usually pronounced "sequel," is an industry standard for relational database access.) JDBC has since become one of the most commonly used APIs in the Java library.

JDBC has been updated several times. As part of the Java SE 1.2 release in 1998, a second version of JDBC was issued. JDBC 3 is included with Java SE 1.4 and 5.0. As this book is published, JDBC 4.1, the version included with Java SE 7, is the most current version.

In this chapter, we will explain the key ideas behind JDBC. We will introduce you to (or refresh your memory of) SQL, the industry-standard Structured Query

Language for relational databases. We will then provide enough details and examples to let you start using JDBC for common programming situations.

 **NOTE:** According to Oracle, JDBC is a trademarked term and not an acronym for Java Database Connectivity. It was named to be reminiscent of ODBC, a standard database API pioneered by Microsoft and since incorporated into the SQL standard.

## 4.1 The Design of JDBC

From the start, the developers of the Java technology were aware of the potential that Java showed for working with databases. In 1995, they began working on extending the standard Java library to deal with SQL access to databases. What they first hoped to do was to extend Java so that a program could talk to any random database using only "pure" Java. It didn't take them long to realize that this is an impossible task: There are simply too many databases out there, using too many protocols. Moreover, although database vendors were all in favor of Java providing a standard network protocol for database access, they were only in favor of it if Java used *their* network protocol.

What all the database vendors and tool vendors *did* agree on was that it would be useful for Java to provide a pure Java API for SQL access along with a driver manager to allow third-party drivers to connect to specific databases. Database vendors could provide their own drivers to plug in to the driver manager. There would then be a simple mechanism for registering third-party drivers with the driver manager.

This organization follows the very successful model of Microsoft's ODBC which provided a C programming language interface for database access. Both JDBC and ODBC are based on the same idea: Programs written according to the API talk to the driver manager, which, in turn, uses a driver to talk to the actual database.

This means the JDBC API is all that most programmers will ever have to deal with.

### 4.1.1 JDBC Driver Types

The JDBC specification classifies drivers into the following *types*:

• A *type 1 driver* translates JDBC to ODBC and relies on an ODBC driver to communicate with the database. Early versions of Java included one such driver, the *JDBC/ODBC bridge*. However, the bridge requires deployment and proper configuration of an ODBC driver. When JDBC was first released, the bridge was handy for testing, but it was never intended for production use. At this point, many better drivers are available, and we advise against using the JDBC/ODBC bridge.

- A *type 2 driver* is written partly in Java and partly in native code; it communicates with the client API of a database. When using such a driver, you must install some platform-specific code onto the client in addition to a Java library.

- A *type 3 driver* is a pure Java client library that uses a database-independent protocol to communicate database requests to a server component, which then translates the requests into a database-specific protocol. This simplifies deployment because the platform-specific code is located only on the server.

- A *type 4 driver* is a pure Java library that translates JDBC requests directly to a database-specific protocol.

Most database vendors supply either a type 3 or type 4 driver with their database. Furthermore, a number of third-party companies specialize in producing drivers with better standards conformance, support for more platforms, better performance, or, in some cases, simply better reliability than the drivers provided by the database vendors.

In summary, the ultimate goal of JDBC is to make possible the following:

- Programmers can write applications in the Java programming language to access any database, using standard SQL statements (or even specialized extensions of SQL) while still following Java language conventions.

- Database vendors and database tool vendors can supply the low-level drivers. Thus, they can optimize their drivers for their specific products.

---

 **NOTE:** If you are curious as to why Java just didn't adopt the ODBC model, the reason, as given at the JavaOne conference in 1996, was this:

- ODBC is hard to learn.

- ODBC has a few commands with lots of complex options. The preferred style in the Java programming language is to have simple and intuitive methods, but to have lots of them.

- ODBC relies on the use of void* pointers and other C features that are not natural in the Java programming language.

- An ODBC-based solution is inherently less safe and harder to deploy than a pure Java solution.

---

## 4.1.2 Typical Uses of JDBC

The traditional client/server model has a rich GUI on the client and a database on the server (see Figure 4.1). In this model, a JDBC driver is deployed on the client.

However, the world is moving away from client/server and toward a three-tier model or even more advanced *n*-tier models. In the three-tier model, the client does not make database calls. Instead, it calls on a middleware layer on the server that in turn makes the database queries. The three-tier model has a couple of advantages. It separates *visual presentation* (on the client) from the *business logic* (in the middle tier) and the raw data (in the database). Therefore, it becomes possible to access the same data and the same business rules from multiple clients, such as a Java application, an applet, or a web form.

Communication between the client and the middle tier can occur through HTTP (when you use a web browser as the client) or another mechanism such as remote method invocation (RMI, see Chapter 11). JDBC manages the communication between the middle tier and the back-end database. Figure 4.2 shows the basic architecture. There are, of course, many variations of this model. In particular, the Java Enterprise Edition defines a structure for *application servers* that manage code modules called *Enterprise JavaBeans*, and provides valuable services such as load balancing, request caching, security, and object-relational mapping. In that architecture, JDBC still plays an important role for issuing complex database queries. (For more information on the Enterprise Edition, see www.oracle.com/technetwork/java/javaee/overview.)

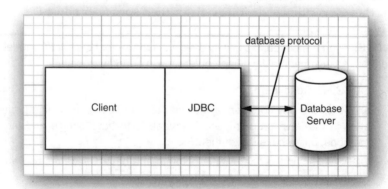

**Figure 4.1** A traditional client/server application

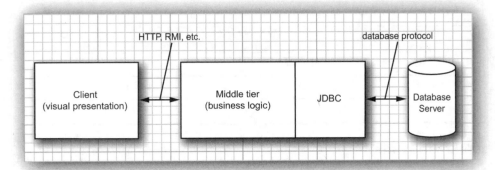

**Figure 4.2** A three-tier application

 **NOTE:** You can use JDBC in applets and Web Start applications, but you probably don't want to. By default, the security manager permits a network connection only to the server from which the applet is downloaded. That means the web server and the database server (or the relay component of a type 3 driver) must be on the same machine, which is not a typical setup. You would need to use code signing to overcome this problem.

## 4.2 The Structured Query Language

JDBC lets you communicate with databases using SQL, which is the command language for essentially all modern relational databases. Desktop databases usually have a GUI that lets users manipulate the data directly, but server-based databases are accessed purely through SQL.

The JDBC package can be thought of as nothing more than an API for communicating SQL statements to databases. We will briefly introduce SQL in this section. If you have never seen SQL before, you might not find this material sufficient. If so, turn to one of the many books on the topic; we recommend *Learning SQL* by Alan Beaulieu (O'Reilly, 2005) or the opinionated classic, *A Guide to the SQL Standard, Fourth Edition*, by C. J. Date and Hugh Darwen (Addison-Wesley, 1997).

You can think of a database as a bunch of named tables with rows and columns. Each column has a *column name*. Each row contains a set of related data.

As an example database for this book, we use a set of database tables that describe a collection of classic computer science books (see Tables 4.1 through 4.4).

**Table 4.1**  The Authors Table

| Author_ID | Name | Fname |
|---|---|---|
| ALEX | Alexander | Christopher |
| BROO | Brooks | Frederick P. |
| . . . | . . . | . . . |

**Table 4.2**  The Books Table

| Title | ISBN | Publisher_ID | Price |
|---|---|---|---|
| A Guide to the SQL Standard | 0-201-96426-0 | 0201 | 47.95 |
| A Pattern Language: Towns, Buildings, Construction | 0-19-501919-9 | 019 | 65.00 |
| . . . | . . . | . . . | . . . |

**Table 4.3**  The BooksAuthors Table

| ISBN | Author_ID | Seq_No |
|---|---|---|
| 0-201-96426-0 | DATE | 1 |
| 0-201-96426-0 | DARW | 2 |
| 0-19-501919-9 | ALEX | 1 |
| . . . | . . . | . . . |

**Table 4.4**  The Publishers Table

| Publisher_ID | Name | URL |
|---|---|---|
| 0201 | Addison-Wesley | www.aw-bc.com |
| 0407 | John Wiley & Sons | www.wiley.com |
| . . . | . . . | . . . |

Figure 4.3 shows a view of the Books table. Figure 4.4 shows the result of *joining* this table with the Publishers table. The Books and the Publishers tables each contain an identifier for the publisher. When we join both tables on the publisher code, we obtain a *query result* made up of values from the joined tables. Each row in

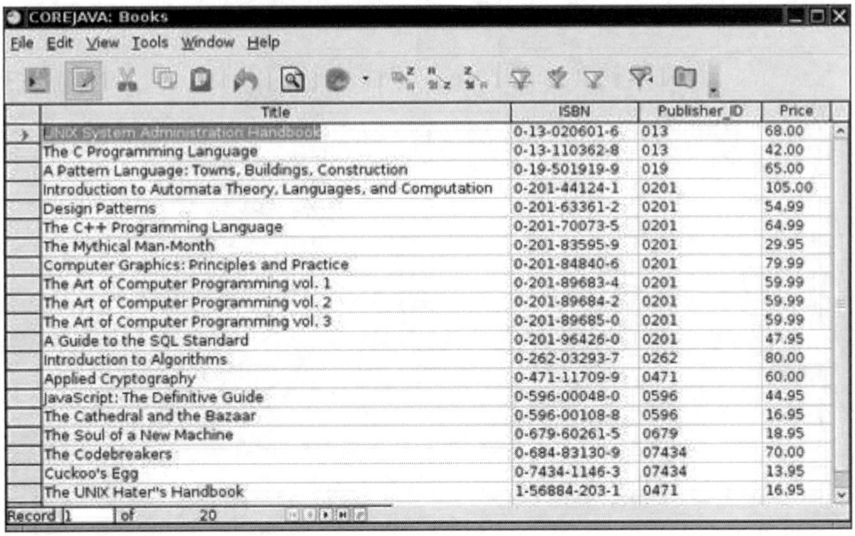


| Title | ISBN | Publisher_ID | Price |
|---|---|---|---|
| UNIX System Administration Handbook | 0-13-020601-6 | 013 | 68.00 |
| The C Programming Language | 0-13-110362-8 | 013 | 42.00 |
| A Pattern Language: Towns, Buildings, Construction | 0-19-501919-9 | 019 | 65.00 |
| Introduction to Automata Theory, Languages, and Computation | 0-201-44124-1 | 0201 | 105.00 |
| Design Patterns | 0-201-63361-2 | 0201 | 54.99 |
| The C++ Programming Language | 0-201-70073-5 | 0201 | 64.99 |
| The Mythical Man-Month | 0-201-83595-9 | 0201 | 29.95 |
| Computer Graphics: Principles and Practice | 0-201-84840-6 | 0201 | 79.99 |
| The Art of Computer Programming vol. 1 | 0-201-89683-4 | 0201 | 59.99 |
| The Art of Computer Programming vol. 2 | 0-201-89684-2 | 0201 | 59.99 |
| The Art of Computer Programming vol. 3 | 0-201-89685-0 | 0201 | 59.99 |
| A Guide to the SQL Standard | 0-201-96426-0 | 0201 | 47.95 |
| Introduction to Algorithms | 0-262-03293-7 | 0262 | 80.00 |
| Applied Cryptography | 0-471-11709-9 | 0471 | 60.00 |
| JavaScript: The Definitive Guide | 0-596-00048-0 | 0596 | 44.95 |
| The Cathedral and the Bazaar | 0-596-00108-8 | 0596 | 16.95 |
| The Soul of a New Machine | 0-679-60261-5 | 0679 | 18.95 |
| The Codebreakers | 0-684-83130-9 | 07434 | 70.00 |
| Cuckoo's Egg | 0-7434-1146-3 | 07434 | 13.95 |
| The UNIX Hater"s Handbook | 1-56884-203-1 | 0471 | 16.95 |

**Figure 4.3** Sample table containing books

the result contains the information about a book, together with the publisher name and web page URL. Note that the publisher names and URLs are duplicated across several rows because we have several rows with the same publisher.

The benefit of joining tables is avoiding unnecessary duplication of data in the database tables. For example, a naive database design might have had columns for the publisher name and URL right in the `Books` table. But then the database itself, and not just the query result, would have many duplicates of these entries. If a publisher's web address changed, *all* entries would need to be updated. Clearly, this is somewhat error-prone. In the relational model, we distribute data into multiple tables so that no information is ever unnecessarily duplicated. For example, each publisher's URL is contained only once in the publisher table. If the information needs to be combined, the tables are joined.

In the figures, you can see a graphical tool to inspect and link the tables. Many vendors have tools to express queries in a simple form by connecting column names and filling information into forms. Such tools are often called *query by example* (QBE) tools. In contrast, a query that uses SQL is written out in text, using SQL syntax, for example:

```
SELECT Books.Title, Books.Publisher_Id, Books.Price, Publishers.Name, Publishers.URL
FROM Books, Publishers
WHERE Books.Publisher_Id = Publishers.Publisher_Id
```

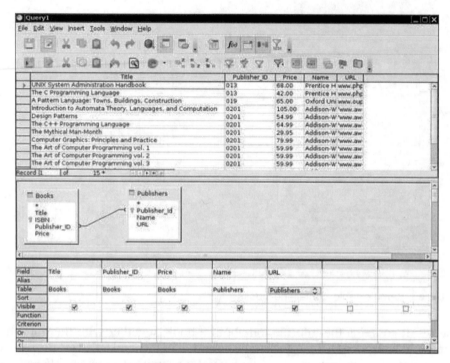

**Figure 4.4** Two tables joined together

In the remainder of this section, you will learn how to write such queries. If you are already familiar with SQL, just skip this section.

By convention, SQL keywords are written in capital letters, although this is not necessary.

The SELECT statement is quite flexible. You can simply select all rows in the Books table with the following query:

```
SELECT * FROM Books
```

The FROM clause is required in every SQL SELECT statement. It tells the database which tables to examine to find the data.

You can choose the columns that you want:

```
SELECT ISBN, Price, Title
FROM Books
```

You can restrict the rows in the answer with the WHERE clause:

```
SELECT ISBN, Price, Title
FROM Books
WHERE Price <= 29.95
```

Be careful with the "equals" comparison. SQL uses = and <>, rather than == or != as in the Java programming language, for equality testing.

 **NOTE:** Some database vendors support the use of != for inequality testing. This is not standard SQL, so we recommend against such use.

The WHERE clause can also use pattern matching by means of the LIKE operator. The wildcard characters are not the usual * and ?, however. Use a % for zero or more characters and an underscore for a single character. For example,

```
SELECT ISBN, Price, Title
FROM Books
WHERE Title NOT LIKE '%n_x%'
```

excludes books with titles that contain words such as Unix or Linux.

Note that strings are enclosed in single quotes, not double quotes. A single quote inside a string is represented by a pair of single quotes. For example,

```
SELECT Title
FROM Books
WHERE Title LIKE '%''%'
```

reports all titles that contain a single quote.

You can select data from multiple tables:

```
SELECT * FROM Books, Publishers
```

Without a WHERE clause, this query is not very interesting. It lists *all combinations* of rows from both tables. In our case, where Books has 20 rows and Publishers has 8 rows, the result is a set of rows with 20 × 8 entries and lots of duplications. We really want to constrain the query to say that we are only interested in *matching* books with their publishers:

```
SELECT * FROM Books, Publishers
WHERE Books.Publisher_Id = Publishers.Publisher_Id
```

This query result has 20 rows, one for each book, because each book has one publisher in the Publisher table.

Whenever you have multiple tables in a query, the same column name can occur in two different places. That happened in our example. There is a column called Publisher_Id in both the Books and the Publishers tables. When an ambiguity would otherwise result, you must prefix each column name with the name of the table to which it belongs, such as Books.Publisher_Id.

You can use SQL to change the data inside a database as well. For example, suppose you want to reduce by $5.00 the current price of all books that have "C++" in their title:

```
UPDATE Books
SET Price = Price - 5.00
WHERE Title LIKE '%C++%'
```

Similarly, to delete all C++ books, use a DELETE query:

```
DELETE FROM Books
WHERE Title LIKE '%C++%'
```

Moreover, SQL comes with built-in functions for taking averages, finding maximums and minimums in a column, and much more. A good source for this information is http://sqlzoo.net. (That site also contains a nifty interactive SQL tutorial.)

Typically, to insert values into a table, you can use the INSERT statement:

```
INSERT INTO Books
VALUES ('A Guide to the SQL Standard', '0-201-96426-0', '0201', 47.95)
```

You need a separate INSERT statement for every row being inserted in the table.

Of course, before you can query, modify, and insert data, you must have a place to store data. Use the CREATE TABLE statement to make a new table. Specify the name and data type for each column. For example,

```
CREATE TABLE Books
(
    Title CHAR(60),
    ISBN CHAR(13),
    Publisher_Id CHAR(6),
    Price DECIMAL(10,2)
)
```

Table 4.5 shows the most common SQL data types.

In this book, we do not discuss the additional clauses, such as keys and constraints, that you can use with the CREATE TABLE statement.

**Table 4.5** Common SQL Data Types

| Data Types | Description |
| --- | --- |
| INTEGER or INT | Typically, a 32-bit integer |
| SMALLINT | Typically, a 16-bit integer |
| NUMERIC($m$,$n$), DECIMAL($m$,$n$) or DEC($m$,$n$) | Fixed-point decimal number with $m$ total digits and $n$ digits after the decimal point |
| FLOAT($n$) | A floating-point number with $n$ binary digits of precision |
| REAL | Typically, a 32-bit floating-point number |
| DOUBLE | Typically, a 64-bit floating-point number |
| CHARACTER($n$) or CHAR($n$) | Fixed-length string of length $n$ |
| VARCHAR(n) | Variable-length strings of maximum length n |
| BOOLEAN | A Boolean value |
| DATE | Calendar date, implementation-dependent |
| TIME | Time of day, implementation-dependent |
| TIMESTAMP | Date and time of day, implementation-dependent |
| BLOB | A binary large object |
| CLOB | A character large object |

# 4.3 JDBC Configuration

Of course, you need a database program for which a JDBC driver is available. There are many excellent choices, such as IBM DB2, Microsoft SQL Server, MySQL, Oracle, and PostgreSQL.

You must also create a database for your experimental use. We assume you name it COREJAVA. Create a new database, or have your database administrator create one with the appropriate permissions. You need to be able to create, update, and drop tables in the database.

If you have never installed a client/server database before, you might find that setting up the database is somewhat complex and that diagnosing the cause for failure can be difficult. It might be best to seek expert help if your setup is not working correctly.

If this is your first experience with databases, we recommend that you use the Apache Derby database that is a part of most versions of JDK 7. (If you use a JDK that doesn't include it, download Apache Derby from http://db.apache.org/derby.)

---

 **NOTE:** The version of Apache Derby that is included in the JDK is officially called JavaDB. We don't think that's particularly helpful, and we will call it Derby in this chapter.

---

You need to gather a number of items before you can write your first database program. The following sections cover these items.

## 4.3.1 Database URLs

When connecting to a database, you must use various database-specific parameters such as host names, port numbers, and database names.

JDBC uses a syntax similar to that of ordinary URLs to describe data sources. Here are examples of the syntax:

```
jdbc:derby://localhost:1527/COREJAVA;create=true
jdbc:postgresql:COREJAVA
```

These JDBC URLs specify a Derby database and a PostgreSQL database named COREJAVA.

The general syntax is

```
jdbc:subprotocol:other stuff
```

where a subprotocol selects the specific driver for connecting to the database.

The format for the *other stuff* parameter depends on the subprotocol used. You will need to look up your vendor's documentation for the specific format.

## 4.3.2 Driver JAR Files

You need to obtain the JAR file in which the driver for your database is located. If you use Derby, you need the file derbyclient.jar. With another database, you need to locate the appropriate driver. For example, the PostgreSQL drivers are available at http://jdbc.postgresql.org.

Include the driver JAR file on the class path when running a program that accesses the database. (You don't need the JAR file for compiling.)

When you launch programs from the command line, simply use the command

```
java -classpath driverPath:. ProgramName
```

On Windows, use a semicolon to separate the current directory (denoted by the
. character) from the driver JAR location.

### 4.3.3 Starting the Database

The database server needs to be started before you can connect to it. The details
depend on your database.

With the Derby database, follow these steps:

1.  Open a command shell and change to a directory that will hold the database
    files.

2.  Locate the file derbyrun.jar. With some versions of the JDK, it is contained in
    the *jdk*/db/lib directory, with others in a separate JavaDB installation directory.
    We will denote the directory containing lib/derbyrun.jar with *derby*.

3.  Run the command

    ```
    java -jar derby/lib/derbyrun.jar server start
    ```

4.  Double-check that the database is working correctly. Create a file ij.properties
    that contains these lines:

    ```
    ij.driver=org.apache.derby.jdbc.ClientDriver
    ij.protocol=jdbc:derby://localhost:1527/
    ij.database=COREJAVA;create=true
    ```

    From another command shell, run Derby's interactive scripting tool
    (called ij) by executing

    ```
    java -jar derby/lib/derbyrun.jar ij -p ij.properties
    ```

    Now you can issue SQL commands such as

    ```
    CREATE TABLE Greetings (Message CHAR(20));
    INSERT INTO Greetings VALUES ('Hello, World!');
    SELECT * FROM Greetings;
    DROP TABLE Greetings;
    ```

    Note that each command must be terminated by a semicolon. To exit, type

    ```
    EXIT;
    ```

5.  When you are done using the database, stop the server with the command

    ```
    java -jar derby/lib/derbyrun.jar server shutdown
    ```

If you use another database, you need to consult the documentation to find out how to start and stop your database server, and how to connect to it and issue SQL commands.

## 4.3.4  Registering the Driver Class

Many JDBC JAR files (such as the Derby driver included with Java SE 7) automatically register the driver class. In that case, you can skip the manual registration step that we describe in this section. A JAR file can automatically register the driver class if it contains a file `META-INF/services/java.sql.Driver`. You can simply unzip your driver's JAR file to check.

**NOTE:** This registration mechanism uses a little-known part of the JAR specification; see http://docs.oracle.com/javase/7/docs/technotes/guides/jar/jar.html#Service%20Provider. Automatic registration is a requirement for a JDBC4-compliant driver.

If your driver's JAR file doesn't support automatic registration, you need to find out the name of the JDBC driver classes used by your vendor. Typical driver names are

```
org.apache.derby.jdbc.ClientDriver
org.postgresql.Driver
```

There are two ways to register the driver with the `DriverManager`. One way is to load the driver class in your Java program. For example,

```
Class.forName("org.postgresql.Driver"); // force loading of driver class
```

This statement causes the driver class to be loaded, thereby executing a static initializer that registers the driver.

Alternatively, you can set the `jdbc.drivers` property. You can specify the property with a command-line argument, such as

```
java -Djdbc.drivers=org.postgresql.Driver ProgramName
```

Or, your application can set the system property with a call such as

```
System.setProperty("jdbc.drivers", "org.postgresql.Driver");
```

You can also supply multiple drivers; separate them with colons, such as

```
org.postgresql.Driver:org.apache.derby.jdbc.ClientDriver
```

### 4.3.5 Connecting to the Database

In your Java program, you can open a database connection like this:

```
String url = "jdbc:postgresql:COREJAVA";
String username = "dbuser";
String password = "secret";
Connection conn = DriverManager.getConnection(url, username, password);
```

The driver manager iterates through the registered drivers to find a driver that can use the subprotocol specified in the database URL.

The getConnection method returns a Connection object. In the following sections, you will see how to use the Connection object to execute SQL statements.

To connect to the database, you will need to have a user name and password for your database.

 **NOTE:** By default, Derby lets you connect with any user name, and it does not check passwords. A separate set of tables is generated for each user. The default user name is app.

The test program in Listing 4.1 puts these steps to work. It loads connection parameters from a file named database.properties and connects to the database. The database.properties file supplied with the sample code contains connection information for the Derby database. If you use a different database, put your database-specific connection information into that file. Here is an example for connecting to a PostgreSQL database:

```
jdbc.drivers=org.postgresql.Driver
jdbc.url=jdbc:postgresql:COREJAVA
jdbc.username=dbuser
jdbc.password=secret
```

After connecting to the database, the test program executes the following SQL statements:

```
CREATE TABLE Greetings (Message CHAR(20))
INSERT INTO Greetings VALUES ('Hello, World!')
SELECT * FROM Greetings
```

The result of the SELECT statement is printed, and you should see an output of

```
Hello, World!
```

Then the table is removed by executing the statement

```
DROP TABLE Greetings
```

To run this test, start your database, as described previously, and launch the program as

```
java -classpath .:driverJAR test.TestDB
```

(As always, Windows users need to use ; instead of : to separate the path elements.)

---

 **TIP:** One way to debug JDBC-related problems is to enable JDBC tracing. Call the `DriverManager.setLogWriter` method to send trace messages to a `PrintWriter`. The trace output contains a detailed listing of the JDBC activity. Most JDBC driver implementations provide additional mechanisms for tracing. For example, with Derby, you can add a `traceFile` option to the JDBC URL: `jdbc:derby://localhost:1527/COREJAVA;create=true;traceFile=trace.out`.

---

**Listing 4.1** test/TestDB.java

```java
1  package test;
2
3  import java.nio.file.*;
4  import java.sql.*;
5  import java.io.*;
6  import java.util.*;
7
8  /**
9   * This program tests that the database and the JDBC driver are correctly configured.
10  * @version 1.02 2012-06-05
11  * @author Cay Horstmann
12  */
13 public class TestDB
14 {
15    public static void main(String args[]) throws IOException
16    {
17       try
18       {
19          runTest();
20       }
21       catch (SQLException ex)
22       {
23          for (Throwable t : ex)
24             t.printStackTrace();
25       }
26    }
27    /**
28     * Runs a test by creating a table, adding a value, showing the table contents, and removing
29     * the table.
30     */
```

```
31   public static void runTest() throws SQLException, IOException
32   {
33      try (Connection conn = getConnection())
34      {
35         Statement stat = conn.createStatement();
36
37         stat.executeUpdate("CREATE TABLE Greetings (Message CHAR(20))");
38         stat.executeUpdate("INSERT INTO Greetings VALUES ('Hello, World!')");
39
40         try (ResultSet result = stat.executeQuery("SELECT * FROM Greetings"))
41         {
42            if (result.next())
43               System.out.println(result.getString(1));
44         }
45         stat.executeUpdate("DROP TABLE Greetings");
46      }
47   }
48
49   /**
50    * Gets a connection from the properties specified in the file database.properties.
51    * @return the database connection
52    */
53   public static Connection getConnection() throws SQLException, IOException
54   {
55      Properties props = new Properties();
56      try (InputStream in = Files.newInputStream(Paths.get("database.properties")))
57      {
58         props.load(in);
59      }
60      String drivers = props.getProperty("jdbc.drivers");
61      if (drivers != null) System.setProperty("jdbc.drivers", drivers);
62      String url = props.getProperty("jdbc.url");
63      String username = props.getProperty("jdbc.username");
64      String password = props.getProperty("jdbc.password");
65
66      return DriverManager.getConnection(url, username, password);
67   }
68 }
```

---

**java.sql.DriverManager** 1.1

- static Connection getConnection(String url, String user, String password)
  establishes a connection to the given database and returns a Connection object.

## 4.4 Executing SQL Statements

To execute a SQL statement, you first create a Statement object. To create statement objects, use the Connection object that you obtained from the call to DriverManager.getConnection.

```
Statement stat = conn.createStatement();
```

Next, place the statement that you want to execute into a string, for example

```
String command = "UPDATE Books"
   + " SET Price = Price - 5.00"
   + " WHERE Title NOT LIKE '%Introduction%'";
```

Then call the executeUpdate method of the Statement interface:

```
stat.executeUpdate(command);
```

The executeUpdate method returns a count of the rows that were affected by the SQL statement, or zero for statements that do not return a row count. For example, the call to executeUpdate in the preceding example returns the number of rows whose price was lowered by $5.00.

The executeUpdate method can execute actions such as INSERT, UPDATE, and DELETE, as well as data definition statements such as CREATE TABLE and DROP TABLE. However, you need to use the executeQuery method to execute SELECT queries. There is also a catch-all execute statement to execute arbitrary SQL statements. It's commonly used only for queries that a user supplies interactively.

When you execute a query, you are interested in the result. The executeQuery object returns an object of type ResultSet that you can use to walk through the result one row at a time.

```
ResultSet rs = stat.executeQuery("SELECT * FROM Books")
```

The basic loop for analyzing a result set looks like this:

```
while (rs.next())
{
   look at a row of the result set
}
```

**CAUTION:** The iteration protocol of the ResultSet interface is subtly different from the protocol of the java.util.Iterator interface. Here, the iterator is initialized to a position *before* the first row. You must call the next method once to move the iterator to the first row. Also, there is no hasNext method; keep calling next until it returns false.

The order of the rows in a result set is completely arbitrary. Unless you specifi-cally ordered the result with an ORDER BY clause, you should not attach any significance to the row order.

When inspecting an individual row, you will want to know the contents of the fields. A large number of accessor methods give you this information.

```
String isbn = rs.getString(1);
double price = rs.getDouble("Price");
```

There are accessors for various *types*, such as getString and getDouble. Each accessor has two forms: one that takes a numeric argument and one that takes a string argument. When you supply a numeric argument, you refer to the column with that number. For example, rs.getString(1) returns the value of the first column in the current row.

---

 **CAUTION:** Unlike array indexes, database column numbers start at 1.

---

When you supply a string argument, you refer to the column in the result set with that name. For example, rs.getDouble("Price") returns the value of the column with label Price. Using the numeric argument is a bit more efficient, but the string arguments make the code easier to read and maintain.

Each get method makes reasonable type conversions when the type of the method doesn't match the type of the column. For example, the call rs.getString("Price") converts the floating-point value of the Price column to a string.

---

*java.sql.Connection* 1.1

- Statement createStatement()
  creates a Statement object that can be used to execute SQL queries and updates without parameters.
- void close()
  immediately closes the current connection and the JDBC resources that it created.

---

*java.sql.Statement* 1.1

- ResultSet executeQuery(String sqlQuery)
  executes the SQL statement given in the string and returns a ResultSet object to view the query result.

*(Continues)*

---

**java.sql.Statement** 1.1 *(Continued)*

- `int executeUpdate(String sqlStatement)`

  executes the SQL INSERT, UPDATE, or DELETE statement specified by the string. Also executes Data Definition Language (DDL) statements such as CREATE TABLE. Returns the number of rows affected, or 0 for a statement without an update count.

- `boolean execute(String sqlStatement)`

  executes the SQL statement specified by the string. Multiple result sets and update counts may be produced. Returns true if the first result is a result set, false otherwise. Call getResultSet or getUpdateCount to retrieve the first result. See Section 4.5.4, "Multiple Results," for details on processing multiple results.

- `ResultSet getResultSet()`

  returns the result set of the preceding query statement, or null if the preceding statement did not have a result set. Call this method only once per executed statement.

- `int getUpdateCount()`

  returns the number of rows affected by the preceding update statement, or -1 if the preceding statement was a statement without an update count. Call this method only once per executed statement.

- `void close()`

  closes this statement object and its associated result set.

- `boolean isClosed()` 6

  returns true if this statement is closed.

- `void closeOnCompletion()` 7

  causes this statement to be closed once all of its result sets have been closed.

---

**java.sql.ResultSet** 1.1

- `boolean next()`

  makes the current row in the result set move forward by one. Returns false after the last row. Note that you must call this method to advance to the first row.

- *Xxx* get*Xxx*`(int columnNumber)`
- *Xxx* get*Xxx*`(String columnLabel)`

  (*Xxx* is a type such as int, double, String, Date, etc.)

- `<T> T getObject(int columnNumber, Class<T> type)` 7
- `<T> T getObject(String columnLabel, Class<T> type)` 7

  returns the value of the column with the given column number or label, converted to the specified type. The column label is the label specified in the SQL AS clause or the column name if AS is not used.

*(Continues)*

---

**java.sql.ResultSet** 1.1 *(Continued)*

- int findColumn(String columnName)
  gives the column index associated with a column name.
- void close()
  immediately closes the current result set.
- boolean isClosed() 6
  returns true if this statement is closed.

---

## 4.4.1 Managing Connections, Statements, and Result Sets

Every Connection object can create one or more Statement objects. You can use the same Statement object for multiple, unrelated commands and queries. However, a statement has *at most one* open result set. If you issue multiple queries whose results you analyze concurrently, you need multiple Statement objects.

Be forewarned, though, that at least one commonly used database (Microsoft SQL Server) has a JDBC driver that allows only one active statement at a time. Use the getMaxStatements method of the DatabaseMetaData interface to find out the number of concurrently open statements that your JDBC driver supports.

This sounds restrictive, but in practice, you should probably not fuss with multiple concurrent result sets. If the result sets are related, you should be able to issue a combined query and analyze a single result. It is much more efficient to let the database combine queries than it is for a Java program to iterate through multiple result sets.

When you are done using a ResultSet, Statement, or Connection, you should call the close method immediately. These objects use large data structures and finite resources on the database server.

The close method of a Statement object automatically closes the associated result set if the statement has an open result set. Similarly, the close method of the Connection class closes all statements of the connection.

Conversely, as of Java SE 7, you can call the closeOnCompletion method on a Statement, and it will close automatically as soon as all its result sets have closed.

If your connections are short-lived, you don't have to worry about closing statements and result sets. To make absolutely sure that a connection object cannot possibly remain open, use a try-with-resources statement:

```
try (Connection conn = . . .)
{
    Statement stat = conn.createStatement();
    ResultSet result = stat.executeQuery(queryString);
    process query result
}
```

**TIP:** Use the try-with-resources block just to close the connection, and use a separate try/catch block to handle exceptions. Separating the try blocks makes your code easier to read and maintain.

## 4.4.2 Analyzing SQL Exceptions

Each SQLException has a chain of SQLException objects that are retrieved with the getNextException method. This exception chain is in addition to the "cause" chain of Throwable objects that every exception has. (See Volume I, Chapter 11 for details about Java exceptions.) One would need two nested loops to fully enumerate all these exceptions. Fortunately, Java SE 6 enhanced the SQLException class to implement the Iterable<Throwable> interface. The iterator() method yields an Iterator<Throwable> that iterates through both chains: starts by going through the cause chain of the first SQLException, then moves on to the next SQLException, and so on. You can simply use an enhanced for loop:

```
for (Throwable t : sqlException)
{
    do something with t
}
```

You can call getSQLState and getErrorCode on an SQLException to analyze it further. The first method yields a string that is standardized by either X/Open or SQL:2003. (Call the getSQLStateType method of the DatabaseMetaData interface to find out which standard is used by your driver.) The error code is vendor-specific.

The SQL exceptions are organized into an inheritance tree (shown in Figure 4.5). This allows you to catch specific error types in a vendor-independent way.

In addition, the database driver can report nonfatal conditions as warnings. You can retrieve warnings from connections, statements, and result sets. The SQLWarning class is a subclass of SQLException (even though a SQLWarning is not thrown as an exception). Call getSQLState and getErrorCode to get further information about the warnings. Similar to SQL exceptions, warnings are chained. To retrieve all warnings, use this loop:

```
SQLWarning w = stat.getWarning();
while (w != null)
```

```
{
    do something with w
    w = w.nextWarning();
}
```

The DataTruncation subclass of SQLWarning is used when data are read from the database and unexpectedly truncated. If data truncation happens in an update statement, a DataTruncation is thrown as an exception.

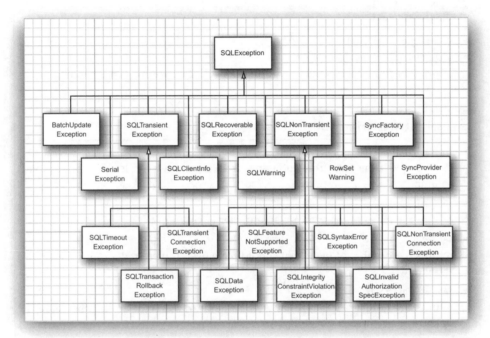

**Figure 4.5** SQL exception types

---

**java.sql.SQLException** 1.1

- SQLException getNextException()
  gets the next SQL exception chained to this one, or null at the end of the chain.

- Iterator<Throwable> iterator() 6
  gets an iterator that yields the chained SQL exceptions and their causes.

- String getSQLState()
  gets the "SQL state," a standardized error code.

- int getErrorCode()
  gets the vendor-specific error code.

---

**java.sql.SQLWarning** 1.1

- SQLWarning getNextWarning()
  returns the next warning chained to this one, or null at the end of the chain.

---

**java.sql.Connection** 1.1
**java.sql.Statement** 1.1
**java.sql.ResultSet** 1.1

- QLWarning getWarnings()
- SQLWarning getWarnings()
  returns the first of the pending warnings, or null if no warnings are pending.

---

**java.sql.DataTruncation** 1.1

- boolean getParameter()
  returns true if the data truncation applies to a parameter, false if it applies to a column.
- int getIndex()
  returns the index of the truncated parameter or column.
- int getDataSize()
  returns the number of bytes that should have been transferred, or -1 if the value is unknown.
- int getTransferSize()
  returns the number of bytes that were actually transferred, or -1 if the value is unknown.

## 4.4.3 Populating a Database

We now want to write our first real JDBC program. Of course, it would be nice if we could execute some of the fancy queries that we discussed earlier. Unfortunately, we have a problem: Right now, there are no data in the database. We need to populate the database, and there is a simple way of doing that with a set of SQL instructions to create tables and insert data into them. Most database programs can process a set of SQL instructions from a text file, but there are pesky differences about statement terminators and other syntactical issues.

For that reason, we will use JDBC to create a simple program that reads a file with SQL instructions, one instruction per line, and executes them.

Specifically, the program reads data from a text file in a format such as

```
CREATE TABLE Publishers (Publisher_Id CHAR(6), Name CHAR(30), URL CHAR(80));
INSERT INTO Publishers VALUES ('0201', 'Addison-Wesley', 'www.aw-bc.com');
INSERT INTO Publishers VALUES ('0471', 'John Wiley & Sons', 'www.wiley.com');
. . .
```

Listing 4.2 contains the code for the program that reads the SQL statement file and executes the statements. It is not important that you read through the code; we merely provide the program so that you can populate your database and run the examples in the remainder of this chapter.

Make sure that your database server is running, and run the program as follows:

```
java -classpath driverPath:. exec.ExecSQL Books.sql
java -classpath driverPath:. exec.ExecSQL Authors.sql
java -classpath driverPath:. exec.ExecSQL Publishers.sql
java -classpath driverPath:. exec.ExecSQL BooksAuthors.sql
```

Before running the program, check that the file database.properties is set up properly for your environment (see Section 4.3.5, "Connecting to the Database," on p. 249).

---

 **NOTE:** Your database may also have a utility to read the SQL files directly. For example, with Derby, you can run

```
java -jar derby/lib/derbyrun.jar ij -p ij.properties Books.sql
```

(The ij.properties file is described in Section 4.3.3, "Starting the Database," on p. 247.)

In the data format for the ExecSQL command, we allow an optional semicolon at the end of each line because most database utilities expect this format.

---

The following steps briefly describe the ExecSQL program:

1. Connect to the database. The getConnection method reads the properties in the file database.properties and adds the jdbc.drivers property to the system properties. The driver manager uses the jdbc.drivers property to load the appropriate database driver. The getConnection method uses the jdbc.url, jdbc.username, and jdbc.password properties to open the database connection.

2. Open the file with the SQL statements. If no file name was supplied, prompt the user to enter the statements on the console.

3. Execute each statement with the generic execute method. If it returns true, the statement had a result set. The four SQL files that we provide for the book database all end in a SELECT * statement so that you can see that the data were successfully inserted.

4. If there was a result set, print out the result. Since this is a generic result set, we need to use metadata to find out how many columns the result has. For more information, see Section 4.8, "Metadata," on p. 286.

5. If there is any SQL exception, print the exception and any chained exceptions that may be contained in it.

6. Close the connection to the database.

Listing 4.2 shows the code for the program.

**Listing 4.2** exec/ExecSQL.java

```java
1  package exec;
2
3  import java.io.*;
4  import java.nio.file.*;
5  import java.util.*;
6  import java.sql.*;
7
8  /**
9   * Executes all SQL statements in a file. Call this program as <br>
10  * java -classpath driverPath:. ExecSQL commandFile
11  * @version 1.31 2012-06-05
12  * @author Cay Horstmann
13  */
14 class ExecSQL
15 {
16    public static void main(String args[]) throws IOException
17    {
18       try
19       {
20          Scanner in = args.length == 0 ? new Scanner(System.in) : new Scanner(Paths.get(args[0]));
21
22          try (Connection conn = getConnection())
23          {
24             Statement stat = conn.createStatement();
25
26             while (true)
27             {
28                if (args.length == 0) System.out.println("Enter command or EXIT to exit:");
29
30                if (!in.hasNextLine()) return;
31
32                String line = in.nextLine();
33                if (line.equalsIgnoreCase("EXIT")) return;
34                if (line.trim().endsWith(";")) // remove trailing semicolon
35                {
36                   line = line.trim();
```

```
37              line = line.substring(0, line.length() - 1);
38          }
39          try
40          {
41              boolean isResult = stat.execute(line);
42              if (isResult)
43              {
44                  ResultSet rs = stat.getResultSet();
45                  showResultSet(rs);
46              }
47              else
48              {
49                  int updateCount = stat.getUpdateCount();
50                  System.out.println(updateCount + " rows updated");
51              }
52          }
53          catch (SQLException ex)
54          {
55              for (Throwable e : ex)
56                  e.printStackTrace();
57          }
58      }
59  }
60  }
61  catch (SQLException e)
62  {
63      for (Throwable t : e)
64          t.printStackTrace();
65  }
66  }
67
68  /**
69   * Gets a connection from the properties specified in the file database.properties.
70   * @return the database connection
71   */
72  public static Connection getConnection() throws SQLException, IOException
73  {
74      Properties props = new Properties();
75      try (InputStream in = Files.newInputStream(Paths.get("database.properties")))
76      {
77          props.load(in);
78      }
79
80      String drivers = props.getProperty("jdbc.drivers");
81      if (drivers != null) System.setProperty("jdbc.drivers", drivers);
82
83      String url = props.getProperty("jdbc.url");
84      String username = props.getProperty("jdbc.username");
```

*(Continues)*

---

**Listing 4.2** *(Continued)*

```
85        String password = props.getProperty("jdbc.password");
86
87        return DriverManager.getConnection(url, username, password);
88    }
89
90    /**
91     * Prints a result set.
92     * @param result the result set to be printed
93     */
94    public static void showResultSet(ResultSet result) throws SQLException
95    {
96        ResultSetMetaData metaData = result.getMetaData();
97        int columnCount = metaData.getColumnCount();
98
99        for (int i = 1; i <= columnCount; i++)
100       {
101           if (i > 1) System.out.print(", ");
102           System.out.print(metaData.getColumnLabel(i));
103       }
104       System.out.println();
105
106       while (result.next())
107       {
108           for (int i = 1; i <= columnCount; i++)
109           {
110               if (i > 1) System.out.print(", ");
111               System.out.print(result.getString(i));
112           }
113           System.out.println();
114       }
115   }
116 }
```

---

## 4.5 Query Execution

In this section, we write a program that executes queries against the COREJAVA database. For this program to work, you must have populated the COREJAVA database with tables, as described in the preceding section.

When querying the database, you can select the author and the publisher or leave either of them as Any.

You can also change the data in the database. Select a publisher and type an amount. All prices of that publisher are adjusted by the amount you entered, and the program displays how many rows were changed. After a price change, you might want to run a query to verify the new prices.

## 4.5.1 Prepared Statements

In this program, we use one new feature, *prepared statements*. Consider the query for all books by a particular publisher, independent of the author. The SQL query is

```
SELECT Books.Price, Books.Title
FROM Books, Publishers
WHERE Books.Publisher_Id = Publishers.Publisher_Id
AND Publishers.Name = the name from the list box
```

Instead of building a separate query statement every time the user launches such a query, we can *prepare* a query with a host variable and use it many times, each time filling in a different string for the variable. That technique benefits performance. Whenever the database executes a query, it first computes a strategy of how to do it efficiently. By preparing the query and reusing it, you ensure that the planning step is done only once.

Each host variable in a prepared query is indicated with a ?. If there is more than one variable, you must keep track of the positions of the ? when setting the values. For example, our prepared query becomes

```
String publisherQuery =
   "SELECT Books.Price, Books.Title" +
   " FROM Books, Publishers" +
   " WHERE Books.Publisher_Id = Publishers.Publisher_Id AND Publishers.Name = ?";
PreparedStatement stat = conn.prepareStatement(publisherQuery);
```

Before executing the prepared statement, you must bind the host variables to actual values with a set method. As with the get methods of the ResultSet interface, there are different set methods for the various types. Here, we want to set a string to a publisher name.

```
stat.setString(1, publisher);
```

The first argument is the position number of the host variable that we want to set. The position 1 denotes the first ?. The second argument is the value that we want to assign to the host variable.

If you reuse a prepared query that you have already executed, all host variables stay bound unless you change them with a set method or call the clearParameters method. That means you only need to call a setXxx method on those host variables that change from one query to the next.

Once all variables have been bound to values, you can execute the prepared statement:

```
ResultSet rs = stat.executeQuery();
```

 **TIP:** Building a query manually, by concatenating strings, is tedious and potentially dangerous. You have to worry about special characters such as quotes, and, if your query involves user input, you have to guard against injection attacks. Therefore, you should use prepared statements whenever your query involves variables.

The price update feature is implemented as an UPDATE statement. Note that we call executeUpdate, not executeQuery, because the UPDATE statement does not return a result set. The return value of executeUpdate is the count of changed rows.

```
int r = stat.executeUpdate();
System.out.println(r + " rows updated");
```

 **NOTE:** A PreparedStatement object becomes invalid after the associated Connection object is closed. However, many databases automatically *cache* prepared statements. If the same query is prepared twice, the database simply reuses the query strategy. Therefore, don't worry about the overhead of calling prepareStatement.

The following list briefly describes the structure of the example program.

- The author and publisher array lists are populated by running two queries that return all author and publisher names in the database.

- The queries involving authors are complex. A book can have multiple authors, so the BooksAuthors table stores the correspondence between authors and books. For example, the book with ISBN 0-201-96426-0 has two authors with codes DATE and DARW. The BooksAuthors table has the rows

```
0-201-96426-0, DATE, 1
0-201-96426-0, DARW, 2
```

to indicate this fact. The third column lists the order of the authors. (We can't just use the position of the rows in the table. There is no fixed row ordering in a relational table.) Thus, the query has to join the Books, BooksAuthors, and Authors tables to compare the author name with the one selected by the user.

```
SELECT Books.Price, Books.Title FROM Books, BooksAuthors, Authors, Publishers
WHERE Authors.Author_Id = BooksAuthors.Author_Id AND BooksAuthors.ISBN = Books.ISBN
AND Books.Publisher_Id = Publishers.Publisher_Id AND Authors.Name = ? AND Publishers.Name = ?
```

**TIP:** Some Java programmers avoid complex SQL statements such as this one. A surprisingly common, but very inefficient, workaround is to write lots of Java code that iterates through multiple result sets. But the database is *a lot* better at executing query code than a Java program can be—that's the core competency of a database. A rule of thumb: If you can do it in SQL, don't do it in Java.

- The `changePrices` method executes an UPDATE statement. Note that the WHERE clause of the UPDATE statement needs the publisher *code* and we know only the publisher *name*. This problem is solved with a nested subquery:

```
UPDATE Books
SET Price = Price + ?
WHERE Books.Publisher_Id = (SELECT Publisher_Id FROM Publishers WHERE Name = ?)
```

Listing 4.3 is the complete program code.

**Listing 4.3** query/QueryTest.java

```java
1  package query;
2
3  import java.io.*;
4  import java.nio.file.*;
5  import java.sql.*;
6  import java.util.*;
7
8  /**
9   * This program demonstrates several complex database queries.
10  * @version 1.30 2012-06-05
11  * @author Cay Horstmann
12  */
13 public class QueryTest
14 {
15    private static final String allQuery = "SELECT Books.Price, Books.Title FROM Books";
16
17    private static final String authorPublisherQuery = "SELECT Books.Price, Books.Title"
18       + " FROM Books, BooksAuthors, Authors, Publishers"
19       + " WHERE Authors.Author_Id = BooksAuthors.Author_Id AND BooksAuthors.ISBN = Books.ISBN"
20       + " AND Books.Publisher_Id = Publishers.Publisher_Id AND Authors.Name = ?"
21       + " AND Publishers.Name = ?";
22
23    private static final String authorQuery =
24       "SELECT Books.Price, Books.Title FROM Books, BooksAuthors, Authors"
25       + " WHERE Authors.Author_Id = BooksAuthors.Author_Id AND BooksAuthors.ISBN = Books.ISBN"
26       + " AND Authors.Name = ?";
```

*(Continues)*

**Listing 4.3** *(Continued)*

```java
27  private static final String publisherQuery =
28      "SELECT Books.Price, Books.Title FROM Books, Publishers"
29      + " WHERE Books.Publisher_Id = Publishers.Publisher_Id AND Publishers.Name = ?";
30
31  private static final String priceUpdate = "UPDATE Books " + "SET Price = Price + ? "
32      + " WHERE Books.Publisher_Id = (SELECT Publisher_Id FROM Publishers WHERE Name = ?)";
33
34  private static Scanner in;
35  private static Connection conn;
36  private static ArrayList<String> authors = new ArrayList<>();
37  private static ArrayList<String> publishers = new ArrayList<>();
38
39  public static void main(String[] args) throws IOException
40  {
41      try
42      {
43          conn = getConnection();
44          in = new Scanner(System.in);
45          authors.add("Any");
46          publishers.add("Any");
47          try (Statement stat = conn.createStatement())
48          {
49              // Fill the authors array list
50              String query = "SELECT Name FROM Authors";
51              try (ResultSet rs = stat.executeQuery(query))
52              {
53                  while (rs.next())
54                      authors.add(rs.getString(1));
55              }
56              // Fill the publishers array list
57              query = "SELECT Name FROM Publishers";
58              try (ResultSet rs = stat.executeQuery(query))
59              {
60                  while (rs.next())
61                      publishers.add(rs.getString(1));
62              }
63          }
64          boolean done = false;
65          while (!done)
66          {
67              System.out.print("Q)uery C)hange prices E)xit: ");
68              String input = in.next().toUpperCase();
69              if (input.equals("Q"))
70                  executeQuery();
71              else if (input.equals("C"))
72                  changePrices();
```

```
73            else
74                done = true;
75        }
76    }
77    catch (SQLException e)
78    {
79        for (Throwable t : e)
80            System.out.println(t.getMessage());
81    }
82 }
83
84 /**
85  * Executes the selected query.
86  */
87 private static void executeQuery() throws SQLException
88 {
89    String author = select("Authors:", authors);
90    String publisher = select("Publishers:", publishers);
91    PreparedStatement stat;
92    if (!author.equals("Any") && !publisher.equals("Any"))
93    {
94        stat = conn.prepareStatement(authorPublisherQuery);
95        stat.setString(1, author);
96        stat.setString(2, publisher);
97    }
98    else if (!author.equals("Any") && publisher.equals("Any"))
99    {
100        stat = conn.prepareStatement(authorQuery);
101        stat.setString(1, author);
102    }
103    else if (author.equals("Any") && !publisher.equals("Any"))
104    {
105        stat = conn.prepareStatement(publisherQuery);
106        stat.setString(1, publisher);
107    }
108    else
109        stat = conn.prepareStatement(allQuery);
110
111    try (ResultSet rs = stat.executeQuery())
112    {
113        while (rs.next())
114            System.out.println(rs.getString(1) + ", " + rs.getString(2));
115    }
116 }
117
118 /**
119  * Executes an update statement to change prices.
120  */
```

*(Continues)*

**Listing 4.3** *(Continued)*

```java
121  public static void changePrices() throws SQLException
122  {
123     String publisher = select("Publishers:", publishers.subList(1, publishers.size()));
124     System.out.print("Change prices by: ");
125     double priceChange = in.nextDouble();
126     PreparedStatement stat = conn.prepareStatement(priceUpdate);
127     stat.setDouble(1, priceChange);
128     stat.setString(2, publisher);
129     int r = stat.executeUpdate();
130     System.out.println(r + " records updated.");
131  }
132
133  /**
134   * Asks the user to select a string.
135   * @param prompt the prompt to display
136   * @param options the options from which the user can choose
137   * @return the option that the user chose
138   */
139  public static String select(String prompt, List<String> options)
140  {
141     while (true)
142     {
143        System.out.println(prompt);
144        for (int i = 0; i < options.size(); i++)
145           System.out.printf("%2d) %s%n", i + 1, options.get(i));
146        int sel = in.nextInt();
147        if (sel > 0 && sel <= options.size())
148           return options.get(sel - 1);
149     }
150  }
151
152  /**
153   * Gets a connection from the properties specified in the file database.properties.
154   * @return the database connection
155   */
156  public static Connection getConnection() throws SQLException, IOException
157  {
158     Properties props = new Properties();
159     try (InputStream in = Files.newInputStream(Paths.get("database.properties")))
160     {
161        props.load(in);
162     }
163
164     String drivers = props.getProperty("jdbc.drivers");
165     if (drivers != null) System.setProperty("jdbc.drivers", drivers);
166     String url = props.getProperty("jdbc.url");
```

```
167     String username = props.getProperty("jdbc.username");
168     String password = props.getProperty("jdbc.password");
169
170     return DriverManager.getConnection(url, username, password);
171   }
172 }
```

---

**java.sql.Connection  1.1**

- PreparedStatement prepareStatement(String sql)

  returns a PreparedStatement object containing the precompiled statement. The string sql contains a SQL statement that can contain one or more parameter placeholders denoted by ? characters.

---

**java.sql.PreparedStatement  1.1**

- void setXxx(int n, Xxx x)

  (Xxx is a type such as int, double, String, Date, etc.)

  sets the value of the nth parameter to x.

- void clearParameters()

  clears all current parameters in the prepared statement.

- ResultSet executeQuery()

  executes a prepared SQL query and returns a ResultSet object.

- int executeUpdate()

  executes the prepared SQL INSERT, UPDATE, or DELETE statement represented by the PreparedStatement object. Returns the number of rows affected, or 0 for DDL statements such as CREATE TABLE.

## 4.5.2 Reading and Writing LOBs

In addition to numbers, strings, and dates, many databases can store *large objects* (LOBs) such as images or other data. In SQL, binary large objects are called BLOBs, and character large objects are called CLOBs.

To read a LOB, execute a SELECT statement and call the getBlob or getClob method on the ResultSet. You will get an object of type Blob or Clob. To get the binary data from a Blob, call the getBytes or getBinaryStream. For example, if you have a table with book cover images, you can retrieve an image like this:

```
PreparedStatement stat = conn.prepareStatement("SELECT Cover FROM BookCovers WHERE ISBN=?");
stat.set(1, isbn);
ResultSet result = stat.executeQuery();
```

```
if (result.next())
{
   Blob coverBlob = result.getBlob(1);
   Image coverImage = ImageIO.read(coverBlob.getBinaryStream());
}
```

Similarly, if you retrieve a `Clob` object, you can get character data by calling the `getSubString` or `getCharacterStream` method.

To place a LOB into a database, call `createBlob` or `createClob` on your `Connection` object, get an output stream or writer to the LOB, write the data, and store the object in the database. For example, here is how you store an image:

```
Blob coverBlob = connection.createBlob();
int offset = 0;
OutputStream out = coverBlob.setBinaryStream(offset);
ImageIO.write(coverImage, "PNG", out);
PreparedStatement stat = conn.prepareStatement("INSERT INTO Cover VALUES (?, ?)");
stat.set(1, isbn);
stat.set(2, coverBlob);
stat.executeUpdate();
```

---

***java.sql.ResultSet*** 1.1

- `Blob getBlob(int columnIndex)` 1.2
- `Blob getBlob(String columnLabel)` 1.2
- `Clob getClob(int columnIndex)` 1.2
- `Clob getClob(String columnLabel)` 1.2
  gets the BLOB or CLOB at the given column.

---

***java.sql.Blob*** 1.2

- `long length()`
  gets the length of this BLOB.
- `byte[] getBytes(long startPosition, long length)`
  gets the data in the given range from this BLOB.
- `InputStream getBinaryStream()`
- `InputStream getBinaryStream(long startPosition, long length)`
  returns a stream to read the data from this BLOB or from the given range.
- `OutputStream setBinaryStream(long startPosition)` 1.4
  returns an output stream for writing into this BLOB, starting at the given position.

---

**java.sql.Clob** 1.4

- `long length()`
  gets the number of characters of this CLOB.
- `String getSubString(long startPosition, long length)`
  gets the characters in the given range from this BLOB.
- `Reader getCharacterStream()`
- `Reader getCharacterStream(long startPosition, long length)`
  returns a reader (not a stream) to read the characters from this CLOB or from the given range.
- `Writer setCharacterStream(long startPosition)` 1.4
  returns a writer (not a stream) for writing into this CLOB, starting at the given position.

---

**java.sql.Connection** 1.1

- `Blob createBlob()` 6
- `Clob createClob()` 6
  creates an empty BLOB or CLOB.

---

## 4.5.3 SQL Escapes

The "escape" syntax supports features that are commonly supported by databases but use database-specific syntax variations. It is the job of the JDBC driver to translate the escape syntax to the syntax of a particular database.

Escapes are provided for the following features:

- Date and time literals
- Calling scalar functions
- Calling stored procedures
- Outer joins
- The escape character in LIKE clauses

Date and time literals vary widely among databases. To embed a date or time literal, specify the value in ISO 8601 format (www.cl.cam.ac.uk/~mgk25/iso-time.html). The driver will then translate it into the native format. Use d, t, ts for DATE, TIME, or TIMESTAMP values:

```
{d '2008-01-24'}
{t '23:59:59'}
{ts '2008-01-24 23:59:59.999'}
```

A *scalar function* is a function that returns a single value. Many functions are widely available in databases, but with varying names. The JDBC specification provides standard names and translates them into the database-specific names. To call a function, embed the standard function name and arguments like this:

```
{fn left(?, 20)}
{fn user()}
```

You can find a complete list of supported function names in the JDBC specification.

A *stored procedure* is a procedure that executes in the database, written in a database-specific language. To call a stored procedure, use the call escape. You need not supply parentheses if the procedure has no parameters. Use = to capture a return value:

```
{call PROC1(?, ?)}
{call PROC2}
{call ? = PROC3(?)}
```

An *outer join* of two tables does not require that the rows of each table match according to the join condition. For example, the query

```
SELECT * FROM {oj Books LEFT OUTER JOIN Publishers ON Books.Publisher_Id = Publisher.Publisher_Id}
```

contains books for which Publisher_Id has no match in the Publishers table, with NULL values to indicate that no match exists. You would need a RIGHT OUTER JOIN to include publishers without matching books, or a FULL OUTER JOIN to return both. The escape syntax is needed because not all databases use a standard notation for these joins.

Finally, the _ and % characters have special meanings in a LIKE clause—to match a single character or a sequence of characters. There is no standard way to use them literally. If you want to match all strings containing a _, use this construct:

```
... WHERE ? LIKE %!_% {escape '!'}
```

Here we define ! as the escape character. The combination !_ denotes a literal underscore.

## 4.5.4 Multiple Results

It is possible for a query to return multiple results. This can happen when executing a stored procedure, or with databases that also allow submission of multiple SELECT statements in a single query. Here is how you retrieve all result sets.

1. Use the execute method to execute the SQL statement.
2. Retrieve the first result or update count.
3. Repeatedly call the getMoreResults method to move on to the next result set.
4. Finish when there are no more result sets or update counts.

The execute and getMoreResults methods return true if the next item in the chain is a result set. The getUpdateCount method returns -1 if the next item in the chain is not an update count.

The following loop traverses all results:

```
boolean isResult = stat.execute(command);
boolean done = false;
while (!done)
{
   if (isResult)
   {
      ResultSet result = stat.getResultSet();
      do something with result
   }
   else
   {
      int updateCount = stat.getUpdateCount();
      if (updateCount >= 0)
         do something with updateCount
      else
         done = true;
   }
   if (!done) isResult = stat.getMoreResults();
}
```

---

**java.sql.Statement** 1.1

- boolean getMoreResults()
- boolean getMoreResults(int current) 6

  gets the next result for this statement. The current parameter is one of CLOSE_CURRENT_RESULT (default), KEEP_CURRENT_RESULT, or CLOSE_ALL_RESULTS. Returns true if the next result exists and is a result set.

---

## 4.5.5 Retrieving Autogenerated Keys

Most databases support some mechanism for autonumbering rows in a database. Unfortunately, the mechanisms differ widely among vendors. These automatic numbers are often used as primary keys. Although JDBC doesn't offer a vendor-independent solution for generating keys, it does provide an efficient way of retrieving them. When you insert a new row into a table and a key is automatically generated, you can retrieve it with the following code:

```
stmt.executeUpdate(insertStatement, Statement.RETURN_GENERATED_KEYS);
ResultSet rs = stmt.getGeneratedKeys();
if (rs.next())
{
   int key = rs.getInt(1);
   . . .
}
```

---

**_java.sql.Statement_** 1.1

- `boolean execute(String statement, int autogenerated)` **1.4**
- `int executeUpdate(String statement, int autogenerated)` **1.4**

  executes the given SQL statement, as previously described. If `autogenerated` is set to `Statement.RETURN_GENERATED_KEYS` and the statement is an `INSERT` statement, the first column contains the autogenerated key.

---

## 4.6 Scrollable and Updatable Result Sets

As you have seen, the `next` method of the `ResultSet` interface iterates over the rows in a result set. That is certainly adequate for a program that needs to analyze the data. However, consider a visual data display that shows a table or query results (such as Figure 4.4 on p. 242). You usually want the user to be able to move both forward and backward in the result set. In a *scrollable* result, you can move forward and backward through a result set and even jump to any position.

Furthermore, once users see the contents of a result set displayed, they may be tempted to edit it. In an *updatable* result set, you can programmatically update entries so that the database is automatically updated. We discuss these capabilities in the following sections.

### 4.6.1 Scrollable Result Sets

By default, result sets are not scrollable or updatable. To obtain scrollable result sets from your queries, you must obtain a different `Statement` object with the method

```
Statement stat = conn.createStatement(type, concurrency);
```

For a prepared statement, use the call

```
PreparedStatement stat = conn.prepareStatement(command, type, concurrency);
```

The possible values of type and concurrency are listed in Tables 4.6 and 4.7. You have the following choices:

- Do you want the result set to be scrollable? If not, use ResultSet.TYPE_FORWARD_ONLY.
- If the result set is scrollable, do you want it to be able to reflect changes in the database that occurred after the query that yielded it? (In our discussion, we assume the ResultSet.TYPE_SCROLL_INSENSITIVE setting for scrollable result sets. This assumes that the result set does not "sense" database changes that occurred after execution of the query.)
- Do you want to be able to update the database by editing the result set? (See the next section for details.)

For example, if you simply want to be able to scroll through a result set but don't want to edit its data, use:

```
Statement stat = conn.createStatement(
    ResultSet.TYPE_SCROLL_INSENSITIVE, ResultSet.CONCUR_READ_ONLY);
```

All result sets that are returned by method calls

```
ResultSet rs = stat.executeQuery(query)
```

are now scrollable. A scrollable result set has a *cursor* that indicates the current position.

**Table 4.6** ResultSet Type Values

| Value | Explanation |
|---|---|
| TYPE_FORWARD_ONLY | The result set is not scrollable (default). |
| TYPE_SCROLL_INSENSITIVE | The result set is scrollable but not sensitive to database changes. |
| TYPE_SCROLL_SENSITIVE | The result set is scrollable and sensitive to database changes. |

**Table 4.7** ResultSet Concurrency Values

| Value | Explanation |
|---|---|
| CONCUR_READ_ONLY | The result set cannot be used to update the database (default). |
| CONCUR_UPDATABLE | The result set can be used to update the database. |

**NOTE:** Not all database drivers support scrollable or updatable result sets. (The `supportsResultSetType` and `supportsResultSetConcurrency` methods of the `DatabaseMetaData` interface will tell you which types and concurrency modes are supported by a particular database using a particular driver.) Even if a database supports all result set modes, a particular query might not be able to yield a result set with all the properties that you requested. (For example, the result set of a complex query might not be updatable.) In that case, the `executeQuery` method returns a `ResultSet` of lesser capabilities and adds an `SQLWarning` to the connection object. (Section 4.4.2, "Analyzing SQL Exceptions," on p. 256 shows how to retrieve the warning.) Alternatively, you can use the `getType` and `getConcurrency` methods of the `ResultSet` interface to find out what mode a result set actually has. If you do not check the result set capabilities and issue an unsupported operation, such as `previous` on a result set that is not scrollable, the operation will throw a `SQLException`.

Scrolling is very simple. Use

```
if (rs.previous()) . . .
```

to scroll backward. The method returns `true` if the cursor is positioned on an actual row, or `false` if it is now positioned before the first row.

You can move the cursor backward or forward by a number of rows with the call

```
rs.relative(n);
```

If $n$ is positive, the cursor moves forward. If $n$ is negative, it moves backward. If $n$ is zero, the call has no effect. If you attempt to move the cursor outside the current set of rows, it is set to point either after the last row or before the first row, depending on the sign of $n$. Then, the method returns `false` and the cursor does not move. The method returns `true` if the cursor is positioned on an actual row.

Alternatively, you can set the cursor to a particular row number:

```
rs.absolute(n);
```

To get the current row number, call

```
int currentRow = rs.getRow();
```

The first row in the result set has number 1. If the return value is 0, the cursor is not currently on a row—it is either before the first row or after the last row.

The convenience methods `first`, `last`, `beforeFirst`, and `afterLast` move the cursor to the first, to the last, before the first, or after the last position.

Finally, the methods isFirst, isLast, isBeforeFirst, and isAfterLast test whether the cursor is at one of these special positions.

Using a scrollable result set is very simple. The hard work of caching the query data is carried out behind the scenes by the database driver.

## 4.6.2  Updatable Result Sets

If you want to edit the result set data and have the changes automatically reflected in the database, create an updatable result set. Updatable result sets don't have to be scrollable, but if you present data to a user for editing, you usually want to allow scrolling as well.

To obtain updatable result sets, create a statement as follows:

```
Statement stat = conn.createStatement(
    ResultSet.TYPE_SCROLL_INSENSITIVE, ResultSet.CONCUR_UPDATABLE);
```

The result sets returned by a call to executeQuery are then updatable.

**NOTE:** Not all queries return updatable result sets. If your query is a join that involves multiple tables, the result might not be updatable. However, if your query involves only a single table or if it joins multiple tables by their primary keys, you should expect the result set to be updatable. Call the getConcurrency method of the ResultSet interface to find out for sure.

For example, suppose you want to raise the prices of some books, but you don't have a simple criterion for issuing an UPDATE statement. Then, you can iterate through all books and update prices, based on arbitrary conditions.

```
String query = "SELECT * FROM Books";
ResultSet rs = stat.executeQuery(query);
while (rs.next())
{
   if (. . .)
   {
      double increase = . . .
      double price = rs.getDouble("Price");
      rs.updateDouble("Price", price + increase);
      rs.updateRow(); // make sure to call updateRow after updating fields
   }
}
```

There are updateXxx methods for all data types that correspond to SQL types, such as updateDouble, updateString, and so on; specify the name or the number of the column (as with the getXxx methods), then the new value for the field.

**NOTE:** If you use the update*Xxx* method whose first parameter is the column number, be aware that this is the column number in the *result set*. It could well be different from the column number in the database.

The update*Xxx* method changes only the row values, not the database. When you are done with the field updates in a row, you must call the updateRow method. That method sends all updates in the current row to the database. If you move the cursor to another row without calling updateRow, this row's updates are discarded from the row set and never communicated to the database. You can also call the cancelRowUpdates method to cancel the updates to the current row.

The preceding example shows how to modify an existing row. If you want to add a new row to the database, first use the moveToInsertRow method to move the cursor to a special position, called the *insert row*. Then, build up a new row in the insert row position by issuing update*Xxx* instructions. When you are done, call the insertRow method to deliver the new row to the database. When you are done inserting, call moveToCurrentRow to move the cursor back to the position before the call to moveToInsertRow. Here is an example:

```
rs.moveToInsertRow();
rs.updateString("Title", title);
rs.updateString("ISBN", isbn);
rs.updateString("Publisher_Id", pubid);
rs.updateDouble("Price", price);
rs.insertRow();
rs.moveToCurrentRow();
```

Note that you cannot influence *where* the new data is added in the result set or the database.

If you don't specify a column value in the insert row, it is set to a SQL NULL. However, if the column has a NOT NULL constraint, an exception is thrown and the row is not inserted.

Finally, you can delete the row under the cursor:

```
rs.deleteRow();
```

The deleteRow method immediately removes the row from both the result set and the database.

The updateRow, insertRow, and deleteRow methods of the ResultSet interface give you the same power as executing UPDATE, INSERT, and DELETE SQL statements. However, Java programmers might find it more natural to manipulate the database contents through result sets than by constructing SQL statements.

**CAUTION:** If you are not careful, you can write staggeringly inefficient code with updatable result sets. It is *much* more efficient to execute an UPDATE statement than to make a query and iterate through the result, changing data along the way. Updatable result sets make sense for interactive programs in which a user can make arbitrary changes, but for most programmatic changes, a SQL UPDATE is more appropriate.

 **NOTE:** JDBC 2 delivered further enhancements to result sets, such as the capability of updating a result set with the most recent data if the data have been modified by another concurrent database connection. JDBC 3 added yet another refinement, specifying the behavior of result sets when a transaction is committed. However, these advanced features are outside the scope of this introductory chapter. We refer you to the *JDBC™ API Tutorial and Reference, Third Edition*, by Maydene Fisher, Jon Ellis, and Jonathan Bruce (Addison-Wesley, 2003) and the JDBC specification documents at www.oracle.com/technetwork/java/javase/tech/index-jsp-136101.html for more information.

---

*java.sql.Connection* 1.1

---

- Statement createStatement(int type, int concurrency) **1.2**
- PreparedStatement prepareStatement(String command, int type, int concurrency) **1.2**
  creates a statement or prepared statement that yields result sets with the given type and concurrency.

  | *Parameters:* | command | The command to prepare |
  | --- | --- | --- |
  | | type | One of the constants TYPE_FORWARD_ONLY, TYPE_SCROLL_INSENSITIVE, or TYPE_SCROLL_SENSITIVE of the ResultSet interface |
  | | concurrency | One of the constants CONCUR_READ_ONLY or CONCUR_UPDATABLE of the ResultSet interface |

---

*java.sql.ResultSet* 1.1

---

- int getType() **1.2**
  returns the type of this result set—one of TYPE_FORWARD_ONLY, TYPE_SCROLL_INSENSITIVE, or TYPE_SCROLL_SENSITIVE.

*(Continues)*

---

*java.sql.ResultSet* **1.1** *(Continued)*

---

- `int getConcurrency()` **1.2**

  returns the concurrency setting of this result set—one of `CONCUR_READ_ONLY` or `CONCUR_UPDATABLE`.

- `boolean previous()` **1.2**

  moves the cursor to the preceding row. Returns `true` if the cursor is positioned on a row, or `false` if the cursor is positioned before the first row.

- `int getRow()` **1.2**

  gets the number of the current row. Rows are numbered starting with 1.

- `boolean absolute(int r)` **1.2**

  moves the cursor to row `r`. Returns `true` if the cursor is positioned on a row.

- `boolean relative(int d)` **1.2**

  moves the cursor by `d` rows. If `d` is negative, the cursor is moved backward. Returns `true` if the cursor is positioned on a row.

- `boolean first()` **1.2**
- `boolean last()` **1.2**

  moves the cursor to the first or last row. Returns `true` if the cursor is positioned on a row.

- `void beforeFirst()` **1.2**
- `void afterLast()` **1.2**

  moves the cursor before the first or after the last row.

- `boolean isFirst()` **1.2**
- `boolean isLast()` **1.2**

  tests whether the cursor is at the first or last row.

- `boolean isBeforeFirst()` **1.2**
- `boolean isAfterLast()` **1.2**

  tests whether the cursor is before the first or after the last row.

- `void moveToInsertRow()` **1.2**

  moves the cursor to the insert row. The insert row is a special row for inserting new data with the update*Xxx* and `insertRow` methods.

- `void moveToCurrentRow()` **1.2**

  moves the cursor back from the insert row to the row that it occupied when the `moveToInsertRow` method was called.

- `void insertRow()` **1.2**

  inserts the contents of the insert row into the database and the result set.

---

*(Continues)*

---

*java.sql.ResultSet*  1.1  *(Continued)*

- void deleteRow() **1.2**
  deletes the current row from the database and the result set.
- void update*Xxx*(int column, *Xxx* data) **1.2**
- void update*Xxx*(String columnName, *Xxx* data) **1.2**
  (*Xxx* is a type such as int, double, String, Date, etc.)

  updates a field in the current row of the result set.

- void updateRow() **1.2**
  sends the current row updates to the database.
- void cancelRowUpdates() **1.2**
  cancels the current row updates.

---

*java.sql.DatabaseMetaData*  1.1

- boolean supportsResultSetType(int type) **1.2**
  returns true if the database can support result sets of the given type; type is one of the constants TYPE_FORWARD_ONLY, TYPE_SCROLL_INSENSITIVE, or TYPE_SCROLL_SENSITIVE of the ResultSet interface.
- boolean supportsResultSetConcurrency(int type, int concurrency) **1.2**
  returns true if the database can support result sets of the given combination of type and concurrency.

  | *Parameters:* | type | One of the constants TYPE_FORWARD_ONLY, TYPE_SCROLL_INSENSITIVE, or TYPE_SCROLL_SENSITIVE of the ResultSet interface |
  | --- | --- | --- |
  | | concurrency | One of the constants CONCUR_READ_ONLY or CONCUR_UPDATABLE of the ResultSet interface |

# 4.7  Row Sets

Scrollable result sets are powerful, but they have a major drawback. You need to keep the database connection open during the entire user interaction. However, a user can walk away from the computer for a long time, leaving the connection occupied. That is not good—database connections are scarce resources. In this situation, use a *row set*. The RowSet interface extends the ResultSet interface, but row sets don't have to be tied to a database connection.

Row sets are also suitable if you need to move a query result to a different tier of a complex application, or to another device such as a cell phone. You would never want to move a result set—its data structures can be huge, and it is tethered to the database connection.

## 4.7.1 Constructing Row Sets

The `javax.sql.rowset` package provides the following interfaces that extend the `RowSet` interface:

- A `CachedRowSet` allows disconnected operation. We will discuss cached row sets in the following section.

- A `WebRowSet` is a cached row set that can be saved to an XML file. The XML file can be moved to another tier of a web application where it is opened by another `WebRowSet` object.

- The `FilteredRowSet` and `JoinRowSet` interfaces support lightweight operations on row sets that are equivalent to SQL `SELECT` and `JOIN` operations. These operations are carried out on the data stored in row sets, without having to make a database connection.

- A `JdbcRowSet` is a thin wrapper around a `ResultSet`. It adds useful getters and setters from the `RowSet` interface, turning a result set into a "bean." (See Chapter 8 for more information on beans.)

As of Java 7, there is a standard way for obtaining a row set:

```
RowSetFactory factory = RowSetProvider.newFactory();
CachedRowSet crs = factory.createCachedRowSet();
```

There are similar methods for obtaining the other row set types.

Before Java 7, there were vendor-specific methods for creating row sets. In addition, the JDK supplies reference implementations in the package `com.sun.rowset`. The class names end in `Impl`, for example, `CachedRowSetImpl`. If you can't use the `RowSetProvider`, you can instead use those classes:

```
CachedRowSet crs = new com.sun.rowset.CachedRowSetImpl();
```

## 4.7.2 Cached Row Sets

A cached row set contains all data from a result set. Since `CachedRowSet` is a subinterface of the `ResultSet` interface, you can use a cached row set exactly as you would use a result set. Cached row sets confer an important benefit: You can close the connection and still use the row set. As you will see in our sample program in Listing 4.4, this greatly simplifies the implementation of interactive applications. Each user command simply opens the database connection, issues a query, puts the result in a cached row set, and then closes the database connection.

It is even possible to modify the data in a cached row set. Of course, the modifications are not immediately reflected in the database. Instead, you need to make an explicit request to accept the accumulated changes. The CachedRowSet then reconnects to the database and issues SQL statements to write the accumulated changes.

You can populate a CachedRowSet from a result set:

```
ResultSet result = . . .;
CachedRowSet crs = new com.sun.rowset.CachedRowSetImpl();
   // or use an implementation from your database vendor
crs.populate(result);
conn.close(); // now OK to close the database connection
```

Alternatively, you can let the CachedRowSet object establish a connection automatically. Set up the database parameters:

```
crs.setURL("jdbc:derby://localhost:1527/COREJAVA");
crs.setUsername("dbuser");
crs.setPassword("secret");
```

Then set the query statement and any parameters.

```
crs.setCommand("SELECT * FROM Books WHERE PUBLISHER = ?");
crs.setString(1, publisherName);
```

Finally, populate the row set with the query result:

```
crs.execute();
```

This call establishes a database connection, issues the query, populates the row set, and disconnects.

If your query result is very large, you would not want to put it into the row set in its entirety. After all, your users will probably only look at a few rows. In that case, specify a page size:

```
CachedRowSet crs = . . .;
crs.setCommand(command);
crs.setPageSize(20);
. . .
crs.execute();
```

Now you will only get 20 rows. To get the next batch of rows, call

```
crs.nextPage();
```

You can inspect and modify the row set with the same methods you use for result sets. If you modified the row set contents, you must write it back to the database by calling

```
crs.acceptChanges(conn);
```

or

```
crs.acceptChanges();
```

The second call works only if you configured the row set with the information required to connect to a database (such as URL, user name, and password).

In Section 4.6.2, "Updatable Result Sets," on p. 277, you saw that not all result sets are updatable. Similarly, a row set that contains the result of a complex query will not be able to write its changes back to the database. You should be safe if your row set contains data from a single table.

 **CAUTION:** If you populated the row set from a result set, the row set does not know the name of the table to update. You need to call setTableName to set the table name.

Another complexity arises if the data in the database have changed after you populated the row set. This is clearly a sign of trouble that could lead to inconsistent data. The reference implementation checks whether the original row set values (that is, the values before editing) are identical to the current values in the database. If so, they are replaced with the edited values; otherwise, a SyncProviderException is thrown and none of the changes are written. Other implementations may use other strategies for synchronization.

---

**javax.sql.RowSet** 1.4

- String getURL()
- void setURL(String url)
  gets or sets the database URL.

- String getUsername()
- void setUsername(String username)
  gets or sets the user name for connecting to the database.

- String getPassword()
- void setPassword(String password)
  gets or sets the password for connecting to the database.

---

*(Continues)*

---

**javax.sql.RowSet** 1.4 *(Continued)*

- String getCommand()
- void setCommand(String command)

  gets or sets the command that is executed to populate this row set.

- void execute()

  populates this row set by issuing the statement set with setCommand. For the driver manager to obtain a connection, the URL, user name, and password must be set.

---

**javax.sql.rowset.CachedRowSet** 5.0

- void execute(Connection conn)

  populates this row set by issuing the statement set with setCommand. This method uses the given connection *and closes it.*

- void populate(ResultSet result)

  populates this cached row set with the data from the given result set.

- String getTableName()
- void setTableName(String tableName)

  gets or sets the name of the table from which this cached row set was populated.

- int getPageSize()
- void setPageSize(int size)

  gets or sets the page size.

- boolean nextPage()
- boolean previousPage()

  loads the next or previous page of rows. Returns true if there is a next or previous page.

- void acceptChanges()
- void acceptChanges(Connection conn)

  reconnects to the database and writes the changes that are the result of editing the row set. May throw a SyncProviderException if the data cannot be written back because the database data have changed.

---

**javax.sql.rowset.RowSetProvider** 7

- static RowSetFactory newFactory()

  creates a row set factory.

---

*javax.sql.rowset.RowSetFactory* 7

---

- CachedRowSet createCachedRowSet()
- FilteredRowSet createFilteredRowSet()
- JdbcRowSet createJdbcRowSet()
- JoinRowSet createJoinRowSet()
- WebRowSet createWebRowSet()

  creates a row set of the specified type.

---

## 4.8 Metadata

In the preceding sections, you saw how to populate, query, and update database tables. However, JDBC can give you additional information about the *structure* of a database and its tables. For example, you can get a list of the tables in a particular database or the column names and types of a table. This information is not useful when you are implementing a business application with a predefined database. After all, if you design the tables, you know their structure. Structural information is, however, extremely useful for programmers who write tools that work with any database.

In SQL, data that describe the database or one of its parts are called *metadata* (to distinguish them from the actual data stored in the database). You can get three kinds of metadata: about a database, about a result set, and about parameters of prepared statements.

To find out more about the database, request an object of type DatabaseMetaData from the database connection.

```
DatabaseMetaData meta = conn.getMetaData();
```

Now you are ready to get some metadata. For example, the call

```
ResultSet mrs = meta.getTables(null, null, null, new String[] { "TABLE" });
```

returns a result set that contains information about all tables in the database. (See the API note at the end of this section for other parameters to this method.)

Each row in the result set contains information about a table in the database. The third column is the name of the table. (Again, see the API note for the other columns.) The following loop gathers all table names:

```
while (mrs.next())
    tableNames.addItem(mrs.getString(3));
```

There is a second important use for database metadata. Databases are complex, and the SQL standard leaves plenty of room for variability. Well over a hundred methods in the DatabaseMetaData interface can inquire about the database, including calls with such exotic names as

```
meta.supportsCatalogsInPrivilegeDefinitions()
```

and

```
meta.nullPlusNonNullIsNull()
```

Clearly, these are geared toward advanced users with special needs—in particular, those who need to write highly portable code that works with multiple databases.

The DatabaseMetaData interface gives data about the database. A second metadata interface, ResultSetMetaData, reports information about a result set. Whenever you have a result set from a query, you can inquire about the number of columns and each column's name, type, and field width. Here is a typical loop:

```
ResultSet mrs = stat.executeQuery("SELECT * FROM " + tableName);
ResultSetMetaData meta = mrs.getMetaData();
for (int i = 1; i <= meta.getColumnCount(); i++)
{
   String columnName = meta.getColumnLabel(i);
   int columnWidth = meta.getColumnDisplaySize(i);
   . . .
}
```

In this section, we will show you how to write such a simple tool. The program in Listing 4.4 uses metadata to let you browse all tables in a database. The program also illustrates the use of a cached row set.

The combo box on top displays all tables in the database. Select one of them, and the center of the frame is filled with the field names of that table and the values of the first row, as shown in Figure 4.6. Click Next and Previous to scroll through the rows in the table. You can also delete a row and edit the row values. Click the Save button to save the changes to the database.

 **NOTE:** Many databases come with much more sophisticated tools for viewing and editing tables. If your database doesn't, check out iSQL-Viewer (http://isql.sourceforge.net) or SQuirreL (http://squirrel-sql.sourceforge.net). These programs can view the tables in any JDBC database. Our example program is not intended as a replacement for these tools, but it shows you how to implement a tool for working with arbitrary tables.

**Listing 4.4** view/ViewDB.java

```java
1  package view;
2
3  import java.awt.*;
4  import java.awt.event.*;
5  import java.io.*;
6  import java.nio.file.*;
7  import java.sql.*;
8  import java.util.*;
9  import javax.sql.*;
10 import javax.sql.rowset.*;
11 import javax.swing.*;
12
13 /**
14  * This program uses metadata to display arbitrary tables in a database.
15  * @version 1.32 2012-01-26
16  * @author Cay Horstmann
17  */
18 public class ViewDB
19 {
20    public static void main(String[] args)
21    {
22       EventQueue.invokeLater(new Runnable()
23          {
24             public void run()
25             {
26                JFrame frame = new ViewDBFrame();
27                frame.setTitle("ViewDB");
28                frame.setDefaultCloseOperation(JFrame.EXIT_ON_CLOSE);
29                frame.setVisible(true);
30             }
31          });
32    }
33 }
34
35 /**
36  * The frame that holds the data panel and the navigation buttons.
37  */
38 class ViewDBFrame extends JFrame
39 {
40    private JButton previousButton;
41    private JButton nextButton;
42    private JButton deleteButton;
43    private JButton saveButton;
44    private DataPanel dataPanel;
45    private Component scrollPane;
46    private JComboBox<String> tableNames;
```

```
47    private Properties props;
48    private CachedRowSet crs;
49
50    public ViewDBFrame()
51    {
52       tableNames = new JComboBox<String>();
53       tableNames.addActionListener(new ActionListener()
54          {
55             public void actionPerformed(ActionEvent event)
56             {
57                showTable((String) tableNames.getSelectedItem());
58             }
59          });
60       add(tableNames, BorderLayout.NORTH);
61
62       try
63       {
64          readDatabaseProperties();
65          try (Connection conn = getConnection())
66          {
67             DatabaseMetaData meta = conn.getMetaData();
68             ResultSet mrs = meta.getTables(null, null, null, new String[] { "TABLE" });
69             while (mrs.next())
70                tableNames.addItem(mrs.getString(3));
71          }
72       }
73       catch (SQLException e)
74       {
75          JOptionPane.showMessageDialog(this, e);
76       }
77       catch (IOException e)
78       {
79          JOptionPane.showMessageDialog(this, e);
80       }
81
82       JPanel buttonPanel = new JPanel();
83       add(buttonPanel, BorderLayout.SOUTH);
84
85       previousButton = new JButton("Previous");
86       previousButton.addActionListener(new ActionListener()
87          {
88             public void actionPerformed(ActionEvent event)
89             {
90                showPreviousRow();
91             }
92          });
93       buttonPanel.add(previousButton);
```

*(Continues)*

**Listing 4.4** *(Continued)*

```
 94        nextButton = new JButton("Next");
 95        nextButton.addActionListener(new ActionListener()
 96           {
 97              public void actionPerformed(ActionEvent event)
 98              {
 99                 showNextRow();
100              }
101           });
102        buttonPanel.add(nextButton);
103
104        deleteButton = new JButton("Delete");
105        deleteButton.addActionListener(new ActionListener()
106           {
107              public void actionPerformed(ActionEvent event)
108              {
109                 deleteRow();
110              }
111           });
112        buttonPanel.add(deleteButton);
113
114        saveButton = new JButton("Save");
115        saveButton.addActionListener(new ActionListener()
116           {
117              public void actionPerformed(ActionEvent event)
118              {
119                 saveChanges();
120              }
121           });
122        buttonPanel.add(saveButton);
123        pack();
124     }
125
126     /**
127      * Prepares the text fields for showing a new table, and shows the first row.
128      * @param tableName the name of the table to display
129      */
130     public void showTable(String tableName)
131     {
132        try
133        {
134           try (Connection conn = getConnection())
135           {
136              // get result set
137              Statement stat = conn.createStatement();
138              ResultSet result = stat.executeQuery("SELECT * FROM " + tableName);
```

```
139            // copy into cached row set
140            RowSetFactory factory = RowSetProvider.newFactory();
141            crs = factory.createCachedRowSet();
142            crs.setTableName(tableName);
143            crs.populate(result);
144         }
145
146         if (scrollPane != null) remove(scrollPane);
147         dataPanel = new DataPanel(crs);
148         scrollPane = new JScrollPane(dataPanel);
149         add(scrollPane, BorderLayout.CENTER);
150         validate();
151         showNextRow();
152      }
153      catch (SQLException e)
154      {
155         JOptionPane.showMessageDialog(this, e);
156      }
157   }
158
159   /**
160    * Moves to the previous table row.
161    */
162   public void showPreviousRow()
163   {
164      try
165      {
166         if (crs == null || crs.isFirst()) return;
167         crs.previous();
168         dataPanel.showRow(crs);
169      }
170      catch (SQLException e)
171      {
172         for (Throwable t : e)
173            t.printStackTrace();
174      }
175   }
176
177   /**
178    * Moves to the next table row.
179    */
180   public void showNextRow()
181   {
182      try
183      {
184         if (crs == null || crs.isLast()) return;
185         crs.next();
186         dataPanel.showRow(crs);
187      }
```

*(Continues)*

**Listing 4.4** (Continued)

```
188       catch (SQLException e)
189       {
190          JOptionPane.showMessageDialog(this, e);
191       }
192    }
193
194    /**
195     * Deletes current table row.
196     */
197    public void deleteRow()
198    {
199       try
200       {
201          try (Connection conn = getConnection())
202          {
203             crs.deleteRow();
204             crs.acceptChanges(conn);
205             if (crs.isAfterLast())
206                if (!crs.last()) crs = null;
207             dataPanel.showRow(crs);
208          }
209       }
210       catch (SQLException e)
211       {
212          JOptionPane.showMessageDialog(this, e);
213       }
214    }
215
216    /**
217     * Saves all changes.
218     */
219    public void saveChanges()
220    {
221       try
222       {
223          try (Connection conn = getConnection())
224          {
225             dataPanel.setRow(crs);
226             crs.acceptChanges(conn);
227          }
228       }
229       catch (SQLException e)
230       {
231          JOptionPane.showMessageDialog(this, e);
232       }
233    }
```

```
234    private void readDatabaseProperties() throws IOException
235    {
236       props = new Properties();
237       try (InputStream in = Files.newInputStream(Paths.get("database.properties")))
238       {
239          props.load(in);
240       }
241       String drivers = props.getProperty("jdbc.drivers");
242       if (drivers != null) System.setProperty("jdbc.drivers", drivers);
243    }
244
245    /**
246     * Gets a connection from the properties specified in the file database.properties.
247     * @return the database connection
248     */
249    private Connection getConnection() throws SQLException
250    {
251       String url = props.getProperty("jdbc.url");
252       String username = props.getProperty("jdbc.username");
253       String password = props.getProperty("jdbc.password");
254
255       return DriverManager.getConnection(url, username, password);
256    }
257 }
258
259 /**
260  * This panel displays the contents of a result set.
261  */
262 class DataPanel extends JPanel
263 {
264    private java.util.List<JTextField> fields;
265
266    /**
267     * Constructs the data panel.
268     * @param rs the result set whose contents this panel displays
269     */
270    public DataPanel(RowSet rs) throws SQLException
271    {
272       fields = new ArrayList<>();
273       setLayout(new GridBagLayout());
274       GridBagConstraints gbc = new GridBagConstraints();
275       gbc.gridwidth = 1;
276       gbc.gridheight = 1;
277
278       ResultSetMetaData rsmd = rs.getMetaData();
279       for (int i = 1; i <= rsmd.getColumnCount(); i++)
280       {
281          gbc.gridy = i - 1;
```

*(Continues)*

**Listing 4.4** *(Continued)*

```
282         String columnName = rsmd.getColumnLabel(i);
283         gbc.gridx = 0;
284         gbc.anchor = GridBagConstraints.EAST;
285         add(new JLabel(columnName), gbc);
286
287         int columnWidth = rsmd.getColumnDisplaySize(i);
288         JTextField tb = new JTextField(columnWidth);
289         if (!rsmd.getColumnClassName(i).equals("java.lang.String"))
290            tb.setEditable(false);
291
292         fields.add(tb);
293
294         gbc.gridx = 1;
295         gbc.anchor = GridBagConstraints.WEST;
296         add(tb, gbc);
297      }
298   }
299
300   /**
301    * Shows a database row by populating all text fields with the column values.
302    */
303   public void showRow(ResultSet rs) throws SQLException
304   {
305      for (int i = 1; i <= fields.size(); i++)
306      {
307         String field = rs == null ? "" : rs.getString(i);
308         JTextField tb = fields.get(i - 1);
309         tb.setText(field);
310      }
311   }
312
313   /**
314    * Updates changed data into the current row of the row set.
315    */
316   public void setRow(RowSet rs) throws SQLException
317   {
318      for (int i = 1; i <= fields.size(); i++)
319      {
320         String field = rs.getString(i);
321         JTextField tb = fields.get(i - 1);
322         if (!field.equals(tb.getText()))
323            rs.updateString(i, tb.getText());
324      }
325      rs.updateRow();
326   }
327 }
```

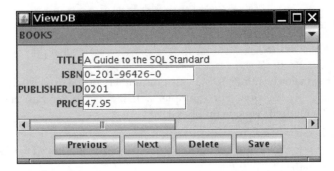

**Figure 4.6** The ViewDB application

---

**java.sql.Connection** 1.1

- DatabaseMetaData getMetaData()
  returns the metadata for the connection as a DatabaseMetaData object.

---

**java.sql.DatabaseMetaData** 1.1

- ResultSet getTables(String catalog, String schemaPattern, String tableNamePattern, String types[])
  returns a description of all tables in a catalog that match the schema and table name patterns and the type criteria. (A *schema* describes a group of related tables and access permissions. A *catalog* describes a related group of schemas. These concepts are important for structuring large databases.)

  The catalog and schemaPattern parameters can be "" to retrieve those tables without a catalog or schema, or null to return tables regardless of catalog or schema.

  The types array contains the names of the table types to include. Typical types are TABLE, VIEW, SYSTEM TABLE, GLOBAL TEMPORARY, LOCAL TEMPORARY, ALIAS, and SYNONYM. If types is null, tables of all types are returned.

  The result set has five columns, all of which are of type String.

| Column | Name | Explanation |
| --- | --- | --- |
| 1 | TABLE_CAT | Table catalog (may be null) |
| 2 | TABLE_SCHEM | Table schema (may be null) |
| 3 | TABLE_NAME | Table name |
| 4 | TABLE_TYPE | Table type |
| 5 | REMARKS | Comment on the table |

*(Continues)*

---

*java.sql.DatabaseMetaData* 1.1 *(Continued)*

- int getJDBCMajorVersion() **1.4**
- int getJDBCMinorVersion() **1.4**

  returns the major or minor JDBC version numbers of the driver that established the database connection. For example, a JDBC 3.0 driver has major version number 3 and minor version number 0.

- int getMaxConnections()

  returns the maximum number of concurrent connections allowed to this database.

- int getMaxStatements()

  returns the maximum number of concurrently open statements allowed per database connection, or 0 if the number is unlimited or unknown.

---

*java.sql.ResultSet* 1.1

- ResultSetMetaData getMetaData()

  returns the metadata associated with the current ResultSet columns.

---

*java.sql.ResultSetMetaData* 1.1

- int getColumnCount()

  returns the number of columns in the current ResultSet object.

- int getColumnDisplaySize(int column)

  returns the maximum width of the column specified by the index parameter.

  *Parameters:*    column          The column number

- String getColumnLabel(int column)

  returns the suggested title for the column.

  *Parameters:*    column          The column number

- String getColumnName(int column)

  returns the column name associated with the column index specified.

  *Parameters:*    column          The column number

---

## 4.9 Transactions

You can group a set of statements to form a *transaction*. The transaction can be *committed* when all has gone well. Or, if an error has occurred in one of them, it can be *rolled back* as if none of the statements had been issued.

The major reason for grouping statements into transactions is *database integrity*. For example, suppose we want to transfer money from one bank account to another. Then, it is important that we simultaneously debit one account and credit another. If the system fails after debiting the first account but before crediting the other account, the debit needs to be undone.

If you group update statements into a transaction, the transaction either succeeds in its entirety and can be *committed*, or it fails somewhere in the middle. In that case, you can carry out a *rollback* and the database automatically undoes the effect of all updates that occurred since the last committed transaction.

By default, a database connection is in *autocommit mode*, and each SQL statement is committed to the database as soon as it is executed. Once a statement is committed, you cannot roll it back. Turn off this default so you can use transactions:

```
conn.setAutoCommit(false);
```

Create a statement object in the normal way:

```
Statement stat = conn.createStatement();
```

Call `executeUpdate` any number of times:

```
stat.executeUpdate(command1);
stat.executeUpdate(command2);
stat.executeUpdate(command3);
. . .
```

If all statements have been executed without error, call the `commit` method:

```
conn.commit();
```

However, if an error occurred, call

```
conn.rollback();
```

Then, all statements since the last commit are automatically reversed. You typically issue a rollback when your transaction was interrupted by a `SQLException`.

## 4.9.1 Save Points

With some drivers, you can gain finer-grained control over the rollback process by using *save points*. Creating a save point marks a point to which you can later return without having to abandon the entire transaction. For example,

```
Statement stat = conn.createStatement(); // start transaction; rollback() goes here
stat.executeUpdate(command1);
Savepoint svpt = conn.setSavepoint(); // set savepoint; rollback(svpt) goes here
stat.executeUpdate(command2);
```

```
if (. . .) conn.rollback(svpt); // undo effect of command2
. . .
conn.commit();
```

When you no longer need a save point, you should release it:

```
conn.releaseSavepoint(svpt);
```

## 4.9.2 Batch Updates

Suppose a program needs to execute many INSERT statements to populate a database table. You can improve the performance of the program by using a *batch update*. In a batch update, a sequence of statements is collected and submitted as a batch.

---

 **NOTE:** Use the supportsBatchUpdates method of the DatabaseMetaData interface to find out if your database supports this feature.

---

The statements in a batch can be actions such as INSERT, UPDATE, or DELETE as well as data definition statements such as CREATE TABLE or DROP TABLE. An exception is thrown if you add a SELECT statement to a batch. (Conceptually, a SELECT statement makes no sense in a batch because it returns a result set without updating the database.)

To execute a batch, first create a Statement object in the usual way:

```
Statement stat = conn.createStatement();
```

Now, instead of calling executeUpdate, call the addBatch method:

```
String command = "CREATE TABLE . . ."
stat.addBatch(command);

while (. . .)
{
   command = "INSERT INTO . . . VALUES (" + . . . + ")";
   stat.addBatch(command);
}
```

Finally, submit the entire batch:

```
int[] counts = stat.executeBatch();
```

The call to executeBatch returns an array of the row counts for all submitted statements.

For proper error handling in batch mode, treat the batch execution as a single transaction. If a batch fails in the middle, you want to roll back to the state before the beginning of the batch.

First, turn the autocommit mode off, then collect the batch, execute it, commit it, and finally restore the original autocommit mode:

```
boolean autoCommit = conn.getAutoCommit();
conn.setAutoCommit(false);
Statement stat = conn.getStatement();
. . .
// keep calling stat.addBatch(. . .);
. . .
stat.executeBatch();
conn.commit();
conn.setAutoCommit(autoCommit);
```

---

*java.sql.Connection* 1.1

- boolean getAutoCommit()
- void setAutoCommit(boolean b)

  gets or sets the autocommit mode of this connection to b. If autocommit is true, all statements are committed as soon as their execution is completed.

- void commit()

  commits all statements that were issued since the last commit.

- void rollback()

  undoes the effect of all statements that were issued since the last commit.

- Savepoint setSavepoint() 1.4
- Savepoint setSavepoint(String name) 1.4

  sets an unnamed or named save point.

- void rollback(Savepoint svpt) 1.4

  rolls back until the given save point.

- void releaseSavepoint(Savepoint svpt) 1.4

  releases the given save point.

---

*java.sql.Savepoint* 1.4

- int getSavepointId()

  gets the ID of this unnamed save point, or throws a SQLException if this is a named save point.

- String getSavepointName()

  gets the name of this save point, or throws a SQLException if this is an unnamed save point.

---

*java.sql.Statement* 1.1

- void addBatch(String command) 1.2
  adds the command to the current batch of commands for this statement.

- int[] executeBatch() 1.2
  executes all commands in the current batch. Each value in the returned array corresponds to one of the batch statements. If it is non-negative, it is a row count. If it is the value SUCCESS_NO_INFO, the statement succeeded, but no row count is available. If it is EXECUTE_FAILED, the statement failed.

---

*java.sql.DatabaseMetaData* 1.1

- boolean supportsBatchUpdates() 1.2
  returns true if the driver supports batch updates.

---

## 4.9.3 Advanced SQL Types

Table 4.8 lists the SQL data types supported by JDBC and their equivalents in the Java programming language.

A SQL ARRAY is a sequence of values. For example, in a Student table, you can have a Scores column that is an ARRAY OF INTEGER. The getArray method returns an object of the interface type java.sql.Array. That interface has methods to fetch the array values.

When you get a LOB or an array from a database, the actual contents are fetched from the database only when you request individual values. This is a useful performance enhancement, as the data can be quite voluminous.

Some databases support ROWID values that describe the location of a row so that it can be retrieved very rapidly. JDBC 4 introduced an interface java.sql.RowId and the methods to supply the row ID in queries and retrieve it from results.

A *national character string* (NCHAR and its variants) stores strings in a local character encoding and sorts them using a local sorting convention. JDBC 4 provided methods for converting between Java String objects and national character strings in queries and results.

Some databases can store user-defined structured types. JDBC 3 provided a mechanism for automatically mapping structured SQL types to Java objects.

**Table 4.8** SQL Data Types and Their Corresponding Java Types

| SQL Data Type | Java Data Type |
| --- | --- |
| INTEGER or INT | int |
| SMALLINT | short |
| NUMERIC($m$,$n$),<br>DECIMAL($m$,$n$) or DEC($m$,$n$) | java.math.BigDecimal |
| FLOAT($n$) | double |
| REAL | float |
| DOUBLE | double |
| CHARACTER($n$) or CHAR($n$) | String |
| VARCHAR($n$), LONG VARCHAR | String |
| BOOLEAN | boolean |
| DATE | java.sql.Date |
| TIME | java.sql.Time |
| TIMESTAMP | java.sql.Timestamp |
| BLOB | java.sql.Blob |
| CLOB | java.sql.Clob |
| ARRAY | java.sql.Array |
| ROWID | java.sql.RowId |
| NCHAR($n$), NVARCHAR($n$), LONG NVARCHAR | String |
| NCLOB | java.sql.NClob |
| SQLXML | java.sql.SQLXML |

Some databases provide native storage for XML data. JDBC 4 introduced a SQLXML interface that can mediate between the internal XML representation and the DOM Source/Result interfaces, as well as binary streams. See the API documentation for the SQLXML class for details.

We do not discuss these advanced SQL types any further. You can find more information on these topics in the *JDBC API Tutorial and Reference* and the JDBC 4 specifications.

## 4.10 Connection Management in Web and Enterprise Applications

The simplistic database connection setup with a database.properties file, as described in the preceding sections, is suitable for small test programs but won't scale for larger applications.

When a JDBC application is deployed in a web or enterprise environment, the management of database connections is integrated with the JNDI. The properties of data sources across the enterprise can be stored in a directory. Using a directory allows for centralized management of user names, passwords, database names, and JDBC URLs.

In such an environment, you can use the following code to establish a database connection:

```
Context jndiContext = new InitialContext();
DataSource source = (DataSource) jndiContext.lookup("java:comp/env/jdbc/corejava");
Connection conn = source.getConnection();
```

Note that the DriverManager is no longer involved. Instead, the JNDI service locates a *data source*. A data source is an interface that allows for simple JDBC connections as well as more advanced services, such as executing distributed transactions that involve multiple databases. The DataSource interface is defined in the javax.sql standard extension package.

---

 **NOTE:** In a Java EE container, you don't even have to program the JNDI lookup. Simply use the Resource annotation on a DataSource field, and the data source reference will be set when your application is loaded:

```
@Resource(name="jdbc/corejava")
private DataSource source;
```

---

Of course, the data source needs to be configured somewhere. If you write database programs that execute in a servlet container such as Apache Tomcat or in an application server such as GlassFish, then you place the database configuration (including the JNDI name, JDBC URL, user name, and password) in a configuration file, or you set it in an admin GUI.

Management of user names and logins is just one of the issues that require special attention. Another issue involves the cost of establishing database connections. Our sample database programs used two strategies for obtaining a database connection. The QueryDB program in Listing 4.3 established a single database connection at the start of the program and closed it at the end of the program. The ViewDB program in Listing 4.4 opened a new connection whenever one was needed.

However, neither of these approaches is satisfactory. Database connections are a finite resource. If a user walks away from an application for some time, the connection should not be left open. Conversely, obtaining a connection for each query and closing it afterward is very costly.

The solution is to *pool* the connections. This means that database connections are not physically closed but are kept in a queue and reused. Connection pooling is an important service, and the JDBC specification provides hooks for implementors to supply it. However, the JDK itself does not provide any implementation, and database vendors don't usually include one with their JDBC drivers either. Instead, vendors of web containers and application servers supply connection pool implementations.

Using a connection pool is completely transparent to the programmer. Acquire a connection from a source of pooled connections by obtaining a data source and calling getConnection. When you are done using the connection, call close. That doesn't close the physical connection but tells the pool that you are done using it. The connection pool typically makes an effort to pool prepared statements as well.

You have now learned about the JDBC fundamentals and know enough to implement simple database applications. However, as we mentioned at the beginning of this chapter, databases are complex and quite a few advanced topics are beyond the scope of this introductory chapter. For an overview of advanced JDBC capabilities, refer to the *JDBC API Tutorial and Reference* or the JDBC specifications.

In this chapter, you have learned how to work with relational databases in Java. The next chapter covers the important topic of internationalization, showing you how to make your software usable for customers around the world.

# Internationalization

## In this chapter:

There's a big world out there; we hope that lots of its inhabitants will be interested in your software. The Internet, after all, effortlessly spans the barriers between countries. On the other hand, when you pay no attention to an international audience, *you* are putting up a barrier.

The Java programming language was the first language designed from the ground up to support internationalization. From the beginning, it had the one essential feature needed for effective internationalization: It used Unicode for all strings. Unicode support makes it easy to write Java programs that manipulate strings in any one of multiple languages.

Many programmers believe that all they need to do to internationalize their application is to support Unicode and to translate the messages in the user interface. However, as this chapter demonstrates, there is a lot more to internationalizing programs than just Unicode support. Dates, times, currencies, even numbers are formatted differently in different parts of the world. You need an easy way to configure menu and button names, message strings, and keyboard shortcuts for different languages.

In this chapter, we will show you how to write internationalized Java programs and how to localize dates, times, numbers, text, and GUIs. We will show you the tools that Java offers for writing internationalized programs. We will close this chapter with a complete example—a retirement calculator with a user interface in English, German, and Chinese.

## 5.1 Locales

When you look at an application that is adapted to an international market, the most obvious difference you notice is the language. This observation is actually a bit too limiting for true internationalization, since countries can share a common language, but you might still need to do some work to make computer users of both countries happy. As Oscar Wilde famously said: "We have really everything in common with America nowadays, except, of course, language."

In all cases, menus, button labels, and program messages will need to be translated to the local language; they might also need to be rendered in a different script. There are many more subtle differences; for example, numbers are formatted quite differently in English and in German. The number

123,456.78

should be displayed as

123.456,78

for a German user—that is, the roles of the decimal point and the decimal comma separator are reversed. There are similar variations in the display of dates. In the United States, dates are somewhat irrationally displayed as month/day/year. Germany uses the more sensible order of day/month/year, whereas in China, the usage is year/month/day. Thus, the date

3/22/61

should be presented as

22.03.1961

to a German user. Of course, if the month names are written out explicitly, then the difference in languages becomes apparent. The English

March 22, 1961

should be presented as

22. März 1961

in German, or

1961年3月22日

in Chinese.

There are several formatter classes that take these differences into account. To control the formatting, use the Locale class. A *locale* describes

- A language
- Commonly, a location
- Optionally, a script (supported since Java SE 7)
- Optionally, a variant, specifying miscellaneous features such as dialects or spelling rules

For example, in the United States, you use a locale with

  language=English, location=United States

In Germany, you use a locale with

  language=German, location=Germany

Switzerland has four official languages (German, French, Italian, and Rhaeto-Romance). A German speaker in Switzerland would want to use a locale with

  language=German, location=Switzerland

This locale would make formatting work similarly to how it works for the German locale, but currency values would be expressed in Swiss francs, not Euros.

If you only specify the language, say,

  language=German

then the locale cannot be used for country-specific issues such as currencies.

To express the language and location in a concise and standardized manner, the Java programming language uses codes that were defined by the International Organization for Standardization (ISO). The local language is expressed as a lowercase two-letter code, following ISO 639-1, and the country code is expressed as an uppercase two-letter code, following ISO 3166-1. Tables 5.1 and 5.2 show some of the most common codes.

These codes do seem a bit random, in part because some of them are derived from local languages (German = Deutsch = de, Chinese = zhongwen = zh), but at least they are standardized.

**Table 5.1** Common ISO 639-1 Language Codes

| Language | Code | Language | Code |
|----------|------|----------|------|
| Chinese | zh | Italian | it |
| Danish | da | Japanese | ja |
| Dutch | nl | Korean | ko |
| English | en | Norwegian | no |
| French | fr | Portuguese | pt |
| Finnish | fi | Spanish | es |
| German | de | Swedish | sv |
| Greek | el | Turkish | tr |

**Table 5.2** Common ISO 3166-1 Country Codes

| Country | Code | Country | Code |
|---------|------|---------|------|
| Austria | AT | Japan | JP |
| Belgium | BE | Korea | KR |
| Canada | CA | The Netherlands | NL |
| China | CN | Norway | NO |
| Denmark | DK | Portugal | PT |
| Finland | FI | Spain | ES |
| Germany | DE | Sweden | SE |
| Great Britain | GB | Switzerland | CH |
| Greece | GR | Taiwan | TW |
| Ireland | IE | Turkey | TR |
| Italy | IT | United States | US |

Given a language code, or a language and country code, you can construct a Locale object:

```
Locale german = new Locale("de");
Locale germanGermany = new Locale("de", "DE");
Locale germanSwitzerland = new Locale("de", "CH");
```

For your convenience, Java SE predefines a number of locale objects:

```
Locale.CANADA
Locale.CANADA_FRENCH
Locale.CHINA
Locale.FRANCE
Locale.GERMANY
Locale.ITALY
Locale.JAPAN
Locale.KOREA
Locale.PRC
Locale.TAIWAN
Locale.UK
Locale.US
```

Java SE also predefines a number of language locales that specify just a language without a location:

```
Locale.CHINESE
Locale.ENGLISH
Locale.FRENCH
Locale.GERMAN
Locale.ITALIAN
Locale.JAPANESE
Locale.KOREAN
Locale.SIMPLIFIED_CHINESE
Locale.TRADITIONAL_CHINESE
```

**NOTE:** If you want to go beyond specifying language and country, you should have a good understanding of the IETF BCP 47 standard (see www.w3.org/International/articles/language-tags for a nice introduction). Since Java SE 7, Java supports IETF BCP 47 language tags. For example, you can construct a locale from a language tag with the call

```
Locale chineseTraditionalCharactersHongKong = Locale.forLanguageTag("zh-Hant-HK");
```

Besides constructing a locale or using a predefined one, you have two other methods for obtaining a locale object.

The static getDefault method of the Locale class initially gets the default locale as stored by the local operating system. You can change the default Java locale by calling setDefault; however, that change only affects your program, not the operating system.

Finally, all locale-dependent utility classes can return an array of the locales they support. For example,

```
Locale[] supportedLocales = DateFormat.getAvailableLocales();
```

returns all locales that the DateFormat class can handle.

**TIP:** For testing, you might want to switch the default locale of your program. Supply the language and region properties when you launch your program. For example, here we set the default locale to German (Switzerland):

```
java -Duser.language=de -Duser.region=CH MyProgram
```

Once you have a locale, what can you do with it? Not much, as it turns out. The only useful methods in the Locale class are those for identifying the language and country codes. The most important one is getDisplayName. It returns a string describing the locale. This string does not contain the cryptic two-letter codes, but is in a form that can be presented to a user, such as

```
German (Switzerland)
```

Actually, there is a problem here. The display name is issued in the default locale. That might not be appropriate. If your user already selected German as the preferred language, you probably want to present the string in German. You can do just that by giving the German locale as a parameter. The code

```
Locale loc = new Locale("de", "CH");
System.out.println(loc.getDisplayName(Locale.GERMAN));
```

prints

```
Deutsch (Schweiz)
```

This example shows why you need Locale objects. You feed them to locale-aware methods that produce text that is presented to users in different locations. You can see many examples in the following sections.

---

**java.util.Locale** 1.1

- Locale(String language)
- Locale(String language, String country)
- Locale(String language, String country, String variant)
  constructs a locale with the given language, country, and variant. Don't use variants in new code—use the IETF BCP 47 language tags instead.
- static Locale forLanguageTag(String languageTag) 7
  constructs a locale corresponding to the given language tag.
- static Locale getDefault()
  returns the default locale.
- static void setDefault(Locale loc)
  sets the default locale.

---

*(Continues)*

---

**java.util.Locale** 1.1 *(Continued)*

- `String getDisplayName()`
  returns a name describing the locale, expressed in the current locale.
- `String getDisplayName(Locale loc)`
  returns a name describing the locale, expressed in the given locale.
- `String getLanguage()`
  returns the language code, a lowercase two-letter ISO 639 code.
- `String getDisplayLanguage()`
  returns the name of the language, expressed in the current locale.
- `String getDisplayLanguage(Locale loc)`
  returns the name of the language, expressed in the given locale.
- `String getCountry()`
  returns the country code as an uppercase two-letter ISO 3166 code.
- `String getDisplayCountry()`
  returns the name of the country, expressed in the current locale.
- `String getDisplayCountry(Locale loc)`
  returns the name of the country, expressed in the given locale.
- `String toLanguageTag()` 7
  returns the IETF BCP 47 language tag for this locale, e.g., "de-CH".
- `String toString()`
  returns a description of the locale, with the language and country separated by underscores (e.g., "de_CH"). Use this method only for debugging.

---

## 5.2 Number Formats

We already mentioned how number and currency formatting is highly locale-dependent. The Java library supplies a collection of formatter objects that can format and parse numeric values in the `java.text` package. Go through the following steps to format a number for a particular locale:

1. Get the locale object, as described in the preceding section.
2. Use a "factory method" to obtain a formatter object.
3. Use the formatter object for formatting and parsing.

The factory methods are static methods of the `NumberFormat` class that take a `Locale` argument. There are three factory methods: `getNumberInstance`, `getCurrencyInstance`, and `getPercentInstance`. These methods return objects that can format and parse numbers, currency amounts, and percentages, respectively. For example, here is how you can format a currency value in German:

```
Locale loc = new Locale("de", "DE");
NumberFormat currFmt = NumberFormat.getCurrencyInstance(loc);
double amt = 123456.78;
String result = currFmt.format(amt);
```

The result is

123.456,78€

Note that the currency symbol is € and that it is placed at the end of the string. Also, note the reversal of decimal points and decimal commas.

Conversely, to read in a number that was entered or stored with the conventions of a certain locale, use the parse method. For example, the following code parses the value that the user typed into a text field. The parse method can deal with decimal points and commas, as well as digits in other languages.

```
TextField inputField;
. . .
NumberFormat fmt = NumberFormat.getNumberInstance();
// get the number formatter for default locale
Number input = fmt.parse(inputField.getText().trim());
double x = input.doubleValue();
```

The return type of parse is the abstract type Number. The returned object is either a Double or a Long wrapper object, depending on whether the parsed number was a floating-point number. If you don't care about the distinction, you can simply use the doubleValue method of the Number class to retrieve the wrapped number.

 **CAUTION:** Objects of type Number are not automatically unboxed—you cannot simply assign a Number object to a primitive type. Instead, use the doubleValue or intValue method.

If the text for the number is not in the correct form, the method throws a ParseException. For example, leading whitespace in the string is *not* allowed. (Call trim to remove it.) However, any characters that follow the number in the string are simply ignored, so no exception is thrown.

Note that the classes returned by the get*Xxx*Instance factory methods are not actually of type NumberFormat. The NumberFormat type is an abstract class, and the actual formatters belong to one of its subclasses. The factory methods merely know how to locate the object that belongs to a particular locale.

You can get a list of the currently supported locales with the static getAvailableLocales method. That method returns an array of the locales for which number formatter objects can be obtained.

The sample program for this section lets you experiment with number formatters (see Figure 5.1). The combo box at the top of the figure contains all locales with number formatters. You can choose between number, currency, and percentage formatters. Each time you make another choice, the number in the text field is reformatted. If you go through a few locales, you can get a good impression of how many ways a number or currency value can be formatted. You can also type a different number and click the Parse button to call the parse method, which tries to parse what you entered. If your input is successfully parsed, it is passed to format and the result is displayed. If parsing fails, then a "Parse error" message is displayed in the text field.

The code, shown in Listing 5.1, is fairly straightforward. In the constructor, we call NumberFormat.getAvailableLocales. For each locale, we call getDisplayName and fill a combo box with the strings that the getDisplayName method returns. (The strings are not sorted; we tackle this issue in Section 5.4, "Collation," on p. 328.) Whenever the user selects another locale or clicks one of the radio buttons, we create a new formatter object and update the text field. When the user clicks the Parse button, we call the parse method to do the actual parsing, based on the locale selected.

**Figure 5.1** The NumberFormatTest program

**Listing 5.1** numberFormat/NumberFormatTest.java

```
1  package numberFormat;
2
3  import java.awt.*;
4  import java.awt.event.*;
5  import java.text.*;
6  import java.util.*;
7
8  import javax.swing.*;
```

*(Continues)*

**Listing 5.1** *(Continued)*

```
 9  /**
10   * This program demonstrates formatting numbers under various locales.
11   * @version 1.13 2007-07-25
12   * @author Cay Horstmann
13   */
14  public class NumberFormatTest
15  {
16     public static void main(String[] args)
17     {
18        EventQueue.invokeLater(new Runnable()
19           {
20              public void run()
21              {
22                 JFrame frame = new NumberFormatFrame();
23                 frame.setTitle("NumberFormatTest");
24                 frame.setDefaultCloseOperation(JFrame.EXIT_ON_CLOSE);
25                 frame.setVisible(true);
26              }
27           });
28     }
29  }
30
31  /**
32   * This frame contains radio buttons to select a number format, a combo box to pick a locale, a
33   * text field to display a formatted number, and a button to parse the text field contents.
34   */
35  class NumberFormatFrame extends JFrame
36  {
37     private Locale[] locales;
38     private double currentNumber;
39     private JComboBox<String> localeCombo = new JComboBox<>();
40     private JButton parseButton = new JButton("Parse");
41     private JTextField numberText = new JTextField(30);
42     private JRadioButton numberRadioButton = new JRadioButton("Number");
43     private JRadioButton currencyRadioButton = new JRadioButton("Currency");
44     private JRadioButton percentRadioButton = new JRadioButton("Percent");
45     private ButtonGroup rbGroup = new ButtonGroup();
46     private NumberFormat currentNumberFormat;
47
48     public NumberFormatFrame()
49     {
50        setLayout(new GridBagLayout());
51
52        ActionListener listener = new ActionListener()
53           {
54              public void actionPerformed(ActionEvent event)
55              {
```

```
56              updateDisplay();
57          }
58      };
59
60      JPanel p = new JPanel();
61      addRadioButton(p, numberRadioButton, rbGroup, listener);
62      addRadioButton(p, currencyRadioButton, rbGroup, listener);
63      addRadioButton(p, percentRadioButton, rbGroup, listener);
64
65      add(new JLabel("Locale:"), new GBC(0, 0).setAnchor(GBC.EAST));
66      add(p, new GBC(1, 1));
67      add(parseButton, new GBC(0, 2).setInsets(2));
68      add(localeCombo, new GBC(1, 0).setAnchor(GBC.WEST));
69      add(numberText, new GBC(1, 2).setFill(GBC.HORIZONTAL));
70      locales = (Locale[]) NumberFormat.getAvailableLocales().clone();
71      Arrays.sort(locales, new Comparator<Locale>()
72          {
73              public int compare(Locale l1, Locale l2)
74              {
75                  return l1.getDisplayName().compareTo(l2.getDisplayName());
76              }
77          });
78      for (Locale loc : locales)
79          localeCombo.addItem(loc.getDisplayName());
80      localeCombo.setSelectedItem(Locale.getDefault().getDisplayName());
81      currentNumber = 123456.78;
82      updateDisplay();
83
84      localeCombo.addActionListener(listener);
85
86      parseButton.addActionListener(new ActionListener()
87          {
88              public void actionPerformed(ActionEvent event)
89              {
90                  String s = numberText.getText().trim();
91                  try
92                  {
93                      Number n = currentNumberFormat.parse(s);
94                      if (n != null)
95                      {
96                          currentNumber = n.doubleValue();
97                          updateDisplay();
98                      }
99                      else
100                     {
101                         numberText.setText("Parse error: " + s);
102                     }
103                 }
```

*(Continues)*

**Listing 5.1** *(Continued)*

```
104                catch (ParseException e)
105                {
106                    numberText.setText("Parse error: " + s);
107                }
108            }
109        });
110        pack();
111    }
112
113    /**
114     * Adds a radio button to a container.
115     * @param p the container into which to place the button
116     * @param b the button
117     * @param g the button group
118     * @param listener the button listener
119     */
120    public void addRadioButton(Container p, JRadioButton b, ButtonGroup g, ActionListener listener)
121    {
122        b.setSelected(g.getButtonCount() == 0);
123        b.addActionListener(listener);
124        g.add(b);
125        p.add(b);
126    }
127
128    /**
129     * Updates the display and formats the number according to the user settings.
130     */
131    public void updateDisplay()
132    {
133        Locale currentLocale = locales[localeCombo.getSelectedIndex()];
134        currentNumberFormat = null;
135        if (numberRadioButton.isSelected()) currentNumberFormat = NumberFormat
136            .getNumberInstance(currentLocale);
137        else if (currencyRadioButton.isSelected()) currentNumberFormat = NumberFormat
138            .getCurrencyInstance(currentLocale);
139        else if (percentRadioButton.isSelected()) currentNumberFormat = NumberFormat
140            .getPercentInstance(currentLocale);
141        String n = currentNumberFormat.format(currentNumber);
142        numberText.setText(n);
143    }
144 }
```

---

**java.text.NumberFormat** 1.1

- static Locale[] getAvailableLocales()
returns an array of Locale objects for which NumberFormat formatters are available.

- static NumberFormat getNumberInstance()
- static NumberFormat getNumberInstance(Locale l)
- static NumberFormat getCurrencyInstance()
- static NumberFormat getCurrencyInstance(Locale l)
- static NumberFormat getPercentInstance()
- static NumberFormat getPercentInstance(Locale l)
returns a formatter for numbers, currency amounts, or percentage values for the current locale or for the given locale.

- String format(double x)
- String format(long x)
returns the string resulting from formatting the given floating-point number or integer.

- Number parse(String s)
parses the given string and returns the number value, as a Double if the input string described a floating-point number and as a Long otherwise. The beginning of the string must contain a number; no leading whitespace is allowed. The number can be followed by other characters, which are ignored. Throws ParseException if parsing was not successful.

- void setParseIntegerOnly(boolean b)
- boolean isParseIntegerOnly()
sets or gets a flag to indicate whether this formatter should parse only integer values.

- void setGroupingUsed(boolean b)
- boolean isGroupingUsed()
sets or gets a flag to indicate whether this formatter emits and recognizes decimal separators (such as 100,000).

- void setMinimumIntegerDigits(int n)
- int getMinimumIntegerDigits()
- void setMaximumIntegerDigits(int n)
- int getMaximumIntegerDigits()
- void setMinimumFractionDigits(int n)
- int getMinimumFractionDigits()
- void setMaximumFractionDigits(int n)
- int getMaximumFractionDigits()
sets or gets the maximum or minimum number of digits allowed in the integer or fractional part of a number.

## 5.2.1 Currencies

To format a currency value, you can use the `NumberFormat.getCurrencyInstance` method. However, that method is not very flexible—it returns a formatter for a single currency. Suppose you prepare an invoice for an American customer in which some amounts are in dollars and others are in Euros. You can't just use two formatters

```
NumberFormat dollarFormatter = NumberFormat.getCurrencyInstance(Locale.US);
NumberFormat euroFormatter = NumberFormat.getCurrencyInstance(Locale.GERMANY);
```

Your invoice would look very strange, with some values formatted like $100,000 and others like 100.000 €. (Note that the Euro value uses a decimal point, not a comma.)

Instead, use the `Currency` class to control the currency used by the formatters. You can get a `Currency` object by passing a currency identifier to the static `Currency.getInstance` method. Then call the `setCurrency` method for each formatter. Here is how you would set up the Euro formatter for your American customer:

```
NumberFormat euroFormatter = NumberFormat.getCurrencyInstance(Locale.US);
euroFormatter.setCurrency(Currency.getInstance("EUR"));
```

The currency identifiers are defined by ISO 4217 (see www.currency-iso.org/iso_index/iso_tables/iso_tables_a1.htm). Table 5.3 provides a partial list.

**Table 5.3** Currency Identifiers

| Currency Value | Identifier |
| --- | --- |
| U.S. Dollar | USD |
| Euro | EUR |
| British Pound | GBP |
| Japanese Yen | JPY |
| Chinese Renminbi (Yuan) | CNY |
| Indian Rupee | INR |
| Russian Ruble | RUB |

---

**java.util.Currency** 1.4

- static Currency getInstance(String currencyCode)
- static Currency getInstance(Locale locale)
  returns the Currency instance for the given ISO 4217 currency code or the country of the given locale.
- String toString()
- String getCurrencyCode()
  gets the ISO 4217 currency code of this currency.
- String getSymbol()
- String getSymbol(Locale locale)
  gets the formatting symbol of this currency for the default locale or the given locale. For example, the symbol for USD can be "$" or "US$", depending on the locale.
- int getDefaultFractionDigits()
  gets the default number of fraction digits of this currency.
- static Set<Currency> getAvailableCurrencies() 7
  gets all available currencies.

---

## 5.3 Date and Time

When you are formatting date and time, you should be concerned with four locale-dependent issues:

- The names of months and weekdays should be presented in the local language.
- There will be local preferences for the order of year, month, and day.
- The Gregorian calendar might not be the local preference for expressing dates.
- The time zone of the location must be taken into account.

The Java DateFormat class handles these issues. It is easy to use and quite similar to the NumberFormat class. First, get a locale. You can use the default locale or call the static getAvailableLocales method to obtain an array of locales that support date formatting. Then, call one of the three factory methods:

```
fmt = DateFormat.getDateInstance(dateStyle, loc);
fmt = DateFormat.getTimeInstance(timeStyle, loc);
fmt = DateFormat.getDateTimeInstance(dateStyle, timeStyle, loc);
```

To specify the desired style, these factory methods have a parameter that is one of the following constants:

1.  DateFormat.DEFAULT
2.  DateFormat.FULL (e.g., Wednesday, September 12, 2007 8:51:03 PM PDT for the U.S. locale)
3.  DateFormat.LONG (e.g., September 12, 2007 8:51:03 PM PDT for the U.S. locale)
4.  DateFormat.MEDIUM (e.g., Sep 12, 2007 8:51:03 PM for the U.S. locale)
5.  DateFormat.SHORT (e.g., 9/12/07 8:51 PM for the U.S. locale)

The factory method returns a formatting object that you can then use to format dates.

```
Date now = new Date();
String s = fmt.format(now);
```

Just as with the NumberFormat class, you can use the parse method to parse a date that the user typed. For example, the following code parses the value that the user typed into a text field, using the default locale:

```
TextField inputField;
. . .
DateFormat fmt = DateFormat.getDateInstance(DateFormat.MEDIUM);
Date input = fmt.parse(inputField.getText().trim());
```

Unfortunately, the user must type the date exactly in the expected format. For example, if the format is set to MEDIUM in the U.S. locale, then dates are expected to look like

Sep 12, 2007

If the user types

Sep 12 2007

(without the comma) or the short format

9/12/07

then a ParseException results.

A lenient flag interprets dates leniently. For example, February 30, 2007 will be automatically converted to March 2, 2007. This seems dangerous, but, unfortunately, it is the default. You should probably turn off this feature. The calendar object that interprets the parsed date will throw IllegalArgumentException when the user enters an invalid day/month/year combination.

Listing 5.2 shows the DateFormat class in action. You can select a locale and see how the date and time are formatted in different places around the world. If you see question mark characters in the output, then you don't have the fonts installed for displaying characters in the local language. For example, if you pick a Chinese locale, the date might be expressed as

2007年3月9日12

Figure 5.2 shows the program (after Chinese fonts were installed). As you can see, it correctly displays the output.

**Figure 5.2** The DateFormatTest program

---

**Listing 5.2** dateFormat/DateFormatTest.java

```java
1  package dateFormat;
2
3  import java.awt.*;
4  import java.awt.event.*;
5  import java.text.*;
6  import java.util.*;
7  import javax.swing.*;
8
9  /**
10  * This program demonstrates formatting dates under various locales.
11  * @version 1.13 2007-07-25
12  * @author Cay Horstmann
13  */
14  public class DateFormatTest
15  {
16     public static void main(String[] args)
17     {
18        EventQueue.invokeLater(new Runnable()
19           {
20              public void run()
21              {
22                 JFrame frame = new DateFormatFrame();
23                 frame.setTitle("DateFormatTest");
```

*(Continues)*

---

**Listing 5.2** *(Continued)*

```
24                  frame.setDefaultCloseOperation(JFrame.EXIT_ON_CLOSE);
25                  frame.setVisible(true);
26              }
27          });
28      }
29  }
30
31  /**
32   * This frame contains combo boxes to pick a locale, date and time formats, text fields to display
33   * formatted date and time, buttons to parse the text field contents, and a "lenient" check box.
34   */
35  class DateFormatFrame extends JFrame
36  {
37      private Locale[] locales;
38      private Date currentDate;
39      private Date currentTime;
40      private DateFormat currentDateFormat;
41      private DateFormat currentTimeFormat;
42      private JComboBox<String> localeCombo = new JComboBox<>();
43      private JButton dateParseButton = new JButton("Parse date");
44      private JButton timeParseButton = new JButton("Parse time");
45      private JTextField dateText = new JTextField(30);
46      private JTextField timeText = new JTextField(30);
47      private JCheckBox lenientCheckbox = new JCheckBox("Parse lenient", true);
48      private EnumCombo dateStyleCombo = new EnumCombo(DateFormat.class, "Default",
49          "Full", "Long", "Medium", "Short");
50      private EnumCombo timeStyleCombo = new EnumCombo(DateFormat.class, "Default",
51          "Full", "Long", "Medium", "Short");
52
53      public DateFormatFrame()
54      {
55          setLayout(new GridBagLayout());
56          add(new JLabel("Locale"), new GBC(0, 0).setAnchor(GBC.EAST));
57          add(new JLabel("Date style"), new GBC(0, 1).setAnchor(GBC.EAST));
58          add(new JLabel("Time style"), new GBC(2, 1).setAnchor(GBC.EAST));
59          add(new JLabel("Date"), new GBC(0, 2).setAnchor(GBC.EAST));
60          add(new JLabel("Time"), new GBC(0, 3).setAnchor(GBC.EAST));
61          add(localeCombo, new GBC(1, 0, 2, 1).setAnchor(GBC.WEST));
62          add(dateStyleCombo, new GBC(1, 1).setAnchor(GBC.WEST));
63          add(timeStyleCombo, new GBC(3, 1).setAnchor(GBC.WEST));
64          add(dateParseButton, new GBC(3, 2).setAnchor(GBC.WEST));
65          add(timeParseButton, new GBC(3, 3).setAnchor(GBC.WEST));
66          add(lenientCheckbox, new GBC(0, 4, 2, 1).setAnchor(GBC.WEST));
67          add(dateText, new GBC(1, 2, 2, 1).setFill(GBC.HORIZONTAL));
68          add(timeText, new GBC(1, 3, 2, 1).setFill(GBC.HORIZONTAL));
69
70          locales = (Locale[]) DateFormat.getAvailableLocales().clone();
```

```
71      Arrays.sort(locales, new Comparator<Locale>()
72         {
73            public int compare(Locale l1, Locale l2)
74            {
75               return l1.getDisplayName().compareTo(l2.getDisplayName());
76            }
77         });
78      for (Locale loc : locales)
79         localeCombo.addItem(loc.getDisplayName());
80      localeCombo.setSelectedItem(Locale.getDefault().getDisplayName());
81      currentDate = new Date();
82      currentTime = new Date();
83      updateDisplay();
84
85      ActionListener listener = new ActionListener()
86         {
87            public void actionPerformed(ActionEvent event)
88            {
89               updateDisplay();
90            }
91         };
92
93      localeCombo.addActionListener(listener);
94      dateStyleCombo.addActionListener(listener);
95      timeStyleCombo.addActionListener(listener);
96
97      dateParseButton.addActionListener(new ActionListener()
98         {
99            public void actionPerformed(ActionEvent event)
100           {
101              String d = dateText.getText().trim();
102              try
103              {
104                 currentDateFormat.setLenient(lenientCheckbox.isSelected());
105                 Date date = currentDateFormat.parse(d);
106                 currentDate = date;
107                 updateDisplay();
108              }
109              catch (ParseException e)
110              {
111                 dateText.setText("Parse error: " + d);
112              }
113              catch (IllegalArgumentException e)
114              {
115                 dateText.setText("Argument error: " + d);
116              }
117           }
118        });
```

*(Continues)*

**Listing 5.2** *(Continued)*

```
119    timeParseButton.addActionListener(new ActionListener()
120        {
121            public void actionPerformed(ActionEvent event)
122            {
123                String t = timeText.getText().trim();
124                try
125                {
126                    currentDateFormat.setLenient(lenientCheckbox.isSelected());
127                    Date date = currentTimeFormat.parse(t);
128                    currentTime = date;
129                    updateDisplay();
130                }
131                catch (ParseException e)
132                {
133                    timeText.setText("Parse error: " + t);
134                }
135                catch (IllegalArgumentException e)
136                {
137                    timeText.setText("Argument error: " + t);
138                }
139            }
140        });
141    pack();
142    }
143
144    /**
145     * Updates the display and formats the date according to the user settings.
146     */
147    public void updateDisplay()
148    {
149        Locale currentLocale = locales[localeCombo.getSelectedIndex()];
150        int dateStyle = dateStyleCombo.getValue();
151        currentDateFormat = DateFormat.getDateInstance(dateStyle, currentLocale);
152        String d = currentDateFormat.format(currentDate);
153        dateText.setText(d);
154        int timeStyle = timeStyleCombo.getValue();
155        currentTimeFormat = DateFormat.getTimeInstance(timeStyle, currentLocale);
156        String t = currentTimeFormat.format(currentTime);
157        timeText.setText(t);
158    }
159 }
```

You can also experiment with parsing. Enter a date or time, click the "Parse lenient" checkbox if desired, and click the "Parse date" or "Parse time" button.

We use a helper class EnumCombo to solve a technical problem (see Listing 5.3). We wanted to fill a combo with values such as Short, Medium, and Long and then automatically convert the user's selection to integer values DateFormat.SHORT, DateFormat.MEDIUM, and DateFormat.LONG. Instead of writing repetitive code, we use reflection: We convert the user's choice to upper case, replace all spaces with underscores, and then find the value of the static field with that name. (See Volume I, Chapter 5 for more details about reflection.)

**Listing 5.3**  dateFormat/EnumCombo.java

```
 1  package dateFormat;
 2
 3  import java.util.*;
 4  import javax.swing.*;
 5  /**
 6     A combo box that lets users choose from among static field
 7     values whose names are given in the constructor.
 8     @version 1.14 2012-01-26
 9     @author Cay Horstmann
10  */
11  public class EnumCombo extends JComboBox<String>
12  {
13     private Map<String, Integer> table = new TreeMap<>();
14
15     /**
16        Constructs an EnumCombo.
17        @param cl a class
18        @param labels an array of static field names of cl
19     */
20     public EnumCombo(Class<?> cl, String... labels)
21     {
22        for (String label : labels)
23        {
24           String name = label.toUpperCase().replace(' ', '_');
25           int value = 0;
26           try
27           {
28              java.lang.reflect.Field f = cl.getField(name);
29              value = f.getInt(cl);
30           }
31           catch (Exception e)
32           {
33              label = "(" + label + ")";
34           }
35           table.put(label, value);
36           addItem(label);
37        }
38        setSelectedItem(labels[0]);
39     }
```

*(Continues)*

**Listing 5.3** *(Continued)*

```
40     /**
41         Returns the value of the field that the user selected.
42         @return the static field value
43     */
44     public int getValue()
45     {
46         return table.get(getSelectedItem());
47     }
48 }
```

---

**java.text.DateFormat** 1.1

- static Locale[] getAvailableLocales()
  returns an array of Locale objects for which DateFormat formatters are available.

- static DateFormat getDateInstance(int dateStyle)
- static DateFormat getDateInstance(int dateStyle, Locale l)
- static DateFormat getTimeInstance(int timeStyle)
- static DateFormat getTimeInstance(int timeStyle, Locale l)
- static DateFormat getDateTimeInstance(int dateStyle, int timeStyle)
- static DateFormat getDateTimeInstance(int dateStyle, int timeStyle, Locale l)
  returns a formatter for date, time, or date and time for the default locale or the given locale.

  *Parameters:*    dateStyle, timeStyle    One of DEFAULT, FULL, LONG, MEDIUM, SHORT

- String format(Date d)
  returns the string resulting from formatting the given date/time.

- Date parse(String s)
  parses the given string and returns the date/time described in it. The beginning of the string must contain a date or time; no leading whitespace is allowed. The date can be followed by other characters, which are ignored. Throws a ParseException if parsing was not successful.

- void setLenient(boolean b)
- boolean isLenient()
  sets or gets a flag to indicate whether parsing should be lenient or strict. In the lenient mode, dates such as February 30, 1999 will be automatically converted to March 2, 1999. The default is lenient mode.

*(Continues)*

---

**java.text.DateFormat** 1.1 *(Continued)*

- void setCalendar(Calendar cal)
- Calendar getCalendar()

  sets or gets the calendar object used for extracting year, month, day, hour, minute, and second from the Date object. Use this method if you do not want to use the default calendar for the locale (usually the Gregorian calendar).

- void setTimeZone(TimeZone tz)
- TimeZone getTimeZone()

  sets or gets the time zone object used for formatting the time. Use this method if you do not want to use the default time zone for the locale. The default time zone is the time zone of the default locale, as obtained from the operating system. For the other locales, it is the preferred time zone in the geographical location.

- void setNumberFormat(NumberFormat f)
- NumberFormat getNumberFormat()

  sets or gets the number format used for formatting the numbers used for representing year, month, day, hour, minute, and second.

---

**java.util.TimeZone** 1.1

- static String[] getAvailableIDs()

  gets all supported time zone IDs.

- static TimeZone getDefault()

  gets the default TimeZone for this computer.

- static TimeZone getTimeZone(String timeZoneId)

  gets the TimeZone for the given ID.

- String getID()

  gets the ID of this time zone.

- String getDisplayName()
- String getDisplayName(Locale locale)
- String getDisplayName(boolean daylight, int style)
- String getDisplayName(boolean daylight, int style, Locale locale)

  gets the display name of this time zone in the default locale or in the given locale. If the daylight parameter is true, the daylight savings name is returned. The style parameter can be SHORT or LONG.

*(Continues)*

---

**java.util.TimeZone** 1.1 *(Continued)*

- `boolean useDaylightTime()`
  returns `true` if this `TimeZone` uses daylight savings time.

- `boolean inDaylightTime(Date date)`
  returns `true` if the given date is in daylight savings time in this `TimeZone`.

---

## 5.4 Collation

Most programmers know how to compare strings with the `compareTo` method of the `String` class. The value of `a.compareTo(b)` is a negative number if `a` is lexicographically less than `b`, zero if they are identical, and positive otherwise.

Unfortunately, this method is useless unless all your words are in uppercase ASCII characters. The problem is that the `compareTo` method in the Java programming language uses the values of the Unicode character to determine the ordering. For example, lowercase characters have a higher Unicode value than uppercase characters, and accented characters have even higher values. This leads to absurd results; for example, the following five strings are ordered according to the `compareTo` method:

```
America
Zulu
able
zebra
Ångström
```

For dictionary ordering, you would want to consider upper case and lower case to be equivalent. To an English speaker, the sample list of words would be ordered as

```
able
America
Ångström
zebra
Zulu
```

However, that order would not be acceptable to a Swedish user. In Swedish, the letter Å is different from the letter A, and it is collated *after* the letter Z! That is, a Swedish user would want the words to be sorted as

```
able
America
zebra
```

```
Zulu
Ångström
```

Fortunately, once you are aware of the problem, collation is quite easy. As always, start by obtaining a `Locale` object. Then, call the `getInstance` factory method to obtain a `Collator` object. Finally, use the `compare` method of the collator, *not* the `compareTo` method of the `String` class, whenever you want to sort strings.

```
Locale loc = . . .;
Collator coll = Collator.getInstance(loc);
if (coll.compare(a, b) < 0) // a comes before b . . .;
```

Most importantly, the `Collator` class implements the `Comparator` interface. Therefore, you can pass a `Collator` object to the `Collections.sort` method to sort a list of strings:

```
Collections.sort(strings, coll);
```

## 5.4.1 Collation Strength

You can set a collator's *strength* to select how selective it should be. Character differences are classified as *primary*, *secondary*, *tertiary*, and *identical*. For example, in English, the difference between "A" and "Z" is considered primary, the difference between "A" and "Å" is secondary, and between "A" and "a" is tertiary.

By setting the strength of the collator to `Collator.PRIMARY`, you tell it to pay attention only to primary differences. By setting the strength to `Collator.SECONDARY`, you instruct the collator to take secondary differences into account. That is, two strings will be more likely to be considered different when the strength is set to "secondary" or "tertiary," as shown in Table 5.4.

When the strength has been set to `Collator.IDENTICAL`, no differences are allowed. This setting is mainly useful in conjunction with the second, rather technical, collator setting, the *decomposition mode*, which we discuss in the next section.

**Table 5.4** Collations with Different Strengths (English Locale)

| Primary | Secondary | Tertiary |
|---|---|---|
| Angstrom = Ångström | Angstrom ≠ Ångström | Angstrom ≠ Ångström |
| Able = able | Able = able | Able ≠ able |

## 5.4.2 Decomposition

Occasionally, a character or sequence of characters can be described in more than one way in Unicode. For example, an "Å" can be Unicode character U+00C5, or it can be expressed as a plain A (U+0065) followed by a ° ("combining ring above"; U+030A). Perhaps more surprisingly, the letter sequence "ffi" can be described with a single character "Latin small ligature ffi" with code U+FB03. (One could argue that this is a presentation issue that should not have resulted in different Unicode characters, but we don't make the rules.)

The Unicode standard defines four *normalization forms* (D, KD, C, and KC) for strings. See www.unicode.org/unicode/reports/tr15/tr15-23.html for the details. Two of them are used for collation. In the normalization form D, accented characters are decomposed into their base letters and combining accents. For example, Å is turned into a sequence of an A and a combining ring above °. Normalization form KD goes further and decomposes *compatibility characters* such as the ffi ligature or the trademark symbol ™.

You can choose the degree of normalization that you want the collator to use. The value Collator.NO_DECOMPOSITION does not normalize strings at all. This option is faster, but it might not be appropriate for text that expresses characters in multiple forms. The default, Collator.CANONICAL_DECOMPOSITION, uses the normalization form D. This is the most useful form for text that contains accents but not ligatures. Finally, "full decomposition" uses normalization form KD. See Table 5.5 for examples.

It is wasteful to have the collator decompose a string many times. If one string is compared many times against other strings, you can save the decomposition in a *collation* key object. The getCollationKey method returns a CollationKey object that you can use for further, faster comparisons. Here is an example:

```
String a = . . .;
CollationKey aKey = coll.getCollationKey(a);
if(aKey.compareTo(coll.getCollationKey(b)) == 0) // fast comparison
   . . .
```

Finally, you might want to convert strings into their normalized forms even when you don't do collation—for example, when storing strings in a database or communicating with another program. The java.text.Normalizer class carries out the normalization process. For example,

```
String name = "Ångström";
String normalized = Normalizer.normalize(name, Normalizer.Form.NFD); // uses normalization form D
```

**Table 5.5** Differences between Decomposition Modes

| No Decomposition | Canonical Decomposition | Full Decomposition |
| --- | --- | --- |
| Å ≠ A° | Å = A° | Å = A° |
| ™ ≠ TM | ™ ≠ TM | ™ = TM |

The normalized string contains ten characters. The "Å" and "ö" are replaced by "A°" and "o¨" sequences.

However, that is not usually the best form for storage and transmission. Normalization form C first applies decomposition and then combines the accents back in a standardized order. According to the W3C, this is the recommended mode for transferring data over the Internet.

The program in Listing 5.4 lets you experiment with collation order. Type a word into the text field and click the Add button to add it to the list of words. Each time you add another word, or change the locale, strength, or decomposition mode, the list of words is sorted again. An = sign indicates words that are considered identical (see Figure 5.3).

The locale names in the combo box are displayed in sorted order, using the collator of the default locale. If you run this program with the US English locale, note that "Norwegian (Norway,Nynorsk)" comes before "Norwegian (Norway)", even though the Unicode value of the comma character is greater than the Unicode value of the closing parenthesis.

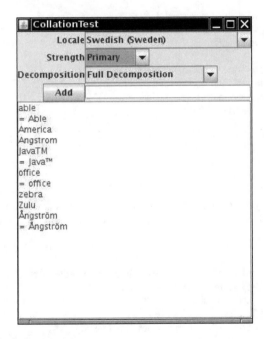

**Figure 5.3** The CollationTest program

**Listing 5.4** collation/CollationTest.java

```
1  package collation;
2
3  import java.awt.*;
4  import java.awt.event.*;
5  import java.text.*;
6  import java.util.*;
7  import java.util.List;
8
9  import javax.swing.*;
10
11 /**
12  * This program demonstrates collating strings under various locales.
13  * @version 1.14 2012-01-26
14  * @author Cay Horstmann
15  */
16 public class CollationTest
17 {
18    public static void main(String[] args)
19    {
20       EventQueue.invokeLater(new Runnable()
21          {
22             public void run()
23             {
24                JFrame frame = new CollationFrame();
25                frame.setTitle("CollationTest");
26                frame.setDefaultCloseOperation(JFrame.EXIT_ON_CLOSE);
27                frame.setVisible(true);
28             }
29          });
30    }
31 }
32
33 /**
34  * This frame contains combo boxes to pick a locale, collation strength and decomposition rules,
35  * a text field and button to add new strings, and a text area to list the collated strings.
36  */
37 class CollationFrame extends JFrame
38 {
39    private Collator collator = Collator.getInstance(Locale.getDefault());
40    private List<String> strings = new ArrayList<>();
41    private Collator currentCollator;
42    private Locale[] locales;
43    private JComboBox<String> localeCombo = new JComboBox<>();
44    private JTextField newWord = new JTextField(20);
45    private JTextArea sortedWords = new JTextArea(20, 20);
46    private JButton addButton = new JButton("Add");
```

```
47   private EnumCombo strengthCombo = new EnumCombo(Collator.class, "Primary",
48       "Secondary", "Tertiary", "Identical");
49   private EnumCombo decompositionCombo = new EnumCombo(Collator.class,
50       "Canonical Decomposition", "Full Decomposition", "No Decomposition");
51
52   public CollationFrame()
53   {
54      setLayout(new GridBagLayout());
55      add(new JLabel("Locale"), new GBC(0, 0).setAnchor(GBC.EAST));
56      add(new JLabel("Strength"), new GBC(0, 1).setAnchor(GBC.EAST));
57      add(new JLabel("Decomposition"), new GBC(0, 2).setAnchor(GBC.EAST));
58      add(addButton, new GBC(0, 3).setAnchor(GBC.EAST));
59      add(localeCombo, new GBC(1, 0).setAnchor(GBC.WEST));
60      add(strengthCombo, new GBC(1, 1).setAnchor(GBC.WEST));
61      add(decompositionCombo, new GBC(1, 2).setAnchor(GBC.WEST));
62      add(newWord, new GBC(1, 3).setFill(GBC.HORIZONTAL));
63      add(new JScrollPane(sortedWords), new GBC(0, 4, 2, 1).setFill(GBC.BOTH));
64
65      locales = (Locale[]) Collator.getAvailableLocales().clone();
66      Arrays.sort(locales, new Comparator<Locale>()
67         {
68            public int compare(Locale l1, Locale l2)
69            {
70               return collator.compare(l1.getDisplayName(), l2.getDisplayName());
71            }
72         });
73      for (Locale loc : locales)
74         localeCombo.addItem(loc.getDisplayName());
75      localeCombo.setSelectedItem(Locale.getDefault().getDisplayName());
76
77      strings.add("America");
78      strings.add("able");
79      strings.add("Zulu");
80      strings.add("zebra");
81      strings.add("\u00C5ngstr\u00F6m");
82      strings.add("A\u030angstro\u0308m");
83      strings.add("Angstrom");
84      strings.add("Able");
85      strings.add("office");
86      strings.add("o\uFB03ce");
87      strings.add("Java\u2122");
88      strings.add("JavaTM");
89      updateDisplay();
90
91      addButton.addActionListener(new ActionListener()
92         {
93            public void actionPerformed(ActionEvent event)
94            {
```

*(Continues)*

**Listing 5.4** *(Continued)*

```
95              strings.add(newWord.getText());
96              updateDisplay();
97           }
98        });
99
100     ActionListener listener = new ActionListener()
101        {
102           public void actionPerformed(ActionEvent event)
103           {
104              updateDisplay();
105           }
106        };
107
108     localeCombo.addActionListener(listener);
109     strengthCombo.addActionListener(listener);
110     decompositionCombo.addActionListener(listener);
111     pack();
112  }
113
114  /**
115   * Updates the display and collates the strings according to the user settings.
116   */
117  public void updateDisplay()
118  {
119     Locale currentLocale = locales[localeCombo.getSelectedIndex()];
120     localeCombo.setLocale(currentLocale);
121
122     currentCollator = Collator.getInstance(currentLocale);
123     currentCollator.setStrength(strengthCombo.getValue());
124     currentCollator.setDecomposition(decompositionCombo.getValue());
125
126     Collections.sort(strings, currentCollator);
127
128     sortedWords.setText("");
129     for (int i = 0; i < strings.size(); i++)
130     {
131        String s = strings.get(i);
132        if (i > 0 && currentCollator.compare(s, strings.get(i - 1)) == 0) sortedWords
133              .append("= ");
134        sortedWords.append(s + "\n");
135     }
136     pack();
137  }
138 }
```

---

**java.text.Collator** 1.1

- static Locale[] getAvailableLocales()
  returns an array of Locale objects for which Collator objects are available.

- static Collator getInstance()
- static Collator getInstance(Locale l)
  returns a collator for the default locale or the given locale.

- int compare(String a, String b)
  returns a negative value if a comes before b, 0 if they are considered identical, and a positive value otherwise.

- boolean equals(String a, String b)
  returns true if they are considered identical, false otherwise.

- void setStrength(int strength)
- int getStrength()
  sets or gets the strength of the collator. Stronger collators tell more words apart. Strength values are Collator.PRIMARY, Collator.SECONDARY, and Collator.TERTIARY.

- void setDecomposition(int decomp)
- int getDecompositon()
  sets or gets the decomposition mode of the collator. The more a collator decomposes a string, the more strict it will be in deciding whether two strings should be considered identical. Decomposition values are Collator.NO_DECOMPOSITION, Collator.CANONICAL_DECOMPOSITION, and Collator.FULL_DECOMPOSITION.

- CollationKey getCollationKey(String a)
  returns a collation key that contains a decomposition of the characters in a form that can be quickly compared against another collation key.

---

**java.text.CollationKey** 1.1

- int compareTo(CollationKey b)
  returns a negative value if this key comes before b, 0 if they are considered identical, and a positive value otherwise.

---

**java.text.Normalizer** 6

- static String normalize(CharSequence str, Normalizer.Form form)
  returns the normalized form of str. The form value is one of ND, NKD, NC, or NKC.

## 5.5 Message Formatting

The Java library has a MessageFormat class that formats text with variable parts, like this:

```
"On {2}, a {0} destroyed {1} houses and caused {3} of damage."
```

The numbers in braces are placeholders for actual names and values. The static method MessageFormat.format lets you substitute values for the variables. As of JDK 5.0, it is a "varargs" method, so you can simply supply the parameters as follows:

```
String msg = MessageFormat.format("On {2}, a {0} destroyed {1} houses and caused {3} of damage.",
    "hurricane", 99, new GregorianCalendar(1999, 0, 1).getTime(), 10.0E8);
```

In this example, the placeholder {0} is replaced with "hurricane", {1} is replaced with 99, and so on.

The result of our example is the string

```
On 1/1/99 12:00 AM, a hurricane destroyed 99 houses and caused 100,000,000 of damage.
```

That is a start, but it is not perfect. We don't want to display the time "12:00 AM," and we want the damage amount printed as a currency value. The way we do this is by supplying an optional format for some of the placeholders:

```
"On {2,date,long}, a {0} destroyed {1} houses and caused {3,number,currency} of damage."
```

This example code prints:

```
On January 1, 1999, a hurricane destroyed 99 houses and caused $100,000,000 of damage.
```

In general, the placeholder index can be followed by a *type* and a *style*. Separate the index, type, and style by commas. The type can be any of

```
number
time
date
choice
```

If the type is number, then the style can be

```
integer
currency
percent
```

or it can be a number format pattern such as $,##0. (See the documentation of the DecimalFormat class for more information about the possible formats.)

If the type is either time or date, then the style can be

```
short
medium
```

```
long
full
```

or a date format pattern such as yyyy-MM-dd. (See the documentation of the SimpleDateFormat class for more information about the possible formats.)

Choice formats are more complex, and we will take them up in the next section.

 **CAUTION:** The static MessageFormat.format method uses the current locale to format the values. To format with an arbitrary locale, you have to work a bit harder because there is no "varargs" method that you can use. You need to place the values to be formatted into an Object[] array, like this:

```
MessageFormat mf = new MessageFormat(pattern, loc);
String msg = mf.format(new Object[] { values });
```

---

**java.text.MessageFormat** 1.1

- MessageFormat(String pattern)
- MessageFormat(String pattern, Locale loc)
  constructs a message format object with the specified pattern and locale.

- void applyPattern(String pattern)
  sets the pattern of a message format object to the specified pattern.

- void setLocale(Locale loc)
- Locale getLocale()
  sets or gets the locale to be used for the placeholders in the message. The locale is *only* used for subsequent patterns that you set by calling the applyPattern method.

- static String format(String pattern, Object... args)
  formats the pattern string by using args[i] as input for placeholder {i}.

- StringBuffer format(Object args, StringBuffer result, FieldPosition pos)
  formats the pattern of this MessageFormat. The args parameter must be an array of objects. The formatted string is appended to result, and result is returned. If pos equals new FieldPosition(MessageFormat.Field.ARGUMENT), its beginIndex and endIndex properties are set to the location of the text that replaces the {1} placeholder. Supply null if you are not interested in position information.

---

**java.text.Format** 1.1

- String format(Object obj)
  formats the given object, according to the rules of this formatter. This method calls format(obj, new StringBuffer(), new FieldPosition(1)).toString().

## 5.5.1 Choice Formats

Let's look closer at the pattern of the preceding section:

```
"On {2}, a {0} destroyed {1} houses and caused {3} of damage."
```

If we replace the disaster placeholder {0} with "earthquake", the sentence is not grammatically correct in English:

```
On January 1, 1999, a earthquake destroyed . . .
```

That means what we really want to do is integrate the article "a" into the placeholder:

```
"On {2}, {0} destroyed {1} houses and caused {3} of damage."
```

The {0} would then be replaced with "a hurricane" or "an earthquake". That is especially appropriate if this message needs to be translated into a language where the gender of a word affects the article. For example, in German, the pattern would be

```
"{0} zerstörte am {2} {1} Häuser und richtete einen Schaden von {3} an."
```

The placeholder would then be replaced with the grammatically correct combination of article and noun, such as "Ein Wirbelsturm" or "Eine Naturkatastrophe".

Now let us turn to the {1} parameter. If the disaster wasn't all that catastrophic, {1} might be replaced with the number 1, and the message would read:

```
On January 1, 1999, a mudslide destroyed 1 houses and . . .
```

Ideally, we would like the message to vary according to the placeholder value, so it would read

```
no houses
one house
2 houses
 . . .
```

depending on the placeholder value. The choice formatting option was designed for this purpose.

A choice format is a sequence of pairs, each containing

- A *lower limit*
- A *format string*

The lower limit and format string are separated by a # character, and the pairs are separated by | characters.

**Table 5.6** String Formatted by Choice Format

| {1} | Result | {1} | Result |
|---|---|---|---|
| 0 | "no houses" | 3 | "3 houses" |
| 1 | "one house" | -1 | "no houses" |

For example,

   `{1,choice,0#no houses|1#one house|2#{1} houses}`

Table 5.6 shows the effect of this format string for various values of {1}.

Why do we use {1} twice in the format string? When the message format applies the choice format to the {1} placeholder and the value is $2, the choice format returns "{1} houses". That string is then formatted again by the message format, and the answer is spliced into the result.

> **NOTE:** This example shows that the designer of the choice format was a bit muddleheaded. If you have three format strings, you need two limits to separate them. In general, you need *one fewer limit* than you have format strings. As you saw in Table 5.6, the `MessageFormat` class ignores the first limit.
>
> The syntax would have been a lot clearer if the designer of this class realized that the limits belong *between* the choices, such as
>
>    `no houses|1|one house|2|{1} houses // not the actual format`

You can use the < symbol to denote that a choice should be selected if the lower bound is strictly less than the value.

You can also use the ≤ symbol (expressed as the Unicode character code \u2264) as a synonym for #. If you like, you can even specify a lower bound of −∞ as -\u221E for the first value.

For example,

   `-∞<no houses|0<one house|2≤{1} houses`

or, using Unicode escapes,

   `-\u221E<no houses|0<one house|2\u2264{1} houses`

Let's finish our natural disaster scenario. If we put the choice string inside the original message string, we get the following format instruction:

```
String pattern = "On {2,date,long}, {0} destroyed {1,choice,0#no houses|1#one house|2#{1}
    houses}" + "and caused {3,number,currency} of damage.";
```

Or, in German,

```
String pattern = "{0} zerstörte am {2,date,long} {1,choice,0#kein Haus|1#ein Haus|2#{1} Häuser}"
    + "und richtete einen Schaden von {3,number,currency} an.";
```

Note that the ordering of the words is different in German, but the array of objects you pass to the `format` method is the *same*. The order of the placeholders in the format string takes care of the changes in the word ordering.

## 5.6 Text Files and Character Sets

As you know, the Java programming language itself is fully Unicode-based. However, operating systems typically have their own character encoding, such as ISO 8859-1 (an 8-bit code sometimes called the "ANSI" code) in the United States, or Big5 in Taiwan.

When you save data to a text file, you should respect the local character encoding so that the users of your program can open the text file in their other applications. Specify the character encoding in the `FileWriter` constructor:

```
out = new FileWriter(filename, "ISO-8859-1");
```

You can find a complete list of the supported encodings in Table 1.1 on p. 22.

Unfortunately, there is currently no connection between locales and character encodings. For example, if your user has selected the Taiwanese locale `zh-TW`, no method in the Java programming language tells you that the Big5 character encoding would be the most appropriate.

### 5.6.1 Character Encoding of Source Files

It is worth keeping in mind that you, the programmer, will need to communicate with the Java compiler. And *you do that with tools on your local system*. For example, you can use the Chinese version of Notepad to write your Java source code files. The resulting source code files are *not portable* because they use the local character encoding (GB or Big5, depending on which Chinese operating system you use). Only the compiled class files are portable—they will automatically use the "modified UTF-8" encoding for identifiers and strings. That means that when a program is compiling and running, three character encodings are involved:

- Source files: local encoding
- Class files: modified UTF-8

- Virtual machine: UTF-16

(See Chapter 1 for a definition of the modified UTF-8 and UTF-16 formats.)

**TIP:** You can specify the character encoding of your source files with the `-encoding` flag, for example,

```
javac -encoding Big5 Myfile.java
```

To make your source files portable, restrict yourself to using the plain ASCII encoding. That is, you should change all non-ASCII characters to their equivalent Unicode encodings. For example, instead of using the string `"Häuser"`, use `"H\u0084user"`. The JDK contains a utility, `native2ascii`, that you can use to convert the native character encoding to plain ASCII. This utility simply replaces every non-ASCII character in the input with a `\u` followed by the four hex digits of the Unicode value. To use the `native2ascii` program, provide the input and output file names.

```
native2ascii Myfile.java Myfile.temp
```

You can convert the other way with the `-reverse` option:

```
native2ascii -reverse Myfile.temp Myfile.java
```

You can specify another encoding with the `-encoding` option. The encoding name must be one of those listed in Table 1.1 on p. 22.

```
native2ascii -encoding Big5 Myfile.java Myfile.temp
```

**TIP:** It is a good idea to restrict yourself to plain ASCII class names. Since the name of the class also turns into the name of the *class file*, you are at the mercy of the local file system to handle any non-ASCII names. Here is a depressing example. Windows 95 used the so-called Code Page 437, or original PC encoding, for its file names. If you compiled a class Bär and tried to run it in Windows 95, you got an error message "cannot find class BΣr."

## 5.7 Resource Bundles

When localizing an application, you'll probably have a dauntingly large number of message strings, button labels, and so on, that all need to be translated. To make this task feasible, you'll want to define the message strings in an external location, usually called a *resource*. The person carrying out the translation can then simply edit the resource files without having to touch the source code of the program.

In Java, you can use property files to specify string resources, and you can implement classes for resources of other types.

**NOTE:** Java technology resources are not the same as Windows or Macintosh resources. A Macintosh or Windows executable program stores resources, such as menus, dialog boxes, icons, and messages, in a section separate from the program code. A resource editor can inspect and update these resources without affecting the program code.

**NOTE:** Volume I, Chapter 10 describes a concept of JAR file resources, whereby data files, sounds, and images can be placed in a JAR file. The `getResource` method of the class `Class` finds the file, opens it, and returns a URL to the resource. By placing the files into the JAR file, you leave the job of finding the files to the class loader, which already knows how to locate items in a JAR file. However, that mechanism has no locale support.

## 5.7.1 Locating Resource Bundles

When localizing an application, you produce a set of *resource bundles*. Each bundle is a property file or a class that describes locale-specific items (such as messages, labels, and so on). For each bundle, you have to provide versions for all locales that you want to support.

You need to use a specific naming convention for these bundles. For example, resources specific to Germany go into a file *bundleName_*de_DE, whereas those shared by all German-speaking countries go into *bundleName_*de. In general, use

   *bundleName_language_country*

for all country-specific resources, and use

   *bundleName_language*

for all language-specific resources. Finally, as a fallback, you can put defaults into a file without any suffix.

To load a bundle, use the command

```
ResourceBundle currentResources = ResourceBundle.getBundle(bundleName, currentLocale);
```

The getBundle method attempts to load the bundle that matches the current locale by language and country. If it is not successful, the country and the language are dropped in turn. Then the same search is applied to the default locale, and finally, the default bundle file is consulted. If even that attempt fails, the method throws a MissingResourceException.

That is, the getBundle method tries to load the following bundles:

*bundleName_currentLocaleLanguage_currentLocaleCountry*
*bundleName_currentLocaleLanguage*
*bundleName_currentLocaleLanguage_defaultLocaleCountry*
*bundleName_defaultLocaleLanguage*
*bundleName*

Once the getBundle method has located a bundle (say, *bundleName_*de_DE), it will still keep looking for *bundleName_*de and *bundleName*. If these bundles exist, they become the *parents* of the *bundleName_*de_DE bundle in a *resource hierarchy*. Later, when looking up a resource, the parents are searched if a lookup was not successful in the current bundle. That is, if a particular resource was not found in *bundleName_*de_DE, then the *bundleName_*de and *bundleName* will be queried as well.

This is clearly a very useful service—and one that would be tedious to program by hand. The resource bundle mechanism of the Java programming language automatically locates the items that are the best match for a given locale. It is easy to add more and more localizations to an existing program—all you have to do is create additional resource bundles.

 **NOTE:** We simplified the discussion of resource bundle lookup. If a locale has a script or variant, the lookup is quite a bit more complex. See the documentation of the method ResourceBundle.Control.getCandidateLocales for the gory details.

 **TIP:** You need not place all resources for your application into a single bundle. You could have one bundle for button labels, one for error messages, and so on.

## 5.7.2 Property Files

Internationalizing strings is quite straightforward. You place all your strings into a property file such as MyProgramStrings.properties. This is simply a text file with one key/value pair per line. A typical file would look like this:

```
computeButton=Rechnen
colorName=black
defaultPaperSize=210x297
```

Then you name your property files as described in the preceding section, for example:

```
MyProgramStrings.properties
MyProgramStrings_en.properties
MyProgramStrings_de_DE.properties
```

You can load the bundle simply as

```
ResourceBundle bundle = ResourceBundle.getBundle("MyProgramStrings", locale);
```

To look up a specific string, call

```
String computeButtonLabel = bundle.getString("computeButton");
```

 **CAUTION:** Files for storing properties are always ASCII files. If you need to place a Unicode character into a property file, encode it using the \uxxxx encoding. For example, to specify "colorName=Grün", use

```
colorName=Gr\u00FCn
```

You can use the native2ascii tool to generate these files.

### 5.7.3 Bundle Classes

To provide resources that are not strings, define classes that extend the ResourceBundle class. Use the standard naming convention to name your classes, for example

```
MyProgramResources.java
MyProgramResources_en.java
MyProgramResources_de_DE.java
```

Load the class with the same getBundle method that you use to load a property file:

```
ResourceBundle bundle = ResourceBundle.getBundle("MyProgramResources", locale);
```

 **CAUTION:** When searching for bundles, a bundle in a class is given preference over a property file when the two bundles have the same base names.

Each resource bundle class implements a lookup table. You need to provide a key string for each setting you want to localize, and use that key string to retrieve the setting. For example,

```
Color backgroundColor = (Color) bundle.getObject("backgroundColor");
double[] paperSize = (double[]) bundle.getObject("defaultPaperSize");
```

The simplest way of implementing resource bundle classes is to extend the
ListResourceBundle class. The ListResourceBundle lets you place all your resources into an
object array and then does the lookup for you. Follow this code outline:

```
public class bundleName_language_country extends ListResourceBundle
{
    private static final Object[][] contents =
    {
        { key1, value2 },
        { key2, value2 },
        . . .
    }
    public Object[][] getContents() { return contents; }
}
```

For example,

```
public class ProgramResources_de extends ListResourceBundle
{
    private static final Object[][] contents =
    {
        { "backgroundColor", Color.black },
        { "defaultPaperSize", new double[] { 210, 297 } }
    }
    public Object[][] getContents() { return contents; }
}
```

```
public class ProgramResources_en_US extends ListResourceBundle
{
    private static final Object[][] contents =
    {
        { "backgroundColor", Color.blue },
        { "defaultPaperSize", new double[] { 216, 279 } }
    }
    public Object[][] getContents() { return contents; }
}
```

 **NOTE:** The paper sizes are given in millimeters. Everyone on the planet, with
the exception of the United States and Canada, uses ISO 216 paper sizes. For
more information, see www.cl.cam.ac.uk/~mgk25/iso-paper.html. According
to the U.S. Metric Association (http://lamar.colostate.edu/~hillger), only three
countries in the world have not yet officially adopted the metric system: Liberia,
Myanmar (Burma), and the United States of America.

Alternatively, your resource bundle classes can extend the ResourceBundle class. Then
you need to implement two methods, to enumerate all keys and to look up the
value for a given key:

```
Enumeration<String> getKeys()
Object handleGetObject(String key)
```

The getObject method of the ResourceBundle class calls the handleGetObject method that you supply.

---

**java.util.ResourceBundle** 1.1

- static ResourceBundle getBundle(String baseName, Locale loc)
- static ResourceBundle getBundle(String baseName)

  loads the resource bundle class with the given name, for the given locale or the default locale, and its parent classes. If the resource bundle classes are located in a package, the base name must contain the full package name, such as "intl.ProgramResources". The resource bundle classes must be public so that the getBundle method can access them.

- Object getObject(String name)

  looks up an object from the resource bundle or its parents.

- String getString(String name)

  looks up an object from the resource bundle or its parents and casts it as a string.

- String[] getStringArray(String name)

  looks up an object from the resource bundle or its parents and casts it as a string array.

- Enumeration<String> getKeys()

  returns an enumeration object to enumerate the keys of this resource bundle. It enumerates the keys in the parent bundles as well.

- Object handleGetObject(String key)

  should be overridden to look up the resource value associated with the given key if you define your own resource lookup mechanism.

---

## 5.8 A Complete Example

In this section, we apply the material of this chapter to localize a retirement calculator. The program calculates whether or not you are saving enough money for your retirement. You enter your age, how much money you save every month, and so on (see Figure 5.4).

The text area and the graph show the balance of the retirement account for every year. If the numbers turn negative toward the later part of your life and the bars in the graph appear below the *x* axis, you need to do something—for example, save more money, postpone your retirement, die earlier, or be younger.

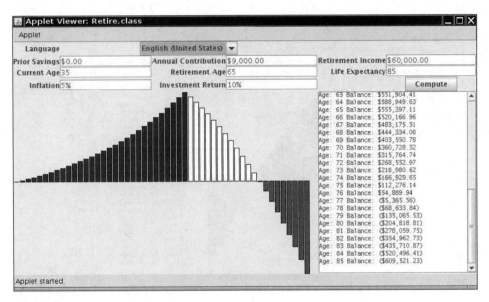

**Figure 5.4** The retirement calculator in English

The retirement calculator works in three locales (English, German, and Chinese). Here are some of the highlights of the internationalization:

- The labels, buttons, and messages are translated into German and Chinese. You can find them in the classes RetireResources_de, RetireResources_zh. English is used as the fallback—see the RetireResources file. To generate the Chinese messages, we first typed the file, using Notepad running in Chinese Windows, and then we used the native2ascii utility to convert the characters to Unicode.

- Whenever the locale changes, we reset the labels and reformat the contents of the text fields.

- The text fields handle numbers, currency amounts, and percentages in the local format.

- The computation field uses a MessageFormat. The format string is stored in the resource bundle of each language.

- Just to show that it can be done, we use different colors for the bar graph, depending on the language chosen by the user.

Listings 5.5 through 5.8 show the code. Listings 5.9 through 5.11 are the property files for the localized strings. Figures 5.5 and 5.6 show the outputs in German and Chinese, respectively. To see Chinese characters, be sure you have Chinese fonts installed and configured with your Java runtime. Otherwise, all Chinese characters will show up as "missing character" icons.

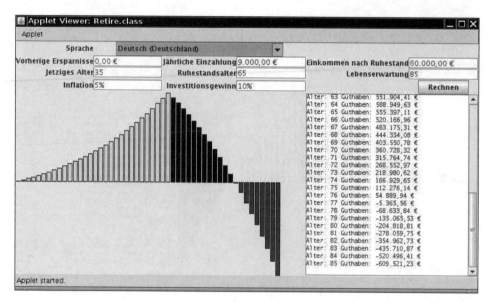

**Figure 5.5** The retirement calculator in German

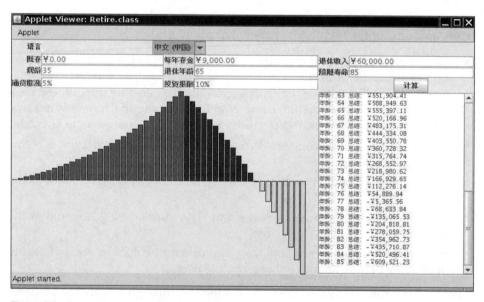

**Figure 5.6** The retirement calculator in Chinese

**Listing 5.5**  retire/Retire.java

```
1  package retire;
2
3  import java.awt.*;
4  import java.awt.event.*;
5  import java.awt.geom.*;
6  import java.util.*;
7  import java.text.*;
8  import javax.swing.*;
9
10  /**
11   * This program shows a retirement calculator. The UI is displayed in English, German, and Chinese.
12   * @version 1.23 2012-06-07
13   * @author Cay Horstmann
14   */
15  public class Retire
16  {
17     public static void main(String[] args)
18     {
19        EventQueue.invokeLater(new Runnable()
20           {
21              public void run()
22              {
23                 JFrame frame = new RetireFrame();
24                 frame.setDefaultCloseOperation(JFrame.EXIT_ON_CLOSE);
25                 frame.setVisible(true);
26              }
27           });
28     }
29  }
30
31  class RetireFrame extends JFrame
32  {
33     private JTextField savingsField = new JTextField(10);
34     private JTextField contribField = new JTextField(10);
35     private JTextField incomeField = new JTextField(10);
36     private JTextField currentAgeField = new JTextField(4);
37     private JTextField retireAgeField = new JTextField(4);
38     private JTextField deathAgeField = new JTextField(4);
39     private JTextField inflationPercentField = new JTextField(6);
40     private JTextField investPercentField = new JTextField(6);
41     private JTextArea retireText = new JTextArea(10, 25);
42     private RetireComponent retireCanvas = new RetireComponent();
43     private JButton computeButton = new JButton();
44     private JLabel languageLabel = new JLabel();
45     private JLabel savingsLabel = new JLabel();
```

*(Continues)*

**Listing 5.5** *(Continued)*

```
46    private JLabel contribLabel = new JLabel();
47    private JLabel incomeLabel = new JLabel();
48    private JLabel currentAgeLabel = new JLabel();
49    private JLabel retireAgeLabel = new JLabel();
50    private JLabel deathAgeLabel = new JLabel();
51    private JLabel inflationPercentLabel = new JLabel();
52    private JLabel investPercentLabel = new JLabel();
53    private RetireInfo info = new RetireInfo();
54    private Locale[] locales = { Locale.US, Locale.CHINA, Locale.GERMANY };
55    private Locale currentLocale;
56    private JComboBox<Locale> localeCombo = new LocaleCombo(locales);
57    private ResourceBundle res;
58    private ResourceBundle resStrings;
59    private NumberFormat currencyFmt;
60    private NumberFormat numberFmt;
61    private NumberFormat percentFmt;
62
63    public RetireFrame()
64    {
65       setLayout(new GridBagLayout());
66       add(languageLabel, new GBC(0, 0).setAnchor(GBC.EAST));
67       add(savingsLabel, new GBC(0, 1).setAnchor(GBC.EAST));
68       add(contribLabel, new GBC(2, 1).setAnchor(GBC.EAST));
69       add(incomeLabel, new GBC(4, 1).setAnchor(GBC.EAST));
70       add(currentAgeLabel, new GBC(0, 2).setAnchor(GBC.EAST));
71       add(retireAgeLabel, new GBC(2, 2).setAnchor(GBC.EAST));
72       add(deathAgeLabel, new GBC(4, 2).setAnchor(GBC.EAST));
73       add(inflationPercentLabel, new GBC(0, 3).setAnchor(GBC.EAST));
74       add(investPercentLabel, new GBC(2, 3).setAnchor(GBC.EAST));
75       add(localeCombo, new GBC(1, 0, 3, 1));
76       add(savingsField, new GBC(1, 1).setWeight(100, 0).setFill(GBC.HORIZONTAL));
77       add(contribField, new GBC(3, 1).setWeight(100, 0).setFill(GBC.HORIZONTAL));
78       add(incomeField, new GBC(5, 1).setWeight(100, 0).setFill(GBC.HORIZONTAL));
79       add(currentAgeField, new GBC(1, 2).setWeight(100, 0).setFill(GBC.HORIZONTAL));
80       add(retireAgeField, new GBC(3, 2).setWeight(100, 0).setFill(GBC.HORIZONTAL));
81       add(deathAgeField, new GBC(5, 2).setWeight(100, 0).setFill(GBC.HORIZONTAL));
82       add(inflationPercentField, new GBC(1, 3).setWeight(100, 0).setFill(GBC.HORIZONTAL));
83       add(investPercentField, new GBC(3, 3).setWeight(100, 0).setFill(GBC.HORIZONTAL));
84       add(retireCanvas, new GBC(0, 4, 4, 1).setWeight(100, 100).setFill(GBC.BOTH));
85       add(new JScrollPane(retireText), new GBC(4, 4, 2, 1).setWeight(0, 100).setFill(GBC.BOTH));
86
87       computeButton.setName("computeButton");
88       computeButton.addActionListener(new ActionListener()
89          {
90             public void actionPerformed(ActionEvent event)
91             {
92                getInfo();
```

```
93              updateData();
94              updateGraph();
95           }
96        });
97     add(computeButton, new GBC(5, 3));
98
99     retireText.setEditable(false);
100    retireText.setFont(new Font("Monospaced", Font.PLAIN, 10));
101
102    info.setSavings(0);
103    info.setContrib(9000);
104    info.setIncome(60000);
105    info.setCurrentAge(35);
106    info.setRetireAge(65);
107    info.setDeathAge(85);
108    info.setInvestPercent(0.1);
109    info.setInflationPercent(0.05);
110
111    int localeIndex = 0; // US locale is default selection
112    for (int i = 0; i < locales.length; i++)
113       // if current locale one of the choices, select it
114       if (getLocale().equals(locales[i])) localeIndex = i;
115    setCurrentLocale(locales[localeIndex]);
116
117    localeCombo.addActionListener(new ActionListener()
118       {
119          public void actionPerformed(ActionEvent event)
120          {
121             setCurrentLocale((Locale) localeCombo.getSelectedItem());
122             validate();
123          }
124       });
125    pack();
126 }
127
128 /**
129  * Sets the current locale.
130  * @param locale the desired locale
131  */
132 public void setCurrentLocale(Locale locale)
133 {
134    currentLocale = locale;
135    localeCombo.setSelectedItem(currentLocale);
136    localeCombo.setLocale(currentLocale);
137
138    res = ResourceBundle.getBundle("retire.RetireResources", currentLocale);
139    resStrings = ResourceBundle.getBundle("retire.RetireStrings", currentLocale);
140    currencyFmt = NumberFormat.getCurrencyInstance(currentLocale);
141    numberFmt = NumberFormat.getNumberInstance(currentLocale);
```

*(Continues)*

**Listing 5.5** *(Continued)*

```
142        percentFmt = NumberFormat.getPercentInstance(currentLocale);
143
144        updateDisplay();
145        updateInfo();
146        updateData();
147        updateGraph();
148     }
149
150     /**
151      * Updates all labels in the display.
152      */
153     public void updateDisplay()
154     {
155        languageLabel.setText(resStrings.getString("language"));
156        savingsLabel.setText(resStrings.getString("savings"));
157        contribLabel.setText(resStrings.getString("contrib"));
158        incomeLabel.setText(resStrings.getString("income"));
159        currentAgeLabel.setText(resStrings.getString("currentAge"));
160        retireAgeLabel.setText(resStrings.getString("retireAge"));
161        deathAgeLabel.setText(resStrings.getString("deathAge"));
162        inflationPercentLabel.setText(resStrings.getString("inflationPercent"));
163        investPercentLabel.setText(resStrings.getString("investPercent"));
164        computeButton.setText(resStrings.getString("computeButton"));
165     }
166
167     /**
168      * Updates the information in the text fields.
169      */
170     public void updateInfo()
171     {
172        savingsField.setText(currencyFmt.format(info.getSavings()));
173        contribField.setText(currencyFmt.format(info.getContrib()));
174        incomeField.setText(currencyFmt.format(info.getIncome()));
175        currentAgeField.setText(numberFmt.format(info.getCurrentAge()));
176        retireAgeField.setText(numberFmt.format(info.getRetireAge()));
177        deathAgeField.setText(numberFmt.format(info.getDeathAge()));
178        investPercentField.setText(percentFmt.format(info.getInvestPercent()));
179        inflationPercentField.setText(percentFmt.format(info.getInflationPercent()));
180     }
181
182     /**
183      * Updates the data displayed in the text area.
184      */
185     public void updateData()
186     {
187        retireText.setText("");
188        MessageFormat retireMsg = new MessageFormat("");
```

```
189        retireMsg.setLocale(currentLocale);
190        retireMsg.applyPattern(resStrings.getString("retire"));
191
192        for (int i = info.getCurrentAge(); i <= info.getDeathAge(); i++)
193        {
194           Object[] args = { i, info.getBalance(i) };
195           retireText.append(retireMsg.format(args) + "\n");
196        }
197     }
198
199     /**
200      * Updates the graph.
201      */
202     public void updateGraph()
203     {
204        retireCanvas.setColorPre((Color) res.getObject("colorPre"));
205        retireCanvas.setColorGain((Color) res.getObject("colorGain"));
206        retireCanvas.setColorLoss((Color) res.getObject("colorLoss"));
207        retireCanvas.setInfo(info);
208        repaint();
209     }
210
211     /**
212      * Reads the user input from the text fields.
213      */
214     public void getInfo()
215     {
216        try
217        {
218           info.setSavings(currencyFmt.parse(savingsField.getText()).doubleValue());
219           info.setContrib(currencyFmt.parse(contribField.getText()).doubleValue());
220           info.setIncome(currencyFmt.parse(incomeField.getText()).doubleValue());
221           info.setCurrentAge(numberFmt.parse(currentAgeField.getText()).intValue());
222           info.setRetireAge(numberFmt.parse(retireAgeField.getText()).intValue());
223           info.setDeathAge(numberFmt.parse(deathAgeField.getText()).intValue());
224           info.setInvestPercent(percentFmt.parse(investPercentField.getText()).doubleValue());
225           info.setInflationPercent(percentFmt.parse(inflationPercentField.getText()).doubleValue());
226        }
227        catch (ParseException ex)
228        {
229           ex.printStackTrace();
230        }
231     }
232  }
233
234  /**
235   * The information required to compute retirement income data.
236   */
```

*(Continues)*

**Listing 5.5**  *(Continued)*

```
237 class RetireInfo
238 {
239    private double savings;
240    private double contrib;
241    private double income;
242    private int currentAge;
243    private int retireAge;
244    private int deathAge;
245    private double inflationPercent;
246    private double investPercent;
247    private int age;
248    private double balance;
249
250    /**
251     * Gets the available balance for a given year.
252     * @param year the year for which to compute the balance
253     * @return the amount of money available (or required) in that year
254     */
255    public double getBalance(int year)
256    {
257       if (year < currentAge) return 0;
258       else if (year == currentAge)
259       {
260          age = year;
261          balance = savings;
262          return balance;
263       }
264       else if (year == age) return balance;
265       if (year != age + 1) getBalance(year - 1);
266       age = year;
267       if (age < retireAge) balance += contrib;
268       else balance -= income;
269       balance = balance * (1 + (investPercent - inflationPercent));
270       return balance;
271    }
272
273    /**
274     * Gets the amount of prior savings.
275     * @return the savings amount
276     */
277    public double getSavings()
278    {
279       return savings;
280    }
```

```
281    /**
282     * Sets the amount of prior savings.
283     * @param newValue the savings amount
284     */
285    public void setSavings(double newValue)
286    {
287       savings = newValue;
288    }
289
290    /**
291     * Gets the annual contribution to the retirement account.
292     * @return the contribution amount
293     */
294    public double getContrib()
295    {
296       return contrib;
297    }
298
299    /**
300     * Sets the annual contribution to the retirement account.
301     * @param newValue the contribution amount
302     */
303    public void setContrib(double newValue)
304    {
305       contrib = newValue;
306    }
307
308    /**
309     * Gets the annual income.
310     * @return the income amount
311     */
312    public double getIncome()
313    {
314       return income;
315    }
316
317    /**
318     * Sets the annual income.
319     * @param newValue the income amount
320     */
321    public void setIncome(double newValue)
322    {
323       income = newValue;
324    }
325
326    /**
327     * Gets the current age.
328     * @return the age
329     */
```

*(Continues)*

---

**Listing 5.5** *(Continued)*

```
330    public int getCurrentAge()
331    {
332        return currentAge;
333    }
334
335    /**
336     * Sets the current age.
337     * @param newValue the age
338     */
339    public void setCurrentAge(int newValue)
340    {
341        currentAge = newValue;
342    }
343
344    /**
345     * Gets the desired retirement age.
346     * @return the age
347     */
348    public int getRetireAge()
349    {
350        return retireAge;
351    }
352
353    /**
354     * Sets the desired retirement age.
355     * @param newValue the age
356     */
357    public void setRetireAge(int newValue)
358    {
359        retireAge = newValue;
360    }
361
362    /**
363     * Gets the expected age of death.
364     * @return the age
365     */
366    public int getDeathAge()
367    {
368        return deathAge;
369    }
370
371    /**
372     * Sets the expected age of death.
373     * @param newValue the age
374     */
```

```
375    public void setDeathAge(int newValue)
376    {
377       deathAge = newValue;
378    }
379
380    /**
381     * Gets the estimated percentage of inflation.
382     * @return the percentage
383     */
384    public double getInflationPercent()
385    {
386       return inflationPercent;
387    }
388
389    /**
390     * Sets the estimated percentage of inflation.
391     * @param newValue the percentage
392     */
393    public void setInflationPercent(double newValue)
394    {
395       inflationPercent = newValue;
396    }
397
398    /**
399     * Gets the estimated yield of the investment.
400     * @return the percentage
401     */
402    public double getInvestPercent()
403    {
404       return investPercent;
405    }
406
407    /**
408     * Sets the estimated yield of the investment.
409     * @param newValue the percentage
410     */
411    public void setInvestPercent(double newValue)
412    {
413       investPercent = newValue;
414    }
415 }
416
417 /**
418  * This component draws a graph of the investment result.
419  */
420 class RetireComponent extends JComponent
421 {
```

*(Continues)*

**Listing 5.5** *(Continued)*

```
422    private static final int DEFAULT_WIDTH = 800;
423    private static final int DEFAULT_HEIGHT = 600;
424    private static final int PANEL_WIDTH = 400;
425    private static final int PANEL_HEIGHT = 200;
426
427    private RetireInfo info = null;
428    private Color colorPre;
429    private Color colorGain;
430    private Color colorLoss;
431
432    public RetireComponent()
433    {
434       setSize(PANEL_WIDTH, PANEL_HEIGHT);
435    }
436
437    /**
438     * Sets the retirement information to be plotted.
439     * @param newInfo the new retirement info.
440     */
441    public void setInfo(RetireInfo newInfo)
442    {
443       info = newInfo;
444       repaint();
445    }
446
447    public void paintComponent(Graphics g)
448    {
449       Graphics2D g2 = (Graphics2D) g;
450       if (info == null) return;
451
452       double minValue = 0;
453       double maxValue = 0;
454       int i;
455       for (i = info.getCurrentAge(); i <= info.getDeathAge(); i++)
456       {
457          double v = info.getBalance(i);
458          if (minValue > v) minValue = v;
459          if (maxValue < v) maxValue = v;
460       }
461       if (maxValue == minValue) return;
462
463       int barWidth = getWidth() / (info.getDeathAge() - info.getCurrentAge() + 1);
464       double scale = getHeight() / (maxValue - minValue);
465
466       for (i = info.getCurrentAge(); i <= info.getDeathAge(); i++)
467       {
468          int x1 = (i - info.getCurrentAge()) * barWidth + 1;
469          int y1;
```

```
470        double v = info.getBalance(i);
471        int height;
472        int yOrigin = (int) (maxValue * scale);
473
474        if (v >= 0)
475        {
476           y1 = (int) ((maxValue - v) * scale);
477           height = yOrigin - y1;
478        }
479        else
480        {
481           y1 = yOrigin;
482           height = (int) (-v * scale);
483        }
484
485        if (i < info.getRetireAge()) g2.setPaint(colorPre);
486        else if (v >= 0) g2.setPaint(colorGain);
487        else g2.setPaint(colorLoss);
488        Rectangle2D bar = new Rectangle2D.Double(x1, y1, barWidth - 2, height);
489        g2.fill(bar);
490        g2.setPaint(Color.black);
491        g2.draw(bar);
492     }
493   }
494
495   /**
496    * Sets the color to be used before retirement.
497    * @param color the desired color
498    */
499   public void setColorPre(Color color)
500   {
501      colorPre = color;
502      repaint();
503   }
504
505   /**
506    * Sets the color to be used after retirement while the account balance is positive.
507    * @param color the desired color
508    */
509   public void setColorGain(Color color)
510   {
511      colorGain = color;
512      repaint();
513   }
514
515   /**
516    * Sets the color to be used after retirement when the account balance is negative.
517    * @param color the desired color
518    */
```

*(Continues)*

**Listing 5.5** *(Continued)*

```
519    public void setColorLoss(Color color)
520    {
521       colorLoss = color;
522       repaint();
523    }
524
525    public Dimension getPreferredSize() { return new Dimension(DEFAULT_WIDTH, DEFAULT_HEIGHT); }
526 }
```

**Listing 5.6** retire/RetireResources.java

```
1  package retire;
2
3  import java.awt.*;
4
5  /**
6   * These are the English non-string resources for the retirement calculator.
7   * @version 1.21 2001-08-27
8   * @author Cay Horstmann
9   */
10 public class RetireResources extends java.util.ListResourceBundle
11 {
12    private static final Object[][] contents = {
13    // BEGIN LOCALIZE
14       { "colorPre", Color.blue }, { "colorGain", Color.white }, { "colorLoss", Color.red }
15    // END LOCALIZE
16    };
17
18    public Object[][] getContents()
19    {
20       return contents;
21    }
22 }
```

**Listing 5.7** retire/RetireResources_de.java

```
1  package retire;
2
3  import java.awt.*;
4
5  /**
6   * These are the German non-string resources for the retirement calculator.
7   * @version 1.21 2001-08-27
8   * @author Cay Horstmann
9   */
```

```
10  public class RetireResources_de extends java.util.ListResourceBundle
11  {
12      private static final Object[][] contents = {
13      // BEGIN LOCALIZE
14          { "colorPre", Color.yellow }, { "colorGain", Color.black }, { "colorLoss", Color.red }
15      // END LOCALIZE
16      };
17
18      public Object[][] getContents()
19      {
20          return contents;
21      }
22  }
```

**Listing 5.8** retire/RetireResources_zh.java

```
1   package retire;
2
3   import java.awt.*;
4
5   /**
6    * These are the Chinese non-string resources for the retirement calculator.
7    * @version 1.21 2001-08-27
8    * @author Cay Horstmann
9    */
10  public class RetireResources_zh extends java.util.ListResourceBundle
11  {
12      private static final Object[][] contents = {
13      // BEGIN LOCALIZE
14          { "colorPre", Color.red }, { "colorGain", Color.blue }, { "colorLoss", Color.yellow }
15      // END LOCALIZE
16      };
17
18      public Object[][] getContents()
19      {
20          return contents;
21      }
22  }
```

**Listing 5.9** retire/RetireStrings.properties

```
1   language=Language
2   computeButton=Compute
3   savings=Prior Savings
4   contrib=Annual Contribution
5   income=Retirement Income
6   currentAge=Current Age
```

*(Continues)*

**Listing 5.9** *(Continued)*

```
 7  retireAge=Retirement Age
 8  deathAge=Life Expectancy
 9  inflationPercent=Inflation
10  investPercent=Investment Return
11  retire=Age: {0,number} Balance: {1,number,currency}
```

**Listing 5.10** retire/RetireStrings_de.properties

```
 1  language=Sprache
 2  computeButton=Rechnen
 3  savings=Vorherige Ersparnisse
 4  contrib=J\u00e4hrliche Einzahlung
 5  income=Einkommen nach Ruhestand
 6  currentAge=Jetziges Alter
 7  retireAge=Ruhestandsalter
 8  deathAge=Lebenserwartung
 9  inflationPercent=Inflation
10  investPercent=Investitionsgewinn
11  retire=Alter: {0,number} Guthaben: {1,number,currency}
```

**Listing 5.11** retire/RetireStrings_zh.properties

```
 1  language=\u8bed\u8a00
 2  computeButton=\u8ba1\u7b97
 3  savings=\u65e2\u5b58
 4  contrib=\u6bcf\u5e74\u5b58\u91d1
 5  income=\u9000\u4f11\u6536\u5165
 6  currentAge=\u73b0\u9f84
 7  retireAge=\u9000\u4f11\u5e74\u9f84
 8  deathAge=\u9884\u671f\u5bff\u547d
 9  inflationPercent=\u901a\u8d27\u81a8\u6da8
10  investPercent=\u6295\u8d44\u62a5\u916c
11  retire=\u5e74\u9f84: {0,number} \u603b\u7ed3: {1,number,currency}
```

You have seen how to use the internationalization features of the Java language. You can now use resource bundles to provide translations into multiple languages, and use formatters and collators for locale-specific text processing.

In the next chapter, we will delve into advanced Swing programming.

# CHAPTER 6

# Advanced Swing

## In this chapter:

In this chapter, we continue our discussion of the Swing user interface toolkit from Volume I. Swing is a rich toolkit, and Volume I covered only the basic and commonly used components. That leaves us with three significantly more complex components for lists, tables, and trees, the exploration of which occupies a large part of this chapter. We will then turn to text components and go beyond the simple text fields and text areas that you have seen in Volume I. We will show you how to add validations and spinners to text fields and how you can display structured text such as HTML. Next, you will see a number of components for displaying progress of a slow activity. We will finish the chapter by covering component organizers, such as tabbed panes and desktop panes with internal frames.

## 6.1 Lists

If you want to present a set of choices to a user, and a radio button or checkbox set consumes too much space, you can use a combo box or a list. Combo boxes were covered in Volume I because they are relatively simple. The JList component has many more features, and its design is similar to that of the tree and table components. For that reason, it is our starting point for the discussion of complex Swing components.

You can have lists of strings, of course, but you can also have lists of arbitrary objects, with full control of how they appear. The internal architecture of the list component that makes this generality possible is rather elegant. Unfortunately, the designers at Sun felt that they needed to show off that elegance, instead of hiding it from the programmer who just wants to use the component. You will find that the list control is somewhat awkward to use for common cases because you need to manipulate some of the machinery that makes the general cases possible. We will walk you through the simple and most common case—a list box of strings—and then give a more complex example that shows off the flexibility of the list component.

### 6.1.1 The JList Component

The JList component shows a number of items inside a single box. Figure 6.1 shows an admittedly silly example. The user can select the attributes for the fox, such as "quick," "brown," "hungry," "wild," and, because we ran out of attributes, "static," "private," and "final." You can thus have the *private static final* fox jump over the lazy dog.

As of Java SE 7, JList is a generic type. The type parameter is the type of the values the user can select. In this example, we use a JList<String>.

To construct this list component, start out with an array of strings and pass that array to the JList constructor:

```
String[] words= { "quick", "brown", "hungry", "wild", . . . };
JList<String> wordList = new JList<>(words);
```

List boxes do not scroll automatically. To make a list box scroll, you must insert it into a scroll pane:

```
JScrollPane scrollPane = new JScrollPane(wordList);
```

Then, add the scroll pane, not the list, into the surrounding panel.

We have to admit that the separation of the list display and the scrolling mechanism is elegant in theory, but a pain in practice. Essentially all lists that we ever

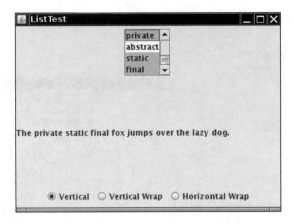

**Figure 6.1** A list box

encountered needed scrolling. It seems cruel to force programmers to go through the hoops in the default case just so they can appreciate that elegance.

By default, the list component displays eight items; use the setVisibleRowCount method to change that value:

```
wordList.setVisibleRowCount(4); // display 4 items
```

You can set the *layout orientation* to one of three values:

- JList.VERTICAL *(the default):* Arrange all items vertically.
- JList.VERTICAL_WRAP: Start new columns if there are more items than the visible row count (see Figure 6.2).
- JList.HORIZONTAL_WRAP: Start new columns if there are more items than the visible row count, but fill them horizontally. Look at the placement of the words "quick," "brown," and "hungry" in Figure 6.2 to see the difference between vertical and horizontal wrap.

By default, a user can select multiple items. To add more items to a selection, press the Ctrl key while clicking on each item. To select a contiguous range of items, click on the first one, then hold down the Shift key and click on the last one.

You can also restrict the user to a more limited selection mode with the setSelectionMode method:

```
wordList.setSelectionMode(ListSelectionModel.SINGLE_SELECTION);
   // select one item at a time
wordList.setSelectionMode(ListSelectionModel.SINGLE_INTERVAL_SELECTION);
   // select one item or one range of items
```

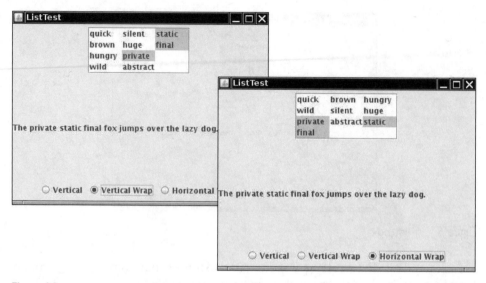

**Figure 6.2** Lists with vertical and horizontal wrap

You might recall from Volume I that the basic user interface components send out action events when the user activates them. List boxes use a different notification mechanism. Rather than listening to action events, you need to listen to list selection events. Add a list selection listener to the list component, and implement the method

```
public void valueChanged(ListSelectionEvent evt)
```

in the listener.

When the user selects items, a flurry of list selection events is generated. For example, suppose the user clicks on a new item. When the mouse button goes down, an event reports a change in selection. This is a transitional event—the call

```
event.getValueIsAdjusting()
```

returns true if the selection is not yet final. Then, when the mouse button goes up, there is another event, this time with getValueIsAdjusting returning false. If you are not interested in the transitional events, you can wait for the event for which getValueIsAdjusting is false. However, if you want to give the user instant feedback as soon as the mouse button is clicked, you need to process all events.

Once you are notified that an event has happened, you will want to find out what items are currently selected. If your list is in single-selection mode, call getSelectedValue to get the value as the list element type. Otherwise, call the

getSelectedValuesList method which returns a list containing all selected items. You
can process it in the usual way:

```
for (String value : wordList.getSelectedValuesList())
    // do something with value
```

---

 **NOTE:** List components do not react to double clicks from a mouse. As envi-
sioned by the designers of Swing, you use a list to select an item, then click a
button to make something happen. However, some interfaces allow a user to
double-click on a list item as a shortcut for selecting the item and invoking
the default action. If you want to implement this behavior, you have to add a
mouse listener to the list box, then trap the mouse event as follows:

```
public void mouseClicked(MouseEvent evt)
{
    if (evt.getClickCount() == 2)
    {
        JList source = (JList) evt.getSource();
        Object[] selection = source.getSelectedValues();
        doAction(selection);
    }
}
```

---

Listing 6.1 is the listing of the frame containing a list box filled with strings. Notice
how the valueChanged method builds up the message string from the selected items.

---

**Listing 6.1** list/ListFrame.java

```
1  package list;
2
3  import java.awt.*;
4  import java.awt.event.*;
5  import javax.swing.*;
6  import javax.swing.event.*;
7
8  /**
9   * This frame contains a word list and a label that shows a sentence made up from the chosen words.
10  * Note that you can select multiple words with Ctrl+click and Shift+click.
11  */
12 class ListFrame extends JFrame
13 {
14     private static final int DEFAULT_WIDTH = 400;
15     private static final int DEFAULT_HEIGHT = 300;
16
17     private JPanel listPanel;
```

*(Continues)*

**Listing 6.1** *(Continued)*

```
18   private JList<String> wordList;
19   private JLabel label;
20   private JPanel buttonPanel;
21   private ButtonGroup group;
22   private String prefix = "The ";
23   private String suffix = "fox jumps over the lazy dog.";
24
25   public ListFrame()
26   {
27      setSize(DEFAULT_WIDTH, DEFAULT_HEIGHT);
28
29      String[] words = { "quick", "brown", "hungry", "wild", "silent", "huge", "private",
30            "abstract", "static", "final" };
31
32      wordList = new JList<>(words);
33      wordList.setVisibleRowCount(4);
34      JScrollPane scrollPane = new JScrollPane(wordList);
35
36      listPanel = new JPanel();
37      listPanel.add(scrollPane);
38      wordList.addListSelectionListener(new ListSelectionListener()
39         {
40            public void valueChanged(ListSelectionEvent event)
41            {
42               StringBuilder text = new StringBuilder(prefix);
43               for (String value : wordList.getSelectedValuesList())
44               {
45                  text.append(value);
46                  text.append(" ");
47               }
48               text.append(suffix);
49
50               label.setText(text.toString());
51            }
52         });
53
54      buttonPanel = new JPanel();
55      group = new ButtonGroup();
56      makeButton("Vertical", JList.VERTICAL);
57      makeButton("Vertical Wrap", JList.VERTICAL_WRAP);
58      makeButton("Horizontal Wrap", JList.HORIZONTAL_WRAP);
59
60      add(listPanel, BorderLayout.NORTH);
61      label = new JLabel(prefix + suffix);
62      add(label, BorderLayout.CENTER);
63      add(buttonPanel, BorderLayout.SOUTH);
64   }
```

```
65   /**
66    * Makes a radio button to set the layout orientation.
67    * @param label the button label
68    * @param orientation the orientation for the list
69    */
70   private void makeButton(String label, final int orientation)
71   {
72      JRadioButton button = new JRadioButton(label);
73      buttonPanel.add(button);
74      if (group.getButtonCount() == 0) button.setSelected(true);
75      group.add(button);
76      button.addActionListener(new ActionListener()
77         {
78            public void actionPerformed(ActionEvent event)
79            {
80               wordList.setLayoutOrientation(orientation);
81               listPanel.revalidate();
82            }
83         });
84   }
85 }
```

---

**javax.swing.JList<E>** 1.2

- JList(E[] items)
  constructs a list that displays these items.

- int getVisibleRowCount()
- void setVisibleRowCount(int c)
  gets or sets the preferred number of rows in the list that can be displayed without a scroll bar.

- int getLayoutOrientation() 1.4
- void setLayoutOrientation(int orientation) 1.4
  gets or sets the layout orientation

  *Parameters:*    orientation    One of VERTICAL, VERTICAL_WRAP, HORIZONTAL_WRAP

- int getSelectionMode()
- void setSelectionMode(int mode)
  gets or sets the mode that determines whether single-item or multiple-item selections are allowed.

  *Parameters:*    mode    One of SINGLE_SELECTION, SINGLE_INTERVAL_SELECTION, MULTIPLE_INTERVAL_SELECTION

- void addListSelectionListener(ListSelectionListener listener)
  adds to the list a listener that's notified each time a change to the selection occurs.

*(Continues)*

---

`javax.swing.JList<E>` 1.2 *(Continued)*

- `List<E> getSelectedValues()` **7**
  returns the selected values or an empty list if the selection is empty.
- `E getSelectedValue()`
  returns the first selected value or `null` if the selection is empty.

---

*`javax.swing.event.ListSelectionListener`* 1.2

- `void valueChanged(ListSelectionEvent e)`
  is called whenever the list selection changes.

---

## 6.1.2 List Models

In the preceding section, you saw the most common method for using a list component:

1. Specify a fixed set of strings for display in the list.
2. Place the list inside a scroll pane.
3. Trap the list selection events.

In the remainder of the section on lists, we cover more complex situations that require a bit more finesse:

- Very long lists
- Lists with changing contents
- Lists that don't contain strings

In the first example, we constructed a `JList` component that held a fixed collection of strings. However, the collection of choices in a list box is not always fixed. How do we add or remove items in the list box? Somewhat surprisingly, there are no methods in the `JList` class to achieve this. Instead, you have to understand a little more about the internal design of the list component. The list component uses the model-view-controller design pattern to separate the visual appearance (a column of items that are rendered in some way) from the underlying data (a collection of objects).

The `JList` class is responsible for the visual appearance of the data. It actually knows very little about how the data are stored—all it knows is that it can retrieve the data through some object that implements the `ListModel` interface:

```
public interface ListModel<E>
{
   int getSize();
   E getElementAt(int i);
   void addListDataListener(ListDataListener l);
   void removeListDataListener(ListDataListener l);
}
```

Through this interface, the JList can get a count of elements and retrieve any of them. Also, the JList object can add itself as a ListDataListener. That way, if the collection of elements changes, the JList gets notified so it can repaint itself.

Why is this generality useful? Why doesn't the JList object simply store an array of objects?

Note that the interface doesn't specify how the objects are stored. In particular, it doesn't force them to be stored at all! The getElementAt method is free to recompute each value whenever it is called. This is potentially useful if you want to show a very large collection without having to store the values.

Here is a somewhat silly example: We let the user choose among *all three-letter words* in a list box (see Figure 6.3).

There are $26 \times 26 \times 26 = 17{,}576$ three-letter combinations. Instead of storing all these combinations, we recompute them as requested when the user scrolls through them.

This turns out to be easy to implement. The tedious part, adding and removing listeners, has been done for us in the AbstractListModel class, which we extend. We only need to supply the getSize and getElementAt methods:

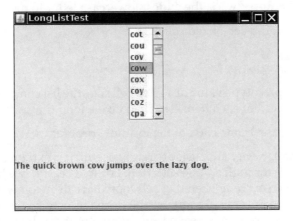

**Figure 6.3** Choosing from a very long list of selections

```
class WordListModel extends AbstractListModel<String>
{
   public WordListModel(int n) { length = n; }
   public int getSize() { return (int) Math.pow(26, length); }
   public String getElementAt(int n)
   {
      // compute nth string
      . . .
   }
   . . .
}
```

The computation of the *n*th string is a bit technical—you'll find the details in Listing 6.3.

Now that we have a model, we can simply build a list that lets the user scroll through the elements supplied by the model:

```
JList<String> wordList = new JList<>(new WordListModel(3));
wordList.setSelectionMode(ListSelectionModel.SINGLE_SELECTION);
JScrollPane scrollPane = new JScrollPane(wordList);
```

The point is that the strings are never *stored*. Only those strings that the user actually requests to see are generated.

We must make one other setting: tell the list component that all items have a fixed width and height. The easiest way to set the cell dimensions is to specify a *prototype cell value*:

```
wordList.setPrototypeCellValue("www");
```

The prototype cell value is used to determine the size for all cells. (We use the string "www" because "w" is the widest lowercase letter in most fonts.)

Alternatively, you can set a fixed cell size:

```
wordList.setFixedCellWidth(50);
wordList.setFixedCellHeight(15);
```

If you don't set a prototype value or a fixed cell size, the list component computes the width and height of each item. That can take a long time.

Listing 6.2 shows the frame class of the example program.

As a practical matter, very long lists are rarely useful. It is extremely cumbersome for a user to scroll through a huge selection. For that reason, we believe that the list control has been overengineered. A selection that can be comfortably managed on the screen is certainly small enough to be stored directly in the list component. That arrangement would have saved programmers from the pain of having to deal with the list model as a separate entity. On the other hand, the JList class is consistent with the JTree and JTable classes where this generality is useful.

**Listing 6.2** longList/LongListFrame.java

```java
1  package longList;
2
3  import java.awt.*;
4  import javax.swing.*;
5  import javax.swing.event.*;
6
7  /**
8   * This frame contains a long word list and a label that shows a sentence made up from the chosen
9   * word.
10  */
11 public class LongListFrame extends JFrame
12 {
13    private JList<String> wordList;
14    private JLabel label;
15    private String prefix = "The quick brown ";
16    private String suffix = " jumps over the lazy dog.";
17
18    public LongListFrame()
19    {
20       wordList = new JList<String>(new WordListModel(3));
21       wordList.setSelectionMode(ListSelectionModel.SINGLE_SELECTION);
22       wordList.setPrototypeCellValue("www");
23       JScrollPane scrollPane = new JScrollPane(wordList);
24
25       JPanel p = new JPanel();
26       p.add(scrollPane);
27       wordList.addListSelectionListener(new ListSelectionListener()
28          {
29             public void valueChanged(ListSelectionEvent evt)
30             {
31                setSubject(wordList.getSelectedValue());
32             }
33          });
34
35       Container contentPane = getContentPane();
36       contentPane.add(p, BorderLayout.NORTH);
37       label = new JLabel(prefix + suffix);
38       contentPane.add(label, BorderLayout.CENTER);
39       setSubject("fox");
40       pack();
41    }
```

*(Continues)*

**Listing 6.2** *(Continued)*

```
42   /**
43    * Sets the subject in the label.
44    * @param word the new subject that jumps over the lazy dog
45    */
46   public void setSubject(String word)
47   {
48      StringBuilder text = new StringBuilder(prefix);
49      text.append(word);
50      text.append(suffix);
51      label.setText(text.toString());
52   }
53 }
```

**Listing 6.3** longList/WordListModel.java

```
1  package longList;
2
3  import javax.swing.*;
4
5  /**
6   * A model that dynamically generates n-letter words.
7   */
8  public class WordListModel extends AbstractListModel<String>
9  {
10     private int length;
11     public static final char FIRST = 'a';
12     public static final char LAST = 'z';
13
14     /**
15      * Constructs the model.
16      * @param n the word length
17      */
18     public WordListModel(int n)
19     {
20        length = n;
21     }
22
23     public int getSize()
24     {
25        return (int) Math.pow(LAST - FIRST + 1, length);
26     }
27
28     public String getElementAt(int n)
29     {
30        StringBuilder r = new StringBuilder();
```

```
31        for (int i = 0; i < length; i++)
32        {
33           char c = (char) (FIRST + n % (LAST - FIRST + 1));
34           r.insert(0, c);
35           n = n / (LAST - FIRST + 1);
36        }
37        return r.toString();
38     }
39  }
```

---

**javax.swing.JList<E>** 1.2

- JList(ListModel<E> dataModel)
  constructs a list that displays the elements in the specified model.

- E getPrototypeCellValue()
- void setPrototypeCellValue(E newValue)
  gets or sets the prototype cell value used to determine the width and height of each cell in the list. The default is null, which forces the size of each cell to be measured.

- void setFixedCellWidth(int width)
  void setFixedCellHeight(int height)

  if the width or height is greater than zero, specifies the width or height (in pixels) of every cell in the list. The default value is -1, which forces the size of each cell to be measured.

---

**javax.swing.ListModel<E>** 1.2

- int getSize()
  returns the number of elements of the model.

- E getElementAt(int position)
  returns an element of the model at the given position.

## 6.1.3 Inserting and Removing Values

You cannot directly edit the collection of list values. Instead, you must access the *model* and then add or remove elements. That, too, is easier said than done. Suppose you want to add more values to a list. You can obtain a reference to the model:

```
ListModel<String> model = list.getModel();
```

But that does you no good—as you saw in the preceding section, the ListModel interface has no methods to insert or remove elements because, after all, the whole point of having a list model is that it does not need to *store* the elements.

Let's try it the other way around. One of the constructors of JList takes a vector of objects:

```
Vector<String> values = new Vector<String>();
values.addElement("quick");
values.addElement("brown");
. . .
JList<String> list = new JList<>(values);
```

You can now edit the vector and add or remove elements, but the list does not know that this is happening, so it cannot react to the changes. In particular, the list does not update its view when you add the values. Therefore, this constructor is not very useful.

Instead, you should construct a DefaultListModel object, fill it with the initial values, and associate it with the list. The DefaultListModel class implements the ListModel interface and manages a collection of objects.

```
DefaultListModel<String> model = new DefaultListModel<>();
model.addElement("quick");
model.addElement("brown");
. . .
JList<String> list = new JList<>(model);
```

Now you can add or remove values from the model object. The model object then notifies the list of the changes, and the list repaints itself.

```
model.removeElement("quick");
model.addElement("slow");
```

For historical reasons, the DefaultListModel class doesn't use the same method names as the collection classes.

Internally, the default list model uses a vector to store the values.

 **CAUTION:** There are JList constructors that construct a list from an array or vector of objects or strings. You might think that these constructors use a DefaultListModel to store these values. That is not the case—the constructors build a trivial model that can access the values without any provisions for notification if the content changes. For example, here is the code for the constructor that constructs a JList from a Vector:

```
public JList(final Vector<? extends E> listData)
{
   this (new AbstractListModel<E>()
   {
      public int getSize() { return listData.size(); }
      public E getElementAt(int i) { return listData.elementAt(i); }
   });
}
```

That means, if you change the contents of the vector after the list is constructed, the list might show a confusing mix of old and new values until it is completely repainted. (The keyword final in the preceding constructor does not prevent you from changing the vector elsewhere—it only means that the constructor itself won't modify the value of the listData reference; the keyword is required because the listData object is used in the inner class.)

---

**javax.swing.JList<E>** 1.2

- ListModel<E> getModel()
  gets the model of this list.

---

**javax.swing.DefaultListModel<E>** 1.2

- void addElement(E obj)
  adds the object to the end of the model.

- boolean removeElement(Object obj)
  removes the first occurrence of the object from the model. Returns true if the object was contained in the model, false otherwise.

## 6.1.4 Rendering Values

So far, all lists you have seen in this chapter contained strings. It is actually just as easy to show a list of icons—simply pass an array or vector filled with Icon objects. More interestingly, you can easily represent your list values with any drawing whatsoever.

Although the JList class can display strings and icons automatically, you need to install a *list cell renderer* into the JList object for all custom drawing. A list cell renderer is any class that implements the following interface:

```
interface ListCellRenderer<E>
{
    Component getListCellRendererComponent(JList<? extends E> list,
        E value, int index, boolean isSelected, boolean cellHasFocus);
}
```

This method is called for each cell. It returns a component that paints the cell contents. The component is placed at the appropriate location whenever a cell needs to be rendered.

One way to implement a cell renderer is to create a class that extends JComponent, like this:

```
class MyCellRenderer extends JComponent implements ListCellRenderer<Type>
{
    public Component getListCellRendererComponent(JList<? extends Type> list,
        Type value, int index, boolean isSelected, boolean cellHasFocus)
    {
        stash away information needed for painting and size measurement
        return this;
    }
    public void paintComponent(Graphics g)
    {
        paint code
    }
    public Dimension getPreferredSize()
    {
        size measurement code
    }
    instance fields
}
```

In Listing 6.4, we display the font choices graphically by showing the actual appearance of each font (see Figure 6.4). In the paintComponent method, we display each name in its own font. We also need to make sure to match the usual colors of the look-and-feel of the JList class. We obtain these colors by calling the getForeground/getBackground and getSelectionForeground/getSelectionBackground methods of the JList class. In the getPreferredSize method, we need to measure the size of the string, using the techniques that you saw in Volume I, Chapter 7.

To install the cell renderer, simply call the setCellRenderer method:

```
fontList.setCellRenderer(new FontCellRenderer());
```

Now all list cells are drawn with the custom renderer.

Actually, a simpler method for writing custom renderers works in many cases. If the rendered image just contains text, an icon, and possibly a change of color,

**Figure 6.4** A list box with rendered cells

you can get by with configuring a JLabel. For example, to show the font name in its own font, we can use the following renderer:

```
class FontCellRenderer extends JLabel implements ListCellRenderer<Font>
{
    public Component getListCellRendererComponent(JList<? extends Font> list,
        Font value, int index, boolean isSelected, boolean cellHasFocus)
    {
        Font font = (Font) value;
        setText(font.getFamily());
        setFont(font);
        setOpaque(true);
        setBackground(isSelected ? list.getSelectionBackground() : list.getBackground());
        setForeground(isSelected ? list.getSelectionForeground() : list.getForeground());
        return this;
    }
}
```

Note that here we don't write any paintComponent or getPreferredSize methods; the JLabel class already implements these methods to our satisfaction. All we do is configure the label appropriately by setting its text, font, and color.

This code is a convenient shortcut for those cases where an existing component—in this case, JLabel—already provides all functionality needed to render a cell value.

We could have used a JLabel in our sample program, but we gave you the more general code so you can modify it when you need to do arbitrary drawings in list cells.

**CAUTION:** It is not a good idea to construct a new component in each call to `getListCellRendererComponent`. If the user scrolls through many list entries, a new component would be constructed every time. Reconfiguring an existing component is safe and much more efficient.

---

**Listing 6.4**   `listRendering/FontCellRenderer.java`

```java
 1  package listRendering;
 2
 3  import java.awt.*;
 4  import javax.swing.*;
 5  /**
 6   * A cell renderer for Font objects that renders the font name in its own font.
 7   */
 8  public class FontCellRenderer extends JComponent implements ListCellRenderer<Font>
 9  {
10     private Font font;
11     private Color background;
12     private Color foreground;
13
14     public Component getListCellRendererComponent(JList<? extends Font> list,
15           Font value, int index, boolean isSelected, boolean cellHasFocus)
16     {
17        font = value;
18        background = isSelected ? list.getSelectionBackground() : list.getBackground();
19        foreground = isSelected ? list.getSelectionForeground() : list.getForeground();
20        return this;
21     }
22
23     public void paintComponent(Graphics g)
24     {
25        String text = font.getFamily();
26        FontMetrics fm = g.getFontMetrics(font);
27        g.setColor(background);
28        g.fillRect(0, 0, getWidth(), getHeight());
29        g.setColor(foreground);
30        g.setFont(font);
31        g.drawString(text, 0, fm.getAscent());
32     }
33
34     public Dimension getPreferredSize()
35     {
36        String text = font.getFamily();
37        Graphics g = getGraphics();
38        FontMetrics fm = g.getFontMetrics(font);
39        return new Dimension(fm.stringWidth(text), fm.getHeight());
40     }
41  }
```

---

**javax.swing.JList<E>**  1.2

- Color getBackground()
  returns the background color for unselected cells.
- Color getSelectionBackground()
  returns the background color for selected cells.
- Color getForeground()
  returns the foreground color for unselected cells.
- Color getSelectionForeground()
  returns the foreground color for selected cells.
- void setCellRenderer(ListCellRenderer<? super E> cellRenderer)
  sets the renderer that paints the cells in the list.

---

*javax.swing.ListCellRenderer<E>*  1.2

- Component getListCellRendererComponent(JList<? extends E> list, E item, int index, boolean isSelected, boolean hasFocus)
  returns a component whose paint method draws the cell contents. If the list cells do not have fixed size, that component must also implement getPreferredSize.

  | *Parameters:* | list | The list whose cell is being drawn |
  |---|---|---|
  | | item | The item to be drawn |
  | | index | The index where the item is stored in the model |
  | | isSelected | true if the specified cell was selected |
  | | hasFocus | true if the specified cell has the focus |

---

## 6.2 Tables

The JTable component displays a two-dimensional grid of objects. Tables are common in user interfaces, and the Swing team has put a lot of effort into the table control. Tables are inherently complex, but—perhaps more successfully than other Swing classes—the JTable component hides much of that complexity. You can produce fully functional tables with rich behavior by writing a few lines of code. You can also write more code and customize the display and behavior for your specific applications.

In the following sections, we will explain how to make simple tables, how the user interacts with them, and how to make some of the most common adjustments. As with the other complex Swing controls, it is impossible to cover all aspects in complete detail. For more information, look in *Graphic Java™, Third Edition*, by David M. Geary (Prentice Hall, 1999), or *Core Swing* by Kim Topley (Prentice Hall, 1999).

## 6.2.1 A Simple Table

Similar to the JList component, a JTable does not store its own data but obtains them from a *table model*. The JTable class has a constructor that wraps a two-dimensional array of objects into a default model. That is the strategy that we use in our first example; later in this chapter, we will turn to table models.

Figure 6.5 shows a typical table, describing the properties of the planets of the solar system. (A planet is *gaseous* if it consists mostly of hydrogen and helium. You should take the "Color" entries with a grain of salt—that column was added because it will be useful in later code examples.)

As you can see from the code in Listing 6.5, the data of the table is stored as a two-dimensional array of Object values:

```
Object[][] cells =
{
   { "Mercury", 2440.0, 0, false, Color.YELLOW },
   { "Venus", 6052.0, 0, false, Color.YELLOW },
   . . .
}
```

**NOTE:** Here, we take advantage of autoboxing. The entries in the second, third, and fourth columns are automatically converted into objects of type Double, Integer, and Boolean.

The table simply invokes the toString method on each object to display it. That's why the colors show up as java.awt.Color[r=...,g=...,b=...].

Supply the column names in a separate array of strings:

```
String[] columnNames = { "Planet", "Radius", "Moons", "Gaseous", "Color" };
```

Then, construct a table from the cell and column name arrays:

```
JTable table = new JTable(cells, columnNames);
```

**NOTE:** Note that a JTable, unlike a JList, is not a generic type. There is a good reason for that. Elements in a list are expected to be of a uniform type—but, in general, there is no single element type for the entire table. In our example, the planet name is a string, the color is a java.awt.Color, and so on.

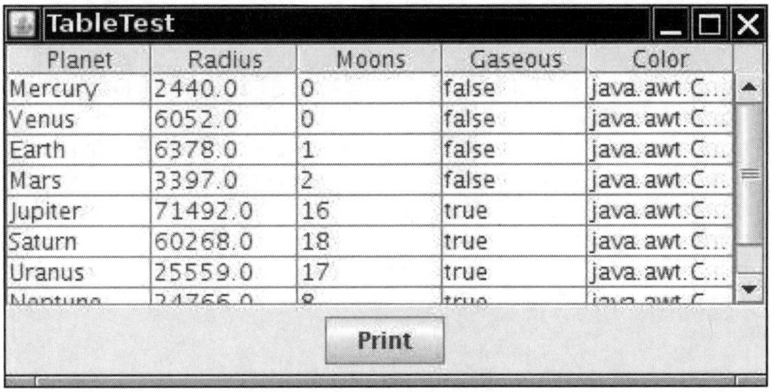

**Figure 6.5** A simple table

You can add scroll bars in the usual way—by wrapping the table in a JScrollPane:

```
JScrollPane pane = new JScrollPane(table);
```

The resulting table already has surprisingly rich behavior. Resize the table vertically until the scroll bar shows up. Then, scroll the table. Note that the column headers don't scroll out of view!

Next, click on one of the column headers and drag it to the left or right. See how the entire column becomes detached (see Figure 6.6). You can drop it in a different location. This rearranges the columns *in the view only*. The data model is not affected.

To *resize* columns, simply place the cursor between two columns until the cursor shape changes to an arrow. Then, drag the column boundary to the desired place (see Figure 6.7).

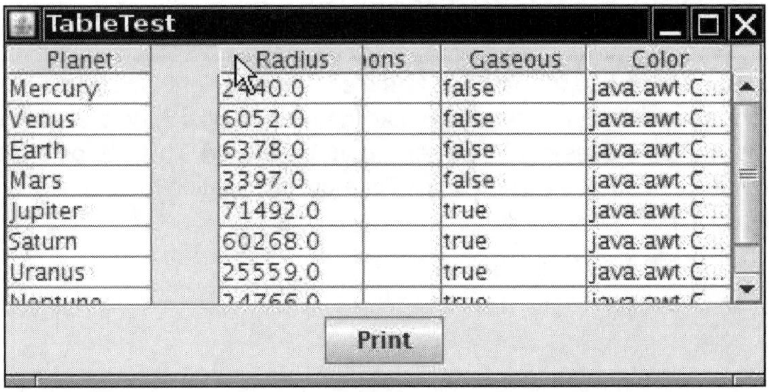

**Figure 6.6** Moving a column

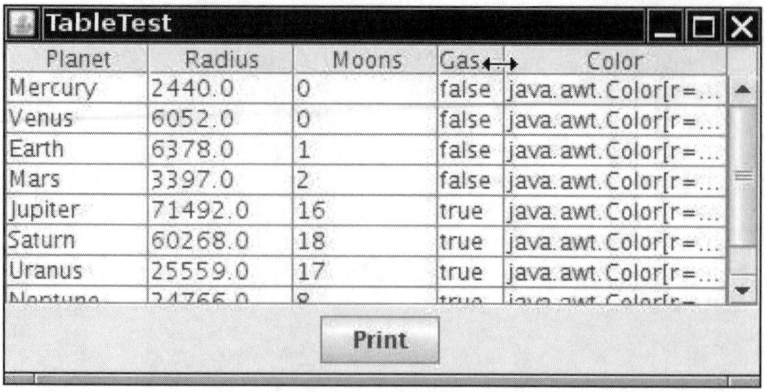

**Figure 6.7** Resizing columns

Users can select rows by clicking anywhere in a row. The selected rows are highlighted; you will see later how to get selection events. Users can also edit the table entries by clicking on a cell and typing into it. However, in this code example, the edits do not change the underlying data. In your programs, you should either make cells uneditable or handle cell editing events and update your model. We will discuss those topics later in this section.

Finally, click on a column header. The rows are automatically sorted. Click again, and the sort order is reversed. This behavior is activated by the call

```
table.setAutoCreateRowSorter(true);
```

You can print a table with the call

```
table.print();
```

A print dialog box appears, and the table is sent to the printer. We will discuss custom printing options in Chapter 7.

---

**NOTE:** If you resize the TableTest frame so that its height is taller than the table height, you will see a gray area below the table. Unlike JList and JTree components, the table does not fill the scroll pane's viewport. This can be a problem if you want to support drag and drop. (For more information on drag and drop, see Chapter 7.) In that case, call

```
table.setFillsViewportHeight(true);
```

---

**Listing 6.5**  table/TableTest.java

```
1  package table;
2
3  import java.awt.*;
4  import java.awt.event.*;
5  import java.beans.*;
6  import javax.swing.*;
7
8  /**
9   * This program demonstrates how to show a simple table.
10  * @version 1.12 2012-06-09
11  * @author Cay Horstmann
12  */
13 public class TableTest
14 {
15    public static void main(String[] args)
16    {
17       EventQueue.invokeLater(new Runnable()
18          {
19             public void run()
20             {
21                JFrame frame = new PlanetTableFrame();
22                frame.setTitle("TableTest");
23                frame.setDefaultCloseOperation(JFrame.EXIT_ON_CLOSE);
24                frame.setVisible(true);
25             }
26          });
27    }
28 }
29
30 /**
31  * This frame contains a table of planet data.
32  */
33 class PlanetTableFrame extends JFrame
34 {
35    private String[] columnNames = { "Planet", "Radius", "Moons", "Gaseous", "Color" };
36    private Object[][] cells = { { "Mercury", 2440.0, 0, false, Color.YELLOW },
37          { "Venus", 6052.0, 0, false, Color.YELLOW }, { "Earth", 6378.0, 1, false, Color.BLUE },
38          { "Mars", 3397.0, 2, false, Color.RED }, { "Jupiter", 71492.0, 16, true, Color.ORANGE },
39          { "Saturn", 60268.0, 18, true, Color.ORANGE },
40          { "Uranus", 25559.0, 17, true, Color.BLUE }, { "Neptune", 24766.0, 8, true, Color.BLUE },
41          { "Pluto", 1137.0, 1, false, Color.BLACK } };
42
43    public PlanetTableFrame()
44    {
```

*(Continues)*

**Listing 6.5** *(Continued)*

```
45        final JTable table = new JTable(cells, columnNames);
46        table.setAutoCreateRowSorter(true);
47        add(table, BorderLayout.CENTER);
48        JButton printButton = new JButton("Print");
49        printButton.addActionListener(EventHandler.create(ActionListener.class, table, "print"));
50        JPanel buttonPanel = new JPanel();
51        buttonPanel.add(printButton);
52        add(buttonPanel, BorderLayout.SOUTH);
53        pack();
54    }
55 }
```

---

**javax.swing.JTable** 1.2

- JTable(Object[][] entries, Object[] columnNames)
  constructs a table with a default table model.

- void print() **5.0**
  displays a print dialog box and prints the table.

- boolean getAutoCreateRowSorter() **6**
- void setAutoCreateRowSorter(boolean newValue) **6**
  gets or sets the autoCreateRowSorter property. The default is false. When set, a default row sorter is automatically set whenever the model changes.

- boolean getFillsViewportHeight() **6**
- void setFillsViewportHeight(boolean newValue) **6**
  gets or sets the fillsViewportHeight property. The default is false. When set, the table always fills an enclosing viewport.

## 6.2.2 Table Models

In the preceding example, the table data were stored in a two-dimensional array. However, you should generally not use that strategy in your own code. If you find yourself dumping data into an array to display it as a table, you should instead consider implementing your own table model.

Table models are particularly simple to implement because you can take advantage of the AbstractTableModel class that implements most of the required methods. You only need to supply three methods:

```
public int getRowCount();
public int getColumnCount();
public Object getValueAt(int row, int column);
```

There are many ways of implementing the getValueAt method. For example, if you want to display the contents of a RowSet that contains the result of a database query, simply provide this method:

```
public Object getValueAt(int r, int c)
{
   try
   {
      rowSet.absolute(r + 1);
      return rowSet.getObject(c + 1);
   }
   catch (SQLException e)
   {
      e.printStackTrace();
      return null;
   }
}
```

Our sample program is even simpler. We construct a table that shows some computed values—namely, the growth of an investment under different interest rate scenarios (see Figure 6.8).

The getValueAt method computes the appropriate value and formats it:

```
public Object getValueAt(int r, int c)
{
   double rate = (c + minRate) / 100.0;
   int nperiods = r;
   double futureBalance = INITIAL_BALANCE * Math.pow(1 + rate, nperiods);
   return String.format("%.2f", futureBalance);
}
```

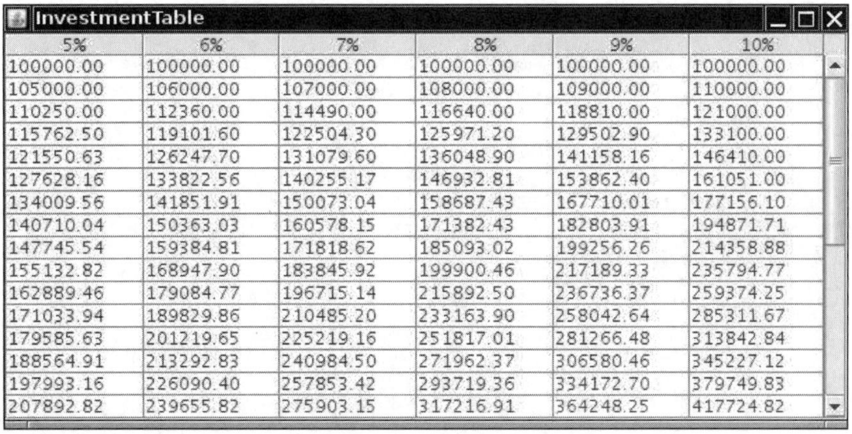

| 5% | 6% | 7% | 8% | 9% | 10% |
|---|---|---|---|---|---|
| 100000.00 | 100000.00 | 100000.00 | 100000.00 | 100000.00 | 100000.00 |
| 105000.00 | 106000.00 | 107000.00 | 108000.00 | 109000.00 | 110000.00 |
| 110250.00 | 112360.00 | 114490.00 | 116640.00 | 118810.00 | 121000.00 |
| 115762.50 | 119101.60 | 122504.30 | 125971.20 | 129502.90 | 133100.00 |
| 121550.63 | 126247.70 | 131079.60 | 136048.90 | 141158.16 | 146410.00 |
| 127628.16 | 133822.56 | 140255.17 | 146932.81 | 153862.40 | 161051.00 |
| 134009.56 | 141851.91 | 150073.04 | 158687.43 | 167710.01 | 177156.10 |
| 140710.04 | 150363.03 | 160578.15 | 171382.43 | 182803.91 | 194871.71 |
| 147745.54 | 159384.81 | 171818.62 | 185093.02 | 199256.26 | 214358.88 |
| 155132.82 | 168947.90 | 183845.92 | 199900.46 | 217189.33 | 235794.77 |
| 162889.46 | 179084.77 | 196715.14 | 215892.50 | 236736.37 | 259374.25 |
| 171033.94 | 189829.86 | 210485.20 | 233163.90 | 258042.64 | 285311.67 |
| 179585.63 | 201219.65 | 225219.16 | 251817.01 | 281266.48 | 313842.84 |
| 188564.91 | 213292.83 | 240984.50 | 271962.37 | 306580.46 | 345227.12 |
| 197993.16 | 226090.40 | 257853.42 | 293719.36 | 334172.70 | 379749.83 |
| 207892.82 | 239655.82 | 275903.15 | 317216.91 | 364248.25 | 417724.82 |

Figure 6.8 Growth of an investment

The getRowCount and getColumnCount methods simply return the number of rows and columns.

```
public int getRowCount() { return years; }
public int getColumnCount() {  return maxRate - minRate + 1; }
```

If you don't supply column names, the getColumnName method of the AbstractTableModel names the columns A, B, C, and so on. You will usually want to override that default behavior. To change column names, override the getColumnName method. In this example, we simply label each column with the interest rate.

```
public String getColumnName(int c) { return (c + minRate) + "%"; }
```

You can find the complete source code in Listing 6.6.

**Listing 6.6** tableModel/InvestmentTable.java

```
 1  package tableModel;
 2
 3  import java.awt.*;
 4
 5  import javax.swing.*;
 6  import javax.swing.table.*;
 7
 8  /**
 9   * This program shows how to build a table from a table model.
10   * @version 1.02 2007-08-01
11   * @author Cay Horstmann
12   */
13  public class InvestmentTable
14  {
15     public static void main(String[] args)
16     {
17        EventQueue.invokeLater(new Runnable()
18           {
19              public void run()
20              {
21                 JFrame frame = new InvestmentTableFrame();
22                 frame.setTitle("InvestmentTable");
23                 frame.setDefaultCloseOperation(JFrame.EXIT_ON_CLOSE);
24                 frame.setVisible(true);
25              }
26           });
27     }
28  }
29
30  /**
31   * This frame contains the investment table.
32   */
```

```
33  class InvestmentTableFrame extends JFrame
34  {
35     public InvestmentTableFrame()
36     {
37        TableModel model = new InvestmentTableModel(30, 5, 10);
38        JTable table = new JTable(model);
39        add(table);
40        pack();
41     }
42  }
43
44  /**
45   * This table model computes the cell entries each time they are requested. The table contents
46   * shows the growth of an investment for a number of years under different interest rates.
47   */
48  class InvestmentTableModel extends AbstractTableModel
49  {
50     private static double INITIAL_BALANCE = 100000.0;
51
52     private int years;
53     private int minRate;
54     private int maxRate;
55
56     /**
57      * Constructs an investment table model.
58      * @param y the number of years
59      * @param r1 the lowest interest rate to tabulate
60      * @param r2 the highest interest rate to tabulate
61      */
62     public InvestmentTableModel(int y, int r1, int r2)
63     {
64        years = y;
65        minRate = r1;
66        maxRate = r2;
67     }
68
69     public int getRowCount()
70     {
71        return years;
72     }
73
74     public int getColumnCount()
75     {
76        return maxRate - minRate + 1;
77     }
78
79     public Object getValueAt(int r, int c)
80     {
81        double rate = (c + minRate) / 100.0;
```

*(Continues)*

---

**Listing 6.6** *(Continued)*

```
82        int nperiods = r;
83        double futureBalance = INITIAL_BALANCE * Math.pow(1 + rate, nperiods);
84        return String.format("%.2f", futureBalance);
85     }
86
87     public String getColumnName(int c)
88     {
89        return (c + minRate) + "%";
90     }
91  }
```

---

*javax.swing.table.TableModel* 1.2

- int getRowCount()
- int getColumnCount()
  gets the number of rows and columns in the table model.
- Object getValueAt(int row, int column)
  gets the value at the given row and column.
- void setValueAt(Object newValue, int row, int column)
  sets a new value at the given row and column.
- boolean isCellEditable(int row, int column)
  returns true if the cell at the given row and column is editable.
- String getColumnName(int column)
  gets the column title.

## 6.2.3 Working with Rows and Columns

In this subsection, you will see how to manipulate the rows and columns in a table. As you read through this material, keep in mind that a Swing table is quite asymmetric—the operations that you can carry out on rows and columns are different. The table component was optimized to display rows of information with the same structure, such as the result of a database query, not an arbitrary two-dimensional grid of objects. You will see this asymmetry throughout this subsection.

### 6.2.3.1 Column Classes

In the next example, we again display our planet data, but this time we want to give the table more information about the column types. This is achieved by defining the method

```
Class<?> getColumnClass(int columnIndex)
```

of the table model to return the class that describes the column type.

The JTable class uses this information to pick an appropriate renderer for the class. Table 6.1 shows the default rendering actions.

You can see the checkboxes and images in Figure 6.9. (Thanks to Jim Evins, www.snaught.com/JimsCoolIcons/Planets, for providing the planet images!)

To render other types, you can install a custom renderer—see Section 6.2.4, "Cell Rendering and Editing," on p. 408.

**Table 6.1** Default Rendering Actions

| Type | Rendered As |
|------|-------------|
| Boolean | Checkbox |
| Icon | Image |
| Object | String |

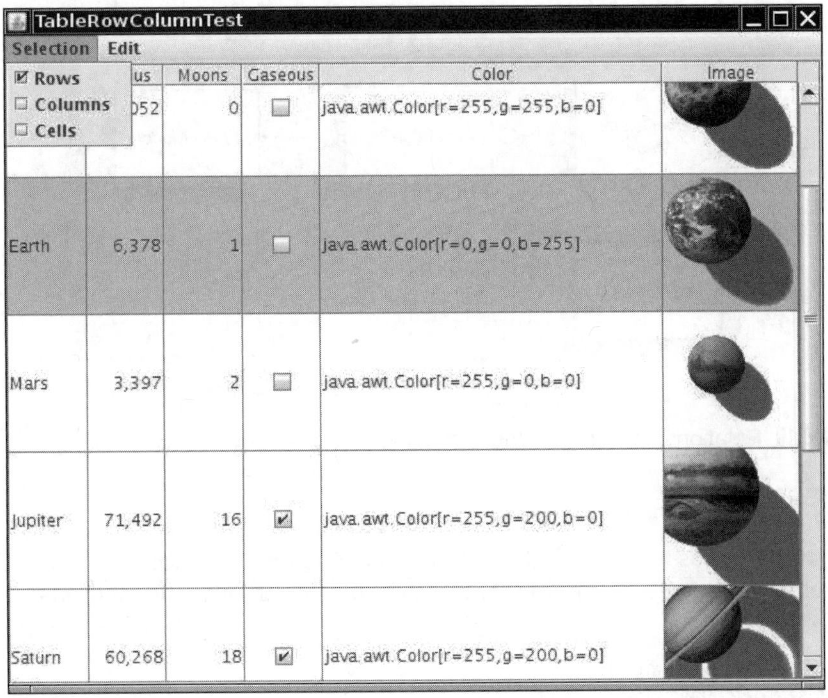

**Figure 6.9** A table with planet data

### 6.2.3.2 Accessing Table Columns

The `JTable` class stores information about table columns in objects of type `TableColumn`. A `TableColumnModel` object manages the columns. (Figure 6.10 shows the relationships among the most important table classes.) If you don't want to insert or remove columns dynamically, you won't use the column model much. The most common use for the column model is simply to get a `TableColumn` object:

```
int columnIndex = . . .;
TableColumn column = table.getColumnModel().getColumn(columnIndex);
```

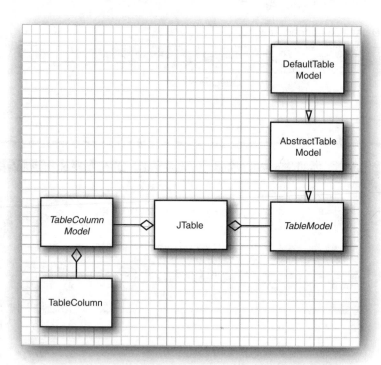

**Figure 6.10** Relationship between table classes

### 6.2.3.3 Resizing Columns

The `TableColumn` class gives you control over the resizing behavior of columns. You can set the preferred, minimum, and maximum width with the methods

```
void setPreferredWidth(int width)
void setMinWidth(int width)
void setMaxWidth(int width)
```

This information is used by the table component to lay out the columns.

Use the method

```
void setResizable(boolean resizable)
```

to control whether the user is allowed to resize the column.

You can programmatically resize a column with the method

```
void setWidth(int width)
```

When a column is resized, the default is to leave the total size of the table unchanged. Of course, the width increase or decrease of the resized column must then be distributed over other columns. The default behavior is to change the size of all columns to the right of the resized column. That's a good default because it allows a user to adjust all columns to a desired width, moving from left to right.

You can set another behavior from Table 6.2 by using the method

```
void setAutoResizeMode(int mode)
```

of the JTable class.

**Table 6.2** Resize Modes

| Mode | Behavior |
| --- | --- |
| AUTO_RESIZE_OFF | Don't resize other columns; change the table width. |
| AUTO_RESIZE_NEXT_COLUMN | Resize the next column only. |
| AUTO_RESIZE_SUBSEQUENT_COLUMNS | Resize all subsequent columns equally; this is the default behavior. |
| AUTO_RESIZE_LAST_COLUMN | Resize the last column only. |
| AUTO_RESIZE_ALL_COLUMNS | Resize all columns in the table; this is not a good choice because it prevents the user from adjusting multiple columns to a desired size. |

### 6.2.3.4 Resizing Rows

Row heights are managed directly by the JTable class. If your cells are taller than the default, you may want to set the row height:

```
table.setRowHeight(height);
```

By default, all rows of the table have the same height. You can set the heights of individual rows with the call

```
table.setRowHeight(row, height);
```

The actual row height equals the row height set with these methods, reduced by the row margin. The default row margin is 1 pixel, but you can change it with the call

```
table.setRowMargin(margin);
```

### 6.2.3.5 Selecting Rows, Columns, and Cells

Depending on the selection mode, the user can select rows, columns, or individual cells in the table. By default, row selection is enabled. Clicking inside a cell selects the entire row (see Figure 6.9 on p. 391). Call

```
table.setRowSelectionAllowed(false)
```

to disable row selection.

When row selection is enabled, you can control whether the user is allowed to select a single row, a contiguous set of rows, or any set of rows. You need to retrieve the *selection model* and use its setSelectionMode method:

```
table.getSelectionModel().setSelectionMode(mode);
```

Here, mode is one of the three values:

```
ListSelectionModel.SINGLE_SELECTION
ListSelectionModel.SINGLE_INTERVAL_SELECTION
ListSelectionModel.MULTIPLE_INTERVAL_SELECTION
```

Column selection is disabled by default. You can turn it on with the call

```
table.setColumnSelectionAllowed(true)
```

Enabling both row and column selection is equivalent to enabling cell selection. The user then selects ranges of cells (see Figure 6.11). You can also enable that setting with the call

```
table.setCellSelectionEnabled(true)
```

Run the program in Listing 6.7 to watch cell selection in action. Enable row, column, or cell selection in the Selection menu and watch how the selection behavior changes.

You can find out which rows and columns are selected by calling the getSelectedRows and getSelectedColumns methods. Both return an int[] array of the indexes of the selected items. Note that the index values are those of the table view, not the underlying table model. Try selecting rows and columns, then drag columns to different places and sort the rows by clicking on column headers. Use the Print Selection menu item to see which rows and columns are reported as selected.

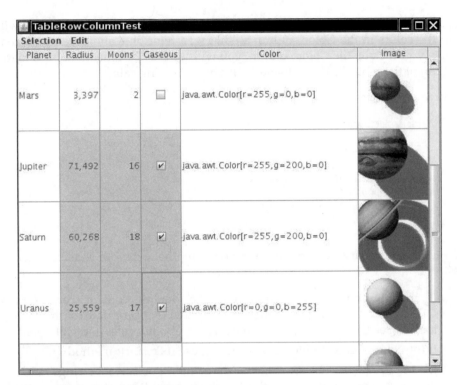

**Figure 6.11** Selecting a range of cells

If you need to translate the table index values to table model index values, use the JTable methods convertRowIndexToModel and convertColumnIndexToModel.

### 6.2.3.6 Sorting Rows

As you have seen in our first table example, it is easy to add row sorting to a JTable simply by calling the setAutoCreateRowSorter method. However, to have finer-grained control over the sorting behavior, install a TableRowSorter<M> object into a JTable and customize it. The type parameter M denotes the table model; it needs to be a subtype of the TableModel interface.

```
TableRowSorter<TableModel> sorter = new TableRowSorter<TableModel>(model);
table.setRowSorter(sorter);
```

Some columns should not be sortable, such as the image column in our planet data. Turn sorting off by calling

```
sorter.setSortable(IMAGE_COLUMN, false);
```

You can install a custom comparator for each column. In our example, we will sort the colors in the Color column so that we prefer blue and green over red. When you click on the Color column, you will see that the blue planets go to the bottom of the table. This is achieved with the following call:

```
sorter.setComparator(COLOR_COLUMN, new Comparator<Color>()
   {
      public int compare(Color c1, Color c2)
      {
         int d = c1.getBlue() - c2.getBlue();
         if (d != 0) return d;
         d = c1.getGreen() - c2.getGreen();
         if (d != 0) return d;
         return c1.getRed() - c2.getRed();
      }
   });
```

If you do not specify a comparator for a column, the sort order is determined as follows:

1.  If the column class is String, use the default collator returned by Collator.getInstance(). It sorts strings in a way that is appropriate for the current locale. (See Chapter 5 for more information about locales and collators.)

2.  If the column class implements Comparable, use its compareTo method.

3.  If a TableStringConverter has been set for the comparator, sort the strings returned by the converter's toString method with the default collator. If you want to use this approach, define a converter as follows:

```
orter.setStringConverter(new TableStringConverter()
   {
      public String toString(TableModel model, int row, int column)
      {
         Object value = model.getValueAt(row, column);
         convert value to a string and return it
      }
   });
```

4.  Otherwise, call the toString method on the cell values and sort them with the default collator.

### 6.2.3.7 Filtering Rows

In addition to sorting rows, the TableRowSorter can also selectively hide rows—a process called *filtering*. To activate filtering, set a RowFilter. For example, to include all rows that contain at least one moon, call

```
sorter.setRowFilter(RowFilter.numberFilter(ComparisonType.NOT_EQUAL, 0, MOONS_COLUMN));
```

Here, we use a predefined number filter. To construct a number filter, supply

- The comparison type (one of EQUAL, NOT_EQUAL, AFTER, or BEFORE).
- An object of a subclass of Number (such as an Integer or Double). Only objects that have the same class as the given Number object are considered.
- Zero or more column index values. If no index values are supplied, all columns are searched.

The static RowFilter.dateFilter method constructs a date filter in the same way; you need to supply a Date object instead of the Number object.

Finally, the static RowFilter.regexFilter method constructs a filter that looks for strings matching a regular expression. For example,

```
sorter.setRowFilter(RowFilter.regexFilter(".*[^s]$", PLANET_COLUMN));
```

only displays those planets whose name doesn't end with an "s". (See Chapter 1 for more information on regular expressions.)

You can also combine filters with the andFilter, orFilter, and notFilter methods. To filter for planets not ending in an "s" with at least one moon, you can use this filter combination:

```
sorter.setRowFilter(RowFilter.andFilter(Arrays.asList(
    RowFilter.regexFilter(".*[^s]$", PLANET_COLUMN),
    RowFilter.numberFilter(ComparisonType.NOT_EQUAL, 0, MOONS_COLUMN)));
```

---

 **CAUTION:** Annoyingly, the andFilter and orFilter methods don't use variable arguments but a single parameter of type Iterable.

---

To implement your own filter, provide a subclass of RowFilter and implement an include method to indicate which rows should be displayed. This is easy to do, but the glorious generality of the RowFilter class makes it a bit scary.

The RowFilter<M, I> class has two type parameters—the types for the model and for the row identifier. When dealing with tables, the model is always a subtype of TableModel and the identifier type is Integer. (At some point in the future, other components might also support row filtering. For example, to filter rows in a JTree, one might use a RowFilter<TreeModel, TreePath>.)

A row filter must implement the method

```
public boolean include(RowFilter.Entry<? extends M, ? extends I> entry)
```

The `RowFilter.Entry` class supplies methods to obtain the model, the row identifier, and the value at a given index. Therefore, you can filter both by row identifier and by the contents of the row.

For example, this filter displays every other row:

```
RowFilter<TableModel, Integer> filter = new RowFilter<TableModel, Integer>()
    {
        public boolean include(Entry<? extends TableModel, ? extends Integer> entry)
        {
            return entry.getIdentifier() % 2 == 0;
        }
    };
```

If you wanted to include only those planets with an even number of moons, you would instead test for

```
((Integer) entry.getValue(MOONS_COLUMN)) % 2 == 0
```

In our sample program, we allow the user to hide arbitrary rows. We store the hidden row indexes in a set. The row filter includes all rows whose indexes are not in that set.

The filtering mechanism wasn't designed for filters with criteria changing over time. In our sample program, we keep calling

```
sorter.setRowFilter(filter);
```

whenever the set of hidden rows changes. Setting a filter causes it to be applied immediately.

### 6.2.3.8 Hiding and Displaying Columns

As you saw in the preceding section, you can filter table rows by either their contents or their row identifier. Hiding table columns uses a completely different mechanism.

The `removeColumn` method of the `JTable` class removes a column from the table view. The column data are not actually removed from the model—they are just hidden from view. The `removeColumn` method takes a `TableColumn` argument. If you have the column number (for example, from a call to `getSelectedColumns`), you need to ask the table model for the actual table column object:

```
TableColumnModel columnModel = table.getColumnModel();
TableColumn column = columnModel.getColumn(i);
table.removeColumn(column);
```

If you remember the column, you can later add it back in:

```
table.addColumn(column);
```

This method adds the column to the end. If you want it to appear elsewhere, call the moveColumn method.

You can also add a new column that corresponds to a column index in the table model, by adding a new TableColumn object:

```
table.addColumn(new TableColumn(modelColumnIndex));
```

You can have multiple table columns that view the same column of the model.

The program in Listing 6.7 demonstrates selection and filtering of rows and columns.

**Listing 6.7** tableRowColumn/PlanetTableFrame.java

```
 1 package tableRowColumn;
 2
 3 import java.awt.*;
 4 import java.awt.event.*;
 5 import java.util.*;
 6 import javax.swing.*;
 7 import javax.swing.table.*;
 8
 9 /**
10  * This frame contains a table of planet data.
11  */
12 public class PlanetTableFrame extends JFrame
13 {
14    private static final int DEFAULT_WIDTH = 600;
15    private static final int DEFAULT_HEIGHT = 500;
16
17    public static final int COLOR_COLUMN = 4;
18    public static final int IMAGE_COLUMN = 5;
19
20    private JTable table;
21    private HashSet<Integer> removedRowIndices;
22    private ArrayList<TableColumn> removedColumns;
23    private JCheckBoxMenuItem rowsItem;
24    private JCheckBoxMenuItem columnsItem;
25    private JCheckBoxMenuItem cellsItem;
26
27    private String[] columnNames = { "Planet", "Radius", "Moons", "Gaseous", "Color", "Image" };
28
29    private Object[][] cells = {
30          { "Mercury", 2440.0, 0, false, Color.YELLOW,
31             new ImageIcon(getClass().getResource("Mercury.gif")) },
32          { "Venus", 6052.0, 0, false, Color.YELLOW,
33             new ImageIcon(getClass().getResource("Venus.gif")) },
```

*(Continues)*

---

**Listing 6.7** *(Continued)*

```
34          { "Earth", 6378.0, 1, false, Color.BLUE,
35              new ImageIcon(getClass().getResource("Earth.gif")) },
36          { "Mars", 3397.0, 2, false, Color.RED,
37              new ImageIcon(getClass().getResource("Mars.gif")) },
38          { "Jupiter", 71492.0, 16, true, Color.ORANGE,
39              new ImageIcon(getClass().getResource("Jupiter.gif")) },
40          { "Saturn", 60268.0, 18, true, Color.ORANGE,
41              new ImageIcon(getClass().getResource("Saturn.gif")) },
42          { "Uranus", 25559.0, 17, true, Color.BLUE,
43              new ImageIcon(getClass().getResource("Uranus.gif")) },
44          { "Neptune", 24766.0, 8, true, Color.BLUE,
45              new ImageIcon(getClass().getResource("Neptune.gif")) },
46          { "Pluto", 1137.0, 1, false, Color.BLACK,
47              new ImageIcon(getClass().getResource("Pluto.gif")) } };
48
49   public PlanetTableFrame()
50   {
51      setSize(DEFAULT_WIDTH, DEFAULT_HEIGHT);
52
53      TableModel model = new DefaultTableModel(cells, columnNames)
54         {
55            public Class<?> getColumnClass(int c)
56            {
57               return cells[0][c].getClass();
58            }
59         };
60
61      table = new JTable(model);
62
63      table.setRowHeight(100);
64      table.getColumnModel().getColumn(COLOR_COLUMN).setMinWidth(250);
65      table.getColumnModel().getColumn(IMAGE_COLUMN).setMinWidth(100);
66
67      final TableRowSorter<TableModel> sorter = new TableRowSorter<>(model);
68      table.setRowSorter(sorter);
69      sorter.setComparator(COLOR_COLUMN, new Comparator<Color>()
70         {
71            public int compare(Color c1, Color c2)
72            {
73               int d = c1.getBlue() - c2.getBlue();
74               if (d != 0) return d;
75               d = c1.getGreen() - c2.getGreen();
76               if (d != 0) return d;
77               return c1.getRed() - c2.getRed();
78            }
79         });
80      sorter.setSortable(IMAGE_COLUMN, false);
```

```
81      add(new JScrollPane(table), BorderLayout.CENTER);
82
83      removedRowIndices = new HashSet<>();
84      removedColumns = new ArrayList<>();
85
86      final RowFilter<TableModel, Integer> filter = new RowFilter<TableModel, Integer>()
87      {
88         public boolean include(Entry<? extends TableModel, ? extends Integer> entry)
89         {
90            return !removedRowIndices.contains(entry.getIdentifier());
91         }
92      };
93
94      // create menu
95
96      JMenuBar menuBar = new JMenuBar();
97      setJMenuBar(menuBar);
98
99      JMenu selectionMenu = new JMenu("Selection");
100     menuBar.add(selectionMenu);
101
102     rowsItem = new JCheckBoxMenuItem("Rows");
103     columnsItem = new JCheckBoxMenuItem("Columns");
104     cellsItem = new JCheckBoxMenuItem("Cells");
105
106     rowsItem.setSelected(table.getRowSelectionAllowed());
107     columnsItem.setSelected(table.getColumnSelectionAllowed());
108     cellsItem.setSelected(table.getCellSelectionEnabled());
109
110     rowsItem.addActionListener(new ActionListener()
111        {
112           public void actionPerformed(ActionEvent event)
113           {
114              table.clearSelection();
115              table.setRowSelectionAllowed(rowsItem.isSelected());
116              updateCheckboxMenuItems();
117           }
118        });
119     selectionMenu.add(rowsItem);
120
121     columnsItem.addActionListener(new ActionListener()
122        {
123           public void actionPerformed(ActionEvent event)
124           {
125              table.clearSelection();
126              table.setColumnSelectionAllowed(columnsItem.isSelected());
127              updateCheckboxMenuItems();
128           }
129        });
```

*(Continues)*

**Listing 6.7** *(Continued)*

```java
130         selectionMenu.add(columnsItem);
131
132         cellsItem.addActionListener(new ActionListener()
133            {
134               public void actionPerformed(ActionEvent event)
135               {
136                  table.clearSelection();
137                  table.setCellSelectionEnabled(cellsItem.isSelected());
138                  updateCheckboxMenuItems();
139               }
140            });
141         selectionMenu.add(cellsItem);
142
143         JMenu tableMenu = new JMenu("Edit");
144         menuBar.add(tableMenu);
145
146         JMenuItem hideColumnsItem = new JMenuItem("Hide Columns");
147         hideColumnsItem.addActionListener(new ActionListener()
148            {
149               public void actionPerformed(ActionEvent event)
150               {
151                  int[] selected = table.getSelectedColumns();
152                  TableColumnModel columnModel = table.getColumnModel();
153
154                  // remove columns from view, starting at the last
155                  // index so that column numbers aren't affected
156
157                  for (int i = selected.length - 1; i >= 0; i--)
158                  {
159                     TableColumn column = columnModel.getColumn(selected[i]);
160                     table.removeColumn(column);
161
162                     // store removed columns for "show columns" command
163
164                     removedColumns.add(column);
165                  }
166               }
167            });
168         tableMenu.add(hideColumnsItem);
169
170         JMenuItem showColumnsItem = new JMenuItem("Show Columns");
171         showColumnsItem.addActionListener(new ActionListener()
172            {
173               public void actionPerformed(ActionEvent event)
174               {
```

```
175             // restore all removed columns
176             for (TableColumn tc : removedColumns)
177                 table.addColumn(tc);
178             removedColumns.clear();
179          }
180       });
181    tableMenu.add(showColumnsItem);
182
183    JMenuItem hideRowsItem = new JMenuItem("Hide Rows");
184
185    hideRowsItem.addActionListener(new ActionListener()
186       {
187          public void actionPerformed(ActionEvent event)
188          {
189             int[] selected = table.getSelectedRows();
190             for (int i : selected)
191                removedRowIndices.add(table.convertRowIndexToModel(i));
192             sorter.setRowFilter(filter);
193          }
194       });
195    tableMenu.add(hideRowsItem);
196
197    JMenuItem showRowsItem = new JMenuItem("Show Rows");
198    showRowsItem.addActionListener(new ActionListener()
199       {
200          public void actionPerformed(ActionEvent event)
201          {
202             removedRowIndices.clear();
203             sorter.setRowFilter(filter);
204          }
205       });
206    tableMenu.add(showRowsItem);
207
208    JMenuItem printSelectionItem = new JMenuItem("Print Selection");
209    printSelectionItem.addActionListener(new ActionListener()
210       {
211          public void actionPerformed(ActionEvent event)
212          {
213             int[] selected = table.getSelectedRows();
214             System.out.println("Selected rows: " + Arrays.toString(selected));
215             selected = table.getSelectedColumns();
216             System.out.println("Selected columns: " + Arrays.toString(selected));
217          }
218       });
219    tableMenu.add(printSelectionItem);
220 }
```

*(Continues)*

---

**Listing 6.7** *(Continued)*

```
221    private void updateCheckboxMenuItems()
222    {
223        rowsItem.setSelected(table.getRowSelectionAllowed());
224        columnsItem.setSelected(table.getColumnSelectionAllowed());
225        cellsItem.setSelected(table.getCellSelectionEnabled());
226    }
227 }
```

---

*javax.swing.table.TableModel* 1.2

- Class getColumnClass(int columnIndex)

  gets the class for the values in this column. This information is used for sorting and rendering.

---

*javax.swing.JTable* 1.2

- TableColumnModel getColumnModel()

  gets the "column model" that describes the arrangement of the table columns.

- void setAutoResizeMode(int mode)

  sets the mode for automatic resizing of table columns.

  *Parameters:*     mode          One of AUTO_RESIZE_OFF, AUTO_RESIZE_NEXT_COLUMN,
                                 AUTO_RESIZE_SUBSEQUENT_COLUMNS, AUTO_RESIZE_LAST_COLUMN, and
                                 AUTO_RESIZE_ALL_COLUMNS

- int getRowMargin()
- void setRowMargin(int margin)

  gets or sets the amount of empty space between cells in adjacent rows.

- int getRowHeight()
- void setRowHeight(int height)

  gets or sets the default height of all rows of the table.

- int getRowHeight(int row)
- void setRowHeight(int row, int height)

  gets or sets the height of the given row of the table.

- ListSelectionModel getSelectionModel()

  returns the list selection model. You need that model to choose between row, column, and cell selection.

*(Continues)*

---

**javax.swing.JTable** 1.2 *(Continued)*

---

- boolean getRowSelectionAllowed()
- void setRowSelectionAllowed(boolean b)

  gets or sets the rowSelectionAllowed property. If true, rows are selected when the user clicks on cells.

- boolean getColumnSelectionAllowed()
- void setColumnSelectionAllowed(boolean b)

  gets or sets the columnSelectionAllowed property. If true, columns are selected when the user clicks on cells.

- boolean getCellSelectionEnabled()

  returns true if both rowSelectionAllowed and columnSelectionAllowed are true.

- void setCellSelectionEnabled(boolean b)

  sets both rowSelectionAllowed and columnSelectionAllowed to b.

- void addColumn(TableColumn column)

  adds a column as the last column of the table view.

- void moveColumn(int from, int to)

  moves the column whose table index is from so that its index becomes to. Only the view is affected.

- void removeColumn(TableColumn column)

  removes the given column from the view.

- int convertRowIndexToModel(int index) 6
- int convertColumnIndexToModel(int index)

  returns the model index of the row or column with the given index. This value is different from index when rows are sorted or filtered, or when columns are moved or removed.

- void setRowSorter(RowSorter<? extends TableModel> sorter)

  sets the row sorter.

---

**javax.swing.table.TableColumnModel** 1.2

---

- TableColumn getColumn(int index)

  gets the table column object that describes the column with the given view index.

---

**`javax.swing.table.TableColumn`** 1.2

- `TableColumn(int modelColumnIndex)`
  constructs a table column for viewing the model column with the given index.
- `void setPreferredWidth(int width)`
- `void setMinWidth(int width)`
- `void setMaxWidth(int width)`
  sets the preferred, minimum, and maximum width of this table column to `width`.
- `void setWidth(int width)`
  sets the actual width of this column to `width`.
- `void setResizable(boolean b)`
  If `b` is true, this column is resizable.

---

**`javax.swing.ListSelectionModel`** 1.2

- `void setSelectionMode(int mode)`

  | *Parameters:* | mode | One of `SINGLE_SELECTION`, `SINGLE_INTERVAL_SELECTION`, and `MULTIPLE_INTERVAL_SELECTION` |
  | --- | --- | --- |

---

**`javax.swing.DefaultRowSorter<M, I>`** 6

- `void setComparator(int column, Comparator<?> comparator)`
  sets the comparator to be used with the given column.
- `void setSortable(int column, boolean enabled)`
  enables or disables sorting for the given column.
- `void setRowFilter(RowFilter<? super M,? super I> filter)`
  sets the row filter.

---

**`javax.swing.table.TableRowSorter<M extends TableModel>`** 6

- `void setStringConverter(TableStringConverter stringConverter)`
  sets the string converter used for sorting and filtering.

---

**`javax.swing.table.TableStringConverter<M extends TableModel>`** 6

- `abstract String toString(TableModel model, int row, int column)`
  converts the model value at the given location to a string; you can override this method.

---

**javax.swing.RowFilter<M, I>** 6

- `boolean include(RowFilter.Entry<? extends M,? extends I> entry)`
  specifies the rows that are retained; you can override this method.
- `static <M,I> RowFilter<M,I> numberFilter(RowFilter.ComparisonType type, Number number, int...` `indices)`
- `static <M,I> RowFilter<M,I> dateFilter(RowFilter.ComparisonType type, Date date, int... indices)`
  returns a filter that includes rows containing values that match the given comparison to the given number or date. The comparison type is one of EQUAL, NOT_EQUAL, AFTER, or BEFORE. If any column model indexes are given, only those columns are searched; otherwise, all columns are searched. For the number filter, the class of the cell value must match the class of `number`.
- `static <M,I> RowFilter<M,I> regexFilter(String regex, int... indices)`
  returns a filter that includes rows that have a string value matching the given regular expression. If any column model indexes are given, only those columns are searched; otherwise, all columns are searched. Note that the string returned by the getStringValue method of RowFilter.Entry is matched.
- `static <M,I> RowFilter<M,I> andFilter(Iterable<? extends RowFilter<? super M,? super I>> filters)`
- `static <M,I> RowFilter<M,I> orFilter(Iterable<? extends RowFilter<? super M,? super I>> filters)`
  returns a filter that includes the entries included by all filters or at least one of the filters.
- `static <M,I> RowFilter<M,I> notFilter(RowFilter<M,I> filter)`
  returns a filter that includes the entries not included by the given filter.

---

**javax.swing.RowFilter.Entry<M, I>** 6

- `I getIdentifier()`
  returns the identifier of this row entry.
- `M getModel()`
  returns the model of this row entry.
- `Object getValue(int index)`
  returns the value stored at the given index of this row.
- `int getValueCount()`
  returns the number of values stored in this row.
- `String getStringValue()`
  returns the value stored at the given index of this row, converted to a string. The TableRowSorter produces entries whose getStringValue calls the sorter's string converter.

## 6.2.4 Cell Rendering and Editing

As you saw in Section 6.2.3.2, "Accessing Table Columns," on p. 392, the column type determines how the cells are rendered. There are default renderers for the types `Boolean` and `Icon` that render a checkbox or icon. For all other types, you need to install a custom renderer.

Table cell renderers are similar to the list cell renderers that you saw earlier. They implement the `TableCellRenderer` interface which has a single method:

```
Component getTableCellRendererComponent(JTable table, Object value, boolean isSelected,
    boolean hasFocus, int row, int column)
```

That method is called when the table needs to draw a cell. You return a component whose `paint` method is then invoked to fill the cell area.

The table in Figure 6.12 contains cells of type `Color`. The renderer simply returns a panel with a background color that is the color object stored in the cell. The color is passed as the `value` parameter.

```
class ColorTableCellRenderer extends JPanel implements TableCellRenderer
{
    public Component getTableCellRendererComponent(JTable table, Object value,
        boolean isSelected, boolean hasFocus, int row, int column)
    {
        setBackground((Color) value);
        if (hasFocus)
            setBorder(UIManager.getBorder("Table.focusCellHighlightBorder"));
        else
            setBorder(null);
        return this;
    }
}
```

As you can see, the renderer installs a border when the cell has focus. (We ask the `UIManager` for the correct border. To find the lookup key, we peeked into the source code of the `DefaultTableCellRenderer` class.)

Generally, you will also want to set the background color of the cell to indicate whether it is currently selected. We skip this step because it would interfere with the displayed color. The `ListRenderingTest` example in Listing 6.4 shows how to indicate the selection status in a renderer.

---

 **TIP:** If your renderer simply draws a text string or an icon, you can extend the `DefaultTableCellRenderer` class. It takes care of rendering the focus and selection status for you.

---

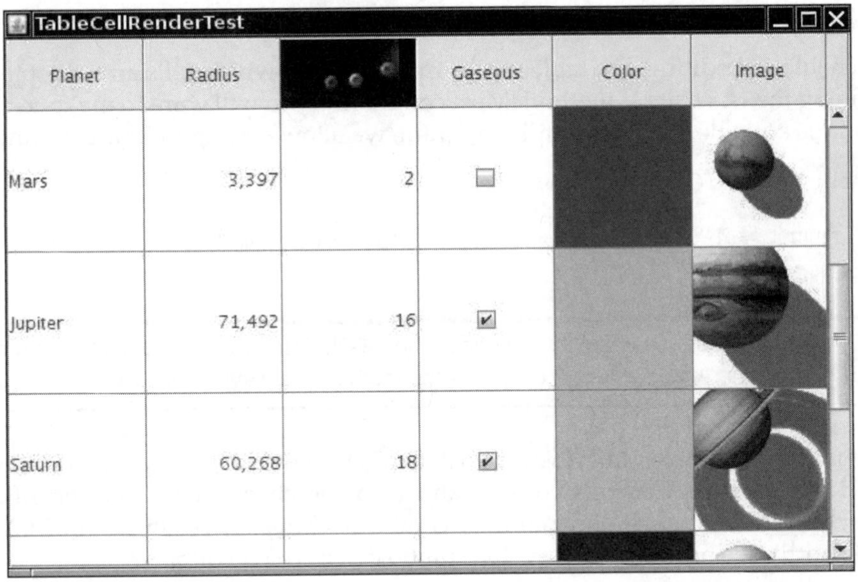

**Figure 6.12** A table with cell renderers

You need to tell the table to use this renderer with all objects of type Color. The setDefaultRenderer method of the JTable class lets you establish this association. Supply a Class object and the renderer:

```
table.setDefaultRenderer(Color.class, new ColorTableCellRenderer());
```

That renderer is now used for all objects of the given type in this table.

If you want to select a renderer based on some other criterion, you need to subclass the JTable class and override the getCellRenderer method.

### 6.2.4.1 Rendering the Header

To display an icon in the header, set the header value:

```
moonColumn.setHeaderValue(new ImageIcon("Moons.gif"));
```

However, the table header isn't smart enough to choose an appropriate renderer for the header value. You have to install the renderer manually. For example, to show an image icon in a column header, call

```
moonColumn.setHeaderRenderer(table.getDefaultRenderer(ImageIcon.class));
```

### 6.2.4.2 Cell Editing

To enable cell editing, the table model must indicate which cells are editable by defining the `isCellEditable` method. Most commonly, you will want to make certain columns editable. In the example program, we allow editing in four columns.

```
public boolean isCellEditable(int r, int c)
{
    return c == PLANET_COLUMN || c == MOONS_COLUMN || c == GASEOUS_COLUMN || c == COLOR_COLUMN;
}
```

 **NOTE:** The `AbstractTableModel` defines the `isCellEditable` method to always return `false`. The `DefaultTableModel` overrides the method to always return `true`.

If you run the program (Listings 6.8 to 6.11), note that you can click the checkboxes in the Gaseous column and turn the check marks on and off. If you click a cell in the Moons column, a combo box appears (see Figure 6.13). You will shortly see how to install such a combo box as a cell editor.

Finally, click a cell in the first column. The cell gains focus. You can start typing, and the cell contents change.

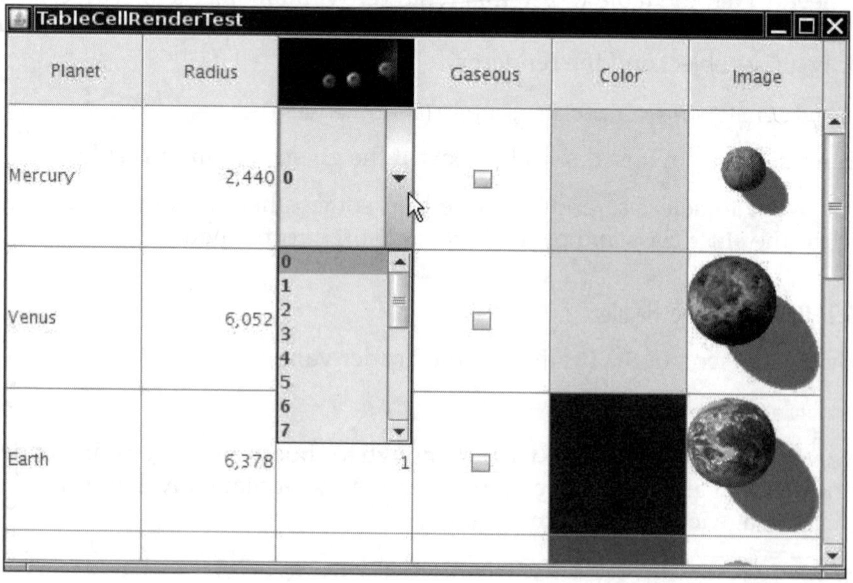

**Figure 6.13** A cell editor

What you just saw in action are the three variations of the DefaultCellEditor class. A DefaultCellEditor can be constructed with a JTextField, a JCheckBox, or a JComboBox. The JTable class automatically installs a checkbox editor for Boolean cells and a text field editor for all editable cells that don't supply their own renderer. The text fields let the user edit the strings that result from applying toString to the return value of the getValueAt method of the table model.

When the edit is complete, the edited value is retrieved by calling the getCellEditorValue method of your editor. That method should return a value of the correct type (that is, the type returned by the getColumnType method of the model).

To get a combo box editor, set a cell editor manually—the JTable component has no idea what values might be appropriate for a particular type. For the Moons column, we wanted to enable the user to pick any value between 0 and 20. Here is the code for initializing the combo box:

```
JComboBox moonCombo = new JComboBox();
for (int i = 0; i <= 20; i++)
   moonCombo.addItem(i);
```

To construct a DefaultCellEditor, supply the combo box in the constructor:

```
TableCellEditor moonEditor = new DefaultCellEditor(moonCombo);
```

Next, we need to install the editor. Unlike the color cell renderer, this editor does not depend on the object *type*—we don't necessarily want to use it for all objects of type Integer. Instead, we need to install it into a particular column:

```
moonColumn.setCellEditor(moonEditor);
```

### 6.2.4.3 Custom Editors

Run the example program again and click a color. A *color chooser* pops up and lets you pick a new color for the planet. Select a color and click OK. The cell color is updated (see Figure 6.14).

The color cell editor is not a standard table cell editor but a custom implementation. To create a custom cell editor, implement the TableCellEditor interface. That interface is a bit tedious, and as of Java SE 1.3, an AbstractCellEditor class is provided to take care of the event handling details.

The getTableCellEditorComponent method of the TableCellEditor interface requests a component to render the cell. It is exactly the same as the getTableCellRendererComponent method of the TableCellRenderer interface, except that there is no focus parameter. When the cell is being edited, it is presumed to have focus. The editor component temporarily *replaces* the renderer when the editing is in progress. In our example, we return a blank panel that is not colored. This is an indication to the user that the cell is currently being edited.

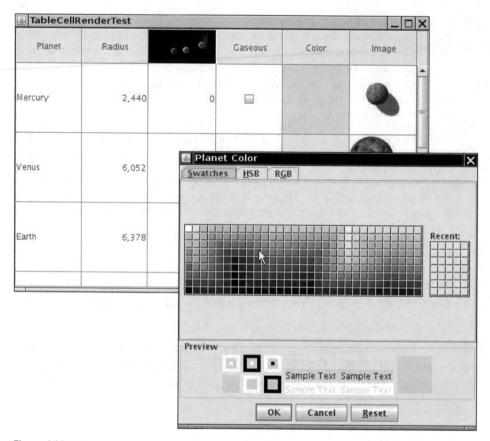

**Figure 6.14** Editing the cell color with a color chooser

Next, you want to have your editor pop up when the user clicks on the cell.

The JTable class calls your editor with an event (such as a mouse click) to find out if that event is acceptable to initiate the editing process. The AbstractCellEditor class defines the method to accept all events.

```
public boolean isCellEditable(EventObject anEvent)
{
    return true;
}
```

However, if you override this method to return false, the table would not go through the trouble of inserting the editor component.

Once the editor component is installed, the shouldSelectCell method is called, presumably with the same event. You should initiate editing in this method—for example, by popping up an external edit dialog box.

```
public boolean shouldSelectCell(EventObject anEvent)
{
   colorDialog.setVisible(true);
   return true;
}
```

If the user cancels the edit, the table calls the cancelCellEditing method. If the user has clicked on another table cell, the table calls the stopCellEditing method. In both cases, you should hide the dialog box. When your stopCellEditing method is called, the table would like to use the partially edited value. You should return true if the current value is valid. In the color chooser, any value is valid. But if you edit other data, you can ensure that only valid data are retrieved from the editor.

Also, you should call the superclass methods that take care of event firing—otherwise, the editing won't be properly canceled.

```
public void cancelCellEditing()
{
   colorDialog.setVisible(false);
   super.cancelCellEditing();
}
```

Finally, you need a method that yields the value that the user supplied in the editing process:

```
public Object getCellEditorValue()
{
   return colorChooser.getColor();
}
```

To summarize, your custom editor should do the following:

1. Extend the AbstractCellEditor class and implement the TableCellEditor interface.

2. Define the getTableCellEditorComponent method to supply a component. This can either be a dummy component (if you pop up a dialog box) or a component for in-place editing such as a combo box or text field.

3. Define the shouldSelectCell, stopCellEditing, and cancelCellEditing methods to handle the start, completion, and cancellation of the editing process. The stopCellEditing and cancelCellEditing methods should call the superclass methods to ensure that listeners are notified.

4. Define the getCellEditorValue method to return the value that is the result of the editing process.

Finally, indicate when the user is finished editing by calling the `stopCellEditing` and `cancelCellEditing` methods. When constructing the color dialog box, we install the accept and cancel callbacks that fire these events.

```
colorDialog = JColorChooser.createDialog(null, "Planet Color", false, colorChooser,
    EventHandler.create(ActionListener.class, this, "stopCellEditing"),
    EventHandler.create(ActionListener.class, this, "cancelCellEditing"));
```

This completes the implementation of the custom editor.

You now know how to make a cell editable and how to install an editor. There is one remaining issue—how to update the model with the value that the user edited. When editing is complete, the `JTable` class calls the following method of the table model:

```
void setValueAt(Object value, int r, int c)
```

You need to override the method to store the new value. The `value` parameter is the object that was returned by the cell editor. If you implemented the cell editor, you know the type of the object you return from the `getCellEditorValue` method. In the case of the `DefaultCellEditor`, there are three possibilities for that value. It is a `Boolean` if the cell editor is a checkbox, a string if it is a text field, and, if the value comes from a combo box, it is the object that the user selected.

If the `value` object does not have the appropriate type, you need to convert it. That happens most commonly when a number is edited in a text field. In our example, we populated the combo box with `Integer` objects so that no conversion is necessary.

---

**Listing 6.8** `tableCellRender/TableCellRenderFrame.java`

---

```
 1  package tableCellRender;
 2
 3  import java.awt.*;
 4  import javax.swing.*;
 5  import javax.swing.table.*;
 6
 7  /**
 8   * This frame contains a table of planet data.
 9   */
10  public class TableCellRenderFrame extends JFrame
11  {
12      private static final int DEFAULT_WIDTH = 600;
13      private static final int DEFAULT_HEIGHT = 400;
14
15      public TableCellRenderFrame()
16      {
```

```
17      setSize(DEFAULT_WIDTH, DEFAULT_HEIGHT);
18
19      TableModel model = new PlanetTableModel();
20      JTable table = new JTable(model);
21      table.setRowSelectionAllowed(false);
22
23      // set up renderers and editors
24      table.setDefaultRenderer(Color.class, new ColorTableCellRenderer());
25      table.setDefaultEditor(Color.class, new ColorTableCellEditor());
26
27      JComboBox<Integer> moonCombo = new JComboBox<>();
28      for (int i = 0; i <= 20; i++)
29         moonCombo.addItem(i);
30
31      TableColumnModel columnModel = table.getColumnModel();
32      TableColumn moonColumn = columnModel.getColumn(PlanetTableModel.MOONS_COLUMN);
33      moonColumn.setCellEditor(new DefaultCellEditor(moonCombo));
34      moonColumn.setHeaderRenderer(table.getDefaultRenderer(ImageIcon.class));
35      moonColumn.setHeaderValue(new ImageIcon(getClass().getResource("Moons.gif")));
36
37      // show table
38      table.setRowHeight(100);
39      add(new JScrollPane(table), BorderLayout.CENTER);
40   }
41 }
```

**Listing 6.9** tableCellRender/PlanetTableModel.java

```
1  package tableCellRender;
2
3  import java.awt.*;
4  import javax.swing.*;
5  import javax.swing.table.*;
6
7  /**
8   * The planet table model specifies the values, rendering and editing properties for the planet
9   * data.
10  */
11 public class PlanetTableModel extends AbstractTableModel
12 {
13     public static final int PLANET_COLUMN = 0;
14     public static final int MOONS_COLUMN = 2;
15     public static final int GASEOUS_COLUMN = 3;
16     public static final int COLOR_COLUMN = 4;
17
18     private Object[][] cells = {
19         { "Mercury", 2440.0, 0, false, Color.YELLOW,
20             new ImageIcon(getClass().getResource("Mercury.gif")) },
```

*(Continues)*

**Listing 6.9** *(Continued)*

```
21          { "Venus", 6052.0, 0, false, Color.YELLOW,
22              new ImageIcon(getClass().getResource("Venus.gif")) },
23          { "Earth", 6378.0, 1, false, Color.BLUE,
24              new ImageIcon(getClass().getResource("Earth.gif")) },
25          { "Mars", 3397.0, 2, false, Color.RED,
26              new ImageIcon(getClass().getResource("Mars.gif")) },
27          { "Jupiter", 71492.0, 16, true, Color.ORANGE,
28              new ImageIcon(getClass().getResource("Jupiter.gif")) },
29          { "Saturn", 60268.0, 18, true, Color.ORANGE,
30              new ImageIcon(getClass().getResource("Saturn.gif")) },
31          { "Uranus", 25559.0, 17, true, Color.BLUE,
32              new ImageIcon(getClass().getResource("Uranus.gif")) },
33          { "Neptune", 24766.0, 8, true, Color.BLUE,
34              new ImageIcon(getClass().getResource("Neptune.gif")) },
35          { "Pluto", 1137.0, 1, false, Color.BLACK,
36              new ImageIcon(getClass().getResource("Pluto.gif")) } };
37
38      private String[] columnNames = { "Planet", "Radius", "Moons", "Gaseous", "Color", "Image" };
39
40      public String getColumnName(int c)
41      {
42          return columnNames[c];
43      }
44
45      public Class<?> getColumnClass(int c)
46      {
47          return cells[0][c].getClass();
48      }
49
50      public int getColumnCount()
51      {
52          return cells[0].length;
53      }
54
55      public int getRowCount()
56      {
57          return cells.length;
58      }
59
60      public Object getValueAt(int r, int c)
61      {
62          return cells[r][c];
63      }
64
65      public void setValueAt(Object obj, int r, int c)
66      {
67          cells[r][c] = obj;
68      }
```

```
69    public boolean isCellEditable(int r, int c)
70    {
71        return c == PLANET_COLUMN || c == MOONS_COLUMN || c == GASEOUS_COLUMN || c == COLOR_COLUMN;
72    }
73 }
```

**Listing 6.10** tableCellRender/ColorTableCellRenderer.java

```
1  package tableCellRender;
2
3  import java.awt.*;
4  import javax.swing.*;
5  import javax.swing.table.*;
6
7  /**
8   * This renderer renders a color value as a panel with the given color.
9   */
10 public class ColorTableCellRenderer extends JPanel implements TableCellRenderer
11 {
12     public Component getTableCellRendererComponent(JTable table, Object value, boolean isSelected,
13            boolean hasFocus, int row, int column)
14     {
15        setBackground((Color) value);
16        if (hasFocus) setBorder(UIManager.getBorder("Table.focusCellHighlightBorder"));
17        else setBorder(null);
18        return this;
19     }
20 }
```

**Listing 6.11** tableCellRender/ColorTableCellEditor.java

```
1  package tableCellRender;
2
3  import java.awt.*;
4  import java.awt.event.*;
5  import java.beans.*;
6  import java.util.*;
7  import javax.swing.*;
8  import javax.swing.table.*;
9
10 /**
11  * This editor pops up a color dialog to edit a cell value.
12  */
13 public class ColorTableCellEditor extends AbstractCellEditor implements TableCellEditor
14 {
15     private JColorChooser colorChooser;
16     private JDialog colorDialog;
17     private JPanel panel;
```

*(Continues)*

Listing 6.11 *(Continued)*

```
18    public ColorTableCellEditor()
19    {
20       panel = new JPanel();
21       // prepare color dialog
22
23       colorChooser = new JColorChooser();
24       colorDialog = JColorChooser.createDialog(null, "Planet Color", false, colorChooser,
25          EventHandler.create(ActionListener.class, this, "stopCellEditing"),
26          EventHandler.create(ActionListener.class, this, "cancelCellEditing"));
27    }
28
29    public Component getTableCellEditorComponent(JTable table, Object value, boolean isSelected,
30          int row, int column)
31    {
32       // This is where we get the current Color value. We store it in the dialog in case the user
33       // starts editing.
34       colorChooser.setColor((Color) value);
35       return panel;
36    }
37
38    public boolean shouldSelectCell(EventObject anEvent)
39    {
40       // start editing
41       colorDialog.setVisible(true);
42
43       // tell caller it is ok to select this cell
44       return true;
45    }
46
47    public void cancelCellEditing()
48    {
49       // editing is canceled--hide dialog
50       colorDialog.setVisible(false);
51       super.cancelCellEditing();
52    }
53
54    public boolean stopCellEditing()
55    {
56       // editing is complete--hide dialog
57       colorDialog.setVisible(false);
58       super.stopCellEditing();
59
60       // tell caller is is ok to use color value
61       return true;
62    }
```

```
63    public Object getCellEditorValue()
64    {
65        return colorChooser.getColor();
66    }
67  }
```

---

**javax.swing.JTable** 1.2

- TableCellRenderer getDefaultRenderer(Class<?> type)
  gets the default renderer for the given type.
- TableCellEditor getDefaultEditor(Class<?> type)
  gets the default editor for the given type.

---

**javax.swing.table.TableCellRenderer** 1.2

- Component getTableCellRendererComponent(JTable table, Object value, boolean selected, boolean hasFocus, int row, int column)
  returns a component whose paint method is invoked to render a table cell.

  | Parameters: | table | The table containing the cell to be rendered |
  | | value | The cell to be rendered |
  | | selected | true if the cell is currently selected |
  | | hasFocus | true if the cell currently has focus |
  | | row, column | The row and column of the cell |

---

**javax.swing.table.TableColumn** 1.2

- void setCellEditor(TableCellEditor editor)
- void setCellRenderer(TableCellRenderer renderer)
  sets the cell editor or renderer for all cells in this column.
- void setHeaderRenderer(TableCellRenderer renderer)
  sets the cell renderer for the header cell in this column.
- void setHeaderValue(Object value)
  sets the value to be displayed for the header in this column.

---

**javax.swing.DefaultCellEditor** 1.2

- DefaultCellEditor(JComboBox comboBox)
  constructs a cell editor that presents the combo box for selecting cell values.

---

`javax.swing.table.TableCellEditor` 1.2

- `Component getTableCellEditorComponent(JTable table, Object value, boolean selected, int row, int column)`

  returns a component whose paint method renders a table cell.

  | *Parameters:* | table | The table containing the cell to be rendered |
  |---|---|---|
  | | value | The cell to be rendered |
  | | selected | true if the cell is currently selected |
  | | row, column | The row and column of the cell |

---

`javax.swing.CellEditor` 1.2

- `boolean isCellEditable(EventObject event)`

  returns true if the event is suitable for initiating the editing process for this cell.

- `boolean shouldSelectCell(EventObject anEvent)`

  starts the editing process. Returns true if the edited cell should be *selected*. Normally, you want to return true, but you can return false if you don't want the editing process to change the cell selection.

- `void cancelCellEditing()`

  cancels the editing process. You can abandon partial edits.

- `boolean stopCellEditing()`

  stops the editing process, with the intent of using the result. Returns true if the edited value is in a proper state for retrieval.

- `Object getCellEditorValue()`

  returns the edited result.

- `void addCellEditorListener(CellEditorListener l)`
- `void removeCellEditorListener(CellEditorListener l)`

  adds or removes the obligatory cell editor listener.

---

## 6.3 Trees

Every computer user who has worked with a hierarchical file system has seen tree displays. Of course, directories and files form only one of the many examples of tree-like organizations. Many tree structures arise in everyday life, such as the hierarchy of countries, states, and cities shown in Figure 6.15.

As programmers, we often need to display tree structures. Fortunately, the Swing library has a JTree class for this purpose. The JTree class (together with its helper

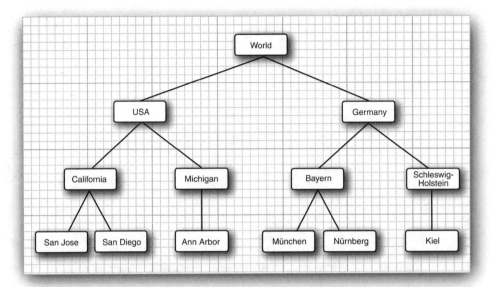

**Figure 6.15** A hierarchy of countries, states, and cities

classes) takes care of laying out the tree and processing user requests for expanding and collapsing nodes. In this section, you will learn how to put the JTree class to use.

As with the other complex Swing components, we must focus on the common and useful cases and cannot cover every nuance. If you want to achieve something unusual, we recommend that you consult *Graphic Java™, Third Edition*, by David M. Geary or *Core Swing* by Kim Topley.

Before going any further, let's settle on some terminology (see Figure 6.16). A *tree* is composed of *nodes*. Every node is either a *leaf* or it has *child nodes*. Every node, with the exception of the root node, has exactly one *parent*. A tree has exactly one root node. Sometimes you have a collection of trees, each with its own root node. Such a collection is called a *forest*.

## 6.3.1 Simple Trees

In our first example program, we will simply display a tree with a few nodes (see Figure 6.18 on p. 424). As with many other Swing components, you need to provide a model of the data, and the component displays it for you. To construct a JTree, supply the tree model in the constructor:

```
TreeModel model = . . .;
JTree tree = new JTree(model);
```

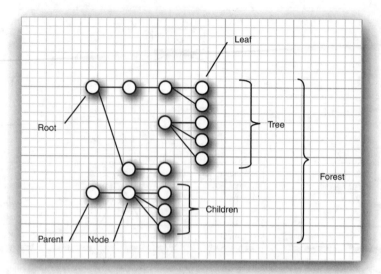

**Figure 6.16** Tree terminology

 **NOTE:** There are also constructors that construct trees out of a collection of elements:

```
JTree(Object[] nodes)
JTree(Vector<?> nodes)
JTree(Hashtable<?, ?> nodes) // the values become the nodes
```

These constructors are not very useful. They merely build a forest of trees, each with a single node. The third constructor seems particularly useless because the nodes appear in the seemingly random order determined by the hash codes of the keys.

How do you obtain a tree model? You can construct your own model by creating a class that implements the TreeModel interface. You will see later in this chapter how to do that. For now, we will stick with the DefaultTreeModel that the Swing library supplies.

To construct a default tree model, you must supply a root node.

```
TreeNode root = . . .;
DefaultTreeModel model = new DefaultTreeModel(root);
```

TreeNode is another interface. Populate the default tree model with objects of any class that implements the interface. For now, we will use the concrete node class

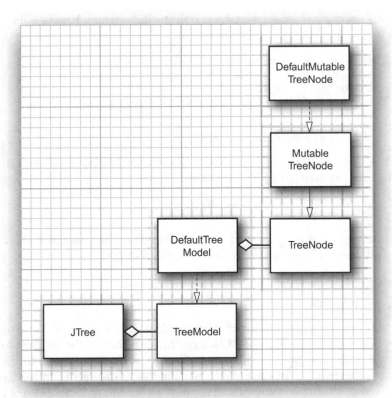

**Figure 6.17** Tree classes

that Swing supplies—namely, DefaultMutableTreeNode. This class implements the MutableTreeNode interface, a subinterface of TreeNode (see Figure 6.17).

A default mutable tree node holds an object—the *user object*. The tree renders the user objects for all nodes. Unless you specify a renderer, the tree displays the string that is the result of the toString method.

In our first example, we use strings as user objects. In practice, you would usually populate a tree with more expressive user objects. For example, when displaying a directory tree, it makes sense to use File objects for the nodes.

You can specify the user object in the constructor, or you can set it later with the setUserObject method.

```
DefaultMutableTreeNode node = new DefaultMutableTreeNode("Texas");
. . .
node.setUserObject("California");
```

Next, you need to establish the parent/child relationships between the nodes. Start with the root node and use the add method to add the children:

```
DefaultMutableTreeNode root = new DefaultMutableTreeNode("World");
DefaultMutableTreeNode country = new DefaultMutableTreeNode("USA");
root.add(country);
DefaultMutableTreeNode state = new DefaultMutableTreeNode("California");
country.add(state);
```

Figure 6.18 illustrates how the tree will look.

Link up all nodes in this fashion. Then, construct a DefaultTreeModel with the root node. Finally, construct a JTree with the tree model.

```
DefaultTreeModel treeModel = new DefaultTreeModel(root);
JTree tree = new JTree(treeModel);
```

Or, as a shortcut, you can simply pass the root node to the JTree constructor. Then the tree automatically constructs a default tree model:

```
JTree tree = new JTree(root);
```

Listing 6.12 contains the complete code.

When you run the program, the tree first looks as in Figure 6.19. Only the root node and its children are visible. Click on the circle icons (the *handles*) to open up the subtrees. The line sticking out from the handle icon points to the right when the subtree is collapsed and down when the subtree is expanded (see Figure 6.20). We don't know what the designers of the Metal look-and-feel had in mind, but we think of the icon as a door handle. You push down on the handle to open the subtree.

**Figure 6.18** A simple tree

**Listing 6.12** tree/SimpleTreeFrame.java

```java
1  package tree;
2
3  import javax.swing.*;
4  import javax.swing.tree.*;
5
6  /**
7   * This frame contains a simple tree that displays a manually constructed tree model.
8   */
9  public class SimpleTreeFrame extends JFrame
10 {
11    private static final int DEFAULT_WIDTH = 300;
12    private static final int DEFAULT_HEIGHT = 200;
13
14    public SimpleTreeFrame()
15    {
16       setSize(DEFAULT_WIDTH, DEFAULT_HEIGHT);
17
18       // set up tree model data
19
20       DefaultMutableTreeNode root = new DefaultMutableTreeNode("World");
21       DefaultMutableTreeNode country = new DefaultMutableTreeNode("USA");
22       root.add(country);
23       DefaultMutableTreeNode state = new DefaultMutableTreeNode("California");
24       country.add(state);
25       DefaultMutableTreeNode city = new DefaultMutableTreeNode("San Jose");
26       state.add(city);
27       city = new DefaultMutableTreeNode("Cupertino");
28       state.add(city);
29       state = new DefaultMutableTreeNode("Michigan");
30       country.add(state);
31       city = new DefaultMutableTreeNode("Ann Arbor");
32       state.add(city);
33       country = new DefaultMutableTreeNode("Germany");
34       root.add(country);
35       state = new DefaultMutableTreeNode("Schleswig-Holstein");
36       country.add(state);
37       city = new DefaultMutableTreeNode("Kiel");
38       state.add(city);
39
40       // construct tree and put it in a scroll pane
41
42       JTree tree = new JTree(root);
43       add(new JScrollPane(tree));
44    }
45 }
```

**Figure 6.19** The initial tree display

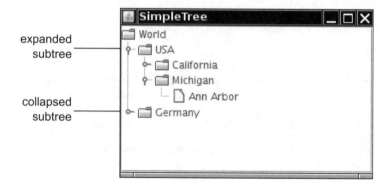

**Figure 6.20** Collapsed and expanded subtrees

 **NOTE:** Of course, the display of the tree depends on the selected look-and-feel. We just described the Metal look-and-feel. In the Windows look-and-feel, the handles have the more familiar look—a "-" or "+" in a box (see Figure 6.21).

You can use the following magic incantation to turn off the lines joining parents and children (see Figure 6.22):

```
tree.putClientProperty("JTree.lineStyle", "None");
```

Conversely, to make sure that the lines are shown, use

```
tree.putClientProperty("JTree.lineStyle", "Angled");
```

Another line style, "Horizontal", is shown in Figure 6.23. The tree is displayed with horizontal lines separating only the children of the root. We aren't quite sure what it is good for.

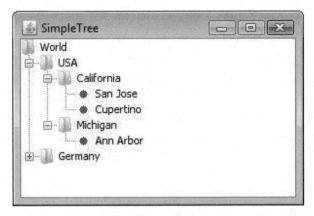

**Figure 6.21** A tree with the Windows look-and-feel

**Figure 6.22** A tree with no connecting lines

**Figure 6.23** A tree with the horizontal line style

By default, there is no handle for collapsing the root of the tree. If you like, you can add one with the call

```
tree.setShowsRootHandles(true);
```

Figure 6.24 shows the result. Now you can collapse the entire tree into the root node.

Conversely, you can hide the root altogether. You will thus display a *forest*—a set of trees, each with its own root. You still must join all trees in the forest to a common root; then, hide the root with the instruction

```
tree.setRootVisible(false);
```

Look at Figure 6.25. There appear to be two roots, labeled "USA" and "Germany." The actual root that joins the two is made invisible.

Let's turn from the root to the leaves of the tree. Note that the leaves have an icon different from the other nodes (see Figure 6.26).

When the tree is displayed, each node is drawn with an icon. There are actually three kinds of icons: a leaf icon, an opened nonleaf icon, and a closed nonleaf icon. For simplicity, we refer to the last two as folder icons.

The node renderer needs to know which icon to use for each node. By default, the decision process works like this: If the isLeaf method of a node returns true, then the leaf icon is used; otherwise, a folder icon is used.

The isLeaf method of the DefaultMutableTreeNode class returns true if the node has no children. Thus, nodes with children get folder icons, and nodes without children get leaf icons.

Sometimes, that behavior is not appropriate. Suppose we added a node "Montana" to our sample tree, but we're at a loss as to what cities to add. We would not want the state node to get a leaf icon because conceptually only the cities are leaves.

The JTree class has no idea which nodes should be leaves. It asks the tree model. If a childless node isn't automatically a conceptual leaf, you can ask the tree model to use a different criterion for leafiness—namely, to query the "allows children" node property.

For those nodes that should not have children, call

```
node.setAllowsChildren(false);
```

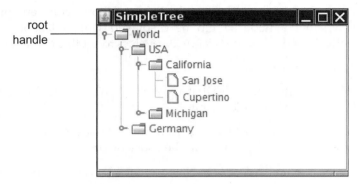

**Figure 6.24** A tree with a root handle

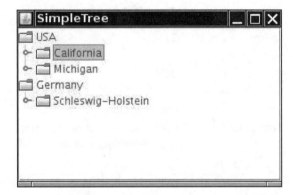

**Figure 6.25** A forest

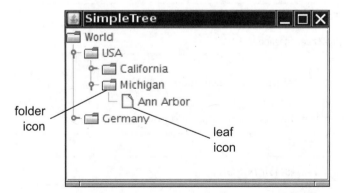

**Figure 6.26** Leaf and folder icons

Then, tell the tree model to ask the value of the "allows children" property to determine whether a node should be displayed with a leaf icon. Use the setAsksAllowsChildren method of the DefaultTreeModel class to set this behavior:

```
model.setAsksAllowsChildren(true);
```

With this decision criterion, nodes that allow children get folder icons, and nodes that don't allow children get leaf icons.

Alternatively, if you construct the tree from the root node, supply the setting for the "asks allows children" property in the constructor.

```
JTree tree = new JTree(root, true); // nodes that don't allow children get leaf icons
```

---

**javax.swing.JTree** 1.2

- JTree(TreeModel model)
  constructs a tree from a tree model.

- JTree(TreeNode root)
- JTree(TreeNode root, boolean asksAllowChildren)
  constructs a tree with a default tree model that displays the root and its children.

  | *Parameters:* | root | The root node |
  | | asksAllowsChildren | true to use the "allows children" node property for determining whether a node is a leaf |

- void setShowsRootHandles(boolean b)
  if b is true, the root node has a handle for collapsing or expanding its children.

- void setRootVisible(boolean b)
  if b is true, then the root node is displayed. Otherwise, it is hidden.

---

**javax.swing.tree.TreeNode** 1.2

- boolean isLeaf()
  returns true if this node is conceptually a leaf.

- boolean getAllowsChildren()
  returns true if this node can have child nodes.

---

**javax.swing.tree.MutableTreeNode** 1.2

- void setUserObject(Object userObject)
  sets the "user object" that the tree node uses for rendering.

---

**javax.swing.tree.TreeModel** 1.2

- `boolean isLeaf(Object node)`
  returns `true` if `node` should be displayed as a leaf node.

---

**javax.swing.tree.DefaultTreeModel** 1.2

- `void setAsksAllowsChildren(boolean b)`
  if `b` is `true`, nodes are displayed as leaves when their `getAllowsChildren` method returns `false`. Otherwise, they are displayed as leaves when their `isLeaf` method returns `true`.

---

**javax.swing.tree.DefaultMutableTreeNode** 1.2

- `DefaultMutableTreeNode(Object userObject)`
  constructs a mutable tree node with the given user object.

- `void add(MutableTreeNode child)`
  adds a node as the last child of this node.

- `void setAllowsChildren(boolean b)`
  if `b` is `true`, children can be added to this node.

---

**javax.swing.JComponent** 1.2

- `void putClientProperty(Object key, Object value)`
  adds a key/value pair to a small table that each component manages. This is an "escape hatch" mechanism that some Swing components use for storing properties specific to a look-and-feel.

---

### 6.3.1.1 Editing Trees and Tree Paths

In the next example program, you will see how to edit a tree. Figure 6.27 shows the user interface. If you click the Add Sibling or Add Child button, the program adds a new node (with title New) to the tree. If you click the Delete button, the program deletes the currently selected node.

To implement this behavior, you need to find out which tree node is currently selected. The `JTree` class has a surprising way of identifying nodes in a tree. It does not deal with tree nodes but with *paths of objects*, called *tree paths*. A tree path starts at the root and consists of a sequence of child nodes (see Figure 6.28).

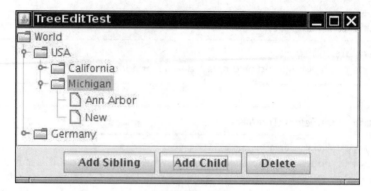

**Figure 6.27** Editing a tree

**Figure 6.28** A tree path

You might wonder why the JTree class needs the whole path. Couldn't it just get a TreeNode and keep calling the getParent method? In fact, the JTree class knows nothing about the TreeNode interface. That interface is never used by the TreeModel interface; it is only used by the DefaultTreeModel implementation. You can have other tree models in which the nodes do not implement the TreeNode interface at all. If you use a tree model that manages other types of objects, those objects might not have getParent and getChild methods. They would of course need to have some other connection to each other. It is the job of the tree model to link nodes together. The JTree class itself has no clue about the nature of their linkage. For that reason, the JTree class always needs to work with complete paths.

The TreePath class manages a sequence of Object (not TreeNode!) references. A number of JTree methods return TreePath objects. When you have a tree path, you usually just need to know the terminal node, which you can get with the getLastPathComponent method. For example, to find out the currently selected node in a tree, use the getSelectionPath method of the JTree class. You will get a TreePath object back, from which you can retrieve the actual node.

```
TreePath selectionPath = tree.getSelectionPath();
DefaultMutableTreeNode selectedNode
   = (DefaultMutableTreeNode) selectionPath.getLastPathComponent();
```

Actually, since this particular query is so common, there is a convenience method that gives the selected node immediately:

```
DefaultMutableTreeNode selectedNode
   = (DefaultMutableTreeNode) tree.getLastSelectedPathComponent();
```

This method is not called getSelectedNode because the tree does not know that it contains nodes—its tree model deals only with paths of objects.

 **NOTE:** Tree paths are one of the two ways in which the JTree class describes nodes. Quite a few JTree methods take or return an integer index—the *row position*. A row position is simply the row number (starting with 0) of the node in the tree display. Only visible nodes have row numbers, and the row number of a node changes if other nodes before it are expanded, collapsed, or modified. For that reason, you should avoid row positions. All JTree methods that use rows have equivalents that use tree paths instead.

Once you have the selected node, you can edit it. However, do not simply add children to a tree node:

```
selectedNode.add(newNode); // No!
```

If you change the structure of the nodes, you change the model but the associated view is not notified. You could send out a notification yourself, but if you use the insertNodeInto method of the DefaultTreeModel class, the model class takes care of that. For example, the following call appends a new node as the last child of the selected node and notifies the tree view:

```
model.insertNodeInto(newNode, selectedNode, selectedNode.getChildCount());
```

The analogous call removeNodeFromParent removes a node and notifies the view:

```
model.removeNodeFromParent(selectedNode);
```

If you keep the node structure in place but change the user object, you should call the following method:

```
model.nodeChanged(changedNode);
```

The automatic notification is a major advantage of using the DefaultTreeModel. If you supply your own tree model, you have to implement automatic notification by hand. (See *Core Swing* by Kim Topley for details.)

 **CAUTION:** The DefaultTreeModel class has a reload method that reloads the entire model. However, don't call reload simply to update the tree after making a few changes. When the tree is regenerated, all nodes beyond the root's children are collapsed again. It will be quite disconcerting to your users if they have to keep expanding the tree after every change.

When the view is notified of a change in the node structure, it updates the display but does not automatically expand a node to show newly added children. In particular, if a user in our sample program adds a new child node to a node for which children are currently collapsed, the new node is silently added to the collapsed subtree. This gives the user no feedback that the command was actually carried out. In such a case, you should make a special effort to expand all parent nodes so that the newly added node becomes visible. Use the makeVisible method of the JTree class for this purpose. The makeVisible method expects a tree path leading to the node that should become visible.

Thus, you need to construct a tree path from the root to the newly inserted node. To get a tree path, first call the getPathToRoot method of the DefaultTreeModel class. It returns a TreeNode[] array of all nodes from a node to the root node. Pass that array to a TreePath constructor.

For example, here is how you make the new node visible:

```
TreeNode[] nodes = model.getPathToRoot(newNode);
TreePath path = new TreePath(nodes);
tree.makeVisible(path);
```

 **NOTE:** It is curious that the DefaultTreeModel class feigns almost complete ignorance of the TreePath class, even though its job is to communicate with a JTree. The JTree class uses tree paths a lot, and it never uses arrays of node objects.

But now suppose your tree is contained inside a scroll pane. After the tree node expansion, the new node might still not be visible because it falls outside the viewport. To overcome that problem, call

```
tree.scrollPathToVisible(path);
```

instead of calling makeVisible. This call expands all nodes along the path and tells the ambient scroll pane to scroll the node at the end of the path into view (see Figure 6.29).

By default, tree nodes cannot be edited. However, if you call

```
tree.setEditable(true);
```

the user can edit a node simply by double-clicking, editing the string, and pressing the Enter key. Double-clicking invokes the *default cell editor*, which is implemented by the DefaultCellEditor class (see Figure 6.30). It is possible to install other cell editors, using the same process that you have seen in our discussion of table cell editors.

Listing 6.13 shows the complete source code of the tree editing program. Run the program, add a few nodes, and edit them by double-clicking them. Observe how collapsed nodes expand to show added children and how the scroll pane keeps added nodes in the viewport.

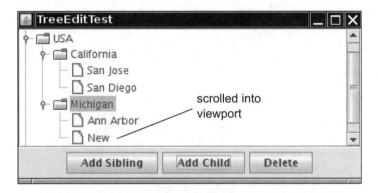

**Figure 6.29** The scroll pane scrolls to display a new node.

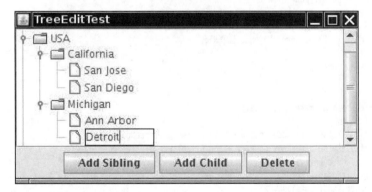

**Figure 6.30** The default cell editor

**Listing 6.13** treeEdit/TreeEditFrame.java

```java
1  package treeEdit;
2
3  import java.awt.*;
4  import java.awt.event.*;
5  import javax.swing.*;
6  import javax.swing.tree.*;
7
8  /**
9   * A frame with a tree and buttons to edit the tree.
10  */
11 public class TreeEditFrame extends JFrame
12 {
13    private static final int DEFAULT_WIDTH = 400;
14    private static final int DEFAULT_HEIGHT = 200;
15
16    private DefaultTreeModel model;
17    private JTree tree;
18
19    public TreeEditFrame()
20    {
21       setSize(DEFAULT_WIDTH, DEFAULT_HEIGHT);
22
23       // construct tree
24
25       TreeNode root = makeSampleTree();
26       model = new DefaultTreeModel(root);
27       tree = new JTree(model);
28       tree.setEditable(true);
29
30       // add scroll pane with tree
31
32       JScrollPane scrollPane = new JScrollPane(tree);
33       add(scrollPane, BorderLayout.CENTER);
34
35       makeButtons();
36    }
37
38    public TreeNode makeSampleTree()
39    {
40       DefaultMutableTreeNode root = new DefaultMutableTreeNode("World");
41       DefaultMutableTreeNode country = new DefaultMutableTreeNode("USA");
42       root.add(country);
43       DefaultMutableTreeNode state = new DefaultMutableTreeNode("California");
44       country.add(state);
45       DefaultMutableTreeNode city = new DefaultMutableTreeNode("San Jose");
46       state.add(city);
```

```
47    city = new DefaultMutableTreeNode("San Diego");
48    state.add(city);
49    state = new DefaultMutableTreeNode("Michigan");
50    country.add(state);
51    city = new DefaultMutableTreeNode("Ann Arbor");
52    state.add(city);
53    country = new DefaultMutableTreeNode("Germany");
54    root.add(country);
55    state = new DefaultMutableTreeNode("Schleswig-Holstein");
56    country.add(state);
57    city = new DefaultMutableTreeNode("Kiel");
58    state.add(city);
59    return root;
60    }
61
62    /**
63     * Makes the buttons to add a sibling, add a child, and delete a node.
64     */
65    public void makeButtons()
66    {
67       JPanel panel = new JPanel();
68       JButton addSiblingButton = new JButton("Add Sibling");
69       addSiblingButton.addActionListener(new ActionListener()
70          {
71             public void actionPerformed(ActionEvent event)
72             {
73                DefaultMutableTreeNode selectedNode = (DefaultMutableTreeNode) tree
74                      .getLastSelectedPathComponent();
75
76                if (selectedNode == null) return;
77
78                DefaultMutableTreeNode parent = (DefaultMutableTreeNode) selectedNode.getParent();
79
80                if (parent == null) return;
81
82                DefaultMutableTreeNode newNode = new DefaultMutableTreeNode("New");
83
84                int selectedIndex = parent.getIndex(selectedNode);
85                model.insertNodeInto(newNode, parent, selectedIndex + 1);
86
87                // now display new node
88
89                TreeNode[] nodes = model.getPathToRoot(newNode);
90                TreePath path = new TreePath(nodes);
91                tree.scrollPathToVisible(path);
92             }
93          });
94       panel.add(addSiblingButton);
```

*(Continues)*

**Listing 6.13**   *(Continued)*

```
 95      JButton addChildButton = new JButton("Add Child");
 96      addChildButton.addActionListener(new ActionListener()
 97         {
 98            public void actionPerformed(ActionEvent event)
 99            {
100               DefaultMutableTreeNode selectedNode = (DefaultMutableTreeNode) tree
101                     .getLastSelectedPathComponent();
102               if (selectedNode == null) return;
103
104               DefaultMutableTreeNode newNode = new DefaultMutableTreeNode("New");
105               model.insertNodeInto(newNode, selectedNode, selectedNode.getChildCount());
106
107               // now display new node
108
109               TreeNode[] nodes = model.getPathToRoot(newNode);
110               TreePath path = new TreePath(nodes);
111               tree.scrollPathToVisible(path);
112            }
113         });
114      panel.add(addChildButton);
115
116      JButton deleteButton = new JButton("Delete");
117      deleteButton.addActionListener(new ActionListener()
118         {
119            public void actionPerformed(ActionEvent event)
120            {
121               DefaultMutableTreeNode selectedNode = (DefaultMutableTreeNode) tree
122                     .getLastSelectedPathComponent();
123
124               if (selectedNode != null && selectedNode.getParent() != null) model
125                     .removeNodeFromParent(selectedNode);
126            }
127         });
128      panel.add(deleteButton);
129      add(panel, BorderLayout.SOUTH);
130   }
131 }
```

---

**javax.swing.JTree**   1.2

- TreePath getSelectionPath()

  gets the path to the currently selected node, or the path to the first selected node if multiple nodes are selected. Returns null if no node is selected.

*(Continues)*

---

**javax.swing.JTree** 1.2 *(Continued)*

- Object getLastSelectedPathComponent()
  gets the node object that represents the currently selected node, or the first node if multiple nodes are selected. Returns null if no node is selected.
- void makeVisible(TreePath path)
  expands all nodes along the path.
- void scrollPathToVisible(TreePath path)
  expands all nodes along the path and, if the tree is contained in a scroll pane, scrolls to ensure that the last node on the path is visible.

---

**javax.swing.tree.TreePath** 1.2

- Object getLastPathComponent()
  gets the last object on this path—that is, the node object that the path represents.

---

**javax.swing.tree.TreeNode** 1.2

- TreeNode getParent()
  returns the parent node of this node.
- TreeNode getChildAt(int index)
  looks up the child node at the given index. The index must be between 0 and getChildCount() - 1.
- int getChildCount()
  returns the number of children of this node.
- Enumeration children()
  returns an enumeration object that iterates through all children of this node.

---

**javax.swing.tree.DefaultTreeModel** 1.2

- void insertNodeInto(MutableTreeNode newChild, MutableTreeNode parent, int index)
  inserts newChild as a new child node of parent at the given index and notifies the tree model listeners.
- void removeNodeFromParent(MutableTreeNode node)
  removes node from this model and notifies the tree model listeners.

*(Continues)*

---

`javax.swing.tree.DefaultTreeModel` **1.2** *(Continued)*

- `void nodeChanged(TreeNode node)`
  notifies the tree model listeners that `node` has changed.

- `void nodesChanged(TreeNode parent, int[] changedChildIndexes)`
  notifies the tree model listeners that all child nodes of `parent` with the given indexes have changed.

- `void reload()`
  reloads all nodes into the model. This is a drastic operation that you should use only if the nodes have changed completely because of some outside influence.

---

## 6.3.2 Node Enumeration

Sometimes you need to find a node in a tree by starting at the root and visiting all children until you have found a match. The `DefaultMutableTreeNode` class has several convenience methods for iterating through nodes.

The `breadthFirstEnumeration` and `depthFirstEnumeration` methods return enumeration objects whose `nextElement` method visits all children of the current node, using either a breadth-first or depth-first traversal. Figure 6.31 shows the traversals for a sample tree—the node labels indicate the order in which the nodes are traversed.

Breadth-first enumeration is the easiest to visualize. The tree is traversed in layers. The root is visited first, followed by all of its children, then the grandchildren, and so on.

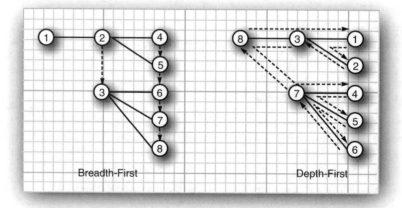

**Figure 6.31** Tree traversal orders

To visualize depth-first enumeration, imagine a rat trapped in a tree-shaped maze. It rushes along the first path until it comes to a leaf. Then, it backtracks and turns around to the next path, and so on.

Computer scientists also call this *postorder traversal* because the search process visits the children before visiting the parents. The `postOrderTraversal` method is a synonym for `depthFirstTraversal`. For completeness, there is also a `preOrderTraversal`, a depth-first search that enumerates parents before the children.

Here is the typical usage pattern:

```
Enumeration breadthFirst = node.breadthFirstEnumeration();
while (breadthFirst.hasMoreElements())
    do something with breadthFirst.nextElement();
```

Finally, a related method, `pathFromAncestorEnumeration`, finds a path from an ancestor to a given node and enumerates the nodes along that path. That's no big deal—it just keeps calling `getParent` until the ancestor is found and then presents the path in reverse order.

In our next example program, we put node enumeration to work. The program displays inheritance trees of classes. Type the name of a class into the text field on the bottom of the frame. The class and all of its superclasses are added to the tree (see Figure 6.32).

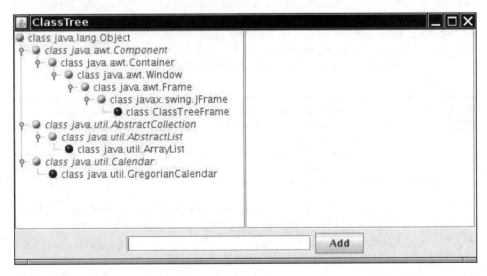

**Figure 6.32** An inheritance tree

In this example, we take advantage of the fact that the user objects of the tree nodes can be objects of any type. Since our nodes describe classes, we store Class objects in the nodes.

We don't want to add the same class object twice, so we need to check whether a class already exists in the tree. The following method finds the node with a given user object if it exists in the tree.

```
public DefaultMutableTreeNode findUserObject(Object obj)
{
   Enumeration e = root.breadthFirstEnumeration();
   while (e.hasMoreElements())
   {
      DefaultMutableTreeNode node = (DefaultMutableTreeNode) e.nextElement();
      if (node.getUserObject().equals(obj))
         return node;
   }
   return null;
}
```

## 6.3.3 Rendering Nodes

In your applications, you will often need to change the way a tree component draws the nodes. The most common change is, of course, to choose different icons for nodes and leaves. Other changes might involve changing the font of the node labels or drawing images at the nodes. All these changes are possible by installing a new *tree cell renderer* into the tree. By default, the JTree class uses DefaultTreeCellRenderer objects to draw each node. The DefaultTreeCellRenderer class extends the JLabel class. The label contains the node icon and the node label.

 **NOTE:** The cell renderer does not draw the "handles" for expanding and collapsing subtrees. The handles are part of the look-and-feel, and it is recommended that you do not change them.

You can customize the display in three ways.

- You can change the icons, font, and background color used by a DefaultTreeCellRenderer. These settings are used for all nodes in the tree.
- You can install a renderer that extends the DefaultTreeCellRenderer class and vary the icons, fonts, and background color for each node.
- You can install a renderer that implements the TreeCellRenderer interface to draw a custom image for each node.

Let us look at these possibilities one by one. The easiest customization is to construct a DefaultTreeCellRenderer object, change the icons, and install it into the tree:

```
DefaultTreeCellRenderer renderer = new DefaultTreeCellRenderer();
renderer.setLeafIcon(new ImageIcon("blue-ball.gif")); // used for leaf nodes
renderer.setClosedIcon(new ImageIcon("red-ball.gif")); // used for collapsed nodes
renderer.setOpenIcon(new ImageIcon("yellow-ball.gif")); // used for expanded nodes
tree.setCellRenderer(renderer);
```

You can see the effect in Figure 6.32. We just use the "ball" icons as placeholders—presumably your user interface designer would supply you with appropriate icons to use for your applications.

We don't recommend that you change the font or background color for an entire tree—that is really the job of the look-and-feel.

However, it can be useful to change the font of some nodes in a tree to highlight them. If you look carefully at Figure 6.32, you will notice that the *abstract* classes are set in italics.

To change the appearance of individual nodes, install a tree cell renderer. Tree cell renderers are very similar to the list cell renderers we discussed earlier in this chapter. The TreeCellRenderer interface has a single method:

```
Component getTreeCellRendererComponent(JTree tree, Object value, boolean selected,
    boolean expanded, boolean leaf, int row, boolean hasFocus)
```

The getTreeCellRendererComponent method of the DefaultTreeCellRenderer class returns this—in other words, a label. (The DefaultTreeCellRenderer class extends the JLabel class.) To customize the component, extend the DefaultTreeCellRenderer class. Override the getTreeCellRendererComponent method as follows: Call the superclass method so it can prepare the label data, customize the label properties, and finally return this.

```
class MyTreeCellRenderer extends DefaultTreeCellRenderer
{
    public Component getTreeCellRendererComponent(JTree tree, Object value, boolean selected,
        boolean expanded, boolean leaf, int row, boolean hasFocus)
    {
        Component comp = super.getTreeCellRendererComponent(tree, value, selected,
                                                    expanded, leaf, row, hasFocus);
        DefaultMutableTreeNode node = (DefaultMutableTreeNode) value;
        look at node.getUserObject();
        Font font = appropriate font;
        comp.setFont(font);
        return comp;
    }
};
```

**CAUTION:** The value parameter of the getTreeCellRendererComponent method is the *node* object, *not* the user object! Recall that the user object is a feature of the DefaultMutableTreeNode, and that a JTree can contain nodes of an arbitrary type. If your tree uses DefaultMutableTreeNode nodes, you must retrieve the user object in a second step, as we did in the preceding code sample.

**CAUTION:** The DefaultTreeCellRenderer uses the *same* label object for all nodes, only changing the label text for each node. If you change the font for a particular node, you must set it back to its default value when the method is called again. Otherwise, all subsequent nodes will be drawn in the changed font! Look at the code in Listing 6.14 to see how to restore the font to the default.

We do not show an example of a tree cell renderer that draws arbitrary graphics. If you need this capability, you can adapt the list cell renderer in Listing 6.4; the technique is entirely analogous.

The ClassNameTreeCellRenderer in Listing 6.14 sets the class name in either the normal or italic font, depending on the ABSTRACT modifier of the Class object. We don't want to set a particular font because we don't want to change whatever font the look-and-feel normally uses for labels. For that reason, we use the font from the label and *derive* an italic font from it. Recall that only a single shared JLabel object is returned by all calls. We need to hang on to the original font and restore it in the next call to the getTreeCellRendererComponent method.

Also, note how we change the node icons in the ClassTreeFrame constructor.

---

**javax.swing.tree.DefaultMutableTreeNode** 1.2

- Enumeration breadthFirstEnumeration()
- Enumeration depthFirstEnumeration()
- Enumeration preOrderEnumeration()
- Enumeration postOrderEnumeration()

  returns enumeration objects for visiting all nodes of the tree model in a particular order. In breadth-first traversal, children that are closer to the root are visited before those that are farther away. In depth-first traversal, all children of a node are completely enumerated before its siblings are visited. The postOrderEnumeration method is a synonym for depthFirstEnumeration. The preorder traversal is identical to the postorder traversal except that parents are enumerated before their children.

---

---

*javax.swing.tree.TreeCellRenderer* 1.2

- Component getTreeCellRendererComponent(JTree tree, Object value, boolean selected, boolean expanded, boolean leaf, int row, boolean hasFocus)
  returns a component whose paint method is invoked to render a tree cell.

  | *Parameters:* | tree | The tree containing the node to be rendered |
  | --- | --- | --- |
  | | value | The node to be rendered |
  | | selected | true if the node is currently selected |
  | | expanded | true if the children of the node are visible |
  | | leaf | true if the node needs to be displayed as a leaf |
  | | row | The display row containing the node |
  | | hasFocus | true if the node currently has input focus |

---

*javax.swing.tree.DefaultTreeCellRenderer* 1.2

- void setLeafIcon(Icon icon)
- void setOpenIcon(Icon icon)
- void setClosedIcon(Icon icon)
  sets the icon to show for a leaf node, an expanded node, and a collapsed node.

## 6.3.4 Listening to Tree Events

Most commonly, a tree component is paired with some other component. When the user selects tree nodes, some information shows up in another window. See Figure 6.33 for an example. When the user selects a class, the instance and static variables of that class are displayed in the text area to the right.

To obtain this behavior, you need to install a *tree selection listener*. The listener must implement the TreeSelectionListener interface—an interface with a single method:

```
void valueChanged(TreeSelectionEvent event)
```

That method is called whenever the user selects or deselects tree nodes.

Add the listener to the tree in the normal way:

```
tree.addTreeSelectionListener(listener);
```

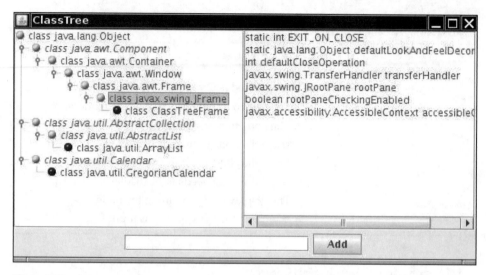

**Figure 6.33** A class browser

You can specify whether the user is allowed to select a single node, a contiguous range of nodes, or an arbitrary, potentially discontiguous, set of nodes. The JTree class uses a TreeSelectionModel to manage node selection. You need to retrieve the model to set the selection state to one of SINGLE_TREE_SELECTION, CONTIGUOUS_TREE_SELECTION, or DISCONTIGUOUS_TREE_SELECTION. (Discontiguous selection mode is the default.) For example, in our class browser, we want to allow selection of only a single class:

```
int mode = TreeSelectionModel.SINGLE_TREE_SELECTION;
tree.getSelectionModel().setSelectionMode(mode);
```

Apart from setting the selection mode, you need not worry about the tree selection model.

 **NOTE:** How the user selects multiple items depends on the look-and-feel. In the Metal look-and-feel, hold down the Ctrl key while clicking an item to add it to the selection, or to remove it if it was currently selected. Hold down the Shift key while clicking an item to select a *range* of items, extending from the previously selected item to the new item.

To find out the current selection, query the tree with the getSelectionPaths method:

```
TreePath[] selectedPaths = tree.getSelectionPaths();
```

If you restricted the user to single-item selection, you can use the convenience method getSelectionPath which returns the first selected path or null if no path was selected.

 **CAUTION:** The TreeSelectionEvent class has a getPaths method that returns an array of TreePath objects, but that array describes *selection changes*, not the current selection.

Listing 6.14 shows the frame class for the class tree program. The program displays inheritance hierarchies and customizes the display to show abstract classes in italics. (See Listing 6.15 for the cell renderer.) The program displays inheritance hierarchies and customizes the display to show abstract classes in italics. You can type the name of any class into the text field at the bottom of the frame. Press the Enter key or click the Add button to add the class and its superclasses to the tree. You must enter the full package name, such as java.util.ArrayList.

This program is a bit tricky because it uses reflection to construct the class tree. This work is done inside the addClass method. (The details are not that important. We use the class tree in this example because inheritance yields a nice supply of trees without laborious coding. When you display trees in your applications, you will have your own source of hierarchical data.) The method uses the breadth-first search algorithm to find whether the current class is already in the tree by calling the findUserObject method that we implemented in the preceding section. If the class is not already in the tree, we add the superclasses to the tree, then make the new class node a child and make that node visible.

When you select a tree node, the text area to the right is filled with the fields of the selected class. In the frame constructor, we restrict the user to single-item selection and add a tree selection listener. When the valueChanged method is called, we ignore its event parameter and simply ask the tree for the current selection path. As always, we need to get the last node of the path and look up its user object. We then call the getFieldDescription method which uses reflection to assemble a string with all fields of the selected class.

**Listing 6.14** treeRender/ClassTreeFrame.java

```
1  package treeRender;
2
3  import java.awt.*;
4  import java.awt.event.*;
5  import java.lang.reflect.*;
6  import java.util.*;
```

*(Continues)*

**Listing 6.14** *(Continued)*

```
 7  import javax.swing.*;
 8  import javax.swing.event.*;
 9  import javax.swing.tree.*;
10
11  /**
12   * This frame displays the class tree, a text field, and an "Add" button to add more classes
13   * into the tree.
14   */
15  public class ClassTreeFrame extends JFrame
16  {
17     private static final int DEFAULT_WIDTH = 400;
18     private static final int DEFAULT_HEIGHT = 300;
19
20     private DefaultMutableTreeNode root;
21     private DefaultTreeModel model;
22     private JTree tree;
23     private JTextField textField;
24     private JTextArea textArea;
25
26     public ClassTreeFrame()
27     {
28        setSize(DEFAULT_WIDTH, DEFAULT_HEIGHT);
29
30        // the root of the class tree is Object
31        root = new DefaultMutableTreeNode(java.lang.Object.class);
32        model = new DefaultTreeModel(root);
33        tree = new JTree(model);
34
35        // add this class to populate the tree with some data
36        addClass(getClass());
37
38        // set up node icons
39        ClassNameTreeCellRenderer renderer = new ClassNameTreeCellRenderer();
40        renderer.setClosedIcon(new ImageIcon(getClass().getResource("red-ball.gif")));
41        renderer.setOpenIcon(new ImageIcon(getClass().getResource("yellow-ball.gif")));
42        renderer.setLeafIcon(new ImageIcon(getClass().getResource("blue-ball.gif")));
43        tree.setCellRenderer(renderer);
44
45        // set up selection mode
46        tree.addTreeSelectionListener(new TreeSelectionListener()
47           {
48              public void valueChanged(TreeSelectionEvent event)
49              {
50                 // the user selected a different node--update description
51                 TreePath path = tree.getSelectionPath();
52                 if (path == null) return;
53                 DefaultMutableTreeNode selectedNode = (DefaultMutableTreeNode) path
54                    .getLastPathComponent();
```

```
55                 Class<?> c = (Class<?>) selectedNode.getUserObject();
56                 String description = getFieldDescription(c);
57                 textArea.setText(description);
58             }
59         });
60      int mode = TreeSelectionModel.SINGLE_TREE_SELECTION;
61      tree.getSelectionModel().setSelectionMode(mode);
62
63      // this text area holds the class description
64      textArea = new JTextArea();
65
66      // add tree and text area
67      JPanel panel = new JPanel();
68      panel.setLayout(new GridLayout(1, 2));
69      panel.add(new JScrollPane(tree));
70      panel.add(new JScrollPane(textArea));
71
72      add(panel, BorderLayout.CENTER);
73
74      addTextField();
75   }
76
77   /**
78    * Add the text field and "Add" button to add a new class.
79    */
80   public void addTextField()
81   {
82      JPanel panel = new JPanel();
83
84      ActionListener addListener = new ActionListener()
85         {
86            public void actionPerformed(ActionEvent event)
87            {
88               // add the class whose name is in the text field
89               try
90               {
91                  String text = textField.getText();
92                  addClass(Class.forName(text)); // clear text field to indicate success
93                  textField.setText("");
94               }
95               catch (ClassNotFoundException e)
96               {
97                  JOptionPane.showMessageDialog(null, "Class not found");
98               }
99            }
100        };
101
102     // new class names are typed into this text field
103     textField = new JTextField(20);
```

*(Continues)*

**Listing 6.14** *(Continued)*

```
104        textField.addActionListener(addListener);
105        panel.add(textField);
106
107        JButton addButton = new JButton("Add");
108        addButton.addActionListener(addListener);
109        panel.add(addButton);
110
111        add(panel, BorderLayout.SOUTH);
112     }
113
114     /**
115      * Finds an object in the tree.
116      * @param obj the object to find
117      * @return the node containing the object or null if the object is not present in the tree
118      */
119     @SuppressWarnings("unchecked")
120     public DefaultMutableTreeNode findUserObject(Object obj)
121     {
122        // find the node containing a user object
123        Enumeration<TreeNode> e = (Enumeration<TreeNode>) root.breadthFirstEnumeration();
124        while (e.hasMoreElements())
125        {
126           DefaultMutableTreeNode node = (DefaultMutableTreeNode) e.nextElement();
127           if (node.getUserObject().equals(obj)) return node;
128        }
129        return null;
130     }
131
132     /**
133      * Adds a new class and any parent classes that aren't yet part of the tree
134      * @param c the class to add
135      * @return the newly added node.
136      */
137     public DefaultMutableTreeNode addClass(Class<?> c)
138     {
139        // add a new class to the tree
140
141        // skip non-class types
142        if (c.isInterface() || c.isPrimitive()) return null;
143
144        // if the class is already in the tree, return its node
145        DefaultMutableTreeNode node = findUserObject(c);
146        if (node != null) return node;
147
148        // class isn't present--first add class parent recursively
149        Class<?> s = c.getSuperclass();
```

```
150        DefaultMutableTreeNode parent;
151        if (s == null) parent = root;
152        else parent = addClass(s);
153
154        // add the class as a child to the parent
155        DefaultMutableTreeNode newNode = new DefaultMutableTreeNode(c);
156        model.insertNodeInto(newNode, parent, parent.getChildCount());
157
158        // make node visible
159        TreePath path = new TreePath(model.getPathToRoot(newNode));
160        tree.makeVisible(path);
161
162        return newNode;
163     }
164
165     /**
166      * Returns a description of the fields of a class.
167      * @param the class to be described
168      * @return a string containing all field types and names
169      */
170     public static String getFieldDescription(Class<?> c)
171     {
172        // use reflection to find types and names of fields
173        StringBuilder r = new StringBuilder();
174        Field[] fields = c.getDeclaredFields();
175        for (int i = 0; i < fields.length; i++)
176        {
177           Field f = fields[i];
178           if ((f.getModifiers() & Modifier.STATIC) != 0) r.append("static ");
179           r.append(f.getType().getName());
180           r.append(" ");
181           r.append(f.getName());
182           r.append("\n");
183        }
184        return r.toString();
185     }
186 }
```

**Listing 6.15**  treeRender/ClassNameTreeCellRenderer.java

```
1 package treeRender;
2
3 import java.awt.*;
4 import java.lang.reflect.*;
5 import javax.swing.*;
6 import javax.swing.tree.*;
```

*(Continues)*

**Listing 6.15** *(Continued)*

```java
7  /**
8   * This class renders a class name either in plain or italic. Abstract classes are italic.
9   */
10 public class ClassNameTreeCellRenderer extends DefaultTreeCellRenderer
11 {
12    private Font plainFont = null;
13    private Font italicFont = null;
14
15    public Component getTreeCellRendererComponent(JTree tree, Object value, boolean selected,
16          boolean expanded, boolean leaf, int row, boolean hasFocus)
17    {
18       super.getTreeCellRendererComponent(tree, value, selected, expanded, leaf, row, hasFocus);
19       // get the user object
20       DefaultMutableTreeNode node = (DefaultMutableTreeNode) value;
21       Class<?> c = (Class<?>) node.getUserObject();
22
23       // the first time, derive italic font from plain font
24       if (plainFont == null)
25       {
26          plainFont = getFont();
27          // the tree cell renderer is sometimes called with a label that has a null font
28          if (plainFont != null) italicFont = plainFont.deriveFont(Font.ITALIC);
29       }
30
31       // set font to italic if the class is abstract, plain otherwise
32       if ((c.getModifiers() & Modifier.ABSTRACT) == 0) setFont(plainFont);
33       else setFont(italicFont);
34       return this;
35    }
36 }
```

---

**javax.swing.JTree** 1.2

- TreePath getSelectionPath()
- TreePath[] getSelectionPaths()
  returns the first selected path, or an array of paths to all selected nodes. If no paths are selected, both methods return null.

---

**javax.swing.event.TreeSelectionListener** 1.2

- void valueChanged(TreeSelectionEvent event)
  is called whenever nodes are selected or deselected.

---

**javax.swing.event.TreeSelectionEvent** 1.2

- TreePath getPath()
- TreePath[] getPaths()

  gets the first path or all paths that have *changed* in this selection event. If you want to know the current selection, not the selection change, you should call JTree.getSelectionPaths instead.

---

## 6.3.5 Custom Tree Models

In the final example, we implement a program that inspects the contents of an object, just like a debugger does (see Figure 6.34).

Before going further, compile and run the example program. Each node corresponds to an instance field. If the field is an object, expand it to see *its* instance fields. The program inspects the contents of the frame window. If you poke around a few of the instance fields, you should be able to find some familiar classes. You'll also gain some respect for how complex the Swing user interface components are under the hood.

What's remarkable about the program is that the tree does not use the DefaultTreeModel. If you already have data that are hierarchically organized, you might not want to build a duplicate tree and worry about keeping both trees

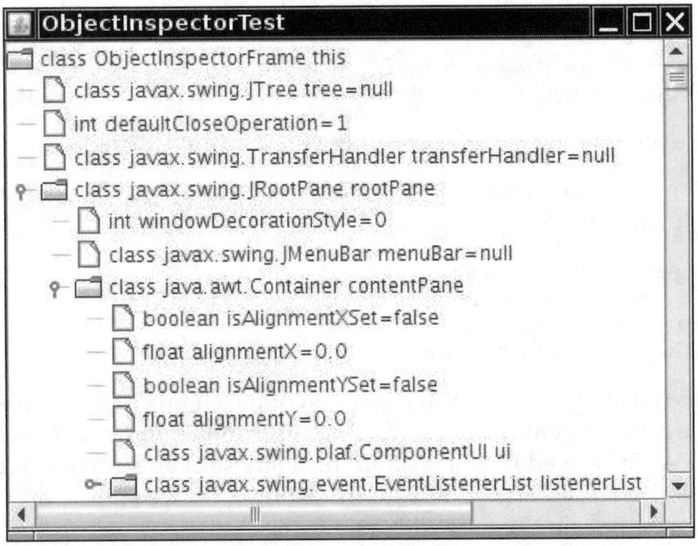

**Figure 6.34** An object inspection tree

synchronized. That is the situation in our case—the inspected objects are already linked to each other through the object references, so there is no need to replicate the linking structure.

The TreeModel interface has only a handful of methods. The first group of methods enables the JTree to find the tree nodes by first getting the root, then the children. The JTree class calls these methods only when the user actually expands a node.

```
Object getRoot()
int getChildCount(Object parent)
Object getChild(Object parent, int index)
```

This example shows why the TreeModel interface, like the JTree class itself, does not need an explicit notion of nodes. The root and its children can be any objects. The TreeModel is responsible for telling the JTree how they are connected.

The next method of the TreeModel interface is the reverse of getChild:

```
int getIndexOfChild(Object parent, Object child)
```

Actually, this method can be implemented in terms of the first three—see the code in Listing 6.16.

The tree model tells the JTree which nodes should be displayed as leaves:

```
boolean isLeaf(Object node)
```

If your code changes the tree model, the tree needs to be notified so that it can redraw itself. The tree adds itself as a TreeModelListener to the model. Thus, the model must support the usual listener management methods:

```
void addTreeModelListener(TreeModelListener l)
void removeTreeModelListener(TreeModelListener l)
```

You can see the implementations for these methods in Listing 6.17.

When the model modifies the tree contents, it calls one of the four methods of the TreeModelListener interface:

```
void treeNodesChanged(TreeModelEvent e)
void treeNodesInserted(TreeModelEvent e)
void treeNodesRemoved(TreeModelEvent e)
void treeStructureChanged(TreeModelEvent e)
```

The TreeModelEvent object describes the location of the change. The details of assembling a tree model event that describes an insertion or removal event are quite technical. You only need to worry about firing these events if your tree can actually have nodes added and removed. In Listing 6.16, we show you how to fire one event by replacing the root with a new object.

**TIP:** To simplify the code for event firing, use the `javax.swing.EventListenerList` convenience class that collects listeners. The last three methods of Listing 6.17 show how to use the class.

Finally, if the user edits a tree node, your model is called with the change:

```
void valueForPathChanged(TreePath path, Object newValue)
```

If you don't allow editing, this method is never called.

If you don't need to support editing, constructing a tree model is easily done. Implement the three methods

```
Object getRoot()
int getChildCount(Object parent)
Object getChild(Object parent, int index)
```

These methods describe the structure of the tree. Supply routine implementations of the other five methods, as in Listing 6.16. You are then ready to display your tree.

Now let's turn to the implementation of the example program. Our tree will contain objects of type `Variable`.

 **NOTE:** Had we used the `DefaultTreeModel`, our nodes would have been objects of type `DefaultMutableTreeNode` with *user objects* of type `Variable`.

For example, suppose you inspect the variable

```
Employee joe;
```

That variable has a *type* `Employee.class`, a *name* "joe", and a *value*—the value of the object reference `joe`. In Listing 6.18, we define a class `Variable` that describes a variable in a program:

```
Variable v = new Variable(Employee.class, "joe", joe);
```

If the type of the variable is a primitive type, you must use an object wrapper for the value.

```
new Variable(double.class, "salary", new Double(salary));
```

If the type of the variable is a class, the variable has *fields*. Using reflection, we enumerate all fields and collect them in an `ArrayList`. Since the `getFields` method of the `Class` class does not return the fields of the superclass, we need to call `getFields` on all superclasses as well. You can find the code in the `Variable` constructor. The getFields method of our Variable class returns the array of fields. Finally, the toString method of the Variable class formats the node label. The label always contains the variable type and name. If the variable is not a class, the label also contains the value.

 **NOTE:** If the type is an array, we do not display the elements of the array. This would not be difficult to do; we leave it as the proverbial "exercise for the reader."

Let's move on to the tree model. The first two methods are simple.

```
public Object getRoot()
{
    return root;
}

public int getChildCount(Object parent)
{
    return ((Variable) parent).getFields().size();
}
```

The getChild method returns a new Variable object that describes the field with the given index. The getType and getName methods of the Field class yield the field type and name. By using reflection, you can read the field value as f.get(parentValue). That method can throw an IllegalAccessException. However, we made all fields accessible in the Variable constructor, so this won't happen in practice.

Here is the complete code of the getChild method:

```
public Object getChild(Object parent, int index)
{
    ArrayList fields = ((Variable) parent).getFields();
    Field f = (Field) fields.get(index);
    Object parentValue = ((Variable) parent).getValue();
    try
    {
        return new Variable(f.getType(), f.getName(), f.get(parentValue));
    }
    catch (IllegalAccessException e)
    {
        return null;
    }
}
```

These three methods reveal the structure of the object tree to the JTree component. The remaining methods are routine—see the source code in Listing 6.17.

There is one remarkable fact about this tree model: It actually describes an *infinite* tree. You can verify this by following one of the WeakReference objects. Click on the variable named referent. It leads you right back to the original object. You get an identical subtree, and you can open its WeakReference object again, ad infinitum. Of course, you cannot *store* an infinite set of nodes; the tree model simply generates the nodes on demand as the user expands the parents. Listing 6.16 shows the frame class of the sample program.

**Listing 6.16** treeModel/ObjectInspectorFrame.java

```java
1  package treeModel;
2
3  import java.awt.*;
4  import javax.swing.*;
5
6  /**
7   * This frame holds the object tree.
8   */
9  public class ObjectInspectorFrame extends JFrame
10 {
11     private JTree tree;
12     private static final int DEFAULT_WIDTH = 400;
13     private static final int DEFAULT_HEIGHT = 300;
14
15     public ObjectInspectorFrame()
16     {
17        setSize(DEFAULT_WIDTH, DEFAULT_HEIGHT);
18
19        // we inspect this frame object
20
21        Variable v = new Variable(getClass(), "this", this);
22        ObjectTreeModel model = new ObjectTreeModel();
23        model.setRoot(v);
24
25        // construct and show tree
26
27        tree = new JTree(model);
28        add(new JScrollPane(tree), BorderLayout.CENTER);
29     }
30 }
```

**Listing 6.17** treeModel/ObjectTreeModel.java

```
1  package treeModel;
2
3  import java.lang.reflect.*;
4  import java.util.*;
5  import javax.swing.event.*;
6  import javax.swing.tree.*;
7
8  /**
9   * This tree model describes the tree structure of a Java object. Children are the objects that
10  * are stored in instance variables.
11  */
12 public class ObjectTreeModel implements TreeModel
13 {
14    private Variable root;
15    private EventListenerList listenerList = new EventListenerList();
16
17    /**
18     * Constructs an empty tree.
19     */
20    public ObjectTreeModel()
21    {
22       root = null;
23    }
24
25    /**
26     * Sets the root to a given variable.
27     * @param v the variable that is being described by this tree
28     */
29    public void setRoot(Variable v)
30    {
31       Variable oldRoot = v;
32       root = v;
33       fireTreeStructureChanged(oldRoot);
34    }
35
36    public Object getRoot()
37    {
38       return root;
39    }
40
41    public int getChildCount(Object parent)
42    {
43       return ((Variable) parent).getFields().size();
44    }
```

```
45    public Object getChild(Object parent, int index)
46    {
47       ArrayList<Field> fields = ((Variable) parent).getFields();
48       Field f = (Field) fields.get(index);
49       Object parentValue = ((Variable) parent).getValue();
50       try
51       {
52          return new Variable(f.getType(), f.getName(), f.get(parentValue));
53       }
54       catch (IllegalAccessException e)
55       {
56          return null;
57       }
58    }
59
60    public int getIndexOfChild(Object parent, Object child)
61    {
62       int n = getChildCount(parent);
63       for (int i = 0; i < n; i++)
64          if (getChild(parent, i).equals(child)) return i;
65       return -1;
66    }
67
68    public boolean isLeaf(Object node)
69    {
70       return getChildCount(node) == 0;
71    }
72
73    public void valueForPathChanged(TreePath path, Object newValue)
74    {
75    }
76
77    public void addTreeModelListener(TreeModelListener l)
78    {
79       listenerList.add(TreeModelListener.class, l);
80    }
81
82    public void removeTreeModelListener(TreeModelListener l)
83    {
84       listenerList.remove(TreeModelListener.class, l);
85    }
86
87    protected void fireTreeStructureChanged(Object oldRoot)
88    {
89       TreeModelEvent event = new TreeModelEvent(this, new Object[] { oldRoot });
90       for (TreeModelListener l : listenerList.getListeners(TreeModelListener.class))
91          l.treeStructureChanged(event);
92    }
93 }
```

**Listing 6.18** treeModel/Variable.java

```java
1  package treeModel;
2
3  import java.lang.reflect.*;
4  import java.util.*;
5
6  /**
7   * A variable with a type, name, and value.
8   */
9  public class Variable
10 {
11    private Class<?> type;
12    private String name;
13    private Object value;
14    private ArrayList<Field> fields;
15
16    /**
17     * Construct a variable.
18     * @param aType the type
19     * @param aName the name
20     * @param aValue the value
21     */
22    public Variable(Class<?> aType, String aName, Object aValue)
23    {
24       type = aType;
25       name = aName;
26       value = aValue;
27       fields = new ArrayList<>();
28
29       // find all fields if we have a class type except we don't expand strings and null values
30
31       if (!type.isPrimitive() && !type.isArray() && !type.equals(String.class) && value != null)
32       {
33          // get fields from the class and all superclasses
34          for (Class<?> c = value.getClass(); c != null; c = c.getSuperclass())
35          {
36             Field[] fs = c.getDeclaredFields();
37             AccessibleObject.setAccessible(fs, true);
38
39             // get all nonstatic fields
40             for (Field f : fs)
41                if ((f.getModifiers() & Modifier.STATIC) == 0) fields.add(f);
42          }
43       }
44    }
```

```
45    /**
46     * Gets the value of this variable.
47     * @return the value
48     */
49    public Object getValue()
50    {
51       return value;
52    }
53
54    /**
55     * Gets all nonstatic fields of this variable.
56     * @return an array list of variables describing the fields
57     */
58    public ArrayList<Field> getFields()
59    {
60       return fields;
61    }
62
63    public String toString()
64    {
65       String r = type + " " + name;
66       if (type.isPrimitive()) r += "=" + value;
67       else if (type.equals(String.class)) r += "=" + value;
68       else if (value == null) r += "=null";
69       return r;
70    }
71 }
```

---

**javax.swing.tree.TreeModel** 1.2

- Object getRoot()
  returns the root node.

- int getChildCount(Object parent)
  gets the number of children of the parent node.

- Object getChild(Object parent, int index)
  gets the child node of the parent node at the given index.

- int getIndexOfChild(Object parent, Object child)
  gets the index of the child node in the parent node, or -1 if child is not a child of parent in this tree model.

- boolean isLeaf(Object node)
  returns true if node is conceptually a leaf of the tree.

*(Continues)*

---

**javax.swing.tree.TreeModel** 1.2 *(Continued)*

---

- void addTreeModelListener(TreeModelListener l)
- void removeTreeModelListener(TreeModelListener l)

  adds or removes listeners that are notified when the information in the tree model changes.

- void valueForPathChanged(TreePath path, Object newValue)

  is called when a cell editor has modified the value of a node.

  *Parameters:*    path          The path to the node that has been edited

                  newValue    The replacement value returned by the editor

---

**javax.swing.event.TreeModelListener** 1.2

---

- void treeNodesChanged(TreeModelEvent e)
- void treeNodesInserted(TreeModelEvent e)
- void treeNodesRemoved(TreeModelEvent e)
- void treeStructureChanged(TreeModelEvent e)

  is called by the tree model when the tree has been modified.

---

**javax.swing.event.TreeModelEvent** 1.2

---

- TreeModelEvent(Object eventSource, TreePath node)

  constructs a tree model event.

  *Parameters:*    eventSource    The tree model generating this event

                  node          The path to the node that is being changed

## 6.4 Text Components

Figure 6.35 shows all text components that are included in the Swing library. You already saw the three most commonly used components—JTextField, JPasswordField, and JTextArea—in Volume I, Chapter 9. In the following sections, we will introduce the remaining text components. We will also discuss the JSpinner component that contains a formatted text field together with tiny "up" and "down" buttons to change its contents.

All text components render and edit the data stored in a model object of a class implementing the Document interface. The JTextField and JTextArea components use a

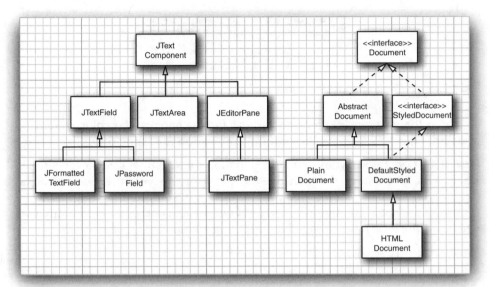

**Figure 6.35** The hierarchy of text components and documents

PlainDocument that simply stores a sequence of lines of plain text without any formatting.

A JEditorPane can show and edit styled text (with fonts, colors, etc.) in a variety of formats, most notably HTML; see Section 6.4.4, "Displaying HTML with the JEditorPane," on p. 494. The StyledDocument interface describes the additional requirements of styles, fonts, and colors. The HTMLDocument class implements this interface.

The subclass JTextPane of JEditorPane also holds styled text as well as embedded Swing components. We do not cover the very complex JTextPane in this book but instead refer you to the detailed description in *Core Swing* by Kim Topley. For a typical use of the JTextPane class, have a look at the StylePad demo that is included in the JDK.

## 6.4.1 Change Tracking in Text Components

Most of the intricacies of the Document interface are of interest only if you implement your own text editor. There is, however, one common use of the interface: tracking changes.

Sometimes, you may want to update a part of your user interface whenever a user edits text, without waiting for the user to click a button. Here is a simple example. We show three text fields for the red, blue, and green component of

**Figure 6.36** Tracking changes in a text field

a color. Whenever the content of the text fields changes, the color should be updated. Figure 6.36 shows the running application of Listing 6.19.

First of all, note that it is not a good idea to monitor keystrokes. Some keystrokes (such as the arrow keys) don't change the text. More importantly, the text can be updated by mouse gestures (such as "middle mouse button pasting" in X11). Instead, you should ask the *document* (and not the text component) to notify you whenever the data have changed by installing a *document listener:*

```
textField.getDocument().addDocumentListener(listener);
```

When the text has changed, one of the following DocumentListener methods is called:

```
void insertUpdate(DocumentEvent event)
void removeUpdate(DocumentEvent event)
void changedUpdate(DocumentEvent event)
```

The first two methods are called when characters have been inserted or removed. The third method is not called at all for text fields. For more complex document types, it would be called when some other change, such as a change in formatting, has occurred. Unfortunately, there is no single callback to tell you that the text has changed—usually you don't much care how it has changed. There is no adapter class, either. Thus, your document listener must implement all three methods. Here is what we do in our sample program:

```
DocumentListener listener = new DocumentListener()
    {
        public void insertUpdate(DocumentEvent event) { setColor(); }
        public void removeUpdate(DocumentEvent event) { setColor(); }
        public void changedUpdate(DocumentEvent event) {}
    }
```

The setColor method uses the getText method to obtain the current user input strings from the text fields and sets the color.

Our program has one limitation. Users can type malformed input, such as "twenty", into the text field, or leave a field blank. For now, we catch the NumberFormatException that the parseInt method throws, and we simply don't update the color when the text field entry is not a number. In the next section, you will see how you can prevent the user from entering invalid input in the first place.

**NOTE:** Instead of listening to document events, you can add an action event listener to a text field. The action listener is notified whenever the user presses the Enter key. We don't recommend this approach, because users don't always remember to press Enter when they are done entering data. If you use an action listener, you should also install a focus listener so that you can track when the user leaves the text field.

**Listing 6.19** textChange/ColorFrame.java

```java
1  package textChange;
2
3  import java.awt.*;
4  import javax.swing.*;
5  import javax.swing.event.*;
6
7  /**
8   * A frame with three text fields to set the background color.
9   */
10 public class ColorFrame extends JFrame
11 {
12    private JPanel panel;
13    private JTextField redField;
14    private JTextField greenField;
15    private JTextField blueField;
16
17    public ColorFrame()
18    {
19       DocumentListener listener = new DocumentListener()
20          {
21             public void insertUpdate(DocumentEvent event) { setColor(); }
22             public void removeUpdate(DocumentEvent event) { setColor(); }
23             public void changedUpdate(DocumentEvent event) {}
24          };
25
26       panel = new JPanel();
27
28       panel.add(new JLabel("Red:"));
29       redField = new JTextField("255", 3);
30       panel.add(redField);
31       redField.getDocument().addDocumentListener(listener);
32
33       panel.add(new JLabel("Green:"));
34       greenField = new JTextField("255", 3);
35       panel.add(greenField);
36       greenField.getDocument().addDocumentListener(listener);
```

*(Continues)*

**Listing 6.19** *(Continued)*

```
37       panel.add(new JLabel("Blue:"));
38       blueField = new JTextField("255", 3);
39       panel.add(blueField);
40       blueField.getDocument().addDocumentListener(listener);
41
42       add(panel);
43       pack();
44    }
45
46    /**
47     * Set the background color to the values stored in the text fields.
48     */
49    public void setColor()
50    {
51       try
52       {
53          int red = Integer.parseInt(redField.getText().trim());
54          int green = Integer.parseInt(greenField.getText().trim());
55          int blue = Integer.parseInt(blueField.getText().trim());
56          panel.setBackground(new Color(red, green, blue));
57       }
58       catch (NumberFormatException e)
59       {
60          // don't set the color if the input can't be parsed
61       }
62    }
63 }
```

---

**javax.swing.JComponent** 1.2

- Dimension getPreferredSize()
- void setPreferredSize(Dimension d)

  gets or sets the preferred size of this component.

---

**javax.swing.text.Document** 1.2

- int getLength()

  returns the number of characters currently in the document.

- String getText(int offset, int length)

  returns the text contained within the given portion of the document.

  | *Parameters:* | offset | The start of the text |
  |---|---|---|
  | | length | The length of the desired string |

---

**javax.swing.text.Document**  1.2  *(Continued)*

---

- void addDocumentListener(DocumentListener listener)
  registers the listener to be notified when the document changes.

---

**javax.swing.event.DocumentEvent**  1.2

---

- Document getDocument()
  gets the document that is the source of the event.

---

**javax.swing.event.DocumentListener**  1.2

---

- void changedUpdate(DocumentEvent event)
  is called whenever an attribute or set of attributes changes.
- void insertUpdate(DocumentEvent event)
  is called whenever an insertion into the document occurs.
- void removeUpdate(DocumentEvent event)
  is called whenever a portion of the document has been removed.

---

## 6.4.2  Formatted Input Fields

In the previous example program, we wanted the program user to type numbers, not arbitrary strings. That is, the user is allowed to enter only digits 0 through 9 and a hyphen (-). The hyphen, if present at all, must be the *first* symbol of the input string.

On the surface, this input validation task sounds simple. We can install a key listener to the text field and consume all key events that aren't digits or a hyphen. Unfortunately, this simple approach, although commonly recommended as a method for input validation, does not work well in practice. First, not every combination of the valid input characters is a valid number. For example, --3 and 3-3 aren't valid, even though they are made up from valid input characters. But more importantly, there are other ways of changing the text that don't involve typing character keys. Depending on the look-and-feel, certain key combinations can be used to cut, copy, and paste text. For example, in the Metal look-and-feel, the Ctrl+V key combination pastes the content of the paste buffer into the text field. That is, we also need to monitor that the user doesn't paste in an invalid character. Clearly, filtering keystrokes to prevent invalid content begins to look like a real chore. This is certainly not something that an application programmer should have to worry about.

Perhaps surprisingly, before Java SE 1.4, there were no components for entering numeric values. Starting with the first edition of Core Java, we supplied an implementation for an IntTextField—a text field for entering a properly formatted integer. In every new edition, we changed the implementation to extract whatever limited advantage we could from the various half-baked validation schemes added in each version of Java. Finally, in Java SE 1.4, the Swing designers faced the issues head-on and supplied a versatile JFormattedTextField class that can be used not just for numeric input but also for dates or even more esoteric formatted values such as IP addresses.

### 6.4.2.1 Integer Input

Let's get started with an easy case: a text field for integer input.

```
JFormattedTextField intField = new JFormattedTextField(NumberFormat.getIntegerInstance());
```

The NumberFormat.getIntegerInstance returns a formatter object that formats integers using the current locale. In the U.S. locale, commas are used as decimal separators, allowing users to enter values such as 1,729. Chapter 5 explains in detail how you can select other locales.

As with any text field, you can set the number of columns:

```
intField.setColumns(6);
```

You can set a default value with the setValue method. That method takes an Object parameter, so you'll need to wrap the default int value in an Integer object:

```
intField.setValue(new Integer(100));
```

Typically, users will supply inputs in multiple text fields and then click a button to read all values. When the button is clicked, you can get the user-supplied value with the getValue method. That method returns an Object result, and you need to cast it into the appropriate type. The JFormattedTextField returns an object of type Long if the user edited the value. However, if the user made no changes, the original Integer object is returned. Therefore, you should cast the return value to the common superclass Number:

```
Number value = (Number) intField.getValue();
int v = value.intValue();
```

The formatted text field is not very interesting until you consider what happens when a user provides illegal input. That is the topic of the next section.

### 6.4.2.2 Behavior on Loss of Focus

Consider what happens when a user supplies input to a text field. The user types input and eventually decides to leave the field, perhaps by clicking on another component with the mouse. Then the text field *loses focus*. The I-beam cursor is no longer visible in the text field, and keystrokes are directed toward a different component.

When the formatted text field loses focus, the formatter looks at the text string that the user produced. If the formatter knows how to convert the text string to an object, the text is valid. Otherwise it is invalid. You can use the isEditValid method to check whether the current content of the text field is valid.

The default behavior on loss of focus is called "commit or revert." If the text string is valid, it is *committed*. The formatter converts it to an object. That object becomes the current value of the field (that is, the return value of the getValue method that you saw in the preceding section). The value is then converted back to a string, which becomes the text string visible in the field. For example, the integer formatter recognizes the input 1729 as valid, sets the current value to new Long(1729), and converts it back into a string with a decimal comma: 1,729.

Conversely, if the text string is invalid, the current value is not changed and the text field *reverts* to the string that represents the old value. For example, if the user enters a bad value, such as x1, the old value is restored when the text field loses focus.

**NOTE:** The integer formatter regards a text string as valid if it starts with an integer. For example, 1729x is a valid string. It is converted to the number 1729, which is then formatted as the string 1,729.

You can set other behaviors with the setFocusLostBehavior method. The "commit" behavior is subtly different from the default. If the text string is invalid, then both the text string and the field value stay unchanged—they are now out of sync. The "persist" behavior is even more conservative. Even if the text string is valid, neither the text field nor the current value are changed. You would need to call commitEdit, setValue, or setText to bring them back in sync. Finally, there is a "revert" behavior that doesn't ever seem to be useful: Whenever focus is lost, the user input is disregarded, and the text string reverts to the old value.

**NOTE:** Generally, the "commit or revert" default behavior is reasonable. There is just one potential problem. Suppose a dialog box contains a text field for an integer value. A user enters a string " 1729", with a leading space, and clicks the OK button. The leading space makes the number invalid, and the field value reverts to the old value. The action listener of the OK button retrieves the field value and closes the dialog box. The user never knows that the new value has been rejected. In this situation, it is appropriate to select the "commit" behavior and have the OK button listener check that all field edits are valid before closing the dialog box.

### 6.4.2.3 Filters

The basic functionality of formatted text fields is straightforward and sufficient for most uses. However, you can add a couple of refinements. Perhaps you want to prevent the user from entering nondigits altogether. You can achieve that behavior with a *document filter*. Recall that in the model-view-controller architecture, the controller translates input events into commands that modify the underlying document of the text field—that is, the text string that is stored in a `PlainDocument` object. For example, whenever the controller processes a command that causes text to be inserted into the document, it calls the "insert string" command. The string to be inserted can be either a single character or the content of the paste buffer. A document filter can intercept this command and modify the string or cancel the insertion altogether. Here is the code for the `insertString` method of a filter that analyzes the string to be inserted and inserts only the characters that are digits or a – sign. (The code handles supplementary Unicode characters, as explained in Volume I, Chapter 3. See Chapter 1 for the `StringBuilder` class.)

```
public void insertString(FilterBypass fb, int offset, String string, AttributeSet attr)
    throws BadLocationException
{
    StringBuilder builder = new StringBuilder(string);
    for (int i = builder.length() - 1; i >= 0; i--)
    {
        int cp = builder.codePointAt(i);
        if (!Character.isDigit(cp) && cp != '-')
        {
            builder.deleteCharAt(i);
            if (Character.isSupplementaryCodePoint(cp))
            {
                i--;
                builder.deleteCharAt(i);
            }
        }
    }
    super.insertString(fb, offset, builder.toString(), attr);
}
```

You should also override the `replace` method of the `DocumentFilter` class—it is called when text is selected and then replaced. The implementation of the `replace` method is straightforward—see Listing 6.21 on p. 480.

Now you need to install the document filter. Unfortunately, there is no straightforward method to do that. You need to override the `getDocumentFilter` method of a formatter class and pass an object of that formatter class to the `JFormattedTextField`. The integer text field uses an `InternationalFormatter` that is initialized with `NumberFormat.getIntegerInstance()`. Here is how you install a formatter to yield the desired filter:

```
JFormattedTextField intField = new JFormattedTextField(new
    InternationalFormatter(NumberFormat.getIntegerInstance())
{
    private DocumentFilter filter = new IntFilter();
    protected DocumentFilter getDocumentFilter()
    {
        return filter;
    }
});
```

> **NOTE:** The Java SE documentation states that the `DocumentFilter` class was invented to avoid subclassing. Until Java SE 1.3, filtering in a text field was achieved by extending the `PlainDocument` class and overriding the `insertString` and `replace` methods. Now the `PlainDocument` class has a pluggable filter instead. That is a splendid improvement. It would have been even more splendid if the filter had also been made pluggable in the formatter class. Alas, it was not, and we must subclass the formatter.

Try out the `FormatTest` example program at the end of this section. The third text field has a filter installed. You can insert only digits or the minus (-) character. Note that you can still enter invalid strings such as "1-2-3". In general, it is impossible to avoid all invalid strings through filtering. For example, the string "-" is invalid, but a filter can't reject it because it is a prefix of a legal string "-1". Even though filters can't give perfect protection, it makes sense to use them to reject inputs that are obviously invalid.

> **TIP:** Another use for filtering is to turn all characters of a string to upper case. Such a filter is easy to write. In the `insertString` and `replace` methods of the filter, convert the string to be inserted to upper case and then invoke the superclass method.

### 6.4.2.4 Verifiers

There is another potentially useful mechanism to alert users to invalid inputs. You can attach a *verifier* to any JComponent. If the component loses focus, the verifier is queried. If the verifier reports the content of the component to be invalid, the component immediately regains focus. The user is thus forced to fix the content before supplying other inputs.

A verifier must extend the abstract `InputVerifier` class and define a `verify` method. It is particularly easy to define a verifier that checks formatted text fields. The `isEditValid` method of the `JFormattedTextField` class calls the formatter and returns true if the formatter can turn the text string into an object. Here is the verifier, attached to a JFormattedTextField:

```
intField.setInputVerifier(new InputVerifier()
   {
      public boolean verify(JComponent component)
      {
         JFormattedTextField field = (JFormattedTextField) component;
         return field.isEditValid();
      }
   });
```

The fourth text field in the example program has this verifier attached. Try entering an invalid number (such as x1729) and press the Tab key or click with the mouse on another text field. Note that the field immediately regains focus. However, if you click the OK button, the action listener calls getValue, which reports the last good value.

A verifier is not entirely foolproof. If you click on a button, the button notifies its action listeners before an invalid component regains focus. The action listeners can then get an invalid result from the component that failed verification. There is a reason for this behavior: Users might want to click a Cancel button without first having to fix an invalid input.

### 6.4.2.5 Other Standard Formatters

Besides the integer formatter, the JFormattedTextField supports several other formatters. The NumberFormat class has static methods

```
getNumberInstance
getCurrencyInstance
getPercentInstance
```

that yield formatters of floating-point numbers, currency values, and percentages. For example, you can obtain a text field for the input of currency values by calling

```
JFormattedTextField currencyField = new JFormattedTextField(NumberFormat.getCurrencyInstance());
```

To edit dates and times, call one of the static methods of the DateFormat class:

```
getDateInstance
getTimeInstance
getDateTimeInstance
```

For example,

```
JFormattedTextField dateField = new JFormattedTextField(DateFormat.getDateInstance());
```

This field edits a date in the default or "medium" format such as

Aug 5, 2007

You can instead choose a "short" format such as

8/5/07

by calling

`DateFormat.getDateInstance(DateFormat.SHORT)`

---

 **NOTE:** By default, the date format is "lenient." That is, an invalid date such as February 31, 2002, is rolled over to the next valid date, March 3, 2002. That behavior might be surprising to your users. In that case, call `setLenient(false)` on the `DateFormat` object.

---

The `DefaultFormatter` can format objects of any class that has a constructor with a string parameter and a matching `toString` method. For example, the `URL` class has a `URL(String)` constructor that can be used to construct a URL from a string, such as

```
URL url = new URL("http://horstmann.com");
```

Therefore, you can use the `DefaultFormatter` to format `URL` objects. The formatter calls `toString` on the field value to initialize the field text. When the field loses focus, the formatter constructs a new object of the same class as the current value, using the constructor with a `String` parameter. If that constructor throws an exception, the edit is not valid. You can try that out in the example program by entering a URL that does not start with a prefix such as `"http:"`.

---

 **NOTE:** By default, the `DefaultFormatter` is in *overwrite mode.* That is different from the other formatters and not very useful. Call `setOverwriteMode(false)` to turn off overwrite mode.

---

Finally, the `MaskFormatter` is useful for fixed-size patterns that contain some constant and some variable characters. For example, Social Security numbers (such as 078-05-1120) can be formatted with a

```
new MaskFormatter("###-##-####")
```

The # symbol denotes a single digit. Table 6.3 shows the symbols that you can use in a mask formatter.

You can restrict the characters that can be typed into the field by calling one of the methods of the `MaskFormatter` class:

**Table 6.3** MaskFormatter Symbols

| Symbol | Explanation |
|--------|-------------|
| # | A digit |
| ? | A letter |
| U | A letter, converted to upper case |
| L | A letter, converted to lower case |
| A | A letter or digit |
| H | A hexadecimal digit [0-9A-Fa-f] |
| * | Any character |
| ' | Escape character to include a symbol in the pattern |

```
setValidCharacters
setInvalidCharacters
```

For example, to read in a letter grade (such as A+ or F), you could use

```
MaskFormatter formatter = new MaskFormatter("U*");
formatter.setValidCharacters("ABCDF+- ");
```

However, there is no way of specifying that the second character cannot be a letter.

Note that the string formatted by the mask formatter has exactly the same length as the pattern. If the user erases characters during editing, they are replaced with the *placeholder character*. The default placeholder character is a space, but you can change it with the setPlaceholderCharacter method, for example,

```
formatter.setPlaceholderCharacter('0');
```

By default, a mask formatter is in overtype mode, which is quite intuitive—try it out in the example program. Also, note that the caret position jumps over the fixed characters in the mask.

The mask formatter is very effective for rigid patterns such as Social Security numbers or American telephone numbers. However, note that no variation at all is permitted in the mask pattern. For example, you cannot use a mask formatter for international telephone numbers that have a variable number of digits.

### 6.4.2.6 Custom Formatters

If none of the standard formatters is appropriate, it is fairly easy to define your own formatter. Consider 4-byte IP addresses such as

```
130.65.86.66
```

You can't use a `MaskFormatter` because each byte might be represented by one, two, or three digits. Also, we want to check in the formatter that each byte's value is at most 255.

To define your own formatter, extend the `DefaultFormatter` class and override the methods

```
String valueToString(Object value)
Object stringToValue(String text)
```

The first method turns the field value into the string that is displayed in the text field. The second method parses the text that the user typed and turns it back into an object. If either method detects an error, it should throw a `ParseException`.

In our example program, we store an IP address in a `byte[]` array of length 4. The `valueToString` method forms a string that separates the bytes with periods. Note that `byte` values are signed quantities between –128 and 127. (For example, in an IP address 130.65.86.66, the first octet is actually the byte with value –126.) To turn negative byte values into unsigned integer values, add 256.

```java
public String valueToString(Object value) throws ParseException
{
    if (!(value instanceof byte[]))
        throw new ParseException("Not a byte[]", 0);
    byte[] a = (byte[]) value;
    if (a.length != 4)
        throw new ParseException("Length != 4", 0);
    StringBuilder builder = new StringBuilder();
    for (int i = 0; i < 4; i++)
    {
        int b = a[i];
        if (b < 0) b += 256;
        builder.append(String.valueOf(b));
        if (i < 3) builder.append('.');
    }
    return builder.toString();
}
```

Conversely, the `stringToValue` method parses the string and produces a `byte[]` object if the string is valid. If not, it throws a `ParseException`.

```java
public Object stringToValue(String text) throws ParseException
{
    StringTokenizer tokenizer = new StringTokenizer(text, ".");
    byte[] a = new byte[4];
```

```
for (int i = 0; i < 4; i++)
{
    int b = 0;
    try
    {
        b = Integer.parseInt(tokenizer.nextToken());
    }
    catch (NumberFormatException e)
    {
        throw new ParseException("Not an integer", 0);
    }
    if (b < 0 || b >= 256)
        throw new ParseException("Byte out of range", 0);
    a[i] = (byte) b;
}
return a;
}
```

Try out the IP address field in the sample program. If you enter an invalid address, the field reverts to the last valid address. The complete formatter is shown in Listing 6.22.

The program in Listing 6.20 shows various formatted text fields in action (see Figure 6.37). Click the OK button to retrieve the current values from the fields.

 **NOTE:** The "Swing Connection" online newsletter has a short article describing a formatter that matches any regular expression. See www.oracle.com/technetwork/java/reftf-138955.html.

| FormatTest | | |
|---|---|---|
| Number: | 100 | 100 |
| Number (Commit behavi... | 100 | 100 |
| Filtered Number | 100 | 100 |
| Verified Number: | 100 | 100 |
| Currency: | $10.00 | 10.0 |
| Date (default): | Aug 5, 2007 | Sun Aug 05 21:03:00 PD... |
| Date (short, not lenient): | 8/5/07 | Sun Aug 05 21:03:00 PD... |
| URL: | http://java.sun.com | http://java.sun.com |
| SSN Mask: | 078-05-1120 | 078-05-1120 |
| IP Address: | 130.65.86.66 | [-126, 65, 86, 66] |

Ok

**Figure 6.37** The FormatTest program

**Listing 6.20** textFormat/FormatTestFrame.java

```
1  package textFormat;
2
3  import java.awt.*;
4  import java.awt.event.*;
5  import java.net.*;
6  import java.text.*;
7  import java.util.*;
8  import javax.swing.*;
9  import javax.swing.text.*;
10 /**
11  * A frame with a collection of formatted text fields and a button that displays the field values.
12  */
13 public class FormatTestFrame extends JFrame
14 {
15    private DocumentFilter filter = new IntFilter();
16    private JButton okButton;
17    private JPanel mainPanel;
18
19    public FormatTestFrame()
20    {
21       JPanel buttonPanel = new JPanel();
22       okButton = new JButton("Ok");
23       buttonPanel.add(okButton);
24       add(buttonPanel, BorderLayout.SOUTH);
25
26       mainPanel = new JPanel();
27       mainPanel.setLayout(new GridLayout(0, 3));
28       add(mainPanel, BorderLayout.CENTER);
29
30       JFormattedTextField intField = new JFormattedTextField(NumberFormat.getIntegerInstance());
31       intField.setValue(new Integer(100));
32       addRow("Number:", intField);
33
34       JFormattedTextField intField2 = new JFormattedTextField(NumberFormat.getIntegerInstance());
35       intField2.setValue(new Integer(100));
36       intField2.setFocusLostBehavior(JFormattedTextField.COMMIT);
37       addRow("Number (Commit behavior):", intField2);
38
39       JFormattedTextField intField3 = new JFormattedTextField(new InternationalFormatter(
40          NumberFormat.getIntegerInstance())
41          {
42             protected DocumentFilter getDocumentFilter()
43             {
44                return filter;
45             }
46          });
```

*(Continues)*

Listing 6.20    *(Continued)*

```
47       intField3.setValue(new Integer(100));
48       addRow("Filtered Number", intField3);
49
50       JFormattedTextField intField4 = new JFormattedTextField(NumberFormat.getIntegerInstance());
51       intField4.setValue(new Integer(100));
52       intField4.setInputVerifier(new InputVerifier()
53          {
54             public boolean verify(JComponent component)
55             {
56                JFormattedTextField field = (JFormattedTextField) component;
57                return field.isEditValid();
58             }
59          });
60       addRow("Verified Number:", intField4);
61
62       JFormattedTextField currencyField = new JFormattedTextField(NumberFormat
63             .getCurrencyInstance());
64       currencyField.setValue(new Double(10));
65       addRow("Currency:", currencyField);
66
67       JFormattedTextField dateField = new JFormattedTextField(DateFormat.getDateInstance());
68       dateField.setValue(new Date());
69       addRow("Date (default):", dateField);
70
71       DateFormat format = DateFormat.getDateInstance(DateFormat.SHORT);
72       format.setLenient(false);
73       JFormattedTextField dateField2 = new JFormattedTextField(format);
74       dateField2.setValue(new Date());
75       addRow("Date (short, not lenient):", dateField2);
76
77       try
78       {
79          DefaultFormatter formatter = new DefaultFormatter();
80          formatter.setOverwriteMode(false);
81          JFormattedTextField urlField = new JFormattedTextField(formatter);
82          urlField.setValue(new URL("http://java.sun.com"));
83          addRow("URL:", urlField);
84       }
85       catch (MalformedURLException ex)
86       {
87          ex.printStackTrace();
88       }
89
90       try
91       {
92          MaskFormatter formatter = new MaskFormatter("###-##-####");
93          formatter.setPlaceholderCharacter('0');
```

```
94       JFormattedTextField ssnField = new JFormattedTextField(formatter);
95       ssnField.setValue("078-05-1120");
96       addRow("SSN Mask:", ssnField);
97    }
98    catch (ParseException ex)
99    {
100      ex.printStackTrace();
101   }
102
103   JFormattedTextField ipField = new JFormattedTextField(new IPAddressFormatter());
104   ipField.setValue(new byte[] { (byte) 130, 65, 86, 66 });
105   addRow("IP Address:", ipField);
106   pack();
107 }
108
109 /**
110  * Adds a row to the main panel.
111  * @param labelText the label of the field
112  * @param field the sample field
113  */
114 public void addRow(String labelText, final JFormattedTextField field)
115 {
116   mainPanel.add(new JLabel(labelText));
117   mainPanel.add(field);
118   final JLabel valueLabel = new JLabel();
119   mainPanel.add(valueLabel);
120   okButton.addActionListener(new ActionListener()
121      {
122         public void actionPerformed(ActionEvent event)
123         {
124            Object value = field.getValue();
125            Class<?> cl = value.getClass();
126            String text = null;
127            if (cl.isArray())
128            {
129               if (cl.getComponentType().isPrimitive())
130               {
131                  try
132                  {
133                     text = Arrays.class.getMethod("toString", cl).invoke(null, value)
134                           .toString();
135                  }
136                  catch (ReflectiveOperationException ex)
137                  {
138                     // ignore reflection exceptions
139                  }
140               }
141               else text = Arrays.toString((Object[]) value);
142            }
```

*(Continues)*

---

**Listing 6.20**   *(Continued)*

```
143              else text = value.toString();
144              valueLabel.setText(text);
145          }
146      });
147  }
148 }
```

---

**Listing 6.21**  textFormat/IntFilter.java

```
1  package textFormat;
2
3  import javax.swing.text.*;
4
5  /**
6   * A filter that restricts input to digits and a '-' sign.
7   */
8  public class IntFilter extends DocumentFilter
9  {
10     public void insertString(FilterBypass fb, int offset, String string, AttributeSet attr)
11           throws BadLocationException
12     {
13        StringBuilder builder = new StringBuilder(string);
14        for (int i = builder.length() - 1; i >= 0; i--)
15        {
16           int cp = builder.codePointAt(i);
17           if (!Character.isDigit(cp) && cp != '-')
18           {
19              builder.deleteCharAt(i);
20              if (Character.isSupplementaryCodePoint(cp))
21              {
22                 i--;
23                 builder.deleteCharAt(i);
24              }
25           }
26        }
27        super.insertString(fb, offset, builder.toString(), attr);
28     }
29
30     public void replace(FilterBypass fb, int offset, int length, String string, AttributeSet attr)
31           throws BadLocationException
32     {
33        if (string != null)
34        {
35           StringBuilder builder = new StringBuilder(string);
```

```
36        for (int i = builder.length() - 1; i >= 0; i--)
37        {
38           int cp = builder.codePointAt(i);
39           if (!Character.isDigit(cp) && cp != '-')
40           {
41              builder.deleteCharAt(i);
42              if (Character.isSupplementaryCodePoint(cp))
43              {
44                 i--;
45                 builder.deleteCharAt(i);
46              }
47           }
48        }
49        string = builder.toString();
50     }
51     super.replace(fb, offset, length, string, attr);
52  }
53 }
```

**Listing 6.22**  textFormat/IPAddressFormatter.java

```
1  package textFormat;
2
3  import java.text.*;
4  import java.util.*;
5  import javax.swing.text.*;
6
7  /**
8   * A formatter for 4-byte IP addresses of the form a.b.c.d
9   */
10 public class IPAddressFormatter extends DefaultFormatter
11 {
12    public String valueToString(Object value) throws ParseException
13    {
14       if (!(value instanceof byte[])) throw new ParseException("Not a byte[]", 0);
15       byte[] a = (byte[]) value;
16       if (a.length != 4) throw new ParseException("Length != 4", 0);
17       StringBuilder builder = new StringBuilder();
18       for (int i = 0; i < 4; i++)
19       {
20          int b = a[i];
21          if (b < 0) b += 256;
22          builder.append(String.valueOf(b));
23          if (i < 3) builder.append('.');
24       }
25       return builder.toString();
26    }
```

*(Continues)*

**Listing 6.22** *(Continued)*

```
27  public Object stringToValue(String text) throws ParseException
28  {
29     StringTokenizer tokenizer = new StringTokenizer(text, ".");
30     byte[] a = new byte[4];
31     for (int i = 0; i < 4; i++)
32     {
33        int b = 0;
34        if (!tokenizer.hasMoreTokens()) throw new ParseException("Too few bytes", 0);
35        try
36        {
37           b = Integer.parseInt(tokenizer.nextToken());
38        }
39        catch (NumberFormatException e)
40        {
41           throw new ParseException("Not an integer", 0);
42        }
43        if (b < 0 || b >= 256) throw new ParseException("Byte out of range", 0);
44        a[i] = (byte) b;
45     }
46     if (tokenizer.hasMoreTokens()) throw new ParseException("Too many bytes", 0);
47     return a;
48  }
49 }
```

---

**javax.swing.JFormattedTextField** 1.4

- JFormattedTextField(Format fmt)

  constructs a text field that uses the specified format.

- JFormattedTextField(JFormattedTextField.AbstractFormatter formatter)

  constructs a text field that uses the specified formatter. Note that DefaultFormatter and InternationalFormatter are subclasses of JFormattedTextField.AbstractFormatter.

- Object getValue()

  returns the current valid value of the field. Note that this might not correspond to the string being edited.

- void setValue(Object value)

  attempts to set the value of the given object. The attempt fails if the formatter cannot convert the object to a string.

- void commitEdit()

  attempts to set the valid value of the field from the edited string. The attempt might fail if the formatter cannot convert the string.

*(Continues)*

---

**javax.swing.JFormattedTextField** 1.4 *(Continued)*

- `boolean isEditValid()`
  checks whether the edited string represents a valid value.

- `int getFocusLostBehavior()`
- `void setFocusLostBehavior(int behavior)`
  gets or sets the "focus lost" behavior. Legal values for `behavior` are the constants `COMMIT_OR_REVERT`, `REVERT`, `COMMIT`, and `PERSIST` of the `JFormattedTextField` class.

---

**javax.swing.JFormattedTextField.AbstractFormatter** 1.4

- `abstract String valueToString(Object value)`
  converts a value to an editable string. Throws a `ParseException` if `value` is not appropriate for this formatter.

- `abstract Object stringToValue(String s)`
  converts a string to a value. Throws a `ParseException` if `s` is not in the appropriate format.

- `DocumentFilter getDocumentFilter()`
  override this method to provide a document filter that restricts inputs into the text field. A return value of `null` indicates that no filtering is needed.

---

**javax.swing.text.DefaultFormatter** 1.3

- `boolean getOverwriteMode()`
- `void setOverwriteMode(boolean mode)`
  gets or sets the overwrite mode. If `mode` is `true`, new characters overwrite existing characters when editing text.

---

**javax.swing.text.DocumentFilter** 1.4

- `void insertString(DocumentFilter.FilterBypass bypass, int offset, String text, AttributeSet attrib)`
  is invoked before a string is inserted into a document. You can override the method and modify the string. You can disable insertion by not calling `super.insertString` or by calling bypass methods to modify the document without filtering.

*(Continues)*

---

**javax.swing.text.DocumentFilter** 1.4 *(Continued)*

---

| *Parameters:* | bypass | An object that allows you to execute edit commands that bypass the filter |
| | offset | The offset at which to insert the text |
| | text | The characters to insert |
| | attrib | The formatting attributes of the inserted text |

- void replace(DocumentFilter.FilterBypass bypass, int offset, int length, String text, AttributeSet attrib)

  is invoked before a part of a document is replaced with a new string. You can override the method and modify the string. You can disable replacement by not calling super.replace or by calling bypass methods to modify the document without filtering.

| *Parameters:* | bypass | An object that allows you to execute edit commands that bypass the filter |
| | offset | The offset at which to insert the text |
| | length | The length of the part to be replaced |
| | text | The characters to insert |
| | attrib | The formatting attributes of the inserted text |

- void remove(DocumentFilter.FilterBypass bypass, int offset, int length)

  is invoked before a part of a document is removed. Get the document by calling bypass.getDocument() if you need to analyze the effect of the removal.

| *Parameters:* | bypass | An object that allows you to execute edit commands that bypass the filter |
| | offset | The offset of the part to be removed |
| | length | The length of the part to be removed |

---

**javax.swing.text.MaskFormatter** 1.4

---

- MaskFormatter(String mask)

  constructs a mask formatter with the given mask. See Table 6.3 on p. 474 for the symbols in a mask.

- String getValidCharacters()
- void setValidCharacters(String characters)

  gets or sets the valid editing characters. Only the characters in the given string are accepted for the variable parts of the mask.

*(Continues)*

---

**javax.swing.text.MaskFormatter**  1.4  *(Continued)*

- String getInvalidCharacters()
- void setInvalidCharacters(String characters)

  gets or sets the invalid editing characters. None of the characters in the given string are accepted as input.

- char getPlaceholderCharacter()
- void setPlaceholderCharacter(char ch)

  gets or sets the placeholder character used for the mask's variable characters that the user has not yet supplied. The default placeholder character is a space.

- String getPlaceholder()
- void setPlaceholder(String s)

  gets or sets the placeholder string. Its tail end is used if the user has not supplied all variable characters in the mask. If it is null or shorter than the mask, the placeholder character fills remaining inputs.

- boolean getValueContainsLiteralCharacters()
- void setValueContainsLiteralCharacters(boolean b)

  gets or sets the "value contains literal characters" flag. If this flag is true, the field value contains the literal (nonvariable) parts of the mask. If it is false, the literal characters are removed. The default is true.

---

## 6.4.3 The JSpinner Component

A JSpinner is a component that contains a text field and two small buttons on the side. When the buttons are clicked, the text field value is incremented or decremented (see Figure 6.38).

The values in the spinner can be numbers, dates, values from a list, or, in the most general case, any sequence of values for which predecessors and successors can be determined. The JSpinner class defines standard data models for the first three cases. You can define your own data model to describe arbitrary sequences.

By default, a spinner manages an integer, and the buttons increment or decrement it by 1. You can get the current value by calling the getValue method. That method returns an Object. Cast it to an Integer and retrieve the wrapped value.

```
JSpinner defaultSpinner = new JSpinner();
. . .
int value = (Integer) defaultSpinner.getValue();
```

You can change the increment to a value other than 1, and you can supply the lower and upper bounds. Here is a spinner with the starting value of 5 and the increment of 0.5, bounded between 0 and 10:

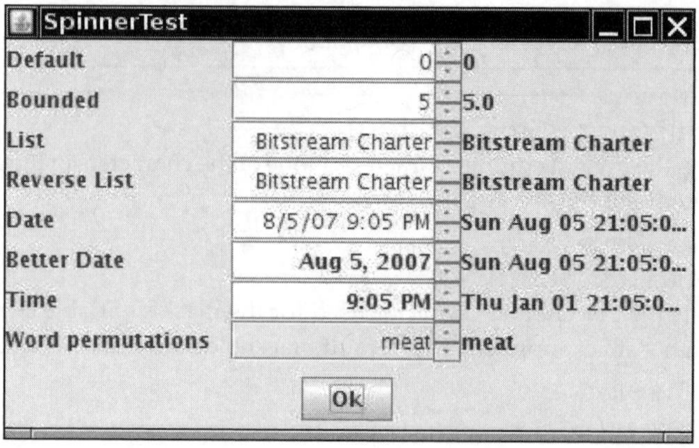

**Figure 6.38** Several variations of the JSpinner component

```
JSpinner boundedSpinner = new JSpinner(new SpinnerNumberModel(5, 0, 10, 0.5));
```

There are two `SpinnerNumberModel` constructors, one with only `int` parameters and one with `double` parameters. If any of the parameters is a floating-point number, the second constructor is used. It sets the spinner value to a `Double` object.

Spinners aren't restricted to numeric values. You can have a spinner iterate through any collection of values. Simply pass a `SpinnerListModel` to the `JSpinner` constructor. You can construct a `SpinnerListModel` from an array or a class implementing the `List` interface (such as an `ArrayList`). In our sample program, we display a spinner control with all available font names.

```
String[] fonts = GraphicsEnvironment.getLocalGraphicsEnvironment().getAvailableFontFamilyNames();
JSpinner listSpinner = new JSpinner(new SpinnerListModel(fonts));
```

However, we found that the direction of the iteration was mildly confusing because it is opposite to that of a combo box. In a combo box, higher values are *below* lower values, so you would expect the downward arrow to navigate toward higher values. But the spinner increments the array index so that the upward arrow yields higher values. There is no provision for reversing the traversal order in the `SpinnerListModel`, but an impromptu anonymous subclass yields the desired result:

```
JSpinner reverseListSpinner = new JSpinner(
    new SpinnerListModel(fonts)
    {
        public Object getNextValue()
        {
            return super.getPreviousValue();
        }
    }
```

```
    public Object getPreviousValue()
    {
        return super.getNextValue();
    }
});
```

Try both versions and see which you find more intuitive.

Another good use for a spinner is for a date that the user can increment or decrement. You can get such a spinner, initialized with today's date, with the call

```
JSpinner dateSpinner = new JSpinner(new SpinnerDateModel());
```

However, if you look carefully at Figure 6.38, you will see that the spinner text shows both date and time, such as

```
8/05/07 9:05 PM
```

The time doesn't make any sense for a date picker. It turns out to be somewhat difficult to make the spinner show just the date. Here is the magic incantation:

```
JSpinner betterDateSpinner = new JSpinner(new SpinnerDateModel());
String pattern = ((SimpleDateFormat) DateFormat.getDateInstance()).toPattern();
betterDateSpinner.setEditor(new JSpinner.DateEditor(betterDateSpinner, pattern));
```

Using the same approach, you can also make a time picker.

```
JSpinner timeSpinner = new JSpinner(new SpinnerDateModel());
pattern = ((SimpleDateFormat) DateFormat.getTimeInstance(DateFormat.SHORT)).toPattern();
timeSpinner.setEditor(new JSpinner.DateEditor(timeSpinner, pattern));
```

You can display arbitrary sequences in a spinner by defining your own spinner model. In our sample program, we have a spinner that iterates through all permutations of the string "meat". You can get to "mate", "meta", "team", and the rest of the total of 24 permutations by clicking the spinner buttons.

When you define your own model, you should extend the AbstractSpinnerModel class and define the following four methods:

```
Object getValue()
void setValue(Object value)
Object getNextValue()
Object getPreviousValue()
```

The getValue method returns the value stored by the model. The setValue method sets a new value. It should throw an IllegalArgumentException if the new value is not appropriate.

---

 **CAUTION:** The setValue method must call the fireStateChanged method after setting the new value. Otherwise, the spinner field won't be updated.

The getNextValue and getPreviousValue methods return the values that should come after or before the current value, or null if the end of the traversal has been reached.

 **CAUTION:** The getNextValue and getPreviousValue methods should *not* change the current value. When a user clicks on the upward arrow of the spinner, the getNextValue method is called. If the return value is not null, it is set by a call to setValue.

In the sample program, we use a standard algorithm to determine the next and previous permutations (see Listing 6.24). The details of the algorithm are not important.

Listing 6.23 shows how to generate the various spinner types. Click the OK button to see the spinner values.

**Listing 6.23** spinner/SpinnerFrame.java

```
1  package spinner;
2
3  import java.awt.*;
4  import java.awt.event.*;
5  import java.text.*;
6  import javax.swing.*;
7
8  /**
9   * A frame with a panel that contains several spinners and a button that displays the spinner
10  * values.
11  */
12  public class SpinnerFrame extends JFrame
13  {
14     private JPanel mainPanel;
15     private JButton okButton;
16
17     public SpinnerFrame()
18     {
19        JPanel buttonPanel = new JPanel();
20        okButton = new JButton("Ok");
21        buttonPanel.add(okButton);
22        add(buttonPanel, BorderLayout.SOUTH);
23
24        mainPanel = new JPanel();
25        mainPanel.setLayout(new GridLayout(0, 3));
26        add(mainPanel, BorderLayout.CENTER);
```

```
27      JSpinner defaultSpinner = new JSpinner();
28      addRow("Default", defaultSpinner);
29
30      JSpinner boundedSpinner = new JSpinner(new SpinnerNumberModel(5, 0, 10, 0.5));
31      addRow("Bounded", boundedSpinner);
32
33      String[] fonts = GraphicsEnvironment.getLocalGraphicsEnvironment()
34          .getAvailableFontFamilyNames();
35
36      JSpinner listSpinner = new JSpinner(new SpinnerListModel(fonts));
37      addRow("List", listSpinner);
38
39      JSpinner reverseListSpinner = new JSpinner(new SpinnerListModel(fonts)
40          {
41              public Object getNextValue() { return super.getPreviousValue(); }
42              public Object getPreviousValue() { return super.getNextValue(); }
43          });
44      addRow("Reverse List", reverseListSpinner);
45
46      JSpinner dateSpinner = new JSpinner(new SpinnerDateModel());
47      addRow("Date", dateSpinner);
48
49      JSpinner betterDateSpinner = new JSpinner(new SpinnerDateModel());
50      String pattern = ((SimpleDateFormat) DateFormat.getDateInstance()).toPattern();
51      betterDateSpinner.setEditor(new JSpinner.DateEditor(betterDateSpinner, pattern));
52      addRow("Better Date", betterDateSpinner);
53
54      JSpinner timeSpinner = new JSpinner(new SpinnerDateModel());
55      pattern = ((SimpleDateFormat) DateFormat.getTimeInstance(DateFormat.SHORT)).toPattern();
56      timeSpinner.setEditor(new JSpinner.DateEditor(timeSpinner, pattern));
57      addRow("Time", timeSpinner);
58
59      JSpinner permSpinner = new JSpinner(new PermutationSpinnerModel("meat"));
60      addRow("Word permutations", permSpinner);
61      pack();
62   }
63
64   /**
65    * Adds a row to the main panel.
66    * @param labelText the label of the spinner
67    * @param spinner the sample spinner
68    */
69   public void addRow(String labelText, final JSpinner spinner)
70   {
71      mainPanel.add(new JLabel(labelText));
72      mainPanel.add(spinner);
73      final JLabel valueLabel = new JLabel();
74      mainPanel.add(valueLabel);
```

*(Continues)*

**Listing 6.23** *(Continued)*

```
75      okButton.addActionListener(new ActionListener()
76         {
77            public void actionPerformed(ActionEvent event)
78            {
79               Object value = spinner.getValue();
80               valueLabel.setText(value.toString());
81            }
82         });
83   }
84 }
```

**Listing 6.24** `spinner/PermutationSpinnerModel.java`

```
1  package spinner;
2
3  import javax.swing.*;
4
5  /**
6   * A model that dynamically generates word permutations.
7   */
8  public class PermutationSpinnerModel extends AbstractSpinnerModel
9  {
10    private String word;
11
12    /**
13     * Constructs the model.
14     * @param w the word to permute
15     */
16    public PermutationSpinnerModel(String w)
17    {
18       word = w;
19    }
20
21    public Object getValue()
22    {
23       return word;
24    }
25
26    public void setValue(Object value)
27    {
28       if (!(value instanceof String)) throw new IllegalArgumentException();
29       word = (String) value;
30       fireStateChanged();
31    }
32
33    public Object getNextValue()
34    {
```

```
35      int[] codePoints = toCodePointArray(word);
36
37      for (int i = codePoints.length - 1; i > 0; i--)
38      {
39         if (codePoints[i - 1] < codePoints[i])
40         {
41            int j = codePoints.length - 1;
42            while (codePoints[i - 1] > codePoints[j])
43               j--;
44            swap(codePoints, i - 1, j);
45            reverse(codePoints, i, codePoints.length - 1);
46            return new String(codePoints, 0, codePoints.length);
47         }
48      }
49      reverse(codePoints, 0, codePoints.length - 1);
50      return new String(codePoints, 0, codePoints.length);
51   }
52
53   public Object getPreviousValue()
54   {
55      int[] codePoints = toCodePointArray(word);
56      for (int i = codePoints.length - 1; i > 0; i--)
57      {
58         if (codePoints[i - 1] > codePoints[i])
59         {
60            int j = codePoints.length - 1;
61            while (codePoints[i - 1] < codePoints[j])
62               j--;
63            swap(codePoints, i - 1, j);
64            reverse(codePoints, i, codePoints.length - 1);
65            return new String(codePoints, 0, codePoints.length);
66         }
67      }
68      reverse(codePoints, 0, codePoints.length - 1);
69      return new String(codePoints, 0, codePoints.length);
70   }
71
72   private static int[] toCodePointArray(String str)
73   {
74      int[] codePoints = new int[str.codePointCount(0, str.length())];
75      for (int i = 0, j = 0; i < str.length(); i++, j++)
76      {
77         int cp = str.codePointAt(i);
78         if (Character.isSupplementaryCodePoint(cp)) i++;
79         codePoints[j] = cp;
80      }
81      return codePoints;
82   }
```

*(Continues)*

**Listing 6.24** *(Continued)*

```
83    private static void swap(int[] a, int i, int j)
84    {
85       int temp = a[i];
86       a[i] = a[j];
87       a[j] = temp;
88    }
89
90    private static void reverse(int[] a, int i, int j)
91    {
92       while (i < j)
93       {
94          swap(a, i, j);
95          i++;
96          j--;
97       }
98    }
99 }
```

---

**javax.swing.JSpinner**  1.4

- JSpinner()
  constructs a spinner that edits an integer with starting value 0, increment 1, and no bounds.

- JSpinner(SpinnerModel model)
  constructs a spinner that uses the given data model.

- Object getValue()
  gets the current value of the spinner.

- void setValue(Object value)
  attempts to set the value of the spinner. Throws an IllegalArgumentException if the model does not accept the value.

- void setEditor(JComponent editor)
  sets the component used for editing the spinner value.

---

**javax.swing.SpinnerNumberModel**  1.4

- SpinnerNumberModel(int initval, int minimum, int maximum, int stepSize)
- SpinnerNumberModel(double initval, double minimum, double maximum, double stepSize)
  these constructors yield number models that manage an Integer or Double value. Use the MIN_VALUE and MAX_VALUE constants of the Integer and Double classes for unbounded values.

*(Continues)*

---

**javax.swing.SpinnerNumberModel** **1.4** *(Continued)*

| *Parameters:* | initval | The initial value |
|---|---|---|
| | minimum | The minimum valid value |
| | maximum | The maximum valid value |
| | stepSize | The increment or decrement of each spin |

---

**javax.swing.SpinnerListModel** **1.4**

- SpinnerListModel(Object[] values)
- SpinnerListModel(List values)
  these constructors yield models that select a value from among the given values.

---

**javax.swing.SpinnerDateModel** **1.4**

- SpinnerDateModel()
  constructs a date model with today's date as the initial value, no lower or upper bounds, and an increment of Calendar.DAY_OF_MONTH.
- SpinnerDateModel(Date initval, Comparable minimum, Comparable maximum, int step)

| *Parameters:* | initval | The initial value |
|---|---|---|
| | minimum | The minimum valid value, or null if no lower bound is desired |
| | maximum | The maximum valid value, or null if no upper bound is desired |
| | step | The date value to increment or decrement on each spin. One of the constants ERA, YEAR, MONTH, WEEK_OF_YEAR, WEEK_OF_MONTH, DAY_OF_MONTH, DAY_OF_YEAR, DAY_OF_WEEK, DAY_OF_WEEK_IN_MONTH, AM_PM, HOUR, HOUR_OF_DAY, MINUTE, SECOND, or MILLISECOND of the Calendar class. |

---

**java.text.SimpleDateFormat** **1.1**

- String toPattern() **1.2**
  gets the editing pattern for this date formatter. A typical pattern is "yyyy-MM-dd". See the Java SE documentation for more details about the pattern.

---

**javax.swing.JSpinner.DateEditor** 1.4

- DateEditor(JSpinner spinner, String pattern)
  constructs a date editor for a spinner.

  *Parameters:*  spinner  The spinner to which this editor belongs

  pattern  The format pattern for the associated SimpleDateFormat

---

**javax.swing.AbstractSpinnerModel** 1.4

- Object getValue()
  gets the current value of the model.

- void setValue(Object value)
  attempts to set a new value for the model. Throws an IllegalArgumentException if the value is not acceptable. When overriding this method, you should call fireStateChanged after setting the new value.

- Object getNextValue()
- Object getPreviousValue()
  computes (but does not set) the next or previous value in the sequence that this model defines.

## 6.4.4 Displaying HTML with the JEditorPane

Unlike the text components discussed up to this point, the JEditorPane can display and edit styled text, in particular HTML and RTF. (RTF is the "Rich Text Format" used by a number of Microsoft applications for document interchange. It is a poorly documented format that doesn't work well even between Microsoft's own applications. We do not cover RTF capabilities in this book.)

Frankly, the JEditorPane is not as functional as one would like it to be. The HTML renderer can display simple files, but it chokes at many complex pages that you typically find on the Web. The HTML editor is limited and unstable.

A plausible application for the JEditorPane is to display program help in HTML format. By having control over the help files you provide, you can stay away from features that the JEditorPane does not display well.

---

 **NOTE:** For more information on an industrial-strength help system, check out JavaHelp at http://javahelp.java.net.

---

The program in Listing 6.25 contains an editor pane that shows the contents of an HTML page. Type a URL into the text field. The URL must start with http: or file:. Then, click the Load button. The selected HTML page is displayed in the editor pane (see Figure 6.39).

The hyperlinks are active: If you click a link, the application loads it. The Back button returns to the previous page.

This program is in fact a very simple browser. Of course, it does not have any of the comfort features, such as page caching or bookmark lists, that you would expect from a commercial browser. The editor pane does not even display applets!

If you click the Editable checkbox, the editor pane becomes editable. You can type in text and use the Backspace key to delete text. The component also understands the Ctrl+X, Ctrl+C, and Ctrl+V shortcuts for cut, copy, and paste. However, you would have to do quite a bit of programming to add support for fonts and formatting.

When the component is editable, hyperlinks are not active. Also, with some web pages you can see JavaScript commands, comments, and other tags when edit

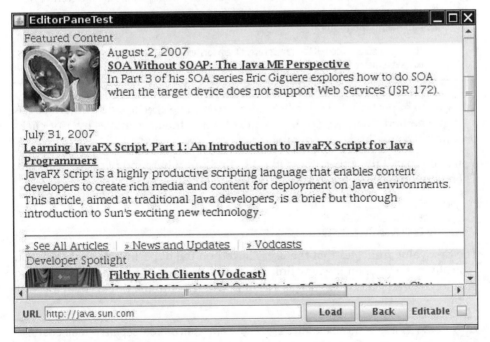

**Figure 6.39** The editor pane displaying an HTML page

mode is turned on (see Figure 6.40). The example program lets you investigate the editing feature, but we recommend that you omit it in your programs.

 **TIP:** By default, the JEditorPane is in edit mode. You should call editorPane. setEditable(false) to turn it off.

The features of the editor pane that you saw in the example program are easy to use. Use the setPage method to load a new document. For example,

```
JEditorPane editorPane = new JEditorPane();
editorPane.setPage(url);
```

The parameter is either a string or a URL object. The JEditorPane class extends the JTextComponent class. Therefore, you can call the setText method as well—it simply displays plain text.

 **TIP:** The API documentation is unclear about whether setPage loads the new document in a separate thread (which is generally what you want—the JEditorPane is no speed demon). However, you can force loading in a separate thread with the following incantation:

```
AbstractDocument doc = (AbstractDocument) editorPane.getDocument();
doc.setAsynchronousLoadPriority(0);
```

To listen to hyperlink clicks, add a HyperlinkListener. The HyperlinkListener interface has a single method, hyperlinkUpdate, that is called when the user moves over or clicks on a link. The method has a parameter of type HyperlinkEvent.

You need to call the getEventType method to find out what kind of event occurred. There are three possible return values:

```
HyperlinkEvent.EventType.ACTIVATED
HyperlinkEvent.EventType.ENTERED
HyperlinkEvent.EventType.EXITED
```

The first value indicates that the user clicked on the hyperlink. In that case, you typically want to open the new link. You can use the second and third values to give some visual feedback, such as a tooltip, when the mouse hovers over the link.

 **NOTE:** It is a complete mystery why there aren't three separate methods to handle activation, entry, and exit in the HyperlinkListener interface.

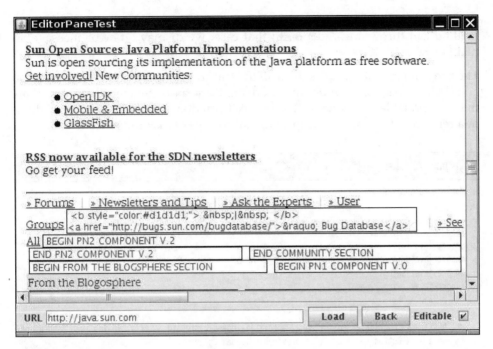

**Figure 6.40** The editor pane in edit mode

The getURL method of the HyperlinkEvent class returns the URL of the hyperlink. For example, here is how you can install a hyperlink listener that follows the links that a user activates:

```
editorPane.addHyperlinkListener(new
   HyperlinkListener()
   {
      public void hyperlinkUpdate(HyperlinkEvent event)
      {
         if (event.getEventType() == HyperlinkEvent.EventType.ACTIVATED)
         {
            try
            {
               editorPane.setPage(event.getURL());
            }
            catch (IOException e)
            {
               editorPane.setText("Exception: " + e);
            }
         }
      }
   });
```

The event handler simply gets the URL and updates the editor pane. The setPage method can throw an IOException. In that case, we display an error message as plain text.

The program in Listing 6.25 shows all the features that you need to put together an HTML help system. Under the hood, the JEditorPane is even more complex than the tree and table components. However, if you don't need to write a text editor or a renderer of a custom text format, that complexity is hidden from you.

**Listing 6.25** editorPane/EditorPaneFrame.java

```java
1  package editorPane;
2
3  import java.awt.*;
4  import java.awt.event.*;
5  import java.io.*;
6  import java.util.*;
7  import javax.swing.*;
8  import javax.swing.event.*;
9
10 /**
11  * This frame contains an editor pane, a text field and button to enter a URL and load a document,
12  * and a Back button to return to a previously loaded document.
13  */
14 public class EditorPaneFrame extends JFrame
15 {
16    private static final int DEFAULT_WIDTH = 600;
17    private static final int DEFAULT_HEIGHT = 400;
18
19    public EditorPaneFrame()
20    {
21       setSize(DEFAULT_WIDTH, DEFAULT_HEIGHT);
22
23       final Stack<String> urlStack = new Stack<>();
24       final JEditorPane editorPane = new JEditorPane();
25       final JTextField url = new JTextField(30);
26
27       // set up hyperlink listener
28
29       editorPane.setEditable(false);
30       editorPane.addHyperlinkListener(new HyperlinkListener()
31          {
32             public void hyperlinkUpdate(HyperlinkEvent event)
33             {
34                if (event.getEventType() == HyperlinkEvent.EventType.ACTIVATED)
35                {
36                   try
37                   {
38                      // remember URL for back button
```

```
39              urlStack.push(event.getURL().toString());
40              // show URL in text field
41              url.setText(event.getURL().toString());
42              editorPane.setPage(event.getURL());
43           }
44           catch (IOException e)
45           {
46              editorPane.setText("Exception: " + e);
47           }
48        }
49     }
50   });
51
52   // set up checkbox for toggling edit mode
53
54   final JCheckBox editable = new JCheckBox();
55   editable.addActionListener(new ActionListener()
56      {
57         public void actionPerformed(ActionEvent event)
58         {
59            editorPane.setEditable(editable.isSelected());
60         }
61      });
62
63   // set up load button for loading URL
64
65   ActionListener listener = new ActionListener()
66      {
67         public void actionPerformed(ActionEvent event)
68         {
69            try
70            {
71               // remember URL for back button
72               urlStack.push(url.getText());
73               editorPane.setPage(url.getText());
74            }
75            catch (IOException e)
76            {
77               editorPane.setText("Exception: " + e);
78            }
79         }
80      };
81
82   JButton loadButton = new JButton("Load");
83   loadButton.addActionListener(listener);
84   url.addActionListener(listener);
85
86   // set up back button and button action
```

*(Continues)*

**Listing 6.25**  *(Continued)*

```
87         JButton backButton = new JButton("Back");
88         backButton.addActionListener(new ActionListener()
89            {
90                public void actionPerformed(ActionEvent event)
91                {
92                   if (urlStack.size() <= 1) return;
93                   try
94                   {
95                      // get URL from back button
96                      urlStack.pop();
97                      // show URL in text field
98                      String urlString = urlStack.peek();
99                      url.setText(urlString);
100                     editorPane.setPage(urlString);
101                  }
102                  catch (IOException e)
103                  {
104                     editorPane.setText("Exception: " + e);
105                  }
106               }
107           });
108
109        add(new JScrollPane(editorPane), BorderLayout.CENTER);
110
111        // put all control components in a panel
112
113        JPanel panel = new JPanel();
114        panel.add(new JLabel("URL"));
115        panel.add(url);
116        panel.add(loadButton);
117        panel.add(backButton);
118        panel.add(new JLabel("Editable"));
119        panel.add(editable);
120
121        add(panel, BorderLayout.SOUTH);
122     }
123  }
```

---

**javax.swing.JEditorPane** 1.2

- void setPage(URL url)

  loads the page from url into the editor pane.

- void addHyperlinkListener(HyperLinkListener listener)

  adds a hyperlink listener to this editor pane.

---

*javax.swing.event.HyperlinkListener* 1.2

- void hyperlinkUpdate(HyperlinkEvent event)
  is called whenever a hyperlink was selected.

---

*javax.swing.event.HyperlinkEvent* 1.2

- URL getURL()
  returns the URL of the selected hyperlink.

---

# 6.5 Progress Indicators

In the following sections, we discuss three classes for indicating the progress of a slow activity. A JProgressBar is a Swing component that indicates progress. A ProgressMonitor is a dialog box that contains a progress bar. A ProgressMonitorInputStream displays a progress monitor dialog box while the stream is read.

## 6.5.1 Progress Bars

A *progress bar* is a simple component—just a rectangle that is partially filled with color to indicate the progress of an operation. By default, progress is indicated by a string "*n%*". You can see a progress bar in the bottom right of Figure 6.41.

You can construct a progress bar much as you construct a slider—by supplying the minimum and maximum value and an optional orientation:

```
progressBar = new JProgressBar(0, 1000);
progressBar = new JProgressBar(SwingConstants.VERTICAL, 0, 1000);
```

**Figure 6.41** A progress bar

You can also set the minimum and maximum with the setMinimum and setMaximum methods.

Unlike a slider, the progress bar cannot be adjusted by the user. Your program needs to call setValue to update it.

If you call

```
progressBar.setStringPainted(true);
```

the progress bar computes the completion percentage and displays a string "$n\%$". If you want to show a different string, you can supply it with the setString method:

```
if (progressBar.getValue() > 900)
    progressBar.setString("Almost Done");
```

The program in Listing 6.26 shows a progress bar that monitors a simulated time-consuming activity.

The SimulatedActivity class increments a value current ten times per second. When it reaches a target value, the activity finishes. We use the SwingWorker class to implement the activity and update the progress bar in the process method. The SwingWorker invokes the method from the event dispatch thread, so that it is safe to update the progress bar. (See Volume I, Chapter 14 for more information about thread safety in Swing.)

Java SE 1.4 added support for an *indeterminate* progress bar that shows an animation indicating some kind of progress, without specifying the percentage of completion. That is the kind of progress bar that you see in your browser—it indicates that the browser is waiting for the server and has no idea how long the wait might be. To display the "indeterminate wait" animation, call the setIndeterminate method.

Listing 6.26 shows the full program code.

**Listing 6.26** progressBar/ProgressBarFrame.java

```
1  package progressBar;
2
3  import java.awt.*;
4  import java.awt.event.*;
5  import java.util.List;
6  import javax.swing.*;
7
8  /**
9   * A frame that contains a button to launch a simulated activity, a progress bar, and a text area
10  * for the activity output.
11  */
```

```
12  public class ProgressBarFrame extends JFrame
13  {
14     public static final int TEXT_ROWS = 10;
15     public static final int TEXT_COLUMNS = 40;
16
17     private JButton startButton;
18     private JProgressBar progressBar;
19     private JCheckBox checkBox;
20     private JTextArea textArea;
21     private SimulatedActivity activity;
22
23     public ProgressBarFrame()
24     {
25        // this text area holds the activity output
26
27        textArea = new JTextArea(TEXT_ROWS, TEXT_COLUMNS);
28
29        // set up panel with button and progress bar
30
31        final int MAX = 1000;
32        JPanel panel = new JPanel();
33        startButton = new JButton("Start");
34        progressBar = new JProgressBar(0, MAX);
35        progressBar.setStringPainted(true);
36        panel.add(startButton);
37        panel.add(progressBar);
38
39        checkBox = new JCheckBox("indeterminate");
40        checkBox.addActionListener(new ActionListener()
41           {
42              public void actionPerformed(ActionEvent event)
43              {
44                 progressBar.setIndeterminate(checkBox.isSelected());
45                 progressBar.setStringPainted(!progressBar.isIndeterminate());
46              }
47           });
48        panel.add(checkBox);
49        add(new JScrollPane(textArea), BorderLayout.CENTER);
50        add(panel, BorderLayout.SOUTH);
51
52        // set up the button action
53
54        startButton.addActionListener(new ActionListener()
55           {
56              public void actionPerformed(ActionEvent event)
57              {
58                 startButton.setEnabled(false);
59                 activity = new SimulatedActivity(MAX);
```

*(Continues)*

**Listing 6.26** *(Continued)*

```
60              activity.execute();
61          }
62      });
63      pack();
64  }
65
66  class SimulatedActivity extends SwingWorker<Void, Integer>
67  {
68      private int current;
69      private int target;
70
71      /**
72       * Constructs the simulated activity that increments a counter from 0 to a
73       * given target.
74       * @param t the target value of the counter.
75       */
76      public SimulatedActivity(int t)
77      {
78          current = 0;
79          target = t;
80      }
81
82      protected Void doInBackground() throws Exception
83      {
84          try
85          {
86              while (current < target)
87              {
88                  Thread.sleep(100);
89                  current++;
90                  publish(current);
91              }
92          }
93          catch (InterruptedException e)
94          {
95          }
96          return null;
97      }
98
99      protected void process(List<Integer> chunks)
100     {
101         for (Integer chunk : chunks)
102         {
103             textArea.append(chunk + "\n");
104             progressBar.setValue(chunk);
105         }
106     }
```

```
107        protected void done()
108        {
109            startButton.setEnabled(true);
110        }
111    }
112 }
```

## 6.5.2 Progress Monitors

A progress bar is a simple component that can be placed inside a window. In contrast, a ProgressMonitor is a complete dialog box that contains a progress bar (see Figure 6.42). The dialog box contains a Cancel button. If you click it, the monitor dialog box is closed. In addition, your program can query whether the user has canceled the dialog box and terminate the monitored action. (Note that the class name does not start with a "J".)

Construct a progress monitor by supplying the following:

- The parent component over which the dialog box should pop up
- An object (which should be a string, icon, or component) that is displayed in the dialog box
- An optional note to display below the object
- The minimum and maximum values

However, the progress monitor cannot measure progress or cancel an activity by itself. You still need to periodically set the progress value by calling the setProgress method. (This is the equivalent of the setValue method of the JProgressBar class.) When the monitored activity has concluded, call the close method to dismiss the dialog box. You can reuse the same dialog box by calling start again.

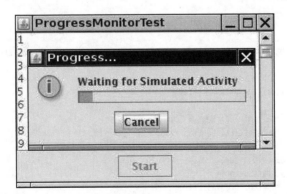

**Figure 6.42** A progress monitor dialog box

The biggest problem with using a progress monitor dialog box is handling the cancellation requests. You cannot attach an event handler to the Cancel button. Instead, you need to periodically call the isCanceled method to see if the user has clicked the Cancel button.

If your worker thread can block indefinitely (for example, when reading input from a network connection), it cannot monitor the Cancel button. In our sample program, we will show you how to use a timer for that purpose. We will also make the timer responsible for updating the progress measurement.

If you run the program in Listing 6.27, you can observe an interesting feature of the progress monitor dialog box. The dialog box doesn't come up immediately. Instead, it waits for a short interval to see if the activity has already been completed or is likely to complete in less time than it would take for the dialog box to appear.

Use the setMillisToDecideToPopup method to set the number of milliseconds to wait between the construction of the dialog object and the decision whether to show the pop-up at all. The default value is 500 milliseconds. The setMillisToPopup is your estimation of the time the dialog box needs to pop up. The Swing designers set this value to a default of 2 seconds. Clearly they were mindful of the fact that Swing dialogs don't always come up as snappily as we all would like. You should probably not touch this value.

**Listing 6.27** progressMonitor/ProgressMonitorFrame.java

```
 1  package progressMonitor;
 2
 3  import java.awt.*;
 4  import java.awt.event.*;
 5  import javax.swing.*;
 6
 7  /**
 8   * A frame that contains a button to launch a simulated activity and a text area for the activity
 9   * output.
10   */
11  class ProgressMonitorFrame extends JFrame
12  {
13     public static final int TEXT_ROWS = 10;
14     public static final int TEXT_COLUMNS = 40;
15
16     private Timer cancelMonitor;
17     private JButton startButton;
18     private ProgressMonitor progressDialog;
19     private JTextArea textArea;
20     private SimulatedActivity activity;
```

```
21    public ProgressMonitorFrame()
22    {
23       // this text area holds the activity output
24       textArea = new JTextArea(TEXT_ROWS, TEXT_COLUMNS);
25
26       // set up a button panel
27       JPanel panel = new JPanel();
28       startButton = new JButton("Start");
29       panel.add(startButton);
30
31       add(new JScrollPane(textArea), BorderLayout.CENTER);
32       add(panel, BorderLayout.SOUTH);
33
34       // set up the button action
35
36       startButton.addActionListener(new ActionListener()
37          {
38             public void actionPerformed(ActionEvent event)
39             {
40                startButton.setEnabled(false);
41                final int MAX = 1000;
42
43                // start activity
44                activity = new SimulatedActivity(MAX);
45                activity.execute();
46
47                // launch progress dialog
48                progressDialog = new ProgressMonitor(ProgressMonitorFrame.this,
49                   "Waiting for Simulated Activity", null, 0, MAX);
50                cancelMonitor.start();
51             }
52          });
53
54       // set up the timer action
55
56       cancelMonitor = new Timer(500, new ActionListener()
57          {
58             public void actionPerformed(ActionEvent event)
59             {
60                if (progressDialog.isCanceled())
61                {
62                   activity.cancel(true);
63                   startButton.setEnabled(true);
64                }
65                else if (activity.isDone())
66                {
67                   progressDialog.close();
68                   startButton.setEnabled(true);
69                }
```

*(Continues)*

**Listing 6.27** *(Continued)*

```
70              else
71              {
72                  progressDialog.setProgress(activity.getProgress());
73              }
74          }
75      });
76      pack();
77  }
78
79  class SimulatedActivity extends SwingWorker<Void, Integer>
80  {
81      private int current;
82      private int target;
83
84      /**
85       * Constructs the simulated activity that increments a counter from 0 to a
86       * given target.
87       * @param t the target value of the counter.
88       */
89      public SimulatedActivity(int t)
90      {
91          current = 0;
92          target = t;
93      }
94
95      protected Void doInBackground() throws Exception
96      {
97          try
98          {
99              while (current < target)
100             {
101                 Thread.sleep(100);
102                 current++;
103                 textArea.append(current + "\n");
104                 setProgress(current);
105             }
106         }
107         catch (InterruptedException e)
108         {
109         }
110         return null;
111     }
112 }
113 }
```

### 6.5.3 Monitoring the Progress of Input Streams

The Swing package contains a useful stream filter, ProgressMonitorInputStream, that automatically pops up a dialog box that monitors how much of the stream has been read.

This filter is extremely easy to use. Insert a ProgressMonitorInputStream into your usual sequence of filtered streams. (See Chapter 1 for more information on streams.)

For example, suppose you read text from a file. You start out with a FileInputStream:

```
FileInputStream in = new FileInputStream(f);
```

Normally, you would convert in to an InputStreamReader:

```
InputStreamReader reader = new InputStreamReader(in);
```

However, to monitor the stream, first turn the file input stream into a stream with a progress monitor:

```
ProgressMonitorInputStream progressIn = new ProgressMonitorInputStream(parent, caption, in);
```

Supply the parent component, a caption, and, of course, the stream to monitor. The read method of the progress monitor stream simply passes along the bytes and updates the progress dialog box.

You can now go on building your filter sequence:

```
InputStreamReader reader = new InputStreamReader(progressIn);
```

That's all there is to it. When the file is read, the progress monitor automatically pops up (see Figure 6.43). This is a very nice application of stream filtering.

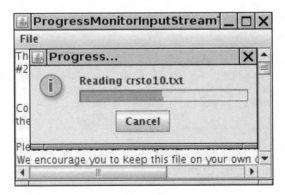

**Figure 6.43** A progress monitor for an input stream

**CAUTION:** The progress monitor stream uses the `available` method of the `InputStream` class to determine the total number of bytes in the stream. However, the `available` method only reports the number of bytes in the stream that are available *without blocking*. Progress monitors work well for files and HTTP URLs because their length is known in advance, but they don't work with all streams.

The program in Listing 6.28 counts the lines in a file. If you read in a large file (such as "The Count of Monte Cristo" in the gutenberg directory of the companion code), the progress dialog box pops up.

If the user clicks the Cancel button, the input stream closes. The code that processes the input already knows how to deal with the end of input, so no change to the programming logic is required to handle cancellation.

Note that the program doesn't use a very efficient way of filling up the text area. It would be faster to first read the file into a StringBuilder and then set the text of the text area to the string builder contents. However, in this example program, we actually like this slow approach—it gives you more time to admire the progress dialog box.

To avoid flicker, we do not display the text area while it is filling up.

**Listing 6.28** progressMonitorInputStream/TextFrame.java

```java
 1  package progressMonitorInputStream;
 2
 3  import java.awt.event.*;
 4  import java.io.*;
 5  import java.nio.file.*;
 6  import java.util.*;
 7  import javax.swing.*;
 8
 9  /**
10   * A frame with a menu to load a text file and a text area to display its contents. The text
11   * area is constructed when the file is loaded and set as the content pane of the frame when
12   * the loading is complete. That avoids flicker during loading.
13   */
14  public class TextFrame extends JFrame
15  {
16     public static final int TEXT_ROWS = 10;
17     public static final int TEXT_COLUMNS = 40;
18
19     private JMenuItem openItem;
20     private JMenuItem exitItem;
21     private JTextArea textArea;
```

```
22    private JFileChooser chooser;
23
24    public TextFrame()
25    {
26       textArea = new JTextArea(TEXT_ROWS, TEXT_COLUMNS);
27       add(new JScrollPane(textArea));
28
29       chooser = new JFileChooser();
30       chooser.setCurrentDirectory(new File("."));
31
32       JMenuBar menuBar = new JMenuBar();
33       setJMenuBar(menuBar);
34       JMenu fileMenu = new JMenu("File");
35       menuBar.add(fileMenu);
36       openItem = new JMenuItem("Open");
37       openItem.addActionListener(new ActionListener()
38          {
39             public void actionPerformed(ActionEvent event)
40             {
41                try
42                {
43                   openFile();
44                }
45                catch (IOException exception)
46                {
47                   exception.printStackTrace();
48                }
49             }
50          });
51
52       fileMenu.add(openItem);
53       exitItem = new JMenuItem("Exit");
54       exitItem.addActionListener(new ActionListener()
55          {
56             public void actionPerformed(ActionEvent event)
57             {
58                System.exit(0);
59             }
60          });
61       fileMenu.add(exitItem);
62       pack();
63    }
64
65    /**
66     * Prompts the user to select a file, loads the file into a text area, and sets it as the
67     * content pane of the frame.
68     */
69    public void openFile() throws IOException
70    {
```

*(Continues)*

**Listing 6.28** *(Continued)*

```
71      int r = chooser.showOpenDialog(this);
72      if (r != JFileChooser.APPROVE_OPTION) return;
73      final File f = chooser.getSelectedFile();
74
75      // set up stream and reader filter sequence
76
77      InputStream fileIn = Files.newInputStream(f.toPath());
78      final ProgressMonitorInputStream progressIn = new ProgressMonitorInputStream(
79         this, "Reading " + f.getName(), fileIn);
80
81      textArea.setText("");
82
83      SwingWorker<Void, Void> worker = new SwingWorker<Void, Void>()
84         {
85            protected Void doInBackground() throws Exception
86            {
87               try (Scanner in = new Scanner(progressIn))
88               {
89                  while (in.hasNextLine())
90                  {
91                     String line = in.nextLine();
92                     textArea.append(line);
93                     textArea.append("\n");
94                  }
95               }
96               return null;
97            }
98         };
99      worker.execute();
100   }
101 }
```

---

**`javax.swing.JProgressBar`** 1.2

- JProgressBar()
- JProgressBar(int direction)
- JProgressBar(int min, int max)
- JProgressBar(int direction, int min, int max)

   constructs a slider with the given direction, minimum, and maximum.

| *Parameters:* | direction | One of SwingConstants.HORIZONTAL or SwingConstants.VERTICAL. The default is horizontal. |
| | min, max | The minimum and maximum for the progress bar values. Defaults are 0 and 100. |

*(Continues)*

---

**javax.swing.JProgressBar** 1.2 *(Continued)*

- `int getMinimum()`
- `int getMaximum()`
- `void setMinimum(int value)`
- `void setMaximum(int value)`

  gets or sets the minimum and maximum values.

- `int getValue()`
- `void setValue(int value)`

  gets or sets the current value.

- `String getString()`
- `void setString(String s)`

  gets or sets the string to be displayed in the progress bar. If the string is `null`, a default string "*n*%" is displayed.

- `boolean isStringPainted()`
- `void setStringPainted(boolean b)`

  gets or sets the "string painted" property. If this property is `true`, a string is painted on top of the progress bar. The default is `false`.

- `boolean isIndeterminate()` 1.4
- `void setIndeterminate(boolean b)` 1.4

  gets or sets the "indeterminate" property. If this property is `true`, the progress bar becomes a block that moves backward and forward, indicating a wait of unknown duration. The default is `false`.

---

**javax.swing.ProgressMonitor** 1.2

- `ProgressMonitor(Component parent, Object message, String note, int min, int max)`

  constructs a progress monitor dialog box.

  | *Parameters:* | `parent` | The parent component over which this dialog box pops up |
  | | `message` | The message object to display in the dialog box |
  | | `note` | The optional string to display under the message. If this value is `null`, no space is set aside for the note, and a later call to `setNote` has no effect. |
  | | `min, max` | The minimum and maximum values of the progress bar |

*(Continues)*

---

`javax.swing.ProgressMonitor` 1.2 *(Continued)*

- `void setNote(String note)`
  changes the note text.
- `void setProgress(int value)`
  sets the progress bar value to the given value.
- `void close()`
  closes this dialog box.
- `boolean isCanceled()`
  returns `true` if the user canceled this dialog box.

---

`javax.swing.ProgressMonitorInputStream` 1.2

- `ProgressMonitorInputStream(Component parent, Object message, InputStream in)`
  constructs an input stream filter with an associated progress monitor dialog box.

  | *Parameters:* | `parent` | The parent component over which this dialog box pops up |
  | | `message` | The message object to display in the dialog box |
  | | `in` | The input stream that is being monitored |

---

## 6.6 Component Organizers and Decorators

We conclude the discussion of advanced Swing features with a presentation of components that help organize other components. These include the *split pane*, a mechanism for splitting an area into multiple parts with boundaries that can be adjusted; the *tabbed pane* which uses tab dividers to allow a user to flip through multiple panels; and the *desktop pane* that can be used to implement applications displaying multiple *internal frames*. We will close with a discussion of *layers*—decorators that can be superimposed over other components.

### 6.6.1 Split Panes

A split pane splits a component into two parts, with an adjustable boundary in between. Figure 6.44 shows a frame with two split panes. The components in the outer split pane are arranged vertically, with a text area on the bottom and another split pane on the top. That split pane's components are arranged horizontally, with a list on the left and a label containing an image on the right.

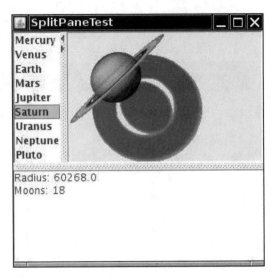

**Figure 6.44** A frame with two nested split panes

Construct a split pane by specifying the orientation—one of JSplitPane.HORIZONTAL_SPLIT or JSplitPane.VERTICAL_SPLIT, followed by the two components. For example,

```
JSplitPane innerPane = new JSplitPane(JSplitPane.HORIZONTAL_SPLIT, planetList, planetImage);
```

That's all you have to do. If you like, you can add "one-touch expand" icons to the splitter bar. You can see those icons in the top pane in Figure 6.44. In the Metal look-and-feel, they are small triangles. If you click one of them, the splitter moves all the way in the direction to which the triangle is pointing, expanding one of the panes completely.

To add this capability, call

```
innerPane.setOneTouchExpandable(true);
```

The "continuous layout" feature continuously repaints the contents of both components as the user adjusts the splitter. That looks classier, but it can be slow. You turn on that feature with the call

```
innerPane.setContinuousLayout(true);
```

In the example program, we left the bottom splitter at the default (no continuous layout). When you drag it, you only move a black outline. When you release the mouse, the components are repainted.

The straightforward program in Listing 6.29 populates a list box with planets. When the user makes a selection, the planet image is displayed to the right and a description is placed in the text area on the bottom. Run the program, adjust the splitters, and try out the one-touch expansion and continuous layout features.

**Listing 6.29** splitPane/SplitPaneFrame.java

```
1  package splitPane;
2
3  import java.awt.*;
4  import javax.swing.*;
5  import javax.swing.event.*;
6
7  /**
8   * This frame consists of two nested split panes to demonstrate planet images and data.
9   */
10 class SplitPaneFrame extends JFrame
11 {
12    private static final int DEFAULT_WIDTH = 300;
13    private static final int DEFAULT_HEIGHT = 300;
14
15    private Planet[] planets = { new Planet("Mercury", 2440, 0), new Planet("Venus", 6052, 0),
16          new Planet("Earth", 6378, 1), new Planet("Mars", 3397, 2),
17          new Planet("Jupiter", 71492, 16), new Planet("Saturn", 60268, 18),
18          new Planet("Uranus", 25559, 17), new Planet("Neptune", 24766, 8),
19          new Planet("Pluto", 1137, 1), };
20
21    public SplitPaneFrame()
22    {
23       setSize(DEFAULT_WIDTH, DEFAULT_HEIGHT);
24
25       // set up components for planet names, images, descriptions
26
27       final JList<Planet> planetList = new JList<>(planets);
28       final JLabel planetImage = new JLabel();
29       final JTextArea planetDescription = new JTextArea();
30
31       planetList.addListSelectionListener(new ListSelectionListener()
32          {
33             public void valueChanged(ListSelectionEvent event)
34             {
35                Planet value = (Planet) planetList.getSelectedValue();
36
37                // update image and description
38
39                planetImage.setIcon(value.getImage());
40                planetDescription.setText(value.getDescription());
41             }
42          });
43
44       // set up split panes
```

```
45      JSplitPane innerPane = new JSplitPane(JSplitPane.HORIZONTAL_SPLIT, planetList, planetImage);
46
47      innerPane.setContinuousLayout(true);
48      innerPane.setOneTouchExpandable(true);
49
50      JSplitPane outerPane = new JSplitPane(JSplitPane.VERTICAL_SPLIT, innerPane,
51          planetDescription);
52
53      add(outerPane, BorderLayout.CENTER);
54   }
55 }
```

---

**javax.swing.JSplitPane** 1.2

- JSplitPane()
- JSplitPane(int direction)
- JSplitPane(int direction, boolean continuousLayout)
- JSplitPane(int direction, Component first, Component second)
- JSplitPane(int direction, boolean continuousLayout, Component first, Component second)
  constructs a new split pane.

  | *Parameters:* | direction | One of HORIZONTAL_SPLIT or VERTICAL_SPLIT |
  |---|---|---|
  | | continousLayout | true if the components are continuously updated when the splitter is moved |
  | | first, second | The components to add |

- boolean isOneTouchExpandable()
- void setOneTouchExpandable(boolean b)
  gets or sets the "one-touch expandable" property. When this property is set, the splitter has two icons to completely expand one or the other component.

- boolean isContinuousLayout()
- void setContinuousLayout(boolean b)
  gets or sets the "continuous layout" property. When this property is set, then the components are continuously updated when the splitter is moved.

- void setLeftComponent(Component c)
- void setTopComponent(Component c)
  These operations have the same effect, setting c as the first component in the split pane.

- void setRightComponent(Component c)
- void setBottomComponent(Component c)
  These operations have the same effect, setting c as the second component in the split pane.

## 6.6.2 Tabbed Panes

Tabbed panes are a familiar user interface device to break up a complex dialog box into subsets of related options. You can also use tabs to let a user flip through a set of documents or images (see Figure 6.45). That is what we do in our sample program.

To create a tabbed pane, first construct a JTabbedPane object, then add tabs to it.

```
JTabbedPane tabbedPane = new JTabbedPane();
tabbedPane.addTab(title, icon, component);
```

The last parameter of the addTab method has type Component. To add multiple components into the same tab, first pack them up in a container, such as a JPanel.

The icon is optional; for example, the addTab method does not require an icon:

```
tabbedPane.addTab(title, component);
```

You can also add a tab in the middle of the tab collection with the insertTab method:

```
tabbedPane.insertTab(title, icon, component, tooltip, index);
```

To remove a tab from the tab collection, use

```
tabPane.removeTabAt(index);
```

When you add a new tab to the tab collection, it is not automatically displayed. You must select it with the setSelectedIndex method. For example, here is how you show a tab that you just added to the end:

```
tabbedPane.setSelectedIndex(tabbedPane.getTabCount() - 1);
```

If you have a lot of tabs, they can take up quite a bit of space. Starting with Java SE 1.4, you can display the tabs in scrolling mode, in which only one row of tabs is displayed, together with a set of arrow buttons that allow the user to scroll through the tab set (see Figure 6.46).

Set the tab layout to wrapped or scrolling mode by calling

```
tabbedPane.setTabLayoutPolicy(JTabbedPane.WRAP_TAB_LAYOUT);
```

or

```
tabbedPane.setTabLayoutPolicy(JTabbedPane.SCROLL_TAB_LAYOUT);
```

The tab labels can have mnemonics, just like menu items. For example,

```
int marsIndex = tabbedPane.indexOfTab("Mars");
tabbedPane.setMnemonicAt(marsIndex, KeyEvent.VK_M);
```

Now the M is underlined, and users can select the tab by pressing Alt+M.

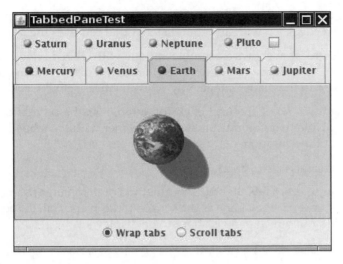

**Figure 6.45** A tabbed pane

**Figure 6.46** A tabbed pane with scrolling tabs

You can add arbitrary components into the tab titles. First, add the tab, then call

```
tabbedPane.setTabComponentAt(index, component);
```

In our sample program, we add a "close box" to the Pluto tab (because, after all, astronomers do not consider Pluto a planet). This is achieved by setting the tab component to a panel containing two components: a label with the icon and tab text, and a checkbox with an action listener that removes the tab.

The example program shows a useful technique with tabbed panes. Sometimes, you may want to update a component just before it is displayed. In our example program, we load the planet image only when the user actually clicks a tab.

To be notified whenever the user clicks on a tab, install a ChangeListener with the tabbed pane. Note that you must install the listener with the tabbed pane itself, not with any of the components.

```
tabbedPane.addChangeListener(listener);
```

When the user selects a tab, the stateChanged method of the change listener is called. You can retrieve the tabbed pane as the source of the event. Call the getSelectedIndex method to find out which pane is about to be displayed.

```
public void stateChanged(ChangeEvent event)
{
   int n = tabbedPane.getSelectedIndex();
   loadTab(n);
}
```

In Listing 6.30, we first set all tab components to null. When a new tab is selected, we test whether its component is still null. If so, we replace it with the image. (This happens instantaneously when you click on the tab. You will not see an empty pane.) Just for fun, we also change the icon from a yellow ball to a red ball to indicate which panes have been visited.

---

**Listing 6.30** tabbedPane/TabbedPaneFrame.java

```
1  package tabbedPane;
2
3  import java.awt.*;
4  import java.awt.event.*;
5  import javax.swing.*;
6  import javax.swing.event.*;
7
8  /**
9   * This frame shows a tabbed pane and radio buttons to switch between wrapped and scrolling tab
10  * layout.
11  */
12 public class TabbedPaneFrame extends JFrame
13 {
14    private static final int DEFAULT_WIDTH = 400;
15    private static final int DEFAULT_HEIGHT = 300;
16
17    private JTabbedPane tabbedPane;
```

```
18    public TabbedPaneFrame()
19    {
20       setSize(DEFAULT_WIDTH, DEFAULT_HEIGHT);
21
22       tabbedPane = new JTabbedPane();
23       // we set the components to null and delay their loading until the tab is shown
24       // for the first time
25
26       ImageIcon icon = new ImageIcon(getClass().getResource("yellow-ball.gif"));
27
28       tabbedPane.addTab("Mercury", icon, null);
29       tabbedPane.addTab("Venus", icon, null);
30       tabbedPane.addTab("Earth", icon, null);
31       tabbedPane.addTab("Mars", icon, null);
32       tabbedPane.addTab("Jupiter", icon, null);
33       tabbedPane.addTab("Saturn", icon, null);
34       tabbedPane.addTab("Uranus", icon, null);
35       tabbedPane.addTab("Neptune", icon, null);
36       tabbedPane.addTab("Pluto", null, null);
37
38       final int plutoIndex = tabbedPane.indexOfTab("Pluto");
39       JPanel plutoPanel = new JPanel();
40       plutoPanel.add(new JLabel("Pluto", icon, SwingConstants.LEADING));
41       JToggleButton plutoCheckBox = new JCheckBox();
42       plutoCheckBox.addActionListener(new ActionListener()
43       {
44          public void actionPerformed(ActionEvent e)
45          {
46             tabbedPane.remove(plutoIndex);
47          }
48       });
49       plutoPanel.add(plutoCheckBox);
50       tabbedPane.setTabComponentAt(plutoIndex, plutoPanel);
51
52       add(tabbedPane, "Center");
53
54       tabbedPane.addChangeListener(new ChangeListener()
55          {
56             public void stateChanged(ChangeEvent event)
57             {
58                // check if this tab still has a null component
59                if (tabbedPane.getSelectedComponent() == null)
60                {
61                   // set the component to the image icon
62                   int n = tabbedPane.getSelectedIndex();
63                   loadTab(n);
64                }
65             }
66          });
```

*(Continues)*

**Listing 6.30** *(Continued)*

```
67         loadTab(0);
68
69         JPanel buttonPanel = new JPanel();
70         ButtonGroup buttonGroup = new ButtonGroup();
71         JRadioButton wrapButton = new JRadioButton("Wrap tabs");
72         wrapButton.addActionListener(new ActionListener()
73            {
74               public void actionPerformed(ActionEvent event)
75               {
76                  tabbedPane.setTabLayoutPolicy(JTabbedPane.WRAP_TAB_LAYOUT);
77               }
78            });
79         buttonPanel.add(wrapButton);
80         buttonGroup.add(wrapButton);
81         wrapButton.setSelected(true);
82         JRadioButton scrollButton = new JRadioButton("Scroll tabs");
83         scrollButton.addActionListener(new ActionListener()
84            {
85               public void actionPerformed(ActionEvent event)
86               {
87                  tabbedPane.setTabLayoutPolicy(JTabbedPane.SCROLL_TAB_LAYOUT);
88               }
89            });
90         buttonPanel.add(scrollButton);
91         buttonGroup.add(scrollButton);
92         add(buttonPanel, BorderLayout.SOUTH);
93      }
94
95      /**
96       * Loads the tab with the given index.
97       * @param n the index of the tab to load
98       */
99      private void loadTab(int n)
100     {
101        String title = tabbedPane.getTitleAt(n);
102        ImageIcon planetIcon = new ImageIcon(getClass().getResource(title + ".gif"));
103        tabbedPane.setComponentAt(n, new JLabel(planetIcon));
104
105        // indicate that this tab has been visited--just for fun
106
107        tabbedPane.setIconAt(n, new ImageIcon(getClass().getResource("red-ball.gif")));
108     }
109  }
```

---

**javax.swing.JTabbedPane** 1.2

- JTabbedPane()
- JTabbedPane(int placement)
  constructs a tabbed pane.

  *Parameters:* placement One of SwingConstants.TOP, SwingConstants.LEFT, SwingConstants.RIGHT, or SwingConstants.BOTTOM

- void addTab(String title, Component c)
- void addTab(String title, Icon icon, Component c)
- void addTab(String title, Icon icon, Component c, String tooltip)
  adds a tab to the end of the tabbed pane.

- void insertTab(String title, Icon icon, Component c, String tooltip, int index)
  inserts a tab to the tabbed pane at the given index.

- void removeTabAt(int index)
  removes the tab at the given index.

- void setSelectedIndex(int index)
  selects the tab at the given index.

- int getSelectedIndex()
  returns the index of the selected tab.

- Component getSelectedComponent()
  returns the component of the selected tab.

- String getTitleAt(int index)
- void setTitleAt(int index, String title)
- Icon getIconAt(int index)
- void setIconAt(int index, Icon icon)
- Component getComponentAt(int index)
- void setComponentAt(int index, Component c)
  gets or sets the title, icon, or component at the given index.

- int indexOfTab(String title)
- int indexOfTab(Icon icon)
- int indexOfComponent(Component c)
  returns the index of the tab with the given title, icon, or component.

- int getTabCount()
  returns the total number of tabs in this tabbed pane.

- int getTabLayoutPolicy()
- void setTabLayoutPolicy(int policy) 1.4
  gets or sets the tab layout policy. policy is one of JTabbedPane.WRAP_TAB_LAYOUT or JTabbedPane.SCROLL_TAB_LAYOUT.

*(Continues)*

---

`javax.swing.JTabbedPane` `1.2` *(Continued)*

- `int getMnemonicAt(int index)` `1.4`
- `void setMnemonicAt(int index, int mnemonic)`

  gets or sets the mnemonic character at a given tab index. The character is specified as a VK_X constant from the KeyEvent class. -1 means that there is no mnemonic.

- `Component getTabComponentAt(int index)` `6`
- `void setTabComponentAt(int index, Component c)` `6`

  gets or sets the component that renders the title of the tab with the given index. If this component is null, the tab icon and title are rendered. Otherwise, only the given component is rendered in the tab.

- `int indexOfTabComponent(Component c)` `6`

  returns the index of the tab with the given title component.

- `void addChangeListener(ChangeListener listener)`

  adds a change listener that is notified when the user selects a different tab.

---

## 6.6.3 Desktop Panes and Internal Frames

Many applications present information in multiple windows that are all contained inside a large frame. If you minimize the application frame, all of its windows are hidden at the same time. In the Windows environment, this user interface is sometimes called the *multiple document interface* (MDI). Figure 6.47 shows a typical application using this interface.

For a time, this user interface style was popular, but it has become less prevalent in recent years. Nowadays, many applications simply display a separate top-level frame for each document. Which is better? MDI reduces window clutter, but having separate top-level windows means that you can use the buttons and hotkeys of the host windowing system to flip through your windows.

In the world of Java, where you can't rely on a rich host windowing system, it makes a lot of sense to have your application manage its frames.

Figure 6.48 shows a Java application with three internal frames. Two of them have decorations on the borders to maximize and iconify them. The third is in its iconified state.

In the Metal look-and-feel, the internal frames have distinctive "grabber" areas that you can use to move the frames around. You can resize the windows by dragging the resize corners.

To achieve this capability, follow these steps:

1. Use a regular JFrame window for the application.

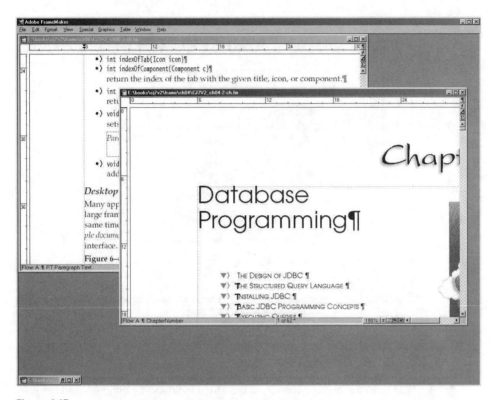

**Figure 6.47** A multiple document interface application

2. Add the `JDesktopPane` to the `JFrame`.

```
desktop = new JDesktopPane();
add(desktop, BorderLayout.CENTER);
```

3. Construct `JInternalFrame` windows. You can specify whether you want the icons for resizing or closing the frame. Normally, you want all icons.

```
JInternalFrame iframe = new JInternalFrame(title,
    true, // resizable
    true, // closable
    true, // maximizable
    true); // iconifiable
```

4. Add components to the frame.

```
iframe.add(c, BorderLayout.CENTER);
```

5. Set a frame icon. The icon is shown in the top left corner of the frame.

```
iframe.setFrameIcon(icon);
```

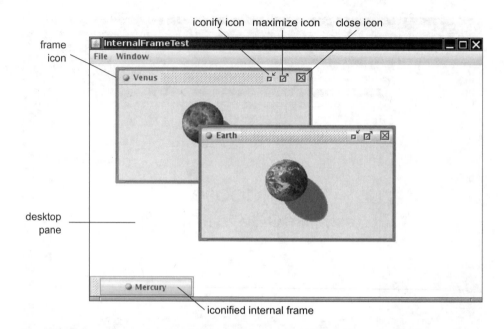

**Figure 6.48** A Java application with three internal frames

---

**NOTE:** In the current version of the Metal look-and-feel, the frame icon is not displayed in iconified frames.

---

6. Set the size of the internal frame. As with regular frames, internal frames initially have a size of 0 by 0 pixels. You don't want internal frames to be displayed on top of each other, so use a variable position for the next frame. Use the `reshape` method to set both the position and size of the frame.

   ```
   iframe.reshape(nextFrameX, nextFrameY, width, height);
   ```

7. As with `JFrame` instances, you need to make the frame visible.

   ```
   iframe.setVisible(true);
   ```

---

**NOTE:** In earlier versions of Swing, internal frames were automatically visible and this call was not necessary.

---

8. Add the frame to the `JDesktopPane`.

   ```
   desktop.add(iframe);
   ```

9. You will probably want to make the new frame the *selected frame*. Of the internal frames on the desktop, only the selected frame receives keyboard focus. In the Metal look-and-feel, the selected frame has a blue title bar, whereas the other frames have gray title bars. Use the setSelected method to select a frame. However, the "selected" property can be *vetoed*—the currently selected frame can refuse to give up focus. In that case, the setSelected method throws a PropertyVetoException that you need to handle.

```
try
{
   iframe.setSelected(true);
}
catch (PropertyVetoException ex)
{
   // attempt was vetoed
}
```

10. You will probably want to move the position of the next internal frame down so that it won't overlay the existing frame. A good distance between frames is the height of the title bar, which you can obtain as

```
int frameDistance = iframe.getHeight() - iframe.getContentPane().getHeight()
```

11. Use that distance to determine the next internal frame's position.

```
nextFrameX += frameDistance;
nextFrameY += frameDistance;
if (nextFrameX + width > desktop.getWidth())
   nextFrameX = 0;
if (nextFrameY + height > desktop.getHeight())
   nextFrameY = 0;
```

## 6.6.4 Cascading and Tiling

In Windows, there are standard commands for *cascading* and *tiling* windows (see Figures 6.49 and 6.50). The Java JDesktopPane and JInternalFrame classes have no built-in support for these operations. In Listing 6.31, we show you how you can implement these operations yourself.

To cascade all windows, reshape windows to the same size and stagger their positions. The getAllFrames method of the JDesktopPane class returns an array of all internal frames.

```
JInternalFrame[] frames = desktop.getAllFrames();
```

However, you need to pay attention to the frame state. An internal frame can be in one of three states:

• Icon

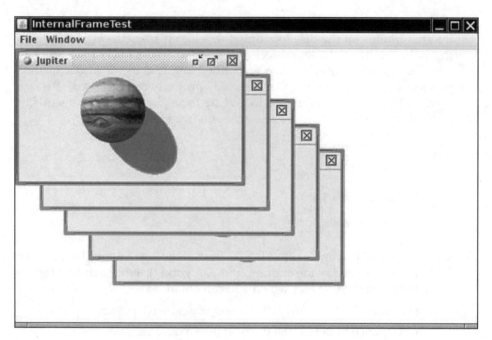

**Figure 6.49** Cascaded internal frames

- Resizable
- Maximum

Use the isIcon method to find out which internal frames are currently icons and should be skipped. However, if a frame is in the maximum state, you first need to set it to be resizable by calling setMaximum(false). This is another property that can be vetoed, so you must catch the PropertyVetoException.

The following loop cascades all internal frames on the desktop:

```
for (JInternalFrame frame : desktop.getAllFrames())
{
   if (!frame.isIcon())
   {
      try
      {
         // try to make maximized frames resizable; this might be vetoed
         frame.setMaximum(false);
         frame.reshape(x, y, width, height);
         x += frameDistance;
         y += frameDistance;
         // wrap around at the desktop edge
```

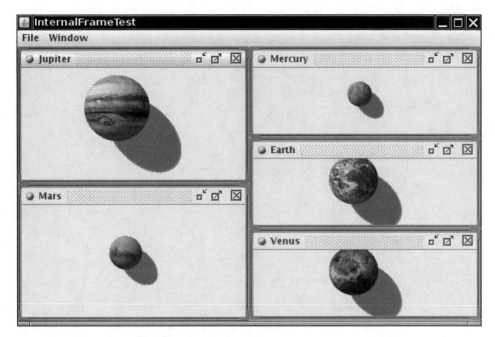

**Figure 6.50** Tiled internal frames

```
         if (x + width > desktop.getWidth()) x = 0;
         if (y + height > desktop.getHeight()) y = 0;
      }
      catch (PropertyVetoException ex)
      {}
   }
}
```

Tiling frames is trickier, particularly if the number of frames is not a perfect square. First, count the number of frames that are not icons. Compute the number of rows in the first column as

```
int rows = (int) Math.sqrt(frameCount);
```

Then the number of columns is

```
int cols = frameCount / rows;
```

The last

```
int extra = frameCount % rows;
```

columns have `rows + 1` rows.

Here is the loop for tiling all frames on the desktop:

```
int width = desktop.getWidth() / cols;
int height = desktop.getHeight() / rows;
int r = 0;
int c = 0;
for (JInternalFrame frame : desktop.getAllFrames())
{
   if (!frame.isIcon())
   {
      try
      {
         frame.setMaximum(false);
         frame.reshape(c * width, r * height, width, height);
         r++;
         if (r == rows)
         {
            r = 0;
            c++;
            if (c == cols - extra)
            {
               // start adding an extra row
               rows++;
               height = desktop.getHeight() / rows;
            }
         }
      }
      catch (PropertyVetoException ex)
      {}
   }
}
```

The example program shows another common frame operation: moving the selection from the current frame to the next frame that isn't an icon. Traverse all frames and call isSelected until you find the currently selected frame. Then, look for the next frame in the sequence that isn't an icon, and try to select it by calling

```
frames[next].setSelected(true);
```

As before, that method can throw a PropertyVetoException, in which case you have to keep looking. If you come back to the original frame, then no other frame was selectable, and you give up. Here is the complete loop:

```
JInternalFrame[] frames = desktop.getAllFrames();
for (int i = 0; i < frames.length; i++)
{
   if (frames[i].isSelected())
   {
      // find next frame that isn't an icon and can be selected
      int next = (i + 1) % frames.length;
```

```
      while (next != i)
      {
         if (!frames[next].isIcon())
         {
            try
            {
               // all other frames are icons or veto selection
               frames[next].setSelected(true);
               frames[next].toFront();
               frames[i].toBack();
               return;
            }
            catch (PropertyVetoException ex)
            {}
         }
         next = (next + 1) % frames.length;
      }
   }
}
```

## 6.6.5 Vetoing Property Settings

Now that you have seen all these veto exceptions, you might wonder how your frames can issue a veto. The JInternalFrame class uses a general *JavaBeans* mechanism for monitoring the setting of properties. We discuss this mechanism in full detail in Chapter 8. For now, we just want to show you how your frames can veto requests for property changes.

Frames don't usually want to use a veto to protest iconization or loss of focus, but it is very common for frames to check whether it is OK to *close* them. You can close a frame with the setClosed method of the JInternalFrame class. Since the method is vetoable, it calls all registered *vetoable change listeners* before proceeding to make the change. That gives each of the listeners the opportunity to throw a PropertyVetoException and thereby terminate the call to setClosed before it changed any settings.

In our example program, we put up a dialog box to ask the user whether it is OK to close the window (see Figure 6.51). If the user doesn't agree, the window stays open.

Here is how you achieve such a notification.

1.  Add a listener object to each frame. The object must belong to some class that implements the VetoableChangeListener interface. It is best to add the listener right after constructing the frame. In our example, we use the frame class

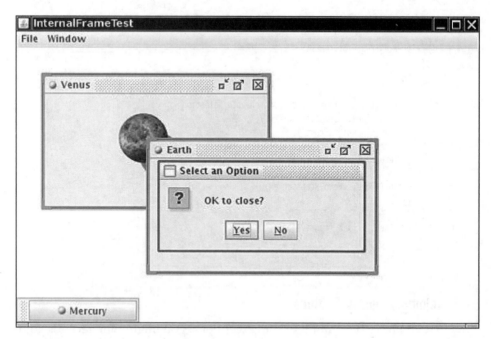

**Figure 6.51** The user can veto the close property.

that constructs the internal frames. Another option would be to use an anonymous inner class.

```
iframe.addVetoableChangeListener(listener);
```

2. Implement the vetoableChange method, the only method required by the VetoableChangeListener interface. The method receives a PropertyChangeEvent object. Use the getName method to find the name of the property that is about to be changed (such as "closed" if the method call to veto is setClosed(true). As you see in Chapter 8, you obtain the property name by removing the "set" prefix from the method name and changing the next letter to lower case.

3. Use the getNewValue method to get the proposed new value.

```
String name = event.getPropertyName();
Object value = event.getNewValue();
if.(name.equals("closed") && value.equals(true))
{
    ask user for confirmation
}
```

4. Simply throw a PropertyVetoException to block the property change. Return normally if you don't want to veto the change.

```
class DesktopFrame extends JFrame
   implements VetoableChangeListener
{
   . . .
   public void vetoableChange(PropertyChangeEvent event)
   throws PropertyVetoException
   {
      . . .
      if (not ok)
         throw new PropertyVetoException(reason, event);
      // return normally if ok
   }
}
```

### 6.6.5.1 Dialogs in Internal Frames

If you use internal frames, you should not use the JDialog class for dialog boxes. Those dialog boxes have two disadvantages:

- They are heavyweight because they create a new frame in the windowing system.
- The windowing system does not know how to position them relative to the internal frame that spawned them.

Instead, for simple dialog boxes, use the showInternal*Xxx*Dialog methods of the JOptionPane class. They work exactly like the show*Xxx*Dialog methods, except they position a lightweight window over an internal frame.

As for more complex dialog boxes, construct them with a JInternalFrame. Unfortunately, you then have no built-in support for modal dialog boxes.

In our sample program, we use an internal dialog box to ask the user whether it is OK to close a frame.

```
int result = JOptionPane.showInternalConfirmDialog(
   iframe, "OK to close?", "Select an Option", JOptionPane.YES_NO_OPTION);
```

**NOTE:** If you simply want to be *notified* when a frame is closed, you should not use the veto mechanism. Instead, install an InternalFrameListener. An internal frame listener works just like a WindowListener. When the internal frame is closing, the internalFrameClosing method is called instead of the familiar windowClosing method. The other six internal frame notifications (opened/closed, iconified/deiconified, activated/deactivated) also correspond to the window listener methods.

### 6.6.5.2 Outline Dragging

One criticism that developers have leveled against internal frames is that performance has not been great. By far the slowest operation is to drag a frame with complex content across the desktop. The desktop manager keeps asking the frame to repaint itself as it is being dragged, which is quite slow.

Actually, if you use Windows or X Windows with a poorly written video driver, you'll experience the same problem. Window dragging appears to be fast on most systems because the video hardware supports the dragging operation by mapping the image inside the frame to a different screen location during the dragging process.

To improve performance without greatly degrading the user experience, you can turn "outline dragging" on. When the user drags the frame, only the outline of the frame is continuously updated. The inside is repainted only when the frame is dropped to its final resting place.

To turn on outline dragging, call

```
desktop.setDragMode(JDesktopPane.OUTLINE_DRAG_MODE);
```

This setting is the equivalent of "continuous layout" in the JSplitPane class.

**NOTE:** In early versions of Swing, you had to use the magic incantation

```
desktop.putClientProperty("JDesktopPane.dragMode", "outline");
```

to turn on outline dragging.

In the sample program, you can use the Window -> Drag Outline checkbox menu selection to toggle outline dragging on or off.

**NOTE:** The internal frames on the desktop are managed by a DesktopManager class. You don't need to know about this class for normal programming. It is possible to implement a different desktop behavior by installing a new desktop manager, but we don't cover that.

Listing 6.31 populates a desktop with internal frames that show HTML pages. The File -> Open menu option pops up a file dialog box for reading a local HTML file into a new internal frame. If you click on any link, the linked document is displayed in another internal frame. Try out the Window -> Cascade and Window -> Tile commands.

---

**Listing 6.31** internalFrame/DesktopFrame.java

```
1  package internalFrame;
2
3  import java.awt.*;
4  import java.awt.event.*;
5  import java.beans.*;
6  import javax.swing.*;
7
8  /**
9   * This desktop frame contains editor panes that show HTML documents.
10  */
11 public class DesktopFrame extends JFrame
12 {
13    private static final int DEFAULT_WIDTH = 600;
14    private static final int DEFAULT_HEIGHT = 400;
15    private static final String[] planets = { "Mercury", "Venus", "Earth", "Mars", "Jupiter",
16       "Saturn", "Uranus", "Neptune", "Pluto", };
17
18    private JDesktopPane desktop;
19    private int nextFrameX;
20    private int nextFrameY;
21    private int frameDistance;
22    private int counter;
23
24    public DesktopFrame()
25    {
26       setSize(DEFAULT_WIDTH, DEFAULT_HEIGHT);
27
28       desktop = new JDesktopPane();
29       add(desktop, BorderLayout.CENTER);
30
31       // set up menus
32
33       JMenuBar menuBar = new JMenuBar();
34       setJMenuBar(menuBar);
35       JMenu fileMenu = new JMenu("File");
36       menuBar.add(fileMenu);
37       JMenuItem openItem = new JMenuItem("New");
38       openItem.addActionListener(new ActionListener()
39          {
40             public void actionPerformed(ActionEvent event)
41             {
42                createInternalFrame(new JLabel(
43                   new ImageIcon(getClass().getResource(planets[counter] + ".gif"))),
44                   planets[counter]);
```

*(Continues)*

**Listing 6.31** *(Continued)*

```
45              counter = (counter + 1) % planets.length;
46            }
47         });
48      fileMenu.add(openItem);
49      JMenuItem exitItem = new JMenuItem("Exit");
50      exitItem.addActionListener(new ActionListener()
51         {
52            public void actionPerformed(ActionEvent event)
53            {
54               System.exit(0);
55            }
56         });
57      fileMenu.add(exitItem);
58      JMenu windowMenu = new JMenu("Window");
59      menuBar.add(windowMenu);
60      JMenuItem nextItem = new JMenuItem("Next");
61      nextItem.addActionListener(new ActionListener()
62         {
63            public void actionPerformed(ActionEvent event)
64            {
65               selectNextWindow();
66            }
67         });
68      windowMenu.add(nextItem);
69      JMenuItem cascadeItem = new JMenuItem("Cascade");
70      cascadeItem.addActionListener(new ActionListener()
71         {
72            public void actionPerformed(ActionEvent event)
73            {
74               cascadeWindows();
75            }
76         });
77      windowMenu.add(cascadeItem);
78      JMenuItem tileItem = new JMenuItem("Tile");
79      tileItem.addActionListener(new ActionListener()
80         {
81            public void actionPerformed(ActionEvent event)
82            {
83               tileWindows();
84            }
85         });
86      windowMenu.add(tileItem);
87      final JCheckBoxMenuItem dragOutlineItem = new JCheckBoxMenuItem("Drag Outline");
```

```
88      dragOutlineItem.addActionListener(new ActionListener()
89         {
90            public void actionPerformed(ActionEvent event)
91            {
92               desktop.setDragMode(dragOutlineItem.isSelected() ? JDesktopPane.OUTLINE_DRAG_MODE
93                     : JDesktopPane.LIVE_DRAG_MODE);
94            }
95         });
96      windowMenu.add(dragOutlineItem);
97   }
98
99   /**
100   * Creates an internal frame on the desktop.
101   * @param c the component to display in the internal frame
102   * @param t the title of the internal frame
103   */
104   public void createInternalFrame(Component c, String t)
105   {
106      final JInternalFrame iframe = new JInternalFrame(t, true, // resizable
107            true, // closable
108            true, // maximizable
109            true); // iconifiable
110
111      iframe.add(c, BorderLayout.CENTER);
112      desktop.add(iframe);
113
114      iframe.setFrameIcon(new ImageIcon(getClass().getResource("document.gif")));
115
116      // add listener to confirm frame closing
117      iframe.addVetoableChangeListener(new VetoableChangeListener()
118         {
119            public void vetoableChange(PropertyChangeEvent event) throws PropertyVetoException
120            {
121               String name = event.getPropertyName();
122               Object value = event.getNewValue();
123
124               // we only want to check attempts to close a frame
125               if (name.equals("closed") && value.equals(true))
126               {
127                  // ask user if it is ok to close
128                  int result = JOptionPane.showInternalConfirmDialog(iframe, "OK to close?",
129                        "Select an Option", JOptionPane.YES_NO_OPTION);
130
131                  // if the user doesn't agree, veto the close
132                  if (result != JOptionPane.YES_OPTION) throw new PropertyVetoException(
133                        "User canceled close", event);
134               }
135            }
136         });
```

*(Continues)*

**Listing 6.31** *(Continued)*

```
137        // position frame
138        int width = desktop.getWidth() / 2;
139        int height = desktop.getHeight() / 2;
140        iframe.reshape(nextFrameX, nextFrameY, width, height);
141
142        iframe.show();
143
144        // select the frame--might be vetoed
145        try
146        {
147           iframe.setSelected(true);
148        }
149        catch (PropertyVetoException ex)
150        {
151        }
152
153        frameDistance = iframe.getHeight() - iframe.getContentPane().getHeight();
154
155        // compute placement for next frame
156
157        nextFrameX += frameDistance;
158        nextFrameY += frameDistance;
159        if (nextFrameX + width > desktop.getWidth()) nextFrameX = 0;
160        if (nextFrameY + height > desktop.getHeight()) nextFrameY = 0;
161     }
162
163     /**
164      * Cascades the noniconified internal frames of the desktop.
165      */
166     public void cascadeWindows()
167     {
168        int x = 0;
169        int y = 0;
170        int width = desktop.getWidth() / 2;
171        int height = desktop.getHeight() / 2;
172
173        for (JInternalFrame frame : desktop.getAllFrames())
174        {
175           if (!frame.isIcon())
176           {
177              try
178              {
179                 // try to make maximized frames resizable; this might be vetoed
180                 frame.setMaximum(false);
181                 frame.reshape(x, y, width, height);
182
183                 x += frameDistance;
184                 y += frameDistance;
```

```
185              // wrap around at the desktop edge
186              if (x + width > desktop.getWidth()) x = 0;
187              if (y + height > desktop.getHeight()) y = 0;
188           }
189           catch (PropertyVetoException ex)
190           {
191           }
192        }
193     }
194  }
195
196  /**
197   * Tiles the noniconified internal frames of the desktop.
198   */
199  public void tileWindows()
200  {
201     // count frames that aren't iconized
202     int frameCount = 0;
203     for (JInternalFrame frame : desktop.getAllFrames())
204        if (!frame.isIcon()) frameCount++;
205     if (frameCount == 0) return;
206
207     int rows = (int) Math.sqrt(frameCount);
208     int cols = frameCount / rows;
209     int extra = frameCount % rows;
210     // number of columns with an extra row
211
212     int width = desktop.getWidth() / cols;
213     int height = desktop.getHeight() / rows;
214     int r = 0;
215     int c = 0;
216     for (JInternalFrame frame : desktop.getAllFrames())
217     {
218        if (!frame.isIcon())
219        {
220           try
221           {
222              frame.setMaximum(false);
223              frame.reshape(c * width, r * height, width, height);
224              r++;
225              if (r == rows)
226              {
227                 r = 0;
228                 c++;
229                 if (c == cols - extra)
230                 {
231                    // start adding an extra row
232                    rows++;
```

*(Continues)*

**Listing 6.31** *(Continued)*

```
233                      height = desktop.getHeight() / rows;
234                   }
235                }
236             }
237          catch (PropertyVetoException ex)
238          {
239          }
240       }
241    }
242  }
243
244  /**
245   * Brings the next noniconified internal frame to the front.
246   */
247  public void selectNextWindow()
248  {
249     JInternalFrame[] frames = desktop.getAllFrames();
250     for (int i = 0; i < frames.length; i++)
251     {
252        if (frames[i].isSelected())
253        {
254           // find next frame that isn't an icon and can be selected
255           int next = (i + 1) % frames.length;
256           while (next != i)
257           {
258              if (!frames[next].isIcon())
259              {
260                 try
261                 {
262                    // all other frames are icons or veto selection
263                    frames[next].setSelected(true);
264                    frames[next].toFront();
265                    frames[i].toBack();
266                    return;
267                 }
268                 catch (PropertyVetoException ex)
269                 {
270                 }
271              }
272              next = (next + 1) % frames.length;
273           }
274        }
275     }
276  }
277 }
```

---

`javax.swing.JDesktopPane`   1.2

---

- `JInternalFrame[] getAllFrames()`
  gets all internal frames in this desktop pane.
- `void setDragMode(int mode)`
  sets the drag mode to live or outline drag mode.

  *Parameters:*     mode          One of `JDesktopPane.LIVE_DRAG_MODE` or
                                  `JDesktopPane.OUTLINE_DRAG_MODE`

---

`javax.swing.JInternalFrame`   1.2

---

- `JInternalFrame()`
- `JInternalFrame(String title)`
- `JInternalFrame(String title, boolean resizable)`
- `JInternalFrame(String title, boolean resizable, boolean closable)`
- `JInternalFrame(String title, boolean resizable, boolean closable, boolean maximizable)`
- `JInternalFrame(String title, boolean resizable, boolean closable, boolean maximizable, boolean iconifiable)`
  constructs a new internal frame.

  *Parameters:*     title          The string to display in the title bar

                    resizable      true if the frame can be resized

                    closable       true if the frame can be closed

                    maximizable    true if the frame can be maximized

                    iconifiable    true if the frame can be iconified

- `boolean isResizable()`
- `void setResizable(boolean b)`
- `boolean isClosable()`
- `void setClosable(boolean b)`
- `boolean isMaximizable()`
- `void setMaximizable(boolean b)`
- `boolean isIconifiable()`
- `void setIconifiable(boolean b)`
  gets or sets the `resizable`, `closable`, `maximizable`, and `iconifiable` properties. When the property is `true`, an icon appears in the frame title to resize, close, maximize, or iconify the internal frame.

*(Continues)*

---

`javax.swing.JInternalFrame` 1.2 *(Continued)*

- `boolean isIcon()`
- `void setIcon(boolean b)`
- `boolean isMaximum()`
- `void setMaximum(boolean b)`
- `boolean isClosed()`
- `void setClosed(boolean b)`

    gets or sets the `icon`, `maximum`, or `closed` property. When this property is `true`, the internal frame is iconified, maximized, or closed.

- `boolean isSelected()`
- `void setSelected(boolean b)`

    gets or sets the `selected` property. When this property is `true`, the current internal frame becomes the selected frame on the desktop.

- `void moveToFront()`
- `void moveToBack()`

    moves this internal frame to the front or the back of the desktop.

- `void reshape(int x, int y, int width, int height)`

    moves and resizes this internal frame.

    *Parameters:*      `x, y`         The top left corner of the frame

    `width, height`     The width and height of the frame

- `Container getContentPane()`
- `void setContentPane(Container c)`

    gets or sets the content pane of this internal frame.

- `JDesktopPane getDesktopPane()`

    gets the desktop pane of this internal frame.

- `Icon getFrameIcon()`
- `void setFrameIcon(Icon anIcon)`

    gets or sets the frame icon that is displayed in the title bar.

- `boolean isVisible()`
- `void setVisible(boolean b)`

    gets or sets the "visible" property.

- `void show()`

    makes this internal frame visible and brings it to the front.

---

**javax.swing.JComponent** 1.2

- void addVetoableChangeListener(VetoableChangeListener listener)
  adds a vetoable change listener that is notified when an attempt is made to change a constrained property.

---

**java.beans.VetoableChangeListener** 1.1

- void vetoableChange(PropertyChangeEvent event)
  is called when the set method of a constrained property notifies the vetoable change listeners.

---

**java.beans.PropertyChangeEvent** 1.1

- String getPropertyName()
  returns the name of the property that is about to be changed.
- Object getNewValue()
  returns the proposed new value for the property.

---

**java.beans.PropertyVetoException** 1.1

- PropertyVetoException(String reason, PropertyChangeEvent event)
  constructs a property veto exception.

  | *Parameters:* | reason | The reason for the veto |
  | | event | The vetoed event |

---

## 6.6.6.3 Layers

Java SE 1.7 introduces a feature that lets you place a layer over another component. You can paint on the layer and listen to events of the underlying component. You can use layers to add visual clues to your user interface. For example, you can decorate the current input, invalid inputs, or disabled components.

The JLayer class associates a component with a LayerUI object that is in charge of painting and event handling. The LayerUI class has a type parameter that must match the associated component. For example, here we add a layer to a JPanel:

```
JPanel panel = new JPanel();
LayerUI<JPanel> layerUI = new PanelLayer();
JLayer layer = new JLayer(panel, layerUI);
frame.add(layer);
```

Note that you add the layer, not the panel, to the parent. Here, PanelLayer is a subclass

```
class PanelLayer extends LayerUI<Panel>
{
    public void paint(Graphics g, JComponent c)
    {
        . . .
    }
    . . .
}
```

In the paint method, you can paint anything you like. Be sure to call super.paint to have the component painted. Here, we draw a transparent color over the entire component:

```
public void paint(Graphics g, JComponent c)
{
    super.paint(g, c);

    Graphics2D g2 = (Graphics2D) g.create();
    g2.setComposite(AlphaComposite.getInstance(AlphaComposite.SRC_OVER, .3f));
    g2.setPaint(color));
    g2.fillRect(0, 0, c.getWidth(), c.getHeight());
    g2.dispose();
}
```

In order to listen to events from the associated component or any of its children, the LayerUI class must set the layer's event mask. This should be done in the installUI method, like this:

```
class PanelLayer extends LayerUI<JPanel>
{
    public void installUI(JComponent c)
    {
        super.installUI(c);
        ((JLayer<?>) c).setLayerEventMask(AWTEvent.KEY_EVENT_MASK | AWTEvent.FOCUS_EVENT_MASK);
    }

    public void uninstallUI(JComponent c)
    {
        ((JLayer<?>) c).setLayerEventMask(0);
        super.uninstallUI(c);
    }
    . . .
}
```

Now you will receive events in the methods named process*Xxx*Event. For example, in our sample application, we repaint the layer after every keystroke:

```java
public class PanelLayer extends LayerUI<JPanel>
{
    protected void processKeyEvent(KeyEvent e, JLayer<? extends JPanel> l)
    {
        l.repaint();
    }
}
```

Our sample program in Listing 6.32 has three input fields for the RGB values of a color. Whenever the user changes the values, the color is shown transparently over the panel. We also trap focus events and show the text of the focused component in a bold font.

**Listing 6.32** layer/ColorFrame.java

```java
1  package layer;
2
3  import java.awt.*;
4  import java.awt.event.*;
5  import javax.swing.*;
6  import javax.swing.plaf.*;
7
8  /**
9   * A frame with three text fields to set the background color.
10  */
11 public class ColorFrame extends JFrame
12 {
13     private JPanel panel;
14     private JTextField redField;
15     private JTextField greenField;
16     private JTextField blueField;
17
18     public ColorFrame()
19     {
20         panel = new JPanel();
21
22         panel.add(new JLabel("Red:"));
23         redField = new JTextField("255", 3);
24         panel.add(redField);
25
26         panel.add(new JLabel("Green:"));
27         greenField = new JTextField("255", 3);
28         panel.add(greenField);
```

*(Continues)*

**Listing 6.32** *(Continued)*

```
29    panel.add(new JLabel("Blue:"));
30    blueField = new JTextField("255", 3);
31    panel.add(blueField);
32
33    LayerUI<JPanel> layerUI = new PanelLayer();
34    JLayer<JPanel> layer = new JLayer<JPanel>(panel, layerUI);
35
36    add(layer);
37    pack();
38    }
39
40    class PanelLayer extends LayerUI<JPanel>
41    {
42       public void installUI(JComponent c)
43       {
44          super.installUI(c);
45          ((JLayer<?>) c).setLayerEventMask(AWTEvent.KEY_EVENT_MASK | AWTEvent.FOCUS_EVENT_MASK);
46       }
47
48       public void uninstallUI(JComponent c)
49       {
50          ((JLayer<?>) c).setLayerEventMask(0);
51          super.uninstallUI(c);
52       }
53
54       protected void processKeyEvent(KeyEvent e, JLayer<? extends JPanel> l)
55       {
56          l.repaint();
57       }
58
59       protected void processFocusEvent(FocusEvent e, JLayer<? extends JPanel> l)
60       {
61          if (e.getID() == FocusEvent.FOCUS_GAINED)
62          {
63             Component c = e.getComponent();
64             c.setFont(getFont().deriveFont(Font.BOLD));
65          }
66          if (e.getID() == FocusEvent.FOCUS_LOST)
67          {
68             Component c = e.getComponent();
69             c.setFont(getFont().deriveFont(Font.PLAIN));
70          }
71       }
72
73       public void paint(Graphics g, JComponent c)
74       {
75          super.paint(g, c);
```

```
76      Graphics2D g2 = (Graphics2D) g.create();
77      g2.setComposite(AlphaComposite.getInstance(AlphaComposite.SRC_OVER, .3f));
78      int red = Integer.parseInt(redField.getText().trim());
79      int green = Integer.parseInt(greenField.getText().trim());
80      int blue = Integer.parseInt(blueField.getText().trim());
81      g2.setPaint(new Color(red, green, blue));
82      g2.fillRect(0, 0, c.getWidth(), c.getHeight());
83      g2.dispose();
84    }
85  }
86 }
```

---

**javax.swing.JLayer<V extends Component>** 7

- JLayer(V view, LayerUI<V> ui)

  constructs a layer over the given view, delegating painting and event handling to the ui object

- void setLayerEventMask(long layerEventMask)

  enables sending of all matching events, sent to the associated component or any of it descendants, to the associated LayerUI. For the event mask, combine any of the constants

  ```
  COMPONENT_EVENT_MASK
  FOCUS_EVENT_MASK
  HIERARCHY_BOUNDS_EVENT_MASK
  HIERARCHY_EVENT_MASK
  INPUT_METHOD_EVENT_MASK
  KEY_EVENT_MASK
  MOUSE_EVENT_MASK
  MOUSE_MOTION_EVENT_MASK
  MOUSE_WHEEL_EVENT_MASK
  ```

  from the AWTEvent class.

---

**javax.swing.plaf.LayerUI<V extends Component>** 7

- void installUI(JComponent c)
- void uninstallUI(JComponent c)

  Called when the LayerUI for the component c is installed or uninstalled. Override to set or clear the layer event mask.

- void paint(Graphics g, JComponent c)

  Called when the decorated component is painted. Override to call super.paint and paint decorations.

*(Continues)*

---

`javax.swing.plaf.LayerUI<V extends Component>` **7** *(Continued)*

- `void processComponentEvent(ComponentEvent e, JLayer<? extends V> l)`
- `void processFocusEvent(FocusEvent e, JLayer<? extends V> l)`
- `void processHierarchyBoundsEvent(HierarchyEvent e, JLayer<? extends V> l)`
- `void processHierarchyEvent(HierarchyEvent e, JLayer<? extends V> l)`
- `void processInputMethodEvent(InputMethodEvent e, JLayer<? extends V> l)`
- `void processKeyEvent(KeyEvent e, JLayer<? extends V> l)`
- `void processMouseEvent(MouseEvent e, JLayer<? extends V> l)`
- `void processMouseMotionEvent(MouseEvent e, JLayer<? extends V> l)`
- `void processMouseWheelEvent(MouseWheelEvent e, JLayer<? extends V> l)`

  Called when the specified event is sent to this `LayerUI`.

---

You have now seen how to use the complex components that the Swing framework offers. In the next chapter, we will turn to advanced AWT issues: complex drawing operations, image manipulation, printing, and interfacing with the native windowing system.

# Advanced AWT

**In this chapter:**

You can use the methods of the Graphics class to create simple drawings. Those methods are sufficient for simple applets and applications, but they fall short when you create complex shapes or when you require complete control over the appearance of the graphics. The Java 2D API is a more sophisticated class library that you can use to produce high-quality drawings. In this chapter, we will give you an overview of that API.

We'll then turn to the topic of printing and show how you can implement printing capabilities in your programs.

We will cover two techniques for transferring data between programs: the system clipboard and the drag-and-drop mechanism. You can use these techniques to transfer data between two Java applications or between a Java application and a native program. Finally, we cover techniques for making Java applications feel more like native applications, such as providing a splash screen and an icon in the system tray.

## 7.1 The Rendering Pipeline

The original JDK 1.0 had a very simple mechanism for drawing shapes. You selected color and paint mode, and called methods of the Graphics class such as drawRect or fillOval. The Java 2D API supports many more options.

- You can easily produce a wide variety of *shapes.*
- You have control over the *stroke*—the pen that traces shape boundaries.
- You can *fill* shapes with solid colors, varying hues, and repeating patterns.
- You can use *transformations* to move, scale, rotate, or stretch shapes.
- You can *clip* shapes to restrict them to arbitrary areas.
- You can select *composition rules* to describe how to combine the pixels of a new shape with existing pixels.
- You can give *rendering hints* to make trade-offs between speed and drawing quality.

To draw a shape, you need to go through the following steps:

1. Obtain an object of the Graphics2D class. This class is a subclass of the Graphics class. Ever since Java SE 1.2, methods such as paint and paintComponent automatically receive an object of the Graphics2D class. Simply use a cast, as follows:

```
public void paintComponent(Graphics g)
{
   Graphics2D g2 = (Graphics2D) g;
   . . .
}
```

2.  Use the `setRenderingHints` method to set *rendering hints*—trade-offs between speed and drawing quality.

    ```
    RenderingHints hints = . . .;
    g2.setRenderingHints(hints);
    ```

3.  Use the `setStroke` method to set the *stroke*. The stroke draws the outline of the shape. You can select the thickness and choose among solid and dotted lines.

    ```
    Stroke stroke = . . .;
    g2.setStroke(stroke);
    ```

4.  Use the `setPaint` method to set the *paint*. The paint fills areas such as the stroke path or the interior of a shape. You can create solid color paint, paint with changing hues, or tiled fill patterns.

    ```
    Paint paint = . . .;
    g2.setPaint(paint);
    ```

5.  Use the `clip` method to set the *clipping region*.

    ```
    Shape clip = . . .;
    g2.clip(clip);
    ```

6.  Use the `transform` method to set a *transformation* from user space to device space. Use transformations if it is easier for you to define your shapes in a custom coordinate system than by using pixel coordinates.

    ```
    AffineTransform transform = . . .;
    g2.transform(transform);
    ```

7.  Use the `setComposite` method to set a *composition rule* that describes how to combine the new pixels with the existing pixels.

    ```
    Composite composite = . . .;
    g2.setComposite(composite);
    ```

8.  Create a shape. The Java 2D API supplies many shape objects and methods to combine shapes.

    ```
    Shape shape = . . .;
    ```

9.  Draw or fill the shape. If you draw the shape, its outline is stroked. If you fill the shape, the interior is painted.

    ```
    g2.draw(shape);
    g2.fill(shape);
    ```

Of course, in many practical circumstances, you don't need all these steps. There are reasonable defaults for the settings of the 2D graphics context; change the settings only if you want to deviate from the defaults.

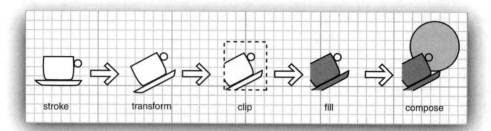

**Figure 7.1** The rendering pipeline

In the following sections, you will see how to describe shapes, strokes, paints, transformations, and composition rules.

The various set methods simply set the state of the 2D graphics context. They don't cause any drawing. Similarly, when you construct Shape objects, no drawing takes place. A shape is only rendered when you call draw or fill. At that time, the new shape is computed in a *rendering pipeline* (see Figure 7.1).

In the rendering pipeline, the following steps take place to render a shape:

1.  The path of the shape is stroked.
2.  The shape is transformed.
3.  The shape is clipped. If there is no intersection between the shape and the clipping area, the process stops.
4.  The remainder of the shape after clipping is filled.
5.  The pixels of the filled shape are composed with the existing pixels. (In Figure 7.1, the circle is part of the existing pixels, and the cup shape is superimposed over it.)

In the next section, you will see how to define shapes. Then, we will turn to the 2D graphics context settings.

---

**java.awt.Graphics2D**  1.2

- void draw(Shape s)
  draws the outline of the given shape with the current paint.
- void fill(Shape s)
  fills the interior of the given shape with the current paint.

---

# 7.2 Shapes

Here are some of the methods in the Graphics class to draw shapes:

```
drawLine
drawRectangle
drawRoundRect
draw3DRect
drawPolygon
drawPolyline
drawOval
drawArc
```

There are also corresponding fill methods. These methods have been in the Graphics class ever since JDK 1.0. The Java 2D API uses a completely different, object-oriented approach. Instead of methods, there are classes:

```
Line2D
Rectangle2D
RoundRectangle2D
Ellipse2D
Arc2D
QuadCurve2D
CubicCurve2D
GeneralPath
```

These classes all implement the Shape interface.

Finally, the Point2D class describes a point with an $x$ and a $y$ coordinate. Points are used to define shapes, but they aren't themselves shapes.

To draw a shape, first create an object of a class that implements the Shape interface and then call the draw method of the Graphics2D class.

The Line2D, Rectangle2D, RoundRectangle2D, Ellipse2D, and Arc2D classes correspond to the drawLine, drawRectangle, drawRoundRect, drawOval, and drawArc methods. (The concept of a "3D rectangle" has died the death that it so richly deserved—there is no analog to the draw3DRect method.) The Java 2D API supplies two additional classes, quadratic and cubic curves, that we will discuss in this section. There is no Polygon2D class; instead, the GeneralPath class describes paths made up from lines, quadratic and cubic curves. You can use a GeneralPath to describe a polygon; we'll show you how later in this section.

The classes

```
Rectangle2D
RoundRectangle2D
```

```
Ellipse2D
Arc2D
```

all inherit from a common superclass RectangularShape. Admittedly, ellipses and arcs are not rectangular, but they have a *bounding rectangle* (see Figure 7.2).

Each of the classes with a name ending in "2D" has two subclasses for specifying coordinates as float or double quantities. In Volume I, you already encountered Rectangle2D.Float and Rectangle2D.Double.

The same scheme is used for the other classes, such as Arc2D.Float and Arc2D.Double.

Internally, all graphics classes use float coordinates because float numbers use less storage space but have sufficient precision for geometric computations. However, the Java programming language makes it a bit more tedious to manipulate float numbers. For that reason, most methods of the graphics classes use double parameters and return values. Only when constructing a 2D object must you choose between the constructors with float and double coordinates. For example,

```
Rectangle2D floatRect = new Rectangle2D.Float(5F, 10F, 7.5F, 15F);
Rectangle2D doubleRect = new Rectangle2D.Double(5, 10, 7.5, 15);
```

The *Xxx*2D.Float and *Xxx*2D.Double classes are subclasses of the *Xxx*2D classes. After object construction, essentially no benefit accrues from remembering the subclass, and you can just store the constructed object in a superclass variable as in the code example above.

As you can see from the curious names, the *Xxx*2D.Float and *Xxx*2D.Double classes are also inner classes of the *Xxx*2D classes. That is just a minor syntactical convenience to avoid inflation of outer class names.

Figure 7.3 shows the relationships between the shape classes. However, the Double and Float subclasses are omitted. Legacy classes from the pre-2D library are marked with a gray fill.

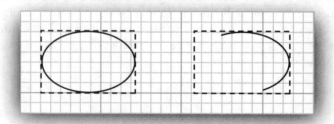

**Figure 7.2** The bounding rectangle of an ellipse and an arc

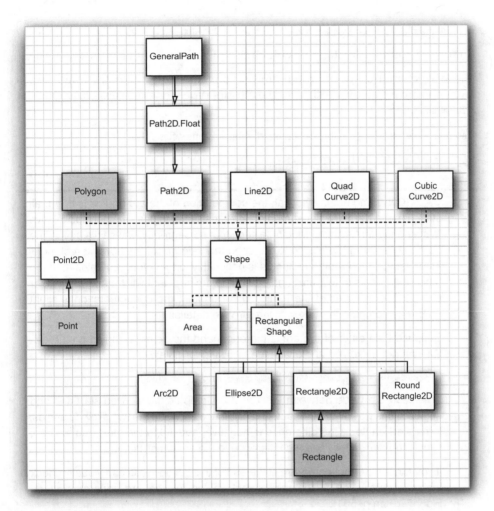

**Figure 7.3** Relationships between the shape classes

## 7.2.1 Using the Shape Classes

You already saw how to use the Rectangle2D, Ellipse2D, and Line2D classes in Volume I, Chapter 7. In this section, you will learn how to work with the remaining 2D shapes.

For the RoundRectangle2D shape, specify the top left corner, width, height, and the $x$ and $y$ dimensions of the corner area that should be rounded (see Figure 7.4). For example, the call

```
RoundRectangle2D r = new RoundRectangle2D.Double(150, 200, 100, 50, 20, 20);
```

produces a rounded rectangle with circles of radius 20 at each of the corners.

To construct an arc, specify the bounding box, the start angle, the angle swept out by the arc (see Figure 7.5), and the closure type—one of Arc2D.OPEN, Arc2D.PIE, or Arc2D.CHORD.

```
Arc2D a = new Arc2D(x, y, width, height, startAngle, arcAngle, closureType);
```

Figure 7.6 illustrates the arc types.

**CAUTION:** If the arc is elliptical, the computation of the arc angles is not at all straightforward. The API documentation states: "The angles are specified relative to the nonsquare framing rectangle such that 45 degrees always falls on the line from the center of the ellipse to the upper right corner of the framing rectangle. As a result, if the framing rectangle is noticeably longer along one axis than the other, the angles to the start and end of the arc segment will be skewed farther along the longer axis of the frame." Unfortunately, the documentation is silent on how to compute this "skew." Here are the details:

Suppose the center of the arc is the origin and the point (*x*, *y*) lies on the arc. You can get a skewed angle with the following formula:

```
skewedAngle = Math.toDegrees(Math.atan2(-y * height, x * width));
```

The result is a value between -180 and 180. Compute the skewed start and end angles in this way. Then, compute the difference between the two skewed angles. If the start angle or the difference is negative, add 360 to the start angle. Then, supply the start angle and the difference to the arc constructor.

If you run the example program at the end of this section, you can visually check that this calculation yields the correct values for the arc constructor (see Figure 7.9 on p. 561).

The Java 2D API supports *quadratic* and *cubic* curves. In this chapter, we do not get into the mathematics of these curves. We suggest you get a feel for how the curves look by running the program in Listing 7.1. As you can see in Figures 7.7 and 7.8, quadratic and cubic curves are specified by two *end points* and one or two *control points*. Moving the control points changes the shape of the curves.

To construct quadratic and cubic curves, give the coordinates of the end points and the control points. For example,

```
QuadCurve2D q = new QuadCurve2D.Double(startX, startY, controlX, controlY, endX, endY);
CubicCurve2D c = new CubicCurve2D.Double(startX, startY, control1X, control1Y,
    control2X, control2Y, endX, endY);
```

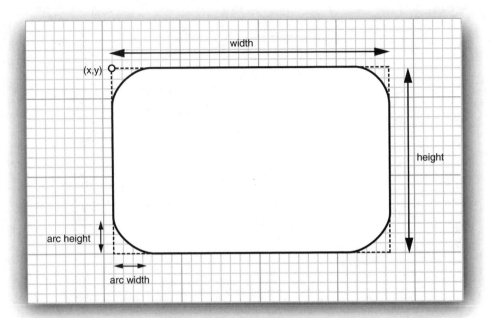

**Figure 7.4** Constructing a RoundRectangle2D

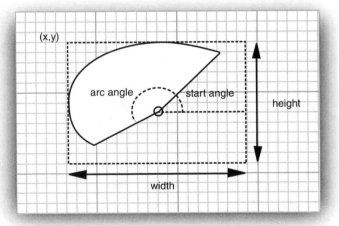

**Figure 7.5** Constructing an elliptical arc

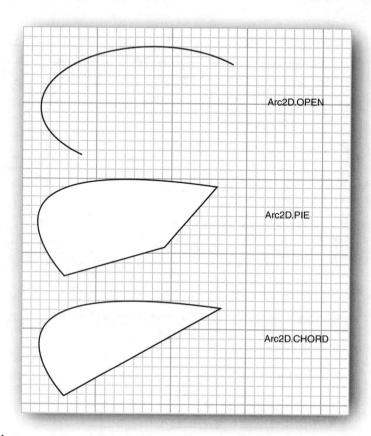

**Figure 7.6** Arc types

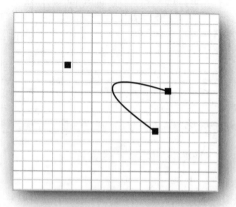

**Figure 7.7** A quadratic curve

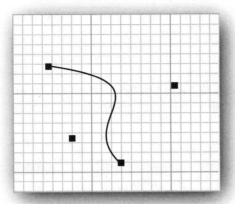

**Figure 7.8** A cubic curve

Quadratic curves are not very flexible, and they are not commonly used in practice. Cubic curves (such as the Bézier curves drawn by the CubicCurve2D class) are, however, very common. By combining many cubic curves so that the slopes at the connection points match, you can create complex, smooth-looking curved shapes. For more information, we refer you to *Computer Graphics: Principles and Practice, Second Edition in C*, by James D. Foley, Andries van Dam, Steven K. Feiner, et al. (Addison-Wesley, 1995).

You can build arbitrary sequences of line segments, quadratic curves, and cubic curves, and store them in a GeneralPath object. Specify the first coordinate of the path with the moveTo method, for example

```
GeneralPath path = new GeneralPath();
path.moveTo(10, 20);
```

You can then extend the path by calling one of the methods lineTo, quadTo, or curveTo. These methods extend the path by a line, a quadratic curve, or a cubic curve. To call lineTo, supply the end point. For the two curve methods, supply the control points, then the end point. For example,

```
path.lineTo(20, 30);
path.curveTo(control1X, control1Y, control2X, control2Y, endX, endY);
```

Close the path by calling the closePath method. It draws a line back to the starting point of the path.

To make a polygon, simply call moveTo to go to the first corner point, followed by repeated calls to lineTo to visit the other corner points. Finally, call closePath to close the polygon. The program in Listing 7.1 shows this in more detail.

A general path does not have to be connected. You can call moveTo at any time to start a new path segment.

Finally, you can use the append method to add arbitrary Shape objects to a general path. The outline of the shape is added to the end to the path. The second parameter of the append method is true if the new shape should be connected to the last point on the path, false otherwise. For example, the call

```
Rectangle2D r = . . .;
path.append(r, false);
```

appends the outline of a rectangle to the path without connecting it to the existing path. But

```
path.append(r, true);
```

adds a straight line from the end point of the path to the starting point of the rectangle, and then adds the rectangle outline to the path.

The program in Listing 7.1 lets you create sample paths. Figures 7.7 and 7.8 show sample runs of the program. You can pick a shape maker from the combo box. The program contains shape makers for

- Straight lines
- Rectangles, rounded rectangles, and ellipses
- Arcs (showing lines for the bounding rectangle and the start and end angles, in addition to the arc itself)
- Polygons (using a GeneralPath)
- Quadratic and cubic curves

Use the mouse to adjust the control points. As you move them, the shape continuously repaints itself.

The program is a bit complex because it handles multiple shapes and supports dragging of the control points.

An abstract superclass ShapeMaker encapsulates the commonality of the shape maker classes. Each shape has a fixed number of control points that the user can move around. The getPointCount method returns that value. The abstract method

```
Shape makeShape(Point2D[] points)
```

computes the actual shape, given the current positions of the control points. The toString method returns the class name so that the ShapeMaker objects can simply be dumped into a JComboBox.

To enable dragging of the control points, the ShapePanel class handles both mouse and mouse motion events. If the mouse is pressed on top of a rectangle, subsequent mouse drags move the rectangle.

The majority of the shape maker classes are simple—their makeShape methods just construct and return the requested shapes. However, the ArcMaker class needs to compute the distorted start and end angles. Furthermore, to demonstrate that the computation is indeed correct, the returned shape is a GeneralPath containing the arc itself, the bounding rectangle, and the lines from the center of the arc to the angle control points (see Figure 7.9).

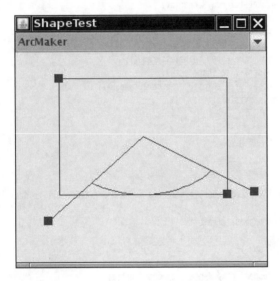

**Figure 7.9** The ShapeTest program

**Listing 7.1** shape/ShapeTest.java

```
1  package shape;
2
3  import java.awt.*;
4  import java.awt.event.*;
5  import java.awt.geom.*;
6  import java.util.*;
7  import javax.swing.*;
```

*(Continues)*

**Listing 7.1** *(Continued)*

```
8    /**
9     * This program demonstrates the various 2D shapes.
10    * @version 1.02 2007-08-16
11    * @author Cay Horstmann
12    */
13   public class ShapeTest
14   {
15      public static void main(String[] args)
16      {
17         EventQueue.invokeLater(new Runnable()
18            {
19               public void run()
20               {
21                  JFrame frame = new ShapeTestFrame();
22                  frame.setTitle("ShapeTest");
23                  frame.setDefaultCloseOperation(JFrame.EXIT_ON_CLOSE);
24                  frame.setVisible(true);
25               }
26            });
27      }
28   }
29
30   /**
31    * This frame contains a combo box to select a shape and a component to draw it.
32    */
33   class ShapeTestFrame extends JFrame
34   {
35      public ShapeTestFrame()
36      {
37         final ShapeComponent comp = new ShapeComponent();
38         add(comp, BorderLayout.CENTER);
39         final JComboBox<ShapeMaker> comboBox = new JComboBox<>();
40         comboBox.addItem(new LineMaker());
41         comboBox.addItem(new RectangleMaker());
42         comboBox.addItem(new RoundRectangleMaker());
43         comboBox.addItem(new EllipseMaker());
44         comboBox.addItem(new ArcMaker());
45         comboBox.addItem(new PolygonMaker());
46         comboBox.addItem(new QuadCurveMaker());
47         comboBox.addItem(new CubicCurveMaker());
48         comboBox.addActionListener(new ActionListener()
49            {
50               public void actionPerformed(ActionEvent event)
51               {
52                  ShapeMaker shapeMaker = comboBox.getItemAt(comboBox.getSelectedIndex());
53                  comp.setShapeMaker(shapeMaker);
54               }
55            });
```

```
56          add(comboBox, BorderLayout.NORTH);
57          comp.setShapeMaker((ShapeMaker) comboBox.getItemAt(0));
58          pack();
59      }
60
61  }
62
63  /**
64   * This component draws a shape and allows the user to move the points that define it.
65   */
66  class ShapeComponent extends JComponent
67  {
68      private static final int DEFAULT_WIDTH = 300;
69      private static final int DEFAULT_HEIGHT = 200;
70
71      private Point2D[] points;
72      private static Random generator = new Random();
73      private static int SIZE = 10;
74      private int current;
75      private ShapeMaker shapeMaker;
76
77      public ShapeComponent()
78      {
79          addMouseListener(new MouseAdapter()
80              {
81                  public void mousePressed(MouseEvent event)
82                  {
83                      Point p = event.getPoint();
84                      for (int i = 0; i < points.length; i++)
85                      {
86                          double x = points[i].getX() - SIZE / 2;
87                          double y = points[i].getY() - SIZE / 2;
88                          Rectangle2D r = new Rectangle2D.Double(x, y, SIZE, SIZE);
89                          if (r.contains(p))
90                          {
91                              current = i;
92                              return;
93                          }
94                      }
95                  }
96
97                  public void mouseReleased(MouseEvent event)
98                  {
99                      current = -1;
100                  }
101              });
```

*(Continues)*

**Listing 7.1** *(Continued)*

```
102        addMouseMotionListener(new MouseMotionAdapter()
103           {
104              public void mouseDragged(MouseEvent event)
105              {
106                 if (current == -1) return;
107                 points[current] = event.getPoint();
108                 repaint();
109              }
110           });
111        current = -1;
112     }
113
114     /**
115      * Set a shape maker and initialize it with a random point set.
116      * @param aShapeMaker a shape maker that defines a shape from a point set
117      */
118     public void setShapeMaker(ShapeMaker aShapeMaker)
119     {
120        shapeMaker = aShapeMaker;
121        int n = shapeMaker.getPointCount();
122        points = new Point2D[n];
123        for (int i = 0; i < n; i++)
124        {
125           double x = generator.nextDouble() * getWidth();
126           double y = generator.nextDouble() * getHeight();
127           points[i] = new Point2D.Double(x, y);
128        }
129        repaint();
130     }
131
132     public void paintComponent(Graphics g)
133     {
134        if (points == null) return;
135        Graphics2D g2 = (Graphics2D) g;
136        for (int i = 0; i < points.length; i++)
137        {
138           double x = points[i].getX() - SIZE / 2;
139           double y = points[i].getY() - SIZE / 2;
140           g2.fill(new Rectangle2D.Double(x, y, SIZE, SIZE));
141        }
142
143        g2.draw(shapeMaker.makeShape(points));
144     }
145
146     public Dimension getPreferredSize() { return new Dimension(DEFAULT_WIDTH, DEFAULT_HEIGHT); }
147  }
```

```
148  /**
149   * A shape maker can make a shape from a point set. Concrete subclasses must return a shape in the
150   * makeShape method.
151   */
152  abstract class ShapeMaker
153  {
154     public abstract Shape makeShape(Point2D[] p);
155     private int pointCount;
156
157     /**
158      * Constructs a shape maker.
159      * @param aPointCount the number of points needed to define this shape.
160      */
161     public ShapeMaker(int aPointCount)
162     {
163        pointCount = aPointCount;
164     }
165
166     /**
167      * Gets the number of points needed to define this shape.
168      * @return the point count
169      */
170     public int getPointCount()
171     {
172        return pointCount;
173     }
174
175     /**
176      * Makes a shape out of the given point set.
177      * @param p the points that define the shape
178      * @return the shape defined by the points
179      */
180
181     public String toString()
182     {
183        return getClass().getName();
184     }
185
186  }
187
188  /**
189   * Makes a line that joins two given points.
190   */
191  class LineMaker extends ShapeMaker
192  {
193     public LineMaker()
194     {
195        super(2);
196     }
```

*(Continues)*

Listing 7.1   *(Continued)*

```
197    public Shape makeShape(Point2D[] p)
198    {
199       return new Line2D.Double(p[0], p[1]);
200    }
201 }
202
203 /**
204  * Makes a rectangle that joins two given corner points.
205  */
206 class RectangleMaker extends ShapeMaker
207 {
208    public RectangleMaker()
209    {
210       super(2);
211    }
212
213    public Shape makeShape(Point2D[] p)
214    {
215       Rectangle2D s = new Rectangle2D.Double();
216       s.setFrameFromDiagonal(p[0], p[1]);
217       return s;
218    }
219 }
220
221 /**
222  * Makes a round rectangle that joins two given corner points.
223  */
224 class RoundRectangleMaker extends ShapeMaker
225 {
226    public RoundRectangleMaker()
227    {
228       super(2);
229    }
230
231    public Shape makeShape(Point2D[] p)
232    {
233       RoundRectangle2D s = new RoundRectangle2D.Double(0, 0, 0, 0, 20, 20);
234       s.setFrameFromDiagonal(p[0], p[1]);
235       return s;
236    }
237 }
238
239 /**
240  * Makes an ellipse contained in a bounding box with two given corner points.
241  */
```

```
242  class EllipseMaker extends ShapeMaker
243  {
244     public EllipseMaker()
245     {
246        super(2);
247     }
248
249     public Shape makeShape(Point2D[] p)
250     {
251        Ellipse2D s = new Ellipse2D.Double();
252        s.setFrameFromDiagonal(p[0], p[1]);
253        return s;
254     }
255  }
256
257  /**
258   * Makes an arc contained in a bounding box with two given corner points, and with starting and
259   * ending angles given by lines emanating from the center of the bounding box and ending in two
260   * given points. To show the correctness of the angle computation, the returned shape contains the
261   * arc, the bounding box, and the lines.
262   */
263  class ArcMaker extends ShapeMaker
264  {
265     public ArcMaker()
266     {
267        super(4);
268     }
269
270     public Shape makeShape(Point2D[] p)
271     {
272        double centerX = (p[0].getX() + p[1].getX()) / 2;
273        double centerY = (p[0].getY() + p[1].getY()) / 2;
274        double width = Math.abs(p[1].getX() - p[0].getX());
275        double height = Math.abs(p[1].getY() - p[0].getY());
276
277        double skewedStartAngle = Math.toDegrees(Math.atan2(-(p[2].getY() - centerY) * width,
278           (p[2].getX() - centerX) * height));
279        double skewedEndAngle = Math.toDegrees(Math.atan2(-(p[3].getY() - centerY) * width,
280           (p[3].getX() - centerX) * height));
281        double skewedAngleDifference = skewedEndAngle - skewedStartAngle;
282        if (skewedStartAngle < 0) skewedStartAngle += 360;
283        if (skewedAngleDifference < 0) skewedAngleDifference += 360;
284
285        Arc2D s = new Arc2D.Double(0, 0, 0, 0, skewedStartAngle, skewedAngleDifference, Arc2D.OPEN);
286        s.setFrameFromDiagonal(p[0], p[1]);
287
288        GeneralPath g = new GeneralPath();
```

*(Continues)*

**Listing 7.1** *(Continued)*

```
289        g.append(s, false);
290        Rectangle2D r = new Rectangle2D.Double();
291        r.setFrameFromDiagonal(p[0], p[1]);
292        g.append(r, false);
293        Point2D center = new Point2D.Double(centerX, centerY);
294        g.append(new Line2D.Double(center, p[2]), false);
295        g.append(new Line2D.Double(center, p[3]), false);
296        return g;
297     }
298  }
299
300  /**
301   * Makes a polygon defined by six corner points.
302   */
303  class PolygonMaker extends ShapeMaker
304  {
305     public PolygonMaker()
306     {
307        super(6);
308     }
309
310     public Shape makeShape(Point2D[] p)
311     {
312        GeneralPath s = new GeneralPath();
313        s.moveTo((float) p[0].getX(), (float) p[0].getY());
314        for (int i = 1; i < p.length; i++)
315           s.lineTo((float) p[i].getX(), (float) p[i].getY());
316        s.closePath();
317        return s;
318     }
319  }
320
321  /**
322   * Makes a quad curve defined by two end points and a control point.
323   */
324  class QuadCurveMaker extends ShapeMaker
325  {
326     public QuadCurveMaker()
327     {
328        super(3);
329     }
330
331     public Shape makeShape(Point2D[] p)
332     {
333        return new QuadCurve2D.Double(p[0].getX(), p[0].getY(), p[1].getX(), p[1].getY(),
334           p[2].getX(), p[2].getY());
335     }
336  }
```

```
337 /**
338  * Makes a cubic curve defined by two end points and two control points.
339  */
340 class CubicCurveMaker extends ShapeMaker
341 {
342    public CubicCurveMaker()
343    {
344       super(4);
345    }
346
347    public Shape makeShape(Point2D[] p)
348    {
349       return new CubicCurve2D.Double(p[0].getX(), p[0].getY(), p[1].getX(), p[1].getY(),
350             p[2].getX(), p[2].getY(), p[3].getX(), p[3].getY());
351    }
352 }
```

---

**java.awt.geom.RoundRectangle2D.Double** 1.2

- RoundRectangle2D.Double(double x, double y, double width, double height, double arcWidth, double arcHeight)
  constructs a rounded rectangle with the given bounding rectangle and arc dimensions. See Figure 7.4 for an explanation of the arcWidth and arcHeight parameters.

---

**java.awt.geom.Arc2D.Double** 1.2

- Arc2D.Double(double x, double y, double w, double h, double startAngle, double arcAngle, int type)
  constructs an arc with the given bounding rectangle, start and arc angle, and arc type. The startAngle and arcAngle are explained on page 557. The type is one of Arc2D.OPEN, Arc2D.PIE, and Arc2D.CHORD.

---

**java.awt.geom.QuadCurve2D.Double** 1.2

- QuadCurve2D.Double(double x1, double y1, double ctrlx, double ctrly, double x2, double y2)
  constructs a quadratic curve from a start point, a control point, and an end point.

---

**java.awt.geom.CubicCurve2D.Double** 1.2

- CubicCurve2D.Double(double x1, double y1, double ctrlx1, double ctrly1, double ctrlx2, double ctrly2, double x2, double y2)
  constructs a cubic curve from a start point, two control points, and an end point.

---

**java.awt.geom.GeneralPath** 1.2

- GeneralPath()
  constructs an empty general path.

---

**java.awt.geom.Path2D.Float** 6

- void moveTo(float x, float y)
  makes (x, y) the *current point*—that is, the starting point of the next segment.
- void lineTo(float x, float y)
- void quadTo(float ctrlx, float ctrly, float x, float y)
- void curveTo(float ctrl1x, float ctrl1y, float ctrl2x, float ctrl2y, float x, float y)
  draws a line, quadratic curve, or cubic curve from the current point to the end point (x, y), and makes that end point the current point.

---

**java.awt.geom.Path2D** 6

- void append(Shape s, boolean connect)
  adds the outline of the given shape to the general path. If connect is true, the current point of the general path is connected to the starting point of the added shape by a straight line.
- void closePath()
  closes the path by drawing a straight line from the current point to the first point in the path.

---

## 7.3 Areas

In the preceding section, you saw how you can specify complex shapes by constructing general paths composed of lines and curves. By using a sufficient number of lines and curves, you can draw essentially any shape. For example, the shapes of characters in the fonts that you see on the screen and on your printouts are all made up of lines and cubic curves.

Occasionally, it is easier to describe a shape by composing it from *areas*, such as rectangles, polygons, or ellipses. The Java 2D API supports four *constructive area geometry* operations that combine two areas into a new area:

- add: The combined area contains all points that are in the first or the second area.

- subtract: The combined area contains all points that are in the first but not the second area.
- intersect: The combined area contains all points that are in the first and the second area.
- exclusiveOr: The combined area contains all points that are in either the first or the second area, but not in both.

Figure 7.10 shows these operations.

To construct a complex area, start with a default area object.

```
Area a = new Area();
```

Then, combine the area with any shape.

```
a.add(new Rectangle2D.Double(. . .));
a.subtract(path);
. . .
```

The Area class implements the Shape interface. You can stroke the boundary of the area with the draw method or paint the interior with the fill method of the Graphics2D class.

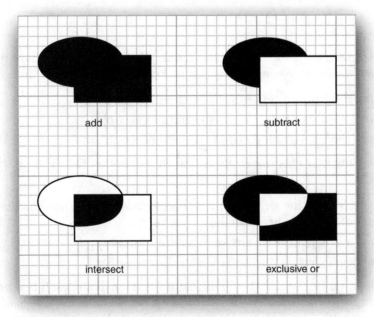

**Figure 7.10** Constructive area geometry operations

---

**java.awt.geom.Area**

---

- void add(Area other)
- void subtract(Area other)
- void intersect(Area other)
- void exclusiveOr(Area other)

  carries out the constructive area geometry operation with this area and the other area and sets this area to the result.

---

## 7.4 Strokes

The draw operation of the Graphics2D class draws the boundary of a shape by using the currently selected *stroke.* By default, the stroke is a solid line that is 1 pixel wide. You can select a different stroke by calling the setStroke method and supplying an object of a class that implements the Stroke interface. The Java 2D API defines only one such class, called BasicStroke. In this section, we'll look at the capabilities of the BasicStroke class.

You can construct strokes of arbitrary thickness. For example, here is how to draw lines that are 10 pixels wide:

```
g2.setStroke(new BasicStroke(10.0F));
g2.draw(new Line2D.Double(. . .));
```

When a stroke is more than a pixel thick, the *end* of the stroke can have different styles. Figure 7.11 shows these so-called end cap styles. You have three choices:

- A *butt cap* simply ends the stroke at its end point.
- A *round cap* adds a half-circle to the end of the stroke.
- A *square cap* adds a half-square to the end of the stroke.

When two thick strokes meet, there are three choices for the *join style* (see Figure 7.12).

- A *bevel join* joins the strokes with a straight line that is perpendicular to the bisector of the angle between the two strokes.
- A *round join* extends each stroke to have a round cap.
- A *miter join* extends both strokes by adding a "spike."

The miter join is not suitable for lines that meet at small angles. If two lines join with an angle that is less than the *miter limit,* a bevel join is used instead, which prevents extremely long spikes. By default, the miter limit is 10 degrees.

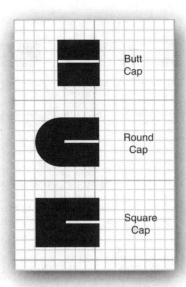

**Figure 7.11** End cap styles

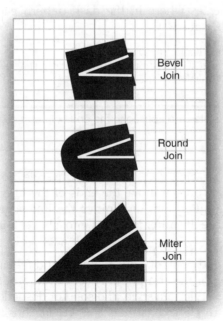

**Figure 7.12** Join styles

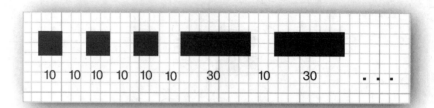

**Figure 7.13** A dash pattern

You can specify these choices in the BasicStroke constructor, for example:

```
g2.setStroke(new BasicStroke(10.0F, BasicStroke.CAP_ROUND, BasicStroke.JOIN_ROUND));
g2.setStroke(new BasicStroke(10.0F, BasicStroke.CAP_BUTT, BasicStroke.JOIN_MITER,
   15.0F /* miter limit */));
```

Finally, you can create dashed lines by setting a *dash pattern*. In the program in Listing 7.2, you can select a dash pattern that spells out SOS in Morse code. The dash pattern is a float[] array of numbers that contains the lengths of the "on" and "off" intervals (see Figure 7.13).

You can specify the dash pattern and a *dash phase* when constructing the BasicStroke. The dash phase indicates where in the dash pattern each line should start. Normally, you set this value to 0.

```
float[] dashPattern = { 10, 10, 10, 10, 10, 10, 30, 10, 30, ... };
g2.setStroke(new BasicStroke(10.0F, BasicStroke.CAP_BUTT, BasicStroke.JOIN_MITER,
   10.0F /* miter limit */, dashPattern, 0 /* dash phase */));
```

 **NOTE:** End cap styles are applied to the ends of *each dash* in a dash pattern.

The program in Listing 7.2 lets you specify end cap styles, join styles, and dashed lines (see Figure 7.14). You can move the ends of the line segments to test the miter limit: Select the miter join, then move the line segment to form a very acute angle. You will see the miter join turn into a bevel join.

The program is similar to the program in Listing 7.1. The mouse listener remembers your click on the end point of a line segment, and the mouse motion listener monitors the dragging of the end point. A set of radio buttons signal the user choices for the end cap style, join style, and solid or dashed line. The paintComponent method of the StrokePanel class constructs a GeneralPath consisting of the two line segments that join the three points that the user can move with the mouse. It then constructs a BasicStroke, according to the selections the user made, and finally draws the path.

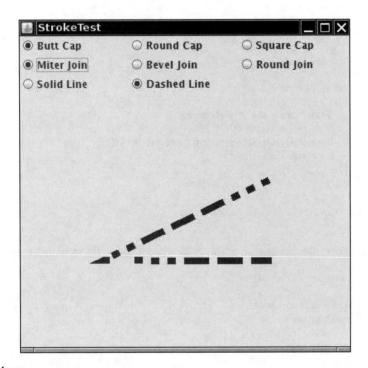

**Figure 7.14** The StrokeTest program

---

**Listing 7.2** stroke/StrokeTest.java

```
 1  package stroke;
 2
 3  import java.awt.*;
 4  import java.awt.event.*;
 5  import java.awt.geom.*;
 6  import javax.swing.*;
 7
 8  /**
 9   * This program demonstrates different stroke types.
10   * @version 1.03 2007-08-16
11   * @author Cay Horstmann
12   */
```

*(Continues)*

**Listing 7.2** *(Continued)*

```
13  public class StrokeTest
14  {
15     public static void main(String[] args)
16     {
17        EventQueue.invokeLater(new Runnable()
18           {
19              public void run()
20              {
21                 JFrame frame = new StrokeTestFrame();
22                 frame.setTitle("StrokeTest");
23                 frame.setDefaultCloseOperation(JFrame.EXIT_ON_CLOSE);
24                 frame.setVisible(true);
25              }
26           });
27     }
28  }
29
30  /**
31   * This frame lets the user choose the cap, join, and line style, and shows the resulting stroke.
32   */
33  class StrokeTestFrame extends JFrame
34  {
35     private StrokeComponent canvas;
36     private JPanel buttonPanel;
37
38     public StrokeTestFrame()
39     {
40        canvas = new StrokeComponent();
41        add(canvas, BorderLayout.CENTER);
42
43        buttonPanel = new JPanel();
44        buttonPanel.setLayout(new GridLayout(3, 3));
45        add(buttonPanel, BorderLayout.NORTH);
46
47        ButtonGroup group1 = new ButtonGroup();
48        makeCapButton("Butt Cap", BasicStroke.CAP_BUTT, group1);
49        makeCapButton("Round Cap", BasicStroke.CAP_ROUND, group1);
50        makeCapButton("Square Cap", BasicStroke.CAP_SQUARE, group1);
51
52        ButtonGroup group2 = new ButtonGroup();
53        makeJoinButton("Miter Join", BasicStroke.JOIN_MITER, group2);
54        makeJoinButton("Bevel Join", BasicStroke.JOIN_BEVEL, group2);
55        makeJoinButton("Round Join", BasicStroke.JOIN_ROUND, group2);
56
57        ButtonGroup group3 = new ButtonGroup();
58        makeDashButton("Solid Line", false, group3);
59        makeDashButton("Dashed Line", true, group3);
60     }
```

```
61   /**
62    * Makes a radio button to change the cap style.
63    * @param label the button label
64    * @param style the cap style
65    * @param group the radio button group
66    */
67   private void makeCapButton(String label, final int style, ButtonGroup group)
68   {
69      // select first button in group
70      boolean selected = group.getButtonCount() == 0;
71      JRadioButton button = new JRadioButton(label, selected);
72      buttonPanel.add(button);
73      group.add(button);
74      button.addActionListener(new ActionListener()
75         {
76            public void actionPerformed(ActionEvent event)
77            {
78               canvas.setCap(style);
79            }
80         });
81      pack();
82   }
83
84   /**
85    * Makes a radio button to change the join style.
86    * @param label the button label
87    * @param style the join style
88    * @param group the radio button group
89    */
90   private void makeJoinButton(String label, final int style, ButtonGroup group)
91   {
92      // select first button in group
93      boolean selected = group.getButtonCount() == 0;
94      JRadioButton button = new JRadioButton(label, selected);
95      buttonPanel.add(button);
96      group.add(button);
97      button.addActionListener(new ActionListener()
98         {
99            public void actionPerformed(ActionEvent event)
100           {
101              canvas.setJoin(style);
102           }
103        });
104  }
105
106  /**
107   * Makes a radio button to set solid or dashed lines
108   * @param label the button label
```

*(Continues)*

**Listing 7.2**  *(Continued)*

```
109      * @param style false for solid, true for dashed lines
110      * @param group the radio button group
111      */
112     private void makeDashButton(String label, final boolean style, ButtonGroup group)
113     {
114        // select first button in group
115        boolean selected = group.getButtonCount() == 0;
116        JRadioButton button = new JRadioButton(label, selected);
117        buttonPanel.add(button);
118        group.add(button);
119        button.addActionListener(new ActionListener()
120           {
121              public void actionPerformed(ActionEvent event)
122              {
123                 canvas.setDash(style);
124              }
125           });
126     }
127  }
128
129  /**
130   * This component draws two joined lines, using different stroke objects, and allows the user to
131   * drag the three points defining the lines.
132   */
133  class StrokeComponent extends JComponent
134  {
135     private static final int DEFAULT_WIDTH = 400;
136     private static final int DEFAULT_HEIGHT = 400;
137     private static int SIZE = 10;
138
139     private Point2D[] points;
140     private int current;
141     private float width;
142     private int cap;
143     private int join;
144     private boolean dash;
145
146     public StrokeComponent()
147     {
148        addMouseListener(new MouseAdapter()
149           {
150              public void mousePressed(MouseEvent event)
151              {
152                 Point p = event.getPoint();
153                 for (int i = 0; i < points.length; i++)
154                 {
155                    double x = points[i].getX() - SIZE / 2;
156                    double y = points[i].getY() - SIZE / 2;
```

```
157              Rectangle2D r = new Rectangle2D.Double(x, y, SIZE, SIZE);
158              if (r.contains(p))
159              {
160                 current = i;
161                 return;
162              }
163           }
164        }
165
166        public void mouseReleased(MouseEvent event)
167        {
168           current = -1;
169        }
170     });
171
172     addMouseMotionListener(new MouseMotionAdapter()
173        {
174           public void mouseDragged(MouseEvent event)
175           {
176              if (current == -1) return;
177              points[current] = event.getPoint();
178              repaint();
179           }
180     });
181
182     points = new Point2D[3];
183     points[0] = new Point2D.Double(200, 100);
184     points[1] = new Point2D.Double(100, 200);
185     points[2] = new Point2D.Double(200, 200);
186     current = -1;
187     width = 8.0F;
188  }
189
190  public void paintComponent(Graphics g)
191  {
192     Graphics2D g2 = (Graphics2D) g;
193     GeneralPath path = new GeneralPath();
194     path.moveTo((float) points[0].getX(), (float) points[0].getY());
195     for (int i = 1; i < points.length; i++)
196        path.lineTo((float) points[i].getX(), (float) points[i].getY());
197     BasicStroke stroke;
198     if (dash)
199     {
200        float miterLimit = 10.0F;
201        float[] dashPattern = { 10F, 10F, 10F, 10F, 10F, 10F, 30F, 10F, 30F, 10F, 30F, 10F, 10F,
202              10F, 10F, 10F, 10F, 30F };
203        float dashPhase = 0;
204        stroke = new BasicStroke(width, cap, join, miterLimit, dashPattern, dashPhase);
205     }
```

*(Continues)*

**Listing 7.2** *(Continued)*

```
206        else stroke = new BasicStroke(width, cap, join);
207        g2.setStroke(stroke);
208        g2.draw(path);
209     }
210
211     /**
212      * Sets the join style.
213      * @param j the join style
214      */
215     public void setJoin(int j)
216     {
217        join = j;
218        repaint();
219     }
220
221     /**
222      * Sets the cap style.
223      * @param c the cap style
224      */
225     public void setCap(int c)
226     {
227        cap = c;
228        repaint();
229     }
230
231     /**
232      * Sets solid or dashed lines.
233      * @param d false for solid, true for dashed lines
234      */
235     public void setDash(boolean d)
236     {
237        dash = d;
238        repaint();
239     }
240
241     public Dimension getPreferredSize() { return new Dimension(DEFAULT_WIDTH, DEFAULT_HEIGHT); }
242 }
```

---

**java.awt.Graphics2D** 1.2

- void setStroke(Stroke s)

  sets the stroke of this graphics context to the given object that implements the Stroke interface.

---

**java.awt.BasicStroke** 1.2

- BasicStroke(float width)
- BasicStroke(float width, int cap, int join)
- BasicStroke(float width, int cap, int join, float miterlimit)
- BasicStroke(float width, int cap, int join, float miterlimit, float[] dash, float dashPhase)
  constructs a stroke object with the given attributes.

  | *Parameters:* | width | The width of the pen |
  |---|---|---|
  | | cap | The end cap style—one of CAP_BUTT, CAP_ROUND, and CAP_SQUARE |
  | | join | The join style—one of JOIN_BEVEL, JOIN_MITER, and JOIN_ROUND |
  | | miterlimit | The angle, in degrees, below which a miter join is rendered as a bevel join |
  | | dash | An array of the lengths of the alternating filled and blank portions of a dashed stroke |
  | | dashPhase | The "phase" of the dash pattern; a segment of this length, preceding the starting point of the stroke, is assumed to have the dash pattern already applied. |

---

# 7.5 Paint

When you fill a shape, its inside is covered with *paint*. Use the setPaint method to set the paint style to an object with a class that implements the Paint interface. The Java 2D API provides three such classes:

- The Color class implements the Paint interface. To fill shapes with a solid color, simply call setPaint with a Color object, such as

  g2.setPaint(Color.red);

- The GradientPaint class varies colors by interpolating between two given color values (see Figure 7.15).

- The TexturePaint class fills an area with repetitions of an image (see Figure 7.16).

You can construct a GradientPaint object by specifying two points and the colors that you want at these two points.

  g2.setPaint(new GradientPaint(p1, Color.RED, p2, Color.YELLOW));

Colors are interpolated along the line joining the two points. Colors are constant along lines perpendicular to that joining line. Points beyond an end point of the line are given the color at the end point.

**Figure 7.15** Gradient paint

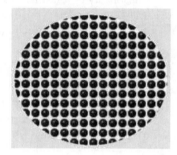

**Figure 7.16** Texture paint

Alternatively, if you call the GradientPaint constructor with true for the cyclic parameter,

```
g2.setPaint(new GradientPaint(p1, Color.RED, p2, Color.YELLOW, true));
```

then the color variation *cycles* and keeps varying beyond the end points.

To construct a TexturePaint object, specify a BufferedImage and an *anchor* rectangle.

```
g2.setPaint(new TexturePaint(bufferedImage, anchorRectangle));
```

We will introduce the BufferedImage class later in this chapter when we discuss images in detail. The simplest way of obtaining a buffered image is to read an image file:

```
bufferedImage = ImageIO.read(new File("blue-ball.gif"));
```

The anchor rectangle is extended indefinitely in *x* and *y* directions to tile the entire coordinate plane. The image is scaled to fit into the anchor and then replicated into each tile.

---

**java.awt.Graphics2D** 1.2

- void setPaint(Paint s)
  sets the paint of this graphics context to the given object that implements the Paint interface.

---

**java.awt.GradientPaint** 1.2

- GradientPaint(float x1, float y1, Color color1, float x2, float y2, Color color2)
- GradientPaint(float x1, float y1, Color color1, float x2, float y2, Color color2, boolean cyclic)
- GradientPaint(Point2D p1, Color color1, Point2D p2, Color color2)
- GradientPaint(Point2D p1, Color color1, Point2D p2, Color color2, boolean cyclic)
  constructs a gradient paint object that fills shapes with color such that the start point is colored with color1, the end point is colored with color2, and the colors in between are linearly interpolated. Colors are constant along lines perpendicular to the line joining the start and the end point. By default, the gradient paint is not cyclic—that is, points beyond the start and end points are colored with the same color as the start and end point. If the gradient paint is *cyclic*, then colors continue to be interpolated, first returning to the starting point color and then repeating indefinitely in both directions.

---

**java.awt.TexturePaint** 1.2

- TexturePaint(BufferedImage texture, Rectangle2D anchor)
  creates a texture paint object. The anchor rectangle defines the tiling of the space to be painted; it is repeated indefinitely in *x* and *y* directions, and the texture image is scaled to fill each tile.

---

# 7.6 Coordinate Transformations

Suppose you need to draw an object, such as an automobile. You know, from the manufacturer's specifications, the height, wheelbase, and total length. You could, of course, figure out all pixel positions, assuming some number of pixels per meter. However, there is an easier way: You can ask the graphics context to carry out the conversion for you.

```
g2.scale(pixelsPerMeter, pixelsPerMeter);
g2.draw(new Line2D.Double(coordinates in meters)); // converts to pixels and draws scaled line
```

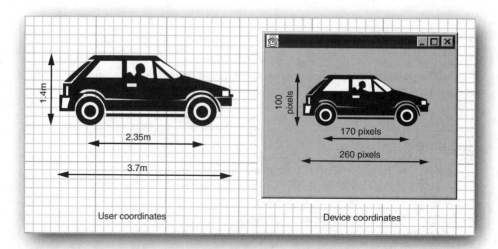

**Figure 7.17** User and device coordinates

The scale method of the Graphics2D class sets the *coordinate transformation* of the graphics context to a scaling transformation. That transformation changes *user coordinates* (user-specified units) to *device coordinates* (pixels). Figure 7.17 shows how the transformation works.

Coordinate transformations are very useful in practice. They allow you to work with convenient coordinate values. The graphics context takes care of the dirty work of transforming them to pixels.

There are four fundamental transformations.

- Scaling: blowing up, or shrinking, all distances from a fixed point.
- Rotation: rotating all points around a fixed center.
- Translation: moving all points by a fixed amount.
- Shear: leaving one line fixed and "sliding" the lines parallel to it by an amount that is proportional to the distance from the fixed line.

Figure 7.18 shows how these four fundamental transformations act on a unit square.

The scale, rotate, translate, and shear methods of the Graphics2D class set the coordinate transformation of the graphics context to one of these fundamental transformations.

You can *compose* the transformations. For example, you might want to rotate shapes *and* double their size; supply both a rotation and a scaling transformation:

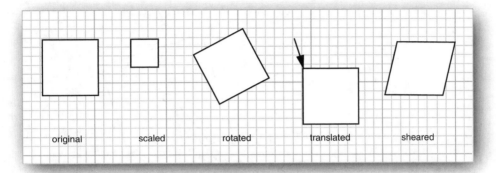

**Figure 7.18** The fundamental transformations

```
g2.rotate(angle);
g2.scale(2, 2);
g2.draw(. . .);
```

In this case, it does not matter in which order you supply the transformations. However, with most transformations, order does matter. For example, if you want to rotate and shear, then it makes a difference which of the transformations you supply first. You need to figure out what your intention is. The graphics context will apply the transformations in the order opposite to that in which you supplied them—that is, the last transformation you supply is applied first.

You can supply as many transformations as you like. For example, consider the following sequence of transformations:

```
g2.translate(x, y);
g2.rotate(a);
g2.translate(-x, -y);
```

The last transformation (which is applied first) moves the point (x, y) to the origin. The second transformation rotates with an angle a around the origin. The final transformation moves the origin back to (x, y). The overall effect is a rotation with center point (x, y)—see Figure 7.19. Since rotating about a point other than the origin is such a common operation, there is a shortcut:

```
g2.rotate(a, x, y);
```

If you know some matrix theory, you are probably aware that all rotations, translations, scalings, shears, and their compositions can be expressed by transformation matrices of the form:

$$
\begin{bmatrix} x_{new} \\ y_{new} \\ 1 \end{bmatrix} = \begin{bmatrix} a & c & e \\ b & d & f \\ 0 & 0 & 1 \end{bmatrix} \cdot \begin{bmatrix} x \\ y \\ 1 \end{bmatrix}
$$

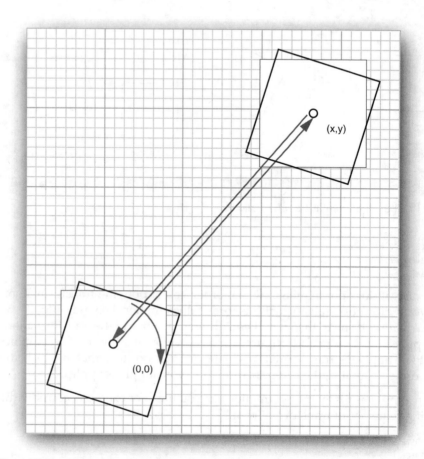

**Figure 7.19** Composing transformations

Such a transformation is called an *affine transformation.* In the Java 2D API, the AffineTransform class describes such a transformation. If you know the components of a particular transformation matrix, you can construct it directly as

```
AffineTransform t = new AffineTransform(a, b, c, d, e, f);
```

Additionally, the factory methods getRotateInstance, getScaleInstance, getTranslateInstance, and getShearInstance construct the matrices that represent these transformation types. For example, the call

```
t = AffineTransform.getScaleInstance(2.0F, 0.5F);
```

returns a transformation that corresponds to the matrix

$$\begin{bmatrix} 2 & 0 & 0 \\ 0 & 0.5 & 0 \\ 0 & 0 & 1 \end{bmatrix}$$

Finally, the instance methods `setToRotation`, `setToScale`, `setToTranslation`, and `setToShear` set a transformation object to a new type. Here is an example:

```
t.setToRotation(angle); // sets t to a rotation
```

You can set the coordinate transformation of the graphics context to an `AffineTransform` object.

```
g2.setTransform(t); // replaces current transformation
```

However, in practice, you shouldn't call the `setTransform` operation, as it replaces any existing transformation that the graphics context may have. For example, a graphics context for printing in landscape mode already contains a 90-degree rotation transformation. If you call `setTransform`, you obliterate that rotation. Instead, call the `transform` method.

```
g2.transform(t); // composes current transformation with t
```

It composes the existing transformation with the new `AffineTransform` object.

If you just want to apply a transformation temporarily, first get the old transformation, compose it with your new transformation, and finally restore the old transformation when you are done.

```
AffineTransform oldTransform = g2.getTransform(); // save old transform
g2.transform(t); // apply temporary transform
draw on g2
g2.setTransform(oldTransform); // restore old transform
```

---

**java.awt.geom.AffineTransform** 1.2

- `AffineTransform(double a, double b, double c, double d, double e, double f)`
- `AffineTransform(float a, float b, float c, float d, float e, float f)`
  constructs the affine transform with matrix

  $$\begin{bmatrix} a & c & e \\ b & d & f \\ 0 & 0 & 1 \end{bmatrix}$$

- `AffineTransform(double[] m)`
- `AffineTransform(float[] m)`
  constructs the affine transform with matrix

---

*(Continues)*

---

`java.awt.geom.AffineTransform` 1.2 *(Continued)*

$$\begin{bmatrix} m[0] & m[2] & m[4] \\ m[1] & m[3] & m[5] \\ 0 & 0 & 1 \end{bmatrix}$$

- static AffineTransform getRotateInstance(double a)

creates a rotation around the origin by the angle a (in radians). The transformation matrix is

$$\begin{bmatrix} \cos(a) & -\sin(a) & 0 \\ \sin(a) & \cos(a) & 0 \\ 0 & 0 & 1 \end{bmatrix}$$

If a is between 0 and $\pi / 2$, the rotation moves the positive $x$ axis toward the positive $y$ axis.

- static AffineTransform getRotateInstance(double a, double x, double y)

creates a rotation around the point (x,y) by the angle a (in radians).

- static AffineTransform getScaleInstance(double sx, double sy)

creates a scaling transformation that scales the $x$ axis by sx and the $y$ axis by sy. The transformation matrix is

$$\begin{bmatrix} sx & 0 & 0 \\ 0 & sy & 0 \\ 0 & 0 & 1 \end{bmatrix}$$

- static AffineTransform getShearInstance(double shx, double shy)

creates a shear transformation that shears the $x$ axis by shx and the $y$ axis by shy. The transformation matrix is

$$\begin{bmatrix} 1 & shx & 0 \\ shy & 1 & 0 \\ 0 & 0 & 1 \end{bmatrix}$$

- static AffineTransform getTranslateInstance(double tx, double ty)

creates a translation that moves the $x$ axis by tx and the $y$ axis by ty. The transformation matrix is

$$\begin{bmatrix} 1 & 0 & tx \\ 0 & 1 & ty \\ 0 & 0 & 1 \end{bmatrix}$$

*(Continues)*

---

**java.awt.geom.AffineTransform** 1.2 *(Continued)*

- void setToRotation(double a)
- void setToRotation(double a, double x, double y)
- void setToScale(double sx, double sy)
- void setToShear(double sx, double sy)
- void setToTranslation(double tx, double ty)

  sets this affine transformation to a basic transformation with the given parameters. See the get*Xxx*Instance methods for an explanation of the basic transformations and their parameters.

---

**java.awt.Graphics2D** 1.2

- void setTransform(AffineTransform t)

  replaces the existing coordinate transformation of this graphics context with t.

- void transform(AffineTransform t)

  composes the existing coordinate transformation of this graphics context with t.

- void rotate(double a)
- void rotate(double a, double x, double y)
- void scale(double sx, double sy)
- void shear(double sx, double sy)
- void translate(double tx, double ty)

  composes the existing coordinate transformation of this graphics context with a basic transformation with the given parameters. See the AffineTransform.get*Xxx*Instance method for an explanation of the basic transformations and their parameters.

## 7.7 Clipping

By setting a *clipping shape* in the graphics context, you constrain all drawing operations to the interior of that clipping shape.

```
g2.setClip(clipShape); // but see below
g2.draw(shape); // draws only the part that falls inside the clipping shape
```

However, in practice, you don't want to call the setClip operation because it replaces any existing clipping shape that the graphics context might have. For example, as you will see later in this chapter, a graphics context for printing comes with a clip rectangle that ensures that you don't draw on the margins. Instead, call the clip method.

```
g2.clip(clipShape); // better
```

The clip method intersects the existing clipping shape with the new one that you supply.

If you just want to apply a clipping area temporarily, you should first get the old clip, add your new clip, and finally restore the old clip when you are done:

```
Shape oldClip = g2.getClip(); // save old clip
g2.clip(clipShape); // apply temporary clip
draw on g2
g2.setClip(oldClip); // restore old clip
```

In Figure 7.20, we show off the clipping capability with a rather dramatic drawing of a line pattern clipped by a complex shape—namely, the outline of a set of letters.

To obtain the character outlines, you need a *font render context*. Use the getFontRenderContext method of the Graphics2D class.

```
FontRenderContext context = g2.getFontRenderContext();
```

Next, using a string, a font, and the font render context, create a TextLayout object:

```
TextLayout layout = new TextLayout("Hello", font, context);
```

This text layout object describes the layout of a sequence of characters, as rendered by a particular font render context. The layout depends on the font render context—the same characters will look different on a screen or on a printer.

More important for our application, the getOutline method returns a Shape object that describes the shape of the outline of the characters in the text layout. The outline shape starts at the origin (0, 0), which might not be what you want. In that case, supply an affine transform to the getOutline operation to specify where you would like the outline to appear.

**Figure 7.20** Using letter shapes to clip a line pattern

```
AffineTransform transform = AffineTransform.getTranslateInstance(0, 100);
Shape outline = layout.getOutline(transform);
```

Then, append the outline to the clipping shape.

```
GeneralPath clipShape = new GeneralPath();
clipShape.append(outline, false);
```

Finally, set the clipping shape and draw a set of lines. The lines appear only inside the character boundaries.

```
g2.setClip(clipShape);
Point2D p = new Point2D.Double(0, 0);
for (int i = 0; i < NLINES; i++)
{
    double x = . . .;
    double y = . . .;
    Point2D q = new Point2D.Double(x, y);
    g2.draw(new Line2D.Double(p, q)); // lines are clipped
}
```

---

**java.awt.Graphics** 1.0

- void setClip(Shape s) **1.2**
  sets the current clipping shape to the shape s.
- Shape getClip() **1.2**
  returns the current clipping shape.

---

**java.awt.Graphics2D** 1.2

- void clip(Shape s)
  intersects the current clipping shape with the shape s.
- FontRenderContext getFontRenderContext()
  returns a font render context that is necessary for constructing TextLayout objects.

---

**java.awt.font.TextLayout** 1.2

- TextLayout(String s, Font f, FontRenderContext context)
  constructs a text layout object from a given string and font, using the font render context to obtain font properties for a particular device.
- float getAdvance()
  returns the width of this text layout.

*(Continues)*

---

`java.awt.font.TextLayout` 1.2 *(Continued)*

---

- `float getAscent()`
- `float getDescent()`
  returns the height of this text layout above and below the baseline.

- `float getLeading()`
  returns the distance between successive lines in the font used by this text layout.

---

# 7.8 Transparency and Composition

In the standard RGB color model, every color is described by its red, green, and blue components. However, it is also convenient to describe areas of an image that are *transparent* or partially transparent. When you superimpose an image onto an existing drawing, the transparent pixels do not obscure the pixels under them at all, whereas partially transparent pixels are mixed with the pixels under them. Figure 7.21 shows the effect of overlaying a partially transparent rectangle on an image. You can still see the details of the image shine through from under the rectangle.

In the Java 2D API, transparency is described by an *alpha channel*. Each pixel has, in addition to its red, green, and blue color components, an alpha value between 0 (fully transparent) and 1 (fully opaque). For example, the rectangle in Figure 7.21 was filled with a pale yellow color with 50% transparency:

```
new Color(0.7F, 0.7F, 0.0F, 0.5F);
```

Now let us look at what happens if you superimpose two shapes. You need to blend or *compose* the colors and alpha values of the source and destination pixels. Porter and Duff, two researchers in the field of computer graphics, have formulated 12 possible *composition rules* for this blending process. The Java 2D API implements all of these rules. Before going any further, we'd like to point out that only two of these rules have practical significance. If you find the rules arcane or

**Figure 7.21** Overlaying a partially transparent rectangle on an image

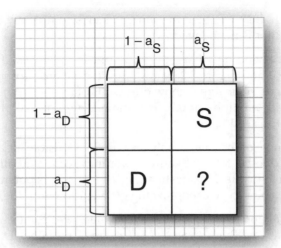

**Figure 7.22** Designing a composition rule

confusing, just use the SRC_OVER rule. It is the default rule for a Graphics2D object, and it gives the most intuitive results.

Here is the theory behind the rules. Suppose you have a *source pixel* with alpha value $a_S$. In the image, there is already a *destination pixel* with alpha value $a_D$. You want to compose the two. The diagram in Figure 7.22 shows how to design a composition rule.

Porter and Duff consider the alpha value as the probability that the pixel color should be used. From the perspective of the source, there is a probability $a_S$ that it wants to use the source color and a probability of $1 - a_S$ that it doesn't care. The same holds for the destination. When composing the colors, let us assume that the probabilities are independent. Then there are four cases, as shown in Figure 7.22. If the source wants to use the source color and the destination doesn't care, then it seems reasonable to let the source have its way. That's why the upper right corner of the diagram is labeled "S". The probability for that event is $a_S \cdot (1 - a_D)$. Similarly, the lower left corner is labeled "D". What should one do if both destination and source would like to select their color? That's where the Porter–Duff rules come in. If we decide that the source is more important, we label the lower right corner with an "S" as well. That rule is called SRC_OVER. In that rule, you combine the source colors with a weight of $a_S$ and the destination colors with a weight of $(1 - a_S) \cdot a_D$.

The visual effect is a blending of the source and destination, with preference given to the source. In particular, if $a_S$ is 1, then the destination color is not taken into account at all. If $a_S$ is 0, then the source pixel is completely transparent and the destination color is unchanged.

The other rules depend on what letters you put in the boxes of the probability diagram. Table 7.1 and Figure 7.23 show all rules that are supported by the Java 2D API. The images in the figure show the results of the rules when a rectangular source region with an alpha of 0.75 is combined with an elliptical destination region with an alpha of 1.0.

As you can see, most of the rules aren't very useful. Consider, as an extreme case, the DST_IN rule. It doesn't take the source color into account at all, but it uses the alpha of the source to affect the destination. The SRC rule is potentially useful—it forces the source color to be used, turning off blending with the destination.

For more information on the Porter–Duff rules, see, for example, *Computer Graphics: Principles and Practice, Second Edition in C*, by James D. Foley, Andries van Dam, Steven K. Feiner, et al.

Use the setComposite method of the Graphics2D class to install an object of a class that implements the Composite interface. The Java 2D API supplies one such class, AlphaComposite, that implements all the Porter–Duff rules in Figure 7.23.

**Table 7.1** The Porter–Duff Composition Rules

| Rule | Explanation |
| --- | --- |
| CLEAR | Source clears destination. |
| SRC | Source overwrites destination and empty pixels. |
| DST | Source does not affect destination. |
| SRC_OVER | Source blends with destination and overwrites empty pixels. |
| DST_OVER | Source does not affect destination and overwrites empty pixels. |
| SRC_IN | Source overwrites destination. |
| SRC_OUT | Source clears destination and overwrites empty pixels. |
| DST_IN | Source alpha modifies destination. |
| DST_OUT | Source alpha complement modifies destination. |
| SRC_ATOP | Source blends with destination. |
| DST_ATOP | Source alpha modifies destination. Source overwrites empty pixels. |
| XOR | Source alpha complement modifies destination. Source overwrites empty pixels. |

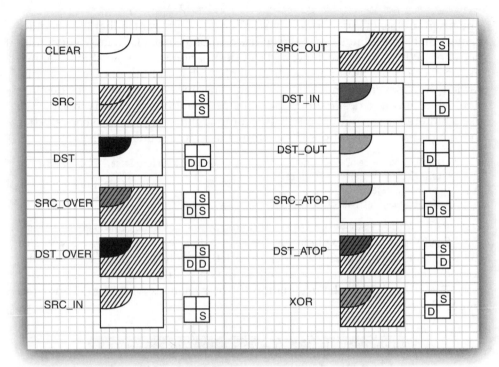

**Figure 7.23** Porter–Duff composition rules

The factory method getInstance of the AlphaComposite class yields an AlphaComposite object. You supply the rule and the alpha value to be used for source pixels. For example, consider the following code:

```
int rule = AlphaComposite.SRC_OVER;
float alpha = 0.5f;
g2.setComposite(AlphaComposite.getInstance(rule, alpha));
g2.setPaint(Color.blue);
g2.fill(rectangle);
```

The rectangle is then painted with blue color and an alpha value of 0.5. Since the composition rule is SRC_OVER, it is transparently overlaid on the existing image.

The program in Listing 7.3 lets you explore these composition rules. Pick a rule from the combo box and use the slider to set the alpha value of the AlphaComposite object.

Furthermore, the program displays a verbal description of each rule. Note that the descriptions are computed from the composition rule diagrams. For example, a "DS" in the second row stands for "blends with destination."

The program has one important twist. There is no guarantee that the graphics context that corresponds to the screen has an alpha channel. (In fact, it generally does not.) When pixels are deposited to a destination without an alpha channel, the pixel colors are multiplied with the alpha value and the alpha value is discarded. Now, several of the Porter–Duff rules use the alpha values of the destination, which means a destination alpha channel is important. For that reason, we use a buffered image with the ARGB color model to compose the shapes. After the images have been composed, we draw the resulting image to the screen.

```
BufferedImage image = new BufferedImage(getWidth(), getHeight(), BufferedImage.TYPE_INT_ARGB);
Graphics2D gImage = image.createGraphics();
// now draw to gImage
g2.drawImage(image, null, 0, 0);
```

Listings 7.3 and 7.4 show the frame and component class. The Rule class in Listing 7.5 provides a brief explanation for each rule—see Figure 7.24. As you run the program, move the alpha slider from left to right to see the effect on the composed shapes. In particular, note that the only difference between the DST_IN and DST_OUT rules is how the destination (!) color changes when you change the source alpha.

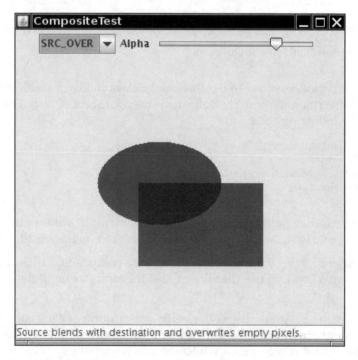

**Figure 7.24** The CompositeTest program

**Listing 7.3** composite/CompositeTestFrame.java

```
1  package composite;
2
3  import java.awt.*;
4  import java.awt.event.*;
5  import javax.swing.*;
6  import javax.swing.event.*;
7
8  /**
9   * This frame contains a combo box to choose a composition rule, a slider to change the source
10  * alpha channel, and a component that shows the composition.
11  */
12  class CompositeTestFrame extends JFrame
13  {
14     private static final int DEFAULT_WIDTH = 400;
15     private static final int DEFAULT_HEIGHT = 400;
16
17     private CompositeComponent canvas;
18     private JComboBox<Rule> ruleCombo;
19     private JSlider alphaSlider;
20     private JTextField explanation;
21
22     public CompositeTestFrame()
23     {
24        setSize(DEFAULT_WIDTH, DEFAULT_HEIGHT);
25
26        canvas = new CompositeComponent();
27        add(canvas, BorderLayout.CENTER);
28
29        ruleCombo = new JComboBox<>(new Rule[] { new Rule("CLEAR", " ", " "),
30              new Rule("SRC", " S", " S"), new Rule("DST", " ", "DD"),
31              new Rule("SRC_OVER", " S", "DS"), new Rule("DST_OVER", " S", "DD"),
32              new Rule("SRC_IN", " ", " S"), new Rule("SRC_OUT", " S", " "),
33              new Rule("DST_IN", " ", " D"), new Rule("DST_OUT", " ", "D "),
34              new Rule("SRC_ATOP", " ", "DS"), new Rule("DST_ATOP", " S", " D"),
35              new Rule("XOR", " S", "D "), });
36        ruleCombo.addActionListener(new ActionListener()
37           {
38              public void actionPerformed(ActionEvent event)
39              {
40                 Rule r = (Rule) ruleCombo.getSelectedItem();
41                 canvas.setRule(r.getValue());
42                 explanation.setText(r.getExplanation());
43              }
44           });
45
46        alphaSlider = new JSlider(0, 100, 75);
```

*(Continues)*

---

**Listing 7.3** *(Continued)*

```
47        alphaSlider.addChangeListener(new ChangeListener()
48           {
49              public void stateChanged(ChangeEvent event)
50              {
51                 canvas.setAlpha(alphaSlider.getValue());
52              }
53           });
54        JPanel panel = new JPanel();
55        panel.add(ruleCombo);
56        panel.add(new JLabel("Alpha"));
57        panel.add(alphaSlider);
58        add(panel, BorderLayout.NORTH);
59
60        explanation = new JTextField();
61        add(explanation, BorderLayout.SOUTH);
62
63        canvas.setAlpha(alphaSlider.getValue());
64        Rule r = ruleCombo.getItemAt(ruleCombo.getSelectedIndex());
65        canvas.setRule(r.getValue());
66        explanation.setText(r.getExplanation());
67     }
68  }
```

---

**Listing 7.4** composite/CompositeComponent.java

```
1  package composite;
2
3  import java.awt.*;
4  import java.awt.geom.*;
5  import java.awt.image.*;
6  import javax.swing.*;
7
8  /**
9   * This component draws two shapes, composed with a composition rule.
10  */
11 class CompositeComponent extends JComponent
12 {
13    private int rule;
14    private Shape shape1;
15    private Shape shape2;
16    private float alpha;
17
18    public CompositeComponent()
19    {
20       shape1 = new Ellipse2D.Double(100, 100, 150, 100);
21       shape2 = new Rectangle2D.Double(150, 150, 150, 100);
22    }
```

```
23    public void paintComponent(Graphics g)
24    {
25       Graphics2D g2 = (Graphics2D) g;
26
27       BufferedImage image = new BufferedImage(getWidth(), getHeight(), BufferedImage.TYPE_INT_ARGB);
28       Graphics2D gImage = image.createGraphics();
29       gImage.setPaint(Color.red);
30       gImage.fill(shape1);
31       AlphaComposite composite = AlphaComposite.getInstance(rule, alpha);
32       gImage.setComposite(composite);
33       gImage.setPaint(Color.blue);
34       gImage.fill(shape2);
35       g2.drawImage(image, null, 0, 0);
36    }
37
38    /**
39     * Sets the composition rule.
40     * @param r the rule (as an AlphaComposite constant)
41     */
42    public void setRule(int r)
43    {
44       rule = r;
45       repaint();
46    }
47
48    /**
49     * Sets the alpha of the source.
50     * @param a the alpha value between 0 and 100
51     */
52    public void setAlpha(int a)
53    {
54       alpha = (float) a / 100.0F;
55       repaint();
56    }
57 }
```

**Listing 7.5** composite/Rule.java

```
1 package composite;
2
3 import java.awt.*;
4
5 /**
6  * This class describes a Porter-Duff rule.
7  */
8 class Rule
9 {
10    private String name;
```

*(Continues)*

**Listing 7.5** *(Continued)*

```
11    private String porterDuff1;
12    private String porterDuff2;
13
14    /**
15     * Constructs a Porter-Duff rule.
16     * @param n the rule name
17     * @param pd1 the first row of the Porter-Duff square
18     * @param pd2 the second row of the Porter-Duff square
19     */
20    public Rule(String n, String pd1, String pd2)
21    {
22       name = n;
23       porterDuff1 = pd1;
24       porterDuff2 = pd2;
25    }
26
27    /**
28     * Gets an explanation of the behavior of this rule.
29     * @return the explanation
30     */
31    public String getExplanation()
32    {
33       StringBuilder r = new StringBuilder("Source ");
34       if (porterDuff2.equals("  ")) r.append("clears");
35       if (porterDuff2.equals(" S")) r.append("overwrites");
36       if (porterDuff2.equals("DS")) r.append("blends with");
37       if (porterDuff2.equals(" D")) r.append("alpha modifies");
38       if (porterDuff2.equals("D ")) r.append("alpha complement modifies");
39       if (porterDuff2.equals("DD")) r.append("does not affect");
40       r.append(" destination");
41       if (porterDuff1.equals(" S")) r.append(" and overwrites empty pixels");
42       r.append(".");
43       return r.toString();
44    }
45
46    public String toString()
47    {
48       return name;
49    }
50
51    /**
52     * Gets the value of this rule in the AlphaComposite class.
53     * @return the AlphaComposite constant value, or -1 if there is no matching constant
54     */
55    public int getValue()
56    {
```

```
57      try
58      {
59          return (Integer) AlphaComposite.class.getField(name).get(null);
60      }
61      catch (Exception e)
62      {
63          return -1;
64      }
65    }
66  }
```

---

**java.awt.Graphics2D** 1.2

- void setComposite(Composite s)
  sets the composite of this graphics context to the given object that implements the
  Composite interface.

---

**java.awt.AlphaComposite** 1.2

- static AlphaComposite getInstance(int rule)
- static AlphaComposite getInstance(int rule, float sourceAlpha)
  constructs an alpha composite object. The rule is one of CLEAR, SRC, SRC_OVER, DST_OVER,
  SRC_IN, SRC_OUT, DST_IN, DST_OUT, DST, DST_ATOP, SRC_ATOP, XOR.

---

# 7.9 Rendering Hints

In the preceding sections you have seen that the rendering process is quite complex. Although the Java 2D API is surprisingly fast in most cases, sometimes you would like to have control over trade-offs between speed and quality. You can achieve this by setting *rendering hints*. The setRenderingHint method of the Graphics2D class lets you set a single hint. The hints' keys and values are declared in the RenderingHints class. Table 7.2 summarizes the choices. The values that end in _DEFAULT denote the defaults that are chosen by a particular implementation as a good trade-off between performance and quality.

The most useful of these settings involves *antialiasing*. This technique removes the "jaggies" from slanted lines and curves. As you can see in Figure 7.25, a slanted line must be drawn as a "staircase" of pixels. Especially on low-resolution screens, this line can look ugly. But if, instead of drawing each pixel completely on or off, you color in the pixels that are partially covered with the color value proportional to the area of the pixel that the line covers, then the result looks much smoother. This technique is called antialiasing. Of course, antialiasing takes a bit longer because it has to compute all those color values.

**Table 7.2** Rendering Hints

| Key | Value | Explanation |
| --- | --- | --- |
| KEY_ANTIALIASING | VALUE_ANTIALIAS_ON<br>VALUE_ANTIALIAS_OFF<br>VALUE_ANTIALIAS_DEFAULT | Turn antialiasing for shapes on or off. |
| KEY_TEXT_ANTIALIASING | VALUE_TEXT_ANTIALIAS_ON<br>VALUE_TEXT_ANTIALIAS_OFF<br>VALUE_TEXT_ANTIALIAS_DEFAULT<br>VALUE_TEXT_ANTIALIAS_GASP 6<br>VALUE_TEXT_ANTIALIAS_LCD_HRGB 6<br>VALUE_TEXT_ANTIALIAS_LCD_HBGR 6<br>VALUE_TEXT_ANTIALIAS_LCD_VRGB 6<br>VALUE_TEXT_ANTIALIAS_LCD_VBGR 6 | Turn antialiasing for fonts on or off. When using the value VALUE_TEXT_ANTIALIAS_GASP, the "gasp table" of the font is consulted to decide whether a particular size of a font should be antialiased. The LCD values force subpixel rendering for a particular display type. |
| KEY_FRACTIONALMETRICS | VALUE_FRACTIONALMETRICS_ON<br>VALUE_FRACTIONALMETRICS_OFF<br>VALUE_FRACTIONALMETRICS_DEFAULT | Turn the computation of fractional character dimensions on or off. Fractional character dimensions lead to better placement of characters. |
| KEY_RENDERING | VALUE_RENDER_QUALITY<br>VALUE_RENDER_SPEED<br>VALUE_RENDER_DEFAULT | When available, select the rendering algorithm for greater quality or speed. |
| KEY_STROKE_CONTROL 1.3 | VALUE_STROKE_NORMALIZE<br>VALUE_STROKE_PURE<br>VALUE_STROKE_DEFAULT | Select whether the placement of strokes is controlled by the graphics accelerator (which may move it by up to half a pixel) or is computed by the "pure" rule that mandates that strokes run through the centers of pixels. |
| KEY_DITHERING | VALUE_DITHER_ENABLE<br>VALUE_DITHER_DISABLE<br>VALUE_DITHER_DEFAULT | Turn dithering for colors on or off. Dithering approximates color values by drawing groups of pixels of similar colors. (Note that antialiasing can interfere with dithering.) |

| Key | Value | Explanation |
|---|---|---|
| KEY_ALPHA_INTERPOLATION | VALUE_ALPHA_INTERPOLATION_QUALITY<br>VALUE_ALPHA_INTERPOLATION_SPEED<br>VALUE_ALPHA_INTERPOLATION_DEFAULT | Turn precise computation of alpha composites on or off. |
| KEY_COLOR_RENDERING | VALUE_COLOR_RENDER_QUALITY<br>VALUE_COLOR_RENDER_SPEED<br>VALUE_COLOR_RENDER_DEFAULT | Select quality or speed for color rendering. This is only an issue when you use different color spaces. |
| KEY_INTERPOLATION | VALUE_INTERPOLATION_NEAREST_NEIGHBOR<br>VALUE_INTERPOLATION_BILINEAR<br>VALUE_INTERPOLATION_BICUBIC | Select a rule for interpolating pixels when scaling or rotating images. |

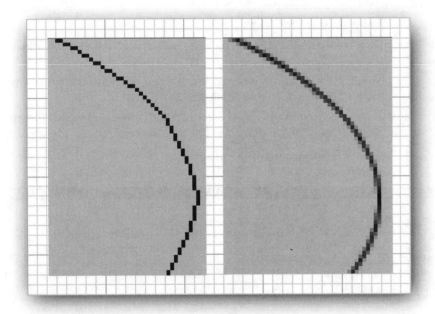

**Figure 7.25** Antialiasing

For example, here is how you can request the use of antialiasing:

```
g2.setRenderingHint(RenderingHints.KEY_ANTIALIASING, RenderingHints.VALUE_ANTIALIAS_ON);
```

It also makes sense to use antialiasing for fonts.

```
g2.setRenderingHint(RenderingHints.KEY_TEXT_ANTIALIASING,
   Rendering-Hints.VALUE_TEXT_ANTIALIAS_ON);
```

The other rendering hints are not as commonly used.

You can also put a bunch of key/value hint pairs into a map and set them all at once by calling the setRenderingHints method. Any collection class implementing the map interface will do, but you might as well use the RenderingHints class itself. It implements the Map interface and supplies a default map implementation if you pass null to the constructor. For example,

```
RenderingHints hints = new RenderingHints(null);
hints.put(RenderingHints.KEY_ANTIALIASING, RenderingHints.VALUE_ANTIALIAS_ON);
hints.put(RenderingHints.KEY_TEXT_ANTIALIASING, RenderingHints.VALUE_TEXT_ANTIALIAS_ON);
g2.setRenderingHints(hints);
```

That is the technique we use in Listing 7.6. The program shows several rendering hints that we found beneficial. Note the following:

- Antialiasing smooths the ellipse.
- Text antialiasing smooths the text.
- On some platforms, fractional text metrics move the letters a bit closer together.
- Selecting VALUE_RENDER_QUALITY smooths the scaled image. (You would get the same effect by setting KEY_INTERPOLATION to VALUE_INTERPOLATION_BICUBIC).
- When antialiasing is turned off, selecting VALUE_STROKE_NORMALIZE changes the appearance of the ellipse and the placement of the diagonal line in the square.

Figure 7.26 shows a screen capture of the program.

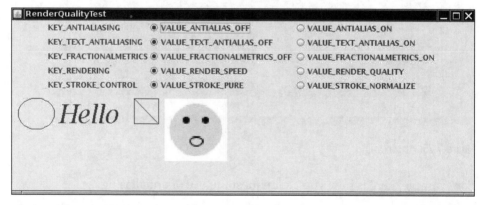

**Figure 7.26** Testing the effect of rendering hints

**Listing 7.6** renderQuality/RenderQualityTestFrame.java

```
 1 package renderQuality;
 2
 3 import java.awt.*;
 4 import java.awt.event.*;
 5 import java.awt.geom.*;
 6 import javax.swing.*;
 7
 8 /**
 9  * This frame contains buttons to set rendering hints and an image that is drawn with the selected
10  * hints.
11  */
12 public class RenderQualityTestFrame extends JFrame
13 {
14    private RenderQualityComponent canvas;
15    private JPanel buttonBox;
16    private RenderingHints hints;
17    private int r;
18
19    public RenderQualityTestFrame()
20    {
21       buttonBox = new JPanel();
22       buttonBox.setLayout(new GridBagLayout());
23       hints = new RenderingHints(null);
24
25       makeButtons("KEY_ANTIALIASING", "VALUE_ANTIALIAS_OFF", "VALUE_ANTIALIAS_ON");
26       makeButtons("KEY_TEXT_ANTIALIASING", "VALUE_TEXT_ANTIALIAS_OFF", "VALUE_TEXT_ANTIALIAS_ON");
27       makeButtons("KEY_FRACTIONALMETRICS", "VALUE_FRACTIONALMETRICS_OFF",
28             "VALUE_FRACTIONALMETRICS_ON");
29       makeButtons("KEY_RENDERING", "VALUE_RENDER_SPEED", "VALUE_RENDER_QUALITY");
30       makeButtons("KEY_STROKE_CONTROL", "VALUE_STROKE_PURE", "VALUE_STROKE_NORMALIZE");
31       canvas = new RenderQualityComponent();
32       canvas.setRenderingHints(hints);
33
34       add(canvas, BorderLayout.CENTER);
35       add(buttonBox, BorderLayout.NORTH);
36       pack();
37    }
38
39    /**
40     * Makes a set of buttons for a rendering hint key and values.
41     * @param key the key name
42     * @param value1 the name of the first value for the key
43     * @param value2 the name of the second value for the key
44     */
45    void makeButtons(String key, String value1, String value2)
46    {
```

*(Continues)*

---

**Listing 7.6** *(Continued)*

```
47      try
48      {
49          final RenderingHints.Key k = (RenderingHints.Key) RenderingHints.class.getField(key).get(
50              null);
51          final Object v1 = RenderingHints.class.getField(value1).get(null);
52          final Object v2 = RenderingHints.class.getField(value2).get(null);
53          JLabel label = new JLabel(key);
54
55          buttonBox.add(label, new GBC(0, r).setAnchor(GBC.WEST));
56          ButtonGroup group = new ButtonGroup();
57          JRadioButton b1 = new JRadioButton(value1, true);
58
59          buttonBox.add(b1, new GBC(1, r).setAnchor(GBC.WEST));
60          group.add(b1);
61          b1.addActionListener(new ActionListener()
62              {
63                  public void actionPerformed(ActionEvent event)
64                  {
65                      hints.put(k, v1);
66                      canvas.setRenderingHints(hints);
67                  }
68              });
69          JRadioButton b2 = new JRadioButton(value2, false);
70
71          buttonBox.add(b2, new GBC(2, r).setAnchor(GBC.WEST));
72          group.add(b2);
73          b2.addActionListener(new ActionListener()
74              {
75                  public void actionPerformed(ActionEvent event)
76                  {
77                      hints.put(k, v2);
78                      canvas.setRenderingHints(hints);
79                  }
80              });
81          hints.put(k, v1);
82          r++;
83      }
84      catch (Exception e)
85      {
86          e.printStackTrace();
87      }
88  }
89 }
90
91 /**
92  * This component produces a drawing that shows the effect of rendering hints.
93  */
```

```
94  class RenderQualityComponent extends JComponent
95  {
96     private static final int DEFAULT_WIDTH = 750;
97     private static final int DEFAULT_HEIGHT = 150;
98
99     private RenderingHints hints = new RenderingHints(null);
100    private Image image;
101
102    public RenderQualityComponent()
103    {
104       image = new ImageIcon(getClass().getResource("face.gif")).getImage();
105    }
106
107    public void paintComponent(Graphics g)
108    {
109       Graphics2D g2 = (Graphics2D) g;
110       g2.setRenderingHints(hints);
111
112       g2.draw(new Ellipse2D.Double(10, 10, 60, 50));
113       g2.setFont(new Font("Serif", Font.ITALIC, 40));
114       g2.drawString("Hello", 75, 50);
115
116       g2.draw(new Rectangle2D.Double(200, 10, 40, 40));
117       g2.draw(new Line2D.Double(201, 11, 239, 49));
118
119       g2.drawImage(image, 250, 10, 100, 100, null);
120    }
121
122    /**
123     * Sets the hints and repaints.
124     * @param h the rendering hints
125     */
126    public void setRenderingHints(RenderingHints h)
127    {
128       hints = h;
129       repaint();
130    }
131
132    public Dimension getPreferredSize() { return new Dimension(DEFAULT_WIDTH, DEFAULT_HEIGHT); }
133 }
```

---

**java.awt.Graphics2D**  1.2

- void setRenderingHint(RenderingHints.Key key, Object value)
  sets a rendering hint for this graphics context.

- void setRenderingHints(Map m)
  sets all rendering hints whose key/value pairs are stored in the map.

---

**`java.awt.RenderingHints`**   **1.2**

- RenderingHints(Map<RenderingHints.Key, ?> m)

  constructs a rendering hints map for storing rendering hints. If m is null, a default map implementation is provided.

---

# 7.10 Readers and Writers for Images

Prior to version 1.4, Java SE had very limited capabilities for reading and writing image files. It was possible to read GIF and JPEG images, but there was no official support for writing images at all.

This situation is now much improved. The javax.imageio package contains "out of the box" support for reading and writing several common file formats, as well as a framework that enables third parties to add readers and writers for other formats. As of Java SE 6, the GIF, JPEG, PNG, BMP (Windows bitmap), and WBMP (wireless bitmap) file formats are supported. In earlier versions, writing of GIF files was not supported because of patent issues.

The basics of the library are extremely straightforward. To load an image, use the static read method of the ImageIO class:

```
File f = . . .;
BufferedImage image = ImageIO.read(f);
```

The ImageIO class picks an appropriate reader, based on the file type. It may consult the file extension and the "magic number" at the beginning of the file for that purpose. If no suitable reader can be found or the reader can't decode the file contents, the read method returns null.

Writing an image to a file is just as simple:

```
File f = . . .;
String format = . . .;
ImageIO.write(image, format, f);
```

Here the format string is a string identifying the image format, such as "JPEG" or "PNG". The ImageIO class picks an appropriate writer and saves the file.

## 7.10.1 Obtaining Readers and Writers for Image File Types

For more advanced image reading and writing operations that go beyond the static read and write methods of the ImageIO class, you first need to get the appropriate ImageReader and ImageWriter objects. The ImageIO class enumerates readers and writers that match one of the following:

- An image format (such as "JPEG")
- A file suffix (such as "jpg")
- A MIME type (such as "image/jpeg")

 **NOTE:** MIME is the Multipurpose Internet Mail Extensions standard. The MIME standard defines common data formats such as "image/jpeg" and "application/pdf". For an HTML version of the Request for Comments (RFC) that defines the MIME format, see http://www.oac.uci.edu/indiv/ehood/MIME.

For example, you can obtain a reader that reads JPEG files as follows:

```
ImageReader reader = null;
Iterator<ImageReader> iter = ImageIO.getImageReadersByFormatName("JPEG");
if (iter.hasNext()) reader = iter.next();
```

The `getImageReadersBySuffix` and `getImageReadersByMIMEType` methods enumerate readers that match a file extension or MIME type.

It is possible that the `ImageIO` class can locate multiple readers that can all read a particular image type. In that case, you have to pick one of them, but it isn't clear how you can decide which one is the best. To find out more information about a reader, obtain its *service provider interface*:

```
ImageReaderSpi spi = reader.getOriginatingProvider();
```

Then you can get the vendor name and version number:

```
String vendor = spi.getVendor();
String version = spi.getVersion();
```

Perhaps that information can help you decide among the choices, or you might just present a list of readers to your program users and let them choose. For now, we assume that the first enumerated reader is adequate.

In the sample program in Listing 7.7, we want to find all file suffixes of all available readers so that we can use them in a file filter. Use the static `ImageIO.getReaderFileSuffixes` method for this purpose:

```
String[] extensions = ImageIO.getWriterFileSuffixes();
chooser.setFileFilter(new FileNameExtensionFilter("Image files", extensions));
```

For saving files, we have to work harder. We'd like to present the user with a menu of all supported image types. Unfortunately, the `getWriterFormatNames` of the `ImageIO` class returns a rather curious list with redundant names, such as

```
jpg, BMP, bmp, JPG, jpeg, wbmp, png, JPEG, PNG, WBMP, GIF, gif
```

That's not something one would want to present in a menu. What is needed is a list of "preferred" format names. We supply a helper method getWriterFormats for this purpose (see Listing 7.7 on p. 613). We look up the first writer associated with each format name. Then we ask it what its format names are, in the hope that it will list the most popular one first. Indeed, for the JPEG writer, this works fine—it lists "JPEG" before the other options. (The PNG writer, on the other hand, lists "png" in lower case before "PNG". We hope this behavior will be addressed at some time in the future. In the meantime, we force all-lowercase names to upper case.) Once we pick a preferred name, we remove all alternate names from the original set. We keep going until all format names are handled.

## 7.10.2 Reading and Writing Files with Multiple Images

Some files—in particular, animated GIF files—contain multiple images. The read method of the ImageIO class reads a single image. To read multiple images, turn the input source (for example, an input stream or file) into an ImageInputStream.

```
InputStream in = . . .;
ImageInputStream imageIn = ImageIO.createImageInputStream(in);
```

Then, attach the image input stream to the reader:

```
reader.setInput(imageIn, true);
```

The second parameter indicates that the input is in "seek forward only" mode. Otherwise, random access is used, either by buffering stream input as it is read or by using random file access. Random access is required for certain operations. For example, to find out the number of images in a GIF file, you need to read the entire file. If you then want to fetch an image, the input must be read again.

This consideration is only important if you read from a stream, if the input contains multiple images, and if the image format doesn't have the information that you request (such as the image count) in the header. If you read from a file, simply use

```
File f = . . .;
ImageInputStream imageIn = ImageIO.createImageInputStream(f);
reader.setInput(imageIn);
```

Once you have a reader, you can read the images in the input by calling

```
BufferedImage image = reader.read(index);
```

where index is the image index, starting with 0.

If the input is in the "seek forward only" mode, you keep reading images until the read method throws an IndexOutOfBoundsException. Otherwise, you can call the getNumImages method:

```
int n = reader.getNumImages(true);
```

Here, the parameter indicates that you allow a search of the input to determine the number of images. That method throws an IllegalStateException if the input is in the "seek forward only" mode. Alternatively, you can set the "allow search" parameter to false. Then the getNumImages method returns -1 if it can't determine the number of images without a search. In that case, you'll have to switch to Plan B and keep reading images until you get an IndexOutOfBoundsException.

Some files contain thumbnails—smaller versions of an image for preview purposes. You can get the number of thumbnails of an image with the call

```
int count = reader.getNumThumbnails(index);
```

Then you get a particular index as

```
BufferedImage thumbnail = reader.getThumbnail(index, thumbnailIndex);
```

Sometimes you may want to get the image size before actually getting the image—in particular, if the image is huge or comes from a slow network connection. Use the calls

```
int width = reader.getWidth(index);
int height = reader.getHeight(index);
```

to get the dimensions of an image with a given index.

To write a file with multiple images, you first need an ImageWriter. The ImageIO class can enumerate the writers capable of writing a particular image format:

```
String format = . . .;
ImageWriter writer = null;
Iterator<ImageWriter> iter =  ImageIO.getImageWritersByFormatName( format );
if (iter.hasNext()) writer = iter.next();
```

Next, turn an output stream or file into an ImageOutputStream and attach it to the writer. For example,

```
File f = . . .;
ImageOutputStream imageOut = ImageIO.createImageOutputStream(f);
writer.setOutput(imageOut);
```

You must wrap each image into an IIOImage object. You can optionally supply a list of thumbnails and image metadata (such as compression algorithms and color information). In this example, we just use null for both; see the API documentation for additional information.

```
IIOImage iioImage = new IIOImage(images[i], null, null);
```

To write out the *first* image, use the write method:

```
writer.write(new IIOImage(images[0], null, null));
```

For subsequent images, use

```
if (writer.canInsertImage(i))
    writer.writeInsert(i, iioImage, null);
```

The third parameter can contain an ImageWriteParam object to set image writing details such as tiling and compression; use null for default values.

Not all file formats can handle multiple images. In that case, the canInsertImage method returns false for i > 0, and only a single image is saved.

The program in Listing 7.7 lets you load and save files in the formats for which the Java library supplies readers and writers. The program displays multiple images (see Figure 7.27), but not thumbnails.

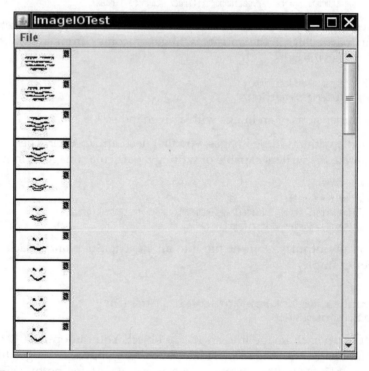

**Figure 7.27** An animated GIF image

**Listing 7.7**  imageIO/ImageIOFrame.java

```java
 1  package imageIO;
 2
 3  import java.awt.event.*;
 4  import java.awt.image.*;
 5  import java.io.*;
 6  import java.util.*;
 7  import javax.imageio.*;
 8  import javax.imageio.stream.*;
 9  import javax.swing.*;
10  import javax.swing.filechooser.*;
11
12  /**
13   * This frame displays the loaded images. The menu has items for loading and saving files.
14   */
15  public class ImageIOFrame extends JFrame
16  {
17     private static final int DEFAULT_WIDTH = 400;
18     private static final int DEFAULT_HEIGHT = 400;
19
20     private static Set<String> writerFormats = getWriterFormats();
21
22     private BufferedImage[] images;
23
24     public ImageIOFrame()
25     {
26        setSize(DEFAULT_WIDTH, DEFAULT_HEIGHT);
27
28        JMenu fileMenu = new JMenu("File");
29        JMenuItem openItem = new JMenuItem("Open");
30        openItem.addActionListener(new ActionListener()
31           {
32              public void actionPerformed(ActionEvent event)
33              {
34                 openFile();
35              }
36           });
37        fileMenu.add(openItem);
38
39        JMenu saveMenu = new JMenu("Save");
40        fileMenu.add(saveMenu);
41        Iterator<String> iter = writerFormats.iterator();
42        while (iter.hasNext())
43        {
44           final String formatName = iter.next();
45           JMenuItem formatItem = new JMenuItem(formatName);
46           saveMenu.add(formatItem);
```

*(Continues)*

---

**Listing 7.7** *(Continued)*

```
47          formatItem.addActionListener(new ActionListener()
48             {
49                public void actionPerformed(ActionEvent event)
50                {
51                   saveFile(formatName);
52                }
53             });
54       }
55
56       JMenuItem exitItem = new JMenuItem("Exit");
57       exitItem.addActionListener(new ActionListener()
58          {
59             public void actionPerformed(ActionEvent event)
60             {
61                System.exit(0);
62             }
63          });
64       fileMenu.add(exitItem);
65
66       JMenuBar menuBar = new JMenuBar();
67       menuBar.add(fileMenu);
68       setJMenuBar(menuBar);
69    }
70
71    /**
72     * Open a file and load the images.
73     */
74    public void openFile()
75    {
76       JFileChooser chooser = new JFileChooser();
77       chooser.setCurrentDirectory(new File("."));
78       String[] extensions = ImageIO.getReaderFileSuffixes();
79       chooser.setFileFilter(new FileNameExtensionFilter("Image files", extensions));
80       int r = chooser.showOpenDialog(this);
81       if (r != JFileChooser.APPROVE_OPTION) return;
82       File f = chooser.getSelectedFile();
83       Box box = Box.createVerticalBox();
84       try
85       {
86          String name = f.getName();
87          String suffix = name.substring(name.lastIndexOf('.') + 1);
88          Iterator<ImageReader> iter = ImageIO.getImageReadersBySuffix(suffix);
89          ImageReader reader = iter.next();
90          ImageInputStream imageIn = ImageIO.createImageInputStream(f);
91          reader.setInput(imageIn);
92          int count = reader.getNumImages(true);
93          images = new BufferedImage[count];
```

```
94          for (int i = 0; i < count; i++)
95          {
96             images[i] = reader.read(i);
97             box.add(new JLabel(new ImageIcon(images[i])));
98          }
99       }
100      catch (IOException e)
101      {
102         JOptionPane.showMessageDialog(this, e);
103      }
104      setContentPane(new JScrollPane(box));
105      validate();
106   }
107
108   /**
109    * Save the current image in a file.
110    * @param formatName the file format
111    */
112   public void saveFile(final String formatName)
113   {
114      if (images == null) return;
115      Iterator<ImageWriter> iter = ImageIO.getImageWritersByFormatName(formatName);
116      ImageWriter writer = iter.next();
117      JFileChooser chooser = new JFileChooser();
118      chooser.setCurrentDirectory(new File("."));
119      String[] extensions = writer.getOriginatingProvider().getFileSuffixes();
120      chooser.setFileFilter(new FileNameExtensionFilter("Image files", extensions));
121
122      int r = chooser.showSaveDialog(this);
123      if (r != JFileChooser.APPROVE_OPTION) return;
124      File f = chooser.getSelectedFile();
125      try
126      {
127         ImageOutputStream imageOut = ImageIO.createImageOutputStream(f);
128         writer.setOutput(imageOut);
129
130         writer.write(new IIOImage(images[0], null, null));
131         for (int i = 1; i < images.length; i++)
132         {
133            IIOImage iioImage = new IIOImage(images[i], null, null);
134            if (writer.canInsertImage(i)) writer.writeInsert(i, iioImage, null);
135         }
136      }
137      catch (IOException e)
138      {
139         JOptionPane.showMessageDialog(this, e);
140      }
141   }
```

*(Continues)*

**Listing 7.7** *(Continued)*

```
142    /**
143     * Gets a set of "preferred" format names of all image writers. The preferred format name is
144     * the first format name that a writer specifies.
145     * @return the format name set
146     */
147    public static Set<String> getWriterFormats()
148    {
149       Set<String> writerFormats = new TreeSet<>();
150       Set<String> formatNames = new TreeSet<>(Arrays.asList(ImageIO
151             .getWriterFormatNames()));
152       while (formatNames.size() > 0)
153       {
154          String name = formatNames.iterator().next();
155          Iterator<ImageWriter> iter = ImageIO.getImageWritersByFormatName(name);
156          ImageWriter writer = iter.next();
157          String[] names = writer.getOriginatingProvider().getFormatNames();
158          String format = names[0];
159          if (format.equals(format.toLowerCase())) format = format.toUpperCase();
160          writerFormats.add(format);
161          formatNames.removeAll(Arrays.asList(names));
162       }
163       return writerFormats;
164    }
165 }
```

---

**javax.imageio.ImageIO** 1.4

- static BufferedImage read(File input)
- static BufferedImage read(InputStream input)
- static BufferedImage read(URL input)
  reads an image from input.

- static boolean write(RenderedImage image, String formatName, File output)
- static boolean write(RenderedImage image, String formatName, OutputStream output)
  writes an image in the given format to output. Returns false if no appropriate writer was found.

- static Iterator<ImageReader> getImageReadersByFormatName(String formatName)
- static Iterator<ImageReader> getImageReadersBySuffix(String fileSuffix)
- static Iterator<ImageReader> getImageReadersByMIMEType(String mimeType)
- static Iterator<ImageWriter> getImageWritersByFormatName(String formatName)
- static Iterator<ImageWriter> getImageWritersBySuffix(String fileSuffix)

*(Continues)*

---

**javax.imageio.ImageIO** 1.4 *(Continued)*

- static Iterator<ImageWriter> getImageWritersByMIMEType(String mimeType)

  gets all readers and writers that are able to handle the given format (e.g., "JPEG"), file suffix (e.g., "jpg"), or MIME type (e.g., "image/jpeg").

- static String[] getReaderFormatNames()
- static String[] getReaderMIMETypes()
- static String[] getWriterFormatNames()
- static String[] getWriterMIMETypes()
- static String[] getReaderFileSuffixes() **6**
- static String[] getWriterFileSuffixes() **6**

  gets all format names, MIME type names, and file suffixes supported by readers and writers.

- ImageInputStream createImageInputStream(Object input)
- ImageOutputStream createImageOutputStream(Object output)

  creates an image input or image output stream from the given object. The object can be a file, a stream, a RandomAccessFile, or another object for which a service provider exists. Returns null if no registered service provider can handle the object.

---

**javax.imageio.ImageReader** 1.4

- void setInput(Object input)
- void setInput(Object input, boolean seekForwardOnly)

  sets the input source of the reader.

  | *Parameters:* | input | An ImageInputStream object or another object that this reader can accept |
  | | seekForwardOnly | true if the reader should read forward only. By default, the reader uses random access and, if necessary, buffers image data. |

- BufferedImage read(int index)

  reads the image with the given image index (starting at 0). Throws an IndexOutOfBoundsException if no such image is available.

- int getNumImages(boolean allowSearch)

  gets the number of images in this reader. If allowSearch is false and the number of images cannot be determined without reading forward, then -1 is returned. If allowSearch is true and the reader is in the "seek forward only" mode, then an IllegalStateException is thrown.

*(Continues)*

---

`javax.imageio.ImageReader` **1.4** *(Continued)*

- `int getNumThumbnails(int index)`
  gets the number of thumbnails of the image with the given index.
- `BufferedImage readThumbnail(int index, int thumbnailIndex)`
  gets the thumbnail with index `thumbnailIndex` of the image with the given index.
- `int getWidth(int index)`
- `int getHeight(int index)`
  gets the image width and height. Throws an `IndexOutOfBoundsException` if no such image is available.
- `ImageReaderSpi getOriginatingProvider()`
  gets the service provider that constructed this reader.

---

`javax.imageio.spi.IIOServiceProvider` **1.4**

- `String getVendorName()`
- `String getVersion()`
  gets the vendor name and version of this service provider.

---

`javax.imageio.spi.ImageReaderWriterSpi` **1.4**

- `String[] getFormatNames()`
- `String[] getFileSuffixes()`
- `String[] getMIMETypes()`
  gets the format names, file suffixes, and MIME types supported by the readers or writers that this service provider creates.

---

`javax.imageio.ImageWriter` **1.4**

- `void setOutput(Object output)`
  sets the output target of this writer.

  *Parameters:*    output        An `ImageOutputStream` object or another object that this writer can accept
- `void write(IIOImage image)`
- `void write(RenderedImage image)`
  writes a single image to the output.

*(Continues)*

---

**javax.imageio.ImageWriter** 1.4 *(Continued)*

---

- void writeInsert(int index, IIOImage image, ImageWriteParam param)
  writes an image into a multi-image file.

- boolean canInsertImage(int index)
  returns true if it is possible to insert an image at the given index.

- ImageWriterSpi getOriginatingProvider()
  gets the service provider that constructed this writer.

---

**javax.imageio.IIOImage** 1.4

---

- IIOImage(RenderedImage image, List thumbnails, IIOMetadata metadata)
  constructs an IIOImage from an image, optional thumbnails, and optional metadata.

---

# 7.11 Image Manipulation

Suppose you have an image and you would like to improve its appearance. You then need to access the individual pixels of the image and replace them with other pixels. Or perhaps you want to compute the pixels of an image from scratch—for example, to show the result of physical measurements or a mathematical computation. The BufferedImage class gives you control over the pixels in an image, and the classes that implement the BufferedImageOp interface let you transform images.

 **NOTE:** JDK 1.0 had a completely different, and far more complex, imaging framework that was optimized for *incremental rendering* of images downloaded from the Web, a scan line at a time. However, it was difficult to manipulate those images. We do not discuss that framework in this book.

## 7.11.1 Constructing Raster Images

Most of the images that you manipulate are simply read in from an image file—they were either produced by a device such as a digital camera or scanner, or constructed by a drawing program. In this section, we'll show you a different technique for constructing an image—namely, building it up a pixel at a time.

To create an image, construct a BufferedImage object in the usual way.

```
image = new BufferedImage(width, height, BufferedImage.TYPE_INT_ARGB);
```

Now, call the getRaster method to obtain an object of type WritableRaster. You will use this object to access and modify the pixels of the image.

```
WritableRaster raster = image.getRaster();
```

The setPixel method lets you set an individual pixel. The complexity here is that you can't simply set the pixel to a Color value. You must know how the buffered image specifies color values. That depends on the *type* of the image. If your image has a type of TYPE_INT_ARGB, then each pixel is described by four values—red, green, blue, and alpha, each between 0 and 255. You have to supply them in an array of four integers:

```
int[] black = { 0, 0, 0, 255 };
raster.setPixel(i, j, black);
```

In the lingo of the Java 2D API, these values are called the *sample values* of the pixel.

---

 **CAUTION:** There are also setPixel methods that take array parameters of types float[] and double[]. However, the values that you need to place into these arrays are *not* normalized color values between 0.0 and 1.0.

```
float[] red = { 1.0F, 0.0F, 0.0F, 1.0F };
raster.setPixel(i, j, red); // ERROR
```

You need to supply values between 0 and 255, no matter what the type of the array is.

---

You can supply batches of pixels with the setPixels method. Specify the starting pixel position and the width and height of the rectangle that you want to set. Then, supply an array that contains the sample values for all pixels. For example, if your buffered image has a type of TYPE_INT_ARGB, supply the red, green, blue, and alpha value of the first pixel, then the red, green, blue, and alpha value for the second pixel, and so on.

```
int[] pixels = new int[4 * width * height];
pixels[0] = . . . // red value for first pixel
pixels[1] = . . . // green value for first pixel
pixels[2] = . . . // blue value for first pixel
pixels[3] = . . . // alpha value for first pixel
. . .
raster.setPixels(x, y, width, height, pixels);
```

Conversely, to read a pixel, use the getPixel method. Supply an array of four integers to hold the sample values.

```
int[] sample = new int[4];
raster.getPixel(x, y, sample);
Color c = new Color(sample[0], sample[1], sample[2], sample[3]);
```

You can read multiple pixels with the getPixels method.

```
raster.getPixels(x, y, width, height, samples);
```

If you use an image type other than TYPE_INT_ARGB and you know how that type represents pixel values, you can still use the getPixel/setPixel methods. However, you have to know the encoding of the sample values in the particular image type.

If you need to manipulate an image with an arbitrary, unknown image type, then you have to work a bit harder. Every image type has a *color model* that can translate between sample value arrays and the standard RGB color model.

---

**NOTE:** The RGB color model isn't as standard as you might think. The exact look of a color value depends on the characteristics of the imaging device. Digital cameras, scanners, monitors, and LCD displays all have their own idiosyncrasies. As a result, the same RGB value can look quite different on different devices. The International Color Consortium (www.color.org) recommends that all color data be accompanied by an *ICC profile* that specifies how the colors map to a standard form such as the 1931 CIE XYZ color specification. That specification was designed by the Commission Internationale de l'Eclairage, or CIE (www.cie.co.at/cie), the international organization in charge of providing technical guidance in all matters of illumination and color. The specification is a standard method for representing any color that the human eye can perceive as a triplet of coordinates called X, Y, Z. (See, for example, *Computer Graphics: Principles and Practice, Second Edition in C*, by James D. Foley, Andries van Dam, Steven K. Feiner, et al., Chapter 13, for more information on the 1931 CIE XYZ specification.)

ICC profiles are complex, however. A simpler proposed standard, called sRGB (www.w3.org/Graphics/Color/sRGB.html), specifies an exact mapping between RGB values and the 1931 CIE XYZ values that was designed to work well with typical color monitors. The Java 2D API uses that mapping when converting between RGB and other color spaces.

---

The getColorModel method returns the color model:

```
ColorModel model = image.getColorModel();
```

To find the color value of a pixel, call the getDataElements method of the Raster class. That call returns an Object that contains a color-model-specific description of the color value.

```
Object data = raster.getDataElements(x, y, null);
```

 **NOTE:** The object that is returned by the getDataElements method is actually an array of sample values. You don't need to know this to process the object, but it explains why the method is called getDataElements.

The color model can translate the object to standard ARGB values. The getRGB method returns an int value that has the alpha, red, green, and blue values packed in four blocks of eight bits each. You can construct a Color value out of that integer with the Color(int argb, boolean hasAlpha) constructor:

```
int argb = model.getRGB(data);
Color color = new Color(argb, true);
```

To set a pixel to a particular color, reverse these steps. The getRGB method of the Color class yields an int value with the alpha, red, green, and blue values. Supply that value to the getDataElements method of the ColorModel class. The return value is an Object that contains the color-model-specific description of the color value. Pass the object to the setDataElements method of the WritableRaster class.

```
int argb = color.getRGB();
Object data = model.getDataElements(argb, null);
raster.setDataElements(x, y, data);
```

To illustrate how to use these methods to build an image from individual pixels, we bow to tradition and draw a Mandelbrot set, as shown in Figure 7.28.

The idea of the Mandelbrot set is that each point of the plane is associated with a sequence of numbers. If that sequence stays bounded, you color the point. If it "escapes to infinity," you leave it transparent.

Here is how you can construct the simplest Mandelbrot set. For each point $(a, b)$, look at sequences that start with $(x, y) = (0, 0)$ and iterate:

$$x_{new} = x^2 - y^2 + a$$

$$y_{new} = 2 \cdot x \cdot y + b$$

It turns out that if $x$ or $y$ ever gets larger than 2, then the sequence escapes to infinity. Only the pixels that correspond to points $(a, b)$ leading to a bounded sequence are colored. (The formulas for the number sequences come ultimately from the mathematics of complex numbers; we'll just take them for granted. For more on the mathematics of fractals, see, for example, http://classes.yale.edu/fractals.)

Listing 7.8 shows the code. In this program, we demonstrate how to use the ColorModel class for translating Color values into pixel data. That process is

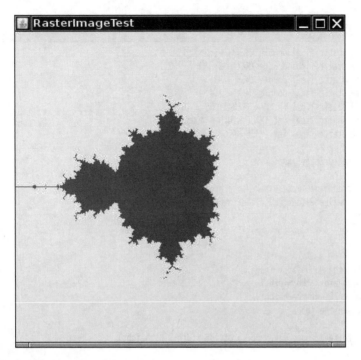

**Figure 7.28** A Mandelbrot set

independent of the image type. Just for fun, change the color type of the buffered image to TYPE_BYTE_GRAY. You don't need to change any other code—the color model of the image automatically takes care of the conversion from colors to sample values.

**Listing 7.8** rasterImage/RasterImageFrame.java

```
1  package rasterImage;
2
3  import java.awt.*;
4  import java.awt.image.*;
5  import javax.swing.*;
6
7  /**
8   * This frame shows an image with a Mandelbrot set.
9   */
10 public class RasterImageFrame extends JFrame
11 {
```

*(Continues)*

**Listing 7.8** *(Continued)*

```java
12   private static final double XMIN = -2;
13   private static final double XMAX = 2;
14   private static final double YMIN = -2;
15   private static final double YMAX = 2;
16   private static final int MAX_ITERATIONS = 16;
17   private static final int IMAGE_WIDTH = 400;
18   private static final int IMAGE_HEIGHT = 400;
19
20   public RasterImageFrame()
21   {
22      BufferedImage image = makeMandelbrot(IMAGE_WIDTH, IMAGE_HEIGHT);
23      add(new JLabel(new ImageIcon(image)));
24      pack();
25   }
26
27   /**
28    * Makes the Mandelbrot image.
29    * @param width the width
30    * @parah height the height
31    * @return the image
32    */
33   public BufferedImage makeMandelbrot(int width, int height)
34   {
35      BufferedImage image = new BufferedImage(width, height, BufferedImage.TYPE_INT_ARGB);
36      WritableRaster raster = image.getRaster();
37      ColorModel model = image.getColorModel();
38
39      Color fractalColor = Color.red;
40      int argb = fractalColor.getRGB();
41      Object colorData = model.getDataElements(argb, null);
42
43      for (int i = 0; i < width; i++)
44         for (int j = 0; j < height; j++)
45         {
46            double a = XMIN + i * (XMAX - XMIN) / width;
47            double b = YMIN + j * (YMAX - YMIN) / height;
48            if (!escapesToInfinity(a, b)) raster.setDataElements(i, j, colorData);
49         }
50      return image;
51   }
52
53   private boolean escapesToInfinity(double a, double b)
54   {
55      double x = 0.0;
56      double y = 0.0;
57      int iterations = 0;
58      while (x <= 2 && y <= 2 && iterations < MAX_ITERATIONS)
59      {
```

```
60          double xnew = x * x - y * y + a;
61          double ynew = 2 * x * y + b;
62          x = xnew;
63          y = ynew;
64          iterations++;
65       }
66       return x > 2 || y > 2;
67    }
68 }
```

---

**java.awt.image.BufferedImage** **1.2**

- BufferedImage(int width, int height, int imageType)
  constructs a buffered image object.

  | *Parameters:* | width, height | The image dimensions |
  |---|---|---|
  | | imageType | The image type. The most common types are TYPE_INT_RGB, TYPE_INT_ARGB, TYPE_BYTE_GRAY, and TYPE_BYTE_INDEXED. |

- ColorModel getColorModel()
  returns the color model of this buffered image.

- WritableRaster getRaster()
  gets the raster for accessing and modifying pixels of this buffered image.

---

**java.awt.image.Raster** **1.2**

- Object getDataElements(int x, int y, Object data)
  returns the sample data for a raster point, in an array whose element type and length depend on the color model. If data is not null, it is assumed to be an array that is appropriate for holding sample data, and it is filled. If data is null, a new array is allocated. Its element type and length depend on the color model.

- int[] getPixel(int x, int y, int[] sampleValues)
- float[] getPixel(int x, int y, float[] sampleValues)
- double[] getPixel(int x, int y, double[] sampleValues)
- int[] getPixels(int x, int y, int width, int height, int[] sampleValues)
- float[] getPixels(int x, int y, int width, int height, float[] sampleValues)
- double[] getPixels(int x, int y, int width, int height, double[] sampleValues)
  returns the sample values for a raster point, or a rectangle of raster points, in an array whose length depends on the color model. If sampleValues is not null, it is assumed to be sufficiently long for holding the sample values, and it is filled. If sampleValues is null, a new array is allocated. These methods are only useful if you know the meaning of the sample values for a color model.

---

`java.awt.image.WritableRaster` **1.2**

- void setDataElements(int x, int y, Object data)
  sets the sample data for a raster point. data is an array filled with the sample data for a pixel. Its element type and length depend on the color model.
- void setPixel(int x, int y, int[] sampleValues)
- void setPixel(int x, int y, float[] sampleValues)
- void setPixel(int x, int y, double[] sampleValues)
- void setPixels(int x, int y, int width, int height, int[] sampleValues)
- void setPixels(int x, int y, int width, int height, float[] sampleValues)
- void setPixels(int x, int y, int width, int height, double[] sampleValues)
  sets the sample values for a raster point or a rectangle of raster points. These methods are only useful if you know the encoding of the sample values for a color model.

---

`java.awt.image.ColorModel` **1.2**

- int getRGB(Object data)
  returns the ARGB value that corresponds to the sample data passed in the data array. Its element type and length depend on the color model.
- Object getDataElements(int argb, Object data);
  returns the sample data for a color value. If data is not null, it is assumed to be an array that is appropriate for holding sample data, and it is filled. If data is null, a new array is allocated. data is an array filled with the sample data for a pixel. Its element type and length depend on the color model.

---

`java.awt.Color` **1.0**

- Color(int argb, boolean hasAlpha) **1.2**
  creates a color with the specified combined ARGB value if hasAlpha is true, or the specified RGB value if hasAlpha is false.
- int getRGB()
  returns the ARGB color value corresponding to this color.

## 7.11.2 Filtering Images

In the preceding section, you saw how to build up an image from scratch. However, often you want to access image data for a different reason: You already have an image and you want to improve it in some way.

Of course, you can use the `getPixel`/`getDataElements` methods that you saw in the preceding section to read the image data, manipulate them, and write them back. But fortunately, the Java 2D API already supplies a number of *filters* that carry out common image processing operations for you.

The image manipulations all implement the `BufferedImageOp` interface. After you construct the operation, you simply call the `filter` method to transform an image into another.

```
BufferedImageOp op = . . .;
BufferedImage filteredImage
   = new BufferedImage(image.getWidth(), image.getHeight(), image.getType());
op.filter(image, filteredImage);
```

Some operations can transform an image in place (`op.filter(image, image)`), but most can't.

Five classes implement the `BufferedImageOp` interface:

```
AffineTransformOp
RescaleOp
LookupOp
ColorConvertOp
ConvolveOp
```

The `AffineTransformOp` carries out an affine transformation on the pixels. For example, here is how you can rotate an image about its center:

```
AffineTransform transform = AffineTransform.getRotateInstance(Math.toRadians(angle),
   image.getWidth() / 2, image.getHeight() / 2);
AffineTransformOp op = new AffineTransformOp(transform, interpolation);
op.filter(image, filteredImage);
```

The `AffineTransformOp` constructor requires an affine transform and an *interpolation* strategy. Interpolation is necessary to determine pixels in the target image if the source pixels are transformed somewhere between target pixels. For example, if you rotate source pixels, then they will generally not fall exactly onto target pixels. There are two interpolation strategies: `AffineTransformOp.TYPE_BILINEAR` and `AffineTransformOp.TYPE_NEAREST_NEIGHBOR`. Bilinear interpolation takes a bit longer but looks better.

The program in Listing 7.9 lets you rotate an image by 5 degrees (see Figure 7.29).

The `RescaleOp` carries out a rescaling operation

$$x_{new} = a \cdot x + b$$

for each of the color components in the image. (Alpha components are not affected.) The effect of rescaling with $a > 1$ is to brighten the image. Construct the

**Figure 7.29** A rotated image

RescaleOp by specifying the scaling parameters and optional rendering hints. In Listing 7.9, we use:

```
float a = 1.1f;
float 20.0f;
RescaleOp op = new RescaleOp(a, b, null);
```

You can also supply separate scaling values for each color component—see the API notes.

The LookupOp operation lets you specify an arbitrary mapping of sample values. Supply a table that specifies how each value should be mapped. In the example program, we compute the *negative* of all colors, changing the color $c$ to $255 - c$.

The LookupOp constructor requires an object of type LookupTable and a map of optional hints. The LookupTable class is abstract, with two concrete subclasses: ByteLookupTable and ShortLookupTable. Since RGB color values are bytes, a ByteLookupTable should suffice. However, because of the bug described in http://bugs.sun.com/bugdatabase/view_bug.do?bug_id=6183251, we will use a ShortLookupTable instead. Here is how we construct the LookupOp for the example program:

```
short negative[] = new short[256];
for (int i = 0; i < 256; i++) negative[i] = (short) (255 - i);
ShortLookupTable table = new ShortLookupTable(0, negative);
LookupOp op = new LookupOp(table, null);
```

The lookup is applied to each color component separately, but not to the alpha component. You can also supply different lookup tables for each color component—see the API notes.

**NOTE:** You cannot apply a LookupOp to an image with an indexed color model. (In those images, each sample value is an offset into a color palette.)

The ColorConvertOp is useful for color space conversions. We do not discuss it here.

The most powerful of the transformations is the ConvolveOp, which carries out a mathematical *convolution*. We do not want to get too deeply into the mathematical details, but the basic idea is simple. Consider, for example, the *blur filter* (see Figure 7.30).

The blurring is achieved by replacing each pixel with the *average* value from the pixel and its eight neighbors. Intuitively, it makes sense why this operation would blur out the picture. Mathematically, the averaging can be expressed as a convolution operation with the following *kernel:*

$$\begin{bmatrix} 1/9 & 1/9 & 1/9 \\ 1/9 & 1/9 & 1/9 \\ 1/9 & 1/9 & 1/9 \end{bmatrix}$$

The kernel of a convolution is a matrix that tells what weights should be applied to the neighboring values. The kernel above leads to a blurred image. A different kernel carries out *edge detection,* locating areas of color changes:

$$\begin{bmatrix} 0 & -1 & 0 \\ -1 & 4 & -1 \\ 0 & -1 & 0 \end{bmatrix}$$

**Figure 7.30** Blurring an image

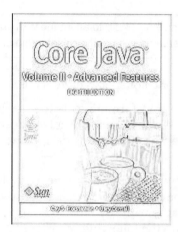

**Figure 7.31** Edge detection and inversion

Edge detection is an important technique for analyzing photographic images (see Figure 7.31).

To construct a convolution operation, you first set up an array of the values for the kernel and construct a `Kernel` object. Then, construct a `ConvolveOp` object from the kernel and use it for filtering.

```
float[] elements =
    {
        0.0f, -1.0f, 0.0f,
        -1.0f,  4.f, -1.0f,
        0.0f, -1.0f, 0.0f
    };
Kernel kernel = new Kernel(3, 3, elements);
ConvolveOp op = new ConvolveOp(kernel);
op.filter(image, filteredImage);
```

The program in Listing 7.9 allows a user to load in a GIF or JPEG image and carry out the image manipulations that we discussed. Thanks to the power of the image operations provided by Java 2D API, the program is very simple.

**Listing 7.9** imageProcessing/ImageProcessingFrame.java

```
1  package imageProcessing;
2
3  import java.awt.*;
4  import java.awt.event.*;
5  import java.awt.geom.*;
6  import java.awt.image.*;
```

```
7   import java.io.*;
8   import javax.imageio.*;
9   import javax.swing.*;
10  import javax.swing.filechooser.*;
11
12  /**
13   * This frame has a menu to load an image and to specify various transformations, and a component
14   * to show the resulting image.
15   */
16  public class ImageProcessingFrame extends JFrame
17  {
18     private static final int DEFAULT_WIDTH = 400;
19     private static final int DEFAULT_HEIGHT = 400;
20
21     private BufferedImage image;
22
23     public ImageProcessingFrame()
24     {
25        setTitle("ImageProcessingTest");
26        setSize(DEFAULT_WIDTH, DEFAULT_HEIGHT);
27
28        add(new JComponent()
29           {
30              public void paintComponent(Graphics g)
31              {
32                 if (image != null) g.drawImage(image, 0, 0, null);
33              }
34           });
35
36        JMenu fileMenu = new JMenu("File");
37        JMenuItem openItem = new JMenuItem("Open");
38        openItem.addActionListener(new ActionListener()
39           {
40              public void actionPerformed(ActionEvent event)
41              {
42                 openFile();
43              }
44           });
45        fileMenu.add(openItem);
46
47        JMenuItem exitItem = new JMenuItem("Exit");
48        exitItem.addActionListener(new ActionListener()
49           {
50              public void actionPerformed(ActionEvent event)
51              {
52                 System.exit(0);
53              }
54           });
```

*(Continues)*

**Listing 7.9** *(Continued)*

```
55       fileMenu.add(exitItem);
56
57       JMenu editMenu = new JMenu("Edit");
58       JMenuItem blurItem = new JMenuItem("Blur");
59       blurItem.addActionListener(new ActionListener()
60          {
61             public void actionPerformed(ActionEvent event)
62             {
63                float weight = 1.0f / 9.0f;
64                float[] elements = new float[9];
65                for (int i = 0; i < 9; i++)
66                   elements[i] = weight;
67                convolve(elements);
68             }
69          });
70       editMenu.add(blurItem);
71
72       JMenuItem sharpenItem = new JMenuItem("Sharpen");
73       sharpenItem.addActionListener(new ActionListener()
74          {
75             public void actionPerformed(ActionEvent event)
76             {
77                float[] elements = { 0.0f, -1.0f, 0.0f, -1.0f, 5.f, -1.0f, 0.0f, -1.0f, 0.0f };
78                convolve(elements);
79             }
80          });
81       editMenu.add(sharpenItem);
82
83       JMenuItem brightenItem = new JMenuItem("Brighten");
84       brightenItem.addActionListener(new ActionListener()
85          {
86             public void actionPerformed(ActionEvent event)
87             {
88                float a = 1.1f;
89                // float b = 20.0f;
90                float b = 0;
91                RescaleOp op = new RescaleOp(a, b, null);
92                filter(op);
93             }
94          });
95       editMenu.add(brightenItem);
96
97       JMenuItem edgeDetectItem = new JMenuItem("Edge detect");
```

```
98      edgeDetectItem.addActionListener(new ActionListener()
99          {
100             public void actionPerformed(ActionEvent event)
101             {
102                 float[] elements = { 0.0f, -1.0f, 0.0f, -1.0f, 4.f, -1.0f, 0.0f, -1.0f, 0.0f };
103                 convolve(elements);
104             }
105         });
106     editMenu.add(edgeDetectItem);
107
108     JMenuItem negativeItem = new JMenuItem("Negative");
109     negativeItem.addActionListener(new ActionListener()
110         {
111             public void actionPerformed(ActionEvent event)
112             {
113                 short[] negative = new short[256 * 1];
114                 for (int i = 0; i < 256; i++)
115                     negative[i] = (short) (255 - i);
116                 ShortLookupTable table = new ShortLookupTable(0, negative);
117                 LookupOp op = new LookupOp(table, null);
118                 filter(op);
119             }
120         });
121     editMenu.add(negativeItem);
122
123     JMenuItem rotateItem = new JMenuItem("Rotate");
124     rotateItem.addActionListener(new ActionListener()
125         {
126             public void actionPerformed(ActionEvent event)
127             {
128                 if (image == null) return;
129                 AffineTransform transform = AffineTransform.getRotateInstance(Math.toRadians(5),
130                         image.getWidth() / 2, image.getHeight() / 2);
131                 AffineTransformOp op = new AffineTransformOp(transform,
132                         AffineTransformOp.TYPE_BICUBIC);
133                 filter(op);
134             }
135         });
136     editMenu.add(rotateItem);
137
138     JMenuBar menuBar = new JMenuBar();
139     menuBar.add(fileMenu);
140     menuBar.add(editMenu);
141     setJMenuBar(menuBar);
142 }
```

*(Continues)*

**Listing 7.9** *(Continued)*

```
143    /**
144     * Open a file and load the image.
145     */
146    public void openFile()
147    {
148       JFileChooser chooser = new JFileChooser(".");
149       chooser.setCurrentDirectory(new File(getClass().getPackage().getName()));
150       String[] extensions = ImageIO.getReaderFileSuffixes();
151       chooser.setFileFilter(new FileNameExtensionFilter("Image files", extensions));
152       int r = chooser.showOpenDialog(this);
153       if (r != JFileChooser.APPROVE_OPTION) return;

154       try
155       {
156          Image img = ImageIO.read(chooser.getSelectedFile());
157          image = new BufferedImage(img.getWidth(null), img.getHeight(null),
158                BufferedImage.TYPE_INT_RGB);
159          image.getGraphics().drawImage(img, 0, 0, null);
160       }
161       catch (IOException e)
162       {
163          JOptionPane.showMessageDialog(this, e);
164       }
165       repaint();
166    }
167
168    /**
169     * Apply a filter and repaint.
170     * @param op the image operation to apply
171     */
172    private void filter(BufferedImageOp op)
173    {
174       if (image == null) return;
175       image = op.filter(image, null);
176       repaint();
177    }
178
179    /**
180     * Apply a convolution and repaint.
181     * @param elements the convolution kernel (an array of 9 matrix elements)
182     */
183    private void convolve(float[] elements)
184    {
185       Kernel kernel = new Kernel(3, 3, elements);
186       ConvolveOp op = new ConvolveOp(kernel);
187       filter(op);
188    }
189 }
```

---

**java.awt.image.BufferedImageOp** 1.2

- BufferedImage filter(BufferedImage source, BufferedImage dest)

  applies the image operation to the source image and stores the result in the destination image. If dest is null, a new destination image is created. The destination image is returned.

---

**java.awt.image.AffineTransformOp** 1.2

- AffineTransformOp(AffineTransform t, int interpolationType)

  constructs an affine transform operator. The interpolation type is one of TYPE_BILINEAR, TYPE_BICUBIC, or TYPE_NEAREST_NEIGHBOR.

---

**java.awt.image.RescaleOp** 1.2

- RescaleOp(float a, float b, RenderingHints hints)
- RescaleOp(float[] as, float[] bs, RenderingHints hints)

  constructs a rescale operator that carries out the scaling operation $x_{new} = a \cdot x + b$. When using the first constructor, all color components (but not the alpha component) are scaled with the same coefficients. When using the second constructor, you supply either the values for each color component, in which case the alpha component is unaffected, or the values for both alpha and color components.

---

**java.awt.image.LookupOp** 1.2

- LookupOp(LookupTable table, RenderingHints hints)

  constructs a lookup operator for the given lookup table.

---

**java.awt.image.ByteLookupTable** 1.2

- ByteLookupTable(int offset, byte[] data)
- ByteLookupTable(int offset, byte[][] data)

  constructs a lookup table for converting byte values. The offset is subtracted from the input before the lookup. The values in the first constructor are applied to all color components but not the alpha component. When using the second constructor, you supply either the values for each color component, in which case the alpha component is unaffected, or the values for both alpha and color components.

---

**java.awt.image.ShortLookupTable** 1.2

- ShortLookupTable(int offset, short[] data)
- ShortLookupTable(int offset, short[][] data)

  constructs a lookup table for converting short values. The offset is subtracted from the input before the lookup. The values in the first constructor are applied to all color components but not the alpha component. When using the second constructor, you supply either the values for each color component, in which case the alpha component is unaffected, or the values for both alpha and color components.

---

**java.awt.image.ConvolveOp** 1.2

- ConvolveOp(Kernel kernel)
- ConvolveOp(Kernel kernel, int edgeCondition, RenderingHints hints)

  constructs a convolution operator. The edge condition specified is one of EDGE_NO_OP and EDGE_ZERO_FILL. Edge values need to be treated specially because they don't have sufficient neighboring values to compute the convolution. The default is EDGE_ZERO_FILL.

---

**java.awt.image.Kernel** 1.2

- Kernel(int width, int height, float[] matrixElements)

  constructs a kernel for the given matrix.

---

# 7.12 Printing

The original JDK had no support for printing at all. It was not possible to print from applets, and you had to get a third-party library if you wanted to print from an application. JDK 1.1 introduced very lightweight printing support, just enough to produce simple printouts, as long as you were not too particular about the print quality. The 1.1 printing model was designed to allow browser vendors to print the surface of an applet as it appears on a web page (which, however, the browser vendors have not embraced).

Java SE 1.2 introduced the beginnings of a robust printing model that is fully integrated with 2D graphics. Java SE 1.4 added important enhancements, such as discovery of printer features and streaming print jobs for server-side print management.

In this section, we will show you how you can easily print a drawing on a single sheet of paper, how you can manage a multipage printout, and how you can benefit from the elegance of the Java 2D imaging model and easily generate a print preview dialog box.

## 7.12.1 Graphics Printing

In this section, we will tackle what is probably the most common printing situation: printing a 2D graphic. Of course, the graphic can contain text in various fonts or even consist entirely of text.

To generate a printout, you have to take care of these two tasks:

* Supply an object that implements the Printable interface
* Start a print job

The Printable interface has a single method:

```
int print(Graphics g, PageFormat format, int page)
```

That method is called whenever the print engine needs to have a page formatted for printing. Your code draws the text and the images to be printed onto the graphics context. The page format tells you the paper size and the print margins. The page number tells you which page to render.

To start a print job, use the PrinterJob class. First, call the static getPrinterJob method to get a print job object. Then set the Printable object that you want to print.

```
Printable canvas = . . .;
PrinterJob job = PrinterJob.getPrinterJob();
job.setPrintable(canvas);
```

**CAUTION:** The class PrintJob handles JDK 1.1-style printing. That class is now obsolete. Do not confuse it with the PrinterJob class.

Before starting the print job, you should call the printDialog method to display a print dialog box (see Figure 7.32). That dialog box gives the user a chance to select the printer to be used (in case multiple printers are available), the page range that should be printed, and various printer settings.

You collect printer settings in an object of a class that implements the PrintRequestAttributeSet interface, such as the HashPrintRequestAttributeSet class.

```
HashPrintRequestAttributeSet attributes = new HashPrintRequestAttributeSet();
```

Add attribute settings and pass the attributes object to the printDialog method.

The printDialog method returns true if the user clicked OK and false if the user canceled the dialog box. If the user accepted, call the print method of the PrinterJob

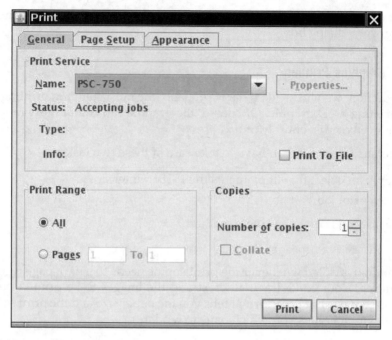

**Figure 7.32** A cross-platform print dialog box

class to start the printing process. The `print` method might throw a `PrinterException`. Here is the outline of the printing code:

```
if (job.printDialog(attributes))
{
   try
   {
      job.print(attributes);
   }
   catch (PrinterException exception)
   {
      . . .
   }
}
```

**NOTE:** Prior to JDK 1.4, the printing system used the native print and page setup dialog boxes of the host platform. To show a native print dialog box, call the `printDialog` method with no parameters. (There is no way to collect user settings in an attribute set.)

During printing, the print method of the PrinterJob class makes repeated calls to the print method of the Printable object associated with the job.

Since the job does not know how many pages you want to print, it simply keeps calling the print method. As long as the print method returns the value Printable.PAGE_EXISTS, the print job keeps producing pages. When the print method returns Printable.NO_SUCH_PAGE, the print job stops.

 **CAUTION:** The page numbers that the print job passes to the print method start with page 0.

Therefore, the print job doesn't have an accurate page count until after the printout is complete. For that reason, the print dialog box can't display the correct page range—instead it displays "Pages 1 to 1." You will see in the next section how to avoid this blemish by supplying a Book object to the print job.

During the printing process, the print job repeatedly calls the print method of the Printable object. The print job is allowed to make multiple calls *for the same page.* You should therefore not count pages inside the print method but always rely on the page number parameter. There is a good reason why the print job might call the print method repeatedly for the same page. Some printers, in particular dot-matrix and inkjet printers, use *banding.* They print one band at a time, advance the paper, and then print the next band. The print job might use banding even for laser printers that print a full page at a time—it gives the print job a way of managing the size of the spool file.

If the print job needs the Printable object to print a band, it sets the clip area of the graphics context to the requested band and calls the print method. Its drawing operations are clipped against the band rectangle, and only those drawing elements that show up in the band are rendered. Your print method need not be aware of that process, with one caveat: It should *not* interfere with the clip area.

 **CAUTION:** The Graphics object that your print method gets is also clipped against the page margins. If you replace the clip area, you can draw outside the margins. Especially in a printer graphics context, the clipping area must be respected. Call clip, not setClip, to further restrict the clipping area. If you must remove a clip area, make sure to call getClip at the beginning of your print method and restore that clip area.

The PageFormat parameter of the print method contains information about the printed page. The methods getWidth and getHeight return the paper size, measured in *points.* One point is 1/72 of an inch. (An inch equals 25.4 millimeters.) For example, A4 paper is approximately 595 × 842 points, and US Letter paper is 612 × 792 points.

Points are a common measurement in the printing trade in the United States. Much to the chagrin of the rest of the world, the printing package uses point units. There are two purposes for that: paper sizes and paper margins are measured in points, and points are the default unit for all print graphics contexts. You can verify that in the example program at the end of this section. The program prints two lines of text that are 72 units apart. Run the example program and measure the distance between the baselines; they are exactly 1 inch or 25.4 millimeters apart.

The getWidth and getHeight methods of the PageFormat class give you the complete paper size. Not all of the paper area is printable. Users typically select margins, and even if they don't, printers need to somehow grip the sheets of paper on which they print and therefore have a small unprintable area around the edges.

The methods getImageableWidth and getImageableHeight tell you the dimensions of the area that you can actually fill. However, the margins need not be symmetrical, so you must also know the top left corner of the imageable area (see Figure 7.33), which you obtain by the methods getImageableX and getImageableY.

**TIP:** The graphics context that you receive in the print method is clipped to exclude the margins, but the origin of the coordinate system is nevertheless the top left corner of the paper. It makes sense to translate the coordinate system to start at the top left corner of the imageable area. Simply start your print method with

```
g.translate(pageFormat.getImageableX(), pageFormat.getImageableY());
```

If you want your users to choose the settings for the page margins or to switch between portrait and landscape orientation without setting other printing attributes, you can call the pageDialog method of the PrinterJob class:

```
PageFormat format = job.pageDialog(attributes);
```

**NOTE:** One of the tabs of the print dialog box contains the page setup dialog (see Figure 7.34). You might still want to give users an option to set the page format before printing, especially if your program presents a "what you see is what you get" display of the pages to be printed. The pageDialog method returns a PageFormat object with the user settings.

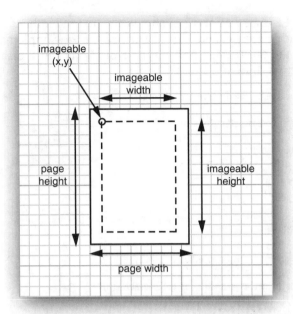

**Figure 7.33** Page format measurements

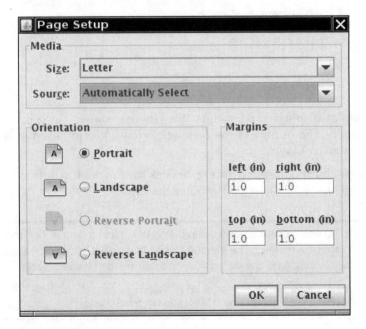

**Figure 7.34** A cross-platform page setup dialog

The program in Listings 7.10 and 7.11 shows how to render the same set of shapes on the screen and on the printed page. A subclass of JPanel implements the Printable interface. Both the paintComponent and the print methods call the same method to carry out the actual drawing.

```
class PrintPanel extends JPanel implements Printable
{
   public void paintComponent(Graphics g)
   {
      super.paintComponent(g);
      Graphics2D g2 = (Graphics2D) g;
      drawPage(g2);
   }

   public int print(Graphics g, PageFormat pf, int page)
      throws PrinterException
   {
      if (page >= 1) return Printable.NO_SUCH_PAGE;
      Graphics2D g2 = (Graphics2D) g;
      g2.translate(pf.getImageableX(), pf.getImageableY());
      drawPage(g2);
      return Printable.PAGE_EXISTS;
   }

   public void drawPage(Graphics2D g2)
   {
      // shared drawing code goes here
      . . .
   }
   . . .
}
```

This example displays and prints the image shown in Figure 7.20 on p. 590—namely, the outline of the message "Hello, World" used as a clipping area for a pattern of lines.

Click the Print button to start printing, or click the Page setup button to open the page setup dialog box. Listing 7.10 shows the code.

---

 **NOTE:** To show a native page setup dialog box, pass a default PageFormat object to the pageDialog method. The method clones that object, modifies it according to the user selections in the dialog box, and returns the cloned object.

```
PageFormat defaultFormat = printJob.defaultPage();
PageFormat selectedFormat = printJob.pageDialog(defaultFormat);
```

---

**Listing 7.10** print/PrintTestFrame.java

```
1  package print;
2
3  import java.awt.*;
4  import java.awt.event.*;
5  import java.awt.print.*;
6  import javax.print.attribute.*;
7  import javax.swing.*;
8
9  /**
10  * This frame shows a panel with 2D graphics and buttons to print the graphics and to set up the
11  * page format.
12  */
13  public class PrintTestFrame extends JFrame
14  {
15     private PrintComponent canvas;
16     private PrintRequestAttributeSet attributes;
17
18     public PrintTestFrame()
19     {
20        canvas = new PrintComponent();
21        add(canvas, BorderLayout.CENTER);
22
23        attributes = new HashPrintRequestAttributeSet();
24
25        JPanel buttonPanel = new JPanel();
26        JButton printButton = new JButton("Print");
27        buttonPanel.add(printButton);
28        printButton.addActionListener(new ActionListener()
29           {
30              public void actionPerformed(ActionEvent event)
31              {
32                 try
33                 {
34                    PrinterJob job = PrinterJob.getPrinterJob();
35                    job.setPrintable(canvas);
36                    if (job.printDialog(attributes)) job.print(attributes);
37                 }
38                 catch (PrinterException e)
39                 {
40                    JOptionPane.showMessageDialog(PrintTestFrame.this, e);
41                 }
42              }
43           });
44
45        JButton pageSetupButton = new JButton("Page setup");
46        buttonPanel.add(pageSetupButton);
```

*(Continues)*

**Listing 7.10** *(Continued)*

```
47        pageSetupButton.addActionListener(new ActionListener()
48           {
49              public void actionPerformed(ActionEvent event)
50              {
51                 PrinterJob job = PrinterJob.getPrinterJob();
52                 job.pageDialog(attributes);
53              }
54           });
55
56        add(buttonPanel, BorderLayout.NORTH);
57        pack();
58     }
59  }
```

**Listing 7.11** print/PrintComponent.java

```
1  package print;
2
3  import java.awt.*;
4  import java.awt.font.*;
5  import java.awt.geom.*;
6  import java.awt.print.*;
7  import javax.swing.*;
8  /**
9   * This component generates a 2D graphics image for screen display and printing.
10  */
11 public class PrintComponent extends JComponent implements Printable
12 {
13    private static final int DEFAULT_WIDTH = 300;
14    private static final int DEFAULT_HEIGHT = 300;
15
16    public void paintComponent(Graphics g)
17    {
18       Graphics2D g2 = (Graphics2D) g;
19       drawPage(g2);
20    }
21
22    public int print(Graphics g, PageFormat pf, int page) throws PrinterException
23    {
24       if (page >= 1) return Printable.NO_SUCH_PAGE;
25       Graphics2D g2 = (Graphics2D) g;
26       g2.translate(pf.getImageableX(), pf.getImageableY());
27       g2.draw(new Rectangle2D.Double(0, 0, pf.getImageableWidth(), pf.getImageableHeight()));
28
29       drawPage(g2);
30       return Printable.PAGE_EXISTS;
31    }
```

```
32    /**
33     * This method draws the page both on the screen and the printer graphics context.
34     * @param g2 the graphics context
35     */
36    public void drawPage(Graphics2D g2)
37    {
38       FontRenderContext context = g2.getFontRenderContext();
39       Font f = new Font("Serif", Font.PLAIN, 72);
40       GeneralPath clipShape = new GeneralPath();
41
42       TextLayout layout = new TextLayout("Hello", f, context);
43       AffineTransform transform = AffineTransform.getTranslateInstance(0, 72);
44       Shape outline = layout.getOutline(transform);
45       clipShape.append(outline, false);
46
47       layout = new TextLayout("World", f, context);
48       transform = AffineTransform.getTranslateInstance(0, 144);
49       outline = layout.getOutline(transform);
50       clipShape.append(outline, false);
51
52       g2.draw(clipShape);
53       g2.clip(clipShape);
54
55       final int NLINES = 50;
56       Point2D p = new Point2D.Double(0, 0);
57       for (int i = 0; i < NLINES; i++)
58       {
59          double x = (2 * getWidth() * i) / NLINES;
60          double y = (2 * getHeight() * (NLINES - 1 - i)) / NLINES;
61          Point2D q = new Point2D.Double(x, y);
62          g2.draw(new Line2D.Double(p, q));
63       }
64    }
65
66    public Dimension getPreferredSize() { return new Dimension(DEFAULT_WIDTH, DEFAULT_HEIGHT); }
67 }
```

---

**java.awt.print.Printable** 1.2

- int print(Graphics g, PageFormat format, int pageNumber)
  renders a page and returns PAGE_EXISTS, or returns NO_SUCH_PAGE.

| *Parameters:* | g | The graphics context onto which the page is rendered |
| --- | --- | --- |
| | format | The format of the page to draw on |
| | pageNumber | The number of the requested page |

---

**java.awt.print.PrinterJob** 1.2

---

- `static PrinterJob getPrinterJob()`
  returns a printer job object.
- `PageFormat defaultPage()`
  returns the default page format for this printer.
- `boolean printDialog(PrintRequestAttributeSet attributes)`
- `boolean printDialog()`
  opens a print dialog box to allow a user to select the pages to be printed and to change print settings. The first method displays a cross-platform dialog box, the second a native dialog box. The first method modifies the `attributes` object to reflect the user settings. Both methods return `true` if the user accepts the dialog box.
- `PageFormat pageDialog(PrintRequestAttributeSet attributes)`
- `PageFormat pageDialog(PageFormat defaults)`
  displays a page setup dialog box. The first method displays a cross-platform dialog box, the second a native dialog box. Both methods return a `PageFormat` object with the format that the user requested in the dialog box. The first method modifies the `attributes` object to reflect the user settings. The second method does not modify the `defaults` object.
- `void setPrintable(Printable p)`
- `void setPrintable(Printable p, PageFormat format)`
  sets the `Printable` of this print job and an optional page format.
- `void print()`
- `void print(PrintRequestAttributeSet attributes)`
  prints the current `Printable` by repeatedly calling its `print` method and sending the rendered pages to the printer, until no more pages are available.

---

**java.awt.print.PageFormat** 1.2

---

- `double getWidth()`
- `double getHeight()`
  returns the width and height of the page.
- `double getImageableWidth()`
- `double getImageableHeight()`
  returns the width and height of the imageable area of the page.
- `double getImageableX()`
- `double getImageableY()`
  returns the position of the top left corner of the imageable area.

*(Continues)*

---

**java.awt.print.PageFormat**  1.2  *(Continued)*

---

- `int getOrientation()`
  returns one of PORTRAIT, LANDSCAPE, or REVERSE_LANDSCAPE. Page orientation is transparent to programmers because the page format and graphics context settings automatically reflect the page orientation.

---

## 7.12.2 Multiple-Page Printing

In practice, you usually shouldn't pass a raw Printable object to a print job. Instead, you should obtain an object of a class that implements the Pageable interface. The Java platform supplies one such class, called Book. A book is made up of sections, each of which is a Printable object. To make a book, add Printable objects and their page counts.

```
Book book = new Book();
Printable coverPage = . . .;
Printable bodyPages = . . .;
book.append(coverPage, pageFormat); // append 1 page
book.append(bodyPages, pageFormat, pageCount);
```

Then, use the setPageable method to pass the Book object to the print job.

```
printJob.setPageable(book);
```

Now the print job knows exactly how many pages to print, so the print dialog box displays an accurate page range and the user can select the entire range or subranges.

---

 **CAUTION:** When the print job calls the print methods of the Printable sections, it passes the current page number of the *book*, and not of each *section*, as the current page number. That is a huge pain—each section must know the page counts of the preceding sections to make sense of the page number parameter.

---

From your perspective as a programmer, the biggest challenge of using the Book class is that you must know how many pages each section will have when you print it. Your Printable class needs a *layout algorithm* that computes the layout of the material on the printed pages. Before printing starts, invoke that algorithm to compute the page breaks and the page count. You can retain the layout information so you have it handy during the printing process.

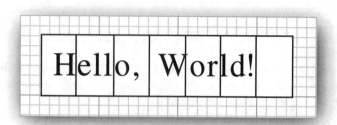

**Figure 7.35** A banner

You must guard against the possibility that the user has changed the page format. If that happens, you must recompute the layout, even if the information that you want to print has not changed.

Listing 7.13 shows how to produce a multipage printout. This program prints a message in very large characters on a number of pages (see Figure 7.35). You can then trim the margins and tape the pages together to form a banner.

The layoutPages method of the Banner class computes the layout. We first lay out the message string in a 72-point font. We then compute the height of the resulting string and compare it with the imageable height of the page. We derive a scale factor from these two measurements. When printing the string, we magnify it by that scale factor.

 **CAUTION:** To lay out your information precisely, you usually need access to the printer graphics context. Unfortunately, there is no way to obtain that graphics context before printing actually starts. In our example program, we make do with the screen graphics context and hope that the font metrics of the screen and printer match.

The getPageCount method of the Banner class first calls the layout method. Then it scales up the width of the string and divides it by the imageable width of each page. The quotient, rounded up to the next integer, is the page count.

It sounds like it might be difficult to print the banner because characters can be broken across multiple pages. However, thanks to the power of the Java 2D API, this turns out not to be a problem at all. When a particular page is requested, we simply use the translate method of the Graphics2D class to shift the top left corner of the string to the left. Then, we set a clip rectangle that equals the current page (see Figure 7.36). Finally, we scale the graphics context with the scale factor that the layout method computed.

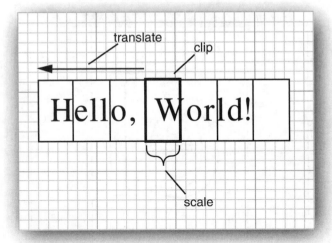

**Figure 7.36** Printing a page of a banner

This example shows the power of transformations. The drawing code is kept simple, and the transformation does all the work of placing the drawing at the appropriate place. Finally, the clip cuts away the part of the image that falls outside the page. In the next section, you will see another compelling use of transformations—to display a print preview.

### 7.12.3 Print Preview

Most professional programs have a print preview mechanism that lets you look at your pages on the screen so that you won't waste paper on a printout that you don't like. The printing classes of the Java platform do not supply a standard "print preview" dialog box, but it is easy to design your own (see Figure 7.37). In this section, we'll show you how. The PrintPreviewDialog class in Listing 7.14 is completely generic—you can reuse it to preview any kind of printout.

To construct a PrintPreviewDialog, you supply either a Printable or a Book, together with a PageFormat object. The dialog box contains a PrintPreviewCanvas (see Listing 7.15). As you use the Next and Previous buttons to flip through the pages, the paintComponent method calls the print method of the Printable object for the requested page.

Normally, the print method draws the page context on a printer graphics context. However, we supply the screen graphics context, suitably scaled so that the entire printed page fits inside a small screen rectangle.

```
float xoff = . . .; // left of page
float yoff = . . .; // top of page
```

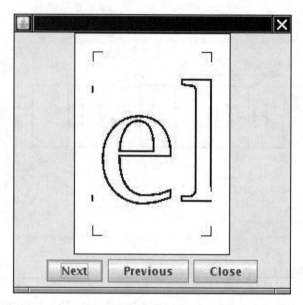

**Figure 7.37** The print preview dialog, showing a banner page

```
float scale = . . .; // to fit printed page onto screen
g2.translate(xoff, yoff);
g2.scale(scale, scale);
Printable printable = book.getPrintable(currentPage);
printable.print(g2, pageFormat, currentPage);
```

The print method never knows that it doesn't actually produce printed pages. It simply draws onto the graphics context, producing a microscopic print preview on the screen. This is a compelling demonstration of the power of the Java 2D imaging model.

Listing 7.12 contains the code for the banner printing program. Type "Hello, World!" into the text field and look at the print preview, then print the banner.

**Listing 7.12** book/BookTestFrame.java

```java
1  package book;
2
3  import java.awt.*;
4  import java.awt.event.*;
5  import java.awt.print.*;
```

```
 6  import javax.print.attribute.*;
 7  import javax.swing.*;
 8
 9  /**
10   * This frame has a text field for the banner text and buttons for printing, page setup, and print
11   * preview.
12   */
13  public class BookTestFrame extends JFrame
14  {
15     private JTextField text;
16     private PageFormat pageFormat;
17     private PrintRequestAttributeSet attributes;
18
19     public BookTestFrame()
20     {
21        text = new JTextField();
22        add(text, BorderLayout.NORTH);
23
24        attributes = new HashPrintRequestAttributeSet();
25
26        JPanel buttonPanel = new JPanel();
27
28        JButton printButton = new JButton("Print");
29        buttonPanel.add(printButton);
30        printButton.addActionListener(new ActionListener()
31           {
32              public void actionPerformed(ActionEvent event)
33              {
34                 try
35                 {
36                    PrinterJob job = PrinterJob.getPrinterJob();
37                    job.setPageable(makeBook());
38                    if (job.printDialog(attributes))
39                    {
40                       job.print(attributes);
41                    }
42                 }
43                 catch (PrinterException e)
44                 {
45                    JOptionPane.showMessageDialog(BookTestFrame.this, e);
46                 }
47              }
48           });
49
50        JButton pageSetupButton = new JButton("Page setup");
51        buttonPanel.add(pageSetupButton);
```

*(Continues)*

**Listing 7.12** *(Continued)*

```
52          pageSetupButton.addActionListener(new ActionListener()
53             {
54                public void actionPerformed(ActionEvent event)
55                {
56                   PrinterJob job = PrinterJob.getPrinterJob();
57                   pageFormat = job.pageDialog(attributes);
58                }
59             });
60
61          JButton printPreviewButton = new JButton("Print preview");
62          buttonPanel.add(printPreviewButton);
63          printPreviewButton.addActionListener(new ActionListener()
64             {
65                public void actionPerformed(ActionEvent event)
66                {
67                   PrintPreviewDialog dialog = new PrintPreviewDialog(makeBook());
68                   dialog.setVisible(true);
69                }
70             });
71
72          add(buttonPanel, BorderLayout.SOUTH);
73          pack();
74       }
75
76       /**
77        * Makes a book that contains a cover page and the pages for the banner.
78        */
79       public Book makeBook()
80       {
81          if (pageFormat == null)
82          {
83             PrinterJob job = PrinterJob.getPrinterJob();
84             pageFormat = job.defaultPage();
85          }
86          Book book = new Book();
87          String message = text.getText();
88          Banner banner = new Banner(message);
89          int pageCount = banner.getPageCount((Graphics2D) getGraphics(), pageFormat);
90          book.append(new CoverPage(message + " (" + pageCount + " pages)"), pageFormat);
91          book.append(banner, pageFormat, pageCount);
92          return book;
93       }
94    }
```

**Listing 7.13** book/Banner.java

```
1  package book;
2
3  import java.awt.*;
4  import java.awt.font.*;
5  import java.awt.geom.*;
6  import java.awt.print.*;
7
8  /**
9   * A banner that prints a text string on multiple pages.
10  */
11 public class Banner implements Printable
12 {
13    private String message;
14    private double scale;
15
16    /**
17     * Constructs a banner.
18     * @param m the message string
19     */
20    public Banner(String m)
21    {
22       message = m;
23    }
24
25    /**
26     * Gets the page count of this section.
27     * @param g2 the graphics context
28     * @param pf the page format
29     * @return the number of pages needed
30     */
31    public int getPageCount(Graphics2D g2, PageFormat pf)
32    {
33       if (message.equals("")) return 0;
34       FontRenderContext context = g2.getFontRenderContext();
35       Font f = new Font("Serif", Font.PLAIN, 72);
36       Rectangle2D bounds = f.getStringBounds(message, context);
37       scale = pf.getImageableHeight() / bounds.getHeight();
38       double width = scale * bounds.getWidth();
39       int pages = (int) Math.ceil(width / pf.getImageableWidth());
40       return pages;
41    }
42
43    public int print(Graphics g, PageFormat pf, int page) throws PrinterException
44    {
45       Graphics2D g2 = (Graphics2D) g;
46       if (page > getPageCount(g2, pf)) return Printable.NO_SUCH_PAGE;
```

*(Continues)*

Listing 7.13   *(Continued)*

```
47        g2.translate(pf.getImageableX(), pf.getImageableY());
48
49        drawPage(g2, pf, page);
50        return Printable.PAGE_EXISTS;
51     }
52
53     public void drawPage(Graphics2D g2, PageFormat pf, int page)
54     {
55        if (message.equals("")) return;
56        page--; // account for cover page
57
58        drawCropMarks(g2, pf);
59        g2.clip(new Rectangle2D.Double(0, 0, pf.getImageableWidth(), pf.getImageableHeight()));
60        g2.translate(-page * pf.getImageableWidth(), 0);
61        g2.scale(scale, scale);
62        FontRenderContext context = g2.getFontRenderContext();
63        Font f = new Font("Serif", Font.PLAIN, 72);
64        TextLayout layout = new TextLayout(message, f, context);
65        AffineTransform transform = AffineTransform.getTranslateInstance(0, layout.getAscent());
66        Shape outline = layout.getOutline(transform);
67        g2.draw(outline);
68     }
69
70     /**
71      * Draws 1/2" crop marks in the corners of the page.
72      * @param g2 the graphics context
73      * @param pf the page format
74      */
75     public void drawCropMarks(Graphics2D g2, PageFormat pf)
76     {
77        final double C = 36; // crop mark length = 1/2 inch
78        double w = pf.getImageableWidth();
79        double h = pf.getImageableHeight();
80        g2.draw(new Line2D.Double(0, 0, 0, C));
81        g2.draw(new Line2D.Double(0, 0, C, 0));
82        g2.draw(new Line2D.Double(w, 0, w, C));
83        g2.draw(new Line2D.Double(w, 0, w - C, 0));
84        g2.draw(new Line2D.Double(0, h, 0, h - C));
85        g2.draw(new Line2D.Double(0, h, C, h));
86        g2.draw(new Line2D.Double(w, h, w, h - C));
87        g2.draw(new Line2D.Double(w, h, w - C, h));
88     }
89  }
90
91  /**
92   * This class prints a cover page with a title.
93   */
```

```
94  class CoverPage implements Printable
95  {
96     private String title;
97
98     /**
99      * Constructs a cover page.
100     * @param t the title
101     */
102    public CoverPage(String t)
103    {
104       title = t;
105    }
106
107    public int print(Graphics g, PageFormat pf, int page) throws PrinterException
108    {
109       if (page >= 1) return Printable.NO_SUCH_PAGE;
110       Graphics2D g2 = (Graphics2D) g;
111       g2.setPaint(Color.black);
112       g2.translate(pf.getImageableX(), pf.getImageableY());
113       FontRenderContext context = g2.getFontRenderContext();
114       Font f = g2.getFont();
115       TextLayout layout = new TextLayout(title, f, context);
116       float ascent = layout.getAscent();
117       g2.drawString(title, 0, ascent);
118       return Printable.PAGE_EXISTS;
119    }
120 }
```

**Listing 7.14** book/PrintPreviewDialog.java

```
1  package book;
2
3  import java.awt.*;
4  import java.awt.event.*;
5  import java.awt.font.*;
6  import java.awt.print.*;
7  import javax.swing.*;
8
9  /**
10  * This class implements a generic print preview dialog.
11  */
12 class PrintPreviewDialog extends JDialog
13 {
14    private static final int DEFAULT_WIDTH = 300;
15    private static final int DEFAULT_HEIGHT = 300;
16
17    private PrintPreviewCanvas canvas;
```

*(Continues)*

**Listing 7.14**  *(Continued)*

```
18    /**
19     * Constructs a print preview dialog.
20     * @param p a Printable
21     * @param pf the page format
22     * @param pages the number of pages in p
23     */
24    public PrintPreviewDialog(Printable p, PageFormat pf, int pages)
25    {
26       Book book = new Book();
27       book.append(p, pf, pages);
28       layoutUI(book);
29    }
30
31    /**
32     * Constructs a print preview dialog.
33     * @param b a Book
34     */
35    public PrintPreviewDialog(Book b)
36    {
37       layoutUI(b);
38    }
39
40    /**
41     * Lays out the UI of the dialog.
42     * @param book the book to be previewed
43     */
44    public void layoutUI(Book book)
45    {
46       setSize(DEFAULT_WIDTH, DEFAULT_HEIGHT);
47
48       canvas = new PrintPreviewCanvas(book);
49       add(canvas, BorderLayout.CENTER);
50
51       JPanel buttonPanel = new JPanel();
52
53       JButton nextButton = new JButton("Next");
54       buttonPanel.add(nextButton);
55       nextButton.addActionListener(new ActionListener()
56          {
57             public void actionPerformed(ActionEvent event)
58             {
59                canvas.flipPage(1);
60             }
61          });
62
63       JButton previousButton = new JButton("Previous");
64       buttonPanel.add(previousButton);
```

```
65      previousButton.addActionListener(new ActionListener()
66         {
67            public void actionPerformed(ActionEvent event)
68            {
69               canvas.flipPage(-1);
70            }
71         });
72
73      JButton closeButton = new JButton("Close");
74      buttonPanel.add(closeButton);
75      closeButton.addActionListener(new ActionListener()
76         {
77            public void actionPerformed(ActionEvent event)
78            {
79               setVisible(false);
80            }
81         });
82
83      add(buttonPanel, BorderLayout.SOUTH);
84   }
85 }
```

**Listing 7.15** book/PrintPreviewCanvas.java

```
1 package book;
2
3 import java.awt.*;
4 import java.awt.geom.*;
5 import java.awt.print.*;
6 import javax.swing.*;
7
8 /**
9  * The canvas for displaying the print preview.
10  */
11 class PrintPreviewCanvas extends JComponent
12 {
13    private Book book;
14    private int currentPage;
15
16    /**
17     * Constructs a print preview canvas.
18     * @param b the book to be previewed
19     */
20    public PrintPreviewCanvas(Book b)
21    {
22       book = b;
23       currentPage = 0;
24    }
```

*(Continues)*

**Listing 7.15** *(Continued)*

```java
25   public void paintComponent(Graphics g)
26   {
27      Graphics2D g2 = (Graphics2D) g;
28      PageFormat pageFormat = book.getPageFormat(currentPage);
29
30      double xoff; // x offset of page start in window
31      double yoff; // y offset of page start in window
32      double scale; // scale factor to fit page in window
33      double px = pageFormat.getWidth();
34      double py = pageFormat.getHeight();
35      double sx = getWidth() - 1;
36      double sy = getHeight() - 1;
37      if (px / py < sx / sy) // center horizontally
38      {
39         scale = sy / py;
40         xoff = 0.5 * (sx - scale * px);
41         yoff = 0;
42      }
43      else
44      // center vertically
45      {
46         scale = sx / px;
47         xoff = 0;
48         yoff = 0.5 * (sy - scale * py);
49      }
50      g2.translate((float) xoff, (float) yoff);
51      g2.scale((float) scale, (float) scale);
52
53      // draw page outline (ignoring margins)
54      Rectangle2D page = new Rectangle2D.Double(0, 0, px, py);
55      g2.setPaint(Color.white);
56      g2.fill(page);
57      g2.setPaint(Color.black);
58      g2.draw(page);
59
60      Printable printable = book.getPrintable(currentPage);
61      try
62      {
63         printable.print(g2, pageFormat, currentPage);
64      }
65      catch (PrinterException e)
66      {
67         g2.draw(new Line2D.Double(0, 0, px, py));
68         g2.draw(new Line2D.Double(px, 0, 0, py));
69      }
70   }
```

```
71   /**
72    * Flip the book by the given number of pages.
73    * @param by the number of pages to flip by. Negative values flip backwards.
74    */
75   public void flipPage(int by)
76   {
77      int newPage = currentPage + by;
78      if (0 <= newPage && newPage < book.getNumberOfPages())
79      {
80         currentPage = newPage;
81         repaint();
82      }
83   }
84 }
```

---

**java.awt.print.PrinterJob** 1.2

- void setPageable(Pageable p)
  sets a Pageable (such as a Book) to be printed.

---

**java.awt.print.Book** 1.2

- void append(Printable p, PageFormat format)
- void append(Printable p, PageFormat format, int pageCount)
  appends a section to this book. If the page count is not specified, the first page
  is added.
- Printable getPrintable(int page)
  gets the printable for the specified page.

## 7.12.4 Print Services

So far, you have seen how to print 2D graphics. However, the printing API introduced in Java SE 1.4 affords far greater flexibility. The API defines a number of data types and lets you find print services that are able to print them. Among the data types are

- Images in GIF, JPEG, or PNG format
- Documents in text, HTML, PostScript, or PDF format
- Raw printer code data
- Objects of a class that implements Printable, Pageable, or RenderableImage

The data themselves can be stored in a source of bytes or characters such as an input stream, a URL, or an array. A *document flavor* describes the combination of a data source and a data type. The DocFlavor class defines a number of inner classes for the various data sources. Each of the inner classes defines constants to specify the flavors. For example, the constant

```
DocFlavor.INPUT_STREAM.GIF
```

describes a GIF image that is read from an input stream. Table 7.3 lists the combinations.

Suppose you want to print a GIF image located in a file. First, find out whether there is a *print service* that is capable of handling the task. The static lookupPrintServices method of the PrintServiceLookup class returns an array of PrintService objects that can handle the given document flavor.

```
DocFlavor flavor = DocFlavor.INPUT_STREAM.GIF;
PrintService[] services = PrintServiceLookup.lookupPrintServices(flavor, null);
```

The second parameter of the lookupPrintServices method is null to indicate that we don't want to constrain the search by specifying printer attributes. We'll cover attributes in the next section.

If the lookup yields an array with more than one element, you select from the listed print services. You can call the getName method of the PrintService class to get the printer names, and then let the user choose.

Next, get a document print job from the service:

```
DocPrintJob job = services[i].createPrintJob();
```

For printing, you need an object that implements the Doc interface. The Java library supplies a class SimpleDoc for that purpose. The SimpleDoc constructor requires the data source object, the document flavor, and an optional attribute set. For example,

```
InputStream in = new FileInputStream(fileName);
Doc doc = new SimpleDoc(in, flavor, null);
```

Finally, you are ready to print:

```
job.print(doc, null);
```

As before, the null parameter can be replaced by an attribute set.

Note that this printing process is quite different from that of the preceding section. There is no user interaction through print dialog boxes. For example, you can implement a server-side printing mechanism in which users submit print jobs through a web form.

**Table 7.3** Document Flavors for Print Services

| Data Source | Data Type | MIME Type |
|---|---|---|
| INPUT_STREAM | GIF | image/gif |
| URL | JPEG | image/jpeg |
| BYTE_ARRAY | PNG | image/png |
| | POSTSCRIPT | application/postscript |
| | PDF | application/pdf |
| | TEXT_HTML_HOST | text/html (using host encoding) |
| | TEXT_HTML_US_ASCII | text/html; charset=us-ascii |
| | TEXT_HTML_UTF_8 | text/html; charset=utf-8 |
| | TEXT_HTML_UTF_16 | text/html; charset=utf-16 |
| | TEXT_HTML_UTF_16LE | text/html; charset=utf-16le (little-endian) |
| | TEXT_HTML_UTF_16BE | text/html; charset=utf-16be (big-endian) |
| | TEXT_PLAIN_HOST | text/plain (using host encoding) |
| | TEXT_PLAIN_US_ASCII | text/plain; charset=us-ascii |
| | TEXT_PLAIN_UTF_8 | text/plain; charset=utf-8 |
| | TEXT_PLAIN_UTF_16 | text/plain; charset=utf-16 |
| | TEXT_PLAIN_UTF_16LE | text/plain; charset=utf-16le (little-endian) |
| | TEXT_PLAIN_UTF_16BE | text/plain; charset=utf-16be (big-endian) |
| | PCL | application/vnd.hp-PCL (Hewlett Packard Printer Control Language) |
| | AUTOSENSE | application/octet-stream (raw printer data) |
| READER | TEXT_HTML | text/html; charset=utf-16 |
| STRING | TEXT_PLAIN | text/plain; charset=utf-16 |
| CHAR_ARRAY | | |
| SERVICE_FORMATTED | PRINTABLE | N/A |
| | PAGEABLE | N/A |
| | RENDERABLE_IMAGE | N/A |

The program in Listing 7.16 demonstrates how to use a print service to print an image file.

---

**javax.print.PrintServiceLookup** 1.4

- `PrintService[] lookupPrintServices(DocFlavor flavor, AttributeSet attributes)`
  looks up the print services that can handle the given document flavor and attributes.

  *Parameters:*     flavor          The document flavor

                        attributes     The required printing attributes, or null if attributes should not be considered

---

**javax.print.PrintService** 1.4

- `DocPrintJob createPrintJob()`
  creates a print job for printing an object of a class that implements the Doc interface, such as a SimpleDoc.

---

**javax.print.DocPrintJob** 1.4

- `void print(Doc doc, PrintRequestAttributeSet attributes)`
  prints the given document with the given attributes.

  *Parameters:*     doc            The Doc to be printed

                        attributes     The required printing attributes, or null if no printing attributes are required

---

**javax.print.SimpleDoc** 1.4

- `SimpleDoc(Object data, DocFlavor flavor, DocAttributeSet attributes)`
  constructs a SimpleDoc object that can be printed with a DocPrintJob.

  *Parameters:*     data           The object with the print data, such as an input stream or a Printable

                        flavor         The document flavor of the print data

                        attributes     Document attributes, or null if attributes are not required

---

**Listing 7.16** printService/PrintServiceTest.java

```java
1  package printService;
2
3  import java.io.*;
4  import java.nio.file.*;
5  import javax.print.*;
6
7  /**
8   * This program demonstrates the use of print services. The program lets you print a GIF image to
9   * any of the print services that support the GIF document flavor.
10  * @version 1.10 2007-08-16
11  * @author Cay Horstmann
12  */
13 public class PrintServiceTest
14 {
15    public static void main(String[] args)
16    {
17       DocFlavor flavor = DocFlavor.URL.GIF;
18       PrintService[] services = PrintServiceLookup.lookupPrintServices(flavor, null);
19       if (args.length == 0)
20       {
21          if (services.length == 0) System.out.println("No printer for flavor " + flavor);
22          else
23          {
24             System.out.println("Specify a file of flavor " + flavor
25                + "\nand optionally the number of the desired printer.");
26             for (int i = 0; i < services.length; i++)
27                System.out.println((i + 1) + ": " + services[i].getName());
28          }
29          System.exit(0);
30       }
31       String fileName = args[0];
32       int p = 1;
33       if (args.length > 1) p = Integer.parseInt(args[1]);
34       if (fileName == null) return;
35       try (InputStream in = Files.newInputStream(Paths.get(fileName)))
36       {
37          Doc doc = new SimpleDoc(in, flavor, null);
38          DocPrintJob job = services[p - 1].createPrintJob();
39          job.print(doc, null);
40       }
41       catch (Exception ex)
42       {
43          ex.printStackTrace();
44       }
45    }
46 }
```

## 7.12.5 Stream Print Services

A print service sends print data to a printer. A stream print service generates the same print data but instead sends them to a stream, perhaps for delayed printing or because the print data format can be interpreted by other programs. In particular, if the print data format is PostScript, it may be useful to save the print data to a file because many programs can process PostScript files. The Java platform includes a stream print service that can produce PostScript output from images and 2D graphics. You can use that service on all systems, even if there are no local printers.

Enumerating stream print services is a bit more tedious than locating regular print services. You need both the DocFlavor of the object to be printed and the MIME type of the stream output. You then get a StreamPrintServiceFactory array of factories.

```
DocFlavor flavor = DocFlavor.SERVICE_FORMATTED.PRINTABLE;
String mimeType = "application/postscript";
StreamPrintServiceFactory[] factories
   = StreamPrintServiceFactory.lookupStreamPrintServiceFactories(flavor, mimeType);
```

The StreamPrintServiceFactory class has no methods that would help us distinguish any one factory from another, so we just take factories[0]. We call the getPrintService method with an output stream parameter to get a StreamPrintService object.

```
OutputStream out = new FileOutputStream(fileName);
StreamPrintService service = factories[0].getPrintService(out);
```

The StreamPrintService class is a subclass of PrintService. To produce a printout, simply follow the steps of the preceding section.

---

**javax.print.StreamPrintServiceFactory** 1.4

- StreamPrintServiceFactory[] lookupStreamPrintServiceFactories(DocFlavor flavor, String mimeType)
  looks up the stream print service factories that can print the given document flavor and produce an output stream of the given MIME type.

- StreamPrintService getPrintService(OutputStream out)
  gets a print service that sends the printing output to the given output stream.

---

## 7.12.6 Printing Attributes

The print service API contains a complex set of interfaces and classes to specify various kinds of attributes. There are four important groups of attributes. The first two specify requests to the printer.

- *Print request attributes* request particular features for all doc objects in a print job, such as two-sided printing or the paper size.
- *Doc attributes* are request attributes that apply only to a single doc object.

The other two attributes contain information about the printer and job status.

- *Print service attributes* give information about the print service, such as the printer make and model or whether the printer is currently accepting jobs.
- *Print job attributes* give information about the status of a particular print job, such as whether the job is already completed.

To describe the various attributes, there is an interface Attribute with subinterfaces:

```
PrintRequestAttribute
DocAttribute
PrintServiceAttribute
PrintJobAttribute
SupportedValuesAttribute
```

Individual attribute classes implement one or more of these interfaces. For example, objects of the Copies class describe the number of copies of a printout. That class implements both the PrintRequestAttribute and the PrintJobAttribute interfaces. Clearly, a print request can contain a request for multiple copies. Conversely, an attribute of the print job might be how many of these copies were actually printed. That number might be lower, perhaps because of printer limitations or because the printer ran out of paper.

The SupportedValuesAttribute interface indicates that an attribute value does not reflect actual request or status data but rather the capability of a service. For example, the CopiesSupported class implements the SupportedValuesAttribute interface. An object of that class might describe that a printer supports 1 through 99 copies of a printout.

Figure 7.38 shows a class diagram of the attribute hierarchy.

In addition to the interfaces and classes for individual attributes, the print service API defines interfaces and classes for attribute sets. A superinterface, AttributeSet, has four subinterfaces:

```
PrintRequestAttributeSet
DocAttributeSet
PrintServiceAttributeSet
PrintJobAttributeSet
```

Each of these interfaces has an implementing class, yielding the five classes:

```
HashAttributeSet
HashPrintRequestAttributeSet
HashDocAttributeSet
```

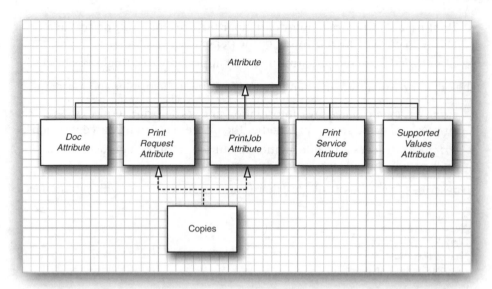

**Figure 7.38** The attribute hierarchy

```
HashPrintServiceAttributeSet
HashPrintJobAttributeSet
```

Figure 7.39 shows a class diagram of the attribute set hierarchy.

For example, you can construct a print request attribute set like this:

```
PrintRequestAttributeSet attributes = new HashPrintRequestAttributeSet();
```

After constructing the set, you are freed from worrying about the Hash prefix.

Why have all these interfaces? They make it possible to check for correct attribute usage. For example, a DocAttributeSet accepts only objects that implement the DocAttribute interface. Any attempt to add another attribute results in a runtime error.

An attribute set is a specialized kind of map where the keys are of type Class and the values belong to a class that implements the Attribute interface. For example, if you insert an object

```
new Copies(10)
```

into an attribute set, then its key is the Class object Copies.class. That key is called the *category* of the attribute. The Attribute interface declares a method

```
Class getCategory()
```

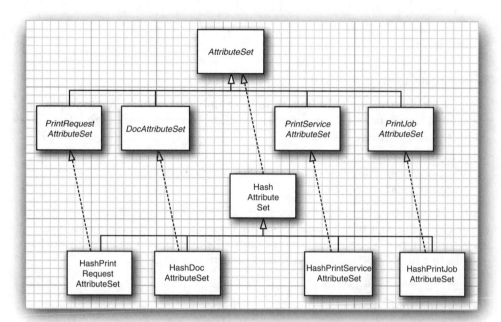

**Figure 7.39** The attribute set hierarchy

that returns the category of an attribute. The Copies class defines the method to return the object Copies.class, but it isn't a requirement that the category be the same as the class of the attribute.

When an attribute is added to an attribute set, the category is extracted automatically. You just add the attribute value:

```
attributes.add(new Copies(10));
```

If you subsequently add another attribute with the same category, it overwrites the first one.

To retrieve an attribute, you need to use the category as the key, for example:

```
AttributeSet attributes = job.getAttributes();
Copies copies = (Copies) attribute.get(Copies.class);
```

Finally, attributes are organized by the values they can have. The Copies attribute can have any integer value. The Copies class extends the IntegerSyntax class that takes care of all integer-valued attributes. The getValue method returns the integer value of the attribute, for example:

```
int n = copies.getValue();
```

The classes

```
TextSyntax
DateTimeSyntax
URISyntax
```

encapsulate a string, date and time value, or a URI.

Finally, many attributes can take a finite number of values. For example, the PrintQuality attribute has three settings: draft, normal, and high. They are represented by three constants:

```
PrintQuality.DRAFT
PrintQuality.NORMAL
PrintQuality.HIGH
```

Attribute classes with a finite number of values extend the EnumSyntax class, which provides a number of convenience methods to set up these enumerations in a typesafe manner. You need not worry about the mechanism when using such an attribute. Simply add the named values to attribute sets:

```
attributes.add(PrintQuality.HIGH);
```

Here is how you check the value of an attribute:

```
if (attributes.get(PrintQuality.class) == PrintQuality.HIGH)
    . . .
```

Table 7.4 lists the printing attributes. The second column lists the superclass of the attribute class (for example, IntegerSyntax for the Copies attribute) or the set of enumeration values for the attributes with a finite set of values. The last four columns indicate whether the attribute class implements the DocAttribute (DA), PrintJobAttribute (PJA), PrintRequestAttribute (PRA), and PrintServiceAttribute (PSA) interfaces.

**Table 7.4** Printing Attributes

| Attribute | Superclass or Enumeration Constants | DA | PJA | PRA | PSA |
|-----------|-------------------------------------|----|-----|-----|-----|
| Chromaticity | MONOCHROME, COLOR | ✓ | ✓ | ✓ | |
| ColorSupported | SUPPORTED, NOT_SUPPORTED | | | | ✓ |
| Compression | COMPRESS, DEFLATE, GZIP, NONE | ✓ | | | |
| Copies | IntegerSyntax | | ✓ | ✓ | |
| DateTimeAtCompleted | DateTimeSyntax | | ✓ | | |
| DateTimeAtCreation | DateTimeSyntax | | ✓ | | |
| DateTimeAtProcessing | DateTimeSyntax | | ✓ | | |

| Attribute | Superclass or Enumeration Constants | DA | PJA | PRA | PSA |
|---|---|:---:|:---:|:---:|:---:|
| Destination | URISyntax | | ✓ | ✓ | |
| DocumentName | TextSyntax | ✓ | | | |
| Fidelity | FIDELITY_TRUE, FIDELITY_FALSE | | ✓ | ✓ | |
| Finishings | NONE, STAPLE, EDGE_STITCH, BIND, SADDLE_STITCH, COVER, . . . | ✓ | ✓ | ✓ | |
| JobHoldUntil | DateTimeSyntax | | ✓ | ✓ | |
| JobImpressions | IntegerSyntax | | ✓ | ✓ | |
| JobImpressionsCompleted | IntegerSyntax | | ✓ | | |
| JobKOctets | IntegerSyntax | | ✓ | ✓ | |
| JobKOctetsProcessed | IntegerSyntax | | ✓ | | |
| JobMediaSheets | IntegerSyntax | | ✓ | ✓ | |
| JobMediaSheetsCompleted | IntegerSyntax | | ✓ | | |
| JobMessageFromOperator | TextSyntax | | ✓ | | |
| JobName | TextSyntax | | ✓ | ✓ | |
| JobOriginatingUserName | TextSyntax | | ✓ | | |
| JobPriority | IntegerSyntax | | ✓ | ✓ | |
| JobSheets | STANDARD, NONE | | ✓ | ✓ | |
| JobState | ABORTED, CANCELED, COMPLETED, PENDING, PENDING_HELD, PROCESSING, PROCESSING_STOPPED | | ✓ | | |
| JobStateReason | ABORTED_BY_SYSTEM, DOCUMENT_FORMAT_ERROR, many others | | | | |
| JobStateReasons | HashSet | | ✓ | | |
| MediaName | ISO_A4_WHITE, ISO_A4_TRANSPARENT, NA_LETTER_WHITE, NA_LETTER_TRANSPARENT | ✓ | ✓ | ✓ | |
| MediaSize | ISO.A0—ISO.A10, ISO.B0—ISO.B10, ISO.C0—ISO.C10, NA.LETTER, NA.LEGAL, various other paper and envelope sizes | | | | |

*(Continues)*

**Table 7.4** *(Continued)*

| Attribute | Superclass or Enumeration Constants | DA | PJA | PRA | PSA |
|-----------|-------------------------------------|:--:|:---:|:---:|:---:|
| MediaSizeName | ISO_A0–ISO_A10, ISO_B0–ISO_B10, ISO_C0–ISO_C10, NA_LETTER, NA_LEGAL, various other paper and envelope size names | ✓ | ✓ | ✓ | |
| MediaTray | TOP, MIDDLE, BOTTOM, SIDE, ENVELOPE, LARGE_CAPACITY, MAIN, MANUAL | ✓ | ✓ | ✓ | |
| MultipleDocumentHandling | SINGLE_DOCUMENT, SINGLE_DOCUMENT_NEW_SHEET, SEPARATE_DOCUMENTS_COLLATED_COPIES, SEPARATE_DOCUMENTS_UNCOLLATED_COPIES | | ✓ | ✓ | |
| NumberOfDocuments | IntegerSyntax | | ✓ | | |
| NumberOfInterveningJobs | IntegerSyntax | | ✓ | | |
| NumberUp | IntegerSyntax | ✓ | ✓ | ✓ | |
| OrientationRequested | PORTRAIT, LANDSCAPE, REVERSE_PORTRAIT, REVERSE_LANDSCAPE | ✓ | ✓ | ✓ | |
| OutputDeviceAssigned | TextSyntax | | ✓ | | |
| PageRanges | SetOfInteger | ✓ | ✓ | ✓ | |
| PagesPerMinute | IntegerSyntax | | | | ✓ |
| PagesPerMinuteColor | IntegerSyntax | | | | ✓ |
| PDLOverrideSupported | ATTEMPTED, NOT_ATTEMPTED | | | | ✓ |
| PresentationDirection | TORIGHT_TOBOTTOM, TORIGHT_TOTOP, TOBOTTOM_TORIGHT, TOBOTTOM_TOLEFT, TOLEFT_TOBOTTOM, TOLEFT_TOTOP, TOTOP_TORIGHT, TOTOP_TOLEFT | | ✓ | ✓ | |
| PrinterInfo | TextSyntax | | | | ✓ |
| PrinterIsAcceptingJobs | ACCEPTING_JOBS, NOT_ACCEPTING_JOBS | | | | ✓ |
| PrinterLocation | TextSyntax | | | | ✓ |
| PrinterMakeAndModel | TextSyntax | | | | ✓ |
| PrinterMessageFromOperator | TextSyntax | | | | ✓ |
| PrinterMoreInfo | URISyntax | | | | ✓ |
| PrinterMoreInfoManufacturer | URISyntax | | | | ✓ |

| Attribute | Superclass or Enumeration Constants | DA | PJA | PRA | PSA |
|-----------|-------------------------------------|:--:|:---:|:---:|:---:|
| PrinterName | TextSyntax | | | | ✓ |
| PrinterResolution | ResolutionSyntax | ✓ | ✓ | ✓ | |
| PrinterState | PROCESSING, IDLE, STOPPED, UNKNOWN | | | | ✓ |
| PrinterStateReason | COVER_OPEN, FUSER_OVER_TEMP, MEDIA_JAM, and many others | | | | |
| PrinterStateReasons | HashMap | | | | |
| PrinterURI | URISyntax | | | | ✓ |
| PrintQuality | DRAFT, NORMAL, HIGH | ✓ | ✓ | ✓ | |
| QueuedJobCount | IntegerSyntax | | | | ✓ |
| ReferenceUriSchemesSupported | FILE, FTP, GOPHER, HTTP, HTTPS, NEWS, NNTP, WAIS | | | | |
| RequestingUserName | TextSyntax | | | ✓ | |
| Severity | ERROR, REPORT, WARNING | | | | |
| SheetCollate | COLLATED, UNCOLLATED | ✓ | ✓ | ✓ | |
| Sides | ONE_SIDED, DUPLEX (= TWO_SIDED_LONG_EDGE), TUMBLE (= TWO_SIDED_SHORT_EDGE) | ✓ | ✓ | ✓ | |

 **NOTE:** As you can see, there are lots of attributes, many of which are quite specialized. The source for most of the attributes is the Internet Printing Protocol 1.1 (RFC 2911).

 **NOTE:** An earlier version of the printing API introduced the JobAttributes and PageAttributes classes, whose purpose was similar to the printing attributes covered in this section. These classes are now obsolete.

---

**javax.print.attribute.Attribute** 1.4

- Class getCategory()
  gets the category of this attribute.
- String getName()
  gets the name of this attribute.

---

*javax.print.attribute.AttributeSet*  1.4

- `boolean add(Attribute attr)`
  adds an attribute to this set. If the set has another attribute with the same category, that attribute is replaced by the given attribute. Returns `true` if the set changed as a result of this operation.
- `Attribute get(Class category)`
  retrieves the attribute with the given category key, or `null` if no such attribute exists.
- `boolean remove(Attribute attr)`
- `boolean remove(Class category)`
  removes the given attribute, or the attribute with the given category, from the set. Returns `true` if the set changed as a result of this operation.
- `Attribute[] toArray()`
  returns an array with all attributes in this set.

---

*javax.print.PrintService*  1.4

- `PrintServiceAttributeSet getAttributes()`
  gets the attributes of this print service.

---

*javax.print.DocPrintJob*  1.4

- `PrintJobAttributeSet getAttributes()`
  gets the attributes of this print job.

---

This concludes our discussion on printing. You now know how to print 2D graphics and other document types, how to enumerate printers and stream print services, and how to set and retrieve attributes. Next, we turn to two important user interface issues: the clipboard and the drag-and-drop mechanism.

## 7.13 The Clipboard

One of the most useful and convenient user interface mechanisms of GUI environments (such as Windows and the X Window System) is *cut and paste*. You select some data in one program and cut or copy them to the clipboard. Then, you switch to another program and paste the clipboard contents into that application. Using the clipboard, you can transfer text, images, or other data from one document to another or, of course, from one place in a document to another in the same document. Cut and paste is so natural that most computer users never think about it.

Even though the clipboard is conceptually simple, implementing clipboard services is actually harder than you might think. Suppose you copy text from a word processor to the clipboard. If you paste that text into another word processor, you expect the fonts and formatting to stay intact. That is, the text in the clipboard needs to retain the formatting information. However, if you paste the text into a plain text field, you expect that just the characters are pasted in, without additional formatting codes. To support this flexibility, the data provider must be able offer the clipboard data in multiple formats, so the data consumer can pick one of them.

The system clipboard implementations of Microsoft Windows and the Macintosh are similar, but, of course, there are slight differences. However, the X Window System clipboard mechanism is much more limited—cutting and pasting of anything but plain text is only sporadically supported. You should consider these limitations when trying out the programs in this section.

---

 **NOTE:** Check out the file *jre*/lib/flavormap.properties on your platform to get an idea about what kinds of objects can be transferred between Java programs and the system clipboard.

---

Often, programs need to support cut and paste of data types that the system clipboard cannot handle. The data transfer API supports the transfer of arbitrary local object references in the same virtual machine. Between different virtual machines, you can transfer serialized objects and references to remote objects.

Table 7.5 summarizes the data transfer capabilities of the clipboard mechanism.

**Table 7.5** Capabilities of the Java Data Transfer Mechanism

| Transfer | Format |
| --- | --- |
| Between a Java program and a native program | Text, images, file lists, . . . (depending on the host platform) |
| Between two cooperating Java programs | Serialized and remote objects |
| Within one Java program | Any object |

## 7.13.1 Classes and Interfaces for Data Transfer

Data transfer in Java is implemented in a package called `java.awt.datatransfer`. Here is an overview of the most important classes and interfaces of that package:

- Objects that can be transferred via a clipboard must implement the `Transferable` interface.

- The `Clipboard` class describes a clipboard. Transferable objects are the only items that can be put on or taken off a clipboard. The system clipboard is a concrete example of a `Clipboard`.

- The `DataFlavor` class describes data flavors that can be placed on the clipboard.

- The `StringSelection` class is a concrete class that implements the `Transferable` interface. It transfers text strings.

- A class must implement the `ClipboardOwner` interface if it wants to be notified when the clipboard contents have been overwritten by someone else. Clipboard ownership enables "delayed formatting" of complex data. If a program transfers simple data (such as a string), it simply sets the clipboard contents and moves on. However, if a program places onto the clipboard complex data that can be formatted in multiple flavors, then it might not actually want to prepare all the flavors, because there is a good chance that most of them will be never needed. However, it then needs to hang on to the clipboard data so it can create the flavors later when they are requested. The clipboard owner is notified (by a call to its `lostOwnership` method) when the contents of the clipboard change. That tells it that the information is no longer needed. In our sample programs, we don't worry about clipboard ownership.

## 7.13.2 Transferring Text

The best way to get comfortable with the data transfer classes is to start with the simplest situation: transferring text to and from the system clipboard. First, get a reference to the system clipboard:

```
Clipboard clipboard = Toolkit.getDefaultToolkit().getSystemClipboard();
```

For strings to be transferred to the clipboard, they must be wrapped into `StringSelection` objects.

```
String text = . . .
StringSelection selection = new StringSelection(text);
```

The actual transfer is done by a call to `setContents`, which takes a `StringSelection` object and a `ClipBoardOwner` as parameters. If you are not interested in designating a clipboard owner, set the second parameter to `null`.

```
clipboard.setContents(selection, null);
```

Here is the reverse operation—reading a string from the clipboard:

```
DataFlavor flavor = DataFlavor.stringFlavor;
if (clipboard.isDataFlavorAvailable(flavor))
    String text = (String) clipboard.getData(flavor);
```

Listing 7.17 is a program that demonstrates cutting and pasting between a Java application and the system clipboard. If you select some text in the text area and click Copy, the selection is copied to the system clipboard. You can then paste it into any text editor (see Figure 7.40). Conversely, when you copy text from the text editor, you can paste it into our sample program.

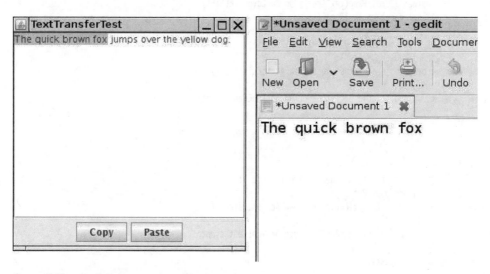

**Figure 7.40** The TextTransferTest program

---

**Listing 7.17** transferText/TextTransferFrame.java

```java
1  package transferText;
2
3  import java.awt.*;
4  import java.awt.datatransfer.*;
5  import java.awt.event.*;
6  import java.io.*;
7  import javax.swing.*;
8
9  /**
10    * This frame has a text area and buttons for copying and pasting text.
11    */
```

*(Continues)*

Listing 7.17    (Continued)

```
12   public class TextTransferFrame extends JFrame
13   {
14      private JTextArea textArea;
15      private static final int TEXT_ROWS = 20;
16      private static final int TEXT_COLUMNS = 60;
17
18      public TextTransferFrame()
19      {
20         textArea = new JTextArea(TEXT_ROWS, TEXT_COLUMNS);
21         add(new JScrollPane(textArea), BorderLayout.CENTER);
22         JPanel panel = new JPanel();
23
24         JButton copyButton = new JButton("Copy");
25         panel.add(copyButton);
26         copyButton.addActionListener(new ActionListener()
27            {
28               public void actionPerformed(ActionEvent event)
29               {
30                  copy();
31               }
32            });
33
34         JButton pasteButton = new JButton("Paste");
35         panel.add(pasteButton);
36         pasteButton.addActionListener(new ActionListener()
37            {
38               public void actionPerformed(ActionEvent event)
39               {
40                  paste();
41               }
42            });
43
44         add(panel, BorderLayout.SOUTH);
45         pack();
46      }
47
48      /**
49       * Copies the selected text to the system clipboard.
50       */
51      private void copy()
52      {
53         Clipboard clipboard = Toolkit.getDefaultToolkit().getSystemClipboard();
54         String text = textArea.getSelectedText();
55         if (text == null) text = textArea.getText();
56         StringSelection selection = new StringSelection(text);
57         clipboard.setContents(selection, null);
58      }
```

```
59    /**
60     * Pastes the text from the system clipboard into the text area.
61     */
62    private void paste()
63    {
64       Clipboard clipboard = Toolkit.getDefaultToolkit().getSystemClipboard();
65       DataFlavor flavor = DataFlavor.stringFlavor;
66       if (clipboard.isDataFlavorAvailable(flavor))
67       {
68          try
69          {
70             String text = (String) clipboard.getData(flavor);
71             textArea.replaceSelection(text);
72          }
73          catch (UnsupportedFlavorException e)
74          {
75             JOptionPane.showMessageDialog(this, e);
76          }
77          catch (IOException e)
78          {
79             JOptionPane.showMessageDialog(this, e);
80          }
81       }
82    }
83 }
```

---

**java.awt.Toolkit**  1.0

- Clipboard getSystemClipboard()  1.1
  gets the system clipboard.

---

**java.awt.datatransfer.Clipboard**  1.1

- Transferable getContents(Object requester)
  gets the clipboard contents.

  | *Parameters:* | requester | The object requesting the clipboard contents; this value is not actually used. |

- void setContents(Transferable contents, ClipboardOwner owner)
  puts contents on the clipboard.

  | *Parameters:* | contents | The Transferable encapsulating the contents |
  | | owner | The object to be notified (via its lostOwnership method) when new information is placed on the clipboard, or null if no notification is desired |

*(Continues)*

---

**java.awt.datatransfer.Clipboard** 1.1 *(Continued)*

---

- boolean isDataFlavorAvailable(DataFlavor flavor) **5.0**
  returns true if the clipboard has data in the given flavor.

- Object getData(DataFlavor flavor) **5.0**
  gets the data in the given flavor, or throws an UnsupportedFlavorException if no data are available in the given flavor.

---

**java.awt.datatransfer.ClipboardOwner** 1.1

---

- void lostOwnership(Clipboard clipboard, Transferable contents)
  notifies this object that it is no longer the owner of the contents of the clipboard.

  *Parameters:*    clipboard     The clipboard onto which the contents were placed

                  contents      The item that this owner had placed onto the clipboard

---

**java.awt.datatransfer.Transferable** 1.1

---

- boolean isDataFlavorSupported(DataFlavor flavor)
  returns true if the specified flavor is one of the supported data flavors, false otherwise.

- Object getTransferData(DataFlavor flavor)
  returns the data, formatted in the requested flavor. Throws an UnsupportedFlavorException if the flavor requested is not supported.

---

## 7.13.3 The Transferable Interface and Data Flavors

A DataFlavor is defined by two characteristics:

- A MIME type name (such as "image/gif")
- A representation class for accessing the data (such as java.awt.Image)

In addition, every data flavor has a human-readable name (such as "GIF Image").

The representation class can be specified with a class parameter in the MIME type, for example,

    image/gif;class=java.awt.Image

---

 **NOTE:** This is just an example to show the syntax. There is no standard data flavor for transferring GIF image data.

---

If no class parameter is given, then the representation class is InputStream.

Three MIME types are defined for transferring local, serialized, and remote Java objects:

```
application/x-java-jvm-local-objectref
application/x-java-serialized-object
application/x-java-remote-object
```

 **NOTE:** The x- prefix indicates that this is an experimental name, not one that is sanctioned by IANA, the organization that assigns standard MIME type names.

For example, the standard stringFlavor data flavor is described by the MIME type

```
application/x-java-serialized-object;class=java.lang.String
```

You can ask the clipboard to list all available flavors:

```
DataFlavor[] flavors = clipboard.getAvailableDataFlavors()
```

You can also install a FlavorListener onto the clipboard. The listener is notified when the collection of data flavors on the clipboard changes. See the API notes for details.

---

**java.awt.datatransfer.DataFlavor** 1.1

- DataFlavor(String mimeType, String humanPresentableName)
  creates a data flavor that describes stream data in a format described by a MIME type.

  | *Parameters:* | mimeType | A MIME type string |
  |---|---|---|
  | | humanPresentableName | A more readable version of the name |

- DataFlavor(Class class, String humanPresentableName)
  creates a data flavor that describes a Java platform class. Its MIME type is application/x-java-serialized-object;class=*className*.

  | *Parameters:* | class | The class that is retrieved from the Transferable |
  |---|---|---|
  | | humanPresentableName | A readable version of the name |

- String getMimeType()
  returns the MIME type string for this data flavor.

- boolean isMimeTypeEqual(String mimeType)
  tests whether this data flavor has the given MIME type.

*(Continues)*

---

`java.awt.datatransfer.DataFlavor` 1.1 *(Continued)*

- `String getHumanPresentableName()`
  returns the human-presentable name for the data format of this data flavor.

- `Class getRepresentationClass()`
  returns a `Class` object that represents the class of the object that a `Transferable` object will return when called with this data flavor. This is either the `class` parameter of the MIME type or `InputStream`.

---

`java.awt.datatransfer.Clipboard` 1.1

- `DataFlavor[] getAvailableDataFlavors()` 5.0
  returns an array of the available flavors.

- `void addFlavorListener(FlavorListener listener)` 5.0
  adds a listener that is notified when the set of available flavors changes.

---

`java.awt.datatransfer.Transferable` 1.1

- `DataFlavor[] getTransferDataFlavors()`
  returns an array of the supported flavors.

---

`java.awt.datatransfer.FlavorListener` 5.0

- `void flavorsChanged(FlavorEvent event)`
  is called when a clipboard's set of available flavors changes.

---

## 7.13.4 Building an Image Transferable

Objects that you want to transfer via the clipboard must implement the `Transferable` interface. The `StringSelection` class is currently the only public class in the Java standard library that implements the `Transferable` interface. In this section, you will see how to transfer images into the clipboard. Since Java does not supply a class for image transfer, you must implement it yourself.

The class is completely trivial. It simply reports that the only available data format is `DataFlavor.imageFlavor`, and it holds an `image` object.

```
class ImageTransferable implements Transferable
{
   private Image theImage;

   public ImageTransferable(Image image)
   {
      theImage = image;
   }

   public DataFlavor[] getTransferDataFlavors()
   {
      return new DataFlavor[] { DataFlavor.imageFlavor };
   }

   public boolean isDataFlavorSupported(DataFlavor flavor)
   {
      return flavor.equals(DataFlavor.imageFlavor);
   }

   public Object getTransferData(DataFlavor flavor)
      throws UnsupportedFlavorException
   {
      if(flavor.equals(DataFlavor.imageFlavor))
      {
         return theImage;
      }
      else
      {
         throw new UnsupportedFlavorException(flavor);
      }
   }
}
```

 **NOTE:** Java SE supplies the DataFlavor.imageFlavor constant and does all the heavy lifting to convert between Java images and native clipboard images. Curiously, however, it does not supply the wrapper class that is necessary to place images onto the clipboard.

The program in Listing 7.18 demonstrates the transfer of images between a Java application and the system clipboard. When the program starts, it generates an image containing a red circle. Click the Copy button to copy the image to the clipboard and then paste it into another application (see Figure 7.41). From another application, copy an image into the system clipboard. Then click the Paste button and see the image being pasted into the example program (see Figure 7.42).

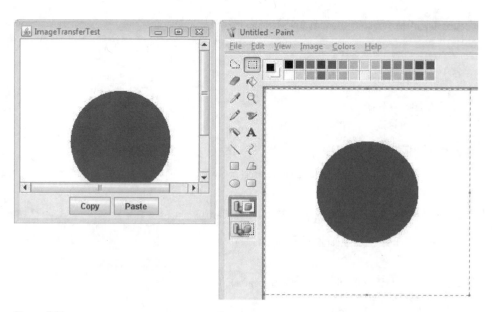

**Figure 7.41** Copying from a Java program to a native program

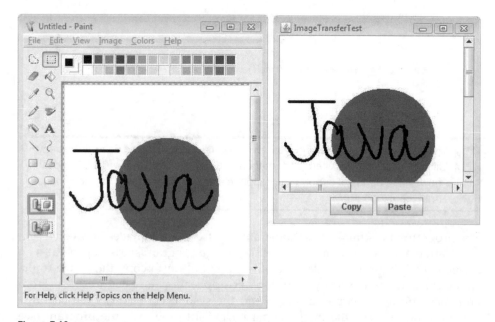

**Figure 7.42** Copying from a native program to a Java program

The program is a straightforward modification of the text transfer program. The data flavor is now DataFlavor.imageFlavor, and we use the ImageTransferable class to transfer an image to the system clipboard.

**Listing 7.18** imageTransfer/ImageTransferFrame.java

```
1  package imageTransfer;
2
3  import java.awt.*;
4  import java.awt.datatransfer.*;
5  import java.awt.event.*;
6  import java.awt.image.*;
7  import java.io.*;
8  import javax.swing.*;
9
10 /**
11  * This frame has an image label and buttons for copying and pasting an image.
12  */
13 class ImageTransferFrame extends JFrame
14 {
15    private JLabel label;
16    private Image image;
17    private static final int IMAGE_WIDTH = 300;
18    private static final int IMAGE_HEIGHT = 300;
19
20    public ImageTransferFrame()
21    {
22       label = new JLabel();
23       image = new BufferedImage(IMAGE_WIDTH, IMAGE_HEIGHT, BufferedImage.TYPE_INT_ARGB);
24       Graphics g = image.getGraphics();
25       g.setColor(Color.WHITE);
26       g.fillRect(0, 0, IMAGE_WIDTH, IMAGE_HEIGHT);
27       g.setColor(Color.RED);
28       g.fillOval(IMAGE_WIDTH / 4, IMAGE_WIDTH / 4, IMAGE_WIDTH / 2, IMAGE_HEIGHT / 2);
29
30       label.setIcon(new ImageIcon(image));
31       add(new JScrollPane(label), BorderLayout.CENTER);
32       JPanel panel = new JPanel();
33
34       JButton copyButton = new JButton("Copy");
35       panel.add(copyButton);
36       copyButton.addActionListener(new ActionListener()
37          {
38             public void actionPerformed(ActionEvent event)
39             {
40                copy();
41             }
42          });
```

*(Continues)*

**Listing 7.18** *(Continued)*

```
43        JButton pasteButton = new JButton("Paste");
44        panel.add(pasteButton);
45        pasteButton.addActionListener(new ActionListener()
46           {
47              public void actionPerformed(ActionEvent event)
48              {
49                 paste();
50              }
51           });
52        add(panel, BorderLayout.SOUTH);
53        pack();
54     }
55
56     /**
57      * Copies the current image to the system clipboard.
58      */
59     private void copy()
60     {
61        Clipboard clipboard = Toolkit.getDefaultToolkit().getSystemClipboard();
62        ImageTransferable selection = new ImageTransferable(image);
63        clipboard.setContents(selection, null);
64     }
65
66     /**
67      * Pastes the image from the system clipboard into the image label.
68      */
69     private void paste()
70     {
71        Clipboard clipboard = Toolkit.getDefaultToolkit().getSystemClipboard();
72        DataFlavor flavor = DataFlavor.imageFlavor;
73        if (clipboard.isDataFlavorAvailable(flavor))
74        {
75           try
76           {
77              image = (Image) clipboard.getData(flavor);
78              label.setIcon(new ImageIcon(image));
79           }
80           catch (UnsupportedFlavorException exception)
81           {
82              JOptionPane.showMessageDialog(this, exception);
83           }
84           catch (IOException exception)
85           {
86              JOptionPane.showMessageDialog(this, exception);
87           }
88        }
89     }
90  }
```

## 7.13.5 Transferring Java Objects via the System Clipboard

Suppose you want to copy and paste objects from one Java application to another. You can accomplish this task by placing serialized Java objects onto the system clipboard.

The program in Listing 7.19 demonstrates this capability. The program shows a color chooser. The Copy button copies the current color to the system clipboard as a serialized Color object. The Paste button checks whether the system clipboard contains a serialized Color object. If so, it fetches the color and sets it as the current choice of the color chooser.

You can transfer the serialized object between two Java applications (see Figure 7.43). Run two copies of the SerialTransferTest program. Click Copy in the first program, then click Paste in the second program. The Color object is transferred from one virtual machine to the other.

To enable data transfer, the Java platform places the binary data of the serialized object on the system clipboard. Another Java program—not necessarily of the same type as the one that generated the clipboard data—can retrieve the clipboard data and deserialize the object.

Of course, a non-Java application will not know what to do with the clipboard data. For that reason, the example program offers the clipboard data in a second flavor—as text. The text is simply the result of the toString method, applied to the

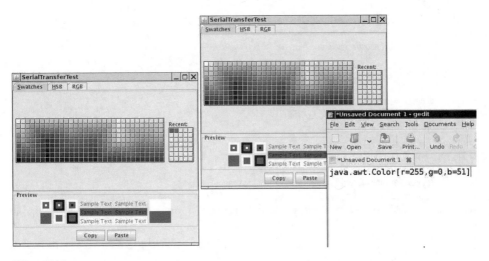

**Figure 7.43** Data are copied between two instances of a Java application.

transferred object. To see the second flavor, run the program, click on a color, and then select the Paste command in your text editor. A string such as

```
java.awt.Color[r=255,g=0,b=51]
```

will be inserted into your document.

Essentially no additional programming is required to transfer a serializable object. Use the MIME type

```
application/x-java-serialized-object;class=className
```

As before, you have to build your own transfer wrapper—see the example code for details.

**Listing 7.19** serialTransfer/SerialTransferFrame.java

```
1  package serialTransfer;
2
3  import java.awt.*;
4  import java.awt.datatransfer.*;
5  import java.awt.event.*;
6  import java.io.*;
7  import javax.swing.*;
8
9  /**
10  * This frame contains a color chooser, and copy and paste buttons.
11  */
12 class SerialTransferFrame extends JFrame
13 {
14    private JColorChooser chooser;
15
16    public SerialTransferFrame()
17    {
18       chooser = new JColorChooser();
19       add(chooser, BorderLayout.CENTER);
20       JPanel panel = new JPanel();
21
22       JButton copyButton = new JButton("Copy");
23       panel.add(copyButton);
24       copyButton.addActionListener(new ActionListener()
25          {
26             public void actionPerformed(ActionEvent event)
27             {
28                copy();
29             }
30          });
```

```
31        JButton pasteButton = new JButton("Paste");
32        panel.add(pasteButton);
33        pasteButton.addActionListener(new ActionListener()
34           {
35              public void actionPerformed(ActionEvent event)
36              {
37                 paste();
38              }
39           });
40
41        add(panel, BorderLayout.SOUTH);
42        pack();
43     }
44
45     /**
46      * Copies the chooser's color into the system clipboard.
47      */
48     private void copy()
49     {
50        Clipboard clipboard = Toolkit.getDefaultToolkit().getSystemClipboard();
51        Color color = chooser.getColor();
52        SerialTransferable selection = new SerialTransferable(color);
53        clipboard.setContents(selection, null);
54     }
55
56     /**
57      * Pastes the color from the system clipboard into the chooser.
58      */
59     private void paste()
60     {
61        Clipboard clipboard = Toolkit.getDefaultToolkit().getSystemClipboard();
62        try
63        {
64           DataFlavor flavor = new DataFlavor(
65              "application/x-java-serialized-object;class=java.awt.Color");
66           if (clipboard.isDataFlavorAvailable(flavor))
67           {
68              Color color = (Color) clipboard.getData(flavor);
69              chooser.setColor(color);
70           }
71        }
72        catch (ClassNotFoundException e)
73        {
74           JOptionPane.showMessageDialog(this, e);
75        }
76        catch (UnsupportedFlavorException e)
77        {
78           JOptionPane.showMessageDialog(this, e);
79        }
```

*(Continues)*

**Listing 7.19** *(Continued)*

```
80        catch (IOException e)
81        {
82           JOptionPane.showMessageDialog(this, e);
83        }
84     }
85  }
86
87  /**
88   * This class is a wrapper for the data transfer of serialized objects.
89   */
90  class SerialTransferable implements Transferable
91  {
92     private Serializable obj;
93
94     /**
95      * Constructs the selection.
96      * @param o any serializable object
97      */
98     SerialTransferable(Serializable o)
99     {
100        obj = o;
101    }
102
103    public DataFlavor[] getTransferDataFlavors()
104    {
105       DataFlavor[] flavors = new DataFlavor[2];
106       Class<?> type = obj.getClass();
107       String mimeType = "application/x-java-serialized-object;class=" + type.getName();
108       try
109       {
110          flavors[0] = new DataFlavor(mimeType);
111          flavors[1] = DataFlavor.stringFlavor;
112          return flavors;
113       }
114       catch (ClassNotFoundException e)
115       {
116          return new DataFlavor[0];
117       }
118    }
119
120    public boolean isDataFlavorSupported(DataFlavor flavor)
121    {
122       return DataFlavor.stringFlavor.equals(flavor)
123             || "application".equals(flavor.getPrimaryType())
124             && "x-java-serialized-object".equals(flavor.getSubType())
125             && flavor.getRepresentationClass().isAssignableFrom(obj.getClass());
126    }
```

```
127   public Object getTransferData(DataFlavor flavor) throws UnsupportedFlavorException
128   {
129      if (!isDataFlavorSupported(flavor)) throw new UnsupportedFlavorException(flavor);
130
131      if (DataFlavor.stringFlavor.equals(flavor)) return obj.toString();
132
133      return obj;
134   }
135 }
```

### 7.13.6  Using a Local Clipboard to Transfer Object References

Occasionally, you might need to copy and paste a data type that isn't one of the data types supported by the system clipboard and that isn't serializable. To transfer an arbitrary Java object reference within the same JVM, use the MIME type

application/x-java-jvm-local-objectref;class=*className*

You need to define a Transferable wrapper for this type. The process is entirely analogous to the SerialTransferable wrapper of the preceding example.

An object reference is only meaningful within a single virtual machine. For that reason, you cannot copy the shape object to the system clipboard. Instead, use a local clipboard:

Clipboard clipboard = new Clipboard("local");

The construction parameter is the clipboard name.

However, using a local clipboard has one major disadvantage. You need to synchronize the local and the system clipboard, so that users don't confuse the two. Currently, the Java platform doesn't do that synchronization for you.

---

**java.awt.datatransfer.Clipboard  1.1**

- Clipboard(String name)
  constructs a local clipboard with the given name.

---

## 7.14  Drag and Drop

When you use cut and paste to transmit information between two programs, the clipboard acts as an intermediary. The *drag and drop* metaphor cuts out the middleman and lets two programs communicate directly. The Java platform offers basic support for drag and drop. You can carry out drag and drop operations between Java applications and native applications. This section shows you how to write a Java application that is a drop target, and an application that is a drag source.

Before going deeper into the Java platform support for drag and drop, let us quickly look at the drag-and-drop user interface. We use the Windows Explorer and WordPad programs as examples—on another platform, you can experiment with locally available programs with drag-and-drop capabilities.

You initiate a *drag operation* with a *gesture* inside a *drag source*—by first selecting one or more elements and then dragging the selection away from its initial location. When you release the mouse button over a drop target that accepts the drop operation, the drop target queries the drag source for information about the dropped elements and carries out an appropriate operation. For example, if you drop a file icon from a file manager on top of a directory icon, the file is moved into that directory. However, if you drag it to a text editor, the text editor opens the file. (This requires, of course, that you use a file manager and text editor that are capable of drag and drop, such as Explorer/WordPad in Windows or Nautilus/gedit in Gnome).

If you hold down the Ctrl key while dragging, the type of the drop action changes from a *move action* to a *copy action,* and a copy of the file is placed into the directory. If you hold down *both* Shift and Ctrl keys, then a *link* to the file is placed into the directory. (Other platforms might use other keyboard combinations for these operations.)

Thus, there are three types of drop actions with different gestures:

- Move
- Copy
- Link

The intention of the link action is to establish a reference to the dropped element. Such links typically require support from the host operating system (such as symbolic links for files, or object links for document components) and don't usually make a lot of sense in cross-platform programs. In this section, we focus on using drag and drop for copying and moving.

There is usually some visual feedback for the drag operation. Minimally, the cursor shape changes. As the cursor moves over possible *drop targets,* the cursor shape indicates whether the drop is possible or not. If a drop is possible, the cursor shape also indicates the type of the drop action. Table 7.6 shows several drop cursor shapes.

**Table 7.6** Drop Cursor Shapes

| Action | Windows Icon | Gnome Icon |
|---|---|---|
| Move | | |
| Copy | | |
| Link | | |
| Drop not allowed | | |

You can also drag other elements besides file icons. For example, you can select text in WordPad or gedit and drag it. Try dropping text fragments into willing drop targets and see how they react.

**NOTE:** This experiment shows a disadvantage of drag and drop as a user interface mechanism. It can be difficult for users to anticipate what they can drag, where they can drop it, and what happens when they do. Because the default "move" action can remove the original, many users are understandably cautious about experimenting with drag and drop.

## 7.14.1 Data Transfer Support in Swing

Starting with Java SE 1.4, several Swing components have built-in support for drag and drop (see Table 7.7). You can drag selected text from a number of components, and you can drop text into text components. For backward compatibility, you must call the setDragEnabled method to activate dragging. Dropping is always enabled.

**NOTE:** The java.awt.dnd package provides a lower-level drag-and-drop API that forms the basis for the Swing drag and drop. We do not discuss that API in this book.

The program in Listing 7.20 demonstrates the behavior. As you run the program, note these points:

- You can select multiple items in the list, table, or tree (see Listing 7.21) and drag them.

**Table 7.7** Data Transfer Support in Swing Components

| Component | Drag Source | Drop Target |
| --- | --- | --- |
| JFileChooser | Exports file list | N/A |
| JColorChooser | Exports color object | Accepts color objects |
| JTextField<br>JFormattedTextField | Exports selected text | Accepts text |
| JPasswordField | N/A (for security) | Accepts text |
| JTextArea<br>JTextPane<br>JEditorPane | Exports selected text | Accepts text and file lists |
| JList<br>JTable<br>JTree | Exports text description of selection (copy only) | N/A |

- Dragging items from the table is a bit awkward. You first select with the mouse, then let go of the mouse button, then click it again, and then you drag.

- When you drop the items in the text area, you can see how the dragged information is formatted. Table cells are separated by tabs, and each selected row is on a separate line (see Figure 7.44).

- You can only copy, not move, items from the list, table, tree, file chooser, or color chooser. Removing items from a list, table, or tree is not possible with all data models. You will see in the next section how to implement this capability when the data model is editable.

- You cannot drag into the list, table, tree, or file chooser.

- If you run two copies of the program, you can drag a color from one color chooser to the other.

- You cannot drag text out of the text area because we didn't call `setDragEnabled` on it.

The Swing package provides a potentially useful mechanism to quickly turn a component into a drag source and drop target. You can install a *transfer handler* for a given property. For example, in our sample program, we call

```
textField.setTransferHandler(new TransferHandler("background"));
```

You can now drag a color into the text field, and its background color changes.

When a drop occurs, then the transfer handler checks whether one of the data flavors has representation class `Color`. If so, it invokes the `setBackground` method.

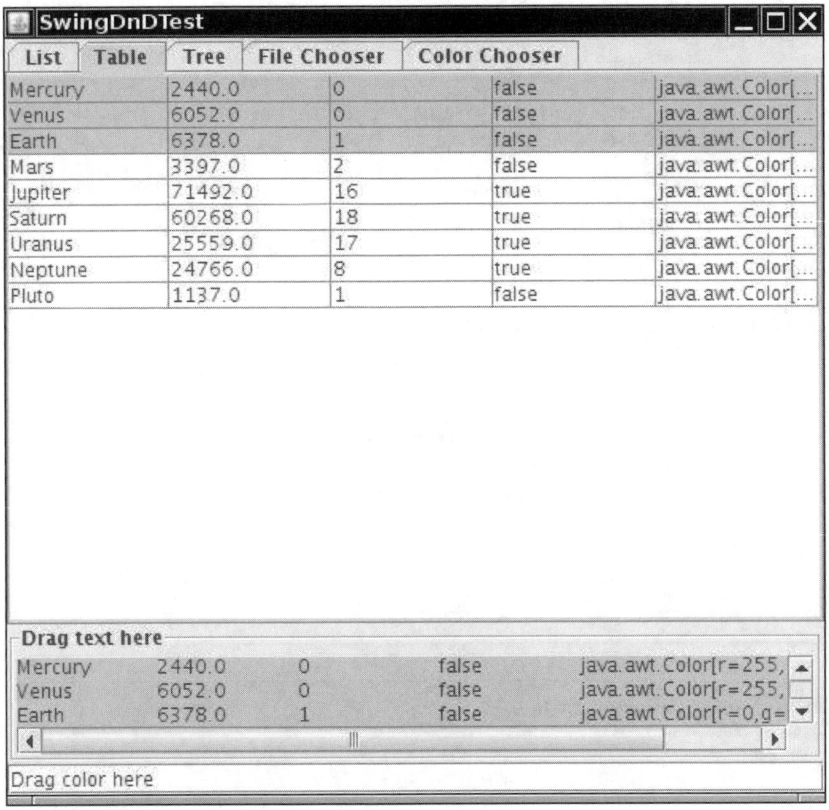

**Figure 7.44** The Swing drag-and-drop test program

By installing this transfer handler into the text field, you disable the standard transfer handler. You can no longer cut, copy, paste, drag, or drop text in the text field. However, you can now drag color out of this text field. You still need to select some text to initiate the drag gesture. When you drag the text, you will find that you can drop it into the color chooser and change its color value to the text field's background color. However, you cannot drop the text into the text area.

**Listing 7.20** dnd/SwingDnDTest.java

```
1 package dnd;
2
3 import java.awt.*;
4 import javax.swing.*;
```

*(Continues)*

---

**Listing 7.20** *(Continued)*

```
5   /**
6    * This program demonstrates the basic Swing support for drag and drop.
7    * @version 1.10 2007-09-20
8    * @author Cay Horstmann
9    */
10  public class SwingDnDTest
11  {
12     public static void main(String[] args)
13     {
14        EventQueue.invokeLater(new Runnable()
15           {
16              public void run()
17              {
18                 JFrame frame = new SwingDnDFrame();
19                 frame.setTitle("SwingDnDTest");
20                 frame.setDefaultCloseOperation(JFrame.EXIT_ON_CLOSE);
21                 frame.setVisible(true);
22              }
23           });
24     }
25  }
```

---

**Listing 7.21** dnd/SampleComponents.java

```
1   package dnd;
2
3   import java.awt.*;
4
5   import javax.swing.*;
6   import javax.swing.tree.*;
7
8   public class SampleComponents
9   {
10     public static JTree tree()
11     {
12        DefaultMutableTreeNode root = new DefaultMutableTreeNode("World");
13        DefaultMutableTreeNode country = new DefaultMutableTreeNode("USA");
14        root.add(country);
15        DefaultMutableTreeNode state = new DefaultMutableTreeNode("California");
16        country.add(state);
17        DefaultMutableTreeNode city = new DefaultMutableTreeNode("San Jose");
18        state.add(city);
19        city = new DefaultMutableTreeNode("Cupertino");
20        state.add(city);
```

```
21        state = new DefaultMutableTreeNode("Michigan");
22        country.add(state);
23        city = new DefaultMutableTreeNode("Ann Arbor");
24        state.add(city);
25        country = new DefaultMutableTreeNode("Germany");
26        root.add(country);
27        state = new DefaultMutableTreeNode("Schleswig-Holstein");
28        country.add(state);
29        city = new DefaultMutableTreeNode("Kiel");
30        state.add(city);
31        return new JTree(root);
32     }
33
34     public static JList<String> list()
35     {
36        String[] words = { "quick", "brown", "hungry", "wild", "silent", "huge", "private",
37           "abstract", "static", "final" };
38
39        DefaultListModel<String> model = new DefaultListModel<>();
40        for (String word : words)
41           model.addElement(word);
42        return new JList<>(model);
43     }
44
45     public static JTable table()
46     {
47        Object[][] cells = { { "Mercury", 2440.0, 0, false, Color.YELLOW },
48           { "Venus", 6052.0, 0, false, Color.YELLOW },
49           { "Earth", 6378.0, 1, false, Color.BLUE }, { "Mars", 3397.0, 2, false, Color.RED },
50           { "Jupiter", 71492.0, 16, true, Color.ORANGE },
51           { "Saturn", 60268.0, 18, true, Color.ORANGE },
52           { "Uranus", 25559.0, 17, true, Color.BLUE },
53           { "Neptune", 24766.0, 8, true, Color.BLUE },
54           { "Pluto", 1137.0, 1, false, Color.BLACK } };
55
56        String[] columnNames = { "Planet", "Radius", "Moons", "Gaseous", "Color" };
57        return new JTable(cells, columnNames);
58     }
59  }
```

---

**javax.swing.JComponent** 1.2

- void setTransferHandler(TransferHandler handler) 1.4

  sets a transfer handler to handle data transfer operations (cut, copy, paste, drag, drop).

---

`javax.swing.TransferHandler` 1.4

---

- `TransferHandler(String propertyName)`
  constructs a transfer handler that reads or writes the JavaBeans component property with the given name when a data transfer operation is executed.

---

`javax.swing.JFileChooser` 1.2
`javax.swing.JColorChooser` 1.2
`javax.swing.text.JTextComponent` 1.2
`javax.swing.JList` 1.2
`javax.swing.JTable` 1.2
`javax.swing.JTree` 1.2

---

- `void setDragEnabled(boolean b)` 1.4
  enables or disables dragging of data out of this component.

---

## 7.14.2 Drag Sources

In the previous section, you saw how to take advantage of the basic drag-and-drop support in Swing. In this section, we'll show you how to configure any component as a drag source. In the next section, we'll discuss drop targets and present a sample component that is both a source and a target for images.

To customize the drag-and-drop behavior of a Swing component, subclass the `TransferHandler` class. First, override the `getSourceActions` method to indicate which actions (copy, move, link) your component supports. Next, override the `createTransferable` method that produces a `Transferable` object, following the same process that you use for copying to the clipboard.

In our sample program, we drag images out of a `JList` that is filled with image icons (see Figure 7.45). Here is the implementation of the `createTransferable` method. The selected image is simply placed into an `ImageTransferable` wrapper.

```
protected Transferable createTransferable(JComponent source)
{
   JList list = (JList) source;
   int index = list.getSelectedIndex();
   if (index < 0) return null;
   ImageIcon icon = (ImageIcon) list.getModel().getElementAt(index);
   return new ImageTransferable(icon.getImage());
}
```

In our example, we are fortunate that a `JList` is already wired for initiating a drag gesture. You simply activate that mechanism by calling the `setDragEnabled` method.

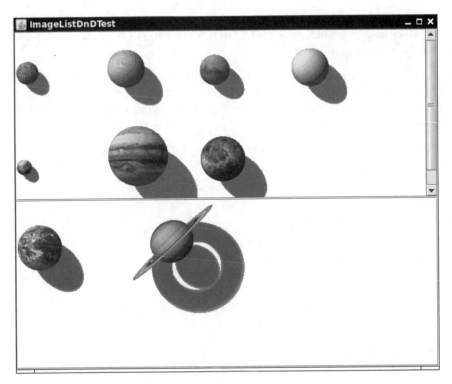

**Figure 7.45** The ImageList drag-and-drop application

If you add drag support to a component that does not recognize a drag gesture, you need to initiate the transfer yourself. For example, here is how you can initiate dragging on a JLabel:

```
label.addMouseListener(new MouseAdapter()
{
   public void mousePressed(MouseEvent evt)
   {
      int mode;
      if ((evt.getModifiers() & (InputEvent.CTRL_MASK | InputEvent.SHIFT_MASK)) != 0)
            mode = TransferHandler.COPY;
      else mode = TransferHandler.MOVE;
      JComponent comp = (JComponent) evt.getSource();
      TransferHandler th = comp.getTransferHandler();
      th.exportAsDrag(comp, evt, mode);
   }
});
```

Here, we simply start the transfer when the user clicks on the label. A more sophisticated implementation would watch for a mouse motion that drags the mouse by a small amount.

When the user completes the drop action, the exportDone method of the source transfer handler is invoked. In that method, you need to remove the transferred object if the user carried out a move action. Here is the implementation for the image list:

```
protected void exportDone(JComponent source, Transferable data, int action)
{
   if (action == MOVE)
   {
      JList list = (JList) source;
      int index = list.getSelectedIndex();
      if (index < 0) return;
      DefaultListModel model = (DefaultListModel) list.getModel();
      model.remove(index);
   }
}
```

To summarize, to turn a component into a drag source, you have to add a transfer handler that specifies the following:

- Which actions are supported
- Which data is transferred
- How the original data is removed after a move action

In addition, if your drag source is a component other than those listed in Table 7.7 on p. 692, you need to watch for a mouse gesture and initiate the transfer.

---

**javax.swing.TransferHandler** 1.4

- int getSourceActions(JComponent c)
  override to return the allowable source actions (bitwise or combination of COPY, MOVE, and LINK) when dragging from the given component.

- protected Transferable createTransferable(JComponent source)
  override to create the Transferable for the data that is to be dragged.

- void exportAsDrag(JComponent comp, InputEvent e, int action)
  starts a drag gesture from the given component. The action is COPY, MOVE, or LINK.

- protected void exportDone(JComponent source, Transferable data, int action)
  override to adjust the drag source after a successful transfer.

## 7.14.3 Drop Targets

In this section, we'll show you how to implement a drop target. Our example is again a JList with image icons. We'll add drop support so that users can drop images into the list.

To make a component into a drop target, set a TransferHandler and implement the canImport and importData methods.

**NOTE:** You can add a transfer handler to a JFrame. This is most commonly used for dropping files into an application. Valid drop locations include the frame decorations and the menu bar, but not components contained in the frame (which have their own transfer handlers).

The canImport method is called continuously as the user moves the mouse over the drop target component. Return true if a drop is allowed. This information affects the cursor icon that gives visual feedback whether the drop is allowed.

The canImport method has a parameter of type TransferHandler.TransferSupport. Through this parameter, you can obtain the drop action chosen by the user, the drop location, and the data to be transferred. (Before Java SE 6, a different canImport method was called that only supplies a list of data flavors.)

In the canImport method, you can also override the user drop action. For example, if a user chose the move action but it would be inappropriate to remove the original, you can force the transfer handler to use a copy action instead.

Here is a typical example. The image list component is willing to accept drops of file lists and images. However, if a file list is dragged into the component, a user-selected MOVE action is changed into a COPY action, so that the image files do not get deleted.

```
public boolean canImport(TransferSupport support)
{
    if (support.isDataFlavorSupported(DataFlavor.javaFileListFlavor))
    {
        if (support.getUserDropAction() == MOVE) support.setDropAction(COPY);
        return true;
    }
    else return support.isDataFlavorSupported(DataFlavor.imageFlavor);
}
```

A more sophisticated implementation could check that the files actually contain images.

The Swing components JList, JTable, JTree, and JTextComponent give visual feedback about insertion positions as the mouse is moved over the drop target. By default, the selection (for JList, JTable, and JTree) or the caret (for JTextComponent) is used to indicate the drop location. That approach is neither user-friendly nor flexible, and it is the default solely for backward compatibility. You should call the setDropMode method to choose a more appropriate visual feedback.

You can control whether the dropped data should overwrite existing items or be inserted between them. For example, in our sample program, we call

```
setDropMode(DropMode.ON_OR_INSERT);
```

to allow the user to drop onto an item (thereby replacing it), or to insert between two items (see Figure 7.46). Table 7.8 shows the drop modes supported by the Swing components.

Once the user completes the drop gesture, the importData method is invoked. You need to obtain the data from the drag source. Invoke the getTransferable method on the TransferSupport parameter to obtain a reference to a Transferable object. This is the same interface that is used for copy and paste.

One data type that is commonly used for drag and drop is the DataFlavor. javaFileListFlavor. A file list describes a set of files that is dropped onto the target. The transfer data is an object of type List<File>. Here is the code for retrieving the files:

```
DataFlavor[] flavors = transferable.getTransferDataFlavors();
if (Arrays.asList(flavors).contains(DataFlavor.javaFileListFlavor))
{
   List<File> fileList = (List<File>) transferable.getTransferData(DataFlavor.javaFileListFlavor);
   for (File f : fileList)
   {
      do something with f;
   }
}
```

When dropping into one of the components listed in Table 7.8, you need to know precisely where to drop the data. Invoke the getDropLocation method on the

**Figure 7.46** Visual indicators for dropping onto an item and between two items

**Table 7.8** Drop Modes

| Component | Supported Drop Modes |
|---|---|
| JList, JTree | ON, INSERT, ON_OR_INSERT, USE_SELECTION |
| JTable | ON, INSERT, ON_OR_INSERT, INSERT_ROWS, INSERT_COLS, ON_OR_INSERT_ROWS, ON_OR_INSERT_COLS, USE_SELECTION |
| JTextComponent | INSERT, USE_SELECTION (actually moves the caret, not the selection) |

TransferSupport parameter to find where the drop occurred. This method returns an object of a subclass of TransferHandler.DropLocation. The JList, JTable, JTree, and JTextComponent classes define subclasses that specify location in the particular data model. For example, a location in a list is simply an integer index, but a location in a tree is a tree path. Here is how we obtain the drop location in our image list:

```
int index;
if (support.isDrop())
{
   JList.DropLocation location = (JList.DropLocation) support.getDropLocation();
   index = location.getIndex();
}
else index = model.size();
```

The JList.DropLocation subclass has a method getIndex that returns the index of the drop. (The JTree.DropLocation subclass has a method getPath instead.)

The importData method is also called when data is pasted into the component with the Ctrl+V keystroke. In that case, the getDropLocation method would throw an IllegalStateException. Therefore, if the isDrop method returns false, we simply append the pasted data to the end of the list.

When inserting into a list, table, or tree, you also need to check whether the data is supposed to be inserted between items or whether it should replace the item at the drop location. For a list, invoke the isInsert method of the JList.DropLocation. For the other components, see the API notes for their drop location classes at the end of this section.

To summarize, to turn a component into a drop target, add a transfer handler that specifies the following:

- When a dragged item can be accepted
- How the dropped data is imported

In addition, if you add drop support to a JList, JTable, JTree, or JTextComponent, you should set the drop mode.

Listing 7.22 shows the frame class of the program. Note that the ImageList class is both a drag source and a drop target. Try dragging images between the two lists. You can also drag image files from a file chooser of another program into the lists.

**Listing 7.22**   dndImage/imageListDnDFrame.java

```java
1  package dndImage;
2
3  import java.awt.*;
4  import java.awt.datatransfer.*;
5  import java.io.*;
6  import java.nio.file.*;
7  import java.util.*;
8  import java.util.List;
9  import javax.imageio.*;
10 import javax.swing.*;
11
12 public class ImageListDnDFrame extends JFrame
13 {
14    private static final int DEFAULT_WIDTH = 600;
15    private static final int DEFAULT_HEIGHT = 500;
16
17    private ImageList list1;
18    private ImageList list2;
19
20    public ImageListDnDFrame()
21    {
22       setSize(DEFAULT_WIDTH, DEFAULT_HEIGHT);
23
24       list1 = new ImageList(Paths.get(getClass().getPackage().getName(), "images1"));
25       list2 = new ImageList(Paths.get(getClass().getPackage().getName(), "images2"));
26
27       setLayout(new GridLayout(2, 1));
28       add(new JScrollPane(list1));
29       add(new JScrollPane(list2));
30    }
31 }
32
33 class ImageList extends JList<ImageIcon>
34 {
35    public ImageList(Path dir)
36    {
37       DefaultListModel<ImageIcon> model = new DefaultListModel<>();
38       try (DirectoryStream<Path> entries = Files.newDirectoryStream(dir))
39       {
40          for (Path entry : entries)
41             model.addElement(new ImageIcon(entry.toString()));
42       }
```

```
43        catch (IOException ex)
44        {
45           ex.printStackTrace();
46        }
47
48        setModel(model);
49        setVisibleRowCount(0);
50        setLayoutOrientation(JList.HORIZONTAL_WRAP);
51        setDragEnabled(true);
52        setDropMode(DropMode.ON_OR_INSERT);
53        setTransferHandler(new ImageListTransferHandler());
54     }
55  }
56
57  class ImageListTransferHandler extends TransferHandler
58  {
59     // support for drag
60
61     public int getSourceActions(JComponent source)
62     {
63        return COPY_OR_MOVE;
64     }
65
66     protected Transferable createTransferable(JComponent source)
67     {
68        ImageList list = (ImageList) source;
69        int index = list.getSelectedIndex();
70        if (index < 0) return null;
71        ImageIcon icon = list.getModel().getElementAt(index);
72        return new ImageTransferable(icon.getImage());
73     }
74
75     protected void exportDone(JComponent source, Transferable data, int action)
76     {
77        if (action == MOVE)
78        {
79           ImageList list = (ImageList) source;
80           int index = list.getSelectedIndex();
81           if (index < 0) return;
82           DefaultListModel<?> model = (DefaultListModel<?>) list.getModel();
83           model.remove(index);
84        }
85     }
86
87     // support for drop
88
89     public boolean canImport(TransferSupport support)
90     {
```

*(Continues)*

**Listing 7.22** *(Continued)*

```
 91        if (support.isDataFlavorSupported(DataFlavor.javaFileListFlavor))
 92        {
 93           if (support.getUserDropAction() == MOVE) support.setDropAction(COPY);
 94           return true;
 95        }
 96        else return support.isDataFlavorSupported(DataFlavor.imageFlavor);
 97     }
 98
 99     public boolean importData(TransferSupport support)
100     {
101        ImageList list = (ImageList) support.getComponent();
102        DefaultListModel<ImageIcon> model = (DefaultListModel<ImageIcon>) list.getModel();
103
104        Transferable transferable = support.getTransferable();
105        List<DataFlavor> flavors = Arrays.asList(transferable.getTransferDataFlavors());
106
107        List<Image> images = new ArrayList<>();
108
109        try
110        {
111           if (flavors.contains(DataFlavor.javaFileListFlavor))
112           {
113              @SuppressWarnings("unchecked") List<File> fileList
114                 = (List<File>) transferable.getTransferData(DataFlavor.javaFileListFlavor);
115              for (File f : fileList)
116              {
117                 try
118                 {
119                    images.add(ImageIO.read(f));
120                 }
121                 catch (IOException ex)
122                 {
123                    // couldn't read image--skip
124                 }
125              }
126           }
127           else if (flavors.contains(DataFlavor.imageFlavor))
128           {
129              images.add((Image) transferable.getTransferData(DataFlavor.imageFlavor));
130           }
131
132           int index;
133           if (support.isDrop())
134           {
135              JList.DropLocation location = (JList.DropLocation) support.getDropLocation();
136              index = location.getIndex();
137              if (!location.isInsert()) model.remove(index); // replace location
138           }
```

```
139        else index = model.size();
140        for (Image image : images)
141        {
142            model.add(index, new ImageIcon(image));
143            index++;
144        }
145        return true;
146    }
147    catch (IOException ex)
148    {
149        return false;
150    }
151    catch (UnsupportedFlavorException ex)
152    {
153        return false;
154    }
155    }
156 }
```

---

**javax.swing.TransferHandler** 1.4

- boolean canImport(TransferSupport support) **6**
  override to indicate whether the target component can accept the drag described by the TransferSupport parameter.

- boolean importData(TransferSupport support) **6**
  override to carry out the drop or paste gesture described by the TransferSupport parameter, and return true if the import was successful.

---

**javax.swing.JFrame** 1.2

- void setTransferHandler(TransferHandler handler) **6**
  sets a transfer handler to handle drop and paste operations only

---

**javax.swing.JList** 1.2
**javax.swing.JTable** 1.2
**javax.swing.JTree** 1.2
**javax.swing.text.JTextComponent** 1.2

- void setDropMode(DropMode mode) **6**
  set the drop mode of this component to one of the values specified in Table 7.8.

---

**javax.swing.TransferHandler.TransferSupport 6**

- Component getComponent()
  gets the target component of this transfer.
- DataFlavor[] getDataFlavors()
  gets the data flavors of the data to be transferred.
- boolean isDrop()
  true if this transfer is a drop, false if it is a paste.
- int getUserDropAction()
  gets the drop action chosen by the user (MOVE, COPY, or LINK).
- getSourceDropActions()
  gets the drop actions that are allowed by the drag source.
- getDropAction()
- setDropAction()
  gets or sets the drop action of this transfer. Initially, this is the user drop action, but it can be overridden by the transfer handler.
- DropLocation getDropLocation()
  gets the location of the drop, or throws an IllegalStateException if this transfer is not a drop.

---

**javax.swing.TransferHandler.DropLocation 6**

- Point getDropPoint()
  gets the mouse location of the drop in the target component.

---

**javax.swing.JList.DropLocation 6**

- boolean isInsert()
  returns true if the data are to be inserted before a given location, false if they are to replace existing data.
- int getIndex()
  gets the model index for the insertion or replacement.

---

`javax.swing.JTable.DropLocation` 6

- boolean isInsertRow()
- boolean isInsertColumn()
  returns true if data are to be inserted before a row or column.
- int getRow()
- int getColumn()
  gets the model row or column index for the insertion or replacement, or -1 if the drop occurred in an empty area.

---

`javax.swing.JTree.DropLocation` 6

- TreePath getPath()
- int getChildIndex()
  returns the tree path and child that, together with the drop mode of the target component, define the drop location, as described below.

| Drop Mode | Tree Edit Action |
|---|---|
| INSERT | Insert as child of the path, before the child index. |
| ON or USE_SELECTION | Replace the data of the path (child index not used). |
| INSERT_OR_ON | If the child index is -1, do as in ON, otherwise as in INSERT. |

---

`javax.swing.text.JTextComponent.DropLocation` 6

- int getIndex()
  the index at which to insert the data.

---

# 7.15 Platform Integration

We finish this chapter with several features for making Java applications feel more like native applications. The splash screen feature allows your application to display a splash screen as the virtual machine starts up. The `java.awt.Desktop` class lets you launch native applications such as the default browser and e-mail program. Finally, you now have access to the system tray and can clutter it up with icons, just like so many native applications do.

## 7.15.1 Splash Screens

A common complaint about Java applications is their long startup time. The Java virtual machine takes some time to load all required classes, particularly for a Swing application that needs to pull in large amounts of Swing and AWT library code. Users dislike applications that take a long time to bring up an initial screen, and they might even try launching the application multiple times if they suspect the first launch was unsuccessful. The remedy is a *splash screen*—a small window that appears quickly, telling the user that the application has been launched successfully.

Of course, you can put up a window as soon as your `main` method starts. However, the `main` method is only launched after the class loader has loaded all dependent classes, which might take a while.

Instead, you can ask the virtual machine to show an image immediately on launch. There are two mechanisms for specifying that image. You can use the `-splash` command-line option:

```
java -splash:myimage.png MyApp
```

Alternatively, you can specify it in the manifest of a JAR file:

```
Main-Class: MyApp
SplashScreen-Image: myimage.gif
```

The image is displayed immediately and automatically disappears when the first AWT window is made visible. You can supply any GIF, JPEG, or PNG image. Animation (in GIF) and transparency (GIF and PNG) are supported.

If your application is ready to go as soon as it reaches `main`, you can skip the remainder of this section. However, many applications use a plug-in architecture in which a small core loads a set of plugins at startup. Eclipse and NetBeans are typical examples. In that case, you can indicate the loading progress on the splash screen.

There are two approaches. You can draw directly on the splash screen, or you can replace it with a borderless frame with identical contents and then draw inside the frame. Our sample program shows both techniques.

To draw directly on the splash screen, get a reference to the splash screen and get its graphics context and dimensions:

```
SplashScreen splash = SplashScreen.getSplashScreen();
Graphics2D g2 = splash.createGraphics();
Rectangle bounds = splash.getBounds();
```

**Figure 7.47** The initial splash screen and a borderless follow-up window

You can now draw in the usual way. When you are done, call update to ensure that the drawing is refreshed. Our sample program draws a simple progress bar, as seen in the left image in Figure 7.47.

```
g.fillRect(x, y, width * percent / 100, height);
splash.update();
```

 **NOTE:** The splash screen is a singleton object. You cannot construct your own. If no splash screen was set on the command line or in the manifest, the getSplashScreen method returns null.

Drawing directly on the splash screen has a drawback. It is tedious to compute all pixel positions, and your progress indicator won't match the native progress bar. To avoid these problems, you can replace the initial splash screen with a follow-up window of the same size and content as soon as the main method starts. That window can contain arbitrary Swing components.

Our sample program in Listing 7.23 demonstrates this technique. The right image in Figure 7.47 shows a borderless frame with a panel that paints the splash screen and contains a JProgressBar. Now we have full access to the Swing API and can easily add message strings without having to fuss with pixel positions.

Note that we do not need to remove the initial splash screen. It is automatically removed as soon as the follow-up window is made visible.

 **CAUTION:** Unfortunately, there is a noticeable flash when the splash screen is replaced by the follow-up window.

**Listing 7.23** splashScreen/SplashScreenTest.java

```
1  package splashScreen;
2
3  import java.awt.*;
4  import java.util.List;
5  import javax.swing.*;
6
7  /**
8   * This program demonstrates the splash screen API.
9   * @version 1.00 2007-09-21
10  * @author Cay Horstmann
11  */
12 public class SplashScreenTest
13 {
14    private static final int DEFAULT_WIDTH = 300;
15    private static final int DEFAULT_HEIGHT = 300;
16
17    private static SplashScreen splash;
18
19    private static void drawOnSplash(int percent)
20    {
21       Rectangle bounds = splash.getBounds();
22       Graphics2D g = splash.createGraphics();
23       int height = 20;
24       int x = 2;
25       int y = bounds.height - height - 2;
26       int width = bounds.width - 4;
27       Color brightPurple = new Color(76, 36, 121);
```

```
28      g.setColor(brightPurple);
29      g.fillRect(x, y, width * percent / 100, height);
30      splash.update();
31   }
32
33   /**
34    * This method draws on the splash screen.
35    */
36   private static void init1()
37   {
38      splash = SplashScreen.getSplashScreen();
39      if (splash == null)
40      {
41         System.err.println("Did you specify a splash image with -splash or in the manifest?");
42         System.exit(1);
43      }
44
45      try
46      {
47         for (int i = 0; i <= 100; i++)
48         {
49            drawOnSplash(i);
50            Thread.sleep(100); // simulate startup work
51         }
52      }
53      catch (InterruptedException e)
54      {
55      }
56   }
57
58   /**
59    * This method displays a frame with the same image as the splash screen.
60    */
61   private static void init2()
62   {
63      final Image img = new ImageIcon(splash.getImageURL()).getImage();
64
65      final JFrame splashFrame = new JFrame();
66      splashFrame.setUndecorated(true);
67
68      final JPanel splashPanel = new JPanel()
69         {
70            public void paintComponent(Graphics g)
71            {
72               g.drawImage(img, 0, 0, null);
73            }
74         };
75
76      final JProgressBar progressBar = new JProgressBar();
```

*(Continues)*

**Listing 7.23** *(Continued)*

```
77      progressBar.setStringPainted(true);
78      splashPanel.setLayout(new BorderLayout());
79      splashPanel.add(progressBar, BorderLayout.SOUTH);
80
81      splashFrame.add(splashPanel);
82      splashFrame.setBounds(splash.getBounds());
83      splashFrame.setVisible(true);
84
85      new SwingWorker<Void, Integer>()
86      {
87         protected Void doInBackground() throws Exception
88         {
89            try
90            {
91               for (int i = 0; i <= 100; i++)
92               {
93                  publish(i);
94                  Thread.sleep(100);
95               }
96            }
97            catch (InterruptedException e)
98            {
99            }
100           return null;
101        }
102
103        protected void process(List<Integer> chunks)
104        {
105           for (Integer chunk : chunks)
106           {
107              progressBar.setString("Loading module " + chunk);
108              progressBar.setValue(chunk);
109              splashPanel.repaint(); // because img is loaded asynchronously
110           }
111        }
112
113        protected void done()
114        {
115           splashFrame.setVisible(false);
116
117           JFrame frame = new JFrame();
118           frame.setSize(DEFAULT_WIDTH, DEFAULT_HEIGHT);
119           frame.setDefaultCloseOperation(JFrame.EXIT_ON_CLOSE);
120           frame.setTitle("SplashScreenTest");
121           frame.setVisible(true);
122        }
```

```
123        }.execute();
124    }
125
126    public static void main(String args[])
127    {
128        init1();
129
130        EventQueue.invokeLater(new Runnable()
131            {
132                public void run()
133                {
134                    init2();
135                }
136            });
137    }
138 }
```

---

**java.awt.SplashScreen** 6

- static SplashScreen getSplashScreen()
  gets a reference to the splash screen, or null if no splash screen is present.
- URL getImageURL()
- void setImageURL(URL imageURL)
  gets or sets the URL of the splash screen image. Setting the image updates the splash screen.
- Rectangle getBounds()
  gets the bounds of the splash screen.
- Graphics2D createGraphics()
  gets a graphics context for drawing on the splash screen.
- void update()
  updates the display of the splash screen.
- void close()
  closes the splash screen. The splash screen is automatically closed when the first AWT window is made visible.

## 7.15.2 Launching Desktop Applications

The java.awt.Desktop class lets you launch the default browser and e-mail program. You can also open, edit, and print files, using the applications that are registered for the file type.

The API is very straightforward. First, call the static isDesktopSupported method. If it returns true, the current platform supports the launching of desktop applications. Then call the static getDesktop method to obtain a Desktop instance.

Not all desktop environments support all API operations. For example, in the Gnome desktop on Linux, it is possible to open files, but you cannot print them. (There is no support for "verbs" in file associations.) To find out what is supported on your platform, call the isSupported method, passing a value in the Desktop.Action enumeration. Our sample program contains tests such as the following:

```
if (desktop.isSupported(Desktop.Action.PRINT)) printButton.setEnabled(true);
```

To open, edit, or print a file, first check that the action is supported, and then call the open, edit, or print method. To launch the browser, pass a URI. (See Chapter 3 for more information on URIs.) You can simply call the URI constructor with a string containing an http or https URL.

To launch the default e-mail program, you need to construct a URI of a particular format, namely

mailto:*recipient*?*query*

Here *recipient* is the e-mail address of the recipient, such as president@whitehouse.gov, and *query* contains &-separated *name=value* pairs, with percent-encoded values. (Percent encoding is essentially the same as the URL encoding algorithm described in Chapter 3, but a space is encoded as %20, not +). An example is subject=dinner%20RSVP&bcc=putin%40kremvax.ru. The format is documented in RFC 2368 (www.ietf.org/rfc/rfc2368.txt). Unfortunately, the URI class does not know anything about mailto URIs, so you have to assemble and encode your own.

Our sample program in Listing 7.24 lets you open, edit, or print a file of your choice, browse a URL, or launch your e-mail program (see Figure 7.48).

**Listing 7.24** desktopApp/DesktopAppFrame.java

```java
1  package desktopApp;
2
3  import java.awt.*;
4  import java.awt.event.*;
5  import java.io.*;
6  import java.net.*;
7  import javax.swing.*;
8
9  class DesktopAppFrame extends JFrame
10 {
```

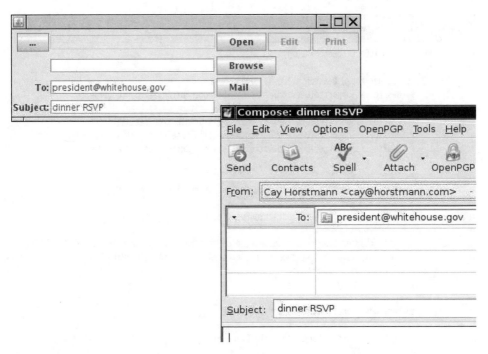

**Figure 7.48** Launching a desktop application

```
11    public DesktopAppFrame()
12    {
13        setLayout(new GridBagLayout());
14        final JFileChooser chooser = new JFileChooser();
15        JButton fileChooserButton = new JButton("...");
16        final JTextField fileField = new JTextField(20);
17        fileField.setEditable(false);
18        JButton openButton = new JButton("Open");
19        JButton editButton = new JButton("Edit");
20        JButton printButton = new JButton("Print");
21        final JTextField browseField = new JTextField();
22        JButton browseButton = new JButton("Browse");
23        final JTextField toField = new JTextField();
24        final JTextField subjectField = new JTextField();
25        JButton mailButton = new JButton("Mail");
26
27        openButton.setEnabled(false);
28        editButton.setEnabled(false);
29        printButton.setEnabled(false);
30        browseButton.setEnabled(false);
31        mailButton.setEnabled(false);
```

*(Continues)*

**Listing 7.24**  *(Continued)*

```
32        if (Desktop.isDesktopSupported())
33        {
34           Desktop desktop = Desktop.getDesktop();
35           if (desktop.isSupported(Desktop.Action.OPEN)) openButton.setEnabled(true);
36           if (desktop.isSupported(Desktop.Action.EDIT)) editButton.setEnabled(true);
37           if (desktop.isSupported(Desktop.Action.PRINT)) printButton.setEnabled(true);
38           if (desktop.isSupported(Desktop.Action.BROWSE)) browseButton.setEnabled(true);
39           if (desktop.isSupported(Desktop.Action.MAIL)) mailButton.setEnabled(true);
40        }
41
42        fileChooserButton.addActionListener(new ActionListener()
43           {
44              public void actionPerformed(ActionEvent e)
45              {
46                 if (chooser.showOpenDialog(DesktopAppFrame.this) == JFileChooser.APPROVE_OPTION)
47                    fileField.setText(chooser.getSelectedFile().getAbsolutePath());
48              }
49           });
50
51        openButton.addActionListener(new ActionListener()
52           {
53              public void actionPerformed(ActionEvent e)
54              {
55                 try
56                 {
57                    Desktop.getDesktop().open(chooser.getSelectedFile());
58                 }
59                 catch (IOException ex)
60                 {
61                    ex.printStackTrace();
62                 }
63              }
64           });
65
66        editButton.addActionListener(new ActionListener()
67           {
68              public void actionPerformed(ActionEvent e)
69              {
70                 try
71                 {
72                    Desktop.getDesktop().edit(chooser.getSelectedFile());
73                 }
74                 catch (IOException ex)
75                 {
76                    ex.printStackTrace();
77                 }
78              }
79           });
```

```
80       printButton.addActionListener(new ActionListener()
81          {
82             public void actionPerformed(ActionEvent e)
83             {
84                try
85                {
86                   Desktop.getDesktop().print(chooser.getSelectedFile());
87                }
88                catch (IOException ex)
89                {
90                   ex.printStackTrace();
91                }
92             }
93          });
94
95       browseButton.addActionListener(new ActionListener()
96          {
97             public void actionPerformed(ActionEvent e)
98             {
99                try
100               {
101                  Desktop.getDesktop().browse(new URI(browseField.getText()));
102               }
103               catch (URISyntaxException ex)
104               {
105                  ex.printStackTrace();
106               }
107               catch (IOException ex)
108               {
109                  ex.printStackTrace();
110               }
111            }
112         });
113
114      mailButton.addActionListener(new ActionListener()
115         {
116            public void actionPerformed(ActionEvent e)
117            {
118               try
119               {
120                  String subject = percentEncode(subjectField.getText());
121                  URI uri = new URI("mailto:" + toField.getText() + "?subject=" + subject);
122
123                  System.out.println(uri);
124                  Desktop.getDesktop().mail(uri);
125               }
```

*(Continues)*

**Listing 7.24** *(Continued)*

```
126              catch (URISyntaxException ex)
127              {
128                  ex.printStackTrace();
129              }
130              catch (IOException ex)
131              {
132                  ex.printStackTrace();
133              }
134          }
135      });
136
137      JPanel buttonPanel = new JPanel();
138      ((FlowLayout) buttonPanel.getLayout()).setHgap(2);
139      buttonPanel.add(openButton);
140      buttonPanel.add(editButton);
141      buttonPanel.add(printButton);
142
143      add(fileChooserButton, new GBC(0, 0).setAnchor(GBC.EAST).setInsets(2));
144      add(fileField, new GBC(1, 0).setFill(GBC.HORIZONTAL));
145      add(buttonPanel, new GBC(2, 0).setAnchor(GBC.WEST).setInsets(0));
146      add(browseField, new GBC(1, 1).setFill(GBC.HORIZONTAL));
147      add(browseButton, new GBC(2, 1).setAnchor(GBC.WEST).setInsets(2));
148      add(new JLabel("To:"), new GBC(0, 2).setAnchor(GBC.EAST).setInsets(5, 2, 5, 2));
149      add(toField, new GBC(1, 2).setFill(GBC.HORIZONTAL));
150      add(mailButton, new GBC(2, 2).setAnchor(GBC.WEST).setInsets(2));
151      add(new JLabel("Subject:"), new GBC(0, 3).setAnchor(GBC.EAST).setInsets(5, 2, 5, 2));
152      add(subjectField, new GBC(1, 3).setFill(GBC.HORIZONTAL));
153
154      pack();
155  }
156
157  private static String percentEncode(String s)
158  {
159      try
160      {
161          return URLEncoder.encode(s, "UTF-8").replaceAll("[+]", "%20");
162      }
163      catch (UnsupportedEncodingException ex)
164      {
165          return null; // UTF-8 is always supported
166      }
167  }
168 }
```

---

**java.awt.Desktop** 6

- `static boolean isDesktopSupported()`
  returns true if launching desktop applications is supported on this platform.

- `static Desktop getDesktop()`
  returns the Desktop object for launching desktop operations. Throws an UnsupportedOperationException if this platform does not support launching desktop operations.

- `boolean isSupported(Desktop.Action action)`
  returns true if the given action is supported. action is one of OPEN, EDIT, PRINT, BROWSE, or MAIL.

- `void open(File file)`
  launches the application that is registered for viewing the given file.

- `void edit(File file)`
  launches the application that is registered for editing the given file.

- `void print(File file)`
  prints the given file.

- `void browse(URI uri)`
  launches the default browser with the given URI.

- `void mail()`
- `void mail(URI uri)`
  launches the default mailer. The second version can be used to fill in parts of the e-mail message.

---

## 7.15.3 The System Tray

Many desktop environments have an area for icons of programs that run in the background and occasionally notify users of events. In Windows, this area is called the *system tray*, and the icons are called *tray icons*. The Java API adopts the same terminology. A typical example of such a program is a monitor that checks for software updates. If new updates are available, the monitor program can change the appearance of the icon or display a message near the icon.

Frankly, the system tray is somewhat overused, and computer users are not usually filled with joy when they discover yet another tray icon. Our sample system tray application—a program that dispenses virtual fortune cookies—is no exception to that rule.

The `java.awt.SystemTray` class is the cross-platform conduit to the system tray. As in the Desktop class discussed in the preceding section, you first call the static `isSupported` method to check that the local Java platform supports the system tray. If so, you get a SystemTray singleton by calling the static getSystemTray method.

The most important method of the SystemTray class is the add method that lets you add a TrayIcon instance. A tray icon has three key properties:

- The icon image
- The tooltip that is visible when the mouse hovers over the icon
- The pop-up menu that is displayed when the user clicks on the icon with the right mouse button

The pop-up menu is an instance of the PopupMenu class of the AWT library, representing a native pop-up menu, not a Swing menu. Fill it out with AWT MenuItem instances, each having an action listener just like the Swing counterpart.

Finally, a tray icon can display notifications to the user (see Figure 7.49). Call the displayMessage method of the TrayIcon class and specify the caption, message, and message type.

```
trayIcon.displayMessage("Your Fortune", fortunes.get(index), TrayIcon.MessageType.INFO);
```

Listing 7.25 shows the application that places a fortune cookie icon into the system tray. The program reads a fortune cookie file (from the venerable UNIX fortune

**Figure 7.49** A notification from a tray icon

program) in which each fortune is terminated by a line containing a % character. It displays a message every ten seconds. Mercifully, there is a pop-up menu with a command to exit the application. If only all tray icons were so considerate!

---

**Listing 7.25** systemTray/SystemTrayTest.java

```java
1  package systemTray;
2
3  import java.awt.*;
4  import java.awt.event.*;
5  import java.io.*;
6  import java.util.*;
7  import java.util.List;
8  import javax.swing.*;
9  import javax.swing.Timer;
10
11 /**
12  * This program demonstrates the system tray API.
13  * @version 1.01 2012-01-26
14  * @author Cay Horstmann
15  */
16 public class SystemTrayTest
17 {
18    public static void main(String[] args)
19    {
20       SystemTrayApp app = new SystemTrayApp();
21       app.init();
22    }
23 }
24
25 class SystemTrayApp
26 {
27    public void init()
28    {
29       final TrayIcon trayIcon;
30
31       if (!SystemTray.isSupported())
32       {
33          System.err.println("System tray is not supported.");
34          return;
35       }
36
37       SystemTray tray = SystemTray.getSystemTray();
38       Image image = new ImageIcon(getClass().getResource("cookie.png")).getImage();
39
40       PopupMenu popup = new PopupMenu();
41       MenuItem exitItem = new MenuItem("Exit");
```

*(Continues)*

**Listing 7.25** *(Continued)*

```
42      exitItem.addActionListener(new ActionListener()
43         {
44            public void actionPerformed(ActionEvent e)
45            {
46               System.exit(0);
47            }
48         });
49      popup.add(exitItem);
50
51      trayIcon = new TrayIcon(image, "Your Fortune", popup);
52
53      trayIcon.setImageAutoSize(true);
54      trayIcon.addActionListener(new ActionListener()
55         {
56            public void actionPerformed(ActionEvent e)
57            {
58               trayIcon.displayMessage("How do I turn this off?",
59                     "Right-click on the fortune cookie and select Exit.",
60                     TrayIcon.MessageType.INFO);
61            }
62         });
63
64      try
65      {
66         tray.add(trayIcon);
67      }
68      catch (AWTException e)
69      {
70         System.err.println("TrayIcon could not be added.");
71         return;
72      }
73
74      final List<String> fortunes = readFortunes();
75      Timer timer = new Timer(10000, new ActionListener()
76         {
77            public void actionPerformed(ActionEvent e)
78            {
79               int index = (int) (fortunes.size() * Math.random());
80               trayIcon.displayMessage("Your Fortune", fortunes.get(index),
81                     TrayIcon.MessageType.INFO);
82            }
83         });
84      timer.start();
85   }
```

```
 86    private List<String> readFortunes()
 87    {
 88       List<String> fortunes = new ArrayList<>();
 89       try (InputStream inStream = getClass().getResourceAsStream("fortunes"))
 90       {
 91          Scanner in = new Scanner(inStream);
 92          StringBuilder fortune = new StringBuilder();
 93          while (in.hasNextLine())
 94          {
 95             String line = in.nextLine();
 96             if (line.equals("%"))
 97             {
 98                fortunes.add(fortune.toString());
 99                fortune = new StringBuilder();
100             }
101             else
102             {
103                fortune.append(line);
104                fortune.append(' ');
105             }
106          }
107       }
108       catch (IOException ex)
109       {
110          ex.printStackTrace();
111       }
112       return fortunes;
113    }
114 }
```

---

**java.awt.SystemTray** 6

- static boolean isSupported()
  returns true if system tray access is supported on this platform.

- static SystemTray getSystemTray()
  returns the SystemTray object for accessing the system tray. Throws an UnsupportedOperationException if this platform does not support system tray access.

- Dimension getTrayIconSize()
  gets the dimensions for an icon in the system tray.

- void add(TrayIcon trayIcon)
- void remove(TrayIcon trayIcon)
  adds or removes a system tray icon.

---

**java.awt.TrayIcon** 6

- TrayIcon(Image image)
- TrayIcon(Image image, String tooltip)
- TrayIcon(Image image, String tooltip, PopupMenu popupMenu)
  constructs a tray icon with the given image, tooltip, and pop-up menu.

- Image getImage()
- void setImage(Image image)
- String getTooltip()
- void setTooltip(String tooltip)
- PopupMenu getPopupMenu()
- void setPopupMenu(PopupMenu popupMenu)
  gets or sets the image, tooltip, or pop-up menu of this tooltip.

- boolean isImageAutoSize()
- void setImageAutoSize(boolean autosize)
  gets or sets the imageAutoSize property. If set, the image is scaled to fit the tooltip icon area; if not (the default), it is cropped (if too large) or centered (if too small).

- void displayMessage(String caption, String text, TrayIcon.MessageType messageType)
  displays a message near the tray icon. The message type is one of INFO, WARNING, ERROR, or NONE.

- public void addActionListener(ActionListener listener)
- public void removeActionListener(ActionListener listener)
  adds or removes an action listener when the listener called is platform-dependent. Typical cases are clicking on a notification or double-clicking on the tray icon.

---

You have now reached the end of this long chapter covering advanced AWT features. In the next chapter, we will discuss the JavaBeans specification and its use for GUI builders.

# CHAPTER 8

# JavaBeans Components

## In this chapter:

The official definition of a bean, as given in the JavaBeans specification, is: "A bean is a reusable software component based on Sun's JavaBeans specification that can be manipulated visually in a builder tool."

Once you implement a bean, others can use it in a builder environment (such as NetBeans). Instead of having to write tedious code, they can simply drop your bean into a GUI form and customize it with dialog boxes.

This chapter explains how you can implement beans so that other developers can use them easily.

**NOTE:** We'd like to address a common confusion before going any further: The JavaBeans that we discuss in this chapter have little in common with Enterprise JavaBeans (EJB). Enterprise JavaBeans are server-side components with support for transactions, persistence, replication, and security. At a very basic level, they too are components that can be manipulated in builder tools. However, the Enterprise JavaBeans technology is quite a bit more complex than the "Standard Edition" JavaBeans technology.

That does not mean that standard JavaBeans components are limited to client-side programming. Web technologies such as JavaServer Faces (JSF) and JavaServer Pages (JSP) rely heavily on the JavaBeans component model.

## 8.1 Why Beans?

Programmers with experience in Visual Basic will immediately recognize why beans are so important. Programmers coming from environments where the tradition is to "roll your own" for everything often find it hard to believe that Visual Basic is one of the most successful examples of reusable object technology. For those who have never worked with Visual Basic, here, in a nutshell, is how you build a Visual Basic application:

1.  Build the interface by dropping components (called *controls* in Visual Basic) onto a form window.

2.  Through *property inspectors*, set the components' properties such as height, color, or behavior.

3.  The property inspectors also list the events to which components can react. Some events can be hooked up through dialog boxes. For other events, you write short snippets of event-handling code.

For example, in Volume I, Chapter 2, we wrote a program that displays an image in a frame. It took over a page of code. Here's what you would do in Visual Basic to create a program with pretty much the same functionality:

1.  Add two controls to a window: an *Image* control for displaying graphics and a *Common Dialog* control for selecting a file.

2.  Set the *Filter* properties of the Common Dialog control so that only the files that the Image control can handle will show up, as shown in Figure 8.1.

3.  Write four lines of Visual Basic code that will be activated when the project first starts running. All the code you need for this sequence looks like this:

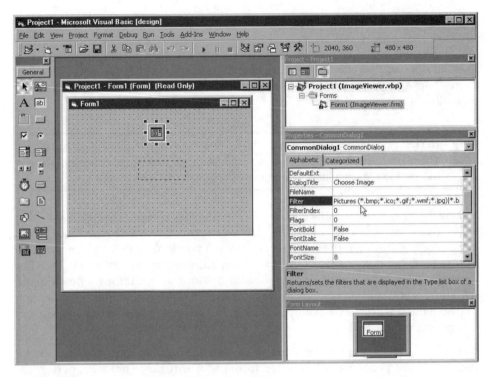

**Figure 8.1** The Properties window in Visual Basic for an image application

```
Private Sub Form_Load()
  CommonDialog1.ShowOpen
  Image1.Picture = LoadPicture(CommonDialog1.FileName)
End Sub
```

The code pops up the file dialog box—but only the files with the right extension are shown because of how we set the filter property. After the user selects an image file, the code tells the Image control to display it.

That's it. The layout activity, combined with these statements, gives essentially the same functionality as a page of Java code. Clearly it is a lot easier to learn how to drop components and set properties than to write a page of code.

We do not want to imply that Visual Basic is a good solution for every problem. It is clearly optimized for a particular kind of problems—the UI-intensive Windows programs. The JavaBeans technology was invented to make Java technology competitive in this arena. It enables vendors to create Visual Basic-style development environments that make it possible to build user interfaces with a minimum of programming.

## 8.2 The Bean-Writing Process

Writing a bean is not technically difficult—there are only a few new classes and interfaces for you to master. In particular, the simplest kind of a bean is nothing more than a Java class that follows some fairly strict naming conventions for its methods.

 **NOTE:** Some authors claim that a bean must have a no-argument constructor. The JavaBeans specification is actually silent on this issue. However, some builder tools do require a no-argument constructor for each bean.

Listing 8.1 at the end of this section shows the code for an ImageViewer bean that could give a Java builder environment the same functionality as the Visual Basic image control from the previous section. When you look at this code, notice that the ImageViewerBean class really doesn't look any different from any other class. For example, all accessor methods begin with get, and all mutator methods begin with set. As you will soon see, builder tools use this standard naming convention to discover *properties*. For example, fileName is a property of this bean because it has get and set methods.

Note that a property is not the same as an instance field. In this particular example, the fileName property is computed from the file instance field. Properties are conceptually at a higher level than instance fields—they are features of the interface, whereas instance fields belong to the implementation of the class.

One point that you need to keep in mind when you read through the examples in this chapter is that real-world beans are much more elaborate and tedious to code than our brief examples—for two reasons:

1. Beans must be usable by less-than-expert programmers. You need to expose *lots of properties* so that your users can access most of your bean's functionality with a visual design tool without programming.

2. The same bean must be usable in a wide *variety of contexts*. Both the behavior and the appearance of your bean must be customizable. Again, this means exposing lots of properties.

A good example of a bean with rich behavior is CalendarBean by Kai Tödter (see Figure 8.2). The bean and its source code are freely available from www.toedter.com/en/jcalendar. This bean gives users a convenient way of entering dates by locating them in a calendar display. This is obviously pretty complex and not something one would want to program from scratch. By using a bean such as this one, you can take advantage of the work of others, simply by dropping the bean into your builder tool.

**Listing 8.1** imageViewer/ImageViewerBean.java

```java
1  package imageViewer;
2
3  import java.awt.*;
4  import java.io.*;
5  import java.nio.file.*;
6  import javax.imageio.*;
7  import javax.swing.*;
8
9  /**
10  * A bean for viewing an image.
11  * @version 1.22 2012-06-10
12  * @author Cay Horstmann
13  */
14  public class ImageViewerBean extends JLabel
15  {
16     private Path path = null;
17     private static final int XPREFSIZE = 200;
18     private static final int YPREFSIZE = 200;
19
20     public ImageViewerBean()
21     {
22        setBorder(BorderFactory.createEtchedBorder());
23     }
24
25     /**
26      * Sets the fileName property.
27      * @param fileName the image file name
28      */
29     public void setFileName(String fileName)
30     {
31        path = Paths.get(fileName);
32        try (InputStream in = Files.newInputStream(path))
33        {
34           setIcon(new ImageIcon(ImageIO.read(in)));
35        }
36        catch (IOException e)
37        {
38           path = null;
39           setIcon(null);
40        }
41     }
42
43     /**
44      * Gets the fileName property.
45      * @return the image file name
46      */
```

*(Continues)*

**Listing 8.1** *(Continued)*

```
47    public String getFileName()
48    {
49       if (path == null) return "";
50       else return path.toString();
51    }
52
53    public Dimension getPreferredSize()
54    {
55       return new Dimension(XPREFSIZE, YPREFSIZE);
56    }
57  }
```

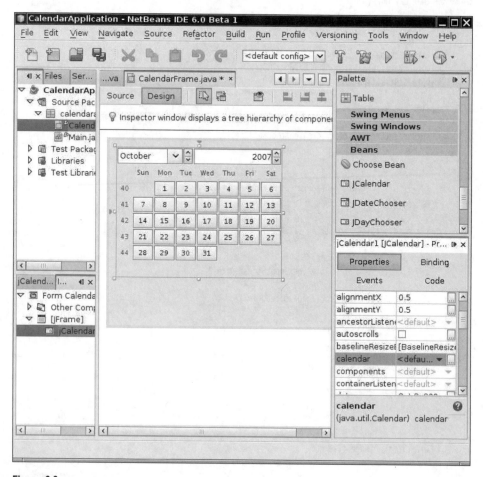

**Figure 8.2** A calendar bean

Fortunately, you need to master only a small number of concepts to write beans with a rich set of behaviors. The example beans in this chapter, although not trivial, are kept simple enough to illustrate the necessary concepts.

## 8.3 Using Beans to Build an Application

Before we get into the mechanics of writing beans, we want you to see how you might use or test them. `ImageViewerBean` is a perfectly usable bean, but outside a builder environment it can't show off its special features.

Each builder environment uses its own set of strategies to ease the programmer's life. We cover one such environment: the NetBeans integrated development environment available from http://netbeans.org.

In this example, we use two beans, `ImageViewerBean` and `FilePickerBean`. You have already seen the code for `ImageViewerBean`. We will analyze the code for `FilePickerBean` later in this chapter. For now, all you have to know is that clicking the button with the ". . ." label opens a file chooser.

### 8.3.1 Packaging Beans in JAR Files

To make any bean usable in a builder tool, package into a JAR file all class files that are used by the bean code. Unlike the JAR files for an applet, a JAR file for a bean needs a manifest file that specifies which class files in the archive are beans and should be included in the builder's toolbox. For example, here is the manifest file `ImageViewerBean.mf` for `ImageViewerBean`:

```
Manifest-Version: 1.0

Name: imageViewer/ImageViewerBean.class
Java-Bean: True
```

Note the blank line between the manifest version and bean name.

 **NOTE:** Some builder environments have problems loading beans from the default package, so you should always place beans into a package.

If your bean contains multiple class files, mention in the manifest which class files are beans that you want to have displayed in the toolbox. For example, you could place `ImageViewerBean` and `FilePickerBean` into the same JAR file and use the manifest

```
Manifest-Version: 1.0

Name: imageViewer/ImageViewerBean.class
Java-Bean: True

Name: filePicker/FilePickerBean.class
Java-Bean: True
```

> **CAUTION:** Some builder tools are extremely fussy about manifests. Make sure that there are no spaces after the ends of each line, that there are blank lines after the version and between bean entries, and that the last line ends in a newline.

To make the JAR file, follow these steps:

1. Edit the manifest file.

2. Gather all needed class files in a directory.

3. Run the jar tool as follows:

    jar cvfm *JarFile ManifestFile ClassFiles*

   For example,

    jar cvfm ImageViewerBean.jar ImageViewerBean.mf imageViewer/*.class

You can also add other items, such as icon images, to the JAR file. We discuss bean icons later in this chapter.

> **CAUTION:** Make sure to include all files that your bean needs in the JAR file. In particular, pay attention to inner class files such as FilePickerBean$1.class.

Builder environments have a mechanism for adding new beans, typically by loading JAR files. Here is what you do to import beans into NetBeans version 7.

Compile the ImageViewerBean and FilePickerBean classes and package them into JAR files. Then start NetBeans and follow these steps:

1. Select Tools -> Palette -> Swing/AWT Components from the menu.

2. Click the Add from JAR button.

3. In the file dialog box, move to the ImageViewerBean directory and select ImageViewerBean.jar.

4. Now a dialog box pops up that lists all the beans found in the JAR file. Select ImageViewerBean.

5. Finally, you are asked into which palette you want to place the beans. Select Beans. (There are other palettes for Swing components, AWT components, and so on.)

6. Have a look at the Beans palette. It now contains an icon representing the new bean. However, the icon is just a default icon—you will see later how to add icons to a bean.

Repeat these steps for `FilePickerBean`. Now you are ready to compose these beans into an application.

## 8.3.2 Composing Beans in a Builder Environment

The promise of component-based development is to compose your application from prefabricated components, with a minimum of programming. In this section, you will see how to compose an application from the `ImageViewerBean` and `FilePickerBean` components.

In NetBeans 6, select File -> New Project from the menu. A dialog box pops up. Select Java, then Java Application (see Figure 8.3).

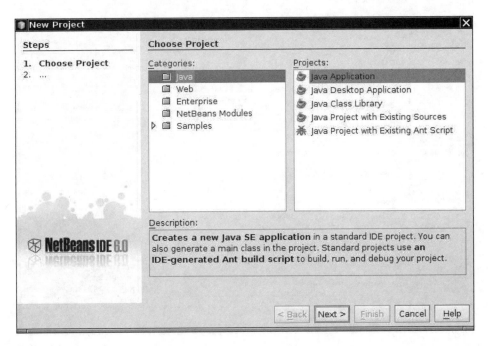

**Figure 8.3** Creating a new project

Click the Next button. On the following screen, set a name for your application (such as ImageViewer), and click the Finish button. Now you see a project viewer on the left and the source code editor in the middle.

Right-click the project name in the project viewer and select New -> JFrame Form from the menu (see Figure 8.4).

A dialog box pops up. Enter a name for the frame class (such as ImageViewerFrame) and click the Finish button. You now get a form editor with a blank frame. To add a bean to the form, select the bean in the palette located to the right of the form editor. Then click the frame.

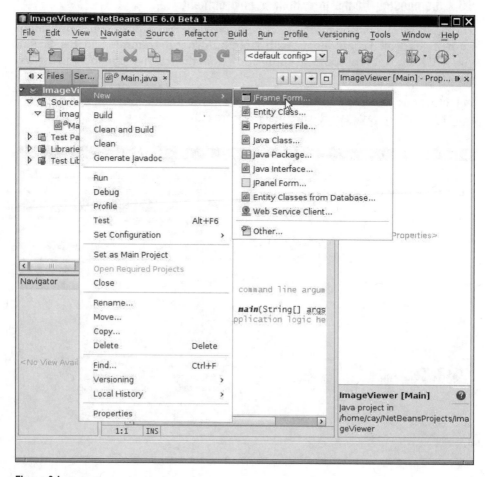

**Figure 8.4** Creating a form view

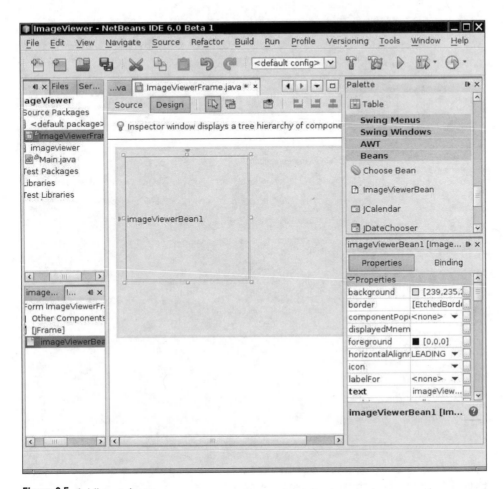

**Figure 8.5** Adding a bean

Figure 8.5 shows the result of adding an ImageViewerBean onto the frame.

If you look into the source window, you will find that the source code now contains the Java instructions to add the bean objects to the frame (see Figure 8.6). The source code is bracketed by dire warnings that you should not edit it. Any edits would be lost when the builder environment updates the code as you modify the form.

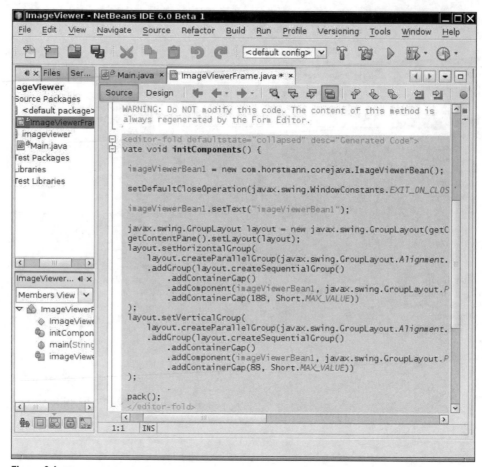

**Figure 8.6** The source code for adding the bean

 **NOTE:** A builder environment is not required to update source code as you build an application. A builder environment can generate source code when you are done editing, serialize the beans you customized, or perhaps produce an entirely different description of your building activity.

For example, the experimental Bean Builder at http://java.net/projects/bean-builder lets you design GUI applications without writing any source code at all.

The JavaBeans mechanism doesn't attempt to force an implementation strategy on a builder tool. Instead, it aims to supply information about beans that the builder tools can take advantage of in one way or another.

Now go back to the design view and click ImageViewerBean in the form. On the right-hand side is a property inspector that lists the bean's property names and their current values. This is a vital part of component-based development tools because setting properties at design time is how you set the initial state of a component.

For example, you can modify the text property of the label used for the image bean simply by typing a new name into the property inspector. To change the text property, just edit a string in a text field. Try it out—set the label text to "Hello". The form is immediately updated to reflect your change (see Figure 8.7).

**NOTE:** When you change the setting of a property, the NetBeans environment updates the source code to reflect your action. For example, if you set the text field to Hello, the instruction

```
imageViewerBean.setText("Hello");
```

is added to the initComponents method. As already mentioned, other builder tools might have different strategies for recording property settings.

Properties don't have to be strings; they can be values of any Java type. To make it possible for users to set values for properties of any type, builder tools use specialized *property editors.* (Property editors either come with the builder or are supplied by the bean developer. You will see how to write your own property editors later in this chapter.)

To see a simple property editor at work, look at the foreground property. The property type is Color. You can see the color editor, with a text field containing a string [0,0,0] and a button labeled "..." that brings up a color chooser. Go ahead and change the foreground color. Notice that you'll immediately see the change to the property value—the label text changes its color.

More interestingly, choose a file name for an image file in the property inspector. Once you do so, ImageViewerBean automatically displays the image.

**NOTE:** If you look closely at the property inspector in NetBeans, you will find a large number of mysterious properties such as focusCycleRoot and paintingForPrint. These are inherited from the JLabel superclass. You will see later in this chapter how you can suppress their visibility in the property inspector.

To complete our application, place a FilePickerBean object into the frame. Now we want the image to be loaded when the fileName property of FilePickerBean is changed. This happens through a PropertyChange event; we'll discuss these kinds of events later in this chapter.

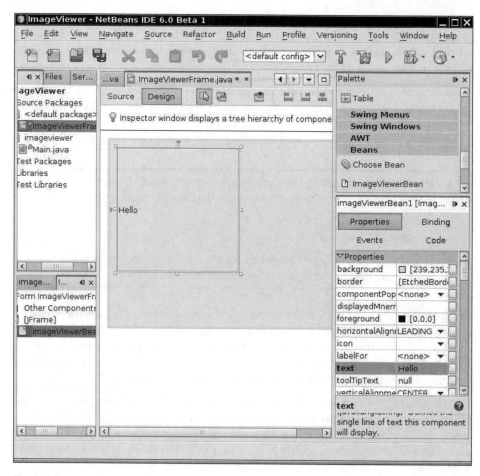

**Figure 8.7** Changing a property in the property inspector

To react to the event, select FilePickerBean and select the Events tab from its property inspector. Then click the " . . . " button next to the propertyChange entry. A dialog box appears that shows that no handlers are currently associated with this event. Click the Add button in the dialog box. You are prompted for a method name (see Figure 8.8). Type loadImage.

Now look at the code editor. Event handling code has been added, and there is a new method:

```
private void loadImage(java.beans.PropertyChange evt)
{
   // TODO add your handling code here
}
```

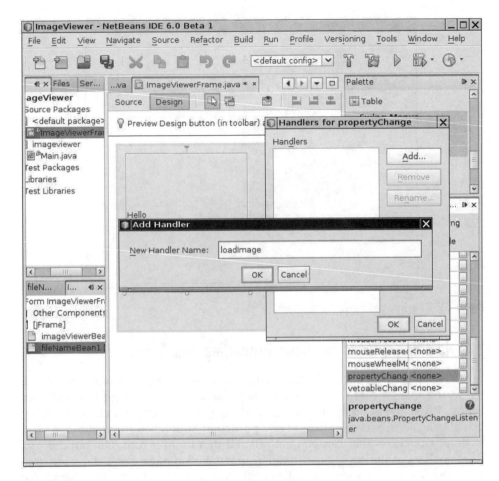

**Figure 8.8** Adding an event to a bean

Add the following line of code to that method:

```
imageViewerBean1.setFileName(filePickerBean1.getFileName());
```

Then compile and execute the frame class. You now have a complete image viewer application. Click the button with the "..." label and select an image file. The image is displayed in the image viewer (see Figure 8.9).

This process demonstrates that you can create a Java application from beans by setting properties and providing a small amount of code for event handlers.

**Figure 8.9** The image viewer application

## 8.4 Naming Patterns for Bean Properties and Events

In this section, we'll cover the basic rules for designing your own beans. First, we want to stress there is *no* cosmic beans class that you extend to build your beans. Visual beans directly or indirectly extend the Component class, but non-visual beans don't have to extend any particular superclass. Remember, a bean is simply *any* class that can be manipulated in a builder tool. The builder tool does not look at the superclass to determine the bean nature of a class, but analyzes the names of its methods. To enable this analysis, the method names for beans must follow certain patterns.

---

**NOTE:** There is a java.beans.Beans class, but all methods in it are static. Extending it would, therefore, be rather pointless, even though you will see it done occasionally, supposedly for greater "clarity." Obviously, since a bean can't extend both Beans and Component, this approach won't work for visual beans. In fact, the Beans class contains methods that are designed to be called by builder tools—for example, to check whether the tool is operating at design time or run time.

---

Other languages for visual design environments, such as Visual Basic and C#, have special keywords such as "Property" and "Event" to express these concepts directly. The designers of the Java specification decided not to add keywords to the language to support visual programming. Therefore, they needed an alternative so that a builder tool could analyze a bean to learn its properties or events. Actually, there are two alternative mechanisms. If the bean writer uses standard naming patterns for properties and events, the builder tool can use the reflection mechanism to understand what properties and events the bean is supposed to expose. Alternatively, the bean writer can supply a *bean information* class that tells the builder tool about the properties and events of the bean. We start by using the naming patterns because they are easier to use. You'll see later in this chapter how to supply a bean information class.

 **NOTE:** Although the documentation calls these standard naming patterns "design patterns," these are really only naming conventions that have nothing to do with the design patterns used in object-oriented programming.

The naming pattern for properties is simple: Any pair of methods

```
public Type getPropertyName()
public void setPropertyName(Type newValue)
```

corresponds to a read/write property.

For example, in our `ImageViewerBean`, there is only one read/write property (for the file name to be viewed), with the following methods:

```
public String getFileName()
public void setFileName(String newValue)
```

If you have a `get` method but not an associated `set` method, you define a read-only property. Conversely, a `set` method without an associated `get` method defines a write-only property.

 **NOTE:** The `get` and `set` methods you create can do more than simply get and set a private data field. Like any Java method, they can carry out arbitrary actions. For example, the `setFileName` method of the `ImageViewerBean` class not only sets the value of the `fileName` data field but also opens the file and loads the image.

**NOTE:** In Visual Basic and C#, properties also come from get and set methods. However, in both these languages, you need to explicitly define properties so that builder tools wouldn't need to second-guess the programmer's intentions by analyzing method names. In these languages, properties have another advantage: Using a property name on the left side of an assignment automatically calls the set method. Using a property name in an expression automatically calls the get method. For example, in Visual Basic you can write

```
imageBean.fileName = "corejava.gif"
```

instead of

```
imageBean.setFileName("corejava.gif");
```

This syntax was considered for Java, but the language designers felt that it was a poor idea to hide a method call behind syntax that looks like field access.

There is one exception to the get/set naming pattern. Properties that have boolean values should use the is/set naming pattern, as in the following examples:

```
public boolean isPropertyName()
public void setPropertyName(boolean b)
```

For example, an animation might have a property running, with two methods

```
public boolean isRunning()
public void setRunning(boolean b)
```

The setRunning method would start and stop the animation. The isRunning method would report its current status.

**NOTE:** It is legal to use a get prefix for a boolean property accessor (such as getRunning), but the is prefix is preferred.

Be careful with capitalization in your method names. The designers of the JavaBeans specification decided that the name of the property in our example would be fileName, with a lowercase f, even though the get and set methods contain an uppercase F (getFileName, setFileName). The bean analyzer performs a process called *decapitalization* to derive the property name. (That is, the first character after get or set is converted to lowercase.) The rationale is that this process results in method and property names that are more natural to programmers.

However, if the first *two* letters are upper case (as in getURL), then the first letter of the property is *not* changed to lower case. After all, a property name of uRL would look ridiculous.

**NOTE:** What do you do if your class has a pair of get and set methods that don't correspond to a property you want users to manipulate in a property inspector? In your own classes, you can of course avoid that situation by renaming your methods. However, if you extend another class, you inherit the method names from the superclass. This happens, for example, when your bean extends JPanel or JLabel—a large number of uninteresting properties show up in the property inspector. You will see later in this chapter how you can override the automatic property discovery process by supplying *bean information*. In the bean information, you can specify exactly which properties your bean should expose.

For events, the naming patterns are equally simple. A bean builder environment will infer that your bean generates events when you supply methods to add and remove event listeners. All event class names must end in Event, and the classes must extend the EventObject class.

Suppose your bean generates events of type *EventName*Event. The listener interface must be called *EventName*Listener, and the methods to manage the listeners must be called

```
public void addEventNameListener(EventNameListener e)
public void removeEventNameListener(EventNameListener e)
public EventNameListener getEventNameListeners()
```

If you look at the code for ImageViewerBean, you'll see that it has no events to expose. However, many Swing components generate events, and they follow this pattern. For example, the AbstractButton class generates ActionEvent objects, and it has the following methods to manage ActionListener objects:

```
public void addActionListener(ActionListener e)
public void removeActionListener(ActionListener e)
ActionListener[] getActionListeners()
```

 **CAUTION:** If your event class doesn't extend EventObject, chances are that your code will compile just fine because none of the methods of the EventObject class are actually needed. However, your bean will mysteriously fail—the introspection mechanism will not recognize the events.

## 8.5 Bean Property Types

A sophisticated bean will expose lots of different properties and events. Properties can be as simple as the fileName property that you saw in ImageViewerBean and FilePickerBean or as sophisticated as a color value or even an array of data points—we'll encounter both of these cases later in this chapter. The JavaBeans specification allows four types of properties, illustrated here by various examples.

## 8.5.1 Simple Properties

A simple property is one that takes a single value such as a string or a number. The `fileName` property of the `ImageViewer` is an example of a simple property. Simple properties are easy to program: Just use the set/get naming convention as described earlier. For example, if you look at the code in Listing 8.1, you can see that all it took to implement a simple string property was the following:

```
public void setFileName(String f)
{
   fileName = f;
   image = . . .
   repaint();
}

public String getFileName()
{
   if (file == null) return "";
   else return file.getPath();
}
```

## 8.5.2 Indexed Properties

An indexed property specifies an array. With an indexed property, you need to supply two pairs of get and set methods: one for the array and one for individual entries. They must follow this pattern:

```
Type[] getPropertyName()
void setPropertyName(Type[] newValue)
Type getPropertyName(int i)
void setPropertyName(int i, Type newValue)
```

For example, the `FilePickerBean` uses an indexed property for the file extensions. It provides these four methods:

```
private String[] extensions;
. . .
public String[] getExtensions() { return extensions; }
public void setExtensions(String[] newValue) { extensions = newValue; }
public String getExtensions(int i)
{
   if (0 <= i && i < extensions.length) return extensions[i];
   else return "";
}
```

```
public void setExtensions(int i, String newValue)
{
    if (0 <= i && i < extensions.length) extensions[i] = value;
}
```

The set*PropertyName*(int, *Type*) method cannot be used to *grow* the array. To grow the array, you must manually build a new array and pass it to the set*PropertyName*(*Type*[]) method.

## 8.5.3 Bound Properties

Bound properties tell interested listeners that their value has changed. For example, the `fileName` property in `FilePickerBean` is a bound property. When the file name changes, then `ImageViewerBean` is automatically notified and loads the new file.

To implement a bound property, you must implement two mechanisms:

1. Whenever the value of the property changes, the bean must send a `PropertyChange` event to all registered listeners. This change can occur when the set method is called or when some other method (such as the action listener of the " . . . " button) changes the value.

2. To enable interested listeners to register themselves, the bean has to implement the following two methods:

   ```
   void addPropertyChangeListener(PropertyChangeListener listener)
   void removePropertyChangeListener(PropertyChangeListener listener)
   ```

   It is also recommended (but not required) to provide the method

   ```
   PropertyChangeListener[] getPropertyChangeListeners()
   ```

The `java.beans` package has a convenience class, called `PropertyChangeSupport`, that manages the listeners for you. To use this convenience class, add an instance field of this class:

```
private PropertyChangeSupport changeSupport = new PropertyChangeSupport(this);
```

Delegate the task of adding and removing property change listeners to that object:

```
public void addPropertyChangeListener(PropertyChangeListener listener)
{
    changeSupport.addPropertyChangeListener(listener);
}

public void removePropertyChangeListener(PropertyChangeListener listener)
{
    changeSupport.removePropertyChangeListener(listener);
}
```

```
public PropertyChangeListener[] getPropertyChangeListeners()
{
    return changeSupport.getPropertyChangeListeners();
}
```

Whenever the value of the property changes, use the firePropertyChange method of the PropertyChangeSupport object to deliver an event to all the registered listeners. That method has three parameters: the name of the property, the old value, and the new value. Here is the boilerplate code for a typical setter of a bound property:

```
public void setValue(Type newValue)
{
    Type oldValue = getValue();
    value = newValue;
    changeSupport.firePropertyChange("propertyName", oldValue, newValue);
}
```

To fire a change of an indexed property, call

```
changeSupport.fireIndexedPropertyChange("propertyName", index, oldValue, newValue);
```

 **TIP:** If your bean extends any class that ultimately extends the Component class, you do *not* need to implement the addPropertyChangeListener, removeProperty-ChangeListener, and getPropertyChangeListeners methods. These methods are already implemented in the Component superclass. To notify the listeners of a property change, simply call the firePropertyChange method of the JComponent superclass. Unfortunately, firing of indexed property changes is not supported.

Other beans that want to be notified when the property value changes must add a PropertyChangeListener. That interface contains only one method:

```
void propertyChange(PropertyChangeEvent event)
```

The PropertyChangeEvent object holds the name of the property and the old and new values, obtainable with the getPropertyName, getOldValue, and getNewValue methods.

If the property type is not a class type, then the property value objects are instances of the usual wrapper classes.

## 8.5.4 Constrained Properties

A *constrained property* is constrained by the fact that *any* listener can "veto" proposed changes, forcing it to revert to the old setting. The Java library contains only a few examples of constrained properties. One of them is the closed property of the JInternalFrame class. If someone tries to call setClosed(true) on an internal frame, all of its VetoableChangeListeners are notified. If any of them throws a PropertyVetoException, the closed property is *not* changed, and the setClosed method throws the same exception. In particular, a VetoableChangeListener may veto closing the frame if its contents have not been saved.

To build a constrained property, your bean must have the following two methods to manage VetoableChangeListener objects:

```
public void addVetoableChangeListener(VetoableChangeListener listener);
public void removeVetoableChangeListener(VetoableChangeListener listener);
```

It also should have a method for getting all listeners:

```
VetoableChangeListener[] getVetoableChangeListeners()
```

Just as there is a convenience class to manage property change listeners, there is a convenience class, called VetoableChangeSupport, that manages vetoable change listeners. Your bean should contain an object of this class.

```
private VetoableChangeSupport vetoSupport = new VetoableChangeSupport(this);
```

Adding and removing listeners should be delegated to this object. For example:

```
public void addVetoableChangeListener(VetoableChangeListener listener)
{
   vetoSupport.addVetoableChangeListener(listener);
}
public void removeVetoableChangeListener(VetoableChangeListener listener)
{
   vetoSupport.removeVetoableChangeListener(listener);
}
```

To update a constrained property value, a bean uses the following three-phase approach:

1.  Notify all vetoable change listeners of the intent to change the property value. (Use the fireVetoableChange method of the VetoableChangeSupport class.)

2.  If none of the vetoable change listeners has thrown a PropertyVetoException, update the value of the property.

3.  Notify all property change listeners to *confirm* that a change has occurred.

For example:

```
public void setValue(Type newValue) throws PropertyVetoException
{
   Type oldValue = getValue();
   vetoSupport.fireVetoableChange("value", oldValue, newValue);
   // survived, therefore no veto
   value = newValue;
   changeSupport.firePropertyChange("value", oldValue, newValue);
}
```

It is important that you don't change the property value until all the registered vetoable change listeners have agreed to the proposed change. Conversely, a vetoable change listener should never assume that a change that it agrees to is actually happening. The only reliable way to get notified when a change is actually happening is through a property change listener.

 **NOTE:** If your bean extends the JComponent class, you do not need a separate VetoableChangeSupport object. Simply call the fireVetoableChange method of the JComponent superclass. Note that you cannot install a vetoable change listener for a specific property into a JComponent. You need to listen to all vetoable changes.

We end our discussion of JavaBeans properties by showing the full code for FilePickerBean (see Listing 8.2). The FilePickerBean has a filename property and an indexed extensions property. Since FilePickerBean extends the JPanel class, we did not have to explicitly use a PropertyChangeSupport object. Instead, we relied on the ability of the JPanel class to manage property change listeners.

**Listing 8.2**   filePicker/FilePickerBean.java

```
1  package filePicker;
2
3  import java.awt.*;
4  import java.awt.event.*;
5  import java.io.*;
6  import java.util.*;
7  import javax.swing.*;
8  import javax.swing.filechooser.*;
9
10 /**
11  * A bean for picking file names.
12  * @version 1.31 2012-06-10
13  * @author Cay Horstmann
14  */
15 public class FilePickerBean extends JPanel
16 {
17    private static final int XPREFSIZE = 200;
18    private static final int YPREFSIZE = 20;
19
20    private JButton dialogButton;
21    private JTextField nameField;
22    private JFileChooser chooser;
23    private String[] extensions = { "gif", "png" };
```

```
24    public FilePickerBean()
25    {
26        dialogButton = new JButton("...");
27        nameField = new JTextField(30);
28
29        chooser = new JFileChooser();
30        setPreferredSize(new Dimension(XPREFSIZE, YPREFSIZE));
31
32        setLayout(new GridBagLayout());
33        GridBagConstraints gbc = new GridBagConstraints();
34        gbc.weightx = 100;
35        gbc.weighty = 100;
36        gbc.anchor = GridBagConstraints.WEST;
37        gbc.fill = GridBagConstraints.BOTH;
38        gbc.gridwidth = 1;
39        gbc.gridheight = 1;
40        add(nameField, gbc);
41
42        dialogButton.addActionListener(new ActionListener()
43            {
44                public void actionPerformed(ActionEvent event)
45                {
46                    chooser.setFileFilter(new FileNameExtensionFilter(Arrays.toString(extensions),
47                        extensions));
48                    int r = chooser.showOpenDialog(null);
49                    if (r == JFileChooser.APPROVE_OPTION)
50                    {
51                        File f = chooser.getSelectedFile();
52                        String name = f.getAbsolutePath();
53                        setFileName(name);
54                    }
55                }
56            });
57        nameField.setEditable(false);
58
59        gbc.weightx = 0;
60        gbc.anchor = GridBagConstraints.EAST;
61        gbc.fill = GridBagConstraints.NONE;
62        gbc.gridx = 1;
63        add(dialogButton, gbc);
64    }
65
66    /**
67     * Sets the fileName property.
68     * @param newValue the new file name
69     */
```

*(Continues)*

**Listing 8.2** *(Continued)*

```
70    public void setFileName(String newValue)
71    {
72       String oldValue = nameField.getText();
73       nameField.setText(newValue);
74       firePropertyChange("fileName", oldValue, newValue);
75    }
76
77    /**
78     * Gets the fileName property.
79     * @return the name of the selected file
80     */
81    public String getFileName()
82    {
83       return nameField.getText();
84    }
85
86    /**
87     * Gets the extensions property.
88     * @return the default extensions in the file chooser
89     */
90    public String[] getExtensions()
91    {
92       return extensions;
93    }
94
95    /**
96     * Sets the extensions property.
97     * @param newValue the new default extensions
98     */
99    public void setExtensions(String[] newValue)
100   {
101      extensions = newValue;
102   }
103
104   /**
105    * Gets one of the extensions property values.
106    * @param i the index of the property value
107    * @return the value at the given index
108    */
109   public String getExtensions(int i)
110   {
111      if (0 <= i && i < extensions.length) return extensions[i];
112      else return "";
113   }
114
115   /**
116    * Sets one of the extensions property values.
```

```
117     * @param i the index of the property value
118     * @param newValue the new value at the given index
119     */
120    public void setExtensions(int i, String newValue)
121    {
122       if (0 <= i && i < extensions.length) extensions[i] = newValue;
123    }
124 }
```

---

**java.beans.PropertyChangeListener** 1.1

- void propertyChange(PropertyChangeEvent event)
  is called when a property change event is fired.

---

**java.beans.PropertyChangeSupport** 1.1

- PropertyChangeSupport(Object sourceBean)
  constructs a PropertyChangeSupport object that manages listeners for the bound property changes of the given bean.
- void addPropertyChangeListener(PropertyChangeListener listener)
- void addPropertyChangeListener(String propertyName, PropertyChangeListener listener) 1.2
  registers an interested listener for changes in all bound properties, or only the named bound property.
- void removePropertyChangeListener(PropertyChangeListener listener)
- void removePropertyChangeListener(String propertyName, PropertyChangeListener listener) 1.2
  removes a previously registered property change listener.
- void firePropertyChange(String propertyName, Object oldValue, Object newValue)
- void firePropertyChange(String propertyName, int oldValue, int newValue) 1.2
- void firePropertyChange(String propertyName, boolean oldValue, boolean newValue) 1.2
  sends a PropertyChangeEvent to registered listeners.
- void fireIndexedPropertyChange(String propertyName, int index, Object oldValue, Object newValue) 5.0
- void fireIndexedPropertyChange(String propertyName, int index, int oldValue, int newValue) 5.0
- void fireIndexedPropertyChange(String propertyName, int index, boolean oldValue, boolean newValue) 5.0
  sends an IndexedPropertyChangeEvent to registered listeners.
- PropertyChangeListener[] getPropertyChangeListeners() 1.4
- PropertyChangeListener[] getPropertyChangeListeners(String propertyName) 1.4
  gets the listeners for changes in all bound properties, or only the named bound property.

---

**java.beans.PropertyChangeEvent** 1.1

- PropertyChangeEvent(Object sourceBean, String propertyName, Object oldValue, Object newValue)
  constructs a new PropertyChangeEvent object informing that the given property has changed from oldValue to newValue.
- String getPropertyName()
  returns the name of the property.
- Object getOldValue();
- Object getNewValue()
  returns the old and the new value of the property.

---

**java.beans.IndexedPropertyChangeEvent** 5.0

- IndexedPropertyChangeEvent(Object sourceBean, String propertyName, Object oldValue, Object newValue, int index)
  constructs a new IndexedPropertyChangeEvent object informing that the given property has changed from oldValue to newValue at the given index.
- int getIndex()
  returns the index at which the change occurred.

---

**java.beans.VetoableChangeListener** 1.1

- void vetoableChange(PropertyChangeEvent event)
  is called when a property is about to be changed. It should throw a PropertyVetoException if the change is not acceptable.

---

**java.beans.VetoableChangeSupport** 1.1

- VetoableChangeSupport(Object sourceBean)
  constructs a PropertyChangeSupport object that manages listeners for the constrained property changes of the given bean.
- void addVetoableChangeListener(VetoableChangeListener listener)
- void addVetoableChangeListener(String propertyName, VetoableChangeListener listener) 1.2
  registers an interested listener for changes in all constrained properties, or only the named constrained property.
- void removeVetoableChangeListener(VetoableChangeListener listener)
- void removeVetoableChangeListener(String propertyName, VetoableChangeListener listener) 1.2
  removes a previously registered vetoable change listener.

*(Continues)*

---

**java.beans.VetoableChangeSupport** 1.1 *(Continued)*

- void fireVetoableChange(String propertyName, Object oldValue, Object newValue)
- void fireVetoableChange(String propertyName, int oldValue, int newValue) 1.2
- void fireVetoableChange(String propertyName, boolean oldValue, boolean newValue) 1.2
  sends a VetoableChangeEvent to registered listeners.
- VetoableChangeListener[] getVetoableChangeListeners() 1.4
- VetoableChangeListener[] getVetoableChangeListeners(String propertyName) 1.4
  gets the listeners for changes in all constrained properties, or only the named bound property.

---

**java.awt.Component** 1.0

- void addPropertyChangeListener(PropertyChangeListener listener) 1.2
- void addPropertyChangeListener(String propertyName, PropertyChangeListener listener) 1.2
  registers an interested listener for changes in all bound properties, or only the named bound property.
- void removePropertyChangeListener(PropertyChangeListener listener) 1.2
- void removePropertyChangeListener(String propertyName, PropertyChangeListener listener) 1.2
  removes a previously registered property change listener.
- void firePropertyChange(String propertyName, Object oldValue, Object newValue) 1.2
  sends a PropertyChangeEvent to registered listeners.

---

**javax.swing.JComponent** 1.2

- void addVetoableChangeListener(VetoableChangeListener listener)
  registers an interested listener for changes in all constrained properties, or only the named constrained property.
- void removeVetoableChangeListener(VetoableChangeListener listener)
  removes a previously registered vetoable change listener.
- void fireVetoableChange(String propertyName, Object oldValue, Object newValue)
  sends a VetoableChangeEvent to registered listeners.

---

**java.beans.PropertyVetoException** 1.1

- PropertyVetoException(String message, PropertyChangeEvent event)
  creates a new PropertyVetoException.
- PropertyChangeEvent getPropertyChangeEvent()
  returns the PropertyChangeEvent that was vetoed.

## 8.6 BeanInfo Classes

If you use the standard naming patterns for the methods of your bean class, a builder tool can use reflection to determine features such as properties and events. This process makes it simple to get started with bean programming, but naming patterns are rather limiting. As your beans become complex, there might be features of your bean that naming patterns will not reveal. Moreover, as we already mentioned, many beans have get/set method pairs that should *not* correspond to bean properties.

If you need a more flexible mechanism for describing information about your bean, define an object that implements the BeanInfo interface. When you provide such an object, a builder tool will consult it about the features that your bean supports.

The name of the bean info class must be formed by adding BeanInfo to the name of the bean. For example, the bean info class associated to the class ImageViewerBean *must* be named ImageViewerBeanBeanInfo. The bean info class must be part of the same package as the bean itself.

You won't normally write a class that implements all methods of the BeanInfo interface. Instead, extend the SimpleBeanInfo convenience class that has default implementations for all the methods in the BeanInfo interface.

The most common reason for supplying a BeanInfo class is to gain control of the bean properties. Construct a PropertyDescriptor for each property by supplying the name of the property and the class of the bean that contains it.

```
PropertyDescriptor descriptor = new PropertyDescriptor("fileName", FilePickerBean.class);
```

Then implement the getPropertyDescriptors method of your BeanInfo class to return an array of all property descriptors.

For example, suppose ImageViewerBean wants to hide all properties it inherits from the JLabel superclass and expose only the fileName property. The following BeanInfo class does just that:

```
// bean info class for ImageViewerBean
public class ImageViewerBeanBeanInfo extends SimpleBeanInfo
{
    private PropertyDescriptor[] propertyDescriptors;

    public ImageViewerBeanBeanInfo()
    {
        try
        {
            propertyDescriptors = new PropertyDescriptor[]
            {
```

```
            new PropertyDescriptor("fileName", FilePickerBean.class);
        }
    }
    catch (IntrospectionException e)
    {
        e.printStackTrace();
    }
}

public PropertyDescriptor[] getPropertyDescriptors()
{
    return propertyDescriptors;
}
}
```

Other methods also return EventSetDescriptor and MethodDescriptor arrays, but they are less commonly used. If one of these methods returns null (as is the case for the SimpleBeanInfo methods), then the standard naming patterns apply. However, if you override a method to return a non-null array, then you must include *all* properties, events, or methods in your array.

 **NOTE:** Sometimes, you might want to write generic code that discovers properties or events of an arbitrary bean. Call the static getBeanInfo method of the Introspector class. The Introspector constructs a BeanInfo class that completely describes the bean, taking into account the information in BeanInfo companion classes.

Another useful method in the BeanInfo interface is the getIcon method that lets you give your bean a custom icon. Builder tools will display the icon in a palette. Actually, you can specify four separate icon bitmaps. The BeanInfo interface has four constants that cover the standard sizes:

```
ICON_COLOR_16x16
ICON_COLOR_32x32
ICON_MONO_16x16
ICON_MONO_32x32
```

In the following class, we use the loadImage convenience method in the SimpleBeanInfo class to load the icon images:

```
public class ImageViewerBeanBeanInfo extends SimpleBeanInfo
{
    private Image iconColor16;
    private Image iconColor32;
    private Image iconMono16;
    private Image iconMono32;
```

```java
public ImageViewerBeanBeanInfo()
{
    iconColor16 = loadImage("ImageViewerBean_COLOR_16x16.gif");
    iconColor32 = loadImage("ImageViewerBean_COLOR_32x32.gif");
    iconMono16 = loadImage("ImageViewerBean_MONO_16x16.gif");
    iconMono32 = loadImage("ImageViewerBean_MONO_32x32.gif");
}

public Image getIcon(int iconType)
{
    if (iconType == BeanInfo.ICON_COLOR_16x16) return iconColor16;
    else if (iconType == BeanInfo.ICON_COLOR_32x32) return iconColor32;
    else if (iconType == BeanInfo.ICON_MONO_16x16) return iconMono16;
    else if (iconType == BeanInfo.ICON_MONO_32x32) return iconMono32;
    else return null;
}
}
```

---

**java.beans.Introspector** 1.1

- static BeanInfo getBeanInfo(Class<?> beanClass)
  gets the bean information of the given class.

---

**java.beans.BeanInfo** 1.1

- PropertyDescriptor[] getPropertyDescriptors()
  returns the descriptors for the bean properties. A return of null indicates that the naming conventions should be used to find the properties.

- Image getIcon(int iconType)
  returns an image object that can represent the bean in toolboxes, tool bars, and the like. There are four constants, as described earlier, for the standard types of icons.

---

**java.beans.SimpleBeanInfo** 1.1

- Image loadImage(String resourceName)
  returns an image object file associated with the resource. The resource name is a path name, taken relative to the directory containing the bean info class.

---

**java.beans.FeatureDescriptor** 1.1

- String getName()
- void setName(String name)

  gets or sets the programmatic name for the feature.

- String getDisplayName()
- void setDisplayName(String displayName)

  gets or sets a display name for the feature. The default value is the value returned by getName. However, currently there is no explicit support for supplying feature names in multiple locales.

- String getShortDescription()
- void setShortDescription(String text)

  gets or sets a string that a builder tool can use to provide a short description for this feature. The default value is the return value of getDisplayName.

- boolean isExpert()
- void setExpert(boolean b)

  gets or sets an expert flag that a builder tool can use to determine whether to hide the feature from a novice user.

- boolean isHidden()
- void setHidden(boolean b)

  gets or sets a flag that a builder tool should hide this feature.

---

**java.beans.PropertyDescriptor** 1.1

- PropertyDescriptor(String propertyName, Class<?> beanClass)
- PropertyDescriptor(String propertyName, Class<?> beanClass, String getMethod, String setMethod)

  constructs a PropertyDescriptor object. The methods throw an IntrospectionException if an error occurred during introspection. The first constructor assumes that you follow the standard convention for the names of the get and set methods.

- Class<?> getPropertyType()

  returns a Class object for the property type.

- Method getReadMethod()
- Method getWriteMethod()

  returns the method to get or set the property.

---

**java.beans.IndexedPropertyDescriptor** 1.1

- IndexedPropertyDescriptor(String propertyName, Class<?> beanClass)
- IndexedPropertyDescriptor(String propertyName, Class<?> beanClass, String getMethod, String setMethod, String indexedGetMethod, String indexedSetMethod)

  constructs an IndexedPropertyDescriptor for the index property. The first constructor assumes that you follow the standard convention for the names of the get and set methods.

- Method getIndexedReadMethod()
- Method getIndexedWriteMethod()

  returns the method to get or set an indexed value in the property.

---

## 8.7 Property Editors

If you add an integer or string property to a bean, that property is automatically displayed in the bean's property inspector. But what happens if you add a property whose values cannot easily be edited in a text field—for example, a Date or a Color? Then, you need to provide a separate component by which the user can specify the property value. Such components are called *property editors*. For example, a property editor for a date object might be a calendar that lets the user scroll through the months and pick a date. A property editor for a Color object would let the user select the red, green, and blue components of the color.

Actually, NetBeans already has a property editor for colors. Also, of course, there are property editors for basic types such as String (a text field) and boolean (a checkbox).

The process for supplying a new property editor is slightly involved. First, you create a bean info class to accompany your bean. Override the getPropertyDescriptors method. That method returns an array of PropertyDescriptor objects. Create one object for each property that should be displayed in a property editor, *even those for which you just want the default editor.*

Construct a PropertyDescriptor by supplying the name of the property and the class of the bean that contains it.

```
PropertyDescriptor descriptor = new PropertyDescriptor("titlePosition", ChartBean.class);
```

Then, call the setPropertyEditorClass method of the PropertyDescriptor class.

```
descriptor.setPropertyEditorClass(TitlePositionEditor.class);
```

Next, build an array of descriptors for properties of your bean. For example, the chart bean that we discuss in this section has five properties:

- A Color property, graphColor
- A String property, title
- An int property, titlePosition
- A double[] property, values
- A boolean property, inverse

The code in Listing 8.3 shows the ChartBeanBeanInfo class that specifies the property editors for these properties. It achieves the following:

1. The getPropertyDescriptors method returns a descriptor for each property. The title and graphColor properties are used with the default editors—that is, the string and color editors that come with the builder tool.

2. The titlePosition, values, and inverse properties use special editors of type TitlePositionEditor, DoubleArrayEditor, and InverseEditor, respectively.

Figure 8.10 shows the chart bean. You can see the title on the top. Its position can be set to left, center, or right. The values property specifies the graph values. If the inverse property is true, then the background is colored and the bars of the chart are white. You can find the code for the chart bean in the book's companion code; the bean is simply a modification of the chart applet in Volume I, Chapter 10.

**Listing 8.3** chart/ChartBeanBeanInfo.java

```
1  package chart;
2
3  import java.awt.*;
4  import java.beans.*;
5
6  /**
7   * The bean info for the chart bean, specifying the property editors.
8   * @version 1.20 2007-10-05
9   * @author Cay Horstmann
10  */
11 public class ChartBeanBeanInfo extends SimpleBeanInfo
12 {
13    private PropertyDescriptor[] propertyDescriptors;
14    private Image iconColor16;
15    private Image iconColor32;
16    private Image iconMono16;
17    private Image iconMono32;
```

(Continues)

**Listing 8.3**    *(Continued)*

```java
18    public ChartBeanBeanInfo()
19    {
20        iconColor16 = loadImage("ChartBean_COLOR_16x16.gif");
21        iconColor32 = loadImage("ChartBean_COLOR_32x32.gif");
22        iconMono16 = loadImage("ChartBean_MONO_16x16.gif");
23        iconMono32 = loadImage("ChartBean_MONO_32x32.gif");
24
25        try
26        {
27            PropertyDescriptor titlePositionDescriptor = new PropertyDescriptor("titlePosition",
28                ChartBean.class);
29            titlePositionDescriptor.setPropertyEditorClass(TitlePositionEditor.class);
30            PropertyDescriptor inverseDescriptor = new PropertyDescriptor("inverse", ChartBean.class);
31            inverseDescriptor.setPropertyEditorClass(InverseEditor.class);
32            PropertyDescriptor valuesDescriptor = new PropertyDescriptor("values", ChartBean.class);
33            valuesDescriptor.setPropertyEditorClass(DoubleArrayEditor.class);
34            propertyDescriptors = new PropertyDescriptor[] {
35                new PropertyDescriptor("title", ChartBean.class), titlePositionDescriptor,
36                valuesDescriptor, new PropertyDescriptor("graphColor", ChartBean.class),
37                inverseDescriptor };
38        }
39        catch (IntrospectionException e)
40        {
41            e.printStackTrace();
42        }
43    }
44
45    public PropertyDescriptor[] getPropertyDescriptors()
46    {
47        return propertyDescriptors;
48    }
49
50    public Image getIcon(int iconType)
51    {
52        if (iconType == BeanInfo.ICON_COLOR_16x16) return iconColor16;
53        else if (iconType == BeanInfo.ICON_COLOR_32x32) return iconColor32;
54        else if (iconType == BeanInfo.ICON_MONO_16x16) return iconMono16;
55        else if (iconType == BeanInfo.ICON_MONO_32x32) return iconMono32;
56        else return null;
57    }
58 }
```

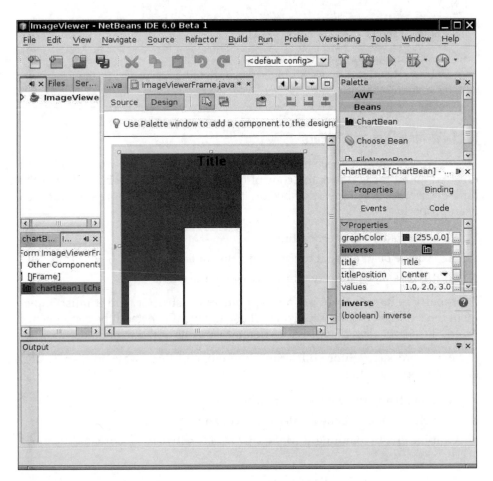

**Figure 8.10** The chart bean

---

**java.beans.PropertyDescriptor** 1.1

- PropertyDescriptor(String name, Class<?> beanClass)
  constructs a PropertyDescriptor object.

  | *Parameters:* | name | The name of the property |
  |---|---|---|
  | | beanClass | The class of the bean to which the property belongs |

- void setPropertyEditorClass(Class<?> editorClass)
  sets the class of the property editor to be used with this property.

---

*java.beans.BeanInfo* 1.1

- PropertyDescriptor[] getPropertyDescriptors()
  returns a descriptor for each property that should be displayed in the property
  inspector for the bean.

---

## 8.7.1 Writing Property Editors

Before we get into the mechanics of writing property editors, we should point out that an editor is under the control of the builder, not the bean. When the builder displays the property inspector, it carries out the following steps for each bean property:

1. It instantiates a property editor.
2. It asks the bean to tell it the current value of the property.
3. It then asks the property editor to display the value.

A property editor must supply a no-argument constructor, and it must implement the PropertyEditor interface. You will usually want to extend the convenience PropertyEditorSupport class that provides default versions of these methods.

For every property editor you write, choose one of three ways to display and edit the property value:

- As a text string (define getAsText and setAsText)
- As a choice field (define getAsText, setAsText, and getTags)
- Graphically, by painting it (define isPaintable, paintValue, supportsCustomEditor, and getCustomEditor)

Let's have a closer look at these choices.

### 8.7.1.1 String-Based Property Editors

Simple property editors work with text strings. Override the setAsText and getAsText methods. For example, our chart bean has a property that lets you choose where the title should be displayed: left, center, or right. These choices are implemented as an enumeration

```
public enum Position { LEFT, CENTER, RIGHT };
```

Of course we don't want them to appear as uppercase strings LEFT, CENTER, RIGHT—unless we are trying to enter the User Interface Hall of Horrors. Instead, we'll define a property editor whose getAsText method picks a string that looks pleasing to the developer:

```
class TitlePositionEditor extends PropertyEditorSupport
{
    private String[] tags = { "Left", "Center", "Right" };
    . . .
    public String getAsText()
    {
        int index = ((ChartBean.Position) getValue()).ordinal();
        return tags[index];
    }
}
```

Ideally, these strings should appear in the current locale, not necessarily in English—but we leave that as an exercise to the reader.

Conversely, we need to supply a method that converts a text string back to the property value:

```
public void setAsText(String s)
{
    int index = Arrays.asList(tags).indexOf(s);
    if (index >= 0) setValue(ChartBean.Position.values()[index]);
}
```

If we simply supply these two methods, the property inspector will provide a text field. It is initialized by a call to getAsText, and the setAsText method is called when we are done editing. Of course, in our situation, this is not a good choice for the titlePosition property—unless, of course, we are also competing for entry into the User Interface Hall of Shame. It is better to display all valid settings in a combo box (see Figure 8.11). The PropertyEditorSupport class gives a simple mechanism for indicating that a combo box is appropriate. Simply write a getTags method that returns an array of strings:

```
public String[] getTags() { return tags; }
```

The default getTags method returns null, indicating that a text field is appropriate for editing the property value.

When supplying the getTags method, you still need to supply the getAsText and setAsText methods. The getTags method simply specifies the strings that should be offered to the user. The getAsText/setAsText methods translate between the strings and the data type of the property (which can be a string, an integer, an enumeration, or a completely different type).

Finally, property editors should implement the getJavaInitializationString method. With this method, you can give to the builder tool the Java code that sets a

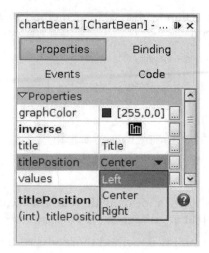

**Figure 8.11** Custom property editors at work

property to its current value. The builder tool uses this string for automatic code generation. Here is the method for the `TitlePositionEditor`:

```
public String getJavaInitializationString()
{
   return ChartBean.Position.class.getName().replace('$', '.') + "." + getValue();
}
```

This method returns a string such as `"chart.ChartBean.Position.LEFT"`. Try it out in NetBeans: If you edit the `titlePosition` property, NetBeans inserts code such as

```
chartBean1.setTitlePosition(chart.ChartBean.Position.LEFT);
```

In our situation, the code is a bit cumbersome because `ChartBean.Position.class.getName()` is the string `"chart.ChartBean$Position"`. We replace the $ with a period, and add the result of invoking `toString` on the enumeration value.

 **NOTE:** If a property has a custom editor that does not implement the `getJavaInitializationString` method, NetBeans does not know how to generate code and produces a setter with parameter ???.

Listing 8.4 shows the code for this property editor.

---

**Listing 8.4**  chart/TitlePositionEditor.java

```
1  package chart;
2
3  import java.beans.*;
4  import java.util.*;
5
6  /**
7   * A custom editor for the titlePosition property of the ChartBean. The editor lets the user
8   * choose between Left, Center, and Right
9   * @version 1.20 2007-12-14
10  * @author Cay Horstmann
11  */
12 public class TitlePositionEditor extends PropertyEditorSupport
13 {
14    private String[] tags = { "Left", "Center", "Right" };
15
16    public String[] getTags()
17    {
18       return tags;
19    }
20
21    public String getJavaInitializationString()
22    {
23       return ChartBean.Position.class.getName().replace('$', '.') + "." + getValue();
24    }
25
26    public String getAsText()
27    {
28       int index = ((ChartBean.Position) getValue()).ordinal();
29       return tags[index];
30    }
31
32    public void setAsText(String s)
33    {
34       int index = Arrays.asList(tags).indexOf(s);
35       if (index >= 0) setValue(ChartBean.Position.values()[index]);
36    }
37 }
```

---

## 8.7.1.2  GUI-Based Property Editors

A sophisticated property may not be editable as text. Instead, a graphical representation is displayed in the property inspector—in the small area that would otherwise hold a text field or combo box. When the user clicks on that area, a custom editor dialog box pops up (see Figure 8.12). The dialog box contains

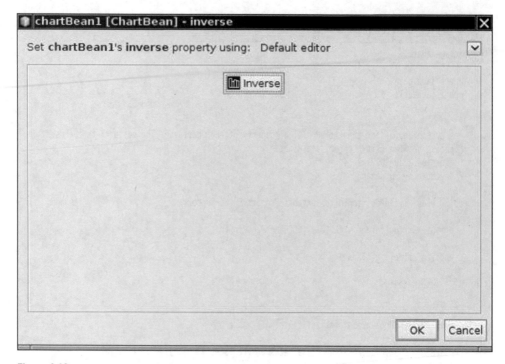

**Figure 8.12** A custom editor dialog box

a component to edit the property values, supplied by the property editor, and various buttons, supplied by the builder environment. In our example, the customizer is rather spare, containing a single button. The book's companion code contains a more elaborate editor for editing chart values.

To build a GUI-based property editor, you first tell the property inspector that you will paint the value and not use a string. Override the getAsText method in the PropertyEditor interface to return null and the isPaintable method to return true.

Then, implement the paintValue method. It receives a Graphics context and the coordinates of the rectangle inside which you can paint. Note that this rectangle is typically small, so you can't have a very elaborate representation. We will simply draw one of two icons (which you can see in Figure 8.11 on p. 764).

```
public void paintValue(Graphics g, Rectangle box)
{
   ImageIcon icon = (Boolean) getValue() ? inverseIcon : normalIcon;
   int x = bounds.x + (bounds.width - icon.getIconWidth()) / 2;
   int y = bounds.y + (bounds.height - icon.getIconHeight()) / 2;
   g.drawImage(icon.getImage(), x, y, null);
}
```

This graphical representation is not editable. The user must click on it to pop up a custom editor.

To indicate that you will have a custom editor, override the supportsCustomEditor in the PropertyEditor interface to return true.

Next, the getCustomEditor method of the PropertyEditor interface constructs and returns an object of the custom editor class.

Listing 8.5 shows the code for the InverseEditor that displays the current property value in the property inspector. Listing 8.6 shows the code for the custom editor panel for changing the value.

**Listing 8.5** chart/InverseEditor.java

```
1  package chart;
2
3  import java.awt.*;
4  import java.beans.*;
5  import javax.swing.*;
6
7  /**
8   * The property editor for the inverse property of the ChartBean. The inverse property toggles
9   * between colored graph bars and colored background.
10  * @version 1.30 2007-10-03
11  * @author Cay Horstmann
12  */
13 public class InverseEditor extends PropertyEditorSupport
14 {
15    private ImageIcon normalIcon = new ImageIcon(getClass().getResource("ChartBean_MONO_16x16.gif"));
16
17    private ImageIcon inverseIcon = new ImageIcon(getClass().getResource(
18       "ChartBean_INVERSE_16x16.gif"));
19
20    public Component getCustomEditor()
21    {
22       return new InverseEditorPanel(this);
23    }
24
25    public boolean supportsCustomEditor()
26    {
27       return true;
28    }
29
30    public boolean isPaintable()
31    {
32       return true;
33    }
```

*(Continues)*

**Listing 8.5** *(Continued)*

```
34    public String getAsText()
35    {
36       return null;
37    }
38
39    public String getJavaInitializationString()
40    {
41       return "" + getValue();
42    }
43
44    public void paintValue(Graphics g, Rectangle bounds)
45    {
46       ImageIcon icon = (Boolean) getValue() ? inverseIcon : normalIcon;
47       int x = bounds.x + (bounds.width - icon.getIconWidth()) / 2;
48       int y = bounds.y + (bounds.height - icon.getIconHeight()) / 2;
49       g.drawImage(icon.getImage(), x, y, null);
50    }
51 }
```

**Listing 8.6** chart/InverseEditorPanel.java

```
1  package chart;
2
3  import java.awt.event.*;
4  import java.beans.*;
5  import javax.swing.*;
6
7  /**
8   * The panel for setting the inverse property. It contains a button to toggle between normal and
9   * inverse coloring.
10  * @version 1.30 2007-10-03
11  * @author Cay Horstmann
12  */
13 public class InverseEditorPanel extends JPanel
14 {
15    private JButton button;
16    private PropertyEditorSupport editor;
17    private ImageIcon normalIcon = new ImageIcon(getClass().getResource("ChartBean_MONO_16x16.gif"));
18
19    public InverseEditorPanel(PropertyEditorSupport ed)
20    {
21       editor = ed;
22       button = new JButton();
23       updateButton();
```

```
24      button.addActionListener(new ActionListener()
25         {
26            public void actionPerformed(ActionEvent event)
27            {
28               editor.setValue(!(Boolean) editor.getValue());
29               updateButton();
30            }
31         });
32      add(button);
33   }
34
35   private void updateButton()
36   {
37      if ((Boolean) editor.getValue())
38      {
39         button.setIcon(inverseIcon);
40         button.setText("Inverse");
41      }
42      else
43      {
44         button.setIcon(normalIcon);
45         button.setText("Normal");
46      }
47   }
48
49   private ImageIcon inverseIcon = new ImageIcon(getClass().getResource(
50         "ChartBean_INVERSE_16x16.gif"));
51 }
```

---

*java.beans.PropertyEditor* 1.1

- Object getValue()
  returns the current value of the property. Basic types are wrapped into object wrappers.

- void setValue(Object newValue)
  sets the property to a new value. Basic types must be wrapped into object wrappers.

  *Parameters:*    newValue    The new value of the object; should be a newly created object that the property can own

- String getAsText()
  override this method to return a string representation of the current value of the property. The default returns null to indicate that the property cannot be represented as a string.

*(Continues)*

---

**java.beans.PropertyEditor**  1.1  *(Continued)*

- void setAsText(String text)

  override this method to set the property to a new value obtained by parsing the text. May throw an IllegalArgumentException if the text does not represent a legal value or if this property cannot be represented as a string.

- String[] getTags()

  override this method to return an array of all possible string representations of the property values so they can be displayed in a choice box. The default returns null to indicate that there is not a finite set of string values.

- boolean isPaintable()

  override this method to return true if the class uses the paintValue method to display the property.

- void paintValue(Graphics g, Rectangle bounds)

  override this method to represent the value by drawing into a graphics context in the specified place on the component used for the property inspector.

- boolean supportsCustomEditor()

  override this method to return true if the property editor has a custom editor.

- Component getCustomEditor()

  override this method to return the component that contains a customized GUI for editing the property value.

- String getJavaInitializationString()

  override this method to return a Java code string that can be used to generate code that initializes the property value. Examples are "0", "new Color(64, 64, 64)".

---

## 8.8  Customizers

A property editor is responsible for allowing the user to set one property at a time. Especially if certain properties of a bean relate to each other, it might be more user-friendly to provide a way to edit multiple properties at the same time. To enable this feature, supply a *customizer* instead of (or in addition to) multiple property editors.

Moreover, some beans might have features that are not exposed as properties and therefore cannot be edited through the property inspector. For those beans, a customizer is essential.

In the example program for this section, we develop a customizer for the chart bean. The customizer lets you set several properties of the chart bean in one dialog box, as shown in Figure 8.13.

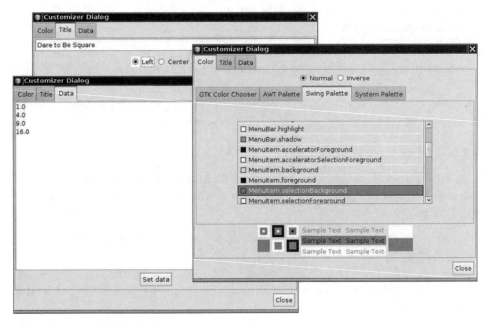

**Figure 8.13** The customizer for the `ChartBean`

To add a customizer to your bean, you must supply a `BeanInfo` class and override the `getBeanDescriptor` method, as shown in the following example.

```
public ChartBean2BeanInfo extends SimpleBeanInfo
{
   private BeanDescriptor beanDescriptor
      = new BeanDescriptor(ChartBean2.class, ChartBean2Customizer.class);
   . . .
   public BeanDescriptor getBeanDescriptor() { return beanDescriptor; }
}
```

Note that you need not follow any naming pattern for the customizer class. Nevertheless, it is the usual practice to name the customizer as *BeanName*`Customizer`.

You will see in the next section how to implement a customizer.

---

**`java.beans.BeanInfo`** 1.1

- `BeanDescriptor getBeanDescriptor()`
  returns a `BeanDescriptor` object that describes features of the bean.

---

**java.beans.BeanDescriptor**   1.1

- BeanDescriptor(Class<?> beanClass, Class<?> customizerClass)
  constructs a BeanDescriptor object for a bean that has a customizer.

  *Parameters:*    beanClass          The Class object for the bean

  customizerClass    The Class object for the bean's customizer

---

## 8.8.1 Writing a Customizer Class

Any customizer class you write must have a no-argument constructor, extend the Component class, and implement the Customizer interface. That interface has only three methods:

- The setObject method taking a parameter that specifies the bean being customized
- The addPropertyChangeListener and removePropertyChangeListener methods which manage the collection of listeners notified when a property is changed in the customizer

It is a good idea to update the visual appearance of the target bean by broadcasting a PropertyChangeEvent whenever the user changes any of the property values, not just when the user is at the end of the customization process.

Unlike property editors, customizers are not automatically displayed. In NetBeans, you must right-click on the bean and select the Customize menu option to pop up the customizer. At that point, the builder calls the setObject method of the customizer. Notice that your customizer is created before it is actually linked to an instance of your bean. Therefore, you cannot assume any information about the state of a bean in the constructor.

Customizers typically present the user with many options, so it may be handy to use the tabbed pane user interface. We use this approach and have the customizer extend the JTabbedPane class.

The customizer gathers the following information in three panes:

- Graph color and inverse mode
- Title and title position
- Data points

Of course, this kind of user interface can be tedious to code—our example devotes over 100 lines just to setting it up in the constructor. However, this task requires only the usual Swing programming skills, and we don't dwell on the details here.

One trick is worth keeping in mind. You will often need to edit property values in a customizer. Instead of implementing a new interface for setting the property value of a particular class, you can simply locate an existing property editor and add it to your user interface! For example, in our ChartBean customizer, we need to set the graph color; we know that NetBeans has a perfectly good property editor for colors, so we locate it as follows:

```
PropertyEditor colorEditor = PropertyEditorManager.findEditor(Color.Class);
Component colorEditorComponent = colorEditor.getCustomEditor();
```

Once we have all components laid out, we initialize their values in the setObject method. The setObject method is called when the customizer is displayed. Its parameter is the bean that is being customized. To proceed, we store that bean reference—we'll need it later to notify the bean of property changes. Then, we initialize each user interface component. Here is a part of the setObject method of the chart bean customizer that does this initialization:

```
public void setObject(Object obj)
{
   bean = (ChartBean) obj;
   titleField.setText(bean.getTitle());
   colorEditor.setValue(bean.getGraphColor());
   . . .
}
```

Finally, we hook up event handlers to track the user's activities. Whenever the user changes the value of a component, the component fires an event that our customizer must handle. The event handler must update the value of the property in the bean and also fire a PropertyChangeEvent so that other listeners (such as the property inspector) can be updated. Let us follow that process with a couple of user interface elements in the chart bean customizer.

When the user types a new title, we want to update the title property. We attach a DocumentListener to the text field into which the user types the title.

```
titleField.getDocument().addDocumentListener(new
   DocumentListener()
   {
      public void changedUpdate(DocumentEvent event)
      {
         setTitle(titleField.getText());
      }
      public void insertUpdate(DocumentEvent event)
      {
         setTitle(titleField.getText());
      }
```

```
    public void removeUpdate(DocumentEvent event)
    {
        setTitle(titleField.getText());
    }
});
```

The three listener methods call the setTitle method of the customizer. That method calls the bean to update the property value and then fires a property change event. (This update is necessary only for properties that are not bound.) Here is the code for the setTitle method.

```
public void setTitle(String newValue)
{
    if (bean == null) return;
    String oldValue = bean.getTitle();
    bean.setTitle(newValue);
    firePropertyChange("title", oldValue, newValue);
}
```

When the color value changes in the color property editor, we want to update the graph color of the bean. We track the color changes by attaching a listener to the property editor. Perhaps confusingly, that editor also sends out property change events.

```
colorEditor.addPropertyChangeListener(new
    PropertyChangeListener()
    {
        public void propertyChange(PropertyChangeEvent event)
        {
            setGraphColor((Color) colorEditor.getValue());
        }
    });
```

Listing 8.7 provides the full code of the chart bean customizer.

---

**Listing 8.7**  chart2/ChartBeanCustomizer.java

```
 1  package chart2;
 2
 3  import java.awt.*;
 4  import java.awt.event.*;
 5  import java.beans.*;
 6  import java.util.*;
 7  import javax.swing.*;
 8  import javax.swing.event.*;
 9
10  /**
11   * A customizer for the chart bean that allows the user to edit all chart properties in a single
12   * tabbed dialog.
```

```
13    * @version 1.12 2007-10-03
14    * @author Cay Horstmann
15    */
16   public class ChartBeanCustomizer extends JTabbedPane implements Customizer
17   {
18      private ChartBean bean;
19      private PropertyEditor colorEditor;
20      private JTextArea data;
21      private JRadioButton normal;
22      private JRadioButton inverse;
23      private JRadioButton[] position;
24      private JTextField titleField;
25
26      public ChartBeanCustomizer()
27      {
28         data = new JTextArea();
29         JPanel dataPane = new JPanel();
30         dataPane.setLayout(new BorderLayout());
31         dataPane.add(new JScrollPane(data), BorderLayout.CENTER);
32         JButton dataButton = new JButton("Set data");
33         dataButton.addActionListener(new ActionListener()
34            {
35               public void actionPerformed(ActionEvent event)
36               {
37                  setData(data.getText());
38               }
39            });
40         JPanel panel = new JPanel();
41         panel.add(dataButton);
42         dataPane.add(panel, BorderLayout.SOUTH);
43
44         JPanel colorPane = new JPanel();
45         colorPane.setLayout(new BorderLayout());
46
47         normal = new JRadioButton("Normal", true);
48         inverse = new JRadioButton("Inverse", false);
49         panel = new JPanel();
50         panel.add(normal);
51         panel.add(inverse);
52         ButtonGroup group = new ButtonGroup();
53         group.add(normal);
54         group.add(inverse);
55         normal.addActionListener(new ActionListener()
56            {
57               public void actionPerformed(ActionEvent event)
58               {
59                  setInverse(false);
60               }
61            });
```

*(Continues)*

**Listing 8.7** *(Continued)*

```
62      inverse.addActionListener(new ActionListener()
63         {
64            public void actionPerformed(ActionEvent event)
65            {
66               setInverse(true);
67            }
68         });
69
70      colorEditor = PropertyEditorManager.findEditor(Color.class);
71      colorEditor.addPropertyChangeListener(new PropertyChangeListener()
72         {
73            public void propertyChange(PropertyChangeEvent event)
74            {
75               setGraphColor((Color) colorEditor.getValue());
76            }
77         });
78
79      colorPane.add(panel, BorderLayout.NORTH);
80      colorPane.add(colorEditor.getCustomEditor(), BorderLayout.CENTER);
81
82      JPanel titlePane = new JPanel();
83      titlePane.setLayout(new BorderLayout());
84
85      group = new ButtonGroup();
86      position = new JRadioButton[3];
87      position[0] = new JRadioButton("Left");
88      position[1] = new JRadioButton("Center");
89      position[2] = new JRadioButton("Right");
90
91      panel = new JPanel();
92      for (int i = 0; i < position.length; i++)
93      {
94         final ChartBean.Position pos = ChartBean.Position.values()[i];
95         panel.add(position[i]);
96         group.add(position[i]);
97         position[i].addActionListener(new ActionListener()
98            {
99               public void actionPerformed(ActionEvent event)
100              {
101                 setTitlePosition(pos);
102              }
103           });
104     }
105
106     titleField = new JTextField();
107     titleField.getDocument().addDocumentListener(new DocumentListener()
108        {
```

```
109        public void changedUpdate(DocumentEvent evt)
110        {
111            setTitle(titleField.getText());
112        }
113
114        public void insertUpdate(DocumentEvent evt)
115        {
116            setTitle(titleField.getText());
117        }
118
119        public void removeUpdate(DocumentEvent evt)
120        {
121            setTitle(titleField.getText());
122        }
123    });
124
125    titlePane.add(titleField, BorderLayout.NORTH);
126    JPanel panel2 = new JPanel();
127    panel2.add(panel);
128    titlePane.add(panel2, BorderLayout.CENTER);
129    addTab("Color", colorPane);
130    addTab("Title", titlePane);
131    addTab("Data", dataPane);
132 }
133
134 /**
135  * Sets the data to be shown in the chart.
136  * @param s a string containing the numbers to be displayed, separated by white space
137  */
138 public void setData(String s)
139 {
140    StringTokenizer tokenizer = new StringTokenizer(s);
141
142    int i = 0;
143    double[] values = new double[tokenizer.countTokens()];
144    while (tokenizer.hasMoreTokens())
145    {
146       String token = tokenizer.nextToken();
147       try
148       {
149          values[i] = Double.parseDouble(token);
150          i++;
151       }
152       catch (NumberFormatException e)
153       {
154       }
155    }
156    setValues(values);
157 }
```

*(Continues)*

**Listing 8.7** *(Continued)*

```
158    /**
159     * Sets the title of the chart.
160     * @param newValue the new title
161     */
162    public void setTitle(String newValue)
163    {
164       if (bean == null) return;
165       String oldValue = bean.getTitle();
166       bean.setTitle(newValue);
167       firePropertyChange("title", oldValue, newValue);
168    }
169
170    /**
171     * Sets the title position of the chart.
172     * @param i the new title position (ChartBean.LEFT, ChartBean.CENTER, or ChartBean.RIGHT)
173     */
174    public void setTitlePosition(ChartBean.Position pos)
175    {
176       if (bean == null) return;
177       ChartBean.Position oldValue = bean.getTitlePosition();
178       bean.setTitlePosition(pos);
179       firePropertyChange("titlePosition", oldValue, pos);
180    }
181
182    /**
183     * Sets the inverse setting of the chart.
184     * @param b true if graph and background color are inverted
185     */
186    public void setInverse(boolean b)
187    {
188       if (bean == null) return;
189       boolean oldValue = bean.isInverse();
190       bean.setInverse(b);
191       firePropertyChange("inverse", oldValue, b);
192    }
193
194    /**
195     * Sets the values to be shown in the chart.
196     * @param newValue the new value array
197     */
198    public void setValues(double[] newValue)
199    {
200       if (bean == null) return;
201       double[] oldValue = bean.getValues();
202       bean.setValues(newValue);
203       firePropertyChange("values", oldValue, newValue);
204    }
```

```
205  /**
206   * Sets the color of the chart
207   * @param newValue the new color
208   */
209  public void setGraphColor(Color newValue)
210  {
211     if (bean == null) return;
212     Color oldValue = bean.getGraphColor();
213     bean.setGraphColor(newValue);
214     firePropertyChange("graphColor", oldValue, newValue);
215  }
216  public void setObject(Object obj)
217  {
218     bean = (ChartBean) obj;
219
220     data.setText("");
221     for (double value : bean.getValues())
222        data.append(value + "\n");
223
224     normal.setSelected(!bean.isInverse());
225     inverse.setSelected(bean.isInverse());
226
227     titleField.setText(bean.getTitle());
228
229     for (int i = 0; i < position.length; i++)
230        position[i].setSelected(i == bean.getTitlePosition().ordinal());
231
232     colorEditor.setValue(bean.getGraphColor());
233  }
234  }
```

---

**java.beans.Customizer** 1.1

* void setObject(Object bean)
  specifies the bean to customize.

---

# 8.9 JavaBeans Persistence

JavaBeans persistence uses JavaBeans properties to save beans to a stream and to read them back at a later time or in a different virtual machine. In this regard, JavaBeans persistence is similar to object serialization. (See Chapter 1 for more on serialization.) However, there is an important difference: JavaBeans persistence is *suitable for long-term storage*.

When an object is serialized, its instance fields are written to a stream. If the implementation of a class changes, its instance fields can change. You cannot simply read files that contain serialized objects of older versions. It is possible to detect version differences and translate between old and new data representations. However, the process is extremely tedious and should only be applied in desperate situations. Plainly, serialization is unsuitable for long-term storage. For that reason, all Swing components have the following message in their documentation: "Warning: Serialized objects of this class will not be compatible with future Swing releases. The current serialization support is appropriate for short term storage or RMI between applications."

The long-term persistence mechanism was invented as a solution for this problem. It was originally intended for drag-and-drop GUI design tools. The design tool saves the result of mouse clicks—a collection of frames, panels, buttons, and other Swing components—in a file, using the long-term persistence format. The running program simply opens that file. This approach cuts out the tedious source code for laying out and wiring up Swing components. Sadly, it has not been widely implemented.

The basic idea behind JavaBeans persistence is simple. Suppose you want to save a JFrame object to a file so that you can retrieve it later. If you look into the source code of the JFrame class and its superclasses, you will see dozens of instance fields. If the frame were to be serialized, all of the field values would need to be written. But think about how a frame is constructed:

```
JFrame frame = new JFrame();
frame.setTitle("My Application");
frame.setVisible(true);
```

The no-argument constructor initializes all instance fields, and a couple of properties are set. If you archive the frame object, the JavaBeans persistence mechanism saves exactly these statements in XML format:

```
<object class="javax.swing.JFrame">
  <void property="title">
    <string>My Application</string>
  </void>
  <void property="visible">
    <boolean>true</boolean>
  </void>
</object>
```

When the object is read back, the statements are *executed*: A JFrame object is constructed, and its title and visible properties are set to the given values. It does not matter if the internal representation of the JFrame has changed in the meantime. All that matters is that you can restore the object by setting properties.

Note that only those properties that are different from the default are archived. The XMLEncoder makes a default JFrame and compares its property with the frame that is being archived. Property setter statements are generated only for properties that are different from the default. This process is called *redundancy elimination*. As a result, the archives are generally smaller than the result of serialization. (When serializing Swing components, the difference is particularly dramatic because Swing objects have a lot of state, most of which is never changed from the default.)

Of course, there are minor technical hurdles with this approach. For example, the call

```
frame.setSize(600, 400);
```

is not a property setter. However, the XMLEncoder can cope with this. It writes the statement

```
<void property="bounds">
    <object class="java.awt.Rectangle">
        <int>0</int>
        <int>0</int>
        <int>600</int>
        <int>400</int>
    </object>
</void>
```

To save an object to a stream, use an XMLEncoder:

```
XMLEncoder out = new XMLEncoder(new FileOutputStream(. . .));
out.writeObject(frame);
out.close();
```

To read it back, use an XMLDecoder:

```
XMLDecoder in = new XMLDecoder(new FileInputStream(. . .));
JFrame newFrame = (JFrame) in.readObject();
in.close();
```

The program in Listing 8.8 shows how a frame can load and save *itself* (see Figure 8.14). When you run the program, first click the Save button and save the frame to a file. Then move the original frame to a different position and click Load to see another frame pop up at the original location. Have a look inside the XML file that the program produces.

If you look closely at the XML output, you will find that the XMLEncoder carries out an amazing amount of work when it saves the frame. It produces statements that carry out the following actions:

- Set various frame properties: size, layout, defaultCloseOperation, title, and so on.
- Add buttons to the frame.
- Add action listeners to the buttons.

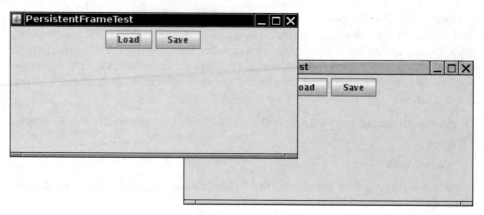

**Figure 8.14** The `PersistentFrameTest` program

Here, we had to construct the action listeners with the `EventHandler` class. The `XMLEncoder` cannot archive arbitrary inner classes, but it knows how to handle `EventHandler` objects.

**Listing 8.8** persistentFrame/PersistentFrameTest.java

```
1  package persistentFrame;
2
3  import java.awt.*;
4  import java.awt.event.*;
5  import java.beans.*;
6  import java.io.*;
7  import javax.swing.*;
8
9  /**
10  * This program demonstrates the use of an XML encoder and decoder to save and restore a frame.
11  * @version 1.01 2007-10-03
12  * @author Cay Horstmann
13  */
14  public class PersistentFrameTest
15  {
16     private static JFileChooser chooser;
17     private JFrame frame;
18
19     public static void main(String[] args)
20     {
21        chooser = new JFileChooser();
22        chooser.setCurrentDirectory(new File("."));
23        PersistentFrameTest test = new PersistentFrameTest();
24        test.init();
25     }
```

```
26    public void init()
27    {
28       frame = new JFrame();
29       frame.setLayout(new FlowLayout());
30       frame.setDefaultCloseOperation(JFrame.EXIT_ON_CLOSE);
31       frame.setTitle("PersistentFrameTest");
32       frame.setSize(400, 200);
33
34       JButton loadButton = new JButton("Load");
35       frame.add(loadButton);
36       loadButton.addActionListener(EventHandler.create(ActionListener.class, this, "load"));
37
38       JButton saveButton = new JButton("Save");
39       frame.add(saveButton);
40       saveButton.addActionListener(EventHandler.create(ActionListener.class, this, "save"));
41
42       frame.setVisible(true);
43    }
44
45    public void load()
46    {
47       // show file chooser dialog
48       int r = chooser.showOpenDialog(null);
49
50       // if file selected, open
51       if(r == JFileChooser.APPROVE_OPTION)
52       {
53          try
54          {
55             File file = chooser.getSelectedFile();
56             XMLDecoder decoder = new XMLDecoder(new FileInputStream(file));
57             decoder.readObject();
58             decoder.close();
59          }
60          catch (IOException e)
61          {
62             JOptionPane.showMessageDialog(null, e);
63          }
64       }
65    }
66
67    public void save()
68    {
69       if (chooser.showSaveDialog(null) == JFileChooser.APPROVE_OPTION)
70       {
71          try
72          {
73             File file = chooser.getSelectedFile();
74             XMLEncoder encoder = new XMLEncoder(new FileOutputStream(file));
```

*(Continues)*

---

**Listing 8.8** *(Continued)*

```
75              encoder.writeObject(frame);
76              encoder.close();
77          }
78          catch (IOException e)
79          {
80              JOptionPane.showMessageDialog(null, e);
81          }
82      }
83  }
84 }
```

---

## 8.9.1 Using JavaBeans Persistence for Arbitrary Data

JavaBeans persistence is not limited to the storage of Swing components. You can use the mechanism to store *any* collection of objects, provided you follow a few simple rules. In the following sections, you will learn how you can use JavaBeans persistence as a long-term storage format for your own data.

The XMLEncoder has built-in support for the following types:

- null
- All primitive types and their wrappers
- Enumerations (since Java SE 6)
- String
- Arrays
- Collections and maps
- The reflection types Class, Field, Method, and Proxy
- The AWT types Color, Cursor, Dimension, Font, Insets, Point, Rectangle, and ImageIcon
- AWT and Swing components, borders, layout managers, and models
- Event handlers

### 8.9.1.1 Writing a Persistence Delegate to Construct an Object

Using JavaBeans persistence is trivial if one can obtain the state of every object by setting properties. But in real programs, there are always a few classes that don't work that way. Consider, for example, the Employee class of Volume I, Chapter 4. Employee isn't a well-behaved bean. It doesn't have a no-argument constructor, and it doesn't have methods setName, setSalary, setHireDay. To overcome this problem, define a *persistence delegate*. Such a delegate is responsible for generating an XML encoding of an object.

The persistence delegate for the Employee class overrides the instantiate method to produce an *expression* that constructs an object.

```
PersistenceDelegate delegate = new
    DefaultPersistenceDelegate()
    {
        protected Expression instantiate(Object oldInstance, Encoder out)
        {
            Employee e = (Employee) oldInstance;
            GregorianCalendar c = new GregorianCalendar();
            c.setTime(e.getHireDay());
            return new Expression(oldInstance, Employee.class, "new",
                new Object[]
                {
                    e.getName(),
                    e.getSalary(),
                    c.get(Calendar.YEAR),
                    c.get(Calendar.MONTH),
                    c.get(Calendar.DATE)
                });
        }
    };
```

This means: "To re-create oldInstance, call the new method (i.e., the constructor) on the Employee.class object, and supply the given parameters." The parameter name oldInstance is a bit misleading—this is simply the instance that is being saved.

To install the persistence delegate, you have two choices. You can associate it with a specific XMLWriter:

```
out.setPersistenceDelegate(Employee.class, delegate);
```

Alternatively, you can set the persistenceDelegate attribute of the *bean descriptor* of the BeanInfo:

```
BeanInfo info = Introspector.getBeanInfo(GregorianCalendar.class);
info.getBeanDescriptor().setValue("persistenceDelegate", delegate);
```

Once the delegate is installed, you can save Employee objects. For example, the statements

```
Object myData = new Employee("Harry Hacker", 50000, 1989, 10, 1);
out.writeObject(myData);
```

generate the following output:

```
<object class="Employee">
  <string>Harry Hacker</string>
  <double>50000.0</double>
  <int>1989</int>
  <int>10</int>
  <int>1</int>
</object>
```

 **NOTE:** You only need to tweak the *encoding* process. There are no special decoding methods. The decoder simply executes the statements and expressions that it finds in its XML input.

### 8.9.1.2 Constructing an Object from Properties

If all constructor parameters can be obtained by accessing properties of oldInstance, then you need not write the instantiate method yourself. Instead, simply construct a DefaultPersistenceDelegate and supply the property names.

For example, the following statement sets the persistence delegate for the Rectangle2D.Double class:

```
out.setPersistenceDelegate(Rectangle2D.Double.class,
    new DefaultPersistenceDelegate(new String[] { "x", "y", "width", "height" }));
```

This tells the encoder: "To encode a Rectangle2D.Double object, get its x, y, width, and height properties and call the constructor with those four values." As a result, the output contains an element such as the following:

```
<object class="java.awt.geom.Rectangle2D$Double">
  <double>5.0</double>
  <double>10.0</double>
  <double>20.0</double>
  <double>30.0</double>
</object>
```

If you are the author of the class, you can do even better. Annotate the constructor with the @ConstructorProperties annotation. Suppose, for example, that the Employee class had a constructor with three parameters (name, salary, and hire day). Then we could annotate the constructor as follows:

```
@ConstructorProperties({"name", "salary", "hireDay"})
public Employee(String n, double s, Date d)
```

This tells the encoder to call the getName, getSalary, and getHireDay property getters and write the resulting values into the object expression.

The @ConstructorProperties annotation was introduced in Java SE 6 and has so far only been used for classes in the Java Management Extensions (JMX) API.

### 8.9.1.3 Constructing an Object with a Factory Method

Sometimes, you need to save objects obtained from factory methods, not constructors. Consider, for example, how you get an InetAddress object:

```
byte[] bytes = new byte[] { 127, 0, 0, 1};
InetAddress address = InetAddress.getByAddress(bytes);
```

The instantiate method of the PersistenceDelegate produces a call to the factory method.

```
protected Expression instantiate(Object oldInstance, Encoder out)
{
    return new Expression(oldInstance, InetAddress.class, "getByAddress",
        new Object[] { ((InetAddress) oldInstance).getAddress() });
}
```

A sample output is

```
<object class="java.net.Inet4Address" method="getByAddress">
    <array class="byte" length="4">
        <void index="0">
            <byte>127</byte>
        </void>
        <void index="3">
            <byte>1</byte>
        </void>
    </array>
</object>
```

**CAUTION:** You must install this delegate with the concrete subclass, such as Inet4Address, not with the abstract InetAddress class!

### 8.9.1.4 Postconstruction Work

The state of some classes is built up by calls to methods that are not property setters. You can cope with that situation by overriding the initialize method of the DefaultPersistenceDelegate. The initialize method is called after the instantiate method. You can generate a sequence of *statements* that are recorded in the archive.

For example, consider the BitSet class. To re-create a BitSet object, you have to set all the bits that were present in the original. The following initialize method generates the necessary statements:

```
protected void initialize(Class<?> type, Object oldInstance, Object newInstance, Encoder out)
{
    super.initialize(type, oldInstance, newInstance, out);
    BitSet bs = (BitSet) oldInstance;
    for (int i = bs.nextSetBit(0); i >= 0; i = bs.nextSetBit(i + 1))
        out.writeStatement(new Statement(bs, "set", new Object[] { i, i + 1, true } ));
}
```

A sample output is

```
<object class="java.util.BitSet">
    <void method="set">
        <int>1</int>
        <int>2</int>
        <boolean>true</boolean>
    </void>
    <void method="set">
        <int>4</int>
        <int>5</int>
        <boolean>true</boolean>
    </void>
</object>
```

**NOTE:** It would make more sense to write `new Statement(bs, "set", new Object[]` `{ i } )`, but then the `XMLWriter` produces an unsightly statement that sets a property with an empty name.

### 8.9.1.5 Transient Properties

Occasionally, a class has a property with a getter and setter that the `XMLDecoder` discovers, but you don't want to include the property value in the archive. To suppress archiving of a property, mark it as *transient* in the property descriptor. For example, the following statement marks the `removeMode` property of the `DamageReporter` class (which you will see in detail in the next section) as transient.

```
BeanInfo info = Introspector.getBeanInfo(DamageReport.class);
for (PropertyDescriptor desc : info.getPropertyDescriptors())
    if (desc.getName().equals("removeMode"))
        desc.setValue("transient", Boolean.TRUE);
```

The program in Listing 8.9 shows the various persistence delegates at work. Keep in mind that this program shows a worst-case scenario—in actual applications, many classes can be archived without the use of delegates.

**Listing 8.9** persistenceDelegate/PersistenceDelegateTest.java

```
1  package persistenceDelegate;
2
3  import java.awt.geom.*;
4  import java.beans.*;
5  import java.net.*;
6  import java.util.*;
7
8  /**
9   * This program demonstrates various persistence delegates.
10  * @version 1.01 2007-10-03
11  * @author Cay Horstmann
12  */
13 public class PersistenceDelegateTest
14 {
15    public static class Point
16    {
17       private final int x, y;
18
19       @ConstructorProperties( { "x", "y" })
20       public Point(int x, int y)
21       {
22          this.x = x;
23          this.y = y;
24       }
25
26       public int getX()
27       {
28          return x;
29       }
30
31       public int getY()
32       {
33          return y;
34       }
35
36    }
37
38    public static void main(String[] args) throws Exception
39    {
40       PersistenceDelegate delegate = new PersistenceDelegate()
41          {
42             protected Expression instantiate(Object oldInstance, Encoder out)
43             {
44                Employee e = (Employee) oldInstance;
45                GregorianCalendar c = new GregorianCalendar();
46                c.setTime(e.getHireDay());
```

*(Continues)*

**Listing 8.9** *(Continued)*

```
47          return new Expression(oldInstance, Employee.class, "new", new Object[] {
48             e.getName(), e.getSalary(), c.get(Calendar.YEAR), c.get(Calendar.MONTH),
49             c.get(Calendar.DATE) });
50       }
51    };
52    BeanInfo info = Introspector.getBeanInfo(Employee.class);
53    info.getBeanDescriptor().setValue("persistenceDelegate", delegate);
54
55    XMLEncoder out = new XMLEncoder(System.out);
56    out.setExceptionListener(new ExceptionListener()
57       {
58          public void exceptionThrown(Exception e)
59          {
60             e.printStackTrace();
61          }
62       });
63
64    out.setPersistenceDelegate(Rectangle2D.Double.class, new DefaultPersistenceDelegate(
65          new String[] { "x", "y", "width", "height" }));
66
67    out.setPersistenceDelegate(Inet4Address.class, new DefaultPersistenceDelegate()
68       {
69          protected Expression instantiate(Object oldInstance, Encoder out)
70          {
71             return new Expression(oldInstance, InetAddress.class, "getByAddress",
72                new Object[] { ((InetAddress) oldInstance).getAddress() });
73          }
74       });
75
76    out.setPersistenceDelegate(BitSet.class, new DefaultPersistenceDelegate()
77       {
78          protected void initialize(Class<?> type, Object oldInstance, Object newInstance,
79             Encoder out)
80          {
81             super.initialize(type, oldInstance, newInstance, out);
82             BitSet bs = (BitSet) oldInstance;
83             for (int i = bs.nextSetBit(0); i >= 0; i = bs.nextSetBit(i + 1))
84                out.writeStatement(new Statement(bs, "set", new Object[] { i, i + 1, true }));
85          }
86       });
87
88    out.writeObject(new Employee("Harry Hacker", 50000, 1989, 10, 1));
89    out.writeObject(new Point(17, 29));
90    out.writeObject(new java.awt.geom.Rectangle2D.Double(5, 10, 20, 30));
91    out.writeObject(InetAddress.getLocalHost());
92    BitSet bs = new BitSet();
93    bs.set(1, 4);
94    bs.clear(2, 3);
```

```
95      out.writeObject(bs);
96      out.close();
97    }
98  }
```

## 8.9.2 A Complete Example for JavaBeans Persistence

We'll end the description of JavaBeans persistence with a complete example (see Figure 8.15). This application writes a damage report for a rental car. The rental car agent enters the rental record, selects the car type, uses the mouse to click on damaged areas on the car, and saves the report. The application can also load existing damage reports. Listing 8.10 contains the code for the program.

The application uses JavaBeans persistence to save and load DamageReport objects (see Listing 8.11). It illustrates the following aspects of the persistence technology:

- Properties are automatically saved and restored. Nothing needs to be done for the rentalRecord and carType properties.

- Postconstruction work is required to restore the damage locations. The persistence delegate generates statements that call the click method.

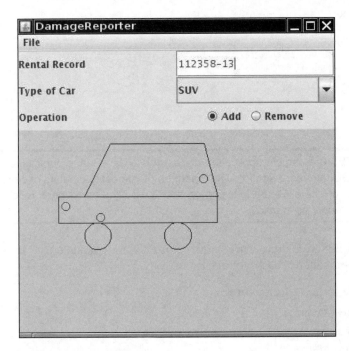

**Figure 8.15** The DamageReporter application

- The `Point2D.Double` class needs a `DefaultPersistenceDelegate` that constructs a point from its x and y properties.
- The `removeMode` property (which specifies whether mouse clicks add or remove damage marks) is transient because it should not be saved in damage reports.

Here is a sample damage report:

```
<?xml version="1.0" encoding="UTF-8"?>
<java version="1.5.0" class="java.beans.XMLDecoder">
   <object class="DamageReport">
      <object class="java.lang.Enum" method="valueOf">
         <class>DamageReport$CarType</class>
         <string>SEDAN</string>
      </object>
      <void property="rentalRecord">
         <string>12443-19</string>
      </void>
      <void method="click">
         <object class="java.awt.geom.Point2D$Double">
            <double>181.0</double>
            <double>84.0</double>
         </object>
      </void>
      <void method="click">
         <object class="java.awt.geom.Point2D$Double">
            <double>162.0</double>
            <double>66.0</double>
         </object>
      </void>
   </object>
</java>
```

 **NOTE:** The sample application does *not* use JavaBeans persistence to save the GUI of the application. That might be of interest to creators of development tools, but here we are focusing on how to use the persistence mechanism to store *application data*.

This example ends our discussion of JavaBeans persistence. In summary, JavaBeans persistence archives are

- Suitable for long-term storage
- Small and fast
- Easy to create
- Human-editable
- A part of standard Java

**Listing 8.10** damageReporter/DamageReporterFrame.java

```java
1   package damageReporter;
2
3   import java.awt.*;
4   import java.awt.event.*;
5   import java.awt.geom.*;
6   import java.beans.*;
7   import java.io.*;
8   import java.util.*;
9   import javax.swing.*;
10
11  public class DamageReporterFrame extends JFrame
12  {
13     private JTextField rentalRecord;
14     private JComboBox<DamageReport.CarType> carType;
15     private JComponent carComponent;
16     private JRadioButton addButton;
17     private JRadioButton removeButton;
18     private DamageReport report;
19     private JFileChooser chooser;
20
21     private static Map<DamageReport.CarType, Shape> shapes = new EnumMap<>(
22        DamageReport.CarType.class);
23
24     public DamageReporterFrame()
25     {
26        chooser = new JFileChooser();
27        chooser.setCurrentDirectory(new File("."));
28
29        report = new DamageReport();
30        report.setCarType(DamageReport.CarType.SEDAN);
31
32        // set up the menu bar
33        JMenuBar menuBar = new JMenuBar();
34        setJMenuBar(menuBar);
35
36        JMenu menu = new JMenu("File");
37        menuBar.add(menu);
38
39        JMenuItem openItem = new JMenuItem("Open");
40        menu.add(openItem);
41        openItem.addActionListener(new ActionListener()
42           {
43              public void actionPerformed(ActionEvent evt)
44              {
45                 // show file chooser dialog
46                 int r = chooser.showOpenDialog(null);
```

*(Continues)*

**Listing 8.10** *(Continued)*

```
47          // if file selected, open
48          if (r == JFileChooser.APPROVE_OPTION)
49          {
50             try
51             {
52                File file = chooser.getSelectedFile();
53                XMLDecoder decoder = new XMLDecoder(new FileInputStream(file));
54                report = (DamageReport) decoder.readObject();
55                decoder.close();
56                rentalRecord.setText(report.getRentalRecord());
57                carType.setSelectedItem(report.getCarType());
58                repaint();
59             }
60             catch (IOException e)
61             {
62                JOptionPane.showMessageDialog(null, e);
63             }
64          }
65       }
66    });
67
68    JMenuItem saveItem = new JMenuItem("Save");
69    menu.add(saveItem);
70    saveItem.addActionListener(new ActionListener()
71       {
72          public void actionPerformed(ActionEvent evt)
73          {
74             report.setRentalRecord(rentalRecord.getText());
75             chooser.setSelectedFile(new File(rentalRecord.getText() + ".xml"));
76
77             // show file chooser dialog
78             int r = chooser.showSaveDialog(null);
79
80             // if file selected, save
81             if (r == JFileChooser.APPROVE_OPTION)
82             {
83                try
84                {
85                   File file = chooser.getSelectedFile();
86                   XMLEncoder encoder = new XMLEncoder(new FileOutputStream(file));
87                   report.configureEncoder(encoder);
88                   encoder.writeObject(report);
89                   encoder.close();
90                }
91                catch (IOException e)
92                {
```

```
 93                     JOptionPane.showMessageDialog(null, e);
 94                  }
 95               }
 96            }
 97         });
 98
 99         JMenuItem exitItem = new JMenuItem("Exit");
100         menu.add(exitItem);
101         exitItem.addActionListener(new ActionListener()
102            {
103               public void actionPerformed(ActionEvent event)
104               {
105                  System.exit(0);
106               }
107            });
108
109         // combo box for car type
110         rentalRecord = new JTextField();
111         carType = new JComboBox<>();
112         carType.addItem(DamageReport.CarType.SEDAN);
113         carType.addItem(DamageReport.CarType.WAGON);
114         carType.addItem(DamageReport.CarType.SUV);
115
116         carType.addActionListener(new ActionListener()
117            {
118               public void actionPerformed(ActionEvent event)
119               {
120                  DamageReport.CarType item = carType.getItemAt(carType.getSelectedIndex());
121                  report.setCarType(item);
122                  repaint();
123               }
124            });
125
126         // component for showing car shape and damage locations
127         carComponent = new JComponent()
128            {
129               private static final int DEFAULT_WIDTH = 400;
130               private static final int DEFAULT_HEIGHT = 200;
131
132               public void paintComponent(Graphics g)
133               {
134                  Graphics2D g2 = (Graphics2D) g;
135                  g2.setColor(new Color(0.9f, 0.9f, 0.45f));
136                  g2.fillRect(0, 0, getWidth(), getHeight());
137                  g2.setColor(Color.BLACK);
138                  g2.draw(shapes.get(report.getCarType()));
139                  report.drawDamage(g2);
140               }
```

*(Continues)*

**Listing 8.10**  *(Continued)*

```
141            public Dimension getPreferredSize()
142            {
143                return new Dimension(DEFAULT_WIDTH, DEFAULT_HEIGHT);
144            }
145         };
146      carComponent.addMouseListener(new MouseAdapter()
147         {
148            public void mousePressed(MouseEvent event)
149            {
150                report.click(new Point2D.Double(event.getX(), event.getY()));
151                repaint();
152            }
153         });
154
155      // radio buttons for click action
156      addButton = new JRadioButton("Add");
157      removeButton = new JRadioButton("Remove");
158      ButtonGroup group = new ButtonGroup();
159      JPanel buttonPanel = new JPanel();
160      group.add(addButton);
161      buttonPanel.add(addButton);
162      group.add(removeButton);
163      buttonPanel.add(removeButton);
164      addButton.setSelected(!report.getRemoveMode());
165      removeButton.setSelected(report.getRemoveMode());
166      addButton.addActionListener(new ActionListener()
167         {
168            public void actionPerformed(ActionEvent event)
169            {
170                report.setRemoveMode(false);
171            }
172         });
173      removeButton.addActionListener(new ActionListener()
174         {
175            public void actionPerformed(ActionEvent event)
176            {
177                report.setRemoveMode(true);
178            }
179         });
180
181      // layout components
182      JPanel gridPanel = new JPanel();
183      gridPanel.setLayout(new GridLayout(0, 2));
184      gridPanel.add(new JLabel("Rental Record"));
185      gridPanel.add(rentalRecord);
186      gridPanel.add(new JLabel("Type of Car"));
187      gridPanel.add(carType);
```

```
188       gridPanel.add(new JLabel("Operation"));
189       gridPanel.add(buttonPanel);
190
191       add(gridPanel, BorderLayout.NORTH);
192       add(carComponent, BorderLayout.CENTER);
193       pack();
194    }
195
196    static
197    {
198       int width = 200;
199       int x = 50;
200       int y = 50;
201       Rectangle2D.Double body = new Rectangle2D.Double(x, y + width / 6, width - 1, width / 6);
202       Ellipse2D.Double frontTire = new Ellipse2D.Double(x + width / 6, y + width / 3, width / 6,
203             width / 6);
204       Ellipse2D.Double rearTire = new Ellipse2D.Double(x + width * 2 / 3, y + width / 3,
205             width / 6, width / 6);
206
207       Point2D.Double p1 = new Point2D.Double(x + width / 6, y + width / 6);
208       Point2D.Double p2 = new Point2D.Double(x + width / 3, y);
209       Point2D.Double p3 = new Point2D.Double(x + width * 2 / 3, y);
210       Point2D.Double p4 = new Point2D.Double(x + width * 5 / 6, y + width / 6);
211
212       Line2D.Double frontWindshield = new Line2D.Double(p1, p2);
213       Line2D.Double roofTop = new Line2D.Double(p2, p3); ·
214       Line2D.Double rearWindshield = new Line2D.Double(p3, p4);
215
216       GeneralPath sedanPath = new GeneralPath();
217       sedanPath.append(frontTire, false);
218       sedanPath.append(rearTire, false);
219       sedanPath.append(body, false);
220       sedanPath.append(frontWindshield, false);
221       sedanPath.append(roofTop, false);
222       sedanPath.append(rearWindshield, false);
223       shapes.put(DamageReport.CarType.SEDAN, sedanPath);
224
225       Point2D.Double p5 = new Point2D.Double(x + width * 11 / 12, y);
226       Point2D.Double p6 = new Point2D.Double(x + width, y + width / 6);
227       roofTop = new Line2D.Double(p2, p5);
228       rearWindshield = new Line2D.Double(p5, p6);
229
230       GeneralPath wagonPath = new GeneralPath();
231       wagonPath.append(frontTire, false);
232       wagonPath.append(rearTire, false);
233       wagonPath.append(body, false);
234       wagonPath.append(frontWindshield, false);
235       wagonPath.append(roofTop, false);
236       wagonPath.append(rearWindshield, false);
```

*(Continues)*

---

**Listing 8.10** *(Continued)*

```
237        shapes.put(DamageReport.CarType.WAGON, wagonPath);
238
239        Point2D.Double p7 = new Point2D.Double(x + width / 3, y - width / 6);
240        Point2D.Double p8 = new Point2D.Double(x + width * 11 / 12, y - width / 6);
241        frontWindshield = new Line2D.Double(p1, p7);
242        roofTop = new Line2D.Double(p7, p8);
243        rearWindshield = new Line2D.Double(p8, p6);
244
245        GeneralPath suvPath = new GeneralPath();
246        suvPath.append(frontTire, false);
247        suvPath.append(rearTire, false);
248        suvPath.append(body, false);
249        suvPath.append(frontWindshield, false);
250        suvPath.append(roofTop, false);
251        suvPath.append(rearWindshield, false);
252        shapes.put(DamageReport.CarType.SUV, suvPath);
253     }
254 }
```

---

**Listing 8.11** damageReporter/DamageReport.java

```
1  package damageReporter;
2
3  import java.awt.*;
4  import java.awt.geom.*;
5  import java.beans.*;
6  import java.util.*;
7
8  /**
9   * This class describes a vehicle damage report that will be saved and loaded with the long-term
10  * persistence mechanism.
11  * @version 1.22 2012-01-26
12  * @author Cay Horstmann
13  */
14 public class DamageReport
15 {
16    private String rentalRecord;
17    private CarType carType;
18    private boolean removeMode;
19    private java.util.List<Point2D> points = new ArrayList<>();
20
21    private static final int MARK_SIZE = 5;
22
23    public enum CarType
24    {
25       SEDAN, WAGON, SUV
26    }
```

```
27    // this property is saved automatically
28    public void setRentalRecord(String newValue)
29    {
30       rentalRecord = newValue;
31    }
32
33    public String getRentalRecord()
34    {
35       return rentalRecord;
36    }
37
38    // this property is saved automatically
39    public void setCarType(CarType newValue)
40    {
41       carType = newValue;
42    }
43
44    public CarType getCarType()
45    {
46       return carType;
47    }
48
49    // this property is set to be transient
50    public void setRemoveMode(boolean newValue)
51    {
52       removeMode = newValue;
53    }
54
55    public boolean getRemoveMode()
56    {
57       return removeMode;
58    }
59
60    public void click(Point2D p)
61    {
62       if (removeMode)
63       {
64          for (Point2D center : points)
65          {
66             Ellipse2D circle = new Ellipse2D.Double(center.getX() - MARK_SIZE, center.getY()
67                - MARK_SIZE, 2 * MARK_SIZE, 2 * MARK_SIZE);
68             if (circle.contains(p))
69             {
70                points.remove(center);
71                return;
72             }
73          }
74       }
75       else points.add(p);
76    }
```

*(Continues)*

**Listing 8.11** *(Continued)*

```java
77      public void drawDamage(Graphics2D g2)
78      {
79         g2.setPaint(Color.RED);
80         for (Point2D center : points)
81         {
82            Ellipse2D circle = new Ellipse2D.Double(center.getX() - MARK_SIZE, center.getY()
83               - MARK_SIZE, 2 * MARK_SIZE, 2 * MARK_SIZE);
84            g2.draw(circle);
85         }
86      }
87
88      public void configureEncoder(XMLEncoder encoder)
89      {
90         // this step is necessary to save Point2D.Double objects
91         encoder.setPersistenceDelegate(Point2D.Double.class, new DefaultPersistenceDelegate(
92            new String[] { "x", "y" }));
93
94         // this step is necessary because the array list of points is not
95         // (and should not be) exposed as a property
96         encoder.setPersistenceDelegate(DamageReport.class, new DefaultPersistenceDelegate()
97            {
98               protected void initialize(Class<?> type, Object oldInstance, Object newInstance,
99                  Encoder out)
100              {
101                 super.initialize(type, oldInstance, newInstance, out);
102                 DamageReport r = (DamageReport) oldInstance;
103
104                 for (Point2D p : r.points)
105                    out.writeStatement(new Statement(oldInstance, "click", new Object[] { p }));
106              }
107           });
108     }
109
110     // this step is necessary to make the removeMode property transient
111     static
112     {
113        try
114        {
115           BeanInfo info = Introspector.getBeanInfo(DamageReport.class);
116           for (PropertyDescriptor desc : info.getPropertyDescriptors())
117              if (desc.getName().equals("removeMode")) desc.setValue("transient", Boolean.TRUE);
118        }
119        catch (IntrospectionException e)
120        {
121           e.printStackTrace();
122        }
123     }
124  }
```

---

**java.beans.XMLEncoder** 1.4

- XMLEncoder(OutputStream out)
  constructs an XMLEncoder that sends its output to the given stream.
- void writeObject(Object obj)
  archives the given object.
- void writeStatement(Statement stat)
  writes the given statement to the archive. This method should only be called from a persistence delegate.

---

**java.beans.Encoder** 1.4

- void setPersistenceDelegate(Class<?> type, PersistenceDelegate delegate)
- PersistenceDelegate getPersistenceDelegate(Class<?> type)
  sets or gets the delegate for archiving objects of the given type.
- void setExceptionListener(ExceptionListener listener)
- ExceptionListener getExceptionListener()
  sets or gets the exception listener that is notified if an exception occurs during the encoding process.

---

**java.beans.ExceptionListener** 1.4

- void exceptionThrown(Exception e)
  is called if an exception was thrown during the encoding or decoding process.

---

**java.beans.XMLDecoder** 1.4

- XMLDecoder(InputStream in)
  constructs an XMLDecoder that reads an archive from the given input stream.
- Object readObject()
  reads the next object from the archive.
- void setExceptionListener(ExceptionListener listener)
- ExceptionListener getExceptionListener()
  sets or gets the exception listener that is notified if an exception occurs during the encoding process.

---

**java.beans.PersistenceDelegate** 1.4

- protected abstract Expression instantiate(Object oldInstance, Encoder out)
  returns an expression for instantiating an object that is equivalent to oldInstance.

- protected void initialize(Class<?> type, Object oldInstance, Object newInstance, Encoder out)
  writes statements to out that turn newInstance into an object equivalent to oldInstance.

---

**java.beans.DefaultPersistenceDelegate** 1.4

- DefaultPersistenceDelegate()
  constructs a persistence delegate for a class with a zero-parameter constructor.

- DefaultPersistenceDelegate(String[] propertyNames)
  constructs a persistence delegate for a class whose construction parameters are the values of the given properties.

- protected Expression instantiate(Object oldInstance, Encoder out)
  returns an expression for invoking the constructor with either no parameters or the values of the properties specified in the constructor.

- protected void initialize(Class<?> type, Object oldInstance, Object newInstance, Encoder out)
  writes statements to out that apply property setters to newInstance, attempting to turn it into an object equivalent to oldInstance.

---

**java.beans.Expression** 1.4

- Expression(Object value, Object target, String methodName, Object[] parameters)
  constructs an expression that calls the given method on target with the given parameters. The result of the expression is assumed to be value. To call a constructor, target should be a Class object and methodName should be "new".

---

**java.beans.Statement** 1.4

- Statement(Object target, String methodName, Object[] parameters)
  constructs a statement that calls the given method on target, with the given parameters.

---

You have now worked your way through three long chapters on GUI programming with Swing, AWT, and JavaBeans. In the next chapter, we'll move on to an entirely different topic: security. Security has always been a core feature of the Java platform. As the world in which we live and compute gets more dangerous, a thorough understanding of Java security will be of increasing importance for many developers.

# Security

## In this chapter:

When Java technology first appeared on the scene, the excitement was not about a well-crafted programming language but about the possibility of safely executing applets delivered over the Internet (see Volume I, Chapter 10 for more on applets). Obviously, delivering executable applets is only practical when the recipients are sure that the code can't wreak havoc on their machines. For this reason, security was and is a major concern of both the designers and the users of Java technology. This means that unlike other languages and systems, where security was implemented as an afterthought or a reaction to break-ins, security mechanisms are an integral part of Java technology.

Three mechanisms help ensure safety:

- Language design features (bounds checking on arrays, no unchecked type conversions, no pointer arithmetic, and so on).
- An access control mechanism that controls what the code can do (such as file access, network access, and so on).

- Code signing, whereby code authors can use standard cryptographic algorithms to authenticate Java code. Then, the users of the code can determine exactly who created the code and whether the code has been altered after it was signed.

We will first discuss *class loaders* that check class files for integrity when they are loaded into the virtual machine. We will demonstrate how that mechanism can detect tampering with class files.

For maximum security, both the default mechanism for loading a class and a custom class loader need to work with a *security manager* class that controls what actions code can perform. You'll see in detail how to configure Java platform security.

Finally, you'll see the cryptographic algorithms supplied in the java.security package, which allow for code signing and user authentication.

As always, we'll focus on those topics that are of greatest interest to application programmers. For an in-depth view, we recommend the book *Inside Java*™ *2 Platform Security: Architecture, API Design, and Implementation, Second Edition*, by Li Gong, Gary Ellison, and Mary Dageforde (Prentice Hall, 2003).

## 9.1 Class Loaders

A Java compiler converts source instructions for the Java virtual machine. The virtual machine code is stored in a class file with a .class extension. Each class file contains the definition and implementation code for one class or interface. These class files must be interpreted by a program that can translate the instruction set of the virtual machine into the machine language of the target platform.

Note that the virtual machine loads only those class files that are needed for the execution of a program. For example, suppose program execution starts with MyProgram.class. Here are the steps that the virtual machine carries out:

1. The virtual machine has a mechanism for loading class files—for example, by reading the files from disk or by requesting them from the Web; it uses this mechanism to load the contents of the MyProgram class file.

2. If the MyProgram class has fields or superclasses of another class type, their class files are loaded as well. (The process of loading all the classes that a given class depends on is called *resolving* the class.)

3. The virtual machine then executes the main method in MyProgram (which is static, so no instance of a class needs to be created).

4. If the main method or a method that main calls requires additional classes, these are loaded next.

The class loading mechanism doesn't just use a single class loader, however. Every Java program has at least three class loaders:

- The bootstrap class loader
- The extension class loader
- The system class loader (sometimes also called the application class loader)

The bootstrap class loader loads the system classes (typically, from the JAR file rt.jar). It is an integral part of the virtual machine and is usually implemented in C. There is no ClassLoader object corresponding to the bootstrap class loader. For example,

```
String.class.getClassLoader()
```

returns null.

The extension class loader loads "standard extensions" from the *jre*/lib/ext directory. You can drop JAR files into that directory, and the extension class loader will find the classes in them, even without any class path. (Some people recommend this mechanism to avoid the "class path hell," but see the next cautionary note.)

The system class loader loads the application classes. It locates classes in the directories and JAR/ZIP files on the class path, as set by the CLASSPATH environment variable or the -classpath command-line option.

In Oracle Java implementation, the extension and system class loaders are implemented in Java. Both are instances of the URLClassLoader class.

**CAUTION:** You can run into grief if you drop a JAR file into the *jre*/lib/ext directory and one of its classes needs to load a class that is not a system or extension class. The extension class loader *does not use the class path*. Keep that in mind before you use the extension directory as a way to manage your class file hassles.

**NOTE:** In addition to all the places already mentioned, classes can be loaded from the *jre*/lib/endorsed directory. This mechanism can only be used to replace certain standard Java libraries (such as those for XML and CORBA support) with newer versions. See http://docs.oracle.com/javase/7/docs/technotes/guides/standards for details.

## 9.1.1 The Class Loader Hierarchy

Class loaders have a *parent/child* relationship. Every class loader except for the bootstrap one has a parent class loader. A class loader is supposed to give its parent a chance to load any given class and only load it if the parent has failed. For example, when the system class loader is asked to load a system class (say, java.util.ArrayList), it first asks the extension class loader. That class loader first asks the bootstrap class loader. The bootstrap class loader finds and loads the class in rt.jar, so neither of the other class loaders searches any further.

Some programs have a plugin architecture in which certain parts of the code are packaged as optional plugins. If the plugins are packaged as JAR files, you can simply load the plugin classes with an instance of URLClassLoader.

```
URL url = new URL("file:///path/to/plugin.jar");
URLClassLoader pluginLoader = new URLClassLoader(new URL[] { url });
Class<?> cl = pluginLoader.loadClass("mypackage.MyClass");
```

Because no parent was specified in the URLClassLoader constructor, the parent of the pluginLoader is the system class loader. Figure 9.1 shows the hierarchy.

Most of the time, you don't have to worry about the class loader hierarchy. Generally, classes are loaded because they are required by other classes, and that process is transparent to you.

Occasionally, you need to intervene and specify a class loader. Consider this example:

- Your application code contains a helper method that calls Class.forName( classNameString).
- That method is called from a plugin class.
- The classNameString specifies a class that is contained in the plugin JAR.

The author of the plugin has reasons to expect that the class should be loaded. However, the helper method's class was loaded by the system class loader, and that is the class loader used by Class.forName. The classes in the plugin JAR are not visible. This phenomenon is called *classloader inversion*.

To overcome this problem, the helper method needs to use the correct class loader. It can require the class loader as a parameter. Alternatively, it can require that the correct class loader is set as the *context class loader* of the current thread. This strategy is used by many frameworks (such as the JAXP and JNDI frameworks that we discussed in Chapters 2 and 4).

Each thread has a reference to a class loader, called the context class loader. The main thread's context class loader is the system class loader. When a new thread is created, its context class loader is set to the creating thread's context class

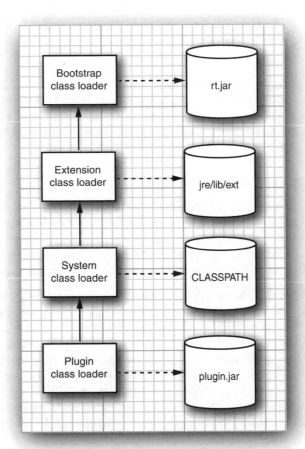

**Figure 9.1** The class loader hierarchy

loader. Thus, if you don't do anything, all threads will have their context class loaders set to the system class loader.

However, you can set any class loader by calling

```
Thread t = Thread.currentThread();
t.setContextClassLoader(loader);
```

The helper method can then retrieve the context class loader:

```
Thread t = Thread.currentThread();
ClassLoader loader = t.getContextClassLoader();
Class cl = loader.loadClass(className);
```

The question remains when the context class loader is set to the plugin class loader. The application designer must make this decision. Generally, it is a good idea to set the context class loader when invoking a method of a plugin class that was loaded with a different class loader. Alternatively, the caller of the helper method can set the context class loader.

 **TIP:** If you write a method that loads a class by name, it is a good idea to offer the caller the choice between passing an explicit class loader and using the context class loader. Don't simply use the class loader of the method's class.

## 9.1.2 Using Class Loaders as Namespaces

Every Java programmer knows that package names are used to eliminate name conflicts. There are two classes called Date in the standard library, but of course their real names are java.util.Date and java.sql.Date. The simple name is only a programmer convenience and requires the inclusion of appropriate import statements. In a running program, all class names contain their package names.

It might surprise you, however, that you can have two classes in the same virtual machine that have the same class *and package* name. A class is determined by its full name *and* the class loader. This technique is useful for loading code from multiple sources. For example, a browser uses separate instances of the applet class loader for each web page. This allows the virtual machine to separate classes from different web pages, no matter what they are named. Figure 9.2 shows an example. Suppose a web page contains two applets, provided by different advertisers, and each applet has a class called Banner. Since each applet is loaded by a separate class loader, these classes are entirely distinct and do not conflict with each other.

 **NOTE:** This technique has other uses as well, such as "hot deployment" of servlets and Enterprise JavaBeans. See http://zeroturnaround.com/labs/rjc301 for more information.

## 9.1.3 Writing Your Own Class Loader

You can write your own class loader for specialized purposes. That lets you carry out custom checks before you pass the bytecodes to the virtual machine. For example, you can write a class loader that can refuse to load a class that has not been marked as "paid for."

To write your own class loader, simply extend the ClassLoader class and override the method

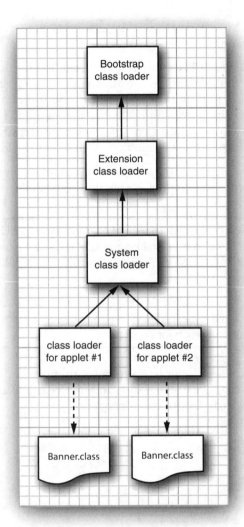

**Figure 9.2** Two class loaders load different classes with the same name.

```
findClass(String className)
```

The `loadClass` method of the `ClassLoader` superclass takes care of the delegation to the parent and calls `findClass` only if the class hasn't already been loaded and if the parent class loader was unable to load the class.

Your implementation of this method must do the following:

1.  Load the bytecodes for the class from the local file system or some other source.

2.  Call the defineClass method of the ClassLoader superclass to present the bytecodes to the virtual machine.

In the program of Listing 9.1, we implement a class loader that loads encrypted class files. The program asks the user for the name of the first class to load (that is, the class containing main) and the decryption key. It then uses a special class loader to load the specified class and calls the main method. The class loader decrypts the specified class and all nonsystem classes that are referenced by it. Finally, the program calls the main method of the loaded class (see Figure 9.3).

For simplicity, we ignore the 2,000 years of progress in the field of cryptography and use the venerable Caesar cipher for encrypting the class files.

 **NOTE:** David Kahn's wonderful book *The Codebreakers* (Macmillan, 1967, p. 84) refers to Suetonius as a historical source for the Caesar cipher. Caesar shifted the 24 letters of the Roman alphabet by 3 letters, which at the time baffled his adversaries.

When this chapter was first written, the U.S. government restricted the export of strong encryption methods. Therefore, we used Caesar's method for our example because it was clearly legal for export.

Our version of the Caesar cipher has as a key a number between 1 and 255. To decrypt, simply add that key to every byte and reduce modulo 256. The Caesar.java program of Listing 9.2 carries out the encryption.

To not confuse the regular class loader, we use a different extension, .caesar, for the encrypted class files.

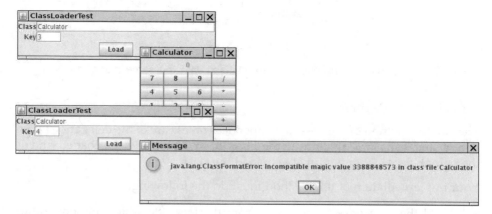

**Figure 9.3** The ClassLoaderTest program

To decrypt, the class loader simply subtracts the key from every byte. In the companion code for this book, you will find four class files, encrypted with a key value of 3—the traditional choice. To run the encrypted program, you'll need the custom class loader defined in our ClassLoaderTest program.

Encrypting class files has a number of practical uses (provided, of course, that you use something stronger than the Caesar cipher). Without the decryption key, the class files are useless. They can neither be executed by a standard virtual machine nor readily disassembled.

This means that you can use a custom class loader to authenticate the user of the class or to ensure that a program has been paid for before it will be allowed to run. Of course, encryption is only one application of a custom class loader. You can use other types of class loaders to solve other problems—for example, storing class files in a database.

---

**Listing 9.1** classLoader/ClassLoaderTest.java

```
 1  package classLoader;
 2
 3  import java.io.*;
 4  import java.lang.reflect.*;
 5  import java.nio.file.*;
 6  import java.awt.*;
 7  import java.awt.event.*;
 8  import javax.swing.*;
 9  /**
10   * This program demonstrates a custom class loader that decrypts class files.
11   * @version 1.23 2012-06-08
12   * @author Cay Horstmann
13   */
14  public class ClassLoaderTest
15  {
16     public static void main(String[] args)
17     {
18        EventQueue.invokeLater(new Runnable()
19           {
20              public void run()
21              {
22                 JFrame frame = new ClassLoaderFrame();
23                 frame.setTitle("ClassLoaderTest");
24                 frame.setDefaultCloseOperation(JFrame.EXIT_ON_CLOSE);
25                 frame.setVisible(true);
26              }
27           });
28     }
29  }
```

*(Continues)*

Listing 9.1 *(Continued)*

```
30  /**
31   * This frame contains two text fields for the name of the class to load and the decryption key.
32   */
33  class ClassLoaderFrame extends JFrame
34  {
35     private JTextField keyField = new JTextField("3", 4);
36     private JTextField nameField = new JTextField("Calculator", 30);
37     private static final int DEFAULT_WIDTH = 300;
38     private static final int DEFAULT_HEIGHT = 200;
39
40     public ClassLoaderFrame()
41     {
42        setSize(DEFAULT_WIDTH, DEFAULT_HEIGHT);
43        setLayout(new GridBagLayout());
44        add(new JLabel("Class"), new GBC(0, 0).setAnchor(GBC.EAST));
45        add(nameField, new GBC(1, 0).setWeight(100, 0).setAnchor(GBC.WEST));
46        add(new JLabel("Key"), new GBC(0, 1).setAnchor(GBC.EAST));
47        add(keyField, new GBC(1, 1).setWeight(100, 0).setAnchor(GBC.WEST));
48        JButton loadButton = new JButton("Load");
49        add(loadButton, new GBC(0, 2, 2, 1));
50        loadButton.addActionListener(new ActionListener()
51           {
52              public void actionPerformed(ActionEvent event)
53              {
54                 runClass(nameField.getText(), keyField.getText());
55              }
56           });
57        pack();
58     }
59
60     /**
61      * Runs the main method of a given class.
62      * @param name the class name.
63      * @param key the decryption key for the class files
64      */
65     public void runClass(String name, String key)
66     {
67        try
68        {
69           ClassLoader loader = new CryptoClassLoader(Integer.parseInt(key));
70           Class<?> c = loader.loadClass(name);
71           Method m = c.getMethod("main", String[].class);
72           m.invoke(null, (Object) new String[] {});
73        }
```

```
74       catch (Throwable e)
75       {
76          JOptionPane.showMessageDialog(this, e);
77       }
78    }
79
80 }
81
82 /**
83  * This class loader loads encrypted class files.
84  */
85 class CryptoClassLoader extends ClassLoader
86 {
87    private int key;
88
89    /**
90     * Constructs a crypto class loader.
91     * @param k the decryption key
92     */
93    public CryptoClassLoader(int k)
94    {
95       key = k;
96    }
97
98    protected Class<?> findClass(String name) throws ClassNotFoundException
99    {
100      try
101      {
102         byte[] classBytes = null;
103         classBytes = loadClassBytes(name);
104         Class<?> cl = defineClass(name, classBytes, 0, classBytes.length);
105         if (cl == null) throw new ClassNotFoundException(name);
106         return cl;
107      }
108      catch (IOException e)
109      {
110         throw new ClassNotFoundException(name);
111      }
112   }
113
114   /**
115    * Loads and decrypt the class file bytes.
116    * @param name the class name
117    * @return an array with the class file bytes
118    */
```

*(Continues)*

**Listing 9.1** *(Continued)*

```java
119    private byte[] loadClassBytes(String name) throws IOException
120    {
121       String cname = name.replace('.', '/') + ".caesar";
122       byte[] bytes = Files.readAllBytes(Paths.get(cname));
123       for (int i = 0; i < bytes.length; i++)
124          bytes[i] = (byte) (bytes[i] - key);
125       return bytes;
126    }
127 }
```

**Listing 9.2** classLoader/Caesar.java

```java
1  package classLoader;
2
3  import java.io.*;
4
5  /**
6   * Encrypts a file using the Caesar cipher.
7   * @version 1.01 2012-06-10
8   * @author Cay Horstmann
9   */
10 public class Caesar
11 {
12    public static void main(String[] args) throws Exception
13    {
14       if (args.length != 3)
15       {
16          System.out.println("USAGE: java classLoader.Caesar in out key");
17          return;
18       }
19
20       try(FileInputStream in = new FileInputStream(args[0]);
21          FileOutputStream out = new FileOutputStream(args[1]))
22       {
23          int key = Integer.parseInt(args[2]);
24          int ch;
25          while ((ch = in.read()) != -1)
26          {
27             byte c = (byte) (ch + key);
28             out.write(c);
29          }
30       }
31    }
32 }
```

---

**java.lang.Class** 1.0

- ClassLoader getClassLoader()
  gets the class loader that loaded this class.

---

**java.lang.ClassLoader** 1.0

- ClassLoader getParent() 1.2
  returns the parent class loader, or null if the parent class loader is the bootstrap class loader.
- static ClassLoader getSystemClassLoader() 1.2
  gets the system class loader—that is, the class loader that was used to load the first application class.
- protected Class findClass(String name) 1.2
  should be overridden by a class loader to find the bytecodes for a class and present them to the virtual machine by calling the defineClass method. In the name of the class, use . as package name separator, and don't use a .class suffix.
- Class defineClass(String name, byte[] byteCodeData, int offset, int length)
  adds a new class to the virtual machine whose bytecodes are provided in the given data range.

---

**java.net.URLClassLoader** 1.2

- URLClassLoader(URL[] urls)
- URLClassLoader(URL[] urls, ClassLoader parent)
  constructs a class loader that loads classes from the given URLs. If a URL ends in a /, it is assumed to be a directory, otherwise it is assumed to be a JAR file.

---

**java.lang.Thread** 1.0

- ClassLoader getContextClassLoader() 1.2
  gets the class loader that the creator of this thread has designated as the most reasonable class loader to use when executing this thread.
- void setContextClassLoader(ClassLoader loader) 1.2
  sets a class loader for code in this thread to retrieve for loading classes. If no context class loader is set explicitly when a thread is started, the parent's context class loader is used.

## 9.2 Bytecode Verification

When a class loader presents the bytecodes of a newly loaded Java platform class to the virtual machine, these bytecodes are first inspected by a *verifier*. The verifier checks that the instructions cannot perform actions that are obviously damaging. All classes except for system classes are verified.

Here are some of the checks that the verifier carries out:

- Variables are initialized before they are used.
- Method calls match the types of object references.
- Rules for accessing private data and methods are not violated.
- Local variable accesses fall within the runtime stack.
- The runtime stack does not overflow.

If any of these checks fails, the class is considered corrupted and will not be loaded.

 **NOTE:** If you are familiar with Gödel's theorem, you might wonder how the verifier can prove that a class file is free from type mismatches, uninitialized variables, and stack overflows. Gödel's theorem states that it is impossible to design algorithms that process program files and decide whether the input programs have a particular property (such as being free from stack overflows). Is this a conflict between the public relations department at Oracle and the laws of logic? No—in fact, the verifier is *not* a decision algorithm in the sense of Gödel. If the verifier accepts a program, it is indeed safe. However, the verifier might reject virtual machine instructions even though they would actually be safe. (You might have run into this issue when you were forced to initialize a variable with a dummy value because the verifier couldn't tell that it was going to be properly initialized.)

This strict verification is an important security consideration. Accidental errors, such as uninitialized variables, can easily wreak havoc if they are not caught. More importantly, in the wide open world of the Internet, you must be protected against malicious programmers who create evil effects on purpose. For example, by modifying values on the runtime stack or by writing to the private data fields of system objects, a program can break through the security system of a browser.

You might wonder, however, why a special verifier checks all these features. After all, the compiler would never allow you to generate a class file in which an uninitialized variable is used or in which a private data field is accessed from another class. Indeed, a class file generated by a compiler for the Java programming language always passes verification. However, the bytecode format used in the class files is well documented, and it is an easy matter for someone with experience in assembly programming and a hex editor to manually produce a class file containing valid but unsafe instructions for the Java virtual machine. Once again, keep in mind that the verifier is always guarding against maliciously altered class files, not just checking the class files produced by a compiler.

Here's an example of how to construct such an altered class file. We start with the program VerifierTest.java of Listing 9.3. This is a simple program that calls a method and displays the method result. The program can be run both as a console program and as an applet. The fun method itself just computes 1 + 2.

```java
static int fun()
{
   int m;
   int n;
   m = 1;
   n = 2;
   int r = m + n;
   return r;
}
```

**Listing 9.3** verifier/VerifierTest.java

```java
1  package verifier;
2
3  import java.applet.*;
4  import java.awt.*;
5  /**
6   * This application demonstrates the bytecode verifier of the virtual machine. If you use a hex
7   * editor to modify the class file, then the virtual machine should detect the tampering.
8   * @version 1.00 1997-09-10
9   * @author Cay Horstmann
10  */
11 public class VerifierTest extends Applet
12 {
13    public static void main(String[] args)
14    {
15       System.out.println("1 + 2 == " + fun());
16    }
17
18    /**
19     * A function that computes 1 + 2.
20     * @return 3, if the code has not been corrupted
21     */
22    public static int fun()
23    {
```

*(Continues)*

| | Listing 9.3 *(Continued)* |
|---|---|
| 24 | int m; |
| 25 | int n; |
| 26 | m = 1; |
| 27 | n = 2; |
| 28 | // use hex editor to change to "m = 2" in class file |
| 29 | int r = m + n; |
| 30 | return r; |
| 31 | } |
| 32 | |
| 33 | public void paint(Graphics g) |
| 34 | { |
| 35 | g.drawString("1 + 2 == " + fun(), 20, 20); |
| 36 | } |
| 37 | } |

As an experiment, try to compile the following modification of this program:

```
static int fun()
{
   int m = 1;
   int n;
   m = 1;
   m = 2;
   int r = m + n;
   return r;
}
```

In this case, n is not initialized, and it could have any random value. Of course, the compiler detects that problem and refuses to compile the program. To create a bad class file, we have to work a little harder. First, run the javap program to find out how the compiler translates the fun method. The command

```
javap -c verifier.VerifierTest
```

shows the bytecodes in the class file in mnemonic form.

```
Method int fun()
   0 iconst_1
   1 istore_0
   2 iconst_2
   3 istore_1
   4 iload_0
   5 iload_1
   6 iadd
   7 istore_2
   8 iload_2
   9 ireturn
```

Use a hex editor to change instruction 3 from istore_1 to istore_0. That is, local variable 0 (which is m) is initialized twice, and local variable 1 (which is n) is not initialized at all. We need to know the hexadecimal values for these instructions; these values are readily available from *The Java™ Virtual Machine Specification, Second Edition*, by Tim Lindholm and Frank Yellin (Prentice Hall, 1999).

```
0 iconst_1 04
1 istore_0 3B
2 iconst_2 05
3 istore_1 3C
4 iload_0  1A
5 iload_1  1B
6 iadd     60
7 istore_2 3D
8 iload_2  1C
9 ireturn  AC
```

You can use any hex editor to carry out the modification. In Figure 9.4, you see the class file VerifierTest.class loaded into the Gnome hex editor, with the bytecodes of the fun method highlighted.

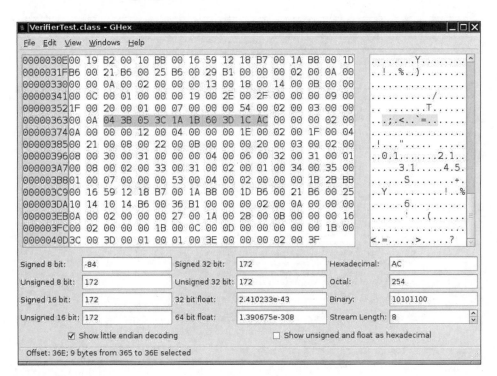

**Figure 9.4** Modifying bytecodes with a hex editor

Change 3C to 3B and save the class file. Then try running the VerifierTest program. You get an error message:

```
Exception in thread "main" java.lang.VerifyError: (class: VerifierTest, method:fun signature:
()I) Accessing value from uninitialized register 1
```

That is good—the virtual machine detected our modification.

Now run the program with the -noverify (or -Xverify:none) option.

```
java -noverify verifier.VerifierTest
```

The fun method returns a seemingly random value. This is actually 2 plus the value that happened to be stored in the variable n, which never was initialized. Here is a typical printout:

```
1 + 2 == 15102330
```

To see how browsers handle verification, we wrote this program to run either as an application or an applet. Load the applet into a browser, using a file URL such as

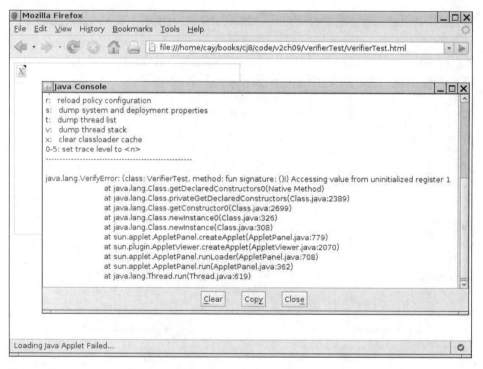

**Figure 9.5** Loading a corrupted class file raises a method verification error.

file:///C:/CoreJavaBook/v2ch9/verifier/VerifierTest.html

You then see an error message displayed indicating that verification has failed (Figure 9.5).

# 9.3 Security Managers and Permissions

Once a class has been loaded into the virtual machine and checked by the verifier, the second security mechanism of the Java platform springs into action: the *security manager*. The security manager is a class that controls whether a specific operation is permitted. Operations checked by the security manager include the following:

* Creating a new class loader
* Exiting the virtual machine
* Accessing a field of another class by using reflection
* Accessing a file
* Opening a socket connection
* Starting a print job
* Accessing the system clipboard
* Accessing the AWT event queue
* Bringing up a top-level window

There are many other checks throughout the Java library.

The default behavior when running Java applications is that *no* security manager is installed, so all these operations are permitted. The applet viewer, on the other hand, enforces a security policy that is quite restrictive.

For example, applets are not allowed to exit the virtual machine. If they try calling the `exit` method, a security exception is thrown. Here is what happens in detail. The `exit` method of the `Runtime` class calls the `checkExit` method of the security manager. Here is the entire code of the `exit` method:

```
public void exit(int status)
{
   SecurityManager security = System.getSecurityManager();
   if (security != null)
       security.checkExit(status);
   exitInternal(status);
}
```

The security manager now checks if the exit request came from the browser or an individual applet. If the security manager agrees with the exit request, the checkExit method simply returns and normal processing continues. However, if the security manager doesn't want to grant the request, the checkExit method throws a SecurityException.

The exit method continues only if no exception occurred. It then calls the *private native* exitInternal method that actually terminates the virtual machine. There is no other way of terminating the virtual machine, and since the exitInternal method is private, it cannot be called from any other class. Thus, any code that attempts to exit the virtual machine must go through the exit method and thus through the checkExit security check without triggering a security exception.

Clearly, the integrity of the security policy depends on careful coding. The providers of system services in the standard library must always consult the security manager before attempting any sensitive operation.

The security manager of the Java platform allows both programmers and system administrators fine-grained control over individual security permissions. We will describe these features in the following section. First, we'll summarize the Java 2 platform security model. We'll then show how you can control permissions with *policy files*. Finally, we'll explain how you can define your own permission types.

---

 **NOTE:** It is possible to implement and install your own security manager, but you should not attempt this unless you are an expert in computer security. It is much safer to configure the standard security manager.

---

## 9.3.1 Java Platform Security

JDK 1.0 had a very simple security model: Local classes had full permissions, and remote classes were confined to the *sandbox*. Just like a child that can only play in a sandbox, remote code was only allowed to paint on the screen and interact with the user. The applet security manager denied all access to local resources. JDK 1.1 implemented a slight modification: Remote code that was signed by a trusted entity was granted the same permissions as local classes. However, both versions of the JDK provided an all-or-nothing approach. Programs either had full access or they had to play in the sandbox.

Starting with Java SE 1.2, the Java platform has a much more flexible mechanism. A *security policy* maps *code sources to permission sets* (see Figure 9.6).

A *code source* is specified by a *code base* and a set of *certificates*. The code base specifies the origin of the code. For example, the code base of remote applet code is the HTTP URL from which the applet is loaded. The code base of code in a JAR

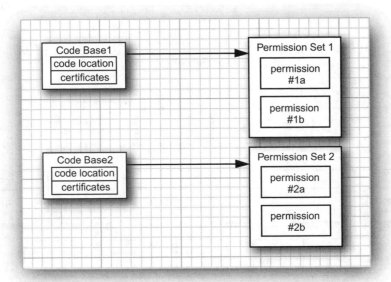

**Figure 9.6** A security policy

file is the file's URL. A certificate, if present, is an assurance by some party that the code has not been tampered with. We cover certificates later in this chapter.

A *permission* is any property that is checked by a security manager. The Java platform supports a number of permission classes, each encapsulating the details of a particular permission. For example, the following instance of the `FilePermission` class states that it is okay to read and write any file in the `/tmp` directory.

```
FilePermission p = new FilePermission("/tmp/*", "read,write");
```

More importantly, the default implementation of the `Policy` class reads permissions from a *permission file*. Inside a permission file, the same read permission is expressed as

```
permission java.io.FilePermission "/tmp/*", "read,write";
```

We'll discuss permission files in the next section.

Figure 9.7 shows the hierarchy of the permission classes that were supplied with Java SE 1.2. Many more permission classes have been added in subsequent Java releases.

In the preceding section, you saw that the `SecurityManager` class has security check methods such as `checkExit`. These methods exist only for the convenience of the programmer and for backward compatibility. They all map into standard permission checks. For example, here is the source code for the `checkExit` method:

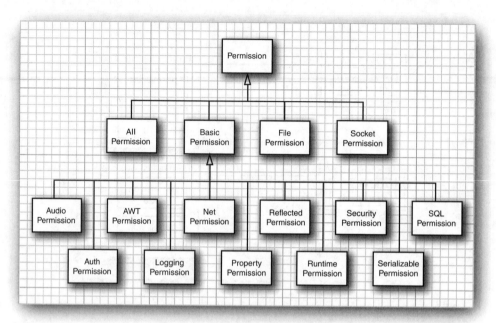

**Figure 9.7** A part of the hierarchy of permission classes

```
public void checkExit()
{
   checkPermission(new RuntimePermission("exitVM"));
}
```

Each class has a *protection domain*—an object that encapsulates both the code source and the collection of permissions of the class. When the SecurityManager needs to check a permission, it looks at the classes of all methods currently on the call stack. It then gets the protection domains of all classes and asks each protection domain if its permission collection allows the operation currently being checked. If all domains agree, the check passes. Otherwise, a SecurityException is thrown.

Why do all methods on the call stack need to allow a particular operation? Let us work through an example. Suppose the init method of an applet wants to open a file. It might call

```
Reader in = new FileReader(name);
```

The FileReader constructor calls the FileInputStream constructor, which calls the checkRead method of the security manager, which finally calls checkPermission with a FilePermission(name, "read") object. Table 9.1 shows the call stack.

**Table 9.1** Call Stack During Permission Checking

| Class | Method | Code Source | Permissions |
|---|---|---|---|
| SecurityManager | checkPermission | null | AllPermission |
| SecurityManager | checkRead | null | AllPermission |
| FileInputStream | Constructor | null | AllPermission |
| FileReader | Constructor | null | AllPermission |
| Applet | init | Applet code source | Applet permissions |
| ... | | | |

The FileInputStream and SecurityManager classes are *system classes* for which CodeSource is null and the permissions consist of an instance of the AllPermission class, which allows all operations. Clearly, their permissions alone can't determine the outcome of the check. As you can see, the checkPermission method must take into account the restricted permissions of the applet class. By checking the entire call stack, the security mechanism ensures that one class can never ask another class to carry out a sensitive operation on its behalf.

 **NOTE:** This brief discussion of permission checking explains the basic concepts. However, we omit a number of technical details here. With security, the devil lies in the details, and we encourage you to read the book by Li Gong for more information. For a more critical view of the Java platform's security model, see the book *Securing Java: Getting Down to Business with Mobile Code, Second Edition*, by Gary McGraw and Ed W. Felten (Wiley, 1999). You can find an online version of that book at www.securingjava.com.

---

**java.lang.SecurityManager 1.0**

- void checkPermission(Permission p) 1.2
  checks whether this security manager grants the given permission. The method throws a SecurityException if the permission is not granted.

---

**java.lang.Class 1.0**

- ProtectionDomain getProtectionDomain() 1.2
  gets the protection domain for this class, or null if this class was loaded without a protection domain.

---

**java.security.ProtectionDomain** 1.2

- ProtectionDomain(CodeSource source, PermissionCollection permissions)
  constructs a protection domain with the given code source and permissions.
- CodeSource getCodeSource()
  gets the code source of this protection domain.
- boolean implies(Permission p)
  returns true if the given permission is allowed by this protection domain.

---

**java.security.CodeSource** 1.2

- Certificate[] getCertificates()
  gets the certificate chain for class file signatures associated with this code source.
- URL getLocation()
  gets the code base of class files associated with this code source.

---

## 9.3.2 Security Policy Files

The *policy manager* reads *policy files* that contain instructions for mapping code sources to permissions. Here is a typical policy file:

```
grant codeBase "http://www.horstmann.com/classes"
{
   permission java.io.FilePermission "/tmp/*", "read,write";
};
```

This file grants permission to read and write files in the /tmp directory to all code that was downloaded from www.horstmann.com/classes.

You can install policy files in standard locations. By default, there are two locations:

- The file java.policy in the Java platform's home directory
- The file .java.policy (notice the period at the beginning of the file name) in the user's home directory

---

 **NOTE:** You can change the locations of these files in the java.security configuration file in the *jre*/lib/security. The defaults are specified as

```
policy.url.1=file:${java.home}/lib/security/java.policy
policy.url.2=file:${user.home}/.java.policy
```

A system administrator can modify the java.security file and specify policy URLs that reside on another server and cannot be edited by users. There can be any number of policy URLs (with consecutive numbers) in the policy file. The permissions of all files are combined.

If you want to store policies outside the file system, you can implement a subclass of the Policy class that gathers the permissions. Then change the line

```
policy.provider=sun.security.provider.PolicyFile
```

in the java.security configuration file.

During testing, we don't like to constantly modify the standard policy files. Therefore, we prefer to explicitly name the policy file required for each application. Place the permissions into a separate file—say, MyApp.policy. To apply the policy, you have two choices. You can set a system property inside your applications' main method:

```
System.setProperty("java.security.policy", "MyApp.policy");
```

Alternatively, you can start the virtual machine as

```
java -Djava.security.policy=MyApp.policy MyApp
```

For applets, you should instead use

```
appletviewer -J-Djava.security.policy=MyApplet.policy MyApplet.html
```

(You can use the -J option of the appletviewer to pass any command-line argument to the virtual machine.)

In these examples, the MyApp.policy file is added to the other policies in effect. If you add a second equal sign, such as

```
java -Djava.security.policy==MyApp.policy MyApp
```

then your application will use *only* the specified policy file, and the standard policy files will be ignored.

 **CAUTION:** An easy mistake during testing is to accidentally leave a .java.policy file that grants a lot of permissions, perhaps even AllPermission, in the home directory. If you find that your application doesn't seem to pay attention to the restrictions in your policy file, check for a left-behind .java.policy file in your home directory. If you use a UNIX system, this is a particularly easy mistake to make because files with names that start with a period are not displayed by default.

As you saw previously, Java applications by default do not install a security manager. Therefore, you won't see the effect of policy files until you install one. You can, of course, add a line

```
System.setSecurityManager(new SecurityManager());
```

into your `main` method. Or you can add the command-line option `-Djava.security.manager` when starting the virtual machine.

```
java -Djava.security.manager -Djava.security.policy=MyApp.policy MyApp
```

In the remainder of this section, we'll show you in detail how to describe permissions in the policy file. We'll describe the entire policy file format, except for code certificates which we cover later in this chapter.

A policy file contains a sequence of `grant` entries. Each entry has the following form:

```
grant codesource
{
    permission1 ;
    permission2 ;
    . . .
};
```

The code source contains a code base (which can be omitted if the entry applies to code from all sources) and the names of trusted principals and certificate signers (which can be omitted if signatures are not required for this entry).

The code base is specified as

```
codeBase "url"
```

If the URL ends in a /, then it refers to a directory. Otherwise, it is taken to be the name of a JAR file. For example,

```
grant codeBase "www.horstmann.com/classes/" { . . . };
grant codeBase "www.horstmann.com/classes/MyApp.jar" { . . . };
```

The code base is a URL and should always contain forward slashes as file separators, even for file URLs in Windows. For example,

```
grant codeBase "file:C:/myapps/classes/" { . . . };
```

---

 **NOTE:** Everyone knows that `http` URLs start with two slashes (`http://`). But there seems enough confusion about `file` URLs that the policy file reader accepts two forms of file URLs, namely, `file://localFile` and `file:localFile`. Furthermore, a slash before a Windows drive letter is optional. That is, all of the following are acceptable:

```
file:C:/dir/filename.ext
file:/C:/dir/filename.ext
file://C:/dir/filename.ext
file:///C:/dir/filename.ext
```

Actually, in our tests, the `file:////C:/dir/filename.ext` is acceptable as well, and we have no explanation for that.

---

The permissions have the following structure:

`permission` *className* *targetName* , *actionList* ;

The *className* is the fully qualified class name of the permission class (such as `java.io.FilePermission`). The *targetName* is a permission-specific value—for example, a file or directory name for the file permission, or a host and port for a socket permission. The *actionList* is also permission-specific. It is a list of actions, such as `read` or `connect`, separated by commas. Some permission classes don't need target names and action lists. Table 9.2 lists the commonly used permission classes and their actions.

As you can see from Table 9.2, most permissions simply permit a particular operation. You can think of the operation as the target with an implied action `"permit"`. These permission classes all extend the `BasicPermission` class (see Figure 9.7 on p. 824). However, the targets for the file, socket, and property permissions are more complex, and we need to investigate them in detail.

File permission targets can have the following form:

| | |
|---|---|
| *file* | A file |
| *directory/* | A directory |
| *directory/\** | All files in the directory |
| * | All files in the current directory |
| *directory/-* | All files in the directory or one of its subdirectories |
| - | All files in the current directory or one of its subdirectories |
| `<<ALL FILES>>` | All files in the file system |

**Table 9.2** Permissions and Their Associated Targets and Actions

| Permission | Target | Action |
|---|---|---|
| `java.io.FilePermission` | File target (see text) | read, write, execute, delete |
| `java.net.SocketPermission` | Socket target (see text) | accept, connect, listen, resolve |

*(Continues)*

**Table 9.2** *(Continued)*

| Permission | Target | Action |
|---|---|---|
| java.util.PropertyPermission | Property target (see text) | read, write |
| java.lang.RuntimePermission | createClassLoader<br>getClassLoader<br>setContextClassLoader<br>enableContextClassLoaderOverride<br>createSecurityManager<br>setSecurityManager<br>exitVM<br>getenv.variableName<br>shutdownHooks<br>setFactory<br>setIO<br>modifyThread<br>stopThread<br>modifyThreadGroup<br>getProtectionDomain<br>readFileDescriptor<br>writeFileDescriptor<br>loadLibrary.libraryName<br>accessClassInPackage.packageName<br>defineClassInPackage.packageName<br>accessDeclaredMembers.className<br>queuePrintJob<br>getStackTrace<br>setDefaultUncaughtExceptionHandler<br>preferences<br>usePolicy | None |
| java.awt.AWTPermission | showWindowWithoutWarningBanner<br>accessClipboard<br>accessEventQueue<br>createRobot<br>fullScreenExclusive<br>listenToAllAWTEvents<br>readDisplayPixels<br>replaceKeyboardFocusManager<br>watchMousePointer<br>setWindowAlwaysOnTop<br>setAppletStub | None |

| Permission | Target | Action |
|---|---|---|
| java.net.NetPermission | setDefaultAuthenticator<br>specifyStreamHandler<br>requestPasswordAuthentication<br>setProxySelector<br>getProxySelector<br>setCookieHandler<br>getCookieHandler<br>setResponseCache<br>getResponseCache | None |
| java.lang.reflect.ReflectPermission | suppressAccessChecks | None |
| java.io.SerializablePermission | enableSubclassImplementation<br>enableSubstitution | None |
| java.security.SecurityPermission | createAccessControlContext<br>getDomainCombiner<br>getPolicy<br>setPolicy<br>getProperty.keyName<br>setProperty.keyName<br>insertProvider.providerName<br>removeProvider.providerName<br>setSystemScope<br>setIdentityPublicKey<br>setIdentityInfo<br>addIdentityCertificate<br>removeIdentityCertificate<br>printIdentity<br>clearProviderProperties.providerName<br>putProviderProperty.providerName<br>removeProviderProperty.providerName<br>getSignerPrivateKey<br>setSignerKeyPair | None |
| java.security.AllPermission | None | None |
| javax.audio.AudioPermission | Play record | None |

*(Continues)*

**Table 9.2**  *(Continued)*

| Permission | Target | Action |
|---|---|---|
| javax.security.auth.AuthPermission | doAs<br>doAsPrivileged<br>getSubject<br>getSubjectFromDomainCombiner<br>setReadOnly<br>modifyPrincipals<br>modifyPublicCredentials<br>modifyPrivateCredentials<br>refreshCredential<br>destroyCredential<br>createLoginContext.contextName<br>getLoginConfiguration<br>setLoginConfiguration<br>refreshLoginConfiguration | None |
| java.util.logging.LoggingPermission | control | None |
| java.sql.SQLPermission | setLog | None |

For example, the following permission entry gives access to all files in the directory /myapp and any of its subdirectories.

```
permission java.io.FilePermission "/myapp/-", "read,write,delete";
```

You must use the \\ escape sequence to denote a backslash in a Windows file name.

```
permission java.io.FilePermission "c:\\myapp\\-", "read,write,delete";
```

Socket permission targets consist of a host and a port range. Host specifications have the following form:

| | |
|---|---|
| *hostname* or *IPaddress* | A single host |
| localhost or the empty string | The local host |
| *.*domainSuffix* | Any host whose domain ends with the given suffix |
| * | All hosts |

Port ranges are optional and have the form:

| | |
|---|---|
| :*n* | A single port |
| :*n*- | All ports numbered *n* and above |

| | |
|---|---|
| *:-n* | All ports numbered *n* and below |
| *:n1-n2* | All ports in the given range |

Here is an example:

```
permission java.net.SocketPermission "*.horstmann.com:8000-8999", "connect";
```

Finally, property permission targets can have one of two forms:

| | |
|---|---|
| *property* | A specific property |
| *propertyPrefix.** | All properties with the given prefix |

Examples are "java.home" and "java.vm.*".

For example, the following permission entry allows a program to read all properties that start with java.vm:

```
permission java.util.PropertyPermission "java.vm.*", "read";
```

You can use system properties in policy files. The token ${*property*} is replaced by the property value. For example, ${user.home} is replaced by the home directory of the user. Here is a typical use of this system property in a permission entry:

```
permission java.io.FilePermission "${user.home}", "read,write";
```

To create platform-independent policy files, it is a good idea to use the file.separator property instead of explicit / or \\ separators. To make this simpler, the special notation ${/} is a shortcut for ${file.separator}. For example,

```
permission java.io.FilePermission "${user.home}${/}-", "read,write";
```

is a portable entry for granting permission to read and write in the user's home directory and any of its subdirectories.

---

 **NOTE:** The JDK comes with a rudimentary tool, called policytool, that you can use to edit policy files (see Figure 9.8). Of course, this tool is not suitable for end users who would be completely mystified by most of the settings. We view it as a proof of concept for an administration tool that might be used by system administrators who prefer point-and-click over syntax. Still, what's missing is a sensible set of categories (such as low, medium, or high security) that is meaningful to nonexperts. As a general observation, we believe that the Java platform certainly contains all the pieces for a fine-grained security model but it could benefit from some polish in delivering these pieces to end users and system administrators.

---

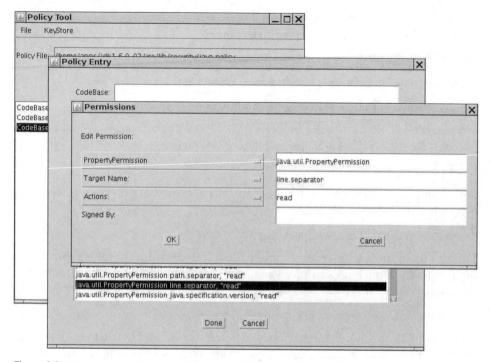

**Figure 9.8** The policy tool

## 9.3.3 Custom Permissions

In this section, you'll see how you can supply your own permission class that users can refer to in their policy files.

To implement your permission class, extend the `Permission` class and supply the following methods:

- A constructor with two `String` parameters, for the target and the action list
- `String getActions()`
- `boolean equals()`
- `int hashCode()`
- `boolean implies(Permission other)`

The last method is the most important. Permissions have an *ordering*, in which more general permissions *imply* more specific ones. Consider the file permission

```
p1 = new FilePermission("/tmp/-", "read, write");
```

This permission allows reading and writing of any file in the /tmp directory and any of its subdirectories.

This permission implies other, more specific permissions:

```
p2 = new FilePermission("/tmp/-", "read");
p3 = new FilePermission("/tmp/aFile", "read, write");
p4 = new FilePermission("/tmp/aDirectory/-", "write");
```

In other words, a file permission p1 implies another file permission p2 if

1.   The target file set of p1 contains the target file set of p2.
2.   The action set of p1 contains the action set of p2.

Consider the following example of the use of the implies method. When the FileInputStream constructor wants to open a file for reading, it checks whether it has permission to do so. For that check, a *specific* file permission object is passed to the checkPermission method:

```
checkPermission(new FilePermission(fileName, "read"));
```

The security manager now asks all applicable permissions whether they imply this permission. If any one of them implies it, the check passes.

In particular, the AllPermission implies all other permissions.

If you define your own permission classes, you need to define a suitable notion of implication for your permission objects. Suppose, for example, that you define a TVPermission for a set-top box powered by Java technology. A permission

```
new TVPermission("Tommy:2-12:1900-2200", "watch,record")
```

might allow Tommy to watch and record television channels 2–12 between 19:00 and 22:00. You need to implement the implies method so that this permission implies a more specific one, such as

```
new TVPermission("Tommy:4:2000-2100", "watch")
```

## 9.3.4 Implementation of a Permission Class

In the next sample program, we implement a new permission for monitoring the insertion of text into a text area. The program ensures that you cannot add "bad words" such as *sex, drugs,* and C++ into a text area. We use a custom permission class so that the list of bad words can be supplied in a policy file.

The following subclass of JTextArea asks the security manager whether it is okay to add new text:

```
class WordCheckTextArea extends JTextArea
{
   public void append(String text)
   {
      WordCheckPermission p = new WordCheckPermission(text, "insert");
      SecurityManager manager = System.getSecurityManager();
      if (manager != null) manager.checkPermission(p);
      super.append(text);
   }
}
```

If the security manager grants the WordCheckPermission, the text is appended. Otherwise, the checkPermission method throws an exception.

Word check permissions have two possible actions: insert (the permission to insert a specific text) and avoid (the permission to add any text that avoids certain bad words). You should run this program with the following policy file:

```
grant
{
   permission permissions.WordCheckPermission "sex,drugs,C++", "avoid";
};
```

This policy file grants the permission to insert any text that avoids the bad words *sex, drugs,* and *C++.*

When designing the WordCheckPermission class, we must pay particular attention to the implies method. Here are the rules that control whether permission p1 implies permission p2.

- If p1 has action avoid and p2 has action insert, then the target of p2 must avoid all words in p1. For example, the permission

  ```
  permissions.WordCheckPermission "sex,drugs,C++", "avoid"
  ```

  implies the permission

  ```
  permissions.WordCheckPermission "Mary had a little lamb", "insert"
  ```

- If p1 and p2 both have action avoid, then the word set of p2 must contain all words in the word set of p1. For example, the permission

  ```
  permissions.WordCheckPermission "sex,drugs", "avoid"
  ```

  implies the permission

  ```
  permissions.WordCheckPermission "sex,drugs,C++", "avoid"
  ```

- If p1 and p2 both have action insert, then the text of p1 must contain the text of p2. For example, the permission

  ```
  permissions.WordCheckPermission "Mary had a little lamb", "insert"
  ```

implies the permission

```
permissions.WordCheckPermission "a little lamb", "insert"
```

You can find the implementation of this class in Listing 9.4.

Note that to retrieve the permission target, you need to use the confusingly named getName method of the Permission class.

Since permissions are described by a pair of strings in policy files, permission classes need to be prepared to parse these strings. In particular, we use the following method to transform the comma-separated list of bad words of an avoid permission into a genuine Set:

```
public Set<String> badWordSet()
{
   Set<String> set = new HashSet<String>();
   set.addAll(Arrays.asList(getName().split(",")));
   return set;
}
```

This code allows us to use the equals and containsAll methods to compare sets. As you saw in Chapter 2, the equals method of a set class finds two sets to be equal if they contain the same elements in any order. For example, the sets resulting from "sex,drugs,C++" and "C++,drugs,sex" are equal.

**CAUTION:** Make sure that your permission class is a public class. The policy file loader cannot load classes with package visibility outside the boot class path, and it silently ignores any classes that it cannot find.

The program in Listing 9.5 shows how the WordCheckPermission class works. Type any text into the text field and click the Insert button. If the security check passes, the text is appended to the text area. If not, an error message is displayed (see Figure 9.9).

**CAUTION:** If you carefully look at Figure 9.9, you will see that the message window has a warning triangle, which is supposed to warn viewers that this window may have been popped up without permission. The warning started out as an ominous "Untrusted Java Applet Window" label, got watered down several times in successive JDK releases, and has now become essentially useless for alerting users. The warning is turned off by the showWindowWithoutWarningBanner target of the java.awt.AWTPermission. If you like, you can edit the policy file to grant that permission.

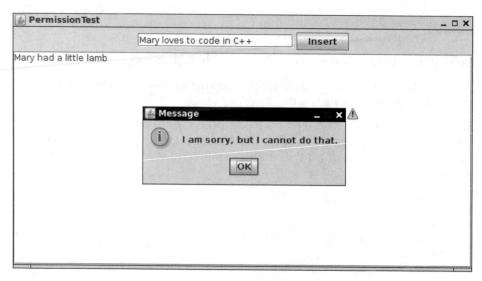

**Figure 9.9** The PermissionTest program

**Listing 9.4** permissions/WordCheckPermission.java

```
1  package permissions;
2
3  import java.security.*;
4  import java.util.*;
5
6  /**
7   * A permission that checks for bad words.
8   */
9  public class WordCheckPermission extends Permission
10 {
11    private String action;
12
13    /**
14     * Constructs a word check permission.
15     * @param target a comma separated word list
16     * @param anAction "insert" or "avoid"
17     */
18    public WordCheckPermission(String target, String anAction)
19    {
20       super(target);
21       action = anAction;
22    }
```

```
23     public String getActions()
24     {
25        return action;
26     }
27
28     public boolean equals(Object other)
29     {
30        if (other == null) return false;
31        if (!getClass().equals(other.getClass())) return false;
32        WordCheckPermission b = (WordCheckPermission) other;
33        if (!Objects.equals(action, b.action)) return false;
34        if ("insert".equals(action)) return Objects.equals(getName(), b.getName());
35        else if ("avoid".equals(action)) return badWordSet().equals(b.badWordSet());
36        else return false;
37     }
38
39     public int hashCode()
40     {
41        return Objects.hash(getName(), action);
42     }
43
44     public boolean implies(Permission other)
45     {
46        if (!(other instanceof WordCheckPermission)) return false;
47        WordCheckPermission b = (WordCheckPermission) other;
48        if (action.equals("insert"))
49        {
50           return b.action.equals("insert") && getName().indexOf(b.getName()) >= 0;
51        }
52        else if (action.equals("avoid"))
53        {
54           if (b.action.equals("avoid")) return b.badWordSet().containsAll(badWordSet());
55           else if (b.action.equals("insert"))
56           {
57              for (String badWord : badWordSet())
58                 if (b.getName().indexOf(badWord) >= 0) return false;
59              return true;
60           }
61           else return false;
62        }
63        else return false;
64     }
65
66     /**
67      * Gets the bad words that this permission rule describes.
68      * @return a set of the bad words
69      */
```

*(Continues)*

---

**Listing 9.4**    *(Continued)*

```
70    public Set<String> badWordSet()
71    {
72       Set<String> set = new HashSet<>();
73       set.addAll(Arrays.asList(getName().split(",")));
74       return set;
75    }
76 }
```

---

**Listing 9.5**    permissions/PermissionTest.java

```
1  package permissions;
2
3  import java.awt.*;
4  import java.awt.event.*;
5  import javax.swing.*;
6
7  /**
8   * This class demonstrates the custom WordCheckPermission.
9   * @version 1.03 2007-10-06
10  * @author Cay Horstmann
11  */
12 public class PermissionTest
13 {
14    public static void main(String[] args)
15    {
16       System.setProperty("java.security.policy", "permissions/PermissionTest.policy");
17       System.setSecurityManager(new SecurityManager());
18       EventQueue.invokeLater(new Runnable()
19          {
20             public void run()
21             {
22                JFrame frame = new PermissionTestFrame();
23                frame.setTitle("PermissionTest");
24                frame.setDefaultCloseOperation(JFrame.EXIT_ON_CLOSE);
25                frame.setVisible(true);
26             }
27          });
28    }
29 }
30
31 /**
32  * This frame contains a text field for inserting words into a text area that is protected from
33  * "bad words".
34  */
```

```
35  class PermissionTestFrame extends JFrame
36  {
37     private JTextField textField;
38     private WordCheckTextArea textArea;
39     private static final int TEXT_ROWS = 20;
40     private static final int TEXT_COLUMNS = 60;
41
42     public PermissionTestFrame()
43     {
44        textField = new JTextField(20);
45        JPanel panel = new JPanel();
46        panel.add(textField);
47        JButton openButton = new JButton("Insert");
48        panel.add(openButton);
49        openButton.addActionListener(new ActionListener()
50           {
51              public void actionPerformed(ActionEvent event)
52              {
53                 insertWords(textField.getText());
54              }
55           });
56
57        add(panel, BorderLayout.NORTH);
58
59        textArea = new WordCheckTextArea();
60        textArea.setRows(TEXT_ROWS);
61        textArea.setColumns(TEXT_COLUMNS);
62        add(new JScrollPane(textArea), BorderLayout.CENTER);
63        pack();
64     }
65
66     /**
67      * Tries to insert words into the text area. Displays a dialog if the attempt fails.
68      * @param words the words to insert
69      */
70     public void insertWords(String words)
71     {
72        try
73        {
74           textArea.append(words + "\n");
75        }
76        catch (SecurityException ex)
77        {
78           JOptionPane.showMessageDialog(this, "I am sorry, but I cannot do that.");
79           ex.printStackTrace();
80        }
81     }
82  }
```

*(Continues)*

**Listing 9.5** *(Continued)*

```
83  /**
84   * A text area whose append method makes a security check to see that no bad words are added.
85   */
86  class WordCheckTextArea extends JTextArea
87  {
88     public void append(String text)
89     {
90        WordCheckPermission p = new WordCheckPermission(text, "insert");
91        SecurityManager manager = System.getSecurityManager();
92        if (manager != null) manager.checkPermission(p);
93        super.append(text);
94     }
95  }
```

You have now seen how to configure Java platform security. Most commonly, you will simply tweak the standard permissions. For additional control, you can define custom permissions that can be configured in the same way as the standard permissions.

---

**java.security.Permission** 1.2

- `Permission(String name)`
  constructs a permission with the given target name.
- `String getName()`
  returns the target name of this permission.
- `boolean implies(Permission other)`
  checks whether this permission implies the other permission. That is the case if the other permission describes a more specific condition that is a consequence of the condition described by this permission.

---

## 9.4 User Authentication

The Java Authentication and Authorization Service (JAAS) has two components. The "authentication" part is concerned with ascertaining the identity of a program user. The "authorization" part maps users to permissions.

JAAS is a "pluggable" API that isolates Java applications from the particular technology used to implement authentication. It supports, among others, UNIX logins, NT logins, Kerberos authentication, and certificate-based authentication.

Once a user has been authenticated, you can attach a set of permissions. For example, here we grant Harry a particular set of permissions that other users do not have:

```
grant principal com.sun.security.auth.UnixPrincipal "harry"
{
    permission java.util.PropertyPermission "user.*", "read";
    . . .
};
```

The com.sun.security.auth.UnixPrincipal class checks the name of the UNIX user who is running this program. Its getName method returns the UNIX login name, and we check whether that name equals "harry".

Use a LoginContext to allow the security manager to check such a grant statement. Here is the basic outline of the login code:

```
try
{
    System.setSecurityManager(new SecurityManager());
    LoginContext context = new LoginContext("Login1"); // defined in JAAS configuration file
    context.login();
    // get the authenticated Subject
    Subject subject = context.getSubject();
    . . .
    context.logout();
}
catch (LoginException exception) // thrown if login was not successful
{
    exception.printStackTrace();
}
```

Now the subject denotes the individual who has been authenticated.

The string parameter "Login1" in the LoginContext constructor refers to an entry with the same name in the JAAS configuration file. Here is a sample configuration file:

```
Login1
{
    com.sun.security.auth.module.UnixLoginModule required;
    com.whizzbang.auth.module.RetinaScanModule sufficient;
};

Login2
{
    . . .
};
```

Of course, the JDK contains no biometric login modules. The following modules are supplied in the com.sun.security.auth.module package:

```
UnixLoginModule
NTLoginModule
Krb5LoginModule
JndiLoginModule
KeyStoreLoginModule
```

A login policy consists of a sequence of login modules, each of which is labeled `required`, `sufficient`, `requisite`, or `optional`. The meaning of these keywords is given by the following algorithm:

A login authenticates a *subject*, which can have multiple *principals*. A principal describes some property of the subject, such as the user name, group ID, or role. As you saw in the `grant` statement, principals govern permissions. The `com.sun.security.auth.UnixPrincipal` describes the UNIX login name, and the `UnixNumericGroupPrincipal` can test for membership in a UNIX group.

A `grant` clause can test for a principal, with the syntax

```
grant principalClass "principalName"
```

For example:

```
grant com.sun.security.auth.UnixPrincipal "harry"
```

When a user has logged in, you then run, in a separate access control context, the code that requires checking of principals. Use the static `doAs` or `doAsPrivileged` method to start a new `PrivilegedAction` whose `run` method executes the code.

Both of those methods execute an action by calling the `run` method of an object that implements the `PrivilegedAction` interface, using the permissions of the subject's principals:

```
PrivilegedAction<T> action = new
   PrivilegedAction()
   {
      public T run()
      {
         // run with permissions of subject principals
         . . .
      }
   };
T result = Subject.doAs(subject, action); // or Subject.doAsPrivileged(subject, action, null)
```

If the actions can throw checked exceptions, you need to implement the `PrivilegedExceptionAction` interface instead.

The difference between the `doAs` and `doAsPrivileged` methods is subtle. The `doAs` method starts out with the current access control context, whereas the `doAsPrivileged` method starts out with a new context. The latter method allows you to separate

the permissions for the login code and the "business logic." In our example
application, the login code has permissions

```
permission javax.security.auth.AuthPermission "createLoginContext.Login1";
permission javax.security.auth.AuthPermission "doAsPrivileged";
```

The authenticated user has a permission

```
permission java.util.PropertyPermission "user.*", "read";
```

If we had used doAs instead of doAsPrivileged, then the login code would have also
needed that permission!

The program in Listings 9.6 and 9.7 demonstrates how to restrict permissions to
certain users. The AuthTest program authenticates a user and runs a simple action
that retrieves a system property.

To make this example work, package the code for the login and the action into
two separate JAR files:

```
javac auth/*.java
jar cvf login.jar auth/AuthTest.class
jar cvf action.jar auth/SysPropAction.class
```

If you look at the policy file in Listing 9.8, you will see that the UNIX user with
the name harry has the permission to read all files. Change harry to your login name.
Then run the command

```
java -classpath login.jar:action.jar
    -Djava.security.policy=auth/AuthTest.policy
    -Djava.security.auth.login.config=auth/jaas.config
    auth.AuthTest
```

Listing 9.9 shows the login configuration.

On Windows, change UnixPrincipal to NTUserPrincipal in AuthTest.policy and UnixLoginModule
to NTLoginModule in jaas.config. When running the program, use a semicolon to separate
the JAR files:

```
java -classpath login.jar;action.jar . . .
```

The AuthTest program should now display the value of the user.home property.
However, if you log in with a different name, a security exception should be
thrown because you no longer have the required permission.

---

 **CAUTION:** Be careful to follow these instructions *exactly*. It is very easy to get
the setup wrong by making seemingly innocuous changes.

---

---

**Listing 9.6** auth/AuthTest.java

```java
1  package auth;
2
3  import java.security.*;
4  import javax.security.auth.*;
5  import javax.security.auth.login.*;
6
7  /**
8   * This program authenticates a user via a custom login and then executes the SysPropAction with
9   * the user's privileges.
10  * @version 1.01 2007-10-06
11  * @author Cay Horstmann
12  */
13 public class AuthTest
14 {
15    public static void main(final String[] args)
16    {
17       System.setSecurityManager(new SecurityManager());
18       try
19       {
20          LoginContext context = new LoginContext("Login1");
21          context.login();
22          System.out.println("Authentication successful.");
23          Subject subject = context.getSubject();
24          System.out.println("subject=" + subject);
25          PrivilegedAction<String> action = new SysPropAction("user.home");
26          String result = Subject.doAsPrivileged(subject, action, null);
27          System.out.println(result);
28          context.logout();
29       }
30       catch (LoginException e)
31       {
32          e.printStackTrace();
33       }
34    }
35 }
```

---

**Listing 9.7** auth/SysPropAction.java

```java
1  package auth;
2
3  import java.security.*;
4
5  /**
6     This action looks up a system property.
7   * @version 1.01 2007-10-06
8   * @author Cay Horstmann
9   */
```

```
10  public class SysPropAction implements PrivilegedAction<String>
11  {
12     private String propertyName;
13
14     /**
15        Constructs an action for looking up a given property.
16        @param propertyName the property name (such as "user.home")
17     */
18     public SysPropAction(String propertyName) { this.propertyName = propertyName; }
19
20     public String run()
21     {
22        return System.getProperty(propertyName);
23     }
24  }
```

**Listing 9.8** auth/AuthTest.policy

```
1  grant codebase "file:login.jar"
2  {
3     permission javax.security.auth.AuthPermission "createLoginContext.Login1";
4     permission javax.security.auth.AuthPermission "doAsPrivileged";
5  };
6
7  grant principal com.sun.security.auth.UnixPrincipal "harry"
8  {
9     permission java.util.PropertyPermission "user.*", "read";
10 };
```

**Listing 9.9** auth/jaas.config

```
1  Login1
2  {
3     com.sun.security.auth.module.UnixLoginModule required;
4  };
```

---

**javax.security.auth.login.LoginContext** `1.4`

- `LoginContext(String name)`
  constructs a login context. The `name` corresponds to the login descriptor in the JAAS configuration file.

- `void login()`
  establishes a login or throws `LoginException` if the login failed. Invokes the `login` method on the managers in the JAAS configuration file.

---

*(Continues)*

---

**javax.security.auth.login.LoginContext** 1.4 *(Continued)*

- void logout()
  logs out the subject. Invokes the logout method on the managers in the JAAS configuration file.
- Subject getSubject()
  returns the authenticated subject.

---

**javax.security.auth.Subject** 1.4

- Set<Principal> getPrincipals()
  gets the principals of this subject.
- static Object doAs(Subject subject, PrivilegedAction action)
- static Object doAs(Subject subject, PrivilegedExceptionAction action)
- static Object doAsPrivileged(Subject subject, PrivilegedAction action, AccessControlContext context)
- static Object doAsPrivileged(Subject subject, PrivilegedExceptionAction action, AccessControlContext context)
  executes the privileged action on behalf of the subject. Returns the return value of the run method. The doAsPrivileged methods execute the action in the given access control context. You can supply a "context snapshot" that you obtained earlier by calling the static method AccessController.getContext(), or you can supply null to execute the code in a new context.

---

**java.security.PrivilegedAction** 1.4

- Object run()
  You must define this method to execute the code that you want to have executed on behalf of a subject.

---

**java.security.PrivilegedExceptionAction** 1.4

- Object run()
  You must define this method to execute the code that you want to have executed on behalf of a subject. This method may throw any checked exceptions.

---

| *java.security.Principal*  1.1 |
|---|
| • String getName()<br>   returns the identifying name of this principal. |

## 9.4.1  JAAS Login Modules

In this section, we'll look at a JAAS example that shows you:

- How to implement your own login module
- How to implement *role-based* authentication

Supplying your own login module is useful if you store login information in a database. Even if you are happy with the default module, studying a custom module will help you understand the JAAS configuration file options.

Role-based authentication is essential if you manage a large number of users. It would be impractical to put the names of all legitimate users into a policy file. Instead, the login module should map users to roles such as "admin" or "HR," and the permissions should be based on these roles.

One job of the login module is to populate the principal set of the subject that is being authenticated. If a login module supports roles, it adds Principal objects that describe roles. The Java library does not provide a class for this purpose, so we wrote our own (see Listing 9.10). The class simply stores a description/value pair, such as role=admin. Its getName method returns that pair, so we can add role-based permissions into a policy file:

```
grant principal SimplePrincipal "role=admin" { . . . }
```

Our login module looks up users, passwords, and roles in a text file that contains lines like this:

```
harry|secret|admin
carl|guessme|HR
```

Of course, in a realistic login module, you would store this information in a database or directory.

You can find the code for the SimpleLoginModule in Listing 9.11. The checkLogin method checks whether the user name and password match a record in the password file. If so, we add two SimplePrincipal objects to the subject's principal set:

```
Set<Principal> principals = subject.getPrincipals();
principals.add(new SimplePrincipal("username", username));
principals.add(new SimplePrincipal("role", role));
```

The remainder of SimpleLoginModule is straightforward plumbing. The initialize method receives

- The Subject that is being authenticated
- A handler to retrieve login information
- A sharedState map that can be used for communication between login modules
- An options map that contains the name/value pairs that are set in the login configuration

For example, we configure our module as follows:

```
SimpleLoginModule required pwfile="password.txt";
```

The login module retrieves the pwfile settings from the options map.

The login module does not gather the user name and password; that is the job of a separate handler. This separation allows you to use the same login module without worrying whether the login information comes from a GUI dialog box, a console prompt, or a configuration file.

The handler is specified when you construct the LoginContext, for example:

```
LoginContext context = new LoginContext("Login1",
    new com.sun.security.auth.callback.DialogCallbackHandler());
```

The DialogCallbackHandler pops up a simple GUI dialog box to retrieve the user name and password. The com.sun.security.auth.callback.TextCallbackHandler class gets the information from the console.

However, in our application, we have our own GUI for collecting the user name and password (see Figure 9.10). We produce a simple handler that merely stores and returns that information (see Listing 9.12).

The handler has a single method, handle, that processes an array of Callback objects. A number of predefined classes, such as NameCallback and PasswordCallback, implement the Callback interface. You could also add your own class, such as RetinaScanCallback. The handler code is a bit unsightly because it needs to analyze the types of the callback objects:

```
public void handle(Callback[] callbacks)
{
    for (Callback callback : callbacks)
    {
        if (callback instanceof NameCallback) . . .
        else if (callback instanceof PasswordCallback) . . .
        else . . .
    }
}
```

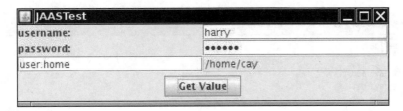

**Figure 9.10** A custom login module

The login module prepares an array of the callbacks that it needs for authentication:

```
NameCallback nameCall = new NameCallback("username: ");
PasswordCallback passCall = new PasswordCallback("password: ", false);
callbackHandler.handle(new Callback[] { nameCall, passCall });
```

Then it retrieves the information from the callbacks.

The program in Listing 9.13 displays a form for entering the login information and the name of a system property. If the user is authenticated, the property value is retrieved in a PrivilegedAction. As you can see from the policy file in Listing 9.14, only users with the admin role have permission to read properties.

As in the preceding section, you must separate the login and action code. Create two JAR files:

```
javac *.java
jar cvf login.jar JAAS*.class Simple*.class
jar cvf action.jar SysPropAction.class
```

Then run the program as

```
java -classpath login.jar:action.jar
    -Djava.security.policy=JAASTest.policy
    -Djava.security.auth.login.config=jaas.config
    JAASTest
```

Listing 9.15 shows the policy file.

**NOTE:** It is possible to support a more complex two-phase protocol, whereby a login is *committed* if all modules in the login configuration were successful. For more information, see the login module developer's guide at http://docs.oracle.com/javase/7/docs/technotes/guides/security/jaas/JAASLMDevGuide.html.

**Listing 9.10** jaas/SimplePrincipal.java

```
1  package jaas;
2
3  import java.security.*;
4  import java.util.*;
5
6  /**
7   * A principal with a named value (such as "role=HR" or "username=harry").
8   */
9  public class SimplePrincipal implements Principal
10 {
11    private String descr;
12    private String value;
13
14    /**
15     * Constructs a SimplePrincipal to hold a description and a value.
16     * @param descr the description
17     * @param value the associated value
18     */
19    public SimplePrincipal(String descr, String value)
20    {
21       this.descr = descr;
22       this.value = value;
23    }
24
25    /**
26     * Returns the role name of this principal.
27     * @return the role name
28     */
29    public String getName()
30    {
31       return descr + "=" + value;
32    }
33
34    public boolean equals(Object otherObject)
35    {
36       if (this == otherObject) return true;
37       if (otherObject == null) return false;
38       if (getClass() != otherObject.getClass()) return false;
39       SimplePrincipal other = (SimplePrincipal) otherObject;
40       return Objects.equals(getName(), other.getName());
41    }
42
43    public int hashCode()
44    {
45       return Objects.hashCode(getName());
46    }
47 }
```

**Listing 9.11**  jaas/SimpleLoginModule.java

```java
 1  package jaas;
 2
 3  import java.io.*;
 4  import java.nio.file.*;
 5  import java.security.*;
 6  import java.util.*;
 7  import javax.security.auth.*;
 8  import javax.security.auth.callback.*;
 9  import javax.security.auth.login.*;
10  import javax.security.auth.spi.*;
11
12  /**
13   * This login module authenticates users by reading usernames, passwords, and roles from a text
14   * file.
15   */
16  public class SimpleLoginModule implements LoginModule
17  {
18     private Subject subject;
19     private CallbackHandler callbackHandler;
20     private Map<String, ?> options;
21
22     public void initialize(Subject subject, CallbackHandler callbackHandler,
23           Map<String, ?> sharedState, Map<String, ?> options)
24     {
25        this.subject = subject;
26        this.callbackHandler = callbackHandler;
27        this.options = options;
28     }
29
30     public boolean login() throws LoginException
31     {
32        if (callbackHandler == null) throw new LoginException("no handler");
33
34        NameCallback nameCall = new NameCallback("username: ");
35        PasswordCallback passCall = new PasswordCallback("password: ", false);
36        try
37        {
38           callbackHandler.handle(new Callback[] { nameCall, passCall });
39        }
40        catch (UnsupportedCallbackException e)
41        {
42           LoginException e2 = new LoginException("Unsupported callback");
43           e2.initCause(e);
44           throw e2;
45        }
```

*(Continues)*

**Listing 9.11** *(Continued)*

```
46        catch (IOException e)
47        {
48           LoginException e2 = new LoginException("I/O exception in callback");
49           e2.initCause(e);
50           throw e2;
51        }
52
53        try
54        {
55           return checkLogin(nameCall.getName(), passCall.getPassword());
56        }
57        catch (IOException ex)
58        {
59           LoginException ex2 = new LoginException();
60           ex2.initCause(ex);
61           throw ex2;
62        }
63     }
64
65     /**
66      * Checks whether the authentication information is valid. If it is, the subject acquires
67      * principals for the user name and role.
68      * @param username the user name
69      * @param password a character array containing the password
70      * @return true if the authentication information is valid
71      */
72     private boolean checkLogin(String username, char[] password) throws LoginException, IOException
73     {
74        try (Scanner in = new Scanner(Paths.get("" + options.get("pwfile"))))
75        {
76           while (in.hasNextLine())
77           {
78              String[] inputs = in.nextLine().split("\\|");
79              if (inputs[0].equals(username) && Arrays.equals(inputs[1].toCharArray(), password))
80              {
81                 String role = inputs[2];
82                 Set<Principal> principals = subject.getPrincipals();
83                 principals.add(new SimplePrincipal("username", username));
84                 principals.add(new SimplePrincipal("role", role));
85                 return true;
86              }
87           }
88           return false;
89        }
90     }
```

```
 91    public boolean logout()
 92    {
 93       return true;
 94    }
 95
 96    public boolean abort()
 97    {
 98       return true;
 99    }
100
101    public boolean commit()
102    {
103       return true;
104    }
105 }
```

---

**Listing 9.12** jaas/SimpleCallbackHandler.java

```
 1 package jaas;
 2
 3 import javax.security.auth.callback.*;
 4
 5 /**
 6  * This simple callback handler presents the given user name and password.
 7  */
 8 public class SimpleCallbackHandler implements CallbackHandler
 9 {
10    private String username;
11    private char[] password;
12
13    /**
14     * Constructs the callback handler.
15     * @param username the user name
16     * @param password a character array containing the password
17     */
18    public SimpleCallbackHandler(String username, char[] password)
19    {
20       this.username = username;
21       this.password = password;
22    }
23
24    public void handle(Callback[] callbacks)
25    {
26       for (Callback callback : callbacks)
27       {
```

*(Continues)*

**Listing 9.12** *(Continued)*

```
28          if (callback instanceof NameCallback)
29          {
30             ((NameCallback) callback).setName(username);
31          }
32          else if (callback instanceof PasswordCallback)
33          {
34             ((PasswordCallback) callback).setPassword(password);
35          }
36       }
37    }
38 }
```

**Listing 9.13** jaas/JAASTest.java

```
1  package jaas;
2
3  import java.awt.*;
4  import javax.swing.*;
5
6  /**
7   * This program authenticates a user via a custom login and then looks up a system property with
8   * the user's privileges.
9   * @version 1.01 2012-06-10
10  * @author Cay Horstmann
11  */
12 public class JAASTest
13 {
14    public static void main(final String[] args)
15    {
16       System.setSecurityManager(new SecurityManager());
17       EventQueue.invokeLater(new Runnable()
18          {
19             public void run()
20             {
21                JFrame frame = new JAASFrame();
22                frame.setDefaultCloseOperation(JFrame.EXIT_ON_CLOSE);
23                frame.setTitle("JAASTest");
24                frame.setVisible(true);
25             }
26          });
27    }
28 }
```

**Listing 9.14**  jaas/JAASTest.policy

```
1  grant codebase "file:login.jar"
2  {
3      permission java.awt.AWTPermission "showWindowWithoutWarningBanner";
4      permission java.awt.AWTPermission "accessEventQueue";
5      permission javax.security.auth.AuthPermission "createLoginContext.Login1";
6      permission javax.security.auth.AuthPermission "doAsPrivileged";
7      permission javax.security.auth.AuthPermission "modifyPrincipals";
8      permission java.io.FilePermission "jaas/password.txt", "read";
9  };
10
11 grant principal jaas.SimplePrincipal "role=admin"
12 {
13     permission java.util.PropertyPermission "*", "read";
14 };
```

**Listing 9.15**  jaas/jaas.config

```
1  Login1
2  {
3      jaas.SimpleLoginModule required pwfile="jaas/password.txt" debug=true;
4  };
```

---

**javax.security.auth.callback.CallbackHandler**  1.4

- void handle(Callback[] callbacks)
  handles the given callbacks, interacting with the user if desired, and stores the security information in the callback objects.

---

**javax.security.auth.callback.NameCallback**  1.4

- NameCallback(String prompt)
- NameCallback(String prompt, String defaultName)
  constructs a NameCallback with the given prompt and default name.
- String getName()
- void setName(String name)
  gets or sets the name gathered by this callback.
- String getPrompt()
  gets the prompt to use when querying this name.
- String getDefaultName()
  gets the default name to use when querying this name.

---

**javax.security.auth.callback.PasswordCallback** 1.4

- PasswordCallback(String prompt, boolean echoOn)
  constructs a PasswordCallback with the given prompt and echo flag.
- char[] getPassword()
- void setPassword(char[] password)
  gets or sets the password gathered by this callback.
- String getPrompt()
  gets the prompt to use when querying this password.
- boolean isEchoOn()
  gets the echo flag to use when querying this password.

---

**javax.security.auth.spi.LoginModule** 1.4

- void initialize(Subject subject, CallbackHandler handler, Map<String,?> sharedState,
  Map<String,?> options)
  initializes this LoginModule for authenticating the given subject. During login processing, uses the given handler to gather login information. Use the sharedState map
  for communicating with other login modules. The options map contains the
  name/value pairs specified in the login configuration for this module instance.
- boolean login()
  carries out the authentication process and populates the subject's principals.
  Returns true if the login was successful.
- boolean commit()
  is called after all login modules were successful, for login scenarios that require a
  two-phase commit. Returns true if the operation was successful.
- boolean abort()
  is called if the failure of another login module caused the login process to abort.
  Returns true if the operation was successful.
- boolean logout()
  logs out this subject. Returns true if the operation was successful.

---

## 9.5 Digital Signatures

As we said earlier, applets were what started the Java craze. In practice, people
discovered that although they could write animated applets (like the famous
"nervous text" applet), applets could not do a whole lot of useful stuff in the
JDK 1.0 security model. For example, since applets under JDK 1.0 were so closely

supervised, they couldn't do much good on a corporate intranet, even though relatively little risk attaches to executing an applet from your company's secure intranet. It quickly became clear to Sun that for applets to become truly useful, it was important for users to be able to assign *different* levels of security, depending on where the applet originated. If an applet comes from a trusted supplier and has not been tampered with, the user of that applet can decide whether to give the applet more privileges.

To give more trust to an applet, we need to know two things:

- Where did the applet come from?
- Was the code corrupted in transit?

In the past 50 years, mathematicians and computer scientists have developed sophisticated algorithms for ensuring the integrity of data and for electronic signatures. The `java.security` package contains implementations of many of these algorithms. Fortunately, you don't need to understand the underlying mathematics to use the algorithms in the `java.security` package. In the next sections, we'll show you how message digests can detect changes in data files and how digital signatures can prove the identity of the signer.

## 9.5.1 Message Digests

A message digest is a digital fingerprint of a block of data. For example, the so-called SHA-1 (Secure Hash Algorithm #1) condenses any data block, no matter how long, into a sequence of 160 bits (20 bytes). As with real fingerprints, one hopes that no two messages have the same SHA-1 fingerprint. Of course, that cannot be true—there are only $2^{160}$ SHA-1 fingerprints, so there must be some messages with the same fingerprint. But $2^{160}$ is so large that the probability of duplication occurring is negligible. How negligible? According to James Walsh in *True Odds: How Risks Affect Your Everyday Life* (Merritt Publishing, 1996), the chance that you will die from being struck by lightning is about one in 30,000. Now, think of nine other people—for example, your nine least favorite managers or professors. The chance that you and *all of them* will die from lightning strikes is higher than that of a forged message having the same SHA-1 fingerprint as the original. (Of course, more than ten people, none of whom you are likely to know, will die from lightning strikes. However, we are talking about the far slimmer chance that *your particular choice* of people will be wiped out.)

A message digest has two essential properties:

- If one bit or several bits of the data are changed, the message digest also changes.

- A forger who is in possession of a given message cannot construct a fake message that has the same message digest as the original.

The second property is again a matter of probabilities, of course. Consider the following message by the billionaire father:

*"Upon my death, my property shall be divided equally among my children; however, my son George shall receive nothing."*

That message (with a final newline) has an SHA-1 fingerprint of

```
12 5F 09 03 E7 31 30 19 2E A6 E7 E4 90 43 84 B4 38 99 8F 67
```

The distrustful father has deposited the message with one attorney and the fingerprint with another. Now, suppose George bribes the lawyer holding the message. He wants to change the message so that Bill gets nothing. Of course, that changes the fingerprint to a completely different bit pattern:

```
7D F6 AB 08 EB 40 EC CD AB 74 ED E9 86 F9 ED 99 D1 45 B1 57
```

Can George find some other wording that matches the fingerprint? If he had been the proud owner of a billion computers from the time the Earth was formed, each computing a million messages a second, he would not yet have found a message he could substitute.

A number of algorithms have been designed to compute such message digests. The two best-known are SHA-1, the secure hash algorithm developed by the National Institute of Standards and Technology, and MD5, an algorithm invented by Ronald Rivest of MIT. Both algorithms scramble the bits of a message in ingenious ways. For details about these algorithms, see, for example, *Cryptography and Network Security, Fifth Edition*, by William Stallings (Prentice Hall, 2011). Note that subtle regularities have been discovered in both algorithms. At this point, most cryptographers recommend avoiding MD5 and using SHA-1 until a stronger alternative becomes available. (See www.rsa.com/rsalabs/node.asp?id=2834 for more information.)

The Java programming language implements both SHA-1 and MD5. The MessageDigest class is a *factory* for creating objects that encapsulate the fingerprinting algorithms. It has a static method, called getInstance, that returns an object of a class that extends the MessageDigest class. This means the MessageDigest class serves double duty:

- As a factory class
- As the superclass for all message digest algorithms

For example, here is how you obtain an object that can compute SHA fingerprints:

```
MessageDigest alg = MessageDigest.getInstance("SHA-1");
```

(To get an object that can compute MD5, use the string "MD5" as the argument to getInstance.)

After you have obtained a MessageDigest object, feed it all the bytes in the message by repeatedly calling the update method. For example, the following code passes all bytes in a file to the alg object just created to do the fingerprinting:

```
InputStream in = . . .
int ch;
while ((ch = in.read()) != -1)
   alg.update((byte) ch);
```

Alternatively, if you have the bytes in an array, you can update the entire array at once:

```
byte[] bytes = . . .;
alg.update(bytes);
```

When you are done, call the digest method. This method pads the input as required by the fingerprinting algorithm, does the computation, and returns the digest as an array of bytes.

```
byte[] hash = alg.digest();
```

The program in Listing 9.16 computes a message digest, using either SHA-1 or MD5. Run it as

```
java hash.Digest hash/input.txt
```

or

```
java hash.Digest hash/input.txt MD5
```

**Listing 9.16**  hash/Digest.java

```
1  package hash;
2
3  import java.io.*;
4  import java.nio.file.*;
5  import java.security.*;
6
7  /**
8   * This program computes the message digest of a file.
9   * @version 1.20 2012-06-16
10  * @author Cay Horstmann
11  */
12 public class Digest
13 {
```

*(Continues)*

---

**Listing 9.16** *(Continued)*

```
14    /**
15     * @param args args[0] is the filename, args[1] is optionally the algorithm (SHA-1 or MD5)
16     */
17    public static void main(String[] args) throws IOException, GeneralSecurityException
18    {
19        String algname = args.length >= 2 ? args[1] : "SHA-1";
20        MessageDigest alg = MessageDigest.getInstance(algname);
21        byte[] input = Files.readAllBytes(Paths.get(args[0]));
22        byte[] hash = alg.digest(input);
23        String d = "";
24        for (int i = 0; i < hash.length; i++)
25        {
26            int v = hash[i] & 0xFF;
27            if (v < 16) d += "0";
28            d += Integer.toString(v, 16).toUpperCase() + " ";
29        }
30        System.out.println(d);
31    }
32 }
```

---

**java.security.MessageDigest** 1.1

- static MessageDigest getInstance(String algorithmName)
  returns a MessageDigest object that implements the specified algorithm. Throws NoSuchAlgorithmException if the algorithm is not provided.

- void update(byte input)
- void update(byte[] input)
- void update(byte[] input, int offset, int len)
  updates the digest, using the specified bytes.

- byte[] digest()
  completes the hash computation, returns the computed digest, and resets the algorithm object.

- void reset()
  resets the digest.

## 9.5.2 Message Signing

In the last section, you saw how to compute a message digest—a fingerprint for the original message. If the message is altered, the fingerprint of the altered message will not match the fingerprint of the original. If the message and its fingerprint are delivered separately, the recipient can check whether the message has been tampered with. However, if both the message and the fingerprint were intercepted, it is an easy matter to modify the message and then recompute the fingerprint. After all, the message digest algorithms are publicly known, and they don't require secret keys. In that case, the recipient of the forged message and the recomputed fingerprint would never know that the message has been altered. Digital signatures solve this problem.

To help you understand how digital signatures work, we'll explain a few concepts from the field called *public key cryptography*. Public key cryptography is based on the notion of a *public* key and *private* key. The idea is that you tell everyone in the world your public key. However, only you hold the private key, and it is important that you safeguard it and don't release it to anyone else. The keys are matched by mathematical relationships, though the exact nature of these relationships is not important to us. (If you are interested, look it up in *The Handbook of Applied Cryptography* at www.cacr.math.uwaterloo.ca/hac.)

The keys are quite long and complex. For example, here is a matching pair of public and private Digital Signature Algorithm (DSA) keys.

Public key:

```
p: fca682ce8e12caba26efccf7110e526db078b05edecbcd1eb4a208f3ae1617ae01f35b91a47e6df63413c5e12ed089
9bcd132acd50d99151bdc43ee737592e17

q: 962eddcc369cba8ebb260ee6b6a126d9346e38c5

g: 678471b27a9cf44ee91a49c5147db1a9aaf244f05a434d6486931d2d14271b9e35030b71fd73da179069b32e293563
0e1c2062354d0da20a6c416e50be794ca4

y: c0b6e67b4ac098eb1a32c5f8c4c1f0e7e6fb9d832532e27d0bdab9ca2d2a8123ce5a8018b8161a760480fadd040b92
7281ddb22cb9bc4df596d7de4d1b977d50
```

Private key:

```
p: fca682ce8e12caba26efccf7110e526db078b05edecbcd1eb4a208f3ae1617ae01f35b91a47e6df63413c5e12ed089
9bcd132acd50d99151bdc43ee737592e17

q: 962eddcc369cba8ebb260ee6b6a126d9346e38c5

g: 678471b27a9cf44ee91a49c5147db1a9aaf244f05a434d6486931d2d14271b9e35030b71fd73da179069b32e293563
0e1c2062354d0da20a6c416e50be794ca4

x: 146c09f881656cc6c51f27ea6c3a91b85ed1d70a
```

It is believed to be practically impossible to compute one key from the other. That is, even though everyone knows your public key, they can't compute your private key in your lifetime, no matter how many computing resources they have available.

It might seem difficult to believe that you can't compute the private key from the public key, but nobody has ever found an algorithm to do this for the encryption algorithms in common use today. If the keys are sufficiently long, brute force—simply trying all possible keys—would require more computers than can be built from all the atoms in the solar system, crunching away for thousands of years. Of course it is possible that someone could come up with algorithms for computing keys that are much more clever than brute force. For example, the RSA algorithm (the encryption algorithm invented by Rivest, Shamir, and Adleman) depends on the difficulty of factoring large numbers. For the last

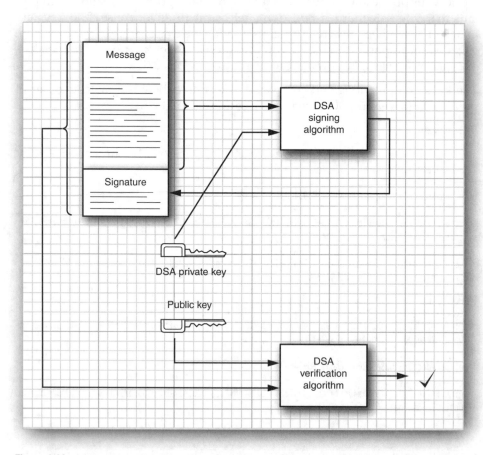

**Figure 9.11** Public key signature exchange with DSA

20 years, many of the best mathematicians have tried to come up with good factoring algorithms, but so far with no success. For that reason, most cryptographers believe that keys with a "modulus" of 2,000 bits or more are currently completely safe from any attack. DSA is believed to be similarly secure.

Figure 9.11 illustrates how the process works in practice.

Suppose Alice wants to send Bob a message, and Bob wants to know this message came from Alice and not an impostor. Alice writes the message and *signs* the message digest with her private key. Bob gets a copy of her public key. Bob then applies the public key to *verify* the signature. If the verification passes, Bob can be assured of two facts:

- The original message has not been altered.
- The message was signed by Alice, the holder of the private key that matches the public key that Bob used for verification.

You can see why the security of private keys is so important. If someone steals Alice's private key, or if a government can require her to turn it over, then she is in trouble. The thief or a government agent can now impersonate her by sending messages, such as money transfer instructions, that others will believe came from Alice.

## 9.5.3 Verifying a Signature

The JDK comes with the `keytool` program, which is a command-line tool to generate and manage a set of certificates. We expect that ultimately the functionality of this tool will be embedded in other, more user-friendly programs. But right now, we'll use `keytool` to show how Alice can sign a document and send it to Bob, and how Bob can verify that the document really was signed by Alice and not an imposter.

The `keytool` program manages *keystores*, databases of certificates and private/public key pairs. Each entry in the keystore has an *alias*. Here is how Alice creates a keystore, `alice.certs`, and generates a key pair with alias `alice`:

```
keytool -genkeypair -keystore alice.certs -alias alice
```

When creating or opening a keystore, you are prompted for a keystore password. For this example, just use `secret`. If you were to use the `keytool`-generated keystore for any serious purpose, you would need to choose a good password and safeguard this file.

When generating a key, you are prompted for the following information:

```
Enter keystore password: secret
Reenter new password: secret
What is your first and last name?
  [Unknown]: Alice Lee
What is the name of your organizational unit?
  [Unknown]: Engineering Department
What is the name of your organization?
  [Unknown]: ACME Software
What is the name of your City or Locality?
  [Unknown]: San Francisco
What is the name of your State or Province?
  [Unknown]: CA
What is the two-letter country code for this unit?
  [Unknown]: US
Is <CN=Alice Lee, OU=Engineering Department, O=ACME Software, L=San Francisco, ST=CA, C=US> cor-
rect?
  [no]: yes
```

The keytool uses names in the X.500 format, whose components are Common Name
(CN), Organizational Unit (OU), Organization (O), Location (L), State (ST), and
Country (C), to identify key owners and certificate issuers.

Finally, specify a key password, or press Enter to use the keystore password as
the key password.

Suppose Alice wants to give her public key to Bob. She needs to export a
certificate file:

```
keytool -exportcert -keystore alice.certs -alias alice -file alice.cer
```

Now Alice can send the certificate to Bob. When Bob receives the certificate, he
can print it:

```
keytool -printcert -file alice.cer
```

The printout looks like this:

```
Owner: CN=Alice Lee, OU=Engineering Department, O=ACME Software, L=San Francisco, ST=CA, C=US
Issuer: CN=Alice Lee, OU=Engineering Department, O=ACME Software, L=San Francisco, ST=CA, C=US
Serial number: 470835ce
Valid from: Sat Oct 06 18:26:38 PDT 2007 until: Fri Jan 04 17:26:38 PST 2008
Certificate fingerprints:
     MD5:  BC:18:15:27:85:69:48:B1:5A:C3:0B:1C:C6:11:B7:81
     SHA1: 31:0A:A0:B8:C2:8B:3B:B6:85:7C:EF:C0:57:E5:94:95:61:47:6D:34
     Signature algorithm name: SHA1withDSA
     Version: 3
```

If Bob wants to check that he got the right certificate, he can call Alice and verify
the certificate fingerprint over the phone.

**NOTE:** Some certificate issuers publish certificate fingerprints on their web sites. For example, to check the VeriSign certificate in the keystore *jre*/lib/security/cacerts directory, use the -list option:

```
keytool -list -v -keystore jre/lib/security/cacerts
```

The password for this keystore is `changeit`. One of the certificates in this keystore is

```
Owner: OU=VeriSign Trust Network, OU="(c) 1998 VeriSign, Inc. - For authorized use only",
OU=Class 1 Public Primary Certification Authority - G2, O="VeriSign, Inc.", C=US
Issuer: OU=VeriSign Trust Network, OU="(c) 1998 VeriSign, Inc. - For authorized
use only", OU=Class 1 Public Primary Certification Authority - G2, O="VeriSign, Inc.",
C=US
Serial number: 4cc7eaaa983e71d39310f83d3a899192
Valid from: Sun May 17 17:00:00 PDT 1998 until: Tue Aug 01 16:59:59 PDT 2028
Certificate fingerprints:
        MD5:  DB:23:3D:F9:69:FA:4B:B9:95:80:44:73:5E:7D:41:83
        SHA1: 27:3E:E1:24:57:FD:C4:F9:0C:55:E8:2B:56:16:7F:62:F5:32:E5:47
```

You can check that your certificate is valid by visiting the web site www.verisign.com/repository/root.html.

Once Bob trusts the certificate, he can import it into his keystore.

```
keytool -importcert -keystore bob.certs -alias alice -file alice.cer
```

**CAUTION:** Never import into a keystore a certificate that you don't fully trust. Once a certificate is added to the keystore, any program that uses the keystore assumes that the certificate can be used to verify signatures.

Now Alice can start sending signed documents to Bob. The jarsigner tool signs and verifies JAR files. Alice simply adds the document to be signed into a JAR file.

```
jar cvf document.jar document.txt
```

She then uses the jarsigner tool to add the signature to the file. She needs to specify the keystore, the JAR file, and the alias of the key to use.

```
jarsigner -keystore alice.certs document.jar alice
```

When Bob receives the file, he uses the -verify option of the jarsigner program.

```
jarsigner -verify -keystore bob.certs document.jar
```

Bob does not need to specify the key alias. The jarsigner program finds the X.500 name of the key owner in the digital signature and looks for a matching certificate in the keystore.

If the JAR file is not corrupted and the signature matches, the jarsigner program prints

```
jar verified.
```

Otherwise, the program displays an error message.

## 9.5.4 The Authentication Problem

Suppose you get a message from your friend Alice, signed with her private key, using the method we just showed you. You might already have her public key, or you can easily get it by asking her for a copy or by getting it from her web page. Then, you can verify that the message was in fact authored by Alice and has not been tampered with. Now, suppose you get a message from a stranger who claims to represent a famous software company, urging you to run a program attached to the message. The stranger even sends you a copy of his public key so you can verify that he authored the message. You check that the signature is valid. This proves that the message was signed with the matching private key and has not been corrupted.

Be careful: *You still have no idea who wrote the message.* Anyone could have generated a pair of public and private keys, signed the message with the private key, and sent the signed message and the public key to you. The problem of determining the identity of the sender is called the *authentication problem.*

The usual way to solve the authentication problem is simple. Suppose the stranger and you have a common acquaintance you both trust. Suppose the stranger meets your acquaintance in person and hands over a disk with the public key. Your acquaintance later meets you, assures you that he met the stranger and that the stranger indeed works for the famous software company, and then gives you the disk (see Figure 9.12). That way, your acquaintance vouches for the authenticity of the stranger.

In fact, your acquaintance does not actually need to meet you. Instead, he can use his private key to sign the stranger's public key file (see Figure 9.13).

When you get the public key file, you verify the signature of your friend, and because you trust him, you are confident that he did check the stranger's credentials before applying his signature.

However, you might not have a common acquaintance. Some trust models assume that there is always a "chain of trust"—a chain of mutual acquaintances—so that you trust every member of that chain. In practice, of course, that isn't always true. You might trust your friend, Alice, and you know that Alice trusts Bob, but you don't know Bob and aren't sure that you trust him. Other trust models

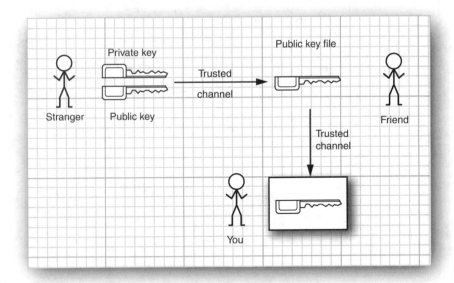

**Figure 9.12** Authentication through a trusted intermediary

assume that there is a benevolent big brother—a company in which we all trust. The best known of such companies is VeriSign, Inc. (www.verisign.com).

You will often encounter digital signatures signed by one or more entities who will vouch for the authenticity, and you will need to evaluate to what degree you trust the authenticators. You might place a great deal of trust in VeriSign, perhaps because you saw their logo on many web pages or because you heard that they require multiple people with black attaché cases to come together into a secure chamber whenever new master keys are to be minted.

However, you should have realistic expectations about what is actually being authenticated. The CEO of VeriSign does not personally meet every individual or company representative when authenticating a public key. You can get a "class 1" ID simply by filling out a web form and paying a small fee. The key is mailed to the e-mail address included in the certificate. Thus, you can be reasonably assured that the e-mail address is genuine, but the requestor could have filled in *any* name and organization. There are more stringent classes of IDs. For example, with a "class 3" ID, VeriSign will require an individual requestor to appear before a notary public, and it will check the financial rating of a corporate requestor. Other authenticators will have different procedures. Thus, when you receive an authenticated message, it is important that you understand what, in fact, is being authenticated.

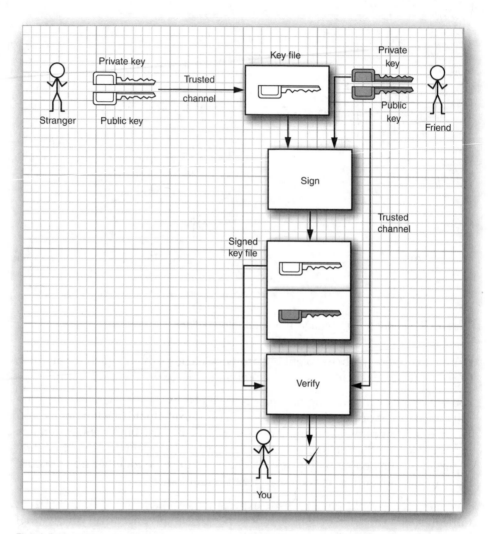

**Figure 9.13** Authentication through a trusted intermediary's signature

## 9.5.5 Certificate Signing

In Section 9.5.3, "Verifying a Signature," on p. 865 you saw how Alice used a self-signed certificate to distribute a public key to Bob. However, Bob needed to ensure that the certificate was valid by verifying the fingerprint with Alice.

Suppose Alice wants to send her colleague Cindy a signed message, but Cindy doesn't want to bother with verifying lots of signature fingerprints. Now suppose there is an entity that Cindy trusts to verify signatures. In this example, Cindy trusts the Information Resources Department at ACME Software.

That department operates a *certificate authority* (CA). Everyone at ACME has the CA's public key in their keystore, installed by a system administrator who carefully checked the key fingerprint. The CA signs the keys of ACME employees. When they install each other's keys, the keystore will trust them implicitly because they are signed by a trusted key.

Here is how you can simulate this process. Create a keystore acmesoft.certs. Generate a key pair and export the public key:

```
keytool -genkeypair -keystore acmesoft.certs -alias acmeroot
keytool -exportcert -keystore acmesoft.certs -alias acmeroot -file acmeroot.cer
```

The public key is exported into a "self-signed" certificate. Then add it to every employee's keystore.

```
keytool -importcert -keystore cindy.certs -alias acmeroot -file acmeroot.cer
```

For Alice to send messages to Cindy and to everyone else at ACME Software, she needs to bring her certificate to the Information Resources Department and have it signed. Unfortunately, this functionality is missing in the keytool program. In the book's companion code, we supply a CertificateSigner class to fill the gap. An authorized staff member at ACME Software would verify Alice's identity and generate a signed certificate as follows:

```
java CertificateSigner -keystore acmesoft.certs -alias acmeroot
    -infile alice.cer -outfile alice_signedby_acmeroot.cer
```

The certificate signer program must have access to the ACME Software keystore, and the staff member must know the keystore password. Clearly, this is a sensitive operation.

Alice gives the file alice_signedby_acmeroot.cer file to Cindy and to anyone else in ACME Software. Alternatively, ACME Software can simply store the file in a company directory. Remember, this file contains Alice's public key and an assertion by ACME Software that this key really belongs to Alice.

Now Cindy imports the signed certificate into her keystore:

```
keytool -importcert -keystore cindy.certs -alias alice -file alice_signedby_acmeroot.cer
```

The keystore verifies that the key was signed by a trusted root key that is already present in the keystore. Cindy is *not* asked to verify the certificate fingerprint.

Once Cindy has added the root certificate and the certificates of the people who regularly send her documents, she never has to worry about the keystore again.

## 9.5.6 Certificate Requests

In the preceding section, we simulated a CA with a keystore and the `CertificateSigner` tool. However, most CAs run more sophisticated software to manage certificates, and they use slightly different formats for certificates. This section shows the added steps required to interact with those software packages.

We will use the OpenSSL software package as an example. The software is preinstalled on many Linux systems and Mac OS X, and a Cygwin port is also available. Alternatively, you can download the software at www.openssl.org.

To create a CA, run the `CA` script. The exact location depends on your operating system. On Ubuntu, run

```
/usr/lib/ssl/misc/CA.pl -newca
```

This script creates a subdirectory called `demoCA` in the current directory. The directory contains a root key pair and storage for certificates and certificate revocation lists.

You will want to import the public key into the Java keystores of all employees, but it is in the Privacy Enhanced Mail (PEM) format, not the DER format that the keystore accepts easily. Copy the file `demoCA/cacert.pem` to a file `acmeroot.pem` and open that file in a text editor. Remove everything before the line

```
-----BEGIN CERTIFICATE-----
```

and after the line

```
-----END CERTIFICATE-----
```

Now you can import `acmeroot.pem` into each keystore in the usual way:

```
keytool -importcert -keystore cindy.certs -alias alice -file acmeroot.pem
```

It seems quite incredible that the keytool cannot carry out this editing operation itself.

To sign Alice's public key, you start by generating a *certificate request* that contains the certificate in the PEM format:

```
keytool -certreq -keystore alice.store -alias alice -file alice.pem
```

To sign the certificate, run

```
openssl ca -in alice.pem -out alice_signedby_acmeroot.pem
```

As before, cut out everything outside the `BEGIN CERTIFICATE`/`END CERTIFICATE` markers from `alice_signedby_acmeroot.pem`. Then import it into the keystore:

```
keytool -importcert -keystore cindy.certs -alias alice -file alice_signedby_acmeroot.pem
```

You can use the same steps to have a certificate signed by a public certificate authority such as VeriSign.

## 9.6 Code Signing

One of the most important uses of authentication technology is signing executable programs. If you download a program, you are naturally concerned about the damage it can do. For example, the program could have been infected by a virus. If you know where the code comes from *and* that it has not been tampered with since it left its origin, your comfort level will be a lot higher than without this knowledge. In fact, if the program was also written in Java, you can use this information to make a rational decision about what privileges you will allow that program to have. You might want it to run just in a sandbox as a regular applet, or you might want to grant it a different set of rights and restrictions. For example, if you download a word processing program, you might want to grant it access to your printer and to files in a certain subdirectory. However, you might not want to give it the right to make network connections so it wouldn't try to send your files to a third party without your knowledge.

You now know how to implement this sophisticated scheme.

### 9.6.1 JAR File Signing

In this section, we'll show you how to sign applets and Web Start applications for use with the Java Plug-in software. There are two scenarios:

- Delivery in an intranet
- Delivery over the public Internet

In the first scenario, a system administrator installs policy files and certificates on local machines. Whenever the Java Plug-in tool loads signed code, it consults the policy file for the permissions and the keystore for signatures. Installing the policies and certificates is straightforward and can be done once per desktop. End users can then run signed corporate code outside the sandbox. Whenever a new program is created or an existing one is updated, it must be signed and deployed on the web server. However, no desktops need to be touched as the programs evolve. We think this is a reasonable scenario that can be an attractive alternative to deploying corporate applications on every desktop.

In the second scenario, software vendors obtain certificates that are signed by CAs such as VeriSign. When an end user visits a web site that contains a signed applet, a pop-up dialog box identifies the software vendor and gives the end user two choices: to run the applet with full privileges or to confine it to the sandbox.

We'll discuss this less desirable scenario in detail in Section 9.6.2, "Software Developer Certificates," on p. 878.

For the remainder of this section, we will describe how you can build policy files that grant specific permissions to code from known sources. Building and deploying these policy files is not for casual end users. However, system administrators can carry out these tasks in preparation for distributing intranet programs.

Suppose ACME Software wants its employees to run certain programs that require local file access, and it wants to deploy these programs through a browser as applets or Web Start applications. Since these programs cannot run inside the sandbox, ACME Software needs to install policy files on the employee machines.

As you saw earlier in this chapter, ACME could identify the programs by their code base. But that means ACME would need to update the policy files each time the programs are moved to a different web server. Instead, ACME decides to *sign* the JAR files that contain the program code.

First, ACME generates a root certificate:

```
keytool -genkeypair -keystore acmesoft.certs -alias acmeroot
```

Of course, the keystore containing the private root key must be kept in a safe place. Therefore, we create a second keystore client.certs for the public certificates and add the public acmeroot certificate into it.

```
keytool -exportcert -keystore acmesoft.certs -alias acmeroot -file acmeroot.cer
keytool -importcert -keystore client.certs -alias acmeroot -file acmeroot.cer
```

To make a signed JAR file, programmers add their class files to a JAR file in the usual way. For example,

```
javac FileReadApplet.java
jar cvf FileReadApplet.jar *.class
```

Then a trusted person at ACME runs the jarsigner tool, specifying the JAR file and the alias of the private key:

```
jarsigner -keystore acmesoft.certs FileReadApplet.jar acmeroot
```

The signed applet is now ready to be deployed on a web server.

Next, let us turn to the client machine configuration. A policy file must be distributed to each client machine.

To reference a keystore, a policy file starts with the line

```
keystore "keystoreURL", "keystoreType";
```

The URL can be absolute or relative. Relative URLs are relative to the location of the policy file. The type is JKS if the keystore was generated by keytool. For example,

```
keystore "client.certs", "JKS";
```

Then `grant` clauses can have suffixes `signedBy` *"alias"*, such as this one:

```
grant signedBy "acmeroot"
{
   . . .
};
```

Any signed code that can be verified with the public key associated with the alias is now granted the permissions inside the `grant` clause.

You can try out the code signing process with the applet in Listing 9.17. The applet tries to read from a local file. The default security policy only lets the applet read files from its code base and any subdirectories. Use `appletviewer` to run the applet and verify that you can view files from the code base directory, but not from other directories.

We provide a policy file `applet.policy` with the contents:

```
keystore "client.certs", "JKS";
grant signedBy "acmeroot"
{
   permission java.lang.RuntimePermission "usePolicy";
   permission java.io.FilePermission "/etc/*", "read";
};
```

The `usePolicy` permission overrides the default "all or nothing" permission for signed applets. Here, we say that any applets signed by `acmeroot` are allowed to read files in the /etc directory. (Windows users: Substitute another directory such as `C:\Windows`.)

Tell the applet viewer to use the policy file:

```
appletviewer -J-Djava.security.policy=applet.policy FileReadApplet.html
```

Now the applet can read files from the /etc directory, thus demonstrating that the signing mechanism works.

 **TIP:** If you have trouble getting this step to work, add the option `-J-Djava.security.debug=policy`, and you will be rewarded with detailed messages that trace how the program establishes the security policy.

As a final test, you can run your applet inside the browser (see Figure 9.14). You need to copy the permission file and the keystore inside the Java deployment directory. If you run UNIX or Linux, that directory is the .java/deployment sub-directory of your home directory. In Windows Vista or Windows 7, it is the

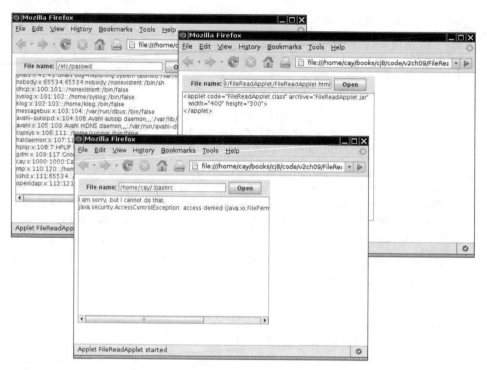

**Figure 9.14** A signed applet can read local files.

C:\Users\\*yourLoginName*\AppData\Sun\Java\Deployment directory. In the following, we'll refer to that directory as *deploydir*.

Copy applet.policy and client.certs to the *deploydir*/security directory. In that directory, rename applet.policy to java.policy. (Double-check that you are not wiping out an existing java.policy file. If there is one, add the applet.policy contents to it.)

---

 **TIP:** For more details on configuring client Java security, read the sections "Deployment Configuration File and Properties" and "Java Control Panel" in the Java deployment guide at http://docs.oracle.com/javase/7/docs/technotes/guides/deployment/deployment-guide/overview.html.

---

Restart your browser and load the FileReadApplet.html. You should *not* be prompted to accept any certificate. Check that you can load any file from the /etc directory and the directory from which the applet was loaded, but not from other directories.

When you are done, remember to clean up your *deploydir*/security directory. Remove the files java.policy and client.certs. Restart your browser. If you load the applet again after cleaning up, you should no longer be able to read files from the local file system. Instead, you will be prompted for a certificate. We'll discuss security certificates in the next section.

**Listing 9.17**  signed/FileReadApplet.java

```
1  package signed;
2
3  import java.awt.*;
4  import java.awt.event.*;
5  import java.io.*;
6  import java.nio.file.*;
7  import javax.swing.*;
8
9  /**
10  * This applet can run "outside the sandbox" and read local files when it is given the right
11  * permissions.
12  * @version 1.12 2012-06-10
13  * @author Cay Horstmann
14  */
15  public class FileReadApplet extends JApplet
16  {
17     private JTextField fileNameField;
18     private JTextArea fileText;
19
20     public void init()
21     {
22        EventQueue.invokeLater(new Runnable()
23           {
24              public void run()
25              {
26                 fileNameField = new JTextField(20);
27                 JPanel panel = new JPanel();
28                 panel.add(new JLabel("File name:"));
29                 panel.add(fileNameField);
30                 JButton openButton = new JButton("Open");
31                 panel.add(openButton);
32                 ActionListener listener = new ActionListener()
33                    {
34                       public void actionPerformed(ActionEvent event)
35                       {
36                          loadFile(fileNameField.getText());
37                       }
38                    };
```

*(Continues)*

---

**Listing 9.17** *(Continued)*

```
39              fileNameField.addActionListener(listener);
40              openButton.addActionListener(listener);
41
42              add(panel, "North");
43
44              fileText = new JTextArea();
45              add(new JScrollPane(fileText), "Center");
46           }
47        });
48     }
49
50     /**
51      * Loads the contents of a file into the text area.
52      * @param filename the file name
53      */
54     public void loadFile(String filename)
55     {
56        fileText.setText("");
57        try
58        {
59           fileText.append(new String(Files.readAllBytes(Paths.get(filename))));
60        }
61        catch (IOException ex)
62        {
63           fileText.append(ex + "\n");
64        }
65        catch (SecurityException ex)
66        {
67           fileText.append("I am sorry, but I cannot do that.\n");
68           fileText.append(ex + "\n");
69           ex.printStackTrace();
70        }
71     }
72  }
```

---

## 9.6.2 Software Developer Certificates

Up to now, we discussed scenarios in which programs are delivered in an intranet and for which a system administrator configures a security policy that controls the privileges of the programs. However, that strategy only works with programs from known sources.

Suppose that while surfing the Internet, you encounter a web site that offers to run an applet or Web Start application from an unfamiliar vendor, provided you grant it the permission to do so (see Figure 9.15). Such a program is signed with

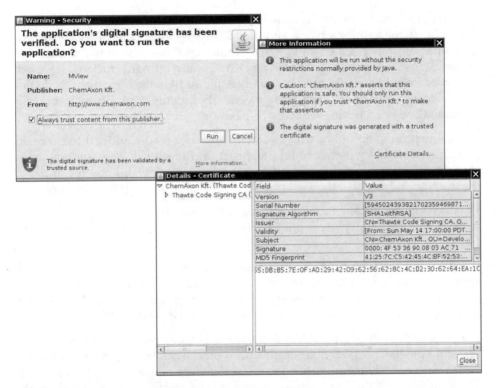

**Figure 9.15** Launching a signed applet

a *software developer* certificate issued by a CA. The pop-up dialog box identifies the software developer and the certificate issuer. You now have two choices:

- Run the program with full privileges.
- Confine the program to the sandbox. (The Cancel button in the dialog box is misleading. If you click that button, the applet is not canceled—instead, it runs in the sandbox.)

What facts do you have at your disposal that might influence your decision? Here is what you know:

- Thawte sold a certificate to the software developer.
- The program really was signed with that certificate, and it hasn't been modified in transit.
- The certificate really was signed by Thawte—it was verified by the public key in the local cacerts file.

Does that tell you whether the code is safe to run? Can you trust a vendor if all you know is the vendor's name and the fact that Thawte sold them a software developer certificate? One would like to think that Thawte went to some degree of trouble to assure itself that ChemAxon Kft. is not an outright cracker. However, no certificate issuer carries out a comprehensive audit of the honesty and competence of software vendors. They merely verify the identity, typically by inspecting a scanned copy of a business license or passport.

In the situation of an unknown vendor, an end user is ill-equipped to make an intelligent decision whether to let this program run outside the sandbox, with all permissions of a local application. If the vendor is a well-known company, the user can at least take the past track record of the company into account.

We don't like situations in which a program demands "give me all rights, or I won't run at all." Naive users are too often cowed into granting access that can put them in danger.

Would it help if each program explained what rights it needs and requested specific permission for those rights? Unfortunately, as you have seen, that can get pretty technical. It doesn't seem reasonable for an end user to have to ponder whether a program should really have the right to inspect the AWT event queue.

We remain unenthusiastic about software developer certificates. It would be better if applets and Web Start applications on the public Internet tried harder to stay within their respective sandboxes, and if those sandboxes were improved. The Web Start API that we discussed in Volume I, Chapter 10 is a step in the right direction.

## 9.7 Encryption

So far, we have discussed one important cryptographic technique implemented in the Java security API—namely, authentication through digital signatures. A second important aspect of security is *encryption*. When information is authenticated, the information itself is plainly visible. The digital signature merely verifies that the information has not been changed. In contrast, when information is encrypted, it is not visible. It can only be decrypted with a matching key.

Authentication is sufficient for code signing—there is no need for hiding the code. However, encryption is necessary when applets or applications transfer confidential information, such as credit card numbers and other personal data.

In the past, patents and export controls prevented many companies from offering strong encryption. Fortunately, export controls are now much less stringent, and the patents for important algorithms have expired. Nowadays, Java SE has excellent encryption support as a part of the standard library.

## 9.7.1 Symmetric Ciphers

The Java cryptographic extensions contain a class `Cipher` that is the superclass of all encryption algorithms. To get a cipher object, call the `getInstance` method:

```
Cipher cipher = Cipher.getInstance(algorithmName);
```

or

```
Cipher cipher = Cipher.getInstance(algorithmName, providerName);
```

The JDK comes with ciphers by the provider named `"SunJCE"`. It is the default provider used if you don't specify another provider name. You might want another provider if you need specialized algorithms that Oracle does not support.

The algorithm name is a string such as `"AES"` or `"DES/CBC/PKCS5Padding"`.

The Data Encryption Standard (DES) is a venerable block cipher with a key length of 56 bits. Nowadays, the DES algorithm is considered obsolete because it can be cracked with brute force (see, for example, http://w2.eff.org/Privacy/Crypto/Crypto_misc/DESCracker). A far better alternative is its successor, the Advanced Encryption Standard (AES). See www.csrc.nist.gov/publications/fips/fips197/fips-197.pdf for a detailed description of the AES algorithm. We use AES for our example.

Once you have a cipher object, initialize it by setting the mode and the key:

```
int mode = . . .;
Key key = . . .;
cipher.init(mode, key);
```

The mode is one of

```
Cipher.ENCRYPT_MODE
Cipher.DECRYPT_MODE
Cipher.WRAP_MODE
Cipher.UNWRAP_MODE
```

The wrap and unwrap modes encrypt one key with another—see the next section for an example.

Now you can repeatedly call the `update` method to encrypt blocks of data:

```
int blockSize = cipher.getBlockSize();
byte[] inBytes = new byte[blockSize];
. . . // read inBytes
int outputSize= cipher.getOutputSize(blockSize);
byte[] outBytes = new byte[outputSize];
int outLength = cipher.update(inBytes, 0, outputSize, outBytes);
. . . // write outBytes
```

When you are done, you must call the doFinal method once. If a final block of input data is available (with fewer than blockSize bytes), call

```
outBytes = cipher.doFinal(inBytes, 0, inLength);
```

If all input data have been encrypted, instead call

```
outBytes = cipher.doFinal();
```

The call to doFinal is necessary to carry out *padding* of the final block. Consider the DES cipher. It has a block size of eight bytes. Suppose the last block of the input data has fewer than eight bytes. Of course, we can fill the remaining bytes with 0, to obtain one final block of eight bytes, and encrypt it. But when the blocks are decrypted, the result will have several trailing 0 bytes appended to it, and therefore will be slightly different from the original input file. That could be a problem; to avoid it, we need a *padding scheme*. A commonly used padding scheme is the one described in the Public Key Cryptography Standard (PKCS) #5 by RSA Security, Inc. (ftp://ftp.rsasecurity.com/pub/pkcs/pkcs-5v2/pkcs5v2-0.pdf).

In this scheme, the last block is not padded with a pad value of zero, but with a pad value that equals the number of pad bytes. In other words, if L is the last (incomplete) block, it is padded as follows:

```
L 01                        if length(L) = 7
L 02 02                     if length(L) = 6
L 03 03 03                  if length(L) = 5
. . .
L 07 07 07 07 07 07 07      if length(L) = 1
```

Finally, if the length of the input is actually divisible by 8, then one block

```
08 08 08 08 08 08 08 08
```

is appended to the input and encrypted. For decryption, the very last byte of the plaintext is a count of the padding characters to discard.

## 9.7.2 Key Generation

To encrypt, you need to generate a key. Each cipher has a different format for keys, and you need to make sure that the key generation is random. Follow these steps:

1. Get a KeyGenerator for your algorithm.
2. Initialize the generator with a source for randomness. If the block length of the cipher is variable, also specify the desired block length.
3. Call the generateKey method.

For example, here is how you generate an AES key:

```
KeyGenerator keygen = KeyGenerator.getInstance("AES");
SecureRandom random = new SecureRandom(); // see below
keygen.init(random);
Key key = keygen.generateKey();
```

Alternatively, you can produce a key from a fixed set of raw data (perhaps derived from a password or the timing of keystrokes). Then construct a SecretKeySpec (which implements the SecretKey interface) like this:

```
byte[] keyData = . . .; // 16 bytes for AES
SecretKey key = new SecretKeySpec(keyData, "AES");
```

When generating keys, make sure you use *truly random* numbers. For example, the regular random number generator in the Random class, seeded by the current date and time, is not random enough. Suppose the computer clock is accurate to 1/10 of a second. Then there are at most 864,000 seeds per day. If an attacker knows the day a key was issued (as can often be deduced from a message date or certificate expiration date), it is an easy matter to generate all possible seeds for that day.

The SecureRandom class generates random numbers that are far more secure than those produced by the Random class. You still need to provide a seed to start the number sequence at a random spot. The best method for doing this is to obtain random input from a hardware device such as a white-noise generator. Another reasonable source for random input is to ask the user to type away aimlessly on the keyboard, with each keystroke contributing only one or two bits to the random seed. Once you gather such random bits in an array of bytes, pass it to the setSeed method:

```
SecureRandom secrand = new SecureRandom();
byte[] b = new byte[20];
// fill with truly random bits
secrand.setSeed(b);
```

If you don't seed the random number generator, it will compute its own 20-byte seed by launching threads, putting them to sleep, and measuring the exact time when they are awakened.

 **NOTE:** This algorithm is *not* known to be safe. In the past, algorithms that relied on timing some components of the computer, such as hard disk access time, were shown not to be completely random.

The sample program at the end of this section puts the AES cipher to work (see Listing 9.18). The crypt utility method in Listing 9.19 will be reused in other examples. To use the program, you first need to generate a secret key. Run

```
java aes.AESTest -genkey secret.key
```

The secret key is saved in the file secret.key.

Now you can encrypt with the command

```
java aes.AESTest -encrypt plaintextFile encryptedFile secret.key
```

Decrypt with the command

```
java aes.AESTest -decrypt encryptedFile decryptedFile secret.key
```

The program is straightforward. The -genkey option produces a new secret key and serializes it in the given file. That operation takes a long time because the initialization of the secure random generator is time-consuming. The -encrypt and -decrypt options both call into the same crypt method that calls the update and doFinal methods of the cipher. Note how the update method is called as long as the input blocks have the full length, and the doFinal method is either called with a partial input block (which is then padded) or with no additional data (to generate one pad block).

---

**Listing 9.18** aes/AESTest.java

```java
 1  package aes;
 2
 3  import java.io.*;
 4  import java.security.*;
 5  import javax.crypto.*;
 6  /**
 7   * This program tests the AES cipher. Usage:<br>
 8   * java aes.AESTest -genkey keyfile<br>
 9   * java aes.AESTest -encrypt plaintext encrypted keyfile<br>
10   * java aes.AESTest -decrypt encrypted decrypted keyfile<br>
11   * @author Cay Horstmann
12   * @version 1.01 2012-06-10
13   */
14  public class AESTest
15  {
16     public static void main(String[] args)
17        throws IOException, GeneralSecurityException, ClassNotFoundException
18     {
19        if (args[0].equals("-genkey"))
20        {
21           KeyGenerator keygen = KeyGenerator.getInstance("AES");
22           SecureRandom random = new SecureRandom();
23           keygen.init(random);
24           SecretKey key = keygen.generateKey();
```

```
25        try (ObjectOutputStream out = new ObjectOutputStream(new FileOutputStream(args[1])))
26        {
27            out.writeObject(key);
28        }
29     }
30     else
31     {
32        int mode;
33        if (args[0].equals("-encrypt")) mode = Cipher.ENCRYPT_MODE;
34        else mode = Cipher.DECRYPT_MODE;
35
36        try (ObjectInputStream keyIn = new ObjectInputStream(new FileInputStream(args[3]));
37            InputStream in = new FileInputStream(args[1]);
38            OutputStream out = new FileOutputStream(args[2]))
39        {
40            Key key = (Key) keyIn.readObject();
41            Cipher cipher = Cipher.getInstance("AES");
42            cipher.init(mode, key);
43            Util.crypt(in, out, cipher);
44        }
45     }
46  }
47 }
```

## Listing 9.19  aes/Util.java

```
1 package aes;
2
3 import java.io.*;
4 import java.security.*;
5 import javax.crypto.*;
6
7 public class Util
8 {
9     /**
10     * Uses a cipher to transform the bytes in an input stream and sends the transformed bytes to
11     * an output stream.
12     * @param in the input stream
13     * @param out the output stream
14     * @param cipher the cipher that transforms the bytes
15     */
16    public static void crypt(InputStream in, OutputStream out, Cipher cipher) throws IOException,
17            GeneralSecurityException
18    {
19        int blockSize = cipher.getBlockSize();
20        int outputSize = cipher.getOutputSize(blockSize);
21        byte[] inBytes = new byte[blockSize];
22        byte[] outBytes = new byte[outputSize];
```

*(Continues)*

---

**Listing 9.19**  *(Continued)*

```
23      int inLength = 0;
24      ;
25      boolean more = true;
26      while (more)
27      {
28         inLength = in.read(inBytes);
29         if (inLength == blockSize)
30         {
31            int outLength = cipher.update(inBytes, 0, blockSize, outBytes);
32            out.write(outBytes, 0, outLength);
33         }
34         else more = false;
35      }
36      if (inLength > 0) outBytes = cipher.doFinal(inBytes, 0, inLength);
37      else outBytes = cipher.doFinal();
38      out.write(outBytes);
39   }
40 }
```

---

**javax.crypto.Cipher**  1.4

- `static Cipher getInstance(String algorithmName)`
- `static Cipher getInstance(String algorithmName, String providerName)`

  returns a Cipher object that implements the specified algorithm. Throws a `NoSuchAlgorithmException` if the algorithm is not provided.

- `int getBlockSize()`

  returns the size (in bytes) of a cipher block, or 0 if the cipher is not a block cipher.

- `int getOutputSize(int inputLength)`

  returns the size of an output buffer that is needed if the next input has the given number of bytes. This method takes into account any buffered bytes in the cipher object.

- `void init(int mode, Key key)`

  initializes the cipher algorithm object. The mode is one of ENCRYPT_MODE, DECRYPT_MODE, WRAP_MODE, or UNWRAP_MODE.

- `byte[] update(byte[] in)`
- `byte[] update(byte[] in, int offset, int length)`
- `int update(byte[] in, int offset, int length, byte[] out)`

  transforms one block of input data. The first two methods return the output. The third method returns the number of bytes placed into out.

*(Continues)*

---

**javax.crypto.Cipher**  1.4  *(Continued)*

- byte[] doFinal()
- byte[] doFinal(byte[] in)
- byte[] doFinal(byte[] in, int offset, int length)
- int doFinal(byte[] in, int offset, int length, byte[] out)

  transforms the last block of input data and flushes the buffer of this algorithm object. The first three methods return the output. The fourth method returns the number of bytes placed into out.

---

**javax.crypto.KeyGenerator**  1.4

- static KeyGenerator getInstance(String algorithmName)

  returns a KeyGenerator object that implements the specified algorithm. Throws a NoSuchAlgorithmException if the algorithm is not provided.

- void init(SecureRandom random)
- void init(int keySize, SecureRandom random)

  initializes the key generator.

- SecretKey generateKey()

  generates a new key.

---

**javax.crypto.spec.SecretKeySpec**  1.4

- SecretKeySpec(byte[] key, String algorithmName)

  constructs a key specification.

---

## 9.7.3 Cipher Streams

The JCE library provides a convenient set of stream classes that automatically encrypt or decrypt stream data. For example, here is how you can encrypt data to a file:

```
Cipher cipher = . . .;
cipher.init(Cipher.ENCRYPT_MODE, key);
CipherOutputStream out = new CipherOutputStream(new FileOutputStream(outputFileName), cipher);
byte[] bytes = new byte[BLOCKSIZE];
int inLength = getData(bytes); // get data from data source
while (inLength != -1)
{
   out.write(bytes, 0, inLength);
   inLength = getData(bytes); // get more data from data source
}
out.flush();
```

Similarly, you can use a CipherInputStream to read and decrypt data from a file:

```
Cipher cipher = . . .;
cipher.init(Cipher.DECRYPT_MODE, key);
CipherInputStream in = new CipherInputStream(new FileInputStream(inputFileName), cipher);
byte[] bytes = new byte[BLOCKSIZE];
int inLength = in.read(bytes);
while (inLength != -1)
{
   putData(bytes, inLength); // put data to destination
   inLength = in.read(bytes);
}
```

The cipher stream classes transparently handle the calls to update and doFinal, which is clearly a convenience.

---

**javax.crypto.CipherInputStream** 1.4

- CipherInputStream(InputStream in, Cipher cipher)
  constructs an input stream that reads data from in and decrypts or encrypts them by using the given cipher.

- int read()
- int read(byte[] b, int off, int len)
  reads data from the input stream, which is automatically decrypted or encrypted.

---

**javax.crypto.CipherOutputStream** 1.4

- CipherOutputStream(OutputStream out, Cipher cipher)
  constructs an output stream that writes data to out and encrypts or decrypts them using the given cipher.

- void write(int ch)
- void write(byte[] b, int off, int len)
  writes data to the output stream, which is automatically encrypted or decrypted.

- void flush()
  flushes the cipher buffer and carries out padding if necessary.

---

## 9.7.4 Public Key Ciphers

The AES cipher that you have seen in the preceding section is a *symmetric* cipher. The same key is used for both encryption and decryption. The Achilles heel of symmetric ciphers is key distribution. If Alice sends Bob an encrypted method, Bob needs the same key that Alice used. If Alice changes the key, she needs to send Bob both the message and, through a secure channel, the new key.

But perhaps she has no secure channel to Bob—which is why she encrypts her messages to him in the first place.

Public key cryptography solves that problem. In a public key cipher, Bob has a key pair consisting of a public key and a matching private key. Bob can publish the public key anywhere, but he must closely guard the private key. Alice simply uses the public key to encrypt her messages to Bob.

Actually, it's not quite that simple. All known public key algorithms are *much* slower than symmetric key algorithms such as DES or AES. It would not be practical to use a public key algorithm to encrypt large amounts of information. However, that problem can easily be overcome by combining a public key cipher with a fast symmetric cipher, like this:

1. Alice generates a random symmetric encryption key. She uses it to encrypt her plaintext.
2. Alice encrypts the symmetric key with Bob's public key.
3. Alice sends Bob both the encrypted symmetric key and the encrypted plaintext.
4. Bob uses his private key to decrypt the symmetric key.
5. Bob uses the decrypted symmetric key to decrypt the message.

Nobody but Bob can decrypt the symmetric key because only Bob has the private key for decryption. Thus, the expensive public key encryption is only applied to a small amount of key data.

The most commonly used public key algorithm is the RSA algorithm invented by Rivest, Shamir, and Adleman. Until October 2000, the algorithm was protected by a patent assigned to RSA Security, Inc. Licenses were not cheap—typically a 3% royalty, with a minimum payment of $50,000 per year. Now the algorithm is in the public domain.

To use the RSA algorithm, you need a public/private key pair. Use a `KeyPairGenerator` like this:

```
KeyPairGenerator pairgen = KeyPairGenerator.getInstance("RSA");
SecureRandom random = new SecureRandom();
pairgen.initialize(KEYSIZE, random);
KeyPair keyPair = pairgen.generateKeyPair();
Key publicKey = keyPair.getPublic();
Key privateKey = keyPair.getPrivate();
```

The program in Listing 9.20 has three options. The `-genkey` option produces a key pair. The `-encrypt` option generates an AES key and *wraps* it with the public key.

```
Key key = . . .; // an AES key
Key publicKey = . . .; // a public RSA key
```

```
Cipher cipher = Cipher.getInstance("RSA");
cipher.init(Cipher.WRAP_MODE, publicKey);
byte[] wrappedKey = cipher.wrap(key);
```

It then produces a file that contains

- The length of the wrapped key
- The wrapped key bytes
- The plaintext encrypted with the AES key

The -decrypt option decrypts such a file. To try the program, first generate the RSA keys:

```
java rsa.RSATest -genkey public.key private.key
```

Then encrypt a file:

```
java rsa.RSATest -encrypt plaintextFile encryptedFile public.key
```

Finally, decrypt it and verify that the decrypted file matches the plaintext:

```
java rsa.RSATest -decrypt encryptedFile decryptedFile private.key
```

**Listing 9.20**  rsa/RSATest.java

```java
1  package rsa;
2
3  import java.io.*;
4  import java.security.*;
5  import javax.crypto.*;
6  /**
7   * This program tests the RSA cipher. Usage:<br>
8   * java rsa.RSATest -genkey public private<br>
9   * java rsa.RSATest -encrypt plaintext encrypted public<br>
10  * java rsa.RSATest -decrypt encrypted decrypted private<br>
11  * @author Cay Horstmann
12  * @version 1.01 2012-06-10
13  */
14 public class RSATest
15 {
16    private static final int KEYSIZE = 512;
17
18    public static void main(String[] args)
19       throws IOException, GeneralSecurityException, ClassNotFoundException
20    {
21       if (args[0].equals("-genkey"))
22       {
23          KeyPairGenerator pairgen = KeyPairGenerator.getInstance("RSA");
24          SecureRandom random = new SecureRandom();
```

```
25        pairgen.initialize(KEYSIZE, random);
26        KeyPair keyPair = pairgen.generateKeyPair();
27        try (ObjectOutputStream out = new ObjectOutputStream(new FileOutputStream(args[1])))
28        {
29           out.writeObject(keyPair.getPublic());
30        }
31        try (ObjectOutputStream out = new ObjectOutputStream(new FileOutputStream(args[2])))
32        {
33           out.writeObject(keyPair.getPrivate());
34        }
35     }
36     else if (args[0].equals("-encrypt"))
37     {
38        KeyGenerator keygen = KeyGenerator.getInstance("AES");
39        SecureRandom random = new SecureRandom();
40        keygen.init(random);
41        SecretKey key = keygen.generateKey();
42
43        // wrap with RSA public key
44        try (ObjectInputStream keyIn = new ObjectInputStream(new FileInputStream(args[3]));
45           DataOutputStream out = new DataOutputStream(new FileOutputStream(args[2]));
46           InputStream in = new FileInputStream(args[1]) )
47        {
48           Key publicKey = (Key) keyIn.readObject();
49           Cipher cipher = Cipher.getInstance("RSA");
50           cipher.init(Cipher.WRAP_MODE, publicKey);
51           byte[] wrappedKey = cipher.wrap(key);
52           out.writeInt(wrappedKey.length);
53           out.write(wrappedKey);
54
55           cipher = Cipher.getInstance("AES");
56           cipher.init(Cipher.ENCRYPT_MODE, key);
57           Util.crypt(in, out, cipher);
58        }
59     }
60     else
61     {
62        try (DataInputStream in = new DataInputStream(new FileInputStream(args[1]));
63           ObjectInputStream keyIn = new ObjectInputStream(new FileInputStream(args[3]));
64           OutputStream out = new FileOutputStream(args[2]))
65        {
66           int length = in.readInt();
67           byte[] wrappedKey = new byte[length];
68           in.read(wrappedKey, 0, length);
69
70           // unwrap with RSA private key
71           Key privateKey = (Key) keyIn.readObject();
72
73           Cipher cipher = Cipher.getInstance("RSA");
```

*(Continues)*

**Listing 9.20** *(Continued)*

```
74              cipher.init(Cipher.UNWRAP_MODE, privateKey);
75              Key key = cipher.unwrap(wrappedKey, "AES", Cipher.SECRET_KEY);
76
77              cipher = Cipher.getInstance("AES");
78              cipher.init(Cipher.DECRYPT_MODE, key);
79
80              Util.crypt(in, out, cipher);
81          }
82      }
83   }
84 }
```

You have now seen how the Java security model allows controlled execution of code, which is a unique and increasingly important aspect of the Java platform. You have also seen the services for authentication and encryption that the Java library provides. We did not cover a number of advanced and specialized issues, among them:

- The GSS-API for "generic security services" that provides support for the Kerberos protocol (and, in principle, other protocols for secure message exchange). There is a tutorial at http://docs.oracle.com/javase/7/docs/technotes/guides/security/jgss/tutorials.

- Support for the Simple Authentication and Security Layer (SASL), used by the Lightweight Directory Access Protocol (LDAP) and Internet Message Access Protocol (IMAP). If you need to implement SASL in your application, look at http://docs.oracle.com/javase/7/docs/technotes/guides/security/sasl/sasl-refguide.html.

- Support for SSL. Using SSL over HTTP is transparent to application programmers; simply use URLs that start with `https`. If you want to add SSL to your application, see the Java Secure Socket Extension (JSSE) reference at http://java.sun.com/javase/6/docs/technotes/guides/security/jsse/JSSERefGuide.html.

Now that we have completed our overview of Java security, we turn, in the next chapter, to scripting, compiling, and annotation processing.

CHAPTER **10**

# Scripting, Compiling, and Annotation Processing

## In this chapter:

This chapter introduces three techniques for processing code. The scripting API lets you invoke code in a scripting language such as JavaScript or Groovy. You can use the compiler API when you want to compile Java code inside your application. Annotation processors operate on Java source or class files that contain annotations. As you will see, there are many applications for annotation processing, ranging from simple diagnostics to "bytecode engineering"—the insertion of bytecodes into class files or even running programs.

## 10.1 Scripting for the Java Platform

A scripting language is a language that avoids the usual edit/compile/link/run cycle by interpreting the program text at runtime. Scripting languages have a number of advantages:

- Rapid turnaround, encouraging experimentation
- Changing the behavior of a running program
- Enabling customization by program users

On the other hand, most scripting languages lack features that are beneficial for programming complex applications, such as strong typing, encapsulation, and modularity.

It is therefore tempting to combine the advantages of scripting and traditional languages. The scripting API lets you do just that for the Java platform. It enables you to invoke scripts written in JavaScript, Groovy, Ruby, and even exotic languages such as Scheme and Haskell, from a Java program. (The other direction—accessing Java from the scripting language—is the responsibility of the scripting language provider. Most scripting languages that run on the Java virtual machine have this capability.)

In the following sections, we'll show you how to select an engine for a particular language, how to execute scripts, and how to take advantage of advanced features that some scripting engines offer.

### 10.1.1 Getting a Scripting Engine

A scripting engine is a library that can execute scripts in a particular language. When the virtual machine starts, it discovers the available scripting engines. To enumerate them, construct a ScriptEngineManager and invoke the getEngineFactories method. You can ask each engine factory for the supported engine names, MIME types, and file extensions. Table 10.1 shows typical values.

Usually, you know which engine you need, and you can simply request it by name, MIME type, or extension. For example:

```
ScriptEngine engine = manager.getEngineByName("JavaScript");
```

Java SE 7 includes a version of Rhino, a JavaScript interpreter developed by the Mozilla foundation. You can add more languages by providing the necessary JAR files on the class path. You will generally need two sets of JAR files. The scripting language itself is implemented by a single JAR file or a set of JARs. The engine that adapts the language to the scripting API usually requires an additional JAR. The site http://java.net/projects/scripting provides engines for a

**Table 10.1** Properties of Scripting Engine Factories

| Engine | Names | MIME types | Extensions |
|---|---|---|---|
| Rhino (included with Java SE) | js, rhino, JavaScript, javascript, ECMAScript, ecmascript | application/javascript, application/ecmascript, text/javascript, text/ecmascript | js |
| Groovy | groovy | None | groovy |
| SISC Scheme | scheme, sisc | None | scc, sce, scm, shp |

wide range of scripting languages. For example, to add support for Groovy, the class path should contain *groovy*/lib/* (from http://groovy.codehaus.org) and groovy-engine.jar (from http://java.net/projects/scripting).

---

`javax.script.ScriptEngineManager`  6

- `List<ScriptEngineFactory> getEngineFactories()`
  gets a list of all discovered engine factories.

- `ScriptEngine getEngineByName(String name)`
- `ScriptEngine getEngineByExtension(String extension)`
- `ScriptEngine getEngineByMimeType(String mimeType)`
  gets the script engine with the given name, script file extension, or MIME type.

---

`javax.script.ScriptEngineFactory`  6

- `List<String> getNames()`
- `List<String> getExtensions()`
- `List<String> getMimeTypes()`
  gets the names, script file extensions, and MIME types under which this factory is known.

---

## 10.1.2 Script Evaluation and Bindings

Once you have an engine, you can call a script simply by invoking

```
Object result = engine.eval(scriptString);
```

If the script is stored in a file, open a `Reader` and call

```
Object result = engine.eval(reader);
```

You can invoke multiple scripts on the same engine. If one script defines variables, functions, or classes, most scripting engines retain the definitions for later use. For example,

```
engine.eval("n = 1728");
Object result = engine.eval("n + 1");
```

will return 1729.

---

 **NOTE:** To find out whether it is safe to concurrently execute scripts in multiple threads, call

```
Object param = factory.getParameter("THREADING");
```

The returned value is one of the following:

- null: Concurrent execution is not safe.
- "MULTITHREADED": Concurrent execution is safe. Effects from one thread might be visible from another thread.
- "THREAD-ISOLATED": In addition to "MULTITHREADED", different variable bindings are maintained for each thread.
- "STATELESS": In addition to "THREAD-ISOLATED", scripts do not alter variable bindings.

---

You will often want to add variable bindings to the engine. A binding consists of a name and an associated Java object. For example, consider these statements:

```
engine.put(k, 1728);
Object result = engine.eval("k + 1");
```

The script code reads the definition of k from the bindings in the "engine scope." This is particularly important because most scripting languages can access Java objects, often with a syntax that is simpler than the Java syntax. For example,

```
engine.put(b, new JButton());
engine.eval("b.text = 'Ok'");
```

Conversely, you can retrieve variables that were bound by scripting statements:

```
engine.eval("n = 1728");
Object result = engine.get("n");
```

In addition to the engine scope, there is also a global scope. Any bindings that you add to the ScriptEngineManager are visible to all engines.

Instead of adding bindings to the engine or global scope, you can collect them in an object of type Bindings and pass it to the eval method:

```
Bindings scope = engine.createBindings();
scope.put(b, new JButton());
engine.eval(scriptString, scope);
```

This is useful if a set of bindings should not persist for future calls to the `eval` method.

> **NOTE:** You might want to have scopes other than the engine and global scopes. For example, a web container might need request and session scopes. However, then you are on your own. You will need to write a class that implements the `ScriptContext` interface, managing a collection of scopes. Each scope is identified by an integer number, and scopes with lower numbers should be searched first. (The standard library provides a `SimpleScriptContext` class, but it only holds global and engine scopes.)

---

*javax.script.ScriptEngine*  6

- `Object eval(String script)`
- `Object eval(Reader reader)`
- `Object eval(String script, Bindings bindings)`
- `Object eval(Reader reader, Bindings bindings)`
  evaluates the script given by the string or reader, subject to the given bindings.
- `Object get(String key)`
- `void put(String key, Object value)`
  gets or puts a binding in the engine scope.
- `Bindings createBindings()`
  creates an empty `Bindings` object suitable for this engine.

---

*javax.script.ScriptEngineManager*  6

- `Object get(String key)`
- `void put(String key, Object value)`
  gets or puts a binding in the global scope.

---

*javax.script.Bindings*  6

- `Object get(String key)`
- `void put(String key, Object value)`
  gets or puts a binding into the scope represented by this `Bindings` object.

## 10.1.3 Redirecting Input and Output

You can redirect the standard input and output of a script by calling the setReader and setWriter methods of the script context. For example,

```
StringWriter writer = new StringWriter();
engine.getContext().setWriter(new PrintWriter(writer, true));
```

Any output written with the JavaScript print or println functions is sent to writer.

 **CAUTION:** You can pass any Writer to the setWriter method, but the Rhino engine throws an exception if it is not a PrintWriter.

The setReader and setWriter methods only affect the scripting engine's standard input and output sources. For example, if you execute the JavaScript code

```
println("Hello");
java.lang.System.out.println("World");
```

only the first output is redirected.

The Rhino engine does not have the notion of a standard input source. Calling setReader has no effect.

---

*javax.script.ScriptEngine* 6

- ScriptContext getContext()
  gets the default script context for this engine.

---

*javax.script.ScriptContext* 6

- Reader getReader()
- void setReader(Reader reader)
- Writer getWriter()
- void setWriter(Writer writer)
- Writer getErrorWriter()
- void setErrorWriter(Writer writer)
  gets or sets the reader for input or writer for normal or error output.

## 10.1.4 Calling Scripting Functions and Methods

With many script engines, you can invoke a function in the scripting language without having to evaluate the actual script code. This is useful if you allow users to implement a service in a scripting language of their choice.

The script engines that offer this functionality implement the `Invocable` interface. In particular, the Rhino engine implements `Invocable`.

To call a function, call the `invokeFunction` method with the function name, followed by the function parameters:

```
if (engine implements Invocable)
    ((Invocable) engine).invokeFunction("aFunction", param1, param2);
```

If the scripting language is object-oriented, you call can a method like this:

```
((Invocable) engine).invokeMethod(implicitParam, "aMethod", explicitParam1, explicitParam2);
```

Here, the `implicitParam` object is a proxy to an object in the scripting language. It must be the result of a prior call to the scripting engine.

---

 **NOTE:** If the script engine does not implement the `Invocable` interface, you might still be able to call a method in a language-independent way. The `getMethodCallSyntax` method of the `ScriptEngineFactory` interface produces a string that you can pass to the `eval` method. However, all method parameters must be bound to names, whereas `invokeMethod` can be called with arbitrary values.

---

You can go a step further and ask the scripting engine to implement a Java interface. Then you can call scripting functions and methods with the Java method call syntax.

The details depend on the scripting engine, but typically you need to supply a function for each method of the interface. For example, consider a Java interface

```
public interface Greeter
{
    String greet(String whom);
}
```

In Rhino, you provide a function

```
function greet(x) { return "Hello, " + x + "!"; }
```

This code must be evaluated first. Then you can call

```
Greeter g = ((Invocable) engine).getInterface(Greeter.class);
```

Now you can make a plain Java method call

```
String result = g.greet("World");
```

Behind the scenes, the JavaScript greet method is invoked. This approach is similar to making a remote method call, as discussed in Chapter 11.

In an object-oriented scripting language, you can access a script class through a matching Java interface. For example, consider this JavaScript code, which defines a SimpleGreeter class.

```
function SimpleGreeter(salutation) { this.salutation = salutation; }
SimpleGreeter.prototype.greet = function(whom) { return this.salutation + ", " + whom + "!"; }
```

You can use this class to construct greeters with different salutations (such as "Hello", "Goodbye", and so on).

---

 **NOTE:** For more information on how to define classes in JavaScript, see *JavaScript—The Definitive Guide, Fifth Edition*, by David Flanagan (O'Reilly, 2006).

---

After evaluating the JavaScript class definition, call

```
Object goodbyeGreeter = engine.eval("new SimpleGreeter('Goodbye')");
Greeter g = ((Invocable) engine).getInterface(goodbyeGreeter, Greeter.class);
```

When you call g.greet("World"), the greet method is invoked on the JavaScript object goodbyeGreeter. The result is a string "Goodbye, World!".

In summary, the Invocable interface is useful if you want to call scripting code from Java without worrying about the scripting language syntax.

---

**javax.script.Invocable** 6

- Object invokeFunction(String name, Object... parameters)
- Object invokeMethod(Object implicitParameter, String name, Object... explicitParameters)
  invokes the function or method with the given name, passing the given parameters.
- <T> T getInterface(Class<T> iface)
  returns an implementation of the given interface, implementing the methods with functions in the scripting engine.
- <T> T getInterface(Object implicitParameter, Class<T> iface)
  returns an implementation of the given interface, implementing the methods with the methods of the given object.

## 10.1.5 Compiling a Script

Some scripting engines can compile scripting code into an intermediate form for efficient execution. Those engines implement the Compilable interface. The following example shows how to compile and evaluate code contained in a script file:

```
Reader reader = new FileReader("myscript.js");
CompiledScript script = null;
if (engine implements Compilable)
   CompiledScript script = ((Compilable) engine).compile(reader);
```

Once the script is compiled, you can execute it. The following code executes the compiled script if compilation was successful, or the original script if the engine didn't support compilation.

```
if (script != null)
   script.eval();
else
   engine.eval(reader);
```

Of course, it only makes sense to compile a script if you need to execute it repeatedly.

---

**javax.script.Compilable  6**

- CompiledScript compile(String script)
- CompiledScript compile(Reader reader)
  compiles the script given by a string or reader.

---

**javax.script.CompiledScript  6**

- Object eval()
- Object eval(Bindings bindings)
  evaluates this script.

---

## 10.1.6 An Example: Scripting GUI Events

To illustrate the scripting API, we will write a sample program that allows users to specify event handlers in a scripting language of their choice.

Have a look at the program in Listing 10.1 that adds scripting to an arbitrary frame class. By default it reads the ButtonFrame class in Listing 10.2, which is similar to the event handling demo in Volume I, with two differences:

- Each component has its `name` property set.
- There are no event handlers.

The event handlers are defined in a property file. Each property definition has the form

    *componentName*.*eventName* = *scriptCode*

For example, if you choose to use JavaScript, supply the event handlers in a file `js.properties`, like this:

```
yellowButton.action=panel.background = java.awt.Color.YELLOW
blueButton.action=panel.background = java.awt.Color.BLUE
redButton.action=panel.background = java.awt.Color.RED
```

The companion code also has files for Groovy and SISC Scheme.

The program starts by loading an engine for the language specified on the command line. If no language is specified, we use JavaScript.

We then process a script `init`.*language* if it is present. This seems like a good idea in general; moreover, the Scheme interpreter needs some cumbersome initializations that we did not want to include in every event handler script.

Next, we recursively traverse all child components and add the bindings (*name*, *object*) into the engine scope.

Then we read the file *language*.`properties`. For each property, we synthesize an event handler proxy that causes the script code to be executed. The details are a bit technical. You might want to read the section on proxies in Volume I, Chapter 6, together with the section on JavaBeans events in Chapter 8 of this volume, if you want to follow the implementation in detail. The essential part, however, is that each event handler calls

```
engine.eval(scriptCode);
```

Let us look at the `yellowButton` in more detail. When the line

```
yellowButton.action=panel.background = java.awt.Color.YELLOW
```

is processed, we find the `JButton` component with the name `"yellowButton"`. We then attach an `ActionListener` with an `actionPerformed` method that executes the script

```
panel.background = java.awt.Color.YELLOW
```

The engine contains a binding that binds the name `"panel"` to the `JPanel` object. When the event occurs, the `setBackground` method of the panel is executed, and the color changes.

You can run this program with the JavaScript event handlers, simply by executing

```
java ScriptTest
```

For the Groovy handlers, use

```
java -classpath .:groovy/lib/*:jsr223-engines/groovy/build/groovy-engine.jar ScriptTest groovy
```

Here, *groovy* is the directory into which you installed Groovy, and *jsr223-engines* is the directory that contains the engine adapters from http://java.net/projects/scripting.

To try out Scheme, download SISC Scheme from http://sisc-scheme.org and run

```
java -classpath .:sisc/*:jsr223-engines/scheme/build/scheme-engine.jar ScriptTest scheme
```

This application demonstrates how to use scripting for Java GUI programming. One could go a step further and describe the GUI with an XML file, as you have seen in Chapter 2. Then our program would become an interpreter for GUIs that have visual presentation defined by XML and behavior defined by a scripting language. Note the similarity to a dynamic HTML page or a dynamic server-side scripting environment.

---

**Listing 10.1** script/ScriptTest.java

```java
1  package script;
2
3  import java.awt.*;
4  import java.beans.*;
5  import java.io.*;
6  import java.lang.reflect.*;
7  import java.util.*;
8  import javax.script.*;
9  import javax.swing.*;
10
11 /**
12  * @version 1.01 2012-01-28
13  * @author Cay Horstmann
14  */
15 public class ScriptTest
16 {
17    public static void main(final String[] args)
18    {
19       EventQueue.invokeLater(new Runnable()
20          {
21             public void run()
22             {
23                try
24                {
25                   ScriptEngineManager manager = new ScriptEngineManager();
```

*(Continues)*

**Listing 10.1** *(Continued)*

```
26              String language;
27              if (args.length == 0)
28              {
29                 System.out.println("Available factories: ");
30                 for (ScriptEngineFactory factory : manager.getEngineFactories())
31                    System.out.println(factory.getEngineName());
32
33                 language = "js";
34              }
35              else language = args[0];
36
37              final ScriptEngine engine = manager.getEngineByName(language);
38              if (engine == null)
39              {
40                 System.err.println("No engine for " + language);
41                 System.exit(1);
42              }
43
44              final String frameClassName = args.length < 2 ? "buttons1.ButtonFrame" : args[1];
45
46              JFrame frame = (JFrame) Class.forName(frameClassName).newInstance();
47              InputStream in = frame.getClass().getResourceAsStream("init." + language);
48              if (in != null) engine.eval(new InputStreamReader(in));
49              getComponentBindings(frame, engine);
50
51              final Properties events = new Properties();
52              in = frame.getClass().getResourceAsStream(language + ".properties");
53              events.load(in);
54
55              for (final Object e : events.keySet())
56              {
57                 String[] s = ((String) e).split("\\.");
58                 addListener(s[0], s[1], (String) events.get(e), engine);
59              }
60              frame.setTitle("ScriptTest");
61              frame.setDefaultCloseOperation(JFrame.EXIT_ON_CLOSE);
62              frame.setVisible(true);
63           }
64           catch (ReflectiveOperationException | IOException
65              | ScriptException | IntrospectionException ex)
66           {
67              ex.printStackTrace();
68           }
69        }
70     });
71  }
```

```
 72    /**
 73     * Gathers all named components in a container.
 74     * @param c the component
 75     * @param namedComponents
 76     */
 77    private static void getComponentBindings(Component c, ScriptEngine engine)
 78    {
 79       String name = c.getName();
 80       if (name != null) engine.put(name, c);
 81       if (c instanceof Container)
 82       {
 83          for (Component child : ((Container) c).getComponents())
 84             getComponentBindings(child, engine);
 85       }
 86    }
 87
 88    /**
 89     * Adds a listener to an object whose listener method executes a script.
 90     * @param beanName the name of the bean to which the listener should be added
 91     * @param eventName the name of the listener type, such as "action" or "change"
 92     * @param scriptCode the script code to be executed
 93     * @param engine the engine that executes the code
 94     * @param bindings the bindings for the execution
 95     * @throws IntrospectionException
 96     */
 97    private static void addListener(String beanName, String eventName, final String scriptCode,
 98       final ScriptEngine engine) throws ReflectiveOperationException, IntrospectionException
 99    {
100       Object bean = engine.get(beanName);
101       EventSetDescriptor descriptor = getEventSetDescriptor(bean, eventName);
102       if (descriptor == null) return;
103       descriptor.getAddListenerMethod().invoke(bean,
104          Proxy.newProxyInstance(null, new Class[] { descriptor.getListenerType() },
105             new InvocationHandler()
106                {
107                   public Object invoke(Object proxy, Method method, Object[] args)
108                      throws Throwable
109                   {
110                      engine.eval(scriptCode);
111                      return null;
112                   }
113             }));
114    }
115
116    private static EventSetDescriptor getEventSetDescriptor(Object bean, String eventName)
117       throws IntrospectionException
118    {
```

*(Continues)*

---

**Listing 10.1** *(Continued)*

```
119     for (EventSetDescriptor descriptor : Introspector.getBeanInfo(bean.getClass())
120             .getEventSetDescriptors())
121         if (descriptor.getName().equals(eventName)) return descriptor;
122     return null;
123   }
124 }
```

---

**Listing 10.2** buttons1/ButtonFrame.java

```
1 package buttons1;
2
3 import javax.swing.*;
4
5 public class ButtonFrame extends JFrame
6 {
7    private static final int DEFAULT_WIDTH = 300;
8    private static final int DEFAULT_HEIGHT = 200;
9
10   private JPanel panel;
11   private JButton yellowButton;
12   private JButton blueButton;
13   private JButton redButton;
14
15   public ButtonFrame()
16   {
17      setSize(DEFAULT_WIDTH, DEFAULT_HEIGHT);
18
19      panel = new JPanel();
20      panel.setName("panel");
21      add(panel);
22
23      yellowButton = new JButton("Yellow");
24      yellowButton.setName("yellowButton");
25      blueButton = new JButton("Blue");
26      blueButton.setName("blueButton");
27      redButton = new JButton("Red");
28      redButton.setName("redButton");
29
30      panel.add(yellowButton);
31      panel.add(blueButton);
32      panel.add(redButton);
33   }
34 }
```

## 10.2  The Compiler API

In the preceding sections, you saw how to interact with code in a scripting language. Now we turn to a different scenario: Java programs that compile Java code. There are quite a few tools that need to invoke the Java compiler, such as:

- Development environments
- Java teaching and tutoring programs
- Build and test automation tools
- Templating tools that process snippets of Java code, such as JavaServer Pages (JSP)

In the past, applications invoked the Java compiler by calling undocumented classes in the *jdk*/lib/tools.jar library. As of Java SE 6, a public API for compilation is a part of the Java platform, and it is no longer necessary to use tools.jar. This section explains the compiler API.

### 10.2.1  Compiling the Easy Way

It is very easy to invoke the compiler. Here is a sample call:

```
JavaCompiler compiler = ToolProvider.getSystemJavaCompiler();
OutputStream outStream = ...;
OutputStream errStream = ...;
int result = compiler.run(null, outStream, errStream, "-sourcepath", "src", "Test.java");
```

A result value of 0 indicates successful compilation.

The compiler sends output and error messages to the provided streams. You can set these parameters to null, in which case System.out and System.err are used. The first parameter of the run method is an input stream. As the compiler takes no console input, you can always leave it as null. (The run method is inherited from a generic Tool interface, which allows for tools that read input.)

The remaining parameters of the run method are simply the arguments that you would pass to javac if you invoked it on the command line. These can be options or file names.

### 10.2.2  Using Compilation Tasks

You can have even more control over the compilation process with a CompilationTask object. In particular, you can

- Control the source of program code—for example, by providing code in a string builder instead of a file.

- Control the placement of class files—for example, by storing them in a database.
- Listen to error and warning messages as they occur during compilation.
- Run the compiler in the background.

The location of source and class files is controlled by a JavaFileManager. It is responsible for determining JavaFileObject instances for source and class files. A JavaFileObject can correspond to a disk file, or it can provide another mechanism for reading and writing its contents.

To listen to error messages, install a DiagnosticListener. The listener receives a Diagnostic object whenever the compiler reports a warning or error message. The DiagnosticCollector class implements this interface. It simply collects all diagnostics so that you can iterate through them after the compilation is complete.

A Diagnostic object contains information about the problem location (including file name, line number, and column number) as well as a human-readable description.

To obtain a CompilationTask object, call the getTask method of the JavaCompiler class. You need to specify:

- A Writer for any compiler output that is not reported as a Diagnostic, or null to use System.err
- A JavaFileManager, or null to use the compiler's standard file manager
- A DiagnosticListener
- Option strings, or null for no options
- Class names for annotation processing, or null if none are specified (we'll discuss annotation processing later in this chapter)
- JavaFileObject instances for source files

You need to provide the last three arguments as Iterable objects. For example, a sequence of options might be specified as

```
Iterable<String> options = Arrays.asList("-g", "-d", "classes");
```

Alternatively, you can use any collection class.

If you want the compiler to read source files from disk, you can ask the StandardJavaFileManager to translate the file name strings or File objects to JavaFileObject instances. For example,

```
StandardJavaFileManager fileManager = compiler.getStandardFileManager(null, null, null);
Iterable<JavaFileObject> fileObjects = fileManager.getJavaFileObjectsFromStrings(fileNames);
```

However, if you want the compiler to read source code from somewhere other than a disk file, you need to supply your own JavaFileObject subclass. Listing 10.3

shows the code for a source file object with data contained in a StringBuilder. The class extends the SimpleJavaFileObject convenience class and overrides the getCharContent method to return the content of the string builder. We'll use this class in our example program in which we dynamically produce the code for a Java class and then compile it.

The CompilationTask interface extends the Callable<Boolean> interface. You can pass it to an Executor for execution in another thread, or you can simply invoke the call method. A return value of Boolean.FALSE indicates failure.

```
Callable<Boolean> task = new JavaCompiler.CompilationTask(null, fileManager, diagnostics,
    options, null, fileObjects);
if (!task.call())
    System.out.println("Compilation failed");
```

If you simply want the compiler to produce class files on disk, you need not customize the JavaFileManager. However, our sample application will generate class files in byte arrays and later read them from memory, using a special class loader. Listing 10.4 defines a class that implements the JavaFileObject interface. Its openOutputStream method returns the ByteArrayOutputStream into which the compiler will deposit the bytecodes.

It turns out a bit tricky to tell the compiler's file manager to use these file objects. The library doesn't supply a class that implements the StandardJavaFileManager interface. Instead, you subclass the ForwardingJavaFileManager class that delegates all calls to a given file manager. In our situation, we only want to change the getJavaFileForOutput method. We achieve this with the following outline:

```
JavaFileManager fileManager = compiler.getStandardFileManager(diagnostics, null, null);
fileManager = new ForwardingJavaFileManager<JavaFileManager>(fileManager)
    {
        public JavaFileObject getJavaFileForOutput(Location location, final String className,
            Kind kind, FileObject sibling) throws IOException
        {
            return custom file object
        }
    };
```

In summary, call the run method of the JavaCompiler task if you simply want to invoke the compiler in the usual way, reading and writing disk files. You can capture the output and error messages, but you need to parse them yourself.

If you want more control over file handling or error reporting, use the CompilationTask interface instead. Its API is quite complex, but you can control every aspect of the compilation process.

**Listing 10.3** compiler/StringBuilderJavaSource.java

```
1  package compiler;
2
3  import java.net.*;
4  import javax.tools.*;
5
6  /**
7   * A Java source that holds the code in a string builder.
8   * @version 1.00 2007-11-02
9   * @author Cay Horstmann
10  */
11 public class StringBuilderJavaSource extends SimpleJavaFileObject
12 {
13    private StringBuilder code;
14
15    /**
16     * Constructs a new StringBuilderJavaSource.
17     * @param name the name of the source file represented by this file object
18     */
19    public StringBuilderJavaSource(String name)
20    {
21       super(URI.create("string:///" + name.replace('.', '/') + Kind.SOURCE.extension),
22          Kind.SOURCE);
23       code = new StringBuilder();
24    }
25
26    public CharSequence getCharContent(boolean ignoreEncodingErrors)
27    {
28       return code;
29    }
30
31    public void append(String str)
32    {
33       code.append(str);
34       code.append('\n');
35    }
36 }
```

**Listing 10.4** compiler/ByteArrayJavaClass.java

```
1  package compiler;
2
3  import java.io.*;
4  import java.net.*;
5  import javax.tools.*;
```

```
6  /**
7   * A Java class that holds the bytecodes in a byte array.
8   * @version 1.00 2007-11-02
9   * @author Cay Horstmann
10  */
11 public class ByteArrayJavaClass extends SimpleJavaFileObject
12 {
13    private ByteArrayOutputStream stream;
14
15    /**
16     * Constructs a new ByteArrayJavaClass.
17     * @param name the name of the class file represented by this file object
18     */
19    public ByteArrayJavaClass(String name)
20    {
21       super(URI.create("bytes:///" + name), Kind.CLASS);
22       stream = new ByteArrayOutputStream();
23    }
24
25    public OutputStream openOutputStream() throws IOException
26    {
27       return stream;
28    }
29
30    public byte[] getBytes()
31    {
32       return stream.toByteArray();
33    }
34 }
```

---

### javax.tools.Tool  6

- int run(InputStream in, OutputStream out, OutputStream err, String... arguments)
  runs the tool with the given input, output, and error streams and the given
  arguments. Returns 0 for success, a nonzero value for failure.

---

### javax.tools.JavaCompiler  6

- StandardJavaFileManager getStandardFileManager(DiagnosticListener<? super JavaFileObject>
  diagnosticListener, Locale locale, Charset charset)
  gets the standard file manager for this compiler. You can supply null for default
  error reporting, locale, and character set.

*(Continues)*

---

*javax.tools.JavaCompiler* 6 *(Continued)*

- JavaCompiler.CompilationTask getTask(Writer out, JavaFileManager fileManager, DiagnosticListener<? super JavaFileObject> diagnosticListener, Iterable<String> options, Iterable<String> classesForAnnotationProcessing, Iterable<? extends JavaFileObject> sourceFiles)

  gets a compilation task that, when called, will compile the given source files. See the discussion in the preceding section for details.

---

*javax.tools.StandardJavaFileManager* 6

- Iterable<? extends JavaFileObject> getJavaFileObjectsFromStrings(Iterable<String> fileNames)
- Iterable<? extends JavaFileObject> getJavaFileObjectsFromFiles(Iterable<? extends File> files)

  translates a sequence of file names or files into a sequence of JavaFileObject instances.

---

*javax.tools.JavaCompiler.CompilationTask* 6

- Boolean call()

  performs the compilation task.

---

*javax.tools.DiagnosticCollector<S>* 6

- DiagnosticCollector()

  constructs an empty collector.

- List<Diagnostic<? extends S>> getDiagnostics()

  gets the collected diagnostics.

---

*javax.tools.Diagnostic<S>* 6

- S getSource()

  gets the source object associated with this diagnostic.

- Diagnostic.Kind getKind()

  gets the type of this diagnostic—one of ERROR, WARNING, MANDATORY_WARNING, NOTE, or OTHER.

- String getMessage(Locale locale)

  gets the message describing the issue raised in this diagnostic. Pass null for the default locale.

- long getLineNumber()
- long getColumnNumber()

  gets the position of the issue raised in this diagnostic.

---

**javax.tools.SimpleJavaFileObject** 6

- CharSequence getCharContent(boolean ignoreEncodingErrors)
  override this method for a file object that represents a source file and produces the source code.

- OutputStream openOutputStream()
  override this method for a file object that represents a class file and produces a stream to which the bytecodes can be written.

---

**javax.tools.ForwardingJavaFileManager<M extends JavaFileManager>** 6

- protected ForwardingJavaFileManager(M fileManager)
  constructs a JavaFileManager that delegates all calls to the given file manager.

- FileObject getFileForOutput(JavaFileManager.Location location, String className, JavaFileObject.Kind kind, FileObject sibling)
  intercept this call if you want to substitute a file object for writing class files; kind is one of SOURCE, CLASS, HTML, or OTHER.

---

## 10.2.3 An Example: Dynamic Java Code Generation

In the JSP technology for dynamic web pages, you can mix HTML with snippets of Java code, such as

```
<p>The current date and time is <b><%= new java.util.Date() %></b>.</p>
```

The JSP engine dynamically compiles the Java code into a servlet. In our sample application, we use a simpler example and generate dynamic Swing code instead. The idea is that you use a GUI builder to lay out the components in a frame and specify the behavior of the components in an external file. Listing 10.5 shows a very simple example of a frame class, and Listing 10.6 shows the code for the button actions. Note that the constructor of the frame class calls an abstract method addEventHandlers. Our code generator will produce a subclass that implements the addEventHandlers method, adding an action listener for each line in the action.properties file. (We leave it as the proverbial exercise to the reader to extend the code generation to other event types.)

We place the subclass into a package with the name x, which we hope is not used anywhere else in the program. The generated code has the form

```
package x;
public class Frame extends SuperclassName {
    protected void addEventHandlers() {
        componentName₁.addActionListener(new java.awt.event.ActionListener() {
            public void actionPerformed(java.awt.event.ActionEvent) {
                code for event handler₁
            } } );
        // repeat for the other event handlers ...
    } }
```

The `buildSource` method in the program of Listing 10.7 builds up this code and places it into a `StringBuilderJavaSource` object. That object is passed to the Java compiler.

We use a `ForwardingJavaFileManager` with a `getJavaFileForOutput` method that constructs a `ByteArrayJavaClass` object for every class in the x package. These objects capture the class files generated when the x.Frame class is compiled. The method adds each file object to a list before returning it so that we can locate the bytecodes later. Note that compiling the x.Frame class produces a class file for the main class and one class file per listener class.

After compilation, we build a map that associates class names with bytecode arrays. A simple class loader (shown in Listing 10.8) loads the classes stored in this map.

We ask the class loader to load the class that we just compiled, and then we construct and display the application's frame class.

```
ClassLoader loader = new MapClassLoader(byteCodeMap);
Class<?> cl = loader.loadClass("x.Frame");
Frame frame = (JFrame) cl.newInstance();
frame.setVisible(true);
```

When you click the buttons, the background color changes in the usual way. To see that the actions are dynamically compiled, change one of the lines in `action.properties`, for example, like this:

```
yellowButton=panel.setBackground(java.awt.Color.YELLOW); yellowButton.setEnabled(false);
```

Run the program again. Now the Yellow button is disabled after you click it. Also have a look at the code directories. You will not find any source or class files for the classes in the x package. This example demonstrates how you can use dynamic compilation with in-memory source and class files.

**Listing 10.5** buttons2/ButtonFrame.java

```
1  package buttons2;
2  import javax.swing.*;
3
4  /**
5   * @version 1.00 2007-11-02
6   * @author Cay Horstmann
7   */
8  public abstract class ButtonFrame extends JFrame
9  {
10     public static final int DEFAULT_WIDTH = 300;
11     public static final int DEFAULT_HEIGHT = 200;
12
13     protected JPanel panel;
14     protected JButton yellowButton;
15     protected JButton blueButton;
16     protected JButton redButton;
17
18     protected abstract void addEventHandlers();
19
20     public ButtonFrame()
21     {
22        setSize(DEFAULT_WIDTH, DEFAULT_HEIGHT);
23
24        panel = new JPanel();
25        add(panel);
26
27        yellowButton = new JButton("Yellow");
28        blueButton = new JButton("Blue");
29        redButton = new JButton("Red");
30
31        panel.add(yellowButton);
32        panel.add(blueButton);
33        panel.add(redButton);
34
35        addEventHandlers();
36     }
37  }
```

**Listing 10.6** buttons2/action.properties

```
1  yellowButton=panel.setBackground(java.awt.Color.YELLOW);
2  blueButton=panel.setBackground(java.awt.Color.BLUE);
```

**Listing 10.7** compiler/CompilerTest.java

```
1  package compiler;
2
3  import java.awt.*;
4  import java.io.*;
5  import java.util.*;
6  import java.util.List;
7  import javax.swing.*;
8  import javax.tools.*;
9  import javax.tools.JavaFileObject.*;
10
11 /**
12  * @version 1.00 2007-10-28
13  * @author Cay Horstmann
14  */
15 public class CompilerTest
16 {
17    public static void main(final String[] args) throws IOException, ClassNotFoundException
18    {
19       JavaCompiler compiler = ToolProvider.getSystemJavaCompiler();
20
21       final List<ByteArrayJavaClass> classFileObjects = new ArrayList<>();
22
23       DiagnosticCollector<JavaFileObject> diagnostics = new DiagnosticCollector<>();
24
25       JavaFileManager fileManager = compiler.getStandardFileManager(diagnostics, null, null);
26       fileManager = new ForwardingJavaFileManager<JavaFileManager>(fileManager)
27          {
28             public JavaFileObject getJavaFileForOutput(Location location, final String className,
29                   Kind kind, FileObject sibling) throws IOException
30             {
31                if (className.startsWith("x."))
32                {
33                   ByteArrayJavaClass fileObject = new ByteArrayJavaClass(className);
34                   classFileObjects.add(fileObject);
35                   return fileObject;
36                }
37                else return super.getJavaFileForOutput(location, className, kind, sibling);
38             }
39          };
40
41
42       String frameClassName = args.length == 0 ? "buttons2.ButtonFrame" : args[0];
43       JavaFileObject source = buildSource(frameClassName);
44       JavaCompiler.CompilationTask task = compiler.getTask(null, fileManager, diagnostics, null,
45             null, Arrays.asList(source));
```

```
46      Boolean result = task.call();
47
48      for (Diagnostic<? extends JavaFileObject> d : diagnostics.getDiagnostics())
49         System.out.println(d.getKind() + ": " + d.getMessage(null));
50      fileManager.close();
51      if (!result)
52      {
53         System.out.println("Compilation failed.");
54         System.exit(1);
55      }
56
57      EventQueue.invokeLater(new Runnable()
58         {
59            public void run()
60            {
61               try
62               {
63                  Map<String, byte[]> byteCodeMap = new HashMap<>();
64                  for (ByteArrayJavaClass cl : classFileObjects)
65                     byteCodeMap.put(cl.getName().substring(1), cl.getBytes());
66                  ClassLoader loader = new MapClassLoader(byteCodeMap);
67                  JFrame frame = (JFrame) loader.loadClass("x.Frame").newInstance();
68                  frame.setDefaultCloseOperation(JFrame.EXIT_ON_CLOSE);
69                  frame.setTitle("CompilerTest");
70                  frame.setVisible(true);
71               }
72               catch (Exception ex)
73               {
74                  ex.printStackTrace();
75               }
76            }
77         });
78   }
79
80   /*
81    * Builds the source for the subclass that implements the addEventHandlers method.
82    * @return a file object containing the source in a string builder
83    */
84   static JavaFileObject buildSource(String superclassName)
85      throws IOException, ClassNotFoundException
86   {
87      StringBuilderJavaSource source = new StringBuilderJavaSource("x.Frame");
88      source.append("package x;\n");
89      source.append("public class Frame extends " + superclassName + " {");
90      source.append("protected void addEventHandlers() {");
91      final Properties props = new Properties();
92      props.load(Class.forName(superclassName).getResourceAsStream("action.properties"));
```

*(Continues)*

**Listing 10.7** *(Continued)*

```
93       for (Map.Entry<Object, Object> e : props.entrySet())
94       {
95          String beanName = (String) e.getKey();
96          String eventCode = (String) e.getValue();
97          source.append(beanName + ".addActionListener(new java.awt.event.ActionListener() {");
98          source.append("public void actionPerformed(java.awt.event.ActionEvent event) {");
99          source.append(eventCode);
100         source.append("} } );");
101      }
102      source.append("} }");
103      return source;
104   }
105 }
```

**Listing 10.8** compiler/MapClassLoader.java

```
1 package compiler;
2
3 import java.util.*;
4
5 /**
6  * A class loader that loads classes from a map whose keys are class names and whose values are
7  * byte code arrays.
8  * @version 1.00 2007-11-02
9  * @author Cay Horstmann
10 */
11 public class MapClassLoader extends ClassLoader
12 {
13    private Map<String, byte[]> classes;
14
15    public MapClassLoader(Map<String, byte[]> classes)
16    {
17       this.classes = classes;
18    }
19
20    protected Class<?> findClass(String name) throws ClassNotFoundException
21    {
22       byte[] classBytes = classes.get(name);
23       if (classBytes == null) throw new ClassNotFoundException(name);
24       Class<?> cl = defineClass(name, classBytes, 0, classBytes.length);
25       if (cl == null) throw new ClassNotFoundException(name);
26       return cl;
27    }
28 }
```

## 10.3  Using Annotations

Annotations are tags that you insert into your source code so that some tool can process them. The tools can operate on the source level, or they can process class files into which the compiler has placed annotations.

Annotations do not change the way in which your programs are compiled. The Java compiler generates the same virtual machine instructions with or without the annotations.

To benefit from annotations, you need to select a *processing tool*. You need to use annotations that your processing tool understands, then apply the processing tool to your code.

There is a wide range of uses for annotations, and that generality can be confusing at first. Here are some uses for annotations:

*   Automatic generation of auxiliary files, such as deployment descriptors or bean information classes
*   Automatic generation of code for testing, logging, transaction semantics, and so on

We'll start our discussion of annotations with the basic concepts and put them to use in a concrete example: We will mark methods as event listeners for AWT components, and show you an annotation processor that analyzes the annotations and hooks up the listeners. We'll then discuss the syntax rules in detail and finish the chapter with two advanced examples for annotation processing. One of them processes source-level annotations, the other uses the Apache Bytecode Engineering Library to process class files, injecting additional bytecodes into annotated methods.

Here is an example of a simple annotation:

```
public class MyClass
{
   . . .
   @Test public void checkRandomInsertions()
}
```

The annotation @Test annotates the checkRandomInsertions method.

In Java, an annotation is used like a *modifier* and is placed before the annotated item *without a semicolon*. (A modifier is a keyword such as public or static.) The name of each annotation is preceded by an @ symbol, similar to Javadoc comments. However, Javadoc comments occur inside /** . . . */ delimiters, whereas annotations are part of the code.

By itself, the @Test annotation does not do anything. It needs a tool to be useful. For example, the JUnit 4 testing tool (available at http://junit.org) calls all methods that are labeled @Test when testing a class. Another tool might remove all test methods from a class file so that they are not shipped with the program after it has been tested.

Annotations can be defined to have *elements*, such as

```
@Test(timeout="10000")
```

These elements can be processed by the tools that read the annotations. Other forms of elements are possible; we'll discuss them later in this chapter.

Besides methods, you can annotate classes, fields, and local variables—an annotation can be anywhere you could put a modifier such as public or static.

Each annotation must be defined by an *annotation interface*. The methods of the interface correspond to the elements of the annotation. For example, the JUnit Test annotation is defined by the following interface:

```
@Target(ElementType.METHOD)
@Retention(RetentionPolicy.RUNTIME)
public @interface Test
{
   long timeout() default 0L;
   . . .
}
```

The @interface declaration creates an actual Java interface. Tools that process annotations receive objects that implement the annotation interface. A tool would call the timeout method to retrieve the timeout element of a particular Test annotation.

The Target and Retention annotations are *meta-annotations*. They annotate the Test annotation, marking it as an annotation that can be applied to methods only and is retained when the class file is loaded into the virtual machine. We'll discuss these in detail in Section 10.5.3, "Meta-Annotations," on p. 933.

You have now seen the basic concepts of program metadata and annotations. In the next section, we'll walk through a concrete example of annotation processing.

## 10.3.1  An Example: Annotating Event Handlers

One of the more boring tasks in user interface programming is the wiring of listeners to event sources. Many listeners are of the form

```
myButton.addActionListener(new
   ActionListener()
   {
      public void actionPerformed(ActionEvent event)
      {
         doSomething();
      }
   });
```

In this section, we'll design an annotation to avoid this drudgery. The annotation, defined in Listing 10.9, is used as follows:

```
@ActionListenerFor(source="myButton") void doSomething() { . . . }
```

The programmer no longer has to make calls to addActionListener. Instead, each method is simply tagged with an annotation. Listing 10.10 shows the ButtonFrame class from Volume I, Chapter 8, reimplemented with these annotations.

We also need to define an annotation interface. The code is in Listing 10.11.

Of course, the annotations don't do anything by themselves. They sit in the source file. The compiler places them in the class file, and the virtual machine loads them. We now need a mechanism to analyze them and install action listeners. That is the job of the ActionListenerInstaller class. The ButtonFrame constructor calls

```
ActionListenerInstaller.processAnnotations(this);
```

The static processAnnotations method enumerates all methods of the object it received. For each method, it gets the ActionListenerFor annotation object and processes it.

```
Class<?> cl = obj.getClass();
for (Method m : cl.getDeclaredMethods())
{
   ActionListenerFor a = m.getAnnotation(ActionListenerFor.class);
   if (a != null) . . .
}
```

Here, we use the getAnnotation method defined in the AnnotatedElement interface. The classes Method, Constructor, Field, Class, and Package implement this interface.

The name of the source field is stored in the annotation object. We retrieve it by calling the source method, and then look up the matching field.

```
String fieldName = a.source();
Field f = cl.getDeclaredField(fieldName);
```

This shows a limitation of our annotation. The source element must be the name of a field. It cannot be a local variable.

The remainder of the code is rather technical. For each annotated method, we construct a proxy object, implementing the `ActionListener` interface, with an `actionPerformed` method that calls the annotated method. (For more information about proxies, see Volume I, Chapter 6.) The details are not important. The key observation is that the functionality of the annotations was established by the `processAnnotations` method.

Figure 10.1 shows how annotations are handled in this example.

In this example, the annotations were processed at runtime. It is also possible to process them at the source level; a source code generator would then produce the code for adding the listeners. Alternatively, the annotations can be processed at the bytecode level; a bytecode editor could inject the calls to `addActionListener` into the frame constructor. This sounds complex, but libraries are available to make this task relatively straightforward. You can see an example in Section 10.7, "Bytecode Engineering," on p. 943.

Our example was not intended as a serious tool for user interface programmers. A utility method for adding a listener could be just as convenient for the programmer as the annotation. (In fact, the `java.beans.EventHandler` class tries to do just that. You could make the class truly useful by supplying a method that adds the event handler instead of just constructing it.)

However, this example shows the mechanics of annotating a program and of analyzing the annotations. Having seen a concrete example, you are now more prepared (we hope) for the following sections that describe the annotation syntax in complete detail.

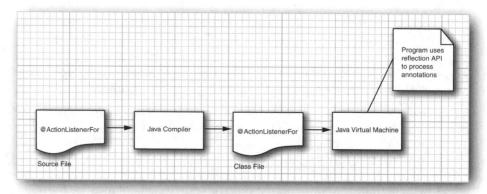

**Figure 10.1** Processing annotations at runtime

---

**Listing 10.9**  runtimeAnnotations/ActionListenerInstaller.java

```
1  package runtimeAnnotations;
2
3  import java.awt.event.*;
4  import java.lang.reflect.*;
5
6  /**
7   * @version 1.00 2004-08-17
8   * @author Cay Horstmann
9   */
10 public class ActionListenerInstaller
11 {
12    /**
13     * Processes all ActionListenerFor annotations in the given object.
14     * @param obj an object whose methods may have ActionListenerFor annotations
15     */
16    public static void processAnnotations(Object obj)
17    {
18       try
19       {
20          Class<?> cl = obj.getClass();
21          for (Method m : cl.getDeclaredMethods())
22          {
23             ActionListenerFor a = m.getAnnotation(ActionListenerFor.class);
24             if (a != null)
25             {
26                Field f = cl.getDeclaredField(a.source());
27                f.setAccessible(true);
28                addListener(f.get(obj), obj, m);
29             }
30          }
31       }
32       catch (ReflectiveOperationException e)
33       {
34          e.printStackTrace();
35       }
36    }
37
38    /**
39     * Adds an action listener that calls a given method.
40     * @param source the event source to which an action listener is added
41     * @param param the implicit parameter of the method that the listener calls
42     * @param m the method that the listener calls
43     */
```

*(Continues)*

---

**Listing 10.9** *(Continued)*

```
44  public static void addListener(Object source, final Object param, final Method m)
45        throws ReflectiveOperationException
46  {
47      InvocationHandler handler = new InvocationHandler()
48        {
49            public Object invoke(Object proxy, Method mm, Object[] args) throws Throwable
50            {
51                return m.invoke(param);
52            }
53        };
54
55      Object listener = Proxy.newProxyInstance(null,
56            new Class[] { java.awt.event.ActionListener.class }, handler);
57      Method adder = source.getClass().getMethod("addActionListener", ActionListener.class);
58      adder.invoke(source, listener);
59  }
60 }
```

---

**Listing 10.10** buttons3/ButtonFrame.java

```
1  package buttons3;
2
3  import java.awt.*;
4  import javax.swing.*;
5  import runtimeAnnotations.*;
6
7  /**
8   * A frame with a button panel.
9   * @version 1.00 2004-08-17
10  * @author Cay Horstmann
11  */
12 public class ButtonFrame extends JFrame
13 {
14    private static final int DEFAULT_WIDTH = 300;
15    private static final int DEFAULT_HEIGHT = 200;
16
17    private JPanel panel;
18    private JButton yellowButton;
19    private JButton blueButton;
20    private JButton redButton;
21
22    public ButtonFrame()
23    {
24       setSize(DEFAULT_WIDTH, DEFAULT_HEIGHT);
25
26       panel = new JPanel();
27       add(panel);
```

```
28        yellowButton = new JButton("Yellow");
29        blueButton = new JButton("Blue");
30        redButton = new JButton("Red");
31
32        panel.add(yellowButton);
33        panel.add(blueButton);
34        panel.add(redButton);
35
36        ActionListenerInstaller.processAnnotations(this);
37     }
38
39     @ActionListenerFor(source = "yellowButton")
40     public void yellowBackground()
41     {
42        panel.setBackground(Color.YELLOW);
43     }
44
45     @ActionListenerFor(source = "blueButton")
46     public void blueBackground()
47     {
48        panel.setBackground(Color.BLUE);
49     }
50
51     @ActionListenerFor(source = "redButton")
52     public void redBackground()
53     {
54        panel.setBackground(Color.RED);
55     }
56  }
```

---

**Listing 10.11** runtimeAnnotations/ActionListenerFor.java

```
1  package runtimeAnnotations;
2
3  import java.lang.annotation.*;
4
5  /**
6   * @version 1.00 2004-08-17
7   * @author Cay Horstmann
8   */
9
10 @Target(ElementType.METHOD)
11 @Retention(RetentionPolicy.RUNTIME)
12 public @interface ActionListenerFor
13 {
14    String source();
15 }
```

---

*java.lang.reflect.AnnotatedElement* 5.0

- `boolean isAnnotationPresent(Class<? extends Annotation> annotationType)`
  returns true if this item has an annotation of the given type.

- `<T extends Annotation> T getAnnotation(Class<T> annotationType)`
  gets the annotation of the given type, or null if this item has no such annotation.

- `Annotation[] getAnnotations()`
  gets all annotations present for this item, including inherited annotations. If no annotations are present, an array of length 0 is returned.

- `Annotation[] getDeclaredAnnotations()`
  gets all annotations declared for this item, excluding inherited annotations. If no annotations are present, an array of length 0 is returned.

---

## 10.4 Annotation Syntax

In this section, we cover everything you need to know about the annotation syntax.

An annotation is defined by an annotation interface:

```
modifiers @interface AnnotationName
{
    elementDeclaration₁
    elementDeclaration₂
    . . .
}
```

Each element declaration has the form

```
type elementName();
```

or

```
type elementName() default value;
```

For example, the following annotation has two elements, `assignedTo` and `severity`:

```
public @interface BugReport
{
    String assignedTo() default "[none]";
    int severity() = 0;
}
```

Each annotation has the format

```
@AnnotationName(elementName₁=value₁, elementName₂=value₂, . . .)
```

For example,

```
@BugReport(assignedTo="Harry", severity=10)
```

The order of the elements does not matter. The annotation

```
@BugReport(severity=10, assignedTo="Harry")
```

is identical to the preceding one.

The default value of the declaration is used if an element value is not specified. For example, consider the annotation

```
@BugReport(severity=10)
```

The value of the `assignedTo` element is the string `"[none]"`.

 **CAUTION:** Defaults are not stored with the annotation; instead, they are dynamically computed. For example, if you change the default for the `assignedTo` element to `"[]"` and recompile the `BugReport` interface, the annotation `@BugReport(severity=10)` will use the new default, even in class files that have been compiled before the default changed.

Two special shortcuts can simplify annotations.

If no elements are specified, either because the annotation doesn't have any or because all of them use the default value, you don't need to use parentheses. For example,

```
@BugReport
```

is the same as

```
@BugReport(assignedTo="[none]", severity=0)
```

Such an annotation is called a *marker annotation*.

The other shortcut is the *single value annotation*. If an element has the special name `value` and no other element is specified, you can omit the element name and the `=` symbol. For example, had we defined the `ActionListenerFor` annotation interface of the preceding section as

```
public @interface ActionListenerFor
{
   String value();
}
```

then the annotations could be written as

```
@ActionListenerFor("yellowButton")
```

instead of

```
@ActionListenerFor(value="yellowButton")
```

All annotation interfaces implicitly extend the `java.lang.annotation.Annotation` interface. That interface is a regular interface, *not* an annotation interface. See the API notes at the end of this section for the methods provided by this interface.

You cannot extend annotation interfaces. In other words, all annotation interfaces directly extend `java.lang.annotation.Annotation`.

You never supply classes that implement annotation interfaces. Instead, the virtual machine generates proxy classes and objects when needed. For example, when requesting an `ActionListenerFor` annotation, the virtual machine carries out an operation similar to the following:

```
return Proxy.newProxyInstance(classLoader, ActionListenerFor.class,
    new
      InvocationHandler()
      {
        public Object invoke(Object proxy, Method m, Object[] args) throws Throwable
        {
          if (m.getName().equals("source")) return value of source annotation;
          . . .
        }
      });
```

The element declarations in the annotation interface are actually method declarations. The methods of an annotation interface can have no parameters and no `throws` clauses, and they cannot be generic.

The type of an annotation element is one of the following:

- A primitive type (`int`, `short`, `long`, `byte`, `char`, `double`, `float`, or `boolean`)
- `String`
- `Class` (with an optional type parameter such as `Class<? extends MyClass>`)
- An `enum` type
- An annotation type
- An array of the preceding types (an array of arrays is not a legal element type)

Here are examples of valid element declarations:

```
public @interface BugReport
{
    enum Status { UNCONFIRMED, CONFIRMED, FIXED, NOTABUG };
    boolean showStopper() default false;
    String assignedTo() default "[none]";
    Class<?> testCase() default Void.class;
```

```
    Status status() default Status.UNCONFIRMED;
    Reference ref() default @Reference(); // an annotation type
    String[] reportedBy();
}
```

Since annotations are evaluated by the compiler, all element values must be compile-time constants. For example,

```
@BugReport(showStopper=true, assignedTo="Harry", testCase=MyTestCase.class,
    status=BugReport.Status.CONFIRMED, . . .)
```

**CAUTION:** An annotation element can never be set to null. Not even a default of null is permissible. This can be rather inconvenient in practice. You will need to find other defaults, such as "" or Void.class.

If an element value is an array, enclose its values in braces:

```
@BugReport(. . ., reportedBy={"Harry", "Carl"})
```

You can omit the braces if the element has a single value:

```
@BugReport(. . ., reportedBy="Joe") // OK, same as {"Joe"}
```

Since an annotation element can be another annotation, you can build arbitrarily complex annotations. For example,

```
@BugReport(ref=@Reference(id="3352627"), . . .)
```

**NOTE:** It is an error to introduce circular dependencies in annotations. For example, BugReport has an element of the annotation type Reference, therefore Reference cannot have an element of type BugReport.

You can add annotations to the following items:

- Packages
- Classes (including enum)
- Interfaces (including annotation interfaces)
- Methods
- Constructors
- Instance fields (including enum constants)
- Local variables
- Parameter variables

However, annotations for local variables can only be processed at the source level. Class files do not describe local variables. Therefore, all local variable annotations are discarded when a class is compiled. Similarly, annotations for packages are not retained beyond the source level.

 **NOTE:** A package is annotated in a file `package-info.java` that contains only the package statement preceded by annotations.

An item can have multiple annotations, provided they belong to different types. You cannot use the same annotation type more than once when annotating a particular item. For example,

```
@BugReport(showStopper=true, reportedBy="Joe")
@BugReport(reportedBy={"Harry", "Carl"})
void myMethod()
```

is a compile-time error. If this is a problem, design an annotation whose value is an array of simpler annotations:

```
@BugReports({
    @BugReport(showStopper=true, reportedBy="Joe"),
    @BugReport(reportedBy={"Harry", "Carl"})})
void myMethod()
```

---

**`java.lang.annotation.Annotation` 5.0**

- `Class<? extends Annotation> annotationType()`
  returns the Class object that represents the annotation interface of this annotation object. Note that calling `getClass` on an annotation object would return the actual class, not the interface.

- `boolean equals(Object other)`
  returns `true` if `other` is an object that implements the same annotation interface as this annotation object and if all elements of this object and `other` are equal.

- `int hashCode()`
  returns a hash code, compatible with the `equals` method, derived from the name of the annotation interface and the element values.

- `String toString()`
  returns a string representation that contains the annotation interface name and the element values; for example, `@BugReport(assignedTo=[none], severity=0)`.

---

## 10.5 Standard Annotations

Java SE defines a number of annotation interfaces in the `java.lang`, `java.lang.annotation`, and `javax.annotation` packages. Four of them are meta-annotations that describe the behavior of annotation interfaces. The others are regular annotations that you can use to annotate items in your source code. Table 10.2 shows these annotations. We'll discuss them in detail in the following two sections.

**Table 10.2** The Standard Annotations

| Annotation Interface | Applicable To | Purpose |
|---|---|---|
| Deprecated | All | Marks item as deprecated. |
| SuppressWarnings | All but packages and annotations | Suppresses warnings of the given type. |
| Override | Methods | Checks that this method overrides a superclass method. |
| PostConstruct PreDestroy | Methods | The marked method should be invoked immediately after construction or before removal. |
| Resource | Classes, interfaces, methods, fields | On a class or interface, marks it as a resource to be used elsewhere. On a method or field, marks it for "injection." |
| Resources | Classes, interfaces | Specifies an array of resources. |
| Generated | All | Marks an item as source code that has been generated by a tool. |
| Target | Annotations | Specifies the items to which this annotation can be applied. |
| Retention | Annotations | Specifies how long this annotation is retained. |
| Documented | Annotations | Specifies that this annotation should be included in the documentation of annotated items. |
| Inherited | Annotations | Specifies that this annotation, when applied to a class, is automatically inherited by its subclasses. |

## 10.5.1 Annotations for Compilation

The `@Deprecated` annotation can be attached to any items for which use is no longer encouraged. The compiler will warn when you use a deprecated item. This annotation has the same role as the `@deprecated` Javadoc tag.

The `@SuppressWarnings` annotation tells the compiler to suppress warnings of a particular type, for example,

```
@SuppressWarnings("unchecked")
```

The `@Override` annotation applies only to methods. The compiler checks that a method with this annotation really overrides a method from the superclass. For example, if you declare

```
public MyClass
{
    @Override public boolean equals(MyClass other);
    . . .
}
```

then the compiler will report an error. After all, the `equals` method does *not* override the `equals` method of the `Object` class because that method has a parameter of type `Object`, not `MyClass`.

The `@Generated` annotation is intended for use by code generator tools. Any generated source code can be annotated to differentiate it from programmer-provided code. For example, a code editor can hide the generated code, or a code generator can remove older versions of generated code. Each annotation must contain a unique identifier for the code generator. A date string (in ISO 8601 format) and a comment string are optional. For example,

```
@Generated("com.horstmann.beanproperty", "2008-01-04T12:08:56.235-0700");
```

## 10.5.2 Annotations for Managing Resources

The `@PostConstruct` and `@PreDestroy` annotations are used in environments that control the lifecycle of objects, such as web containers and application servers. Methods tagged with these annotations should be invoked immediately after an object has been constructed or immediately before it is being removed.

The `@Resource` annotation is intended for resource injection. For example, consider a web application that accesses a database. Of course, the database access information should not be hardwired into the web application. Instead, the web container has some user interface for setting connection parameters and a JNDI name for a data source. In the web application, you can reference the data source like this:

```
@Resource(name="jdbc/mydb")
private DataSource source;
```

When an object containing this field is constructed, the container "injects" a reference to the data source.

## 10.5.3 Meta-Annotations

The @Target meta-annotation is applied to an annotation, restricting the items to which the annotation applies. For example,

```
@Target({ElementType.TYPE, ElementType.METHOD})
public @interface BugReport
```

Table 10.3 shows all possible values. They belong to the enumerated type ElementType. You can specify any number of element types, enclosed in braces.

An annotation without an @Target restriction can be applied to any item. The compiler checks that you apply an annotation only to a permitted item. For example, if you apply @BugReport to a field, a compile-time error results.

The @Retention meta-annotation specifies how long an annotation is retained. You can specify at most one of the values in Table 10.4. The default is RetentionPolicy.CLASS.

In Listing 10.11 on p. 925, the @ActionListenerFor annotation was declared with RetentionPolicy.RUNTIME because we used reflection to process annotations. In the following two sections, you will see examples of processing annotations at the source and class file levels.

**Table 10.3** Element Types for the @Target Annotation

| Element Type | Annotation Applies To |
| --- | --- |
| ANNOTATION_TYPE | Annotation type declarations |
| PACKAGE | Packages |
| TYPE | Classes (including enum) and interfaces (including annotation types) |
| METHOD | Methods |
| CONSTRUCTOR | Constructors |
| FIELD | Fields (including enum constants) |
| PARAMETER | Method or constructor parameters |
| LOCAL_VARIABLE | Local variables |

**Table 10.4** Retention Policies for the @Retention Annotation

| Retention Policy | Description |
|---|---|
| SOURCE | Annotations are not included in class files. |
| CLASS | Annotations are included in class files, but the virtual machine need not load them. |
| RUNTIME | Annotations are included in class files and loaded by the virtual machine. They are available through the reflection API. |

The @Documented meta-annotation gives a hint to documentation tools such as Javadoc. Documented annotations should be treated just like other modifiers such as protected or static for documentation purposes. The use of other annotations is not included in the documentation. For example, suppose we declare @ActionListenerFor as a documented annotation:

```
@Documented
@Target(ElementType.METHOD)
@Retention(RetentionPolicy.RUNTIME)
public @interface ActionListenerFor
```

Now the documentation of each annotated method contains the annotation, as shown in Figure 10.2.

If an annotation is transient (such as @BugReport), you should probably not document its use.

 **NOTE:** It is legal to apply an annotation to itself. For example, the @Documented annotation is itself annotated as @Documented. Therefore, the Javadoc documentation for annotations shows whether they are documented.

The @Inherited meta-annotation applies only to annotations for classes. When a class has an inherited annotation, then all of its subclasses automatically have the same annotation. This makes it easy to create annotations that work as marker interfaces, such as Serializable.

In fact, an annotation @Serializable would be more appropriate than the Serializable marker interface with no methods. A class is serializable because there is runtime support for reading and writing its fields, not because of any principles of object-oriented design. An annotation describes this fact better than does interface inheritance. Of course, the Serializable interface was created in JDK 1.1, long before annotations existed.

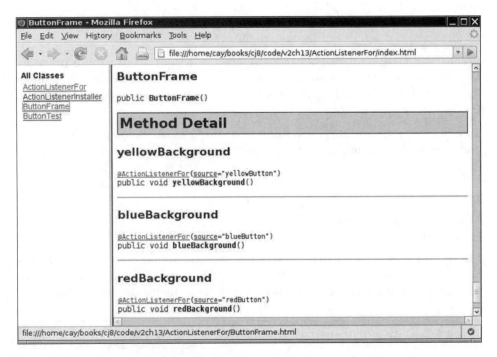

**Figure 10.2** Documented annotations

Suppose you define an inherited annotation @Persistent to indicate that objects of a class can be saved in a database. Then the subclasses of persistent classes are automatically annotated as persistent.

```
@Inherited @interface Persistent { }
@Persistent class Employee { . . . }
class Manager extends Employee { . . . } // also @Persistent
```

When the persistence mechanism searches for objects to store in the database, it will detect both Employee and Manager objects.

## 10.6  Source-Level Annotation Processing

One use for annotation is the automatic generation of "side files" that contain additional information about programs. In the past, the Enterprise Edition of Java was notorious for making programmers fuss with lots of boilerplate code. Modern versions of Java EE use annotations to greatly simplify the programming model.

In this section, we demonstrate this technique with a simpler example. We write a program that automatically produces bean info classes. You tag bean properties with an annotation and then run a tool that parses the source file, analyzes the annotations, and writes out the source file of the bean info class.

Recall from Chapter 8 that a bean info class describes a bean more precisely than the automatic introspection process can. The bean info class lists all of the properties of the bean. Properties can have optional property editors. The ChartBeanBeanInfo class in Chapter 8 is a typical example.

To eliminate the drudgery of writing bean info classes, we supply an @Property annotation. You can tag either the property getter or setter, like this:

```
@Property String getTitle() { return title; }
```

or

```
@Property(editor="TitlePositionEditor")
public void setTitlePosition(int p) { titlePosition = p; }
```

Listing 10.12 contains the definition of the @Property annotation. Note that the annotation has a retention policy of SOURCE. We analyze the annotation at the source level only. It is not included in class files and not available during reflection.

**Listing 10.12**  sourceAnnotations/Property.java

```
 1  package sourceAnnotations;
 2  import java.lang.annotation.*;
 3
 4  @Documented
 5  @Target(ElementType.METHOD)
 6  @Retention(RetentionPolicy.SOURCE)
 7  public @interface Property
 8  {
 9     String editor() default "";
10  }
```

 **NOTE:** It would have made sense to declare the editor element to have type Class. However, the annotation processor cannot retrieve annotations of type Class because the meaning of a class can depend on external factors (such as the class path or class loaders). Therefore, we use a string to specify the editor class name.

To automatically generate the bean info class of a class with name *BeanClass*, we carry out the following tasks:

1.  Write a source file *BeanClass*BeanInfo.java. Declare the *BeanClass*BeanInfo class to extend SimpleBeanInfo, and override the getPropertyDescriptors method.

2. For each annotated method, recover the property name by stripping off the get or set prefix and "decapitalizing" the remainder.

3. For each property, write a statement for constructing a PropertyDescriptor.

4. If the property has an editor, write a method call to setPropertyEditorClass.

5. Write the code for returning an array of all property descriptors.

For example, the annotation

```
@Property(editor="TitlePositionEditor")
public void setTitlePosition(int p) { titlePosition = p; }
```

in the ChartBean class is translated into

```
public class ChartBeanBeanInfo extends java.beans.SimpleBeanInfo
{
    public java.beans.PropertyDescriptor[] getProperties()
    {
        java.beans.PropertyDescriptor titlePositionDescriptor
            = new java.beans.PropertyDescriptor("titlePosition", ChartBean.class);
        titlePositionDescriptor.setPropertyEditorClass(TitlePositionEditor.class)
        . . .
        return new java.beans.PropertyDescriptor[]
        {
            titlePositionDescriptor,
            . . .
        }
    }
}
```

(The boilerplate code is printed in the lighter gray.)

All this is easy enough to do, provided we can locate all methods that have been tagged with the @Property annotation.

As of Java SE 6, you can add *annotation processors* to the Java compiler. (In Java SE 5, a stand-alone tool, called apt, was used for the same purpose.) To invoke annotation processing, run

```
javac -processor ProcessorClassName₁,ProcessorClassName₂,. . . sourceFiles
```

The compiler locates the annotations of the source files. It then selects the annotation processors that should be applied. Each annotation processor is executed in turn. If an annotation processor creates a new source file, then the process is repeated. Once a processing round yields no further source files, all source files are compiled. Figure 10.3 shows how the @Property annotations are processed.

We do not discuss the annotation processing API in detail, but the program in Listing 10.13 will give you a flavor of its capabilities.

An annotation processor implements the Processor interface, generally by extending the AbstractProcessor class. You need to specify which annotations your processor supports. The designers of the API themselves love annotations, so they use an annotation for this purpose:

```
@SupportedAnnotationTypes("com.horstmann.annotations.Property")
public class BeanInfoAnnotationProcessor extends AbstractProcessor
```

A processor can claim specific annotation types, wildcards such as "com.horstmann.*" (all annotations in the com.horstmann package or any subpackage), or even "*" (all annotations).

The BeanInfoAnnotationProcessor has a single public method, process, that is called for each file. The process method has two parameters: the set of annotations that is being processed in this round, and a RoundEnv reference that contains information about the current processing round.

In the process method, we iterate through all annotated methods. For each method, we get the property name by stripping off the get, set, or is prefix and changing the next letter to lower case. Here is the outline of the code:

```
public boolean process(Set<? extends TypeElement> annotations, RoundEnvironment roundEnv)
{
   for (TypeElement t : annotations)
   {
      Map<String, Property> props = new LinkedHashMap<String, Property>();
      for (Element e : roundEnv.getElementsAnnotatedWith(t))
      {
         props.put(property name, e.getAnnotation(Property.class));
      }
   }
   write bean info source file
   return true;
}
```

The process method should return true if it *claims* all the annotations presented to it; that is, if those annotations should not be passed on to other processors.

The code for writing the source file is straightforward—just a sequence of out.print statements. Note that we create the output writer as follows:

```
JavaFileObject sourceFile = processingEnv.getFiler().createSourceFile(beanClassName + "BeanInfo");
PrintWriter out = new PrintWriter(sourceFile.openWriter());
```

The AbstractProcessor class has a protected field processingEnv for accessing various processing services. The Filer interface is responsible for creating new files and tracking them so that they can be processed in subsequent processing rounds.

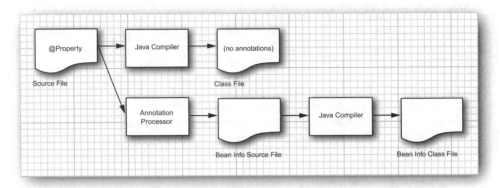

**Figure 10.3** Processing source-level annotations

When an annotation processor detects an error, it uses the Messager to communicate with the user. For example, we issue an error message if a method has been annotated with @Property but its name doesn't start with get, set, or is:

```
if (!found) processingEnv.getMessager().printMessage(Kind.ERROR,
    "@Property must be applied to getXxx, setXxx, or isXxx method", e);
```

In the companion code for this book, we supply an annotated file, ChartBean.java. Compile the annotation processor:

```
javac sourceAnnotations/BeanInfoAnnotationProcessor.java
```

Then run

```
javac -processor sourceAnnotations.BeanInfoAnnotationProcessor chart/ChartBean.java
```

and have a look at the automatically generated file ChartBeanBeanInfo.java.

To see the annotation processing in action, add the command-line option XprintRounds to the javac command. You will get this output:

```
Round 1:
        input files: {com.horstmann.corejava.ChartBean}
        annotations: [com.horstmann.annotations.Property]
        last round: false
Round 2:
        input files: {com.horstmann.corejava.ChartBeanBeanInfo}
        annotations: []
        last round: false
Round 3:
        input files: {}
        annotations: []
        last round: true
```

This example demonstrates how tools can harvest source file annotations to produce other files. The generated files don't have to be source files. Annotation processors may choose to generate XML descriptors, property files, shell scripts, HTML documentation, and so on.

 **NOTE:** Some people have suggested using annotations to remove an even bigger drudgery. Wouldn't it be nice if trivial getters and setters were generated automatically? For example, the annotation

```
@Property private String title;
```

could produce the methods

```
public String getTitle() { return title; }
public void setTitle(String title) { this.title = title; }
```

However, those methods need to be added to the *same class*. This requires editing a source file, not just generating another file, and is beyond the capabilities of annotation processors. It would be possible to build another tool for this purpose, but such a tool would go beyond the mission of annotations. An annotation is intended as a description *about* a code item, not a directive for adding or changing code.

**Listing 10.13** sourceAnnotations/BeanInfoAnnotationProcessor.java

```
1  package sourceAnnotations;
2
3  import java.beans.*;
4  import java.io.*;
5  import java.util.*;
6  import javax.annotation.processing.*;
7  import javax.lang.model.*;
8  import javax.lang.model.element.*;
9  import javax.tools.*;
10 import javax.tools.Diagnostic.*;
11
12 /**
13  * This class is the processor that analyzes Property annotations.
14  * @version 1.11 2012-01-26
15  * @author Cay Horstmann
16  */
17 @SupportedAnnotationTypes("sourceAnnotations.Property")
18 @SupportedSourceVersion(SourceVersion.RELEASE_7)
19 public class BeanInfoAnnotationProcessor extends AbstractProcessor
20 {
```

```
21   @Override
22   public boolean process(Set<? extends TypeElement> annotations, RoundEnvironment roundEnv)
23   {
24      for (TypeElement t : annotations)
25      {
26         Map<String, Property> props = new LinkedHashMap<>();
27         String beanClassName = null;
28         for (Element e : roundEnv.getElementsAnnotatedWith(t))
29         {
30            String mname = e.getSimpleName().toString();
31            String[] prefixes = { "get", "set", "is" };
32            boolean found = false;
33            for (int i = 0; !found && i < prefixes.length; i++)
34               if (mname.startsWith(prefixes[i]))
35               {
36                  found = true;
37                  int start = prefixes[i].length();
38                  String name = Introspector.decapitalize(mname.substring(start));
39                  props.put(name, e.getAnnotation(Property.class));
40               }

42            if (!found) processingEnv.getMessager().printMessage(Kind.ERROR,
43                  "@Property must be applied to getXxx, setXxx, or isXxx method", e);
44            else if (beanClassName == null)
45               beanClassName = ((TypeElement) e.getEnclosingElement()).getQualifiedName()
46                     .toString();
47         }
48         try
49         {
50            if (beanClassName != null) writeBeanInfoFile(beanClassName, props);
51         }
52         catch (IOException e)
53         {
54            e.printStackTrace();
55         }
56      }
57      return true;
58   }

60   /**
61    * Writes the source file for the BeanInfo class.
62    * @param beanClassName the name of the bean class
63    * @param props a map of property names and their annotations
64    */
65   private void writeBeanInfoFile(String beanClassName, Map<String, Property> props)
66      throws IOException
67   {
68      JavaFileObject sourceFile = processingEnv.getFiler().createSourceFile(
69         beanClassName + "BeanInfo");
```

*(Continues)*

Listing 10.13    *(Continued)*

```
70       PrintWriter out = new PrintWriter(sourceFile.openWriter());
71       int i = beanClassName.lastIndexOf(".");
72       if (i > 0)
73       {
74          out.print("package ");
75          out.print(beanClassName.substring(0, i));
76          out.println(";");
77       }
78       out.print("public class ");
79       out.print(beanClassName.substring(i + 1));
80       out.println("BeanInfo extends java.beans.SimpleBeanInfo");
81       out.println("{");
82       out.println("   public java.beans.PropertyDescriptor[] getPropertyDescriptors()");
83       out.println("   {");
84       out.println("      try");
85       out.println("      {");
86       for (Map.Entry<String, Property> e : props.entrySet())
87       {
88          out.print("         java.beans.PropertyDescriptor ");
89          out.print(e.getKey());
90          out.println("Descriptor");
91          out.print("            = new java.beans.PropertyDescriptor(\"");
92          out.print(e.getKey());
93          out.print("\", ");
94          out.print(beanClassName);
95          out.println(".class);");
96          String ed = e.getValue().editor().toString();
97          if (!ed.equals(""))
98          {
99             out.print("         ");
100            out.print(e.getKey());
101            out.print("Descriptor.setPropertyEditorClass(");
102            out.print(ed);
103            out.println(".class);");
104         }
105      }
106      out.println("         return new java.beans.PropertyDescriptor[]");
107      out.print("         {");
108      boolean first = true;
109      for (String p : props.keySet())
110      {
111         if (first) first = false;
112         else out.print(",");
113         out.println();
114         out.print("            ");
115         out.print(p);
116         out.print("Descriptor");
117      }
```

```
118    out.println();
119    out.println("            };");
120    out.println("         }");
121    out.println("         catch (java.beans.IntrospectionException e)");
122    out.println("         {");
123    out.println("            e.printStackTrace();");
124    out.println("            return null;");
125    out.println("         }");
126    out.println("   }");
127    out.println("}");
128    out.close();
129    }
130 }
```

# 10.7  Bytecode Engineering

You have seen how annotations can be processed at runtime or at the source code level. There is a third possibility: processing at the bytecode level. Unless annotations are removed at the source level, they are present in the class files. The class file format is documented (see http://docs.oracle.com/javase/specs/jvms/se7/html). The format is rather complex, and it would be challenging to process class files without special libraries. One such library is the Bytecode Engineering Library (BCEL), available at http://jakarta.apache.org/bcel.

In this section, we use BCEL to add logging messages to annotated methods. If a method is annotated with

```
@LogEntry(logger=loggerName)
```

then we add the bytecodes for the following statement at the beginning of the method:

```
Logger.getLogger(loggerName).entering(className, methodName);
```

For example, if you annotate the hashCode method of the Item class as

```
@LogEntry(logger="global") public int hashCode()
```

then a message similar to the following is printed whenever the method is called:

```
Aug 17, 2004 9:32:59 PM Item hashCode
FINER: ENTRY
```

To achieve this, we do the following:

1.  Load the bytecodes in the class file.
2.  Locate all methods.
3.  For each method, check whether it has a LogEntry annotation.

4. If it does, add the bytecodes for the following instructions at the beginning of the method:

```
ldc loggerName
invokestatic java/util/logging/Logger.getLogger:(Ljava/lang/String;)Ljava/util/logging/Logger;
ldc className
ldc methodName
invokevirtual java/util/logging/Logger.entering:(Ljava/lang/String;Ljava/lang/String;)V
```

Inserting these bytecodes sounds tricky, but BCEL makes it fairly straightforward. We don't describe the process of analyzing and inserting bytecodes in detail. The important point is that the program in Listing 10.14 edits a class file and inserts a logging call at the beginning of the methods annotated with the LogEntry annotation.

 **NOTE:** If you are interested in the details of bytecode engineering, read through the BCEL manual at http://jakarta.apache.org/bcel/manual.html.

You'll need version 6.0 or later of the BCEL library to compile and run the EntryLogger program. (As this chapter was written, that version was still a work in progress. If it isn't finished when you read this, check out the trunk from the Subversion repository.)

For example, here is how you add the logging instructions to Item.java in Listing 10.15:

```
javac set/Item.java
javac -classpath .:bcel-version.jar bytecodeAnnotations/EntryLogger.java
java -classpath .:bcel-version.jar bytecodeAnnotations.EntryLogger set.Item
```

Try running

```
javap -c set.Item
```

before and after modifying the Item class file. You can see the inserted instructions at the beginning of the hashCode, equals, and compareTo methods.

```
public int hashCode();
  Code:
   0:  ldc     #85; //String global
   2:  invokestatic  #80;
      //Method java/util/logging/Logger.getLogger:(Ljava/lang/String;)Ljava/util/logging/Logger;
   5:  ldc     #86; //String Item
   7:  ldc     #88; //String hashCode
   9:  invokevirtual  #84;
      //Method java/util/logging/Logger.entering:(Ljava/lang/String;Ljava/lang/String;)V
  12:  bipush  13
  14:  aload_0
```

```
15:  getfield     #2; //Field description:Ljava/lang/String;
18:  invokevirtual #15; //Method java/lang/String.hashCode:()I
21:  imul
22:  bipush 17
24:  aload_0
25:  getfield     #3; //Field partNumber:I
28:  imul
29:  iadd
30:  ireturn
```

The SetTest program in Listing 10.16 inserts Item objects into a hash set. When you run it with the modified class file, you will see the logging messages.

```
Aug 18, 2004 10:57:59 AM Item hashCode
FINER: ENTRY
Aug 18, 2004 10:57:59 AM Item hashCode
FINER: ENTRY
Aug 18, 2004 10:57:59 AM Item hashCode
FINER: ENTRY
Aug 18, 2004 10:57:59 AM Item equals
FINER: ENTRY
[[description=Toaster, partNumber=1729], [description=Microwave, partNumber=4104]]
```

Note the call to equals when we insert the same item twice.

This example shows the power of bytecode engineering. Annotations are used to add directives to a program, and a bytecode editing tool picks up the directives and modifies the virtual machine instructions.

**Listing 10.14** bytecodeAnnotations/EntryLogger.java

```
1  package bytecodeAnnotations;
2
3  import java.io.*;
4  import org.apache.bcel.*;
5  import org.apache.bcel.classfile.*;
6  import org.apache.bcel.generic.*;
7
8  /**
9   * Adds "entering" logs to all methods of a class that have the LogEntry annotation.
10  * @version 1.10 2007-10-27
11  * @author Cay Horstmann
12  */
13 public class EntryLogger
14 {
15    private ClassGen cg;
16    private ConstantPoolGen cpg;
```

*(Continues)*

**Listing 10.14** *(Continued)*

```
17    /**
18     * Adds entry logging code to the given class.
19     * @param args the name of the class file to patch
20     */
21    public static void main(String[] args)
22    {
23       try
24       {
25          if (args.length == 0)
26             System.out.println("USAGE: java bytecodeAnnotations.EntryLogger classname");
27          else
28          {
29             JavaClass jc = Repository.lookupClass(args[0]);
30             ClassGen cg = new ClassGen(jc);
31             EntryLogger el = new EntryLogger(cg);
32             el.convert();
33             String f = Repository.lookupClassFile(cg.getClassName()).getPath();
34             System.out.println("Dumping " + f);
35             cg.getJavaClass().dump(f);
36          }
37       }
38       catch (Exception e)
39       {
40          e.printStackTrace();
41       }
42    }
43
44    /**
45     * Constructs an EntryLogger that inserts logging into annotated methods of a given class.
46     * @param cg the class
47     */
48    public EntryLogger(ClassGen cg)
49    {
50       this.cg = cg;
51       cpg = cg.getConstantPool();
52    }
53
54    /**
55     * converts the class by inserting the logging calls.
56     */
57    public void convert() throws IOException
58    {
59       for (Method m : cg.getMethods())
60       {
61          AnnotationEntry[] annotations = m.getAnnotationEntries();
```

```
62          for (AnnotationEntry a : annotations)
63          {
64             if (a.getAnnotationType().equals("LbytecodeAnnotations/LogEntry;"))
65             {
66                for (ElementValuePair p : a.getElementValuePairs())
67                {
68                   if (p.getNameString().equals("logger"))
69                   {
70                      String loggerName = p.getValue().stringifyValue();
71                      cg.replaceMethod(m, insertLogEntry(m, loggerName));
72                   }
73                }
74             }
75          }
76       }
77    }
78
79    /**
80     * Adds an "entering" call to the beginning of a method.
81     * @param m the method
82     * @param loggerName the name of the logger to call
83     */
84    private Method insertLogEntry(Method m, String loggerName)
85    {
86       MethodGen mg = new MethodGen(m, cg.getClassName(), cpg);
87       String className = cg.getClassName();
88       String methodName = mg.getMethod().getName();
89       System.out.printf("Adding logging instructions to %s.%s%n", className, methodName);
90
91       int getLoggerIndex = cpg.addMethodref("java.util.logging.Logger", "getLogger",
92          "(Ljava/lang/String;)Ljava/util/logging/Logger;");
93       int enteringIndex = cpg.addMethodref("java.util.logging.Logger", "entering",
94          "(Ljava/lang/String;Ljava/lang/String;)V");
95
96       InstructionList il = mg.getInstructionList();
97       InstructionList patch = new InstructionList();
98       patch.append(new PUSH(cpg, loggerName));
99       patch.append(new INVOKESTATIC(getLoggerIndex));
100      patch.append(new PUSH(cpg, className));
101      patch.append(new PUSH(cpg, methodName));
102      patch.append(new INVOKEVIRTUAL(enteringIndex));
103      InstructionHandle[] ihs = il.getInstructionHandles();
104      il.insert(ihs[0], patch);
105
106      mg.setMaxStack();
107      return mg.getMethod();
108   }
109 }
```

**Listing 10.15** set/Item.java

```java
1  package set;
2
3  import java.util.*;
4  import bytecodeAnnotations.*;
5
6  /**
7   * An item with a description and a part number.
8   * @version 1.01 2012-01-26
9   * @author Cay Horstmann
10  */
11 public class Item
12 {
13    private String description;
14    private int partNumber;
15
16    /**
17     * Constructs an item.
18     * @param aDescription the item's description
19     * @param aPartNumber the item's part number
20     */
21    public Item(String aDescription, int aPartNumber)
22    {
23       description = aDescription;
24       partNumber = aPartNumber;
25    }
26
27    /**
28     * Gets the description of this item.
29     * @return the description
30     */
31    public String getDescription()
32    {
33       return description;
34    }
35
36    public String toString()
37    {
38       return "[description=" + description + ", partNumber=" + partNumber + "]";
39    }
40
41    @LogEntry(logger = "global")
42    public boolean equals(Object otherObject)
43    {
44       if (this == otherObject) return true;
45       if (otherObject == null) return false;
46       if (getClass() != otherObject.getClass()) return false;
```

```
47        Item other = (Item) otherObject;
48        return Objects.equals(description, other.description) && partNumber == other.partNumber;
49     }
50
51     @LogEntry(logger = "global")
52     public int hashCode()
53     {
54        return Objects.hash(description, partNumber);
55     }
56 }
```

**Listing 10.16** set/SetTest.java

```
1 package set;
2
3 import java.util.*;
4 import java.util.logging.*;
5
6 /**
7  * @version 1.02 2012-01-26
8  * @author Cay Horstmann
9  */
10 public class SetTest
11 {
12    public static void main(String[] args)
13    {
14       Logger.getLogger(Logger.GLOBAL_LOGGER_NAME).setLevel(Level.FINEST);
15       Handler handler = new ConsoleHandler();
16       handler.setLevel(Level.FINEST);
17       Logger.getLogger(Logger.GLOBAL_LOGGER_NAME).addHandler(handler);
18
19       Set<Item> parts = new HashSet<>();
20       parts.add(new Item("Toaster", 1279));
21       parts.add(new Item("Microwave", 4104));
22       parts.add(new Item("Toaster", 1279));
23       System.out.println(parts);
24    }
25 }
```

## 10.7.1 Modifying Bytecodes at Load Time

In the preceding section, you saw a tool that edits class files. However, it can be cumbersome to add yet another tool into the build process. An attractive alternative is to defer the bytecode engineering until *load time*, when the class loader loads the class.

Before Java SE 5.0, you had to write a custom class loader to achieve this task. Now, the *instrumentation API* has a hook for installing a bytecode transformer. The transformer must be installed before the main method of the program is called. You can meet this requirement by defining an *agent*, a library that is loaded to monitor a program in some way. The agent code can carry out initializations in a premain method.

Here are the steps required to build an agent:

1.  Implement a class with a method

    ```
    public static void premain(String arg, Instrumentation instr)
    ```

    This method is called when the agent is loaded. The agent can get a single command-line argument, which is passed in the arg parameter. The instr parameter can be used to install various hooks.

2.  Make a manifest file EntryLoggingAgent.mf that sets the Premain-Class attribute, for example:

    ```
    Premain-Class: bytecodeAnnotations.EntryLoggingAgent
    ```

3.  Package the agent code and the manifest into a JAR file, for example:

    ```
    javac -classpath .:bcel-version.jar bytecodeAnnotations.EntryLoggingAgent
    jar cvfm EntryLoggingAgent.jar EntryLoggingAgent.mf bytecodeAnnotations/Entry*.class
    ```

To launch a Java program together with the agent, use the following command-line options:

```
java -javaagent:AgentJARFile=agentArgument . . .
```

For example, to run the SetTest program with the entry logging agent, call

```
javac SetTest.java
java -javaagent:EntryLoggingAgent.jar=set.Item -classpath .:bcel-version.jar set.SetTest
```

The Item argument is the name of the class that the agent should modify.

Listing 10.17 shows the agent code. The agent installs a class file transformer. The transformer first checks whether the class name matches the agent argument. If so, it uses the EntryLogger class from the preceding section to modify the bytecodes. However, the modified bytecodes are not saved to a file. Instead, the transformer returns them for loading into the virtual machine (see Figure 10.4). In other words, this technique carries out "just in time" modification of the bytecodes.

**Listing 10.17** bytecodeAnnotations/EntryLoggingAgent.java

```java
1  package bytecodeAnnotations;
2
3  import java.lang.instrument.*;
4  import java.io.*;
5  import java.security.*;
6  import org.apache.bcel.classfile.*;
7  import org.apache.bcel.generic.*;
8
9  /**
10  * @version 1.00 2004-08-17
11  * @author Cay Horstmann
12  */
13  public class EntryLoggingAgent
14  {
15     public static void premain(final String arg, Instrumentation instr)
16     {
17        instr.addTransformer(new ClassFileTransformer()
18           {
19              public byte[] transform(ClassLoader loader, String className, Class<?> cl,
20                    ProtectionDomain pd, byte[] data)
21              {
22                 if (!className.equals(arg)) return null;
23                 try
24                 {
25                    ClassParser parser = new ClassParser(new ByteArrayInputStream(data), className
26                          + ".java");
27                    JavaClass jc = parser.parse();
28                    ClassGen cg = new ClassGen(jc);
29                    EntryLogger el = new EntryLogger(cg);
30                    el.convert();
31                    return cg.getJavaClass().getBytes();
32                 }
33                 catch (Exception e)
34                 {
35                    e.printStackTrace();
36                    return null;
37                 }
38              }
39           });
40     }
41  }
```

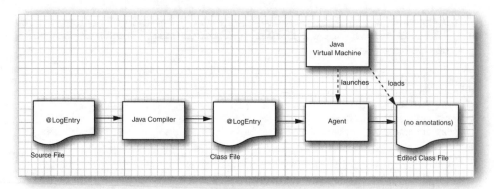

**Figure 10.4** Modifying classes at load time

In this chapter, you have learned how to

- Add annotations to Java programs
- Design your own annotation interfaces
- Implement tools that make use of the annotations

You have seen three technologies for processing code: scripting, compiling Java programs, and processing annotations. The first two were quite straightforward. On the other hand, building annotation tools is undeniably complex and not something that most developers will need to tackle. This chapter gave you the background for understanding the inner workings of the annotation tools you will encounter, and perhaps piqued your interest in developing your own tools.

In the next chapter, you will learn about the RMI mechanism, a distributed object model for Java programs.

# CHAPTER 11

# Distributed Objects

## In this chapter:

Periodically, the programming community starts thinking that the solution to all its problems is "objects everywhere." The idea is to have a happy family of collaborating objects that can be located anywhere. When an object on one computer needs to invoke a method on an object on another computer, it sends a network message that contains the details of the request. The remote object computes a response, perhaps by accessing a database or by communicating with additional objects. Once the remote object has the answer to the client request, it sends the answer back over the network. Conceptually, this process sounds simple, but you need to understand what goes on under the hood to use distributed objects effectively.

In this chapter, we'll focus on the *Remote Method Invocation* (RMI) protocol for communicating between two Java virtual machines which might run on different computers. At one time, RMI was thought to be a viable technology for application programmers, but at this point, RMI is mostly of interest as a case study of a simple distributed object system.

## 11.1 The Roles of Client and Server

The basic idea behind distributed programming is simple. A client computer makes a request and sends the request data across a network to a server. The server processes the request and sends back a response for the client to analyze. Figure 11.1 shows the process.

We would like to say at the outset that these requests and responses are *not* what you would see in a web application. The client is not a web browser. It can be any application that executes business rules of any complexity. The client application might or might not interact with a human user, and if it does, it can

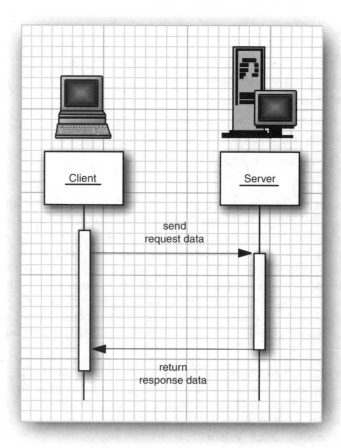

**Figure 11.1** Transmitting objects between client and server

have a command-line or Swing user interface. The protocol for the request and response data allows the transfer of arbitrary objects, whereas traditional web applications are limited by using HTTP for the request and HTML for the response.

What we want is a mechanism by which the client programmer makes a regular method call, without worrying about sending data across the network or parsing the response. The solution is to install a *proxy* object on the client. The proxy is an object located in the client virtual machine that appears to the client program as if it were the remote object. The client calls the proxy, making a regular method call. The client proxy contacts the server, using a network protocol.

Similarly, the programmer who implements the service doesn't want to fuss with client communication. The solution is to install a second proxy object on the server. The server proxy communicates with the client proxy, and it makes regular method calls to the object implementing the service (see Figure 11.2).

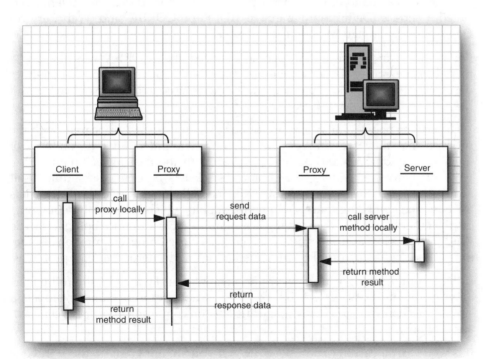

**Figure 11.2** Remote method call with proxies

How do the proxies communicate with each other? That depends on the implementation technology. There are three common choices:

- The Common Object Request Broker Architecture (CORBA) supports method calls between objects of any programming language. CORBA uses the binary Internet Inter-ORB Protocol, or IIOP, to communicate between objects.
- The web services architecture is a collection of protocols, sometimes collectively described as WS-*. It is also programming-language neutral. However, it uses XML-based communication formats. The format for transmitting objects is the Simple Object Access Protocol (SOAP).
- The Java RMI technology supports method calls between distributed Java objects.

CORBA and SOAP are completely language-neutral. Client and server programs can be written in C, C++, C#, Java, or any other language. You supply an *interface description* to specify the signatures of the methods and the types of the data that your objects can handle. These descriptions are formatted in a special language, called Interface Definition Language (IDL) for CORBA and Web Services Description Language (WSDL) for web services.

For many years, quite a few people believed that CORBA was the object model of the future. By now, though, CORBA has a reputation—sometimes deserved—for complex implementations and interoperability problems, and it has only reached modest success.

Web services had a similar amount of buzz when they first appeared, with the promise that they are simpler and, of course, founded on the goodness of the World Wide Web and XML. However, with the passing of time and the work of many committees, the protocol stack has become less simple, as it acquired more of the features that CORBA had all along. The XML protocol has the advantage of being (barely) human-readable, which helps with debugging. On the other hand, XML processing is a significant performance bottleneck. The WS-* stack has lost quite a bit of its luster and is, too, gaining a reputation—sometimes deserved—for complex implementations and interoperability problems.

If the communicating programs are implemented in Java code, the full generality and complexity of CORBA or WS-* is not required. Sun developed a simple mechanism, called RMI, specifically for communication between Java applications.

It is well worth learning about RMI, even if you are not going to use it in your own programs. Using a straightforward architecture, you will learn about the mechanisms essential for programming distributed applications.

## 11.2 Remote Method Calls

The key to distributed computing is the *remote method call*. Some code on one machine (called the *client*) wants to invoke a method on an object on another machine (the *remote object*). To make this possible, the method parameters must somehow be shipped to the other machine, the server must be informed so it can locate the remote object and execute the method, and the return value must be shipped back.

Before looking at this process in detail, we want to point out that the client/server terminology applies only to a single method call. The computer that calls the remote method is the client for *that* call, and the computer hosting the object that processes the call is the server for *that* call. It is entirely possible for the roles to be reversed somewhere down the road. The server of a previous call can itself become the client when it invokes a remote method on an object residing on another computer.

### 11.2.1 Stubs and Parameter Marshalling

When client code wants to invoke a method on a remote object, it actually calls an ordinary method on a proxy object called a *stub*. For example,

```
Warehouse centralWarehouse = get stub object;
double price = centralWarehouse.getPrice("Blackwell Toaster");
```

The stub resides on the client machine, not on the server. It knows how to contact the server over the network. The stub packages the parameters used in the remote method into a block of bytes. The process of encoding the parameters is called *parameter marshalling*. The purpose of parameter marshalling is to convert the parameters into a format suitable for transport from one virtual machine to another. In the RMI protocol, objects are encoded with the serialization mechanism described in Chapter 1. In the SOAP protocol, objects are encoded as XML.

To sum up, the stub method on the client builds an information block that consists of

- An identifier of the remote object to be used
- A description of the method to be called
- The parameters

The stub then sends this information to the server. On the server side, a receiver object performs the following actions:

1. It locates the remote object to be called.
2. It calls the desired method, passing the supplied parameters.

3. It captures the return value or the exception of the call.

4. It sends a package consisting of the marshalled return data back to the stub on the client.

The client stub unmarshals the return value or exception from the server. The value becomes the return value of the stub call; if the remote method threw an exception, the stub rethrows it in the virtual machine of the caller. Figure 11.3 shows the information flow of a remote method invocation.

This process is obviously complex, but the good news is that it is completely automatic and, to a large extent, transparent for the programmer.

The details of implementing remote objects and getting client stubs depend on the technology for distributed objects. In the following sections, we'll have a close look at RMI.

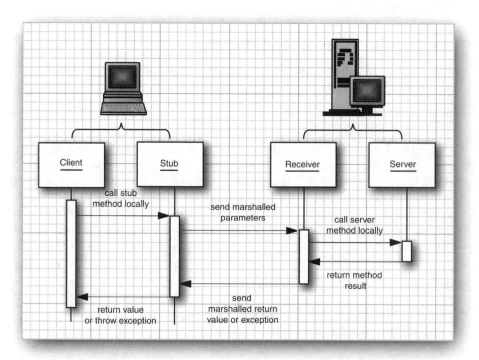

**Figure 11.3** Parameter marshalling

## 11.3 The RMI Programming Model

To introduce the RMI programming model, we'll start with a simple example. A remote object represents a warehouse. The client program asks the warehouse about the price of a product. In the following sections, you will see how to implement and launch the server and client programs.

### 11.3.1 Interfaces and Implementations

The capabilities of remote objects are expressed in interfaces that are shared between the client and server. For example, the interface in Listing 11.1 describes the service provided by a remote warehouse object.

---

**Listing 11.1** warehouse1/Warehouse.java

```
1  import java.rmi.*;
2
3  /**
4     The remote interface for a simple warehouse.
5     @version 1.0 2007-10-09
6     @author Cay Horstmann
7  */
8  public interface Warehouse extends Remote
9  {
10     double getPrice(String description) throws RemoteException;
11 }
```

---

 **NOTE:** In this chapter, we do not use packages. As you will see, deployment of remote applications is complex, and we want to avoid the added complexity of package directories.

---

Interfaces for remote objects must always extend the Remote interface defined in the java.rmi package. All the methods in those interfaces must also declare that they will throw a RemoteException. Remote method calls are inherently less reliable than local calls—it is always possible that a remote call will fail. For example, the server might be temporarily unavailable, or there might be a network problem. Your client code must be prepared to deal with these possibilities. For these reasons, you must handle the RemoteException with *every* remote method call and specify the appropriate action to take when the call does not succeed.

Next, on the server side, you must provide the class that actually carries out the work advertised in the remote interface—see Listing 11.2.

**Listing 11.2** warehouse1/WarehouseImpl.java

```
1  import java.rmi.*;
2  import java.rmi.server.*;
3  import java.util.*;
4
5  /**
6   * This class is the implementation for the remote Warehouse interface.
7   * @version 1.01 2012-01-26
8   * @author Cay Horstmann
9   */
10 public class WarehouseImpl extends UnicastRemoteObject implements Warehouse
11 {
12    private Map<String, Double> prices;
13
14    public WarehouseImpl() throws RemoteException
15    {
16       prices = new HashMap<>();
17       prices.put("Blackwell Toaster", 24.95);
18       prices.put("ZapXpress Microwave Oven", 49.95);
19    }
20
21    public double getPrice(String description) throws RemoteException
22    {
23       Double price = prices.get(description);
24       return price == null ? 0 : price;
25    }
26 }
```

 **NOTE:** The WarehouseImpl constructor is declared to throw a RemoteException because the superclass constructor can throw that exception. This happens when there is a problem connecting to the network service that tracks remote objects.

You can tell that the class is the target of remote method calls if it extends UnicastRemoteObject. The constructor of that class makes objects remotely accessible. The "path of least resistance" is to derive from UnicastRemoteObject, and all service implementation classes in this chapter do so.

Occasionally, you might not want to extend the UnicastRemoteObject class, perhaps because your implementation class already extends another class. In that situation, you need to manually instantiate the remote objects and pass them to the static exportObject method. Instead of extending UnicastRemoteObject, call

```
UnicastRemoteObject.exportObject(this, 0);
```

in the constructor of the remote object. The second parameter is 0 to indicate that any suitable port can be used to listen to client connections.

**NOTE:** The term "unicast" refers to the fact that the remote object is located by making a call to a single IP address and port. This is the only mechanism supported in Java SE. More sophisticated distributed object systems (such as JINI) allow for "multicast" lookup of remote objects that might be on a number of different servers.

## 11.3.2 The RMI Registry

To access a remote object that exists on the server, the client needs a local stub object. How can the client request such a stub? The most common method is to call a remote method of another remote object and get a stub object as a return value. There is, however, a chicken-and-egg problem here: The *first* remote object has to be located some other way. For that purpose, the JDK provides a *bootstrap registry service*.

A server program registers at least one remote object with a bootstrap registry. To register a remote object, you need a RMI URL and a reference to the implementation object.

RMI URLs start with rmi: and contain an optional host name, an optional port number, and the name of the remote object that is (hopefully) unique. An example is:

```
rmi://regserver.mycompany.com:99/central_warehouse
```

By default, the host name is localhost and the port number is 1099. The server tells the registry at the given location to associate or "bind" the name with the object.

Here is the code for registering a WarehouseImpl object with the RMI registry on the same server:

```
WarehouseImpl centralWarehouse = new WarehouseImpl();
Context namingContext = new InitialContext();
namingContext.bind("rmi:central_warehouse", centralWarehouse);
```

The program in Listing 11.3 simply constructs and registers a WarehouseImpl object.

 **NOTE:** For security reasons, an application can bind, unbind, or rebind registry object references only if it runs on the same host as the registry. This prevents hostile clients from changing the registry information. However, any client can look up objects.

A client can enumerate all registered RMI objects by calling:

```
Enumeration<NameClassPair> e = namingContext.list("rmi://regserver.mycompany.com");
```

`NameClassPair` is a helper class that contains both the name of the bound object and the name of its class. For example, the following code displays the names of all registered objects:

```
while (e.hasMoreElements())
   System.out.println(e.nextElement().getName());
```

A client gets a stub to access a remote object by specifying the server and the remote object name in the following way:

```
String url = "rmi://regserver.mycompany.com/central_warehouse";
Warehouse centralWarehouse = (Warehouse) namingContext.lookup(url);
```

 **NOTE:** It is notoriously difficult to keep names unique in a global registry, so you should not use this technique as the general method for locating objects on the server. Instead, there should be relatively few named remote objects registered with the bootstrap service. These should be the objects that can locate other objects for you.

**Listing 11.3** warehouse1/WarehouseServer.java

```
1  import java.rmi.*;
2  import javax.naming.*;
3
4  /**
5   * This server program instantiates a remote warehouse object, registers it with the naming
6   * service, and waits for clients to invoke methods.
7   * @version 1.12 2007-10-09
8   * @author Cay Horstmann
9   */
10 public class WarehouseServer
11 {
12    public static void main(String[] args) throws RemoteException, NamingException
13    {
14       System.out.println("Constructing server implementation...");
15       WarehouseImpl centralWarehouse = new WarehouseImpl();
16
17       System.out.println("Binding server implementation to registry...");
18       Context namingContext = new InitialContext();
19       namingContext.bind("rmi:central_warehouse", centralWarehouse);
20
21       System.out.println("Waiting for invocations from clients...");
22    }
23 }
```

The code in Listing 11.4 shows the client that obtains a stub to the remote warehouse object and invokes the remote getPrice method. Figure 11.4 shows the flow of control. The client obtains a Warehouse stub and invokes the getPrice method on it. Behind the scenes, the stub contacts the server and causes the getPrice method to be invoked on the WarehouseImpl object.

**Listing 11.4**  warehouse1/WarehouseClient.java

```
1  import java.rmi.*;
2  import java.util.*;
3  import javax.naming.*;
4
5  /**
6   * A client that invokes a remote method.
7   * @version 1.0 2007-10-09
8   * @author Cay Horstmann
9   */
10 public class WarehouseClient
11 {
12    public static void main(String[] args) throws NamingException, RemoteException
13    {
14       Context namingContext = new InitialContext();
15
16       System.out.print("RMI registry bindings: ");
17       Enumeration<NameClassPair> e = namingContext.list("rmi://localhost/");
18       while (e.hasMoreElements())
19          System.out.println(e.nextElement().getName());
20
21       String url = "rmi://localhost/central_warehouse";
22       Warehouse centralWarehouse = (Warehouse) namingContext.lookup(url);
23
24       String descr = "Blackwell Toaster";
25       double price = centralWarehouse.getPrice(descr);
26       System.out.println(descr + ": " + price);
27    }
28 }
```

---

**javax.naming.InitialContext**  1.3

- InitialContext()
  constructs a naming context that can be used for accessing the RMI registry.

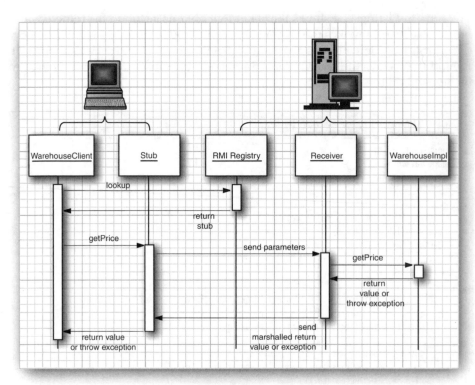

**Figure 11.4** Calling the remote `getPrice` method

---

**`javax.naming.Context`** `1.3`

- `static Object lookup(String name)`
  returns the object for the given name. Throws a `NamingException` if the name is not currently bound.

- `static void bind(String name, Object obj)`
  binds `name` to the object `obj`. Throws a `NameAlreadyBoundException` if the object is already bound.

- `static void unbind(String name)`
  unbinds the name. It is legal to unbind a name that doesn't exist.

- `static void rebind(String name, Object obj)`
  binds `name` to the object `obj`. Replaces any existing binding.

- `NamingEnumeration<NameClassPair> list(String name)`
  returns an enumeration listing all matching bound objects. To list all RMI objects, call with `"rmi:"`.

---

**javax.naming.NameClassPair** 1.3

- String getName()
  gets the name of the named object.
- String getClassName()
  gets the name of the class to which the named object belongs.

---

**java.rmi.Naming** 1.1

- static Remote lookup(String url)
  returns the remote object for the URL. Throws a NotBoundException if the name is not currently bound.
- static void bind(String name, Remote obj)
  binds name to the remote object obj. Throws an AlreadyBoundException if the object is already bound.
- static void unbind(String name)
  unbinds the name. Throws the NotBound exception if the name is not currently bound.
- static void rebind(String name, Remote obj)
  binds name to the remote object obj. Replaces any existing binding.
- static String[] list(String url)
  returns an array of strings of the URLs in the registry located at the given URL. The array contains a snapshot of the names present in the registry.

## 11.3.3 Deploying the Program

Deploying an application that uses RMI can be tricky because so many things can go wrong—and the error messages you get when something goes wrong are so poor. We have found that it really pays off to test the deployment under realistic conditions, separating the classes for client and server.

Make two separate directories to hold the classes for starting the server and client.

```
server/
   WarehouseServer.class
   Warehouse.class
   WarehouseImpl.class

client/
   WarehouseClient.class
   Warehouse.class
```

When deploying RMI applications, one commonly needs to dynamically deliver classes to running programs. One example is the RMI registry. Keep in mind that one instance of the registry will serve many different RMI applications. The RMI registry needs to have access to the class files of the service interfaces that are being registered. When the registry starts, however, one cannot predict all future registration requests. Therefore, the RMI registry dynamically loads the class files of any remote interfaces it has not previously encountered.

Dynamically delivered class files are distributed through standard web servers. In our case, the server program needs to make the Warehouse.class file available to the RMI registry, so we put that file into a third directory that we call download.

```
download/
    Warehouse.class
```

We use a web server to serve the contents of that directory.

When the application is deployed, the server, RMI registry, web server, and client can be located on four different computers—see Figure 11.5. However, for testing purposes, we will use a single computer.

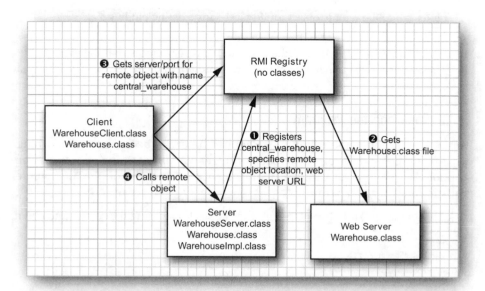

**Figure 11.5** Server calls in the Warehouse application

**NOTE:** For security reasons, the rmiregistry service that is part of the JDK only allows binding calls from the same host. That is, the server and rmiregistry process need to be located on the same computer. However, the RMI architecture allows for a more general RMI registry implementation that supports multiple servers.

To test our sample application, use the NanoHTTPD web server available from http://elonen.iki.fi/code/nanohttpd. This tiny web server is implemented in a single Java source file. Open a new console window, change to the download directory, and copy NanoHTTPD.java to that directory. Compile the source file and start the web server with the command

```
java NanoHTTPD 8080
```

The command-line argument is the port number. Use any other available port if port 8080 is already used on your machine.

Next, open another console window, change to a directory that *contains no class files*, and start the RMI registry:

```
rmiregistry
```

**CAUTION:** Before starting the RMI registry, make sure the CLASSPATH environment variable is not set to anything, and double-check that the current directory contains no class files. Otherwise, the RMI registry might find spurious class files which will confuse it when it should download additional classes from a different source. There is a reason for this behavior; see http://docs.oracle.com/javase/7/docs/technotes/guides/rmi/codebase.html. In a nutshell, each stub object has a *codebase* entry that specifies from where it was loaded. That codebase is used to load dependent classes. If the RMI registry finds a class locally, it will set the wrong codebase.

Now you are ready to start the server. Open a third console window, change to the server directory, and issue the command

```
java -Djava.rmi.server.codebase=http://localhost:8080/ WarehouseServer
```

The java.rmi.server.codebase property points to the URL for serving class files. The server program communicates this URL to the RMI registry.

Have a peek at the console window running NanoHTTPD. You will see a message that demonstrates that the Warehouse.class file has been served to the RMI registry.

**CAUTION:** It is very important to ensure that the codebase URL *ends with a slash* (/).

Note that the server program does not exit. This seems strange—after all, the program just creates a `WarehouseImpl` object and registers it. Actually, the `main` method does exit immediately after registration, as you would expect. However, when you create an object of a class that extends `UnicastRemoteObject`, a separate thread is started that keeps the program alive indefinitely. Thus, the program stays around to allow clients to connect to it.

Finally, open a fourth console window, change to the `client` directory, and run

```
java WarehouseClient
```

You will see a short message, indicating that the remote method was successfully invoked (see Figure 11.6).

 **NOTE:** If you just want to test out basic program logic, you can put your client and server class files into the same directory. Then you can start the RMI registry, server, and client in that directory. However, as RMI class loading is the source of much grief and confusion, we felt it best to show you right away the correct setup for dynamic class loading.

## 11.3.4 Logging RMI Activity

If you start the server with the option

```
-Djava.rmi.server.logCalls=true WarehouseServer &
```

then the server logs all remote method calls on its console. Try it—you'll get a good impression of the RMI traffic.

If you want to see additional logging messages, you have to configure RMI loggers using the standard Java logging API. (See Volume I, Chapter 11 for more information on logging.)

Make a file `logging.properties` with the following content:

```
handlers=java.util.logging.ConsoleHandler
.level=FINE
java.util.logging.ConsoleHandler.level=FINE
java.util.logging.ConsoleHandler.formatter=java.util.logging.SimpleFormatter
```

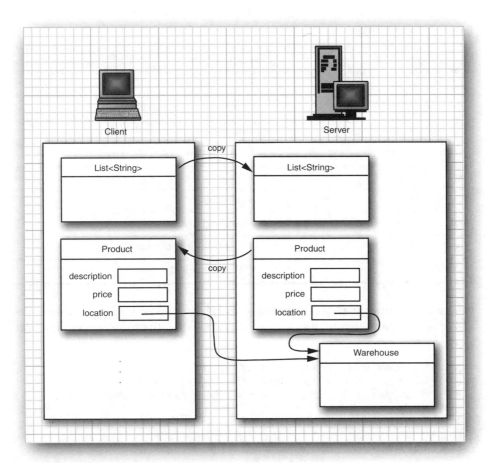

**Figure 11.6** Testing an RMI application

You can fine-tune the settings by adjusting the individual levels for each logger instead of the global level. Table 11.1 lists the RMI loggers. For example, to track the class-loading activity, you can set

```
sun.rmi.loader.level=FINE
```

Start the RMI registry with the option

```
-J-Djava.util.logging.config.file=directory/logging.properties
```

Start the client and server with

```
-Djava.util.logging.config.file=directory/logging.properties
```

**Table 11.1** RMI Loggers

| Logger Name | Logged Activity |
|---|---|
| sun.rmi.server.call | Server-side remote calls |
| sun.rmi.server.ref | Server-side remote references |
| sun.rmi.client.call | Client-side remote calls |
| sun.rmi.client.ref | Client-side remote references |
| sun.rmi.dgc | Distributed garbage collection |
| sun.rmi.loader | RMIClassLoader |
| sun.rmi.transport.misc | Transport layer |
| sun.rmi.transport.tcp | TCP binding and connection |
| sun.rmi.transport.proxy | HTTP tunneling |

Here is an example of a logging message that shows a class loading problem. The RMI registry cannot find the Warehouse class because the web server has been shut down:

```
FINE: RMI TCP Connection(1)-127.0.1.1: (port 1099) op = 80
Oct 13, 2007 4:43:30 PM sun.rmi.server.LoaderHandler loadProxyClass
FINE: RMI TCP Connection(1)-127.0.1.1: interfaces = [java.rmi.Remote, Warehouse], codebase =
"http://localhost:8080/"
Oct 13, 2007 4:43:30 PM sun.rmi.server.LoaderHandler loadProxyClass
FINE: RMI TCP Connection(1)-127.0.1.1: proxy class resolution failed
java.lang.ClassNotFoundException: Warehouse
```

# 11.4 Parameters and Return Values in Remote Methods

At the start of a remote method invocation, the parameters need to be moved from the virtual machine of the client to the virtual machine of the server. After the invocation has completed, the return value needs to be transferred in the other direction. When a value is passed from one virtual machine to another, we distinguish two cases: passing remote objects and passing nonremote objects. For example, suppose that a client of the WarehouseServer passes a Warehouse reference (that is, a stub through which the remote warehouse object can be called) to another remote method. That is an example of passing a remote object. However, most method parameters will be ordinary Java objects, not stubs to remote objects. An example is the String parameter of the getPrice method in our first sample application.

## 11.4.1 Transferring Remote Objects

When a reference to a remote object is passed from one virtual machine to the other, the sender and the recipient of the remote object both hold a reference to the same entity. That reference is not a memory location (which is only meaningful in a single virtual machine); it consists of a network address and a unique identifier for the remote object. This information is encapsulated in a stub object.

Conceptually, passing a remote reference is quite similar to passing local object references within a virtual machine. However, always keep in mind that a method call on a remote reference is significantly slower and potentially less reliable than a method call on a local reference.

## 11.4.2 Transferring Nonremote Objects

Consider the String parameter of the getPrice method. The string value needs to be copied from the client to the server. It is not difficult to imagine how a copy of a string can be transported across a network. The RMI mechanism can also make copies of more complex objects, provided they are *serializable*. RMI uses the serialization mechanism described in Chapter 1 to send objects across a network connection. This means that any classes that implement the Serializable interface can be used as parameter or return types.

Passing parameters by serializing them has a subtle effect on the semantics of remote methods. When you pass objects into a local method, object *references* are transferred. When the method applies a mutator method to a parameter object, the caller will observe that change. But if a remote method mutates a serialized parameter, it changes the copy, and the caller will never notice.

To summarize, there are two mechanisms for transferring values between virtual machines.

- Objects of classes that implement the Remote interface are transferred as remote references.

- Objects of classes that implement the Serializable interface but not the Remote interface are copied using serialization.

All of this is automatic and requires no programmer intervention. Keep in mind that serialization can be slow for large objects, and that the remote method cannot mutate serialized parameters. You can, of course, avoid these issues by passing around remote references. That, too, comes at a cost: Invoking methods on remote references is far more expensive than calling local methods. Being aware of these costs will allow you to make informed choices when designing remote services.

**NOTE:** Remote objects are garbage-collected automatically, just as local objects are. However, the distributed collector is significantly more complex. When the local garbage collector finds that there are no further local uses of a remote reference, it notifies the distributed collector that the server is no longer referenced by this client. When a server is no longer used by any clients, it is marked as garbage.

Our next example program will illustrate the transfer of remote and serializable objects. We change the Warehouse interface as shown in Listing 11.5. Given a list of keywords, the warehouse returns the Product that is the best match.

**Listing 11.5** warehouse2/Warehouse.java

```
1  import java.rmi.*;
2  import java.util.*;
3
4  /**
5     The remote interface for a simple warehouse.
6     @version 1.0 2007-10-09
7     @author Cay Horstmann
8  */
9  public interface Warehouse extends Remote
10 {
11    double getPrice(String description) throws RemoteException;
12    Product getProduct(List<String> keywords) throws RemoteException;
13 }
```

The parameter of the getProduct method has type List<String>. A parameter value must belong to a serializable class that implements the List<String> interface, such as ArrayList<String>. (Our sample client passes a value obtained by a call to Arrays.asList. Fortunately, that method is guaranteed to return a serializable list as well.)

The return type Product encapsulates the description, price, and location of the product (see Listing 11.6).

Note that the Product class is serializable. The server constructs a Product object, and the client gets a copy (see Figure 11.7).

However, there is a subtlety. The Product class has an instance field of type Warehouse—a remote interface. The warehouse object is *not* serialized, which is just as well as it might have a huge amount of state. Instead, the client receives a stub to a remote Warehouse object. That stub might be different from the centralWarehouse stub on which the getProduct method was called. In our implementation, we will have two kinds of products, toasters and books, that are located in different warehouses.

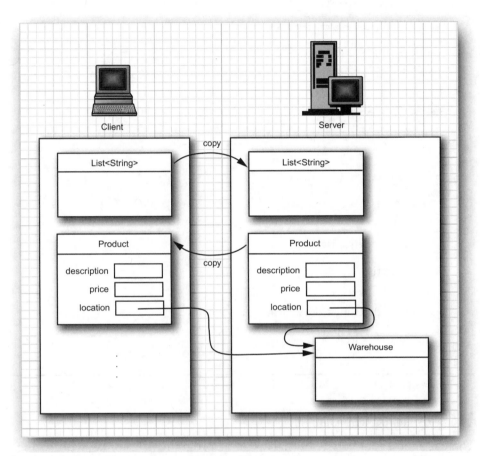

**Figure 11.7** Copying local parameter and result objects

---

**Listing 11.6** warehouse2/Product.java

```java
1  import java.io.*;
2
3  public class Product implements Serializable
4  {
5     private String description;
6     private double price;
```

*(Continues)*

**Listing 11.6**  *(Continued)*

```
 7    private Warehouse location;
 8
 9    public Product(String description, double price)
10    {
11       this.description = description;
12       this.price = price;
13    }
14
15    public String getDescription()
16    {
17       return description;
18    }
19
20    public double getPrice()
21    {
22       return price;
23    }
24
25    public Warehouse getLocation()
26    {
27       return location;
28    }
29
30    public void setLocation(Warehouse location)
31    {
32       this.location = location;
33    }
34 }
```

## 11.4.3  Dynamic Class Loading

There is another subtlety to our next sample program. A list of keyword strings is sent to the server, and the warehouse returns an instance of a class Product. Of course, the client program will need the class file Product.class to compile. However, whenever our server program cannot find a match for the keywords, it returns the one product that is sure to delight everyone: the *Core Java* book. That object is an instance of the Book class, a subclass of Product.

When the client was compiled, it might have never seen the Book class. Yet when it runs, it needs to be able to execute Book methods that override Product methods. This demonstrates that the client needs to have the capability of loading additional classes at runtime. The client uses the same mechanism as the RMI registry. Classes are served by a web server, the RMI server class communicates the URL to the client, and the client makes an HTTP request to download the class files.

Whenever a program loads new code from another network location, there is a security issue. For that reason, you need to use a *security manager* in RMI applications that dynamically load classes. (See Chapter 9 for more information on class loaders and security managers.)

Programs that use RMI should install a security manager to control the activities of the dynamically loaded classes. Install it with the instruction

```
System.setSecurityManager(new SecurityManager());
```

 **NOTE:** If all classes are available locally, you do not actually need a security manager. If you know all class files of your program at deployment time, you can deploy them all locally. However, it often happens that the client or server program evolves and new classes are added over time. Then you can benefit from dynamic class loading. Any time you load code from another source, you need a security manager.

By default, the `SecurityManager` restricts all code in the program from establishing network connections. However, the program needs to make network connections to three remote locations:

- The web server that loads remote classes
- The RMI registry
- Remote objects

To allow these operations, supply a policy file. (We discussed policy files in greater detail in Chapter 9.) Here is a policy file that allows an application to make any network connection to a port with port number of at least 1024. (The RMI port is 1099 by default, and the remote objects also use ports 1024. We use port 8080 for downloading classes.)

```
grant
{
    permission java.net.SocketPermission
        "*:1024-65535", "connect";
};
```

You need to instruct the security manager to read the policy file by setting the `java.security.policy` property to the file name. You can use a call such as

```
System.setProperty("java.security.policy", "rmi.policy");
```

Alternatively, you can specify the system property setting on the command line:

```
-Djava.security.policy=rmi.policy
```

To run the sample application, be sure you have killed the RMI registry, web server, and the server program from the preceding sample. Open four console windows and follow these steps.

1. Compile the source files for the interface, implementation, client, and server classes.

   ```
   javac *.java
   ```

2. Make three directories, client, server, and download, and populate them as follows:

   ```
   client/
       WarehouseClient.class
       Warehouse.class
       Product.class
       client.policy
   server/
       Warehouse.class
       Product.class
       Book.class
       WarehouseImpl.class
       WarehouseServer.class
       server.policy
   download/
       Warehouse.class
       Product.class
       Book.class
   ```

3. In the first console window, change to a directory that has *no* class files. Start the RMI registry.

4. In the second console window, change to the download directory and start NanoHTTPD.

5. In the third console window, change to the server directory and start the server.

   ```
   java -Djava.rmi.server.codebase=http://localhost:8080/ WarehouseServer
   ```

6. In the fourth console window, change to the client directory and run the client.

   ```
   java WarehouseClient
   ```

Listing 11.7 shows the code of the Book class. Note that the getDescription method is overridden to show the ISBN. When the client program runs, it shows the ISBN for the *Core Java* book, which proves that the Book class was loaded dynamically. Listing 11.8 shows the warehouse implementation. A warehouse has a reference to a backup warehouse. If an item cannot be found in the warehouse, the backup warehouse is searched. Listing 11.9 shows the server program. Only the central warehouse is entered into the RMI registry. Note that a remote reference to the backup warehouse can be passed to the client even though it is not included in the RMI registry. This happens whenever no keyword matches and a *Core Java* book (whose location field references the backup warehouse) is sent to the client.

---

**Listing 11.7**  warehouse2/Book.java

```
1  /**
2   * A book is a product with an ISBN number.
3   * @version 1.0 2007-10-09
4   * @author Cay Horstmann
5   */
6  public class Book extends Product
7  {
8     private String isbn;
9
10    public Book(String title, String isbn, double price)
11    {
12       super(title, price);
13       this.isbn = isbn;
14    }
15
16    public String getDescription()
17    {
18       return super.getDescription() + " " + isbn;
19    }
20 }
```

---

**Listing 11.8**  warehouse2/WarehouseImpl.java

```
1  import java.rmi.*;
2  import java.rmi.server.*;
3  import java.util.*;
4
5  /**
6   * This class is the implementation for the remote Warehouse interface.
7   * @version 1.01 2012-01-26
8   * @author Cay Horstmann
9   */
10 public class WarehouseImpl extends UnicastRemoteObject implements Warehouse
11 {
12    private Map<String, Product> products;
13    private Warehouse backup;
14
15    /**
16     * Constructs a warehouse implementation.
17     */
```

*(Continues)*

**Listing 11.8** *(Continued)*

```
18   public WarehouseImpl(Warehouse backup) throws RemoteException
19   {
20      products = new HashMap<>();
21      this.backup = backup;
22   }
23
24   public void add(String keyword, Product product)
25   {
26      product.setLocation(this);
27      products.put(keyword, product);
28   }
29
30   public double getPrice(String description) throws RemoteException
31   {
32      for (Product p : products.values())
33         if (p.getDescription().equals(description)) return p.getPrice();
34      if (backup == null) return 0;
35      else return backup.getPrice(description);
36   }
37
38   public Product getProduct(List<String> keywords) throws RemoteException
39   {
40      for (String keyword : keywords)
41      {
42         Product p = products.get(keyword);
43         if (p != null) return p;
44      }
45      if (backup != null)
46         return backup.getProduct(keywords);
47      else if (products.values().size() > 0)
48         return products.values().iterator().next();
49      else
50         return null;
51   }
52 }
```

**Listing 11.9** warehouse2/WarehouseServer.java

```
1 import java.rmi.*;
2 import javax.naming.*;
3
4 /**
5  * This server program instantiates a remote warehouse objects, registers it with the naming
6  * service, and waits for clients to invoke methods.
7  * @version 1.12 2007-10-09
8  * @author Cay Horstmann
9  */
```

```
10  public class WarehouseServer
11  {
12     public static void main(String[] args) throws RemoteException, NamingException
13     {
14        System.setProperty("java.security.policy", "server.policy");
15        System.setSecurityManager(new SecurityManager());
16
17        System.out.println("Constructing server implementation...");
18        WarehouseImpl backupWarehouse = new WarehouseImpl(null);
19        WarehouseImpl centralWarehouse = new WarehouseImpl(backupWarehouse);
20
21        centralWarehouse.add("toaster", new Product("Blackwell Toaster", 23.95));
22        backupWarehouse.add("java", new Book("Core Java vol. 2", "0132354799", 44.95));
23
24        System.out.println("Binding server implementation to registry...");
25        Context namingContext = new InitialContext();
26        namingContext.bind("rmi:central_warehouse", centralWarehouse);
27
28        System.out.println("Waiting for invocations from clients...");
29     }
30  }
```

## 11.4.4 Remote References with Multiple Interfaces

A remote class can implement multiple interfaces. Consider a remote interface
ServiceCenter.

```
public interface ServiceCenter extends Remote
{
   int getReturnAuthorization(Product prod) throws RemoteException;
}
```

Now suppose a WarehouseImpl class implements this interface as well as the Warehouse
interface. When a remote reference to such a service center is transferred to another virtual machine, the recipient obtains a stub that has access to the remote
methods in both the ServiceCenter and the Warehouse interface. You can use the instanceof
operator to find out whether a particular remote object implements an interface.
Suppose you receive a remote object through a variable of type Warehouse.

```
Warehouse location = product.getLocation();
```

The remote object might or might not be a service center. To find out, use the test

```
if (location instanceof ServiceCenter)
```

If the test passes, you can cast location to the ServiceCenter type and invoke the
getReturnAuthorization method.

## 11.4.5 Remote Objects and the equals, hashCode, and clone Methods

Objects inserted in sets must override the equals method. In the case of a hash set or hash map, the hashCode method must be defined as well. However, there is a problem when trying to compare remote objects. To find out if two remote objects have the same contents, the call to equals would need to contact the servers containing the objects and compare their contents. Like any remote call, that call could fail. But the equals method in the class Object is not declared to throw a RemoteException, whereas all methods in a remote interface must throw that exception. Since a subclass method cannot throw more exceptions than the superclass method it replaces, you cannot define an equals method in a remote interface. The same holds for hashCode.

Instead, the equals and hashCode methods on stub objects simply look at the location of the remote objects. The equals method deems two stubs equal if they refer to the same remote object. Two stubs that refer to different remote objects are never equal, even if those objects have identical contents. Similarly, the hash code is computed only from the object identifier.

For the same technical reasons, remote references do not have a clone method. If clone were to make a remote call to tell the server to clone the implementation object, then the clone method would need to throw a RemoteException. However, the clone method in the Object superclass promised never to throw any exception other than CloneNotSupportedException.

To summarize, you can use remote references in sets and hash tables, but you must remember that equality testing and hashing do not take into account the contents of the remote objects. You simply cannot clone remote references.

# 11.5 Remote Object Activation

In the preceding sample programs, we used a server program to instantiate and register objects so that clients could make remote calls on them. However, in some cases, it might be wasteful to instantiate lots of remote objects and have them wait for connections, whether or not client objects use them. The *activation* mechanism lets you delay the object construction so that a remote object is only constructed when at least one client invokes a remote method on it.

To take advantage of activation, the client code is completely unchanged. The client simply requests a remote reference and makes calls through it.

However, the server program is replaced by an activation program that constructs *activation descriptors* of the objects that are to be constructed at a later time, and binds receivers for remote method calls with the naming service. When a call is made for the first time, the information in the activation descriptor is used to construct the object.

A remote object used in this way should extend the Activatable class instead of the UnicastRemoteObject class. Of course, it also implements one or more remote interfaces. For example,

```
class WarehouseImpl
    extends Activatable
    implements Warehouse
{
    . . .
}
```

Since the object construction is delayed until a later time, it must happen in a standardized form. Therefore, you must provide a constructor that takes two parameters:

- An activation ID (which you simply pass to the superclass constructor).
- A single object containing all construction information, wrapped in a MarshalledObject.

If you need multiple construction parameters, you must package them into a single object. You can always use an Object[] array or an ArrayList for this purpose.

When you build the activation descriptor, you will construct a MarshalledObject from the construction information like this:

```
MarshalledObject<T> param = new MarshalledObject<T>(constructionInfo);
```

In the constructor of the implementation object, use the get method of the MarshalledObject class to obtain the deserialized construction information.

```
T constructionInfo = param.get();
```

To demonstrate activation, we modify the WarehouseImpl class so that the construction information is a map of descriptions and prices. That information is wrapped into a MarshalledObject and unwrapped in the constructor:

```
public WarehouseImpl(ActivationID id, MarshalledObject<Map<String, Double>> param)
        throws RemoteException, ClassNotFoundException, IOException
{
    super(id, 0);
    prices = param.get();
    System.out.println("Warehouse implementation constructed.");
}
```

By passing 0 as the second parameter of the superclass constructor, we indicate that the RMI library should assign a suitable port number to the listener port.

This constructor prints a message so that you can see that the warehouse object is activated on demand.

---

 **NOTE:** Your remote objects don't actually have to extend the `Activatable` class. If they don't, place the static method call

```
Activatable.exportObject(this, id, 0)
```

in the constructor of the server class.

---

Now let us turn to the activation program. First, you need to define an activation group. An activation group describes common parameters for launching the virtual machine that contains the remote objects. The most important parameter is the security policy.

Construct an activation group descriptor as follows:

```
Properties props = new Properties();
props.put("java.security.policy", "/path/to/server.policy");
ActivationGroupDesc group = new ActivationGroupDesc(props, null);
```

The second parameter describes special command options. We don't need any for this example, so we pass a `null` reference.

Next, create a group ID with the call

```
ActivationGroupID id = ActivationGroup.getSystem().registerGroup(group);
```

Now you are ready to construct activation descriptors. For each object that should be constructed on demand, you need the following:

- The activation group ID for the virtual machine in which the object should be constructed.
- The name of the class (such as `"WarehouseImpl"` or `"com.mycompany.MyClassImpl"`).
- The URL string from which to load the class files. This should be the base URL, not including package paths.
- The marshalled construction information.

For example,

```
MarshalledObject param = new MarshalledObject(constructionInfo);
ActivationDesc desc = new ActivationDesc(id, "WarehouseImpl",
                                "http://myserver.com/download/", param);
```

Pass the descriptor to the static `Activatable.register` method. It returns an object of some class that implements the remote interfaces of the implementation class. You can bind that object with the naming service:

```
Warehouse centralWarehouse = (Warehouse) Activatable.register(desc);
namingContext.bind("rmi:central_warehouse", centralWarehouse);
```

Unlike the server programs of the preceding examples, the activation program exits after registering and binding the activation receivers. The remote objects are constructed only when the first remote method call occurs.

Listings 11.10 and 11.11 show the code for the activation program and the activatable warehouse implementation. The warehouse interface and the client program are unchanged.

To launch this program, follow these steps:

1. Compile all source files.

2. Distribute class files as follows:

```
client/
    WarehouseClient.class
    Warehouse.class
server/
    WarehouseActivator.class
    Warehouse.class
    WarehouseImpl.class
    server.policy
download/
    Warehouse.class
    WarehouseImpl.class
rmi/
    rmid.policy
```

3. Start the RMI registry in the `rmi` directory (which contains no class files).

4. Start the RMI activation daemon in the `rmi` directory.

```
rmid -J-Djava.security.policy=rmid.policy
```

The `rmid` program listens to activation requests and activates objects in a separate virtual machine. To launch a virtual machine, the `rmid` program needs certain permissions. These are specified in a policy file (see Listing 11.12). Use the `-J` option to pass an option to the virtual machine running the activation daemon.

5. Start the `NanoHTTPD` web server in the `download` directory.

6. Run the activation program from the `server` directory.

    ```
    java -Djava.rmi.server.codebase=http://localhost:8080/ WarehouseActivator
    ```

    The program exits after the activation receivers have been registered with the naming service. (You might wonder why you need to specify the codebase as it is also provided in the constructor of the activation descriptor. However, that information is only processed by the RMI activation daemon. The RMI registry still needs the codebase to load the remote interface classes.)

7. Run the client program from the `client` directory.

    ```
    java WarehouseClient
    ```

    The client will print the familiar product description. When you run the client for the first time, you will also see the constructor messages in the shell window of the activation daemon.

---

**Listing 11.10** activation/WarehouseActivator.java

```
1  import java.io.*;
2  import java.rmi.*;
3  import java.rmi.activation.*;
4  import java.util.*;
5  import javax.naming.*;
6
7  /**
8   * This server program instantiates a remote warehouse object, registers it with the naming
9   * service, and waits for clients to invoke methods.
10  * @version 1.13 2012-01-26
11  * @author Cay Horstmann
12  */
13 public class WarehouseActivator
14 {
15    public static void main(String[] args) throws RemoteException, NamingException,
16          ActivationException, IOException
17    {
18       System.out.println("Constructing activation descriptors...");
19
20       Properties props = new Properties();
21       // use the server.policy file in the current directory
22       props.put("java.security.policy", new File("server.policy").getCanonicalPath());
23       ActivationGroupDesc group = new ActivationGroupDesc(props, null);
24       ActivationGroupID id = ActivationGroup.getSystem().registerGroup(group);
25
26       Map<String, Double> prices = new HashMap<>();
27       prices.put("Blackwell Toaster", 24.95);
28       prices.put("ZapXpress Microwave Oven", 49.95);
```

```
29    MarshalledObject<Map<String, Double>> param = new MarshalledObject<Map<String, Double>>(
30        prices);
31
32    String codebase = "http://localhost:8080/";
33
34    ActivationDesc desc = new ActivationDesc(id, "WarehouseImpl", codebase, param);
35
36    Warehouse centralWarehouse = (Warehouse) Activatable.register(desc);
37
38    System.out.println("Binding activable implementation to registry...");
39    Context namingContext = new InitialContext();
40    namingContext.bind("rmi:central_warehouse", centralWarehouse);
41    System.out.println("Exiting...");
42  }
43 }
```

**Listing 11.11**  activation/WarehouseImpl.java

```
1  import java.io.*;
2  import java.rmi.*;
3  import java.rmi.activation.*;
4  import java.util.*;
5
6  /**
7   * This class is the implementation for the remote Warehouse interface.
8   * @version 1.0 2007-10-20
9   * @author Cay Horstmann
10  */
11 public class WarehouseImpl extends Activatable implements Warehouse
12 {
13    private Map<String, Double> prices;
14
15    public WarehouseImpl(ActivationID id, MarshalledObject<Map<String, Double>> param)
16        throws RemoteException, ClassNotFoundException, IOException
17    {
18       super(id, 0);
19       prices = param.get();
20       System.out.println("Warehouse implementation constructed.");
21    }
22
23    public double getPrice(String description) throws RemoteException
24    {
25       Double price = prices.get(description);
26       return price == null ? 0 : price;
27    }
28 }
```

---

**Listing 11.12** activation/rmid.policy

```
1  grant
2  {
3      permission com.sun.rmi.rmid.ExecPermission
4          "${java.home}${/}bin${/}java";
5      permission com.sun.rmi.rmid.ExecOptionPermission
6          "-Djava.security.policy=*";
7  };
```

---

**java.rmi.activation.Activatable** 1.2

- `protected Activatable(ActivationID id, int port)`
  constructs the activatable object and establishes a listener on the given port. Use 0 for the port to have a port assigned automatically.

- `static Remote exportObject(Remote obj, ActivationID id, int port)`
  makes a remote object activatable. Returns the activation receiver that should be made available to remote callers. Use 0 for the port to have a port assigned automatically.

- `static Remote register(ActivationDesc desc)`
  registers the descriptor for an activatable object and prepares it for receiving remote calls. Returns the activation receiver that should be made available to remote callers.

---

**java.rmi.MarshalledObject** 1.2

- `MarshalledObject(Object obj)`
  constructs an object containing the serialized data of a given object.

- `Object get()`
  deserializes the stored object data and returns the object.

---

**java.rmi.activation.ActivationGroupDesc** 1.2

- `ActivationGroupDesc(Properties props, ActivationGroupDesc.CommandEnvironment env)`
  constructs an activation group descriptor that specifies virtual machine properties for a virtual machine that hosts activated objects. The `env` parameter contains the path to the virtual machine executable and command-line options, or it is `null` if no special settings are required.

---

**java.rmi.activation.ActivationGroup**  1.2

- static ActivationSystem getSystem()
  returns a reference to the activation system.

---

**java.rmi.activation.ActivationSystem**  1.2

- ActivationGroupID registerGroup(ActivationGroupDesc group)
  registers an activation group and returns the group ID.

---

**java.rmi.activation.ActivationDesc**  1.2

- ActivationDesc(ActivationGroupID id, String className, String classFileURL, MarshalledObject data)
  constructs an activation descriptor.

---

You have now seen the RMI mechanism, a distributed object model for Java programs. In the final chapter, we will turn to a different aspect of Java programming: interacting, on the same machine, with "native" code in a different programming language.

# Native Methods

## In this chapter:

While a "100% Pure Java" solution is nice in principle, there are situations in which you will want to write (or use) code written in another language. (Such code is usually called *native* code.)

Particularly in the early days of Java, many people assumed that it would be a good idea to use C or C++ to speed up critical parts of a Java application. However, in practice, this was rarely useful. A presentation at the 1996 JavaOne conference showed this clearly. The implementors of the cryptography library at Sun Microsystems reported that a pure Java platform implementation of their cryptographic functions was more than adequate. It was true that the code was not as fast as a C implementation would have been, but it turned out not to matter. The

Java platform implementation was far faster than the network I/O. This turned out to be the real bottleneck.

Of course, there are drawbacks to going native. If a part of your application is written in another language, you must supply a separate native library for every platform you want to support. Code written in C or C++ offers no protection against overwriting memory through invalid pointer usage. It is easy to write native methods that corrupt your program or infect the operating system.

Thus, we suggest using native code only when you need to. In particular, there are three reasons why native code might be the right choice:

• Your application requires access to system features or devices that are not accessible through the Java platform.

• You have substantial amounts of tested and debugged code in another language, and you know how to port it to all desired target platforms.

• You have found, through benchmarking, that the Java code is much slower than the equivalent code in another language.

The Java platform has an API for interoperating with native C code called the Java Native Interface (JNI). We'll discuss JNI programming in this chapter.

---

 **C++ NOTE:** You can also use C++ instead of C to write native methods. There are a few advantages—type checking is slightly stricter, and accessing the JNI functions is a bit more convenient. However, JNI does not support any mapping between Java and C++ classes.

---

## 12.1 Calling a C Function from a Java Program

Suppose you have a C function that does something you like and, for one reason or another, you don't want to bother reimplementing it in Java. For the sake of illustration, we'll start with a simple C function that prints a greeting.

The Java programming language uses the keyword native for a native method, and you will obviously need to place a method in a class. The result is shown in Listing 12.1.

The native keyword alerts the compiler that the method will be defined externally. Of course, native methods will contain no code in the Java programming language, and the method header is followed immediately by a terminating semicolon. Therefore, native method declarations look similar to abstract method declarations.

**Listing 12.1** helloNative/HelloNative.java

```
1  /**
2   * @version 1.11 2007-10-26
3   * @author Cay Horstmann
4   */
5  class HelloNative
6  {
7     public static native void greeting();
8  }
```

 **NOTE:** As in the previous chapter, we do not use packages here to keep examples simple.

In this particular example, the native method is also declared as static. Native methods can be both static and nonstatic. We'll start with a static method because we do not yet want to deal with parameter passing.

You can actually compile this class, but if you try to use it in a program, the virtual machine will tell you it doesn't know how to find greeting—reporting an UnsatisfiedLinkError. To implement the native code, write a corresponding C function. You must name that function *exactly* the way the Java virtual machine expects. Here are the rules:

1.  Use the full Java method name, such as HelloNative.greeting. If the class is in a package, prepend the package name, such as com.horstmann.HelloNative.greeting.

2.  Replace every period with an underscore, and append the prefix Java_. For example, Java_HelloNative_greeting or Java_com_horstmann_HelloNative_greeting.

3.  If the class name contains characters that are not ASCII letters or digits—that is, '_', '$', or Unicode characters with codes greater than '\u007F'—replace them with _0xxxx, where xxxx is the sequence of four hexadecimal digits of the character's Unicode value.

 **NOTE:** If you *overload* native methods—that is, if you provide multiple native methods with the same name—you must append a double underscore followed by the encoded argument types. (We'll describe the encoding of the argument types later in this chapter.) For example, if you have a native method greeting and another native method greeting(int repeat), then the first one is called Java_HelloNative_greeting__, and the second, Java_HelloNative_greeting__I.

Actually, nobody does this by hand; instead, run the javah utility which automatically generates the function names. To use javah, first compile the source file in Listing 12.1:

```
javac HelloNative.java
```

Next, call the javah utility, which produces a C header file from the class file. The javah executable can be found in the *jdk*/bin directory. Invoke it with the name of the class, just as you would start a Java program:

```
javah HelloNative
```

This command creates a header file, HelloNative.h, shown in Listing 12.2.

**Listing 12.2** helloNative/HelloNative.h

```
1  /* DO NOT EDIT THIS FILE - it is machine generated */
2  #include <jni.h>
3  /* Header for class HelloNative */
4
5  #ifndef _Included_HelloNative
6  #define _Included_HelloNative
7  #ifdef __cplusplus
8  extern "C" {
9  #endif
10 /*
11  * Class:     HelloNative
12  * Method:    greeting
13  * Signature: ()V
14  */
15 JNIEXPORT void JNICALL Java_HelloNative_greeting
16   (JNIEnv *, jclass);
17
18 #ifdef __cplusplus
19 }
20 #endif
21 #endif
```

As you can see, this file contains the declaration of a function Java_HelloNative_greeting. (The macros JNIEXPORT and JNICALL are defined in the header file jni.h. They denote compiler-dependent specifiers for exported functions that come from a dynamically loaded library.)

Now, simply copy the function prototype from the header file into the source file and give the implementation code for the function, as shown in Listing 12.3.

In this simple function, ignore the env and cl arguments. You'll see their use later.

**Listing 12.3** helloNative/HelloNative.c

```
1  /*
2     @version 1.10 1997-07-01
3     @author Cay Horstmann
4  */
5
6  #include "HelloNative.h"
7  #include <stdio.h>
8
9  JNIEXPORT void JNICALL Java_HelloNative_greeting(JNIEnv* env, jclass cl)
10 {
11    printf("Hello Native World!\n");
12 }
```

 **C++ NOTE:** You can use C++ to implement native methods. However, you must then declare the functions that implement the native methods as extern "C". (This stops the C++ compiler from "mangling" the method name.) For example,

```
extern "C"
JNIEXPORT void JNICALL Java_HelloNative_greeting(JNIEnv* env, jclass cl)
{
    cout << "Hello, Native World!" << endl;
}
```

Compile the native C code into a dynamically loaded library. The details depend on your compiler.

For example, with the Gnu C compiler on Linux, use these commands:

```
gcc -fPIC -I jdk/include -I jdk/include/linux -shared -o libHelloNative.so HelloNative.c
```

With the Sun compiler under the Solaris Operating System, the command is

```
cc -G -I jdk/include -I jdk/include/solaris -o libHelloNative.so HelloNative.c
```

With the Microsoft compiler under Windows, the command is

```
cl -I jdk\include -I jdk\include\win32 -LD HelloNative.c -FeHelloNative.dll
```

Here, *jdk* is the directory that contains the JDK.

 **TIP:** If you use the Microsoft compiler from a command shell, first run the batch file vcvars32.bat or vsvars32.bat. That batch file sets up the path and the environment variables needed by the compiler. You can find it in the directory c:\Program Files\Microsoft Visual Studio .NET 2003\Common7\tools, c:\Program Files\Microsoft Visual Studio 8\VC, or a similar monstrosity.

You can also use the freely available Cygwin programming environment from www.cygwin.com. It contains the Gnu C compiler and libraries for UNIX-style programming on Windows. With Cygwin, use the command

```
gcc -mno-cygwin -D __int64="long long" -I jdk/include/ -I jdk/include/win32
    -shared -Wl,--add-stdcall-alias -o HelloNative.dll HelloNative.c
```

Type the entire command on a single line.

**NOTE:** The Windows version of the header file `jni_md.h` contains the type declaration

```
typedef __int64 jlong;
```

which is specific to the Microsoft compiler. If you use the Gnu compiler, you might want to edit that file, for example,

```
#ifdef __GNUC__
    typedef long long jlong;
#else
    typedef __int64 jlong;
#endif
```

Alternatively, compile with `-D __int64="long long"`, as shown in the sample compiler invocation.

Finally, add a call to the `System.loadLibrary` method in your program. To ensure that the virtual machine will load the library before the first use of the class, use a static initialization block, as in Listing 12.4.

**Listing 12.4** `helloNative/HelloNativeTest.java`

```java
1  /**
2   * @version 1.11 2007-10-26
3   * @author Cay Horstmann
4   */
5  class HelloNativeTest
6  {
7     public static void main(String[] args)
8     {
9        HelloNative.greeting();
10    }
11
12    static
13    {
14       System.loadLibrary("HelloNative");
15    }
16 }
```

Figure 12.1 gives a summary of the native code processing.

After you compile and run this program, the message "Hello, Native World!" is displayed in a terminal window.

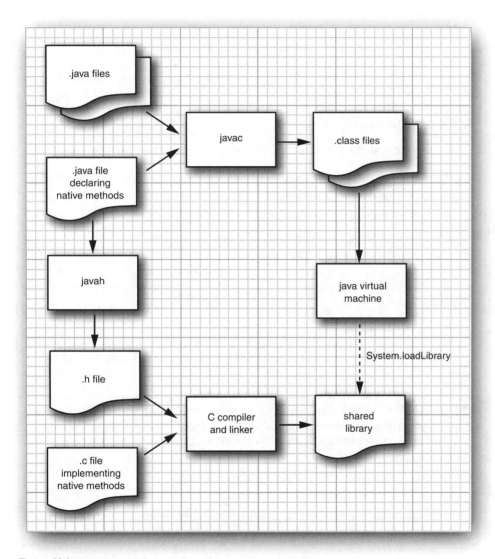

**Figure 12.1** Processing native code

**NOTE:** If you run Linux, you must add the current directory to the library path. Either set the `LD_LIBRARY_PATH` environment variable:

> `export LD_LIBRARY_PATH=.:$LD_LIBRARY_PATH`

or set the `java.library.path` system property:

> `java -Djava.library.path=. HelloNativeTest`

Of course, this is not particularly impressive by itself. However, keep in mind that this message is generated by the C `printf` command and not by any Java programming language code. We have taken the first steps toward bridging the gap between the two languages!

In summary, follow these steps to link a native method to a Java program:

1. Declare a native method in a Java class.
2. Run `javah` to get a header file with a C declaration for the method.
3. Implement the native method in C.
4. Place the code in a shared library.
5. Load that library in your Java program.

---

**`java.lang.System` 1.0**

- `void loadLibrary(String libname)`
  loads the library with the given name. The library is located in the library search path. The exact method for locating the library is operating system dependent.

---

 **NOTE:** Some shared libraries for native code must execute certain initializations. You can place any initialization code into a `JNI_OnLoad` method. Similarly, when the virtual machine (VM) shuts down, it will call the `JNI_OnUnload` method if you provide it. The prototypes are

> `jint JNI_OnLoad(JavaVM* vm, void* reserved);`
> `void JNI_OnUnload(JavaVM* vm, void* reserved);`

The `JNI_OnLoad` method needs to return the minimum version of the VM it requires, such as `JNI_VERSION_1_2`.

## 12.2 Numeric Parameters and Return Values

When passing numbers between C and Java, you should understand which types correspond to each other. For example, although C does have data types called int and long, their implementation is platform-dependent. On some platforms, an int is a 16-bit quantity, on others it is a 32-bit quantity. In the Java platform, of course, an int is *always* a 32-bit integer. For that reason, JNI defines types jint, jlong, and so on.

Table 12.1 shows the correspondence between Java types and C types.

In the header file jni.h, these types are declared with typedef statements as the equivalent types on the target platform. That header file also defines the constants JNI_FALSE = 0 and JNI_TRUE = 1.

**Table 12.1**  Java Types and C Types

| Java Programming Language | C Programming Language | Bytes |
| --- | --- | --- |
| boolean | jboolean | 1 |
| byte | jbyte | 1 |
| char | jchar | 2 |
| short | jshort | 2 |
| int | jint | 4 |
| long | jlong | 8 |
| float | jfloat | 4 |
| double | jdouble | 8 |

### 12.2.1 Using `printf` for Formatting Numbers

Until Java SE 5.0, Java had no direct analog of the C printf function. In the following examples, we will suppose you are stuck with an ancient JDK release and decide to implement the same functionality by calling the C printf function in a native method.

Listing 12.5 shows a class called Printf1 that uses a native method to print a floating-point number with a given field width and precision.

---

**Listing 12.5** printf1/Printf1.java

```
1  /**
2   * @version 1.10 1997-07-01
3   * @author Cay Horstmann
4   */
5  class Printf1
6  {
7     public static native int print(int width, int precision, double x);
8
9     static
10    {
11       System.loadLibrary("Printf1");
12    }
13 }
```

---

Notice that when the method is implemented in C, all int and double parameters are changed to jint and jdouble, as shown in Listing 12.6.

---

**Listing 12.6** printf1/Printf1.c

```
1  /**
2     @version 1.10 1997-07-01
3     @author Cay Horstmann
4  */
5
6  #include "Printf1.h"
7  #include <stdio.h>
8
9  JNIEXPORT jint JNICALL Java_Printf1_print(JNIEnv* env, jclass cl,
10    jint width, jint precision, jdouble x)
11 {
12    char fmt[30];
13    jint ret;
14    sprintf(fmt, "%%%d.%df", width, precision);
15    ret = printf(fmt, x);
16    fflush(stdout);
17    return ret;
18 }
19
```

---

The function simply assembles a format string "%w.pf" in the variable fmt, then calls printf. It returns the number of characters printed.

Listing 12.7 shows the test program that demonstrates the Printf1 class.

---

**Listing 12.7** `printf1/Printf1Test.java`

```java
1  /**
2   * @version 1.10 1997-07-01
3   * @author Cay Horstmann
4   */
5  class Printf1Test
6  {
7     public static void main(String[] args)
8     {
9        int count = Printf1.print(8, 4, 3.14);
10       count += Printf1.print(8, 4, count);
11       System.out.println();
12       for (int i = 0; i < count; i++)
13          System.out.print("-");
14       System.out.println();
15    }
16 }
```

---

## 12.3 String Parameters

Next, we want to consider how to transfer strings to and from native methods. Strings are quite different in the two languages: In Java they are sequences of UTF-16 code points whereas C strings are null-terminated sequences of bytes. JNI has two sets of functions for manipulating strings: One converts Java strings to "modified UTF-8" byte sequences and another converts them to arrays of UTF-16 values—that is, to jchar arrays. (The UTF-8, "modified UTF-8," and UTF-16 formats were discussed in Chapter 1. Recall that the UTF-8 and "modified UTF-8" encodings leave ASCII characters unchanged, but all other Unicode characters are encoded as multibyte sequences.)

---

 **NOTE:** The standard UTF-8 encoding and the "modified UTF-8" encoding differ only for "supplementary" characters with codes higher than 0xFFFF. In the standard UTF-8 encoding, these characters are encoded as 4-byte sequences. In the "modified" encoding, each such character is first encoded as a pair of "surrogates" in the UTF-16 encoding, and then each surrogate is encoded with UTF-8, yielding a total of 6 bytes. This is clumsy, but it is a historical accident—the JVM specification was written when Unicode was still limited to 16 bits.

---

If your C code already uses Unicode, you'll want to use the second set of conversion functions. On the other hand, if all your strings are restricted to ASCII characters, you can use the "modified UTF-8" conversion functions.

A native method with a String parameter actually receives a value of an opaque type called jstring. A native method with a return value of type String must return a value of type jstring. JNI functions read and construct these jstring objects. For example, the NewStringUTF function makes a new jstring object out of a char array that contains ASCII characters or, more generally, "modified UTF-8"-encoded byte sequences.

JNI functions have a somewhat odd calling convention. Here is a call to the NewStringUTF function:

```
JNIEXPORT jstring JNICALL Java_HelloNative_getGreeting(JNIEnv* env, jclass cl)
{
    jstring jstr;
    char greeting[] = "Hello, Native World\n";
    jstr = (*env)->NewStringUTF(env, greeting);
    return jstr;
}
```

 **NOTE:** Unless explicitly mentioned otherwise, all code in this chapter is C code.

All calls to JNI functions use the env pointer that is the first argument of every native method. The env pointer is a pointer to a table of function pointers (see Figure 12.2). Therefore, you must prefix every JNI call with (*env)-> to actually dereference the function pointer. Furthermore, env is the first parameter of every JNI function.

 **C++ NOTE:** It is simpler to access JNI functions in C++. The C++ version of the JNIEnv class has inline member functions that take care of the function pointer lookup for you. For example, you can call the NewStringUTF function as

```
jstr = env->NewStringUTF(greeting);
```

Note that you omit the JNIEnv pointer from the parameter list of the call.

The NewStringUTF function lets you construct a new jstring. To read the contents of an existing jstring object, use the GetStringUTFChars function. This function returns a const jbyte* pointer to the "modified UTF-8" characters that describe the character string. Note that a specific virtual machine is free to choose this character encoding for its internal string representation, so you might get a character pointer into the actual Java string. Since Java strings are meant to be immutable, it is *very* important that you treat the const seriously and do not try to write into this character array. On the other hand, if the virtual machine uses UTF-16 or UTF-32

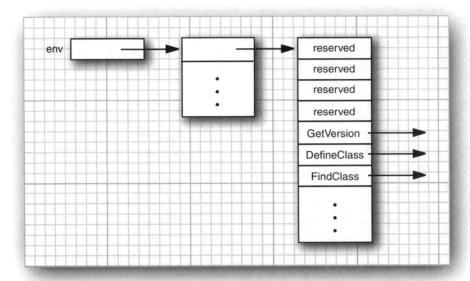

**Figure 12.2** The `env` pointer

characters for its internal string representation, this function call allocates a new memory block that will be filled with the "modified UTF-8" equivalents.

The virtual machine must know when you are finished using the string so that it can garbage-collect it. (The garbage collector runs in a separate thread, and it can interrupt the execution of native methods.) For that reason, you must call the `ReleaseStringUTFChars` function.

Alternatively, you can supply your own buffer to hold the string characters by calling the `GetStringRegion` or `GetStringUTFRegion` methods.

Finally, the `GetStringUTFLength` function returns the number of characters needed for the "modified UTF-8" encoding of the string.

 **NOTE:** You can find the JNI API at http://docs.oracle.com/javase/7/docs/technotes/guides/jni.

---

**Accessing Java Strings from C Code**

- `jstring NewStringUTF(JNIEnv* env, const char bytes[])`
  returns a new Java string object from a zero byte-terminated "modified UTF-8" byte sequence, or `NULL` if the string cannot be constructed.

*(Continues)*

---

**Accessing Java Strings from C Code** *(Continued)*

---

- `jsize GetStringUTFLength(JNIEnv* env, jstring string)`

  returns the number of bytes required for the "modified UTF-8" encoding (not counting the zero byte terminator).

- `const jbyte* GetStringUTFChars(JNIEnv* env, jstring string, jboolean* isCopy)`

  returns a pointer to the "modified UTF-8" encoding of a string, or NULL if the character array cannot be constructed. The pointer is valid until `ReleaseStringUTFChars` is called. `isCopy` points to a `jboolean` filled with `JNI_TRUE` if a copy is made, with `JNI_FALSE` otherwise.

- `void ReleaseStringUTFChars(JNIEnv* env, jstring string, const jbyte bytes[])`

  informs the virtual machine that the native code no longer needs access to the Java string through `bytes` (a pointer returned by `GetStringUTFChars`).

- `void GetStringRegion(JNIEnv *env, jstring string, jsize start, jsize length, jchar *buffer)`

  copies a sequence of UTF-16 double bytes from a string to a user-supplied buffer of size at least 2 × `length`.

- `void GetStringUTFRegion(JNIEnv *env, jstring string, jsize start, jsize length, jbyte *buffer)`

  copies a sequence of "modified UTF-8" bytes from a string to a user-supplied buffer. The buffer must be long enough to hold the bytes. In the worst case, 3 × `length` bytes are copied.

- `jstring NewString(JNIEnv* env, const jchar chars[], jsize length)`

  returns a new Java string object from a Unicode string, or NULL if the string cannot be constructed.

  | *Parameters:* | env | The JNI interface pointer |
  |---|---|---|
  | | chars | The null-terminated UTF-16 string |
  | | length | The number of characters in the string |

- `jsize GetStringLength(JNIEnv* env, jstring string)`

  returns the number of characters in the string.

- `const jchar* GetStringChars(JNIEnv* env, jstring string, jboolean* isCopy)`

  returns a pointer to the Unicode encoding of a string, or NULL if the character array cannot be constructed. The pointer is valid until `ReleaseStringChars` is called. `isCopy` is either NULL or points to a `jboolean` filled with `JNI_TRUE` if a copy is made, with `JNI_FALSE` otherwise.

- `void ReleaseStringChars(JNIEnv* env, jstring string, const jchar chars[])`

  informs the virtual machine that the native code no longer needs access to the Java string through `chars` (a pointer returned by `GetStringChars`).

---

Let us put these functions to work and write a class that calls the C function `sprintf`. We would like to call the function as shown in Listing 12.8.

---

**Listing 12.8** printf2/Printf2Test.java

```java
1  /**
2   * @version 1.10 1997-07-01
3   * @author Cay Horstmann
4   */
5  class Printf2Test
6  {
7     public static void main(String[] args)
8     {
9        double price = 44.95;
10       double tax = 7.75;
11       double amountDue = price * (1 + tax / 100);
12
13       String s = Printf2.sprint("Amount due = %8.2f", amountDue);
14       System.out.println(s);
15    }
16 }
```

---

Listing 12.9 shows the class with the native `sprint` method.

Therefore, the C function that formats a floating-point number has the prototype

```
JNIEXPORT jstring JNICALL Java_Printf2_sprint(JNIEnv* env, jclass cl, jstring format, jdouble x)
```

---

**Listing 12.9** printf2/Printf2.java

```java
1  /**
2   * @version 1.10 1997-07-01
3   * @author Cay Horstmann
4   */
5  class Printf2
6  {
7     public static native String sprint(String format, double x);
8
9     static
10    {
11       System.loadLibrary("Printf2");
12    }
13 }
```

---

Listing 12.10 shows the code for the C implementation. Note the calls to `GetStringUTFChars` to read the format argument, `NewStringUTF` to generate the return value, and `ReleaseStringUTFChars` to inform the virtual machine that access to the string is no longer required.

**Listing 12.10** printf2/Printf2.c

```
 1  /**
 2     @version 1.10 1997-07-01
 3     @author Cay Horstmann
 4  */
 5
 6  #include "Printf2.h"
 7  #include <string.h>
 8  #include <stdlib.h>
 9  #include <float.h>
10
11  /**
12     @param format a string containing a printf format specifier
13     (such as "%8.2f"). Substrings "%%" are skipped.
14     @return a pointer to the format specifier (skipping the '%')
15     or NULL if there wasn't a unique format specifier
16  */
17  char* find_format(const char format[])
18  {
19     char* p;
20     char* q;
21
22     p = strchr(format, '%');
23     while (p != NULL && *(p + 1) == '%') /* skip %% */
24        p = strchr(p + 2, '%');
25     if (p == NULL) return NULL;
26     /* now check that % is unique */
27     p++;
28     q = strchr(p, '%');
29     while (q != NULL && *(q + 1) == '%') /* skip %% */
30        q = strchr(q + 2, '%');
31     if (q != NULL) return NULL; /* % not unique */
32     q = p + strspn(p, " -0+#"); /* skip past flags */
33     q += strspn(q, "0123456789"); /* skip past field width */
34     if (*q == '.') { q++; q += strspn(q, "0123456789"); }
35        /* skip past precision */
36     if (strchr("eEfFgG", *q) == NULL) return NULL;
37        /* not a floating-point format */
38     return p;
39  }
40
41  JNIEXPORT jstring JNICALL Java_Printf2_sprint(JNIEnv* env, jclass cl,
42     jstring format, jdouble x)
43  {
44     const char* cformat;
45     char* fmt;
46     jstring ret;
47
48     cformat = (*env)->GetStringUTFChars(env, format, NULL);
```

```
49     fmt = find_format(cformat);
50     if (fmt == NULL)
51         ret = format;
52     else
53     {
54         char* cret;
55         int width = atoi(fmt);
56         if (width == 0) width = DBL_DIG + 10;
57         cret = (char*) malloc(strlen(cformat) + width);
58         sprintf(cret, cformat, x);
59         ret = (*env)->NewStringUTF(env, cret);
60         free(cret);
61     }
62     (*env)->ReleaseStringUTFChars(env, format, cformat);
63     return ret;
64 }
65
```

In this function, we chose to keep error handling simple. If the format code to print a floating-point number is not of the form %w.pc, where c is one of the characters e, E, f, g, or G, then we simply do not format the number. We'll show you later how to make a native method throw an exception.

# 12.4 Accessing Fields

All the native methods you saw so far were static methods with number and string parameters. We'll now consider native methods that operate on objects. As an exercise, we will reimplement as native a method of the Employee class that was introduced in Volume I, Chapter 4. Again, this is not something you would normally want to do, but it does illustrate how to access fields from a native method when you need to do so.

## 12.4.1 Accessing Instance Fields

To see how to access instance fields from a native method, we will reimplement the raiseSalary method. Here is the code in Java:

```
public void raiseSalary(double byPercent)
{
    salary *= 1 + byPercent / 100;
}
```

Let us rewrite this as a native method. Unlike the previous examples of native methods, this is not a static method. Running javah gives the following prototype:

```
JNIEXPORT void JNICALL Java_Employee_raiseSalary(JNIEnv *, jobject, jdouble);
```

Note the second argument. It is no longer of type `jclass` but of type `jobject`. In fact, it is an equivalent of the `this` reference. Static methods obtain a reference to the class, whereas nonstatic methods obtain a reference to the implicit `this` argument object.

Now we access the `salary` field of the implicit argument. In the "raw" Java-to-C binding of Java 1.0, this was easy—a programmer could directly access object data fields. However, direct access requires all virtual machines to expose their internal data layout. For that reason, the JNI requires programmers to get and set the values of data fields by calling special JNI functions.

In our case, we need to use the `GetDoubleField` and `SetDoubleField` functions because the type of `salary` is `double`. There are other functions—`GetIntField`/`SetIntField`, `GetObjectField`/ `SetObjectField`, and so on for other field types. The general syntax is:

```
x = (*env)->GetXxxField(env, this_obj, fieldID);
(*env)->SetXxxField(env, this_obj, fieldID, x);
```

Here, `fieldID` is a value of a special type, `jfieldID`, that identifies a field in a structure, and *Xxx* represents a Java data type (`Object`, `Boolean`, `Byte`, and so on). To obtain the `fieldID`, you must first get a value representing the class, which you can do in one of two ways. The `GetObjectClass` function returns the class of any object. For example:

```
jclass class_Employee = (*env)->GetObjectClass(env, this_obj);
```

The `FindClass` function lets you specify the class name as a string (curiously, with / characters instead of periods as package name separators).

```
jclass class_String = (*env)->FindClass(env, "java/lang/String");
```

Use the `GetFieldID` function to obtain the `fieldID`. You must supply the name of the field and its *signature*, an encoding of its type. For example, here is the code to obtain the field ID of the `salary` field:

```
jfieldID id_salary = (*env)->GetFieldID(env, class_Employee, "salary", "D");
```

The string `"D"` denotes the type `double`. You'll learn the complete rules for encoding signatures in the next section.

You might be thinking that accessing a data field seems quite convoluted. The designers of the JNI did not want to expose the data fields directly, so they had to supply functions for getting and setting field values. To minimize the cost of these functions, computing the field ID from the field name—which is the most expensive step—is factored out into a separate step. That is, if you repeatedly get and set the value of a particular field, you can incur the cost of computing the field identifier only once.

Let us put all the pieces together. The following code reimplements the raiseSalary method as a native method:

```
JNIEXPORT void JNICALL Java_Employee_raiseSalary(JNIEnv* env, jobject this_obj, jdouble byPercent)
{
   /* get the class */
   jclass class_Employee = (*env)->GetObjectClass(env, this_obj);

   /* get the field ID */
   jfieldID id_salary = (*env)->GetFieldID(env, class_Employee, "salary", "D");

   /* get the field value */
   jdouble salary = (*env)->GetDoubleField(env, this_obj, id_salary);

   salary *= 1 + byPercent / 100;

   /* set the field value */
   (*env)->SetDoubleField(env, this_obj, id_salary, salary);
}
```

**CAUTION:** Class references are only valid until the native method returns. Thus, you cannot cache the return values of GetObjectClass in your code. Do *not* store away a class reference for reuse in a later method call. You must call GetObjectClass every time the native method executes. If this is intolerable, you can lock the reference with a call to NewGlobalRef:

```
static jclass class_X = 0;
static jfieldID id_a;
. . .
if (class_X == 0)
{
   jclass cx = (*env)->GetObjectClass(env, obj);
   class_X = (*env)->NewGlobalRef(env, cx);
   id_a = (*env)->GetFieldID(env, cls, "a", ". . .");
}
```

Now you can use the class reference and field IDs in subsequent calls. When you are done using the class, make sure to call

```
(*env)->DeleteGlobalRef(env, class_X);
```

Listings 12.11 and 12.12 show the Java code for a test program and the Employee class. Listing 12.13 contains the C code for the native raiseSalary method.

**Listing 12.11** employee/EmployeeTest.java

```java
1  /**
2   * @version 1.10 1999-11-13
3   * @author Cay Horstmann
4   */
5
6  public class EmployeeTest
7  {
8     public static void main(String[] args)
9     {
10        Employee[] staff = new Employee[3];
11
12        staff[0] = new Employee("Harry Hacker", 35000);
13        staff[1] = new Employee("Carl Cracker", 75000);
14        staff[2] = new Employee("Tony Tester", 38000);
15
16        for (Employee e : staff)
17           e.raiseSalary(5);
18        for (Employee e : staff)
19           e.print();
20     }
21  }
```

**Listing 12.12** employee/Employee.java

```java
1  /**
2   * @version 1.10 1999-11-13
3   * @author Cay Horstmann
4   */
5
6  public class Employee
7  {
8     private String name;
9     private double salary;
10
11    public native void raiseSalary(double byPercent);
12
13    public Employee(String n, double s)
14    {
15       name = n;
16       salary = s;
17    }
18
19    public void print()
20    {
21       System.out.println(name + " " + salary);
22    }
```

```
23    static
24    {
25        System.loadLibrary("Employee");
26    }
27 }
```

**Listing 12.13** employee/Employee.c

```
1  /**
2     @version 1.10 1999-11-13
3     @author Cay Horstmann
4  */
5
6  #include "Employee.h"
7
8  #include <stdio.h>
9
10 JNIEXPORT void JNICALL Java_Employee_raiseSalary(JNIEnv* env, jobject this_obj, jdouble byPercent)
11 {
12    /* get the class */
13    jclass class_Employee = (*env)->GetObjectClass(env, this_obj);
14
15    /* get the field ID */
16    jfieldID id_salary = (*env)->GetFieldID(env, class_Employee, "salary", "D");
17
18    /* get the field value */
19    jdouble salary = (*env)->GetDoubleField(env, this_obj, id_salary);
20
21    salary *= 1 + byPercent / 100;
22
23    /* set the field value */
24    (*env)->SetDoubleField(env, this_obj, id_salary, salary);
25 }
26
```

## 12.4.2 Accessing Static Fields

Accessing static fields is similar to accessing nonstatic fields. Use the GetStaticFieldID and GetStatic*Xxx*Field/SetStatic*Xxx*Field functions that work almost identically to their nonstatic counterparts, with two differences:

- As you have no object, you must use FindClass instead of GetObjectClass to obtain the class reference.
- You have to supply the class, not the instance object, when accessing the field.

For example, here is how you can get a reference to System.out:

```
/* get the class */
jclass class_System = (*env)->FindClass(env, "java/lang/System");

/* get the field ID */
jfieldID id_out = (*env)->GetStaticFieldID(env, class_System, "out",
    "Ljava/io/PrintStream;");

/* get the field value */
jobject obj_out = (*env)->GetStaticObjectField(env, class_System, id_out);
```

---

**Accessing Fields**

- jfieldID GetFieldID(JNIEnv *env, jclass cl, const char name[], const char fieldSignature[])

  returns the identifier of a field in a class.

- *Xxx* Get*Xxx*Field(JNIEnv *env, jobject obj, jfieldID id)

  returns the value of a field. The field type *Xxx* is one of Object, Boolean, Byte, Char, Short, Int, Long, Float, or Double.

- void Set*Xxx*Field(JNIEnv *env, jobject obj, jfieldID id, *Xxx* value)

  sets a field to a new value. The field type *Xxx* is one of Object, Boolean, Byte, Char, Short, Int, Long, Float, or Double.

- jfieldID GetStaticFieldID(JNIEnv *env, jclass cl, const char name[], const char fieldSignature[])

  returns the identifier of a static field in a class.

- *Xxx* GetStatic*Xxx*Field(JNIEnv *env, jclass cl, jfieldID id)

  returns the value of a static field. The field type *Xxx* is one of Object, Boolean, Byte, Char, Short, Int, Long, Float, or Double.

- void SetStatic*Xxx*Field(JNIEnv *env, jclass cl, jfieldID id, *Xxx* value)

  sets a static field to a new value. The field type *Xxx* is one of Object, Boolean, Byte, Char, Short, Int, Long, Float, or Double.

---

## 12.5 Encoding Signatures

To access instance fields and call methods defined in the Java programming language, you need to learn the rules for "mangling" the names of data types and method signatures. (A method signature describes the parameters and return type of the method.) Here is the encoding scheme:

| B | byte |
|---|------|
| C | char |
| D | double |
| F | float |
| I | int |
| J | long |
| L*classname*; | a class type |
| S | short |
| V | void |
| Z | boolean |

To describe an array type, use a [. For example, an array of strings is

    [Ljava/lang/String;

A `float[][]` is mangled into

    [[F

For the complete signature of a method, list the parameter types inside a pair of parentheses and then list the return type. For example, a method receiving two integers and returning an integer is encoded as

    (II)I

The `print` method that we used in the preceding example has a mangled signature of

    (Ljava/lang/String;)V

That is, the method receives a string and returns `void`.

Note that the semicolon at the end of the L expression is the terminator of the type expression, not a separator between parameters. For example, the constructor

    Employee(java.lang.String, double, java.util.Date)

has a signature

    "(Ljava/lang/String;DLjava/util/Date;)V"

Note that there is no separator between the D and `Ljava/util/Date;`. Also note that in this encoding scheme, you must use / instead of . to separate the package and class names. The V at the end denotes a return type of `void`. Even though you don't specify a return type for constructors in Java, you need to add a V to the virtual machine signature.

**TIP:** You can use the `javap` command with option `-s` to generate the method signatures from class files. For example, run

```
javap -s -private Employee
```

You will get the following output, displaying the signatures of all fields and methods.

```
Compiled from "Employee.java"
public class Employee extends java.lang.Object{
private java.lang.String name;
  Signature: Ljava/lang/String;
private double salary;
  Signature: D
public Employee(java.lang.String, double);
  Signature: (Ljava/lang/String;D)V
public native void raiseSalary(double);
  Signature: (D)V
public void print();
  Signature: ()V
static {};
  Signature: ()V
}
```

**NOTE:** There is no rationale whatsoever for forcing programmers to use this mangling scheme for signatures. The designers of the native calling mechanism could have just as easily written a function that reads signatures in the Java programming language style, such as `void(int,java.lang.String)`, and encodes them into whatever internal representation they prefer. Then again, using the mangled signatures lets you partake in the mystique of programming close to the virtual machine.

# 12.6 Calling Java Methods

Of course, Java programming language functions can call C functions—that is what native methods are for. Can we go the other way? Why would we want to do this anyway? It often happens that a native method needs to request a service from an object that was passed to it. We'll first show you how to do it for instance methods, then for static methods.

## 12.6.1 Instance Methods

As an example of calling a Java method from native code, let's enhance the `Printf` class and add a method that works similarly to the C function `fprintf`. That is, it should be able to print a string on an arbitrary PrintWriter object. Here is the definition of the method in Java:

```
class Printf3
{
    public native static void fprint(PrintWriter out, String s, double x);
    . . .
}
```

We'll first assemble the string to be printed into a String object str, as in the sprint method that we already implemented. Then, from the C function that implements the native method, we'll call the print method of the PrintWriter class.

You can call any Java method from C by using the function call

(*env)->Call XxxMethod(env, *implicit parameter*, *methodID*, *explicit parameters*)

Replace *Xxx* with Void, Int, Object, and so on, depending on the return type of the method. Just as you need a fieldID to access a field of an object, you need a method ID to call a method. To obtain a method ID, call the JNI function GetMethodID and supply the class, the name of the method, and the method signature.

In our example, we want to obtain the ID of the print method of the PrintWriter class. As you saw in Volume I, Chapter 12, the PrintWriter class has several overloaded methods called print. For that reason, you must also supply a string describing the parameters and the return value of the specific function that you want to use. For example, we want to use void print(java.lang.String). As described in the preceding section, we must now "mangle" the signature into the string "(Ljava/lang/String;)V".

Here is the complete code to make the method call, by

1. Obtaining the class of the implicit parameter
2. Obtaining the method ID
3. Making the call

```
/* get the class */
class_PrintWriter = (*env)->GetObjectClass(env, out);

/* get the method ID */
id_print = (*env)->GetMethodID(env, class_PrintWriter, "print", "(Ljava/lang/String;)V");

/* call the method */
(*env)->CallVoidMethod(env, out, id_print, str);
```

Listings 12.14 and 12.15 show the Java code for a test program and the Printf3 class. Listing 12.16 contains the C code for the native fprint method.

**NOTE:** The numerical method IDs and field IDs are conceptually similar to `Method` and `Field` objects in the reflection API. You can convert between them with the following functions:

```
jobject ToReflectedMethod(JNIEnv* env, jclass class, jmethodID methodID);
    // returns Method object
methodID FromReflectedMethod(JNIEnv* env, jobject method);
jobject ToReflectedField(JNIEnv* env, jclass class, jfieldID fieldID);
    // returns Field object
fieldID FromReflectedField(JNIEnv* env, jobject field);
```

---

**Listing 12.14** printf3/Printf3Test.java

```
1  import java.io.*;
2  /**
3   * @version 1.10 1997-07-01
4   * @author Cay Horstmann
5   */
6  class Printf3Test
7  {
8     public static void main(String[] args)
9     {
10        double price = 44.95;
11        double tax = 7.75;
12        double amountDue = price * (1 + tax / 100);
13        PrintWriter out = new PrintWriter(System.out);
14        Printf3.fprint(out, "Amount due = %8.2f\n", amountDue);
15        out.flush();
16     }
17  }
```

---

**Listing 12.15** printf3/Printf3.java

```
1  import java.io.*;
2  /**
3   * @version 1.10 1997-07-01
4   * @author Cay Horstmann
5   */
6  class Printf3
7  {
8     public static native void fprint(PrintWriter out, String format, double x);
9
10    static
11    {
12       System.loadLibrary("Printf3");
13    }
14  }
```

**Listing 12.16**  printf3/Printf3.c

```
1  /**
2     @version 1.10 1997-07-01
3     @author Cay Horstmann
4  */
5  #include "Printf3.h"
6  #include <string.h>
7  #include <stdlib.h>
8  #include <float.h>
9  /**
10     @param format a string containing a printf format specifier
11     (such as "%8.2f"). Substrings "%%" are skipped.
12     @return a pointer to the format specifier (skipping the '%')
13     or NULL if there wasn't a unique format specifier
14  */
15  char* find_format(const char format[])
16  {
17     char* p;
18     char* q;
19
20     p = strchr(format, '%');
21     while (p != NULL && *(p + 1) == '%') /* skip %% */
22        p = strchr(p + 2, '%');
23     if (p == NULL) return NULL;
24     /* now check that % is unique */
25     p++;
26     q = strchr(p, '%');
27     while (q != NULL && *(q + 1) == '%') /* skip %% */
28        q = strchr(q + 2, '%');
29     if (q != NULL) return NULL; /* % not unique */
30     q = p + strspn(p, " -0+#"); /* skip past flags */
31     q += strspn(q, "0123456789"); /* skip past field width */
32     if (*q == '.') { q++; q += strspn(q, "0123456789"); }
33        /* skip past precision */
34     if (strchr("eEfFgG", *q) == NULL) return NULL;
35        /* not a floating-point format */
36     return p;
37  }
38
39  JNIEXPORT void JNICALL Java_Printf3_fprint(JNIEnv* env, jclass cl,
40     jobject out, jstring format, jdouble x)
41  {
42     const char* cformat;
43     char* fmt;
44     jstring str;
45     jclass class_PrintWriter;
46     jmethodID id_print;
```

*(Continues)*

---

**Listing 12.16** *(Continued)*

```
47    cformat = (*env)->GetStringUTFChars(env, format, NULL);
48    fmt = find_format(cformat);
49    if (fmt == NULL)
50       str = format;
51    else
52    {
53       char* cstr;
54       int width = atoi(fmt);
55       if (width == 0) width = DBL_DIG + 10;
56       cstr = (char*) malloc(strlen(cformat) + width);
57       sprintf(cstr, cformat, x);
58       str = (*env)->NewStringUTF(env, cstr);
59       free(cstr);
60    }
61    (*env)->ReleaseStringUTFChars(env, format, cformat);
62
63    /* now call ps.print(str) */
64
65    /* get the class */
66    class_PrintWriter = (*env)->GetObjectClass(env, out);
67
68    /* get the method ID */
69    id_print = (*env)->GetMethodID(env, class_PrintWriter, "print", "(Ljava/lang/String;)V");
70
71    /* call the method */
72    (*env)->CallVoidMethod(env, out, id_print, str);
73 }
```

---

## 12.6.2 Static Methods

Calling static methods from native methods is similar to calling instance methods. There are two differences:

- Use the GetStaticMethodID and CallStatic*Xxx*Method functions
- Supply a class object, not an implicit parameter object, when invoking the method

As an example of this, let's make the call to the static method

```
System.getProperty("java.class.path")
```

from a native method. The return value of this call is a string that gives the current class path.

First, we have to find the class to use. As we have no object of the class System readily available, we use FindClass rather than GetObjectClass.

```
jclass class_System = (*env)->FindClass(env, "java/lang/System");
```

Next, we need the ID of the static getProperty method. The encoded signature of that method is

```
"(Ljava/lang/String;)Ljava/lang/String;"
```

because both the parameter and the return value are strings. Hence, we obtain the method ID as follows:

```
jmethodID id_getProperty = (*env)->GetStaticMethodID(env, class_System, "getProperty",
    "(Ljava/lang/String;)Ljava/lang/String;");
```

Finally, we can make the call. Note that the class object is passed to the CallStaticObjectMethod function.

```
jobject obj_ret = (*env)->CallStaticObjectMethod(env, class_System, id_getProperty,
    (*env)->NewStringUTF(env, "java.class.path"));
```

The return value of this method is of type jobject. If we want to manipulate it as a string, we must cast it to jstring:

```
jstring str_ret = (jstring) obj_ret;
```

**C++ NOTE:** In C, the types jstring and jclass, as well as the array types to be introduced later, are all type-equivalent to jobject. The cast of the preceding example is therefore not strictly necessary in C. But in C++, these types are defined as pointers to "dummy classes" that have the correct inheritance hierarchy. For example, assigning a jstring to a jobject is legal without a cast in C++, but an assignment from a jobject to a jstring requires a cast.

## 12.6.3 Constructors

A native method can create a new Java object by invoking its constructor. Invoke the constructor by calling the NewObject function.

```
jobject obj_new = (*env)->NewObject(env, class, methodID, construction parameters);
```

You can obtain the method ID needed for this call from the GetMethodID function by specifying the method name as "<init>" and the encoded signature of the constructor (with return type void). For example, here is how a native method can create a FileOutputStream object.

```
const char[] fileName = ". . .";
jstring str_fileName = (*env)->NewStringUTF(env, fileName);
jclass class_FileOutputStream = (*env)->FindClass(env, "java/io/FileOutputStream");
jmethodID id_FileOutputStream
    = (*env)->GetMethodID(env, class_FileOutputStream, "<init>", "(Ljava/lang/String;)V");
```

```
jobject obj_stream
  = (*env)->NewObject(env, class_FileOutputStream, id_FileOutputStream, str_fileName);
```

Note that the signature of the constructor takes a parameter of type `java.lang.String` and has a return type of `void`.

## 12.6.4 Alternative Method Invocations

Several variants of the JNI functions can be used to call a Java method from native code. These are not as important as the functions that we already discussed, but they are occasionally useful.

The `CallNonvirtualXxxMethod` functions receive an implicit argument, a method ID, a class object (which must correspond to a superclass of the implicit argument), and explicit arguments. The function calls the version of the method in the specified class, bypassing the normal dynamic dispatch mechanism.

All call functions have versions with suffixes "A" and "V" that receive the explicit parameters in an array or a va_list (as defined in the C header `stdarg.h`).

---

**Executing Java Methods**

- `jmethodID GetMethodID(JNIEnv *env, jclass cl, const char name[], const char methodSignature[])`
  returns the identifier of a method in a class.

- *Xxx* `CallXxxMethod(JNIEnv *env, jobject obj, jmethodID id, args)`
- *Xxx* `CallXxxMethodA(JNIEnv *env, jobject obj, jmethodID id, jvalue args[])`
- *Xxx* `CallXxxMethodV(JNIEnv *env, jobject obj, jmethodID id, va_list args)`
  calls a method. The return type *Xxx* is one of Object, Boolean, Byte, Char, Short, Int, Long, Float, or Double. The first function has a variable number of arguments—simply append the method parameters after the method ID. The second function receives the method arguments in an array of jvalue, where jvalue is a union defined as

  ```
  typedef union jvalue
  {
    jboolean z;
    jbyte b;
    jchar c;
    jshort s;
    jint i;
    jlong j;
    jfloat f;
    jdouble d;
    jobject l;
  } jvalue;
  ```

---

*(Continues)*

---

**Executing Java Methods** *(Continued)*

The third function receives the method parameters in a va_list, as defined in the C header stdarg.h.

- *Xxx* CallNonvirtual*Xxx*Method(JNIEnv *env, jobject obj, jclass cl, jmethodID id, args)
- *Xxx* CallNonvirtual*Xxx*MethodA(JNIEnv *env, jobject obj, jclass cl, jmethodID id, jvalue args[])
- *Xxx* CallNonvirtual*Xxx*MethodV(JNIEnv *env, jobject obj, jclass cl, jmethodID id, va_list args)

  calls a method, bypassing dynamic dispatch. The return type *Xxx* is one of Object, Boolean, Byte, Char, Short, Int, Long, Float, or Double. The first function has a variable number of arguments—simply append the method parameters after the method ID. The second function receives the method arguments in an array of jvalue. The third function receives the method parameters in a va_list, as defined in the C header stdarg.h.

- jmethodID GetStaticMethodID(JNIEnv *env, jclass cl, const char name[], const char methodSignature[])

  returns the identifier of a static method in a class.

- *Xxx* CallStatic*Xxx*Method(JNIEnv *env, jclass cl, jmethodID id, args)
- *Xxx* CallStatic*Xxx*MethodA(JNIEnv *env, jclass cl, jmethodID id, jvalue args[])
- *Xxx* CallStatic*Xxx*MethodV(JNIEnv *env, jclass cl, jmethodID id, va_list args)

  calls a static method. The return type *Xxx* is one of Object, Boolean, Byte, Char, Short, Int, Long, Float, or Double. The first function has a variable number of arguments—simply append the method parameters after the method ID. The second function receives the method arguments in an array of jvalue. The third function receives the method parameters in a va_list, as defined in the C header stdarg.h.

- jobject NewObject(JNIEnv *env, jclass cl, jmethodID id, args)
- jobject NewObjectA(JNIEnv *env, jclass cl, jmethodID id, jvalue args[])
- jobject NewObjectV(JNIEnv *env, jclass cl, jmethodID id, va_list args)

  calls a constructor. The method ID is obtained from GetMethodID with a method name of "<init>" and a return type of void. The first function has a variable number of arguments—simply append the method parameters after the method ID. The second function receives the method arguments in an array of jvalue. The third function receives the method parameters in a va_list, as defined in the C header stdarg.h.

---

# 12.7 Accessing Array Elements

All array types of the Java programming language have corresponding C types, as shown in Table 12.2.

**Table 12.2** Correspondence between Java Array Types and C Types

| Java Type | C Type | Java Type | C Type |
|-----------|--------|-----------|--------|
| boolean[] | jbooleanArray | long[] | jlongArray |
| byte[] | jbyteArray | float[] | jfloatArray |
| char[] | jcharArray | double[] | jdoubleArray |
| int[] | jintArray | Object[] | jobjectArray |
| short[] | jshortArray | | |

> **C++ NOTE:** In C, all these array types are actually type synonyms of jobject. In C++, however, they are arranged in the inheritance hierarchy shown in Figure 12.3. The type jarray denotes a generic array.

The GetArrayLength function returns the length of an array.

```
jarray array = . . .;
jsize length = (*env)->GetArrayLength(env, array);
```

How you access elements in an array depends on whether the array stores objects or a primitive type (bool, char, or a numeric type). To access elements in an object array, use the GetObjectArrayElement and SetObjectArrayElement methods.

```
jobjectArray array = . . .;
int i, j;
jobject x = (*env)->GetObjectArrayElement(env, array, i);
(*env)->SetObjectArrayElement(env, array, j, x);
```

Although simple, this approach is also clearly inefficient; you want to be able to access array elements directly, especially when doing vector and matrix computations.

The Get*Xxx*ArrayElements function returns a C pointer to the starting element of an array. As with ordinary strings, you must remember to call the corresponding Release*Xxx*ArrayElements function to tell the virtual machine when you no longer need that pointer. Here, the type *Xxx* must be a primitive type—that is, not Object. You can then read and write the array elements directly. However, since the pointer *might point to a copy*, any changes that you make are guaranteed to be reflected in the original array only when you call the corresponding Release*Xxx*ArrayElements function!

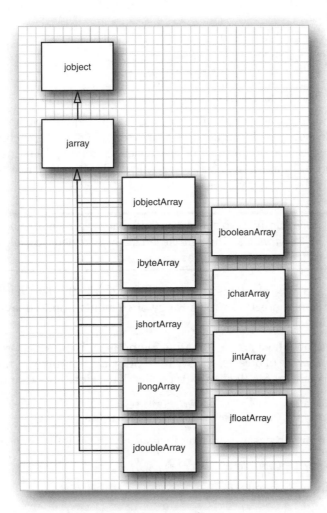

**Figure 12.3** Inheritance hierarchy of array types

---

 **NOTE:** You can find out if an array is a copy by passing a pointer to a `jboolean` variable as the third parameter to a `GetXxxArrayElements` method. The variable is filled with `JNI_TRUE` if the array is a copy. If you aren't interested in that information, just pass a `NULL` pointer.

---

Here is a code sample that multiplies all elements in an array of `double` values by a constant. We obtain a C pointer a into the Java array and then access individual elements as a[i].

```
jdoubleArray array_a = . . .;
double scaleFactor = . . .;
double* a = (*env)->GetDoubleArrayElements(env, array_a, NULL);
for (i = 0; i < (*env)->GetArrayLength(env, array_a); i++)
    a[i] = a[i] * scaleFactor;
(*env)->ReleaseDoubleArrayElements(env, array_a, a, 0);
```

Whether the virtual machine actually copies the array depends on how it allocates arrays and does its garbage collection. Some "copying" garbage collectors routinely move objects around and update object references. That strategy is not compatible with "pinning" an array to a particular location, because the collector cannot update the pointer values in native code.

**NOTE:** In the Sun JVM implementation, `boolean` arrays are represented as packed arrays of 32-bit words. The `GetBooleanArrayElements` method copies them into unpacked arrays of `jboolean` values.

To access just a few elements of a large array, use the `Get`*Xxx*`ArrayRegion` and `Set`*Xxx*`ArrayRegion` methods that copy a range of elements from the Java array into a C array and back.

You can create new Java arrays in native methods with the `New`*Xxx*`Array` function. To create a new array of objects, specify the length, the type of the array elements, and an initial element for all entries (typically, `NULL`). Here is an example:

```
jclass class_Employee = (*env)->FindClass(env, "Employee");
jobjectArray array_e = (*env)->NewObjectArray(env, 100, class_Employee, NULL);
```

Arrays of primitive types are simpler: just supply the length of the array.

```
jdoubleArray array_d = (*env)->NewDoubleArray(env, 100);
```

The array is then filled with zeroes.

**NOTE:** Java SE 1.4 added three methods to the JNI API:

```
jobject NewDirectByteBuffer(JNIEnv* env, void* address, jlong capacity)
void* GetDirectBufferAddress(JNIEnv* env, jobject buf)
jlong GetDirectBufferCapacity(JNIEnv* env, jobject buf)
```

Direct buffers are used in the `java.nio` package to support more efficient input/output operations and to minimize the copying of data between native and Java arrays.

---

**Manipulating Java Arrays**

- jsize GetArrayLength(JNIEnv *env, jarray array)
  returns the number of elements in the array.

- jobject GetObjectArrayElement(JNIEnv *env, jobjectArray array, jsize index)
  returns the value of an array element.

- void SetObjectArrayElement(JNIEnv *env, jobjectArray array, jsize index, jobject value)
  sets an array element to a new value.

- *Xxx** Get*Xxx*ArrayElements(JNIEnv *env, jarray array, jboolean* isCopy)
  yields a C pointer to the elements of a Java array. The field type *Xxx* is one of
  Boolean, Byte, Char, Short, Int, Long, Float, or Double. The pointer must be passed to
  Release*Xxx*ArrayElements when it is no longer needed. isCopy is either NULL or points to
  a jboolean that is filled with JNI_TRUE if a copy is made, with JNI_FALSE otherwise.

- void Release*Xxx*ArrayElements(JNIEnv *env, jarray array, *Xxx* elems[], jint mode)
  notifies the virtual machine that a pointer obtained by Get*Xxx*ArrayElements is no
  longer needed. mode is one of 0 (free the elems buffer after updating the array elements), JNI_COMMIT (do not free the elems buffer after updating the array elements),
  or JNI_ABORT (free the elems buffer without updating the array elements).

- void Get*Xxx*ArrayRegion(JNIEnv *env, jarray array, jint start, jint length, *Xxx* elems[])
  copies elements from a Java array to a C array. The field type *Xxx* is one of Boolean,
  Byte, Char, Short, Int, Long, Float, or Double.

- void Set*Xxx*ArrayRegion(JNIEnv *env, jarray array, jint start, jint length, *Xxx* elems[])
  copies elements from a C array to a Java array. The field type *Xxx* is one of Boolean,
  Byte, Char, Short, Int, Long, Float, or Double.

---

# 12.8 Handling Errors

Native methods are a significant security risk to Java programs. The C runtime
system has no protection against array bounds errors, indirection through bad
pointers, and so on. It is particularly important that programmers of native
methods handle all error conditions to preserve the integrity of the Java platform.
In particular, when your native method diagnoses a problem that it cannot
handle, it should report this problem to the Java virtual machine.

Normally, you would throw an exception in this situation. However, C has no
exceptions. Instead, you must call the Throw or ThrowNew function to create a new exception object. When the native method exits, the Java virtual machine throws
that exception.

To use the Throw function, call NewObject to create an object of a subtype of Throwable.
For example, here we allocate an EOFException object and throw it:

```
jclass class_EOFException = (*env)->FindClass(env, "java/io/EOFException");
jmethodID id_EOFException = (*env)->GetMethodID(env, class_EOFException, "<init>", "()V");
    /* ID of no-argument constructor */
jthrowable obj_exc = (*env)->NewObject(env, class_EOFException, id_EOFException);
(*env)->Throw(env, obj_exc);
```

It is usually more convenient to call ThrowNew, which constructs an exception object, given a class and a "modified UTF-8" byte sequence.

```
(*env)->ThrowNew(env, (*env)->FindClass(env, "java/io/EOFException"), "Unexpected end of file");
```

Both Throw and ThrowNew merely *post* the exception; they do not interrupt the control flow of the native method. Only when the method returns does the Java virtual machine throw the exception. Therefore, every call to Throw and ThrowNew should always be immediately followed by a return statement.

---

 **C++ NOTE:** If you implement native methods in C++, you cannot throw a Java exception object in your C++ code. In a C++ binding, it would be possible to implement a translation between exceptions in the C++ and Java programming languages; however, this is not currently done. Use Throw or ThrowNew to throw a Java exception in a native C++ method, and make sure that your native methods throw no C++ exceptions.

---

Normally, native code need not be concerned with catching Java exceptions. However, when a native method calls a Java method, that method might throw an exception. Moreover, a number of the JNI functions throw exceptions as well. For example, SetObjectArrayElement throws an ArrayIndexOutOfBoundsException if the index is out of bounds, and an ArrayStoreException if the class of the stored object is not a subclass of the element class of the array. In situations like these, a native method should call the ExceptionOccurred method to determine whether an exception has been thrown. The call

```
jthrowable obj_exc = (*env)->ExceptionOccurred(env);
```

returns NULL if no exception is pending, or a reference to the current exception object. If you just want to check whether an exception has been thrown, without obtaining a reference to the exception object, use

```
jboolean occurred = (*env)->ExceptionCheck(env);
```

Normally, a native method should simply return when an exception has occurred so that the virtual machine can propagate it to the Java code. However, a native method *may* analyze the exception object to determine if it can handle the exception. If it can, then the function

```
(*env)->ExceptionClear(env);
```

must be called to turn off the exception.

In our next example, we implement the `fprint` native method with all the paranoia appropriate for a native method. Here are the exceptions that we throw:

- A `NullPointerException` if the format string is `NULL`
- An `IllegalArgumentException` if the format string doesn't contain a `%` specifier that is appropriate for printing a `double`
- An `OutOfMemoryError` if the call to `malloc` fails

Finally, to demonstrate how to check for an exception when calling a Java method from a native method, we send the string to the stream, a character at a time, and call `ExceptionOccurred` after each call. Listing 12.17 shows the code for the native method, and Listing 12.18 shows the definition of the class containing the native method. Notice that the native method does not immediately terminate when an exception occurs in the call to `PrintWriter.print`—it first frees the `cstr` buffer. When the native method returns, the virtual machine again raises the exception. The test program in Listing 12.19 demonstrates how the native method throws an exception when the formatting string is not valid.

**Listing 12.17**  `printf4/Printf4.c`

```
1  /**
2     @version 1.10 1997-07-01
3     @author Cay Horstmann
4  */
5
6  #include "Printf4.h"
7  #include <string.h>
8  #include <stdlib.h>
9  #include <float.h>
10
11 /**
12    @param format a string containing a printf format specifier
13    (such as "%8.2f"). Substrings "%%" are skipped.
14    @return a pointer to the format specifier (skipping the '%')
15    or NULL if there wasn't a unique format specifier
16 */
17 char* find_format(const char format[])
18 {
19    char* p;
20    char* q;
21
22    p = strchr(format, '%');
23    while (p != NULL && *(p + 1) == '%') /* skip %% */
24       p = strchr(p + 2, '%');
```

*(Continues)*

**Listing 12.17** *(Continued)*

```
25    if (p == NULL) return NULL;
26    /* now check that % is unique */
27    p++;
28    q = strchr(p, '%');
29    while (q != NULL && *(q + 1) == '%') /* skip %% */
30       q = strchr(q + 2, '%');
31    if (q != NULL) return NULL; /* % not unique */
32    q = p + strspn(p, " -0+#"); /* skip past flags */
33    q += strspn(q, "0123456789"); /* skip past field width */
34    if (*q == '.') { q++; q += strspn(q, "0123456789"); }
35       /* skip past precision */
36    if (strchr("eEfFgG", *q) == NULL) return NULL;
37       /* not a floating-point format */
38    return p;
39 }
40
41 JNIEXPORT void JNICALL Java_Printf4_fprint(JNIEnv* env, jclass cl,
42    jobject out, jstring format, jdouble x)
43 {
44    const char* cformat;
45    char* fmt;
46    jclass class_PrintWriter;
47    jmethodID id_print;
48    char* cstr;
49    int width;
50    int i;
51
52    if (format == NULL)
53    {
54       (*env)->ThrowNew(env,
55          (*env)->FindClass(env,
56          "java/lang/NullPointerException"),
57          "Printf4.fprint: format is null");
58       return;
59    }
60
61    cformat = (*env)->GetStringUTFChars(env, format, NULL);
62    fmt = find_format(cformat);
63
64    if (fmt == NULL)
65    {
66       (*env)->ThrowNew(env,
67          (*env)->FindClass(env,
68          "java/lang/IllegalArgumentException"),
69          "Printf4.fprint: format is invalid");
70       return;
71    }
```

```
72    width = atoi(fmt);
73    if (width == 0) width = DBL_DIG + 10;
74    cstr = (char*)malloc(strlen(cformat) + width);
75
76    if (cstr == NULL)
77    {
78       (*env)->ThrowNew(env,
79          (*env)->FindClass(env, "java/lang/OutOfMemoryError"),
80          "Printf4.fprint: malloc failed");
81       return;
82    }
83
84    sprintf(cstr, cformat, x);
85
86    (*env)->ReleaseStringUTFChars(env, format, cformat);
87
88    /* now call ps.print(str) */
89
90    /* get the class */
91    class_PrintWriter = (*env)->GetObjectClass(env, out);
92
93    /* get the method ID */
94    id_print = (*env)->GetMethodID(env, class_PrintWriter, "print", "(C)V");
95
96    /* call the method */
97    for (i = 0; cstr[i] != 0 && !(*env)->ExceptionOccurred(env); i++)
98       (*env)->CallVoidMethod(env, out, id_print, cstr[i]);
99
100   free(cstr);
101 }
```

---

**Listing 12.18** printf4/Printf4.java

```
1  import java.io.*;
2
3  /**
4   * @version 1.10 1997-07-01
5   * @author Cay Horstmann
6   */
7  class Printf4
8  {
9     public static native void fprint(PrintWriter ps, String format, double x);
10
11    static
12    {
13       System.loadLibrary("Printf4");
14    }
15 }
```

---

**Listing 12.19** printf4/Printf4Test.java

```java
1  import java.io.*;
2
3  /**
4   * @version 1.10 1997-07-01
5   * @author Cay Horstmann
6   */
7  class Printf4Test
8  {
9     public static void main(String[] args)
10    {
11       double price = 44.95;
12       double tax = 7.75;
13       double amountDue = price * (1 + tax / 100);
14       PrintWriter out = new PrintWriter(System.out);
15       /* This call will throw an exception--note the %% */
16       Printf4.fprint(out, "Amount due = %%8.2f\n", amountDue);
17       out.flush();
18    }
19 }
```

---

**Handling Java Exceptions**

- `jint Throw(JNIEnv *env, jthrowable obj)`

  prepares an exception to be thrown upon exiting from the native code. Returns 0 on success, a negative value on failure.

- `jint ThrowNew(JNIEnv *env, jclass cl, const char msg[])`

  prepares an exception of type `cl` to be thrown upon exiting from the native code. Returns 0 on success, a negative value on failure. `msg` is a "modified UTF-8" byte sequence denoting the String construction argument of the exception object.

- `jthrowable ExceptionOccurred(JNIEnv *env)`

  returns the exception object if an exception is pending, or NULL otherwise.

- `jboolean ExceptionCheck(JNIEnv *env)`

  returns true if an exception is pending.

- `void ExceptionClear(JNIEnv *env)`

  clears any pending exceptions.

## 12.9 Using the Invocation API

Up to now, we have considered programs in the Java programming language that made a few C calls, presumably because C was faster or allowed access to functionality inaccessible from the Java platform. Suppose you are in the opposite situation. You have a C or C++ program and would like to make calls to Java code. The *invocation API* enables you to embed the Java virtual machine into a C or C++ program. Here is the minimal code that you need to initialize a virtual machine:

```
JavaVMOption options[1];
JavaVMInitArgs vm_args;
JavaVM *jvm;
JNIEnv *env;

options[0].optionString = "-Djava.class.path=.";

memset(&vm_args, 0, sizeof(vm_args));
vm_args.version = JNI_VERSION_1_2;
vm_args.nOptions = 1;
vm_args.options = options;

JNI_CreateJavaVM(&jvm, (void**) &env, &vm_args);
```

The call to `JNI_CreateJavaVM` creates the virtual machine and fills in a pointer `jvm` to the virtual machine and a pointer `env` to the execution environment.

You can supply any number of options to the virtual machine. Simply increase the size of the `options` array and the value of `vm_args.nOptions`. For example,

```
options[i].optionString = "-Djava.compiler=NONE";
```

deactivates the just-in-time compiler.

---

 **TIP:** When you run into trouble and your program crashes, refuses to initialize the JVM, or can't load your classes, turn on the JNI debugging mode. Set an option to

```
options[i].optionString = "-verbose:jni";
```

You will see a flurry of messages that indicate the progress in initializing the JVM. If you don't see your classes loaded, check both your path and class path settings.

---

Once you have set up the virtual machine, you can call Java methods as described in the preceding sections. Simply use the `env` pointer in the usual way.

You'll need the `jvm` pointer only to call other functions in the invocation API. Currently, there are only four such functions. The most important one is the function to terminate the virtual machine:

```
(*jvm)->DestroyJavaVM(jvm);
```

Unfortunately, under Windows, it has become difficult to dynamically link to the JNI_CreateJavaVM function in the jre/bin/client/jvm.dll library, due to the changed linking rules in Vista and Oracle's reliance on an older C runtime library. Our sample program overcomes this problem by loading the library manually. This is the same approach used by the java program—see the file launcher/java_md.c in the src.jar file that is a part of the JDK.

The C program in Listing 12.20 sets up a virtual machine and calls the main method of the Welcome class, which was discussed in Volume I, Chapter 2. (Make sure to compile the Welcome.java file before starting the invocation test program.)

**Listing 12.20**   invocation/InvocationTest.c

```c
1  /**
2     @version 1.20 2007-10-26
3     @author Cay Horstmann
4  */
5
6  #include <jni.h>
7  #include <stdlib.h>
8
9  #ifdef _WINDOWS
10
11 #include <windows.h>
12 static HINSTANCE loadJVMLibrary(void);
13 typedef jint (JNICALL *CreateJavaVM_t)(JavaVM **, void **, JavaVMInitArgs *);
14
15 #endif
16
17 int main()
18 {
19    JavaVMOption options[2];
20    JavaVMInitArgs vm_args;
21    JavaVM *jvm;
22    JNIEnv *env;
23    long status;
24
25    jclass class_Welcome;
26    jclass class_String;
27    jobjectArray args;
28    jmethodID id_main;
29
30 #ifdef _WINDOWS
31    HINSTANCE hjvmlib;
32    CreateJavaVM_t createJavaVM;
33 #endif
34
35    options[0].optionString = "-Djava.class.path=.";
```

```
36    memset(&vm_args, 0, sizeof(vm_args));
37    vm_args.version = JNI_VERSION_1_2;
38    vm_args.nOptions = 1;
39    vm_args.options = options;
40
41
42 #ifdef _WINDOWS
43    hjvmlib = loadJVMLibrary();
44    createJavaVM = (CreateJavaVM_t) GetProcAddress(hjvmlib, "JNI_CreateJavaVM");
45    status = (*createJavaVM)(&jvm, (void **) &env, &vm_args);
46 #else
47    status = JNI_CreateJavaVM(&jvm, (void **) &env, &vm_args);
48 #endif
49
50    if (status == JNI_ERR)
51    {
52       fprintf(stderr, "Error creating VM\n");
53       return 1;
54    }
55
56    class_Welcome = (*env)->FindClass(env, "Welcome");
57    id_main = (*env)->GetStaticMethodID(env, class_Welcome, "main", "([Ljava/lang/String;)V");
58
59    class_String = (*env)->FindClass(env, "java/lang/String");
60    args = (*env)->NewObjectArray(env, 0, class_String, NULL);
61    (*env)->CallStaticVoidMethod(env, class_Welcome, id_main, args);
62
63    (*jvm)->DestroyJavaVM(jvm);
64
65    return 0;
66 }
67
68 #ifdef _WINDOWS
69
70 static int GetStringFromRegistry(HKEY key, const char *name, char *buf, jint bufsize)
71 {
72    DWORD type, size;
73
74    return RegQueryValueEx(key, name, 0, &type, 0, &size) == 0
75       && type == REG_SZ
76       && size < (unsigned int) bufsize
77       && RegQueryValueEx(key, name, 0, 0, buf, &size) == 0;
78 }
79
80 static void GetPublicJREHome(char *buf, jint bufsize)
81 {
82    HKEY key, subkey;
83    char version[MAX_PATH];
```

*(Continues)*

**Listing 12.20** *(Continued)*

```
84     /* Find the current version of the JRE */
85     char *JRE_KEY = "Software\\JavaSoft\\Java Runtime Environment";
86     if (RegOpenKeyEx(HKEY_LOCAL_MACHINE, JRE_KEY, 0, KEY_READ, &key) != 0)
87     {
88         fprintf(stderr, "Error opening registry key '%s'\n", JRE_KEY);
89         exit(1);
90     }
91
92     if (!GetStringFromRegistry(key, "CurrentVersion", version, sizeof(version)))
93     {
94         fprintf(stderr, "Failed reading value of registry key:\n\t%s\\CurrentVersion\n", JRE_KEY);
95         RegCloseKey(key);
96         exit(1);
97     }
98
99     /* Find directory where the current version is installed. */
100    if (RegOpenKeyEx(key, version, 0, KEY_READ, &subkey) != 0)
101    {
102      fprintf(stderr, "Error opening registry key '%s\\%s'\n", JRE_KEY, version);
103      RegCloseKey(key);
104      exit(1);
105    }
106
107    if (!GetStringFromRegistry(subkey, "JavaHome", buf, bufsize))
108    {
109        fprintf(stderr, "Failed reading value of registry key:\n\t%s\\%s\\JavaHome\n",
110            JRE_KEY, version);
111        RegCloseKey(key);
112        RegCloseKey(subkey);
113        exit(1);
114    }
115
116    RegCloseKey(key);
117    RegCloseKey(subkey);
118 }
119
120 static HINSTANCE loadJVMLibrary(void)
121 {
122    HINSTANCE h1, h2;
123    char msvcdll[MAX_PATH];
124    char javadll[MAX_PATH];
125    GetPublicJREHome(msvcdll, MAX_PATH);
126    strcpy(javadll, msvcdll);
127    strncat(msvcdll, "\\bin\\msvcr71.dll", MAX_PATH - strlen(msvcdll));
128    msvcdll[MAX_PATH - 1] = '\0';
```

```
129    strncat(javadll, "\\bin\\client\\jvm.dll", MAX_PATH - strlen(javadll));
130    javadll[MAX_PATH - 1] = '\0';
131
132    h1 = LoadLibrary(msvcdll);
133    if (h1 == NULL)
134    {
135       fprintf(stderr, "Can't load library msvcr71.dll\n");
136       exit(1);
137    }
138
139    h2 = LoadLibrary(javadll);
140    if (h2 == NULL)
141    {
142       fprintf(stderr, "Can't load library jvm.dll\n");
143       exit(1);
144    }
145    return h2;
146 }
147
148 #endif
```

To compile this program under Linux, use

```
gcc -I jdk/include -I jdk/include/linux -o InvocationTest
   -L jdk/jre/lib/i386/client -ljvm InvocationTest.c
```

Under Solaris, use

```
cc -I jdk/include -I jdk/include/solaris -o InvocationTest
   -L jdk/jre/lib/sparc -ljvm InvocationTest.c
```

When compiling in Windows with the Microsoft compiler, use the command line

```
cl -D_WINDOWS -I jdk\include -I jdk\include\win32 InvocationTest.c jdk\lib\jvm.lib advapi32.lib
```

You will need to make sure that the INCLUDE and LIB environment variables include the paths to the Windows API header and library files.

With Cygwin, compile with

```
gcc -D_WINDOWS -mno-cygwin -I jdk\include -I jdk\include\win32 -D__int64="long long"
   -I c:\cygwin\usr\include\w32api -o InvocationTest
```

Before you run the program under Linux/UNIX, make sure that the LD_LIBRARY_PATH contains the directories for the shared libraries. For example, if you use the bash shell on Linux, issue the following command:

```
export LD_LIBRARY_PATH=jdk/jre/lib/i386/client:$LD_LIBRARY_PATH
```

---

**Invocation API Functions**

- `jint JNI_CreateJavaVM(JavaVM** p_jvm, void** p_env, JavaVMInitArgs* vm_args)`
  initializes the Java virtual machine. The function returns 0 if successful, `JNI_ERR` on failure.

  *Parameters:*  `p_jvm`   Filled with a pointer to the invocation API function table

  `p_env`   Filled with a pointer to the JNI function table

  `vm_args`  The virtual machine arguments

- `jint DestroyJavaVM(JavaVM* jvm)`
  destroys the virtual machine. Returns 0 on success, a negative number on failure. This function must be called through a virtual machine pointer, i.e., `(*jvm)->DestroyJavaVM(jvm)`.

---

## 12.10 A Complete Example: Accessing the Windows Registry

In this section, we describe a full, working example that covers everything we discussed in this chapter: using native methods with strings, arrays, objects, constructor calls, and error handling. We'll show you how to put a Java platform wrapper around a subset of the ordinary C-based API used to work with the Windows registry. Of course, the Windows registry being a Windows-specific feature, such a program is inherently nonportable. For that reason, the standard Java library has no support for the registry, and it makes sense to use native methods to gain access to it.

### 12.10.1 Overview of the Windows Registry

The Windows registry is a data depository that holds configuration information for the Windows operating system and application programs. It provides a single point for administration and backup of system and application preferences. On the downside, the registry is also a single point of failure—if you mess up the registry, your computer could malfunction or even fail to boot!

We don't suggest that you use the registry to store configuration parameters for your Java programs. The Java preferences API is a better solution (see Volume I, Chapter 10 for more information). We'll simply use the registry to demonstrate how to wrap a nontrivial native API into a Java class.

The principal tool for inspecting the registry is the *registry editor*. Because of the potential for error by naive but enthusiastic users, there is no icon for launching the registry editor. Instead, start a DOS shell (or open the Start -> Run dialog box) and type `regedit`. Figure 12.4 shows the registry editor in action.

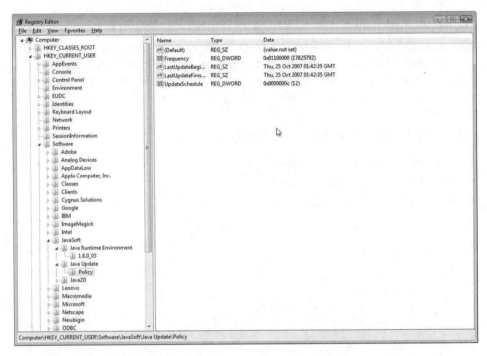

**Figure 12.4** The registry editor

The left side shows the keys, which are arranged in a tree structure. Note that each key starts with one of the HKEY nodes like

```
HKEY_CLASSES_ROOT
HKEY_CURRENT_USER
HKEY_LOCAL_MACHINE
. . .
```

The right side shows the name/value pairs associated with a particular key. For example, if you installed Java SE 7, the key

```
HKEY_LOCAL_MACHINE\Software\JavaSoft\Java Runtime Environment
```

contains a name/value pair such as

```
CurrentVersion="1.7.0_10"
```

In this case, the value is a string. The values can also be integers or arrays of bytes.

## 12.10.2  A Java Platform Interface for Accessing the Registry

We create a simple interface to access the registry from Java code, and then implement this interface with native code. Our interface allows only a few registry operations; to keep the code size down, we omitted some important operations such as adding, deleting, and enumerating keys. (It should be easy to add the remaining registry API functions.)

Even with the limited subset that we supply, you can

- Enumerate all names stored in a key
- Read the value stored with a name
- Set the value stored with a name

Here is the Java class that encapsulates a registry key:

```
public class Win32RegKey
{
    public Win32RegKey(int theRoot, String thePath) { . . . }
    public Enumeration names() { . . . }
    public native Object getValue(String name);
    public native void setValue(String name, Object value);

    public static final int HKEY_CLASSES_ROOT = 0x80000000;
    public static final int HKEY_CURRENT_USER = 0x80000001;
    public static final int HKEY_LOCAL_MACHINE = 0x80000002;
    . . .
}
```

The `names` method returns an enumeration that holds all the names stored with the key. You can get at them with the familiar `hasMoreElements/nextElement` methods. The `getValue` method returns an object that is either a string, an `Integer` object, or a byte array. The value parameter of the `setValue` method must also be of one of these three types.

## 12.10.3  Implementation of Registry Access Functions as Native Methods

We need to implement three actions:

- Get the value of a name
- Set the value of a name
- Iterate through the names of a key

Fortunately, you have seen essentially all the tools that are required, such as the conversion between Java strings and arrays and those of C. You also saw how to raise a Java exception in case something goes wrong.

Two issues make these native methods more complex than the preceding examples. The getValue and setValue methods deal with the type Object, which can be one of String, Integer, or byte[]. The enumeration object stores the state between successive calls to hasMoreElements and nextElement.

Let us first look at the getValue method. The method (shown in Listing 12.22) goes through the following steps:

1. Opens the registry key. To read their values, the registry API requires that keys be open.
2. Queries the type and size of the value associated with the name.
3. Reads the data into a buffer.
4. Calls NewStringUTF to create a new string with the value data if the type is REG_SZ (a string).
5. Invokes the Integer constructor if the type is REG_DWORD (a 32-bit integer).
6. Calls NewByteArray to create a new byte array, then SetByteArrayRegion to copy the value data into the byte array, if the type is REG_BINARY.
7. If the type is none of these or if an error occurred when an API function was called, throws an exception and releases all resources that had been acquired up to that point.
8. Closes the key and returns the object (String, Integer, or byte[]) that had been created.

As you can see, this example illustrates quite nicely how to generate Java objects of different types.

In this native method, coping with the generic return type is not difficult. The jstring, jobject, or jarray reference is simply returned as a jobject. However, the setValue method receives a reference to an Object and must determine the Object's exact type to save the Object as a string, integer, or byte array. We can make this determination by querying the class of the value object, finding the class references for java.lang.String, java.lang.Integer, and byte[], and comparing them with the IsAssignableFrom function.

If class1 and class2 are two class references, then the call

```
(*env)->IsAssignableFrom(env, class1, class2)
```

returns JNI_TRUE when class1 and class2 are the same class or when class1 is a subclass of class2. In either case, references to objects of class1 can be cast to class2. For example, when

```
(*env)->IsAssignableFrom(env, (*env)->GetObjectClass(env, value), (*env)->FindClass(env, "[B"))
```

is true, we know that value is a byte array.

Here is an overview of the steps in the setValue method:

1. Open the registry key for writing.
2. Find the type of the value to write.
3. Call GetStringUTFChars to get a pointer to the characters if the type is String.
4. Call the intValue method to get the integer stored in the wrapper object if the type is Integer.
5. Call GetByteArrayElements to get a pointer to the bytes if the type is byte[].
6. Pass the data and length to the registry.
7. Close the key.
8. Release the pointer to the data if the type is String or byte[].

Finally, let us turn to the native methods that enumerate keys. These are methods of the Win32RegKeyNameEnumeration class (see Listing 12.21). When the enumeration process starts, we must open the key. For the duration of the enumeration, we must retain the key handle—that is, the key handle must be stored with the enumeration object. The key handle is of type DWORD (a 32-bit quantity), so it can be stored in a Java integer. We store it in the hkey field of the enumeration class. When the enumeration starts, the field is initialized with SetIntField. Subsequent calls read the value with GetIntField.

In this example, we store three other data items with the enumeration object. When the enumeration first starts, we can query the registry for the count of name/value pairs and the length of the longest name, which we need so we can allocate C character arrays to hold the names. These values are stored in the count and maxsize fields of the enumeration object. Finally, the index field is initialized with -1 to indicate the start of the enumeration, is set to 0 once the other instance fields are initialized, and is incremented after every enumeration step.

Let's walk through the native methods that support the enumeration. The hasMoreElements method is simple:

1. Retrieve the index and count fields.
2. If the index is -1, call the startNameEnumeration function, which opens the key, queries the count and maximum length, and initializes the hkey, count, maxsize, and index fields.
3. Return JNI_TRUE if index is less than count, and JNI_FALSE otherwise.

The nextElement method needs to work a little harder:

1. Retrieve the index and count fields.

2. If the index is -1, call the `startNameEnumeration` function, which opens the key, queries the count and maximum length, and initializes the `hkey`, `count`, `maxsize`, and `index` fields.

3. If `index` equals `count`, throw a `NoSuchElementException`.

4. Read the next name from the registry.

5. Increment `index`.

6. If `index` equals `count`, close the key.

Before compiling, remember to run `javah` on both `Win32RegKey` and `Win32RegKeyNameEnumeration`. The complete command line for the Microsoft compiler is

```
cl -I jdk\include -I jdk\include\win32 -LD Win32RegKey.c advapi32.lib -FeWin32RegKey.dll
```

With Cygwin, use

```
gcc -mno-cygwin -D _int64="long long" -I jdk\include -I jdk\include\win32
   -I c:\cygwin\usr\include\w32api -shared -Wl,--add-stdcall-alias -o Win32RegKey.dll
Win32RegKey.c
```

As the registry API is specific to Windows, this program will not work on other operating systems.

Listing 12.23 shows a program to test our new registry functions. We add three name/value pairs, a string, an integer, and a byte array to the key

```
HKEY_CURRENT_USER\Software\JavaSoft\Java Runtime Environment
```

We then enumerate all names of that key and retrieve their values. The program will print

```
Default user=Harry Hacker
Lucky number=13
Small primes=2 3 5 7 11 13
```

Although adding these name/value pairs to that key probably does no harm, you might want to use the registry editor to remove them after running this program.

---

**Listing 12.21**  win32reg/Win32RegKey.java

```
1  import java.util.*;
2
3  /**
4   * A Win32RegKey object can be used to get and set values of a registry key in the Windows registry.
5   * @version 1.00 1997-07-01
6   * @author Cay Horstmann
7   */
```

*(Continues)*

**Listing 12.21** *(Continued)*

```
8   public class Win32RegKey
9   {
10     public static final int HKEY_CLASSES_ROOT = 0x80000000;
11     public static final int HKEY_CURRENT_USER = 0x80000001;
12     public static final int HKEY_LOCAL_MACHINE = 0x80000002;
13     public static final int HKEY_USERS = 0x80000003;
14     public static final int HKEY_CURRENT_CONFIG = 0x80000005;
15     public static final int HKEY_DYN_DATA = 0x80000006;
16
17     private int root;
18     private String path;
19
20     /**
21      * Gets the value of a registry entry.
22      * @param name the entry name
23      * @return the associated value
24      */
25     public native Object getValue(String name);
26
27     /**
28      * Sets the value of a registry entry.
29      * @param name the entry name
30      * @param value the new value
31      */
32     public native void setValue(String name, Object value);
33
34     /**
35      * Construct a registry key object.
36      * @param theRoot one of HKEY_CLASSES_ROOT, HKEY_CURRENT_USER, HKEY_LOCAL_MACHINE, HKEY_USERS,
37      * HKEY_CURRENT_CONFIG, HKEY_DYN_DATA
38      * @param thePath the registry key path
39      */
40     public Win32RegKey(int theRoot, String thePath)
41     {
42        root = theRoot;
43        path = thePath;
44     }
45
46     /**
47      * Enumerates all names of registry entries under the path that this object describes.
48      * @return an enumeration listing all entry names
49      */
50     public Enumeration<String> names()
51     {
52        return new Win32RegKeyNameEnumeration(root, path);
53     }
```

```
54     static
55     {
56        System.loadLibrary("Win32RegKey");
57     }
58  }
59
60  class Win32RegKeyNameEnumeration implements Enumeration<String>
61  {
62     public native String nextElement();
63     public native boolean hasMoreElements();
64     private int root;
65     private String path;
66     private int index = -1;
67     private int hkey = 0;
68     private int maxsize;
69     private int count;
70
71     Win32RegKeyNameEnumeration(int theRoot, String thePath)
72     {
73        root = theRoot;
74        path = thePath;
75     }
76  }
77
78  class Win32RegKeyException extends RuntimeException
79  {
80     public Win32RegKeyException()
81     {
82     }
83
84     public Win32RegKeyException(String why)
85     {
86        super(why);
87     }
88  }
```

**Listing 12.22**  win32reg/Win32RegKey.c

```
1  /**
2     @version 1.00 1997-07-01
3     @author Cay Horstmann
4  */
5
6  #include "Win32RegKey.h"
7  #include "Win32RegKeyNameEnumeration.h"
8  #include <string.h>
9  #include <stdlib.h>
10 #include <windows.h>
```

*(Continues)*

**Listing 12.22** *(Continued)*

```
11  JNIEXPORT jobject JNICALL Java_Win32RegKey_getValue(JNIEnv* env, jobject this_obj, jobject name)
12  {
13     const char* cname;
14     jstring path;
15     const char* cpath;
16     HKEY hkey;
17     DWORD type;
18     DWORD size;
19     jclass this_class;
20     jfieldID id_root;
21     jfieldID id_path;
22     HKEY root;
23     jobject ret;
24     char* cret;
25
26     /* get the class */
27     this_class = (*env)->GetObjectClass(env, this_obj);
28
29     /* get the field IDs */
30     id_root = (*env)->GetFieldID(env, this_class, "root", "I");
31     id_path = (*env)->GetFieldID(env, this_class, "path", "Ljava/lang/String;");
32
33     /* get the fields */
34     root = (HKEY) (*env)->GetIntField(env, this_obj, id_root);
35     path = (jstring)(*env)->GetObjectField(env, this_obj, id_path);
36     cpath = (*env)->GetStringUTFChars(env, path, NULL);
37
38     /* open the registry key */
39     if (RegOpenKeyEx(root, cpath, 0, KEY_READ, &hkey) != ERROR_SUCCESS)
40     {
41        (*env)->ThrowNew(env, (*env)->FindClass(env, "Win32RegKeyException"),
42           "Open key failed");
43        (*env)->ReleaseStringUTFChars(env, path, cpath);
44        return NULL;
45     }
46
47     (*env)->ReleaseStringUTFChars(env, path, cpath);
48     cname = (*env)->GetStringUTFChars(env, name, NULL);
49
50     /* find the type and size of the value */
51     if (RegQueryValueEx(hkey, cname, NULL, &type, NULL, &size) != ERROR_SUCCESS)
52     {
53        (*env)->ThrowNew(env, (*env)->FindClass(env, "Win32RegKeyException"),
54           "Query value key failed");
55        RegCloseKey(hkey);
56        (*env)->ReleaseStringUTFChars(env, name, cname);
57        return NULL;
58     }
```

```
59   /* get memory to hold the value */
60   cret = (char*)malloc(size);
61
62   /* read the value */
63   if (RegQueryValueEx(hkey, cname, NULL, &type, cret, &size) != ERROR_SUCCESS)
64   {
65      (*env)->ThrowNew(env, (*env)->FindClass(env, "Win32RegKeyException"),
66         "Query value key failed");
67      free(cret);
68      RegCloseKey(hkey);
69      (*env)->ReleaseStringUTFChars(env, name, cname);
70      return NULL;
71   }
72
73   /* depending on the type, store the value in a string,
74      integer or byte array */
75   if (type == REG_SZ)
76   {
77      ret = (*env)->NewStringUTF(env, cret);
78   }
79   else if (type == REG_DWORD)
80   {
81      jclass class_Integer = (*env)->FindClass(env, "java/lang/Integer");
82      /* get the method ID of the constructor */
83      jmethodID id_Integer = (*env)->GetMethodID(env, class_Integer, "<init>", "(I)V");
84      int value = *(int*) cret;
85      /* invoke the constructor */
86      ret = (*env)->NewObject(env, class_Integer, id_Integer, value);
87   }
88   else if (type == REG_BINARY)
89   {
90      ret = (*env)->NewByteArray(env, size);
91      (*env)->SetByteArrayRegion(env, (jarray) ret, 0, size, cret);
92   }
93   else
94   {
95      (*env)->ThrowNew(env, (*env)->FindClass(env, "Win32RegKeyException"),
96         "Unsupported value type");
97      ret = NULL;
98   }
99
100  free(cret);
101  RegCloseKey(hkey);
102  (*env)->ReleaseStringUTFChars(env, name, cname);
103
104  return ret;
105 }
```

*(Continues)*

**Listing 12.22** *(Continued)*

```
106  JNIEXPORT void JNICALL Java_Win32RegKey_setValue(JNIEnv* env, jobject this_obj,
107     jstring name, jobject value)
108  {
109     const char* cname;
110     jstring path;
111     const char* cpath;
112     HKEY hkey;
113     DWORD type;
114     DWORD size;
115     jclass this_class;
116     jclass class_value;
117     jclass class_Integer;
118     jfieldID id_root;
119     jfieldID id_path;
120     HKEY root;
121     const char* cvalue;
122     int ivalue;
123
124     /* get the class */
125     this_class = (*env)->GetObjectClass(env, this_obj);
126
127     /* get the field IDs */
128     id_root = (*env)->GetFieldID(env, this_class, "root", "I");
129     id_path = (*env)->GetFieldID(env, this_class, "path", "Ljava/lang/String;");
130
131     /* get the fields */
132     root = (HKEY)(*env)->GetIntField(env, this_obj, id_root);
133     path = (jstring)(*env)->GetObjectField(env, this_obj, id_path);
134     cpath = (*env)->GetStringUTFChars(env, path, NULL);
135
136     /* open the registry key */
137     if (RegOpenKeyEx(root, cpath, 0, KEY_WRITE, &hkey) != ERROR_SUCCESS)
138     {
139        (*env)->ThrowNew(env, (*env)->FindClass(env, "Win32RegKeyException"),
140           "Open key failed");
141        (*env)->ReleaseStringUTFChars(env, path, cpath);
142        return;
143     }
144
145     (*env)->ReleaseStringUTFChars(env, path, cpath);
146     cname = (*env)->GetStringUTFChars(env, name, NULL);
147
148     class_value = (*env)->GetObjectClass(env, value);
149     class_Integer = (*env)->FindClass(env, "java/lang/Integer");
150     /* determine the type of the value object */
```

```
151   if ((*env)->IsAssignableFrom(env, class_value, (*env)->FindClass(env, "java/lang/String")))
152   {
153      /* it is a string--get a pointer to the characters */
154      cvalue = (*env)->GetStringUTFChars(env, (jstring) value, NULL);
155      type = REG_SZ;
156      size = (*env)->GetStringLength(env, (jstring) value) + 1;
157   }
158   else if ((*env)->IsAssignableFrom(env, class_value, class_Integer))
159   {
160      /* it is an integer--call intValue to get the value */
161      jmethodID id_intValue = (*env)->GetMethodID(env, class_Integer, "intValue", "()I");
162      ivalue = (*env)->CallIntMethod(env, value, id_intValue);
163      type = REG_DWORD;
164      cvalue = (char*)&ivalue;
165      size = 4;
166   }
167   else if ((*env)->IsAssignableFrom(env, class_value, (*env)->FindClass(env, "[B")))
168   {
169      /* it is a byte array--get a pointer to the bytes */
170      type = REG_BINARY;
171      cvalue = (char*)(*env)->GetByteArrayElements(env, (jarray) value, NULL);
172      size = (*env)->GetArrayLength(env, (jarray) value);
173   }
174   else
175   {
176      /* we don't know how to handle this type */
177      (*env)->ThrowNew(env, (*env)->FindClass(env, "Win32RegKeyException"),
178         "Unsupported value type");
179      RegCloseKey(hkey);
180      (*env)->ReleaseStringUTFChars(env, name, cname);
181      return;
182   }
183
184   /* set the value */
185   if (RegSetValueEx(hkey, cname, 0, type, cvalue, size) != ERROR_SUCCESS)
186   {
187      (*env)->ThrowNew(env, (*env)->FindClass(env, "Win32RegKeyException"),
188         "Set value failed");
189   }
190
191   RegCloseKey(hkey);
192   (*env)->ReleaseStringUTFChars(env, name, cname);
193
194   /* if the value was a string or byte array, release the pointer */
195   if (type == REG_SZ)
196   {
197      (*env)->ReleaseStringUTFChars(env, (jstring) value, cvalue);
198   }
```

*(Continues)*

**Listing 12.22**  *(Continued)*

```
199    else if (type == REG_BINARY)
200    {
201       (*env)->ReleaseByteArrayElements(env, (jarray) value, (jbyte*) cvalue, 0);
202    }
203 }
204
205 /* helper function to start enumeration of names */
206 static int startNameEnumeration(JNIEnv* env, jobject this_obj, jclass this_class)
207 {
208    jfieldID id_index;
209    jfieldID id_count;
210    jfieldID id_root;
211    jfieldID id_path;
212    jfieldID id_hkey;
213    jfieldID id_maxsize;
214
215    HKEY root;
216    jstring path;
217    const char* cpath;
218    HKEY hkey;
219    DWORD maxsize = 0;
220    DWORD count = 0;
221
222    /* get the field IDs */
223    id_root = (*env)->GetFieldID(env, this_class, "root", "I");
224    id_path = (*env)->GetFieldID(env, this_class, "path", "Ljava/lang/String;");
225    id_hkey = (*env)->GetFieldID(env, this_class, "hkey", "I");
226    id_maxsize = (*env)->GetFieldID(env, this_class, "maxsize", "I");
227    id_index = (*env)->GetFieldID(env, this_class, "index", "I");
228    id_count = (*env)->GetFieldID(env, this_class, "count", "I");
229
230    /* get the field values */
231    root = (HKEY)(*env)->GetIntField(env, this_obj, id_root);
232    path = (jstring)(*env)->GetObjectField(env, this_obj, id_path);
233    cpath = (*env)->GetStringUTFChars(env, path, NULL);
234
235    /* open the registry key */
236    if (RegOpenKeyEx(root, cpath, 0, KEY_READ, &hkey) != ERROR_SUCCESS)
237    {
238       (*env)->ThrowNew(env, (*env)->FindClass(env, "Win32RegKeyException"),
239          "Open key failed");
240       (*env)->ReleaseStringUTFChars(env, path, cpath);
241       return -1;
242    }
243    (*env)->ReleaseStringUTFChars(env, path, cpath);
```

```
244    /* query count and max length of names */
245    if (RegQueryInfoKey(hkey, NULL, NULL, NULL, NULL, NULL, NULL, &count, &maxsize,
246           NULL, NULL, NULL) != ERROR_SUCCESS)
247    {
248       (*env)->ThrowNew(env, (*env)->FindClass(env, "Win32RegKeyException"),
249          "Query info key failed");
250       RegCloseKey(hkey);
251       return -1;
252    }
253
254    /* set the field values */
255    (*env)->SetIntField(env, this_obj, id_hkey, (DWORD) hkey);
256    (*env)->SetIntField(env, this_obj, id_maxsize, maxsize + 1);
257    (*env)->SetIntField(env, this_obj, id_index, 0);
258    (*env)->SetIntField(env, this_obj, id_count, count);
259    return count;
260 }
261
262 JNIEXPORT jboolean JNICALL Java_Win32RegKeyNameEnumeration_hasMoreElements(JNIEnv* env,
263    jobject this_obj)
264 { jclass this_class;
265    jfieldID id_index;
266    jfieldID id_count;
267    int index;
268    int count;
269    /* get the class */
270    this_class = (*env)->GetObjectClass(env, this_obj);
271
272    /* get the field IDs */
273    id_index = (*env)->GetFieldID(env, this_class, "index", "I");
274    id_count = (*env)->GetFieldID(env, this_class, "count", "I");
275
276    index = (*env)->GetIntField(env, this_obj, id_index);
277    if (index == -1) /* first time */
278    {
279       count = startNameEnumeration(env, this_obj, this_class);
280       index = 0;
281    }
282    else
283       count = (*env)->GetIntField(env, this_obj, id_count);
284    return index < count;
285 }
286
287 JNIEXPORT jobject JNICALL Java_Win32RegKeyNameEnumeration_nextElement(JNIEnv* env,
288    jobject this_obj)
289 {
290    jclass this_class;
291    jfieldID id_index;
```

*(Continues)*

**Listing 12.22** *(Continued)*

```
292    jfieldID id_hkey;
293    jfieldID id_count;
294    jfieldID id_maxsize;
295
296    HKEY hkey;
297    int index;
298    int count;
299    DWORD maxsize;
300
301    char* cret;
302    jstring ret;
303
304    /* get the class */
305    this_class = (*env)->GetObjectClass(env, this_obj);
306
307    /* get the field IDs */
308    id_index = (*env)->GetFieldID(env, this_class, "index", "I");
309    id_count = (*env)->GetFieldID(env, this_class, "count", "I");
310    id_hkey = (*env)->GetFieldID(env, this_class, "hkey", "I");
311    id_maxsize = (*env)->GetFieldID(env, this_class, "maxsize", "I");
312
313    index = (*env)->GetIntField(env, this_obj, id_index);
314    if (index == -1) /* first time */
315    {
316       count = startNameEnumeration(env, this_obj, this_class);
317       index = 0;
318    }
319    else
320       count = (*env)->GetIntField(env, this_obj, id_count);
321
322    if (index >= count) /* already at end */
323    {
324       (*env)->ThrowNew(env, (*env)->FindClass(env, "java/util/NoSuchElementException"),
325          "past end of enumeration");
326       return NULL;
327    }
328
329    maxsize = (*env)->GetIntField(env, this_obj, id_maxsize);
330    hkey = (HKEY)(*env)->GetIntField(env, this_obj, id_hkey);
331    cret = (char*)malloc(maxsize);
332
333    /* find the next name */
334    if (RegEnumValue(hkey, index, cret, &maxsize, NULL, NULL, NULL, NULL) != ERROR_SUCCESS)
335    {
336       (*env)->ThrowNew(env, (*env)->FindClass(env, "Win32RegKeyException"),
337          "Enum value failed");
```

```
338      free(cret);
339      RegCloseKey(hkey);
340      (*env)->SetIntField(env, this_obj, id_index, count);
341      return NULL;
342   }
343
344   ret = (*env)->NewStringUTF(env, cret);
345   free(cret);
346
347   /* increment index */
348   index++;
349   (*env)->SetIntField(env, this_obj, id_index, index);
350
351   if (index == count) /* at end */
352   {
353      RegCloseKey(hkey);
354   }
355
356   return ret;
357 }
```

---

**Listing 12.23** win32reg/Win32RegKeyTest.java

```
1  import java.util.*;
2
3  /**
4     @version 1.02 2007-10-26
5     @author Cay Horstmann
6  */
7  public class Win32RegKeyTest
8  {
9     public static void main(String[] args)
10    {
11       Win32RegKey key = new Win32RegKey(
12          Win32RegKey.HKEY_CURRENT_USER, "Software\\JavaSoft\\Java Runtime Environment");
13
14       key.setValue("Default user", "Harry Hacker");
15       key.setValue("Lucky number", new Integer(13));
16       key.setValue("Small primes", new byte[] { 2, 3, 5, 7, 11 });
17
18       Enumeration<String> e = key.names();
19
20       while (e.hasMoreElements())
21       {
22          String name = e.nextElement();
23          System.out.print(name + "=");
24
25          Object value = key.getValue(name);
```

*(Continues)*

**Listing 12.23** *(Continued)*

```
26          if (value instanceof byte[])
27              for (byte b : (byte[]) value) System.out.print((b & 0xFF) + " ");
28          else
29              System.out.print(value);
30
31          System.out.println();
32      }
33  }
34 }
```

---

**Type Inquiry Functions**

- jboolean IsAssignableFrom(JNIEnv *env, jclass cl1, jclass cl2)

  returns JNI_TRUE if objects of the first class can be assigned to objects of the second class, and JNI_FALSE otherwise. This tests if the classes are the same, or cl1 is a subclass of cl2, or cl2 represents an interface implemented by cl1 or one of its superclasses.

- jclass GetSuperclass(JNIEnv *env, jclass cl)

  returns the superclass of a class. If cl represents the class Object or an interface, returns NULL.

---

You have now reached the end of the second volume of *Core Java*, completing a long journey in which you encountered many advanced APIs. We started out with topics that every Java programmer needs to know: streams, XML, networking, databases, and internationalization. Three long chapters covered graphics and GUI programming. We concluded with very technical chapters on security, remote methods, annotation processing, and native methods. We hope that you enjoyed your tour through the vast breadth of the Java APIs, and that you will be able to apply your newly gained knowledge in your projects.

# Index

Your purchase of **Core Java™, Volume II—Advanced Features, Ninth Edition,** includes access to a free online edition for 45 days through the **Safari Books Online** subscription service. Nearly every Prentice Hall book is available online through **Safari Books Online,** along with thousands of books and videos from publishers such as Addison-Wesley Professional, Cisco Press, Exam Cram, IBM Press, O'Reilly Media, Que, Sams, and VMware Press.

**Safari Books Online** is a digital library providing searchable, on-demand access to thousands of technology, digital media, and professional development books and videos from leading publishers. With one monthly or yearly subscription price, you get unlimited access to learning tools and information on topics including mobile app and software development, tips and tricks on using your favorite gadgets, networking, project management, graphic design, and much more.

## Activate your FREE Online Edition at
## informit.com/safarifree

**STEP 1:**   Enter the coupon code: HFHANXA.

**STEP 2:**   New Safari users, complete the brief registration form.
Safari subscribers, just log in.

If you have difficulty registering on Safari or accessing the online edition,
please e-mail customer-service@safaribooksonline.com